COLLINS

AUTHORS AND PRINTERS DICTIONARY

AUTHORS
AND
PRINTERS
DICTIONARY

F. HOWARD COLLINS

ELEVENTH EDITION
revised by
STANLEY BEALE

LONDON
OXFORD UNIVERSITY PRESS
NEW YORK   TORONTO
1973

Oxford University Press, Ely House, London W. 1

GLASGOW   NEW YORK   TORONTO   MELBOURNE   WELLINGTON
CAPE TOWN   IBADAN   NAIROBI   DAR ES SALAAM   LUSAKA   ADDIS ABABA
DELHI   BOMBAY   CALCUTTA   MADRAS   KARACHI   LAHORE   DACCA
KUALA LUMPUR   SINGAPORE   HONG KONG   TOKYO

ISBN 0 19 211542 1

© *Oxford University Press 1973*

FIRST EDITION 1905
NEW EDITIONS 1905, 1909, 1912, 1921, 1928,
1933, 1938, 1946, 1956
ELEVENTH EDITION 1973

Printed in Great Britain
at the University Press, Oxford
by Vivian Ridler
Printer to the University

PREFACE TO
THE ELEVENTH EDITION

In his Preface to the First Edition of this work, which appeared in 1905, F. Howard Collins concluded as follows: 'While probably no one will agree with everything contained in this book, I hope it may be found that the number of marginal notes needed to bring it into accordance with the views of those who use it will be as few as could be expected, considering the difficulty of the subject-matter, and the fact that it is, I believe, the first time it has been thoroughly and systematically investigated in any country.'

This 'subject-matter' was not only difficult but varied. Collins included, within the covers of a book of modest size, almost everything to which an author or a printer might wish to refer—spelling, difficult proper names, punctuation, italicization, capitalization, abbreviations, printing technicalities, foreign words and phrases.

In the sixty-eight years that have passed since that first edition there have been dictionaries and specialist reference books in profusion, and many entertaining and instructive volumes on the current use and abuse of English. But there has never been anything quite like *Collins*. Without pretending to rival the length and breadth of the monumental dictionaries, or the detailed information, in narrower fields, of highly technical works, this book does indeed serve the everyday needs of authors and printers. It has been through ten editions, and undergone constant revision. There have been substantial corrections, additions, and subtractions. But the purpose and the style are still the same—a striking tribute to the judgement and prescience of its first editor.

The problems of selection and accuracy which he faced are still with us. This new edition is perhaps the most extensive of the revisions so far. The world is changing rapidly, and the English language with it. Room has had to be found for new ideas, new words, new measurements, new sets of initials, new political and geographical adjustments, and new habits of speech and writing.

In order not to make the book unwieldy, there have had to be excisions. There were obsolescent words, defunct societies, proper names which had lost their importance, abbreviations no longer in use, and a superfluity of foreign printing terms. All these have gone, unless they seemed historically significant or likely to occur in books still in use. There are natural changes of emphasis, too— fewer words from Afrikaans, for instance, and more Americanisms.

This is an English dictionary, and when a foreign word has become anglicized we see no reason to insist on retaining or reverting to the strict foreign form. For instance, 'librettos' is now English, and 'libretti' is not; 'kapellmeister' is sufficiently English to be printed in roman, and therefore does not need the German capital letter; 'mêlée' is so familiar that it no longer needs italic—indeed, we shall soon have to abandon the accents and adopt the American 'melee'. It is the same with geographical names: to use 'Samarqand' instead of 'Samarkand' would be merely pedantic. These judgements recognize that language is a growing, changing thing, and that occasional discrepancies between this latest edition of *Collins* and earlier editions of other dictionaries are inevitable.

Collins, in 1905, made no attempt ever to sit on the fence. His aim was to give a reasonable verdict, in the interests of consistency. To quote from his original Preface: 'Where a choice has been made between two or more forms of any word, it should not be concluded that I consider the other forms wrong, but merely that the weight of evidence has led me to select the one given.'

Pursuing the same policy, I have tried to assess, for example, how far a word has now advanced along the road which leads from 'rear guard', through 'rear-guard', to 'rearguard'. Developments like these are often rapid, and need constant review, so that even the preparation of this eleventh edition, a work of nearly five years, has come to seem like painting the Forth Bridge.

Newspapers are a major source of innovation and change. One usage in particular should be mentioned, the omission of full points between the letters of abbreviations like I.A.A.M. This is understandable in the brief headlines and narrow columns of a newspaper, but need not normally be imitated in a book. However, many organizations are indifferent to the form of their abbreviation, and with some the un-pointed form is well established, especially when the initials make a pronounceable word, like 'Unesco'. Indeed, newly formed societies often choose a name with this in view, like an American feminist 'Society for Cutting Up Men'; here the development, if any, will be from 'S.C.U.M.', through 'SCUM', to 'Scum'.

This new edition contains very brief definitions of all but the simplest words, intended more to identify the words than to give a complete account of their meanings. But an effort has been made to get technical meanings accurate and to bring scientific phrases up to date.

I am indebted to many members of the printing and publishing staffs of the Oxford University Press for their valuable and expert advice, especially on printing terms. R. W. Burchfield, editor of the *Oxford English Dictionary Supplement* (new edition), made very helpful suggestions at an early stage in the revision, and G. N. S. Hunt of the Publisher's staff has been available for consultation throughout my work.

Finally, I want to thank many users of *The Authors and Printers Dictionary* for corrections and suggestions based on the earlier editions. Revisers of this dictionary will always be very grateful for any criticisms or contributions which may add to its usefulness.

STANLEY BEALE

1973

EXTRACTS FROM THE PREFACE
TO THE FIRST EDITION

A SKETCH of the way in which this work was compiled may be of interest. All suitable words, phrases, etc., were copied on to separate slips. These were then arranged alphabetically, duplicates eliminated, and the manuscript copy made. With this my duties as Author ceased, and those of Editor commenced, for from that time I merely co-ordinated the opinions of others upon my work.

In the selection of words, my object has been to insert only those, spelt in more than one way, which are likely to be met with in *general* reading: to deal, in fact, with what are briefly called 'duplicate spellings'. I was compelled to omit many special, unusual, or technical, words and phrases, so that the book might be handy in size.

Where a choice has been made between two or more forms of any word, it should not be concluded that I consider the other forms wrong, but merely that the weight of evidence has led me to select the one given.

Many foreign words and phrases are included on account of the frequent mistakes that are made with the accents. The translations given are usually free ones; literal renderings being generally omitted as often obvious, and as less practically useful. In a few cases an endeavour has been made to correct popular misapprehensions: thus *cui bono?* does not, except in modern incorrect usage, mean 'What is the good of it?' I have also added the pronunciation of some words which are frequently mispronounced. A cursory glance through the book will reveal other special features on which it is unnecessary to dwell: such as the sizes of type, books, and paper; the explanation of printing terms; punctuation; and the spelling of place-names.

That more than twenty thousand separate entries, containing more than one hundred thousand words, and many of these not easily spelt, should have survived without any error, is more than can be hoped for.

It has been a great advantage to have had the proofs read by natives of other countries than England, for they have not only checked the words in their own language, but have also shown where, while the meaning was clear to an Englishman, it was not necessarily so to a foreigner.

The question as to the use of capital or small initial letters for many words was a constant source of trouble during the preparation of the book, for no English authority—not even the *Oxford English Dictionary*—seems specially to have dealt with this point.

Many criticisms may be passed on the different treatment of nearly allied words in the following pages: why one should be hyphened and the other not; or why one should be in italic type and the other in roman. May I, however, point out that the present is *not* an attempt to rationalize the English language, but merely an endeavour to represent the language as it is now used by the people most capable of writing it?

A few observations are called for with reference to the general adoption throughout the book of the suffix *-ize* in place of *-ise*; though the latter is much used. The main reason is, that *-ize* is the form adopted by the Editors of the *Oxford English Dictionary*—the best authority in England.

The general rule for the division of words— 'Never separate a group of letters representing a single sound; and so divide a word that each part retains its present sound'—is the result of a large correspondence on this one point alone. Contrary to what might be supposed, the greater the knowledge of etymology possessed by the writer, the more he would seem to favour this division by sound. As this matter has at first to be dealt with by the compositor alone—for the author cannot tell when writing the copy what word will need division—it is singularly fortunate that so easy a rule, requiring no etymological knowledge, can be framed. The case for the phonetic division of words has been ably put by Professor Skeat: 'The rule for the division of words is not "the rule of the root" by any means, but the rule of the sound or pronunciation. It is much best to ignore the root and go by the sound. Thus it is usual to make such divisions as are seen in impu-dence, solilo-quize, peru-sal, counte-nance, plea-sure, princi-pal; in perfect contempt of the root-forms, which are respectively pud-, loqu-, us-, ten-, plac-, cap-. We simply regard the utterance, writing pe-ruse at one moment and pe-ru-sal at another. Nothing is gained by pretending to keep the root intact, when the spoken utterance does nothing of the kind.'

While probably no one will agree with everything contained in this book, I hope it may be found that the number of marginal notes needed to bring it into accordance with the views of those who use it will be as few as could be expected, considering the difficulty of the subject-matter, and the fact that it is, I believe, the first time it has been thoroughly and systematically investigated in any country.

F. HOWARD COLLINS

1905

AUTHOR AND PRINTER[1]

THE effect of the rise of manufacturing and other
costs upon the book trade is a matter of very
general speculation and concern. Those especially
who are interested in the production of learned
books, technical books, and all books which command a limited market, are asking how such books
are to be published, and how the impoverished
professional man is to buy them. If it were assumed
that the purchasing powers of this class were
stationary, which is a sanguine view, and that the
cost of production were, or might be, no more than
twice what it was, it should still seem that production would be halved and the price (of so many
hundred pages) doubled. For there are only two
ways in which the cost of a book can be substantially
reduced: by increase in the number of copies
printed and sold, or by reduction of bulk. It is
probable, indeed, that the English-reading public
will accustom itself to flimsy, perhaps even to paper
bindings; and the public will certainly have to put
up with smaller and closer type, narrower margins,
fewer pictures. But such economies, though not unimportant, will not make any vital difference. You
cannot make books cheap by making them nasty.
The necessity for limiting prices can only be met
by greater popularity or by fewer words. Novels,
accordingly, may be expected to be shorter, less
numerous, and more widely advertised. It is
enormously more profitable to all concerned to sell

---

[1] This article by Dr. R. W. Chapman, then Secretary to the
Delegates of the Press at Oxford, was first published in the
Athenaeum, 16 July 1920, and was reprinted in Collins's *Authors'
and Printers' Dictionary* in the fifth (1921) and subsequent
editions. It refers to the basic principles of book-production
which, even fifty years after it was written, still hold good in
the main.

one article in tens of thousands than many articles in hundreds; and even before the war it is known that some retailers offered the public nothing but the best-sellers of the season.

But there were very many books, addressed to a public limited and incapable of rapid or artificial expansion, which it was yet possible to publish without subvention and without risk of serious loss. These are books of which the future is doubtful: books on the sciences; books for doctors, chemists, and lawyers; biographies; historical treatises; critical editions of the classics, English and foreign; school-books which must take their chance in free competition with numerous rivals. The prices of such books cannot be advanced beyond a point without ultimate injury to their sale or reduction of their number.

If the effect of economic pressure is to make authors study compression, and readers, attention, the gain will be great. The prolixity of modern writing, fostered by cheap paper and print, by the habit of making books out of articles and lectures, by the use of typewriters and stenographers, is a positive evil; and it has so reacted upon most readers that they have become incapable of assimilating close thought or a terse style.

These are grave ills and heroic remedies. The purpose of the present article is to call attention to some minor palliatives, the application of which may be assisted by information in some degree technical. When an author has made a book, he may study economy in his preparation of the printer's copy and in his treatment of the printer's proof; and these things he often performs indifferently from lack of knowledge which might be made more accessible. Knowledge, however, is not all; some change of heart is required. We have grown accustomed to write so fast, and to supply copy at so short notice, that we are not disposed to treat as a grave responsibility the committal of manuscript to be set up. As such, however, it must be considered. The operation of setting type has always been very much more laborious and costly than that of copying and recopying manuscript or typescript; and it is now more than ever imperative that the writers of learned and scientific books should in their own and their colleagues' interest aim at finality in the copy they furnish to the printer. Books exist which give useful hints on points of typography, such as the use of italic and capitals and the conventional signs used by printers. But with most of these experienced authors are familiar; what is wanted is the resolution to make copy which can be easily set and which will not reveal incongruities and obscurities when exposed to the stronger light which beats upon the printed page. Authors sometimes plead in extenuation that their writings 'look different' when they are printed; but it requires no great mental agility to perceive that a printer must be shown where a paragraph is to begin or a footnote be placed, and that though he may safely enough be left in charge of spelling and punctuation, he must not be expected to make references or abbreviations uniform. A book is not set by a single compositor.

Typewriting is to be recommended not so much because it facilitates the compositor's task as because it approximates more nearly than manuscript to the regularity and uniformity of print; and so enables most writers to view what they have written with a more synoptic eye and to grasp more readily the relation of chapters and paragraphs. But there are other and cheaper tests of good copy. Sentences will bear printing if they will bear reading aloud; transpositions and inter-lineations can be made clear if the writing is not cramped; and it is as easy to italicize references in manuscript as in typescript or in proof. A golden rule is never to spare paper. In a book of any complexity the important thing is that the arrangement should be clear; and nothing is so destructive of clearness as economy in paper. If only one side is used, and ample space left for revision between the lines and in the margin, there is room for alteration, and even for transposition and interlineation, without serious loss of clarity. A manuscript so prepared can, if necessary, be easily read and marked by a second eye, and the compositor's path made smooth. If copy is crabbed, so that it cannot be read without an effort, there is always a temptation to fling it at the printer and see what happens.

Footnotes, it may be mentioned, are in small type, and therefore set by a different compositor. They should be written on the same page as the text (otherwise mistakes in placing them are likely to be made), but at the foot of the page, and clearly marked.

Authors are often unnecessarily costly in their proof correction because they do not understand what kinds of alteration are more or less expensive. In general, correction, if necessary at all, should be regarded as a necessary evil. An author who is tempted by the specious mutability of a printed proof should ask himself, when verbal changes occur, whether the gain in point or elegance is worth the human labour it will occasion.

If a correction is irresistible, it should be considered what will be its result. Even an apparently trifling addition often produces in closely set type a dislocation which ends only with the paragraph, and therefore means shifting hundreds of minute pieces of metal. If the paragraph ends with a full line, the addition may mean a whole new line, and so involve shifting one line from each page to the next until the end of a chapter brings relief. (Meanwhile the page-references in the index are perhaps going wrong; or a footnote may be on the wrong page.) Such dislocation could often be restricted if an author would be careful to make compensatory changes where necessary: it is not difficult, by counting letters and spaces, to guess how much should be removed to make room for an insertion. There are other possibilities: a line may be saved by 'running on' footnotes, by stealing space between quotations, paragraph-headings, or the like. Authors very seldom do this, because they hardly know how; the printer does not complain, because correction is in the day's work and is paid for like the rest; the publisher indeed has an interest in removing costly misunderstandings, and often does intervene; but problems of this kind are unimportant taken singly, and are not readily solved by correspondence.

More serious dislocation is caused by more extensive addition, deletion, or transposition. Suppose that a chapter extends from page 1 to page 20, the next chapter beginning a fresh page, and that a new paragraph is added on page 2. If the new paragraph occupies no more space than the blank on page 20, the correction will affect one chapter only; but it will affect every page of that chapter, in the same way as the intrusive line imagined above, but in a greater degree. This is called *overrunning*.

If, again, the new paragraph is so long that the chapter bursts its banks and overflows on to page 21, then the next chapter will have to begin on page 22 instead of on page 21; and page 23 (the old 22) will, e.g., be found to have the right-hand headline when it should have the left-hand; and every page to the end of the book will have to be moved on. This is a process less simple than shuffling sheets of paper; to understand it, it is necessary to reflect how a book is printed. If the reader will take a piece of paper, fold it three times as an octavo sheet is folded, number the pages from 1 to 16, and then flatten it out again, he will have on each side a map, as it were, of the forme of type, containing eight pages locked together with 'furniture', from which one side of the sheet is printed. In the example supposed, pages 21–32 have to be converted into 22–33 (limiting the problem to the first sheet exploded). Now of these pages, 21, 24, 25, 28, 29, and 32 belong to one forme, pages 22, 23, 26, 27, 30, and 31 to the other. To reconstitute the sheet both formes will have to be broken up, the type pages transferred and rearranged; and since each page is made up of thousands of pieces of lead in unstable equilibrium,[1] the chances of disturbance or loss are such that when the shock is over a reader must go through the whole and make good any damage. This is *reimposition*. All these processes mean the passage from one to another department of the printing house not only of the proof, but of the type; 16 pages of small octavo weigh half a hundredweight.

The practice of giving the author slip or galley proof is designed to mitigate such disturbances. If the author makes his additions and subtractions before the book is paged (and confines his alterations to that stage), the result is certainly much more expensive than if he had finished his book before he sent it to press; two bites have been made of his cherry, and all the elaboration of records and correspondence doubled; the new 'matter' has to be set up and put in its place, read by the readers

---

[1] The principle holds good whether Monotype setting has been used, as envisaged by Chapman; Linotype or Intertype slug-composition; or filmsetting.

and by the author, and two if not three stages of revision by all concerned are substituted for one. At least, however, the disintegrating consequences are avoided of the addition of fresh paragraphs to paged or 'made-up' proof. Many authors unfortunately, having grasped that slips can be added to or shuffled, infer that any kind of correction is venial on slips. But it should be obvious that if the area affected is the paragraph, slips are in no way different from pages. The cost of verbal corrections is the same.

Authors would doubtless treat a proof with more respect if they realized that type-setting is not a purely mechanical act. Words do not arrange themselves; about a quarter of the compositor's time is spent in spacing his letters, after he has picked them up and placed them in order; and a well-set page, in which the spacing strikes the eye as uniform, is a work of art. To disturb it for a trifle is injurious as well as costly.

In a perfect world, perhaps the author would pay for his own corrections—those, that is, that are due to his own taste and not to the error of the printer. (It may be mentioned that printers are entitled to charge, and do charge, for pardonable misreading of an author's illegible copy; and that the term 'printer's error' is far too often applied by authors and the public to such misreadings, not detected in revision, and even to palpable mistakes which could not possibly be due to the compositor.) But it is impossible to determine when a compositor is justified in misreading copy; and for other reasons it is impracticable to make the author pay. Publishers therefore expect to pay something beyond the bare cost of composition; and to protect themselves against incompetence or wantonness they are accustomed to stipulate that a certain limit shall not be exceeded. Unfortunately this precaution, like that of slips, is often interpreted as an indulgence, and an author thinks that if he does not exceed his limit he is free to correct as he pleases. It is very desirable that his conscience should be educated. It should be a point of honour not to inflict upon printer and publisher the burden of irritating afterthoughts and infirm vacillations.

R. W. CHAPMAN

1920

STRESS AND PRONUNCIATION

WHEN necessary these have been indicated in the following way:

The stressed syllable is followed by a stress-mark, e.g. noo'gah (nougat).

Vowel sounds have the value shown by the roman-type letters in: māte, mēte, mīte, mōte, mūte, mo͞ot; răck, rĕck, rĭck, rŏck, rŭck, ro͝ok; caw, cow; bah, boil.

Vowel-combinations with r (the r is not trilled before a consonant or mute e) are as follows:

mār̄e, mēr̄e, mīr̄e, mōr̄e, demūr̄e, moor; dowry; part, pert, port.

Italicized vowels or vowel-combinations have the indistinct sound shown in again, moment, admiral, morose, support, certain, connoisseur, comfort, jealous, murder. ö and ü are used with their German values.

Each consonant or consonant-combination has only one sound; the value of ambiguous or specially used ones is:

ch as in *loch*; **dh** as in *dhen* (= then); **g** as in *get*; **j** as in *jet*; **ng** as in *singer*; **ngg** as in *finger*; **n-g** as in *un-gardĭd* (= unguarded); **r** as in *rat* (and see vowel-combinations above); **s** as in *sister*; **th** as in *thinketh*; **tsh** as in *tship* (= chip); **w** as in *wit* (and see vowel sounds above); **y** as in *yet*; **zh** as in *fūzhn* (= fusion).

A

A, adult (motion-picture certificate), ampere, argon (no point, *now usually* Ar), *avancer* (on timepiece regulator), the first in a series.

A., Academician, Academy, Acting (rank), alto, amateur, anna, artillery, all proper names beginning with this initial.

a., accepted (Fr. *accepté,* Ger. *acceptiert*), on bills of exchange; acre, active, area.

a, *not* **an,** before all words beginning with a consonant (except silent *h*), or with the *sound* of *w* or *y,* as: a eulogy, a euphony, a European, a ewe, a ewer, a herb, -al, a hope, a horse, a hospital, a humble, a one, a oneness, a unanimous, a unicorn, a uniform, a union, a unison, a unit, a univers/e, -al, -ity, a useful, a usurper. *See also* **'an,** *not* **a'.**

Ä, ä, in German, may *not* be replaced by *Ae, ae* (except in some proper names), *A, a,* or *Æ, æ.* The first only of two vowels takes the Umlaut sign, as *äu.*

Å, ångström, q.v.

å, the 'Swedish *a*', used in Scandinavian words, chiefly Norwegian and Swedish, widely interchangeable with *aa,* and pronounced *aw.*

@, at, the 'commercial *a*' used in quoting prices; also as = *from,* in designating sailing of ship.

A₀ ('A nought' or 'A zero'), paper size. *See* **DIN**

A 1, 'first-class' ships in 'Lloyd's Registers'; *see* **Lloyd's.**

A.A., anti-aircraft, Associate in Arts, Automobile Association.

A.A.A., Amateur Athletic Association, American Automobile Association.

A.A.C., *anno ante Christum* (in the year before Christ) (s.caps.).

A.A.C.C.A., Associate of the Association of Certified and Corporate Accountants.

Aachen, Aix-la-Chapelle.

A.A.F., Auxiliary Air Force (till 1957), (U.S.) Army Air Force.

A.A.G., Assistant Adjutant-General.

A.A.I.A., Associate of the Association of International Accountants.

A.A.M.I., Association of Assistant Mistresses, Incorporated (usu. called **A.A.M.**). *See also* **I.A.A.M.**

A. & M., (Hymns) Ancient and Modern.

A. & S. H., Argyll and Sutherland Highlanders.

a.a.O. (Ger.), *am angeführten Orte* (at the place quoted).

A.A.R., against all risks (Ins.).

A.A.S., *Academiae Americanae Socius,* Fellow of the American Academy of Arts and Sciences.

A.A.U. (U.S.), Amateur Athletic Union.

A.B., *Artium Baccalaureus* (Bachelor of Arts); able-bodied [seaman], Army Book.

A.B.A., Amateur Boxing Association, American Bankers' Association, American Bar Association, Association of British Archaeologists.

A.B.A.A., Associate of British Association of Accountants and Auditors.

ab (Lat.), from.

abac/us, *pl.* **-i,** counting-frame, (arch.) plate at top of column.

abalone, shellfish.

ab ante (Lat.), from before.

à bas (Fr.), down with.

abattoir, slaughter-house.

abattu/ (Fr.), *fem.* *-e,* dejected.

abb., abbess, abbey, abbot.

abbé (Fr. m.), title (not ital.).

Abbotsinch Airport, Glasgow.

abbr., abbreviat/ed, -ion.

abbreviat/e, -or.

abbreviation, in Fr. *abré-*.

abbreviations. See the many instances in this book for rulings in individual cases. Subject to these, the following leading types may be noted for guidance:

(*a*) With points, denoting shortening of a word to less than its full form: O.U.P., Esq. This is standard practice.

(*b*) Where last letter of word is retained in short form (contraction) point is sometimes omitted (Mr, Dr for Mister, Doctor) but this is not O.U.P. practice.

(*c*) Without points, as in: mathematical and scientific symbols and abbreviations (mm, Hg); 1st, 2nd, 3rd, 4th, etc.; 4to, 8vo (quarto, octavo); letters not forming abbreviations of anything (*ABC Guide*); Mme, Mlle, Ste, and some others, following French usage; groups of initials pronounced as a word (NATO, Unesco).

(*d*) With one point, not several: MS., MSS. (manuscript(s)); NE., NNW. and all points of the compass (unless otherwise ordered);

PS., PSS. (postscript(s)); ME. (Middle English), OHG. (Old High German), and other specialist forms.

(*e*) Where points would be used according to (*a*), (*b*) and (*d*) above they may be omitted in certain types of work, e.g.: ARIBA, MSIA in publications connected with architecture and industrial artists; KCMG, DSO, OBE, and other honorifics in publications where these occur frequently (often set in small capitals); MA, DD, BSc, and other degrees in publications of some universities and other bodies; Mr, Dr, also Esq in general contexts where specified by typographer or designer. Such omission of normally used points should be limited to definite types of work and within them should be done consistently.

ABC, the alphabet.

A.B.C., Aerated Bread Company('s shop), Argentina, Brazil, and Chile, (U.S.) Audit Bureau of Circulation, Australian Broadcasting Commission.

A.B.C.A., Army Bureau of Current Affairs, *now* **B.C.A.,** Bureau of Current Affairs.

ABC Guide (no points).

A.B.D.A., American–British–Dutch–Australian Command in the Pacific area during Second World War.

abdicat/e, -or.

abecedarian (U.S.), pupil learning alphabet.

à Becket (Thomas), 1118?–70, Abp. (one *t*).

Abendlied (Ger.), evening song (cap.).

Abercrombie, Fife.

Abercromby, Lancs.

Aberdeen Angus (two caps.).

Aberdeen terrier (one cap.).

Aberdonian, (native) of Aberdeen.

Abergavenny, (town) Monmouth, *pron.* as spelt, (title) *pron.* Abergenny.

Abernethy, Inverness and Perth.

Abernethy biscuit (one cap.).

Aberystwyth, Wales, *not* -ith.

abest (Lat.), he, she, *or* it, is absent; *pl.* **absunt.**

abett/er, in law -**or.**

ab extra (Lat.), from outside.

abgk., abk., abgekürzt (Ger.) = abbreviated.

Abhandlungen (Ger. f. pl.), Transactions (of a Society); abbr. *Abh.*

abigail, lady's-maid.

abiit/ ad plures or — ad majores (Lat.), he, *or* she, has gone to the majority; is dead; *pl.* **abierunt — —.**

Abilene, Tex., U.S.

ab incunabulis (Lat.), from the cradle.

Abingdon, Berks. and Va., U.S.

Abington, Northants., Lanark, Limerick, and Mass., U.S.

ab/ initio (Lat.), from the beginning, abbr. *ab init.*; *— intra,* from within.

à bis **(ou)** *à blanc* (Fr.), one way or another.

Abl., Abril (Sp.), April.

abl., ablative.

ablaut, variation in root vowel.

-able (the suffix). Words ending in silent *-e* tend to drop the *e* before *-able*, as conceivable, debatable. It is retained when it serves to prevent the modification of the preceding consonant, as changeable, peaceable. In practice the following words also often retain the *e*: blameable, giveable,

hireable, likeable, nameable, rateable, saleable, sizeable, tameable, unshakeable. See the list in *Hart's Rules,* p. 76.

A-bomb (no point, hyphen).

à bon/ compte (Fr.), cheaply, at a low estimate; *— — droit,* with justice; *— — marché,* cheap.

aboriginal (adj.), indigenous (with init. cap, in tech. sense in Australia); **Aborigin/es** (pl. noun, sing. -**e**) also with init. cap. in Australia.

ab origine (Lat.), from the beginning.

above/-board, *— -mentioned, — -named* (hyphens).

ab ovo (Lat.), from the beginning.

Abp., Archbishop.

abr., abridged, abridgement.

à bras ouverts (Fr.), with open arms.

abrégé (Fr. m.), abridgement.

abréviation (Fr. f.), abbreviation.

abridgement, abbr. **abr.**

abs., absolute(ly), abstract.

abscess.

Abschnitt/ (Ger. typ. m.), section, part, chapter, or division; *pl.* -**e.**

absciss/a (math.), *pl.* -**ae.**

absente reo (Lat.), the defendant being absent; abbr. *abs. re.*

absenter, *not* -**or.**

absent-minded/ (hyphen), -**ness.**

absinth/, a liqueur, in Fr. f. -**e** (U.S. -**e**).

absit/, let him, her, *or* it be absent; *— omen,* let there be no (ill) omen.

absolutely, abbr. **abs.**

absorption, *not* -btion.

abs. re., absente reo, q.v.

abstract, abbr. **abs.**

absurdum (Lat.), absurd.

Abt. (Ger. f.), *Abteilung* (division).

abundance, in Fr. **abond-.**

ab/ uno disce omnes (Lat.), from one (sample) judge the rest; *— urbe condita* (Lat.), **A.U.C.,** from the foundation of Rome, 753 B.C.

Abu Simbel, site of Egyptian rock-temples.

abut/, -ment, -ted, -ting.

abys/s, deep cavity, **-mal.**

abyssal, below 300 fathoms.

Abyssinia, *now* **Ethiopia.**

Ac, actinium (no point).

A.C., Alpine Club, (*or* **A/C**) Aircraftman, Assistant Commissioner.

A.C., *ante Christum* (before Christ) (s.caps.).

A/C, current account.

a.c., alternating current, author's correction; in Fr. *année courante* (current year).

a/c, account; in printing use **acct.**

A.C.A., Associate of the Institute of Chartered Accountants in England and Wales; (*or* Ireland).

Academician, abbr. **A.**

Académie française.

Academy, a learned body; abbr. **A.,** *or* **Acad.** (cap.).

Academy, the, the Platonic school of philosophy.

Acadian, Nova Scotian (Fr. **Acadie**).

a capite ad calcem (Lat.), completely.

a cappella (It.) (mus.), unaccompanied.

A.C.C., Army Catering Corps.

acc., acceptance (bill), accusative.

accabl/é (Fr.), *fem.* **-ée,** overwhelmed.

Accademia (It.), Academy.

acced/e, -er.

accedence, a giving consent.

accelerando (mus.), accelerating; abbr. *accel.*

accelerat/e, -or.

accents and other diacritical marks: acute (´), grave (`), circumflex (ˆ); vowels, long (¯), short (˘), doubtful (˟); diaeresis (¨); cedilla (ç); umlaut (¨); Gr. breathings: asper, rough (’), lenis, smooth (’); Arabic *'ain,* Hebrew *'ayin* (‘), Arabic *hamza,* Hebrew *aleph* (’), ancient Egyptian special sign ‘.

Also: Albanian ç.

Czech č, š, ž; d', ě, ň, ř, ť; ů; ý; (and Slovak l').

Danish å, ø.

Estonian õ or ô; š, ž.

French ç (cedilla).

Hungarian ő, ű (ö, ü lengthened).

Latvian č, š, ž; g', k', l', n', r', sometimes written ģ, ķ, ļ, ņ, ŗ.

Lithuanian ą, ę, į, ų (nasal vowels); č, š, ž; ė.

Norwegian å.

Polish ą, ę (nasal vowels); ć, ń, ś, ź; Ł, ł; ż.

Portuguese ã, õ; ç (comma, not cedilla).

Romanian ă; ş, ţ (commas).

Serbo-Croat ć; č, ž, š; Đ, đ.

Spanish ñ (tilde).

Swedish å.

accep^on, acceptation (Fr.), acceptance (bill).

acceptance, abbr. **acc.**

accept/er, in law **-or.**

accessary (noun *or* adj.), (strictly) (one) privy to an act; *but see* **accessory.**

accessible.

access/it (Lat.), he, she, *or* it, came near; *pl.* **-erunt.**

accessory (noun *or* adj.), (strictly) accompanying (detail). But increasingly used for **accessary.**

acciaccatura (mus.), a grace-note.

accidence, inflexions of words.

accidental (mus.).

accidie, acedia, listlessness.

acclimatize, *not* -ise (U.S. also **acclimate**).

accolade.

accommodate (two *c*'s, two *m*'s).

accompanist, *not* -yist.

accordion, *not* -eon.

accouche/ment, -ur, -use (not ital.).

account, abbr. **a/c**; in printing use **acct.**

Accountant-General, abbr. **A.G.**

Accra, Ghana, *not* Akkra.

accroch/é (Fr.), *fem.* **-ée,** hooked, brought to a deadlock.

A.C.C.S., Associate of the Corporation of Certified Secretaries.

acct., account, *or* account current.

accumulat/e (two *c*'s), **-or.**

accusative, abbrs. **acc., accus.**

A.C.E., after Christian era (Jewish usage in place of A.D.)

ac etiam (Lat.), and also.

acetic (acid).

A.C.F., Automobile Club de France; Army Cadet Force.

A.C.G.B., Arts Council of Great Britain.

A.C.G.B.I., Automobile Club of Great Britain and Ireland.

A.C.G.I., Associate of the City and Guilds of London Institute.

Achaemenes, *not* Achai-.

Acheson (Dean Gooderham), 1893–1971, U.S. diplomat.

à cheval (Fr.), on horseback.

Achin, Sumatra, Indonesia, *not* Atchin.

Achnashellach, Ross.

A.C.I. (Fr.), *assuré contre l'incendie* (insured against fire).

A.C.I., Army Council Instruction.

A.C.I.A., Associate of the Corporation of Insurance Agents.

A.C.I.B., Associate of the Corporation of Insurance Brokers.

A.C.I.I., Associate of the Chartered Insurance Institute.

acknowledgement, *not* -ledgment.

acolyte, *not* -ite.

à/ compte (Fr.), in part payment; — *corps perdu* (Fr.), desperately.

acoustics, (noun sing.) the science of sound, (noun pl.) acoustic properties.

à couvert (Fr.), protected.

A.C.P., Associate of the College of Preceptors; Association of Correctors of the Press, now part of **N.G.A.,** q.v.

acquit/, -tal, -tance.

Acra, *use* **Accra.**

Acre, Palestine, *not* Acca, Accho, Acco.

acre, abbr. **a.**

acre (Fr. f.), acre.

âcre (Fr.), acrid.

Acrilan, regd. trade mark (cap.).

acronym, word formed from initials, as Anzac, q.v.

act., active.

A.C.T., Australian Capital Territory.

Actaeon, a mythical hunter.

acte d'accusation (Fr. m.), indictment.

Actini/a (zool.), *pl.* **-ae.**

actinium, symbol Ac (no point).

actinomy/ces (bot.), *pl.* **-cetes.**

actionnaire (Fr. m.), a shareholder.

active, abbrs. **a., act.**

actor (person), *but* **one-acter** (play).

acts of a play (typ.), cap. A only when the number

acts of a play (*cont.*):
follows, as *Hamlet*, Act I, sc. ii.
See also **authorities**.

Acts of Parliament (cap. A),
cited thus: Factory and
Workshop Act, 1891; use
arabic figures for chapter
numbers in Public (General)
and Private Acts (e.g. 3 & 4
Geo. V, c. 12, ss. 18, 19)
and lower-case roman
numerals in Public (Local)
Acts (e.g. 3 & 4 Geo. V,
c. xii, ss. 18, 19). See also
Hart's Rules, pp. 50–2.

Acts of Sederunt (Scots law).

Acts of the Apostles, abbr.
Acts (no point).

actualité (Fr. f.), present state.

actuel/ (Fr.), *fem. -le*, present.

actum/ agere (Lat.), to do
what has been already done;
— *est*, it is all over.

acute accent (´).

A.C.W., Aircraftwoman.

A.D. (*anno Domini*) should
always be placed *before* the
figures; B.C. *after* (s.caps.).

a.d., *ante diem* (before the day).

a.d., after date.

ad., adapted, adapter,
advertisement.

adagio (mus.), slow.

Adam's Peak, Ceylon.

ad amussim (Lat.), exactly.

adapt/able, -er (person), **-or**
(elec.).

ad/ arbitrium (Lat.), at
pleasure; — *astra*, to the
stars.

a dato (Lat.), from date.

A.D.C., aide-de-camp.

ad/ captandum vulgus
(Lat.), to catch the rabble,
claptrap; — *clerum*, to the
clergy; — *crumenam*, to
the purse.

Addams (Jane), 1860–1935,
American social worker and
writer.

addend/um, something to be
added; *pl.* **-a** (not ital.).

addio (It.), good-bye.

Addis Ababa, capital of
Ethiopia.

additive, (something) in the
nature of an addition.

addorsed (her.), *not* adorsed,
adossed.

adduc/ible, *pref. to* -eable.

Adélie Land, Antarctica.

à demi (Fr.), by halves.

Adenauer (Konrad),
1876–1967, German
statesman, Chancellor of
W. Germany 1949–63.

à dessein (Fr.), on purpose.

ad eundem (gradum)
(Lat.), to the same degree at
another university.

à deux/ (Fr.), of (or between)
two; — *mains*, with
both hands; — *temps*
(*see* valse, etc.).

ad/ extra (Lat.), in an
outward direction; —
extremum, to the last;
— *finem*, near the end,
abbr. **ad fin.**; — *gustum*,
to the taste; — *hoc*, for this
(object); — *hominem*, to
the [interests of the] man;
— *hunc locum*, on this
passage, abbr. *a.h.l.*; —
idem, to the same (point).

a die (Lat.), from that day.

adieu/, *pl.* **-x** (not ital.).

ad/ infinitum (Lat.), to
infinity, *pron.* in-fĭ-nī′tum;
— *interim*, meanwhile,
abbr. **ad int.**; —
internecionem, to
extermination.

adiós (Sp.), adieu.

Adirondack Mountains
(U.S.), *not* -dac.

à discrétion (Fr.), at
discretion.

Adj., Adjutant.

Adj.-Gen., Adjutant-General.

adjectiv/e, abbr. **adj.**; **-al**,
-ally (now more common
than **-ely**).

adjudicator, *not* -er.

adjutage, a nozzle, *not* aj-;
in Fr. *ajoutage* (f.).

Adjutant/, abbr. **Adj.** (rank, cap.); **-General**, abbr. **A.-G.**, or **Adj.-Gen.**

adjuvant.

ad kalendas Graecas (Lat.), never.

Adler (Alfred), 1870–1937, Austrian psychologist.

ad/libitum (Lat.), at pleasure, abbr. *ad lib.*; — *litem*, for a suit.

ad locum, at the place, abbr. **ad loc.** (not ital.).

Adm., Admiral, Admiralty.

ad manum (Lat.), ready.

administrat/or, abbr. **admor.**; **-rix**, abbr. **admix.**

Admiral/, in Fr. *amir/al*, *pl.* **—**, **-ty**, abbr. **Adm.**

Admiralty, the, abbr. **Adm.**; *see* **M.o.D.**

admiration (note of), exclamation mark, ! *See* **punctuation** VII.

ad misericordiam (Lat.), appealing to pity.

admiss/ible, *not* -able.

admix., administratrix.

ad modum (Lat.), after the manner of.

admonitor/, *not* -er; **-y.**

admor., administrator.

ad nauseam (Lat.), to a sickening degree.

ado, work, trouble (one word).

adobe (Sp.), (U.S.) sun-dried brick.

Adonai (Heb.), the Lord.

Adonais, Keats, in Shelley's elegy, 1821.

Adonis (myth.), beloved of Venus.

adopter, *not* -or.

adorsed, *use* add-.

ad/ patres (Lat.), dead; — *quod damnum*, to what damage; — *refer- endum*, for further consideration; — *rem*, to the point.

adrenal/in, *not* -ine.

adresse (Fr. f.), address.

à droite (Fr.), to the right.

adscititious, *not* asci-.

adscriptus glebae (Lat.), bound to the soil (of serfs).

adsorb, adsorption, condensing, condensation, of gases on surface of solid.

adsum (Lat.), I am present.

ad summum (Lat.), to the highest point.

a due (It.), in two parts.

adulator, *not* -er.

ad/ unguem (Lat.), perfectly; — *unum omnes*, all, to a man; — *usum*, according to custom, abbr. *ad us.*

adv., adverb, -ially, advocate.

adv., *adversus* (against).

ad valorem (Lat.), according to value; abbr. *ad val.*

advancement.

adverb/, **-ially**, abbr. **adv.**

ad verbum (Lat.), to a word, verbally.

adversaria (Lat. pl.), jottings.

adversus (Lat.), against; abbr. *adv.*

advertise, *not* -ize.

advertisement, abbr. **ad.**, or **advt.**, *pl.* **ads.**, or **advts.**; in Fr. f. *annonce.*

advis/er, *not* -or; **-ory.**

ad/ vitam aut culpam (Lat.), for lifetime or until fault; — *vivum*, lifelike.

advocaat, liqueur.

advocate, abbr. **adv.**

Advocates (Faculty of), the Bar of Scotland.

advocatus diaboli (Lat.), an adverse critic (not ital.).

advt/., **-s.**, advertisement, -s.

A. E. *or* **AE** (originally Æ), pen-name of George Russell (1867–1935).

Æ, 'third-class' ships in 'Lloyd's Register'; in numismatics = copper (Lat. *aes*).

æ (ligature), *see* **diphthongs.**

A.E.A., Atomic Energy Authority.

A.E.C., Army Educational Corps, (U.S.) Atomic Energy Commission.

aedile, *not* e-.

Aegean Sea, the eastern part of the Mediterranean.

aegis, a shield, protection, *not* e-.

aegrot/*at* (Lat.), he, she is ill (certificate that exam. candidate is ill); *pl.* *-ant.*

Aemilius.

Aeneas; *Aeneid.*

Aeolian, Aeolic (caps.).

aeon, *pref.* to eon.

aepyornis (zool.), *not* epi-, epy-.

aequales (Lat.), equal (pl. adj.), (pl. noun) equals (in age or performance); abbr. *aeq.*

aequo animo (Lat.), with an equable mind.

A.E.R.A., Associate Engraver, Royal Academy.

aer/*ate,* etc., *-ial, -ify, -obic, -onaut,* *not* aë-.

A.E.R.E., Atomic Energy Research Establishment.

aerie, *see* **eyrie.**

aerodrome (U.S. and increasingly Brit., **airfield**).

aero-elastic (hyphen).

aerofoil.

aeronaut/, **-ical.**

aeroplane (U.S. **airplane**), tending to be superseded by **aircraft.**

aerosol.

Aerospace (Minister for) (one word).

aes/ *alienum* (Lat.), debt; *— triplex,* a strong defence.

Aeschylus, Greek playwright.

Aesculapi/*us, -an.*

Aesop.

aesthete, etc. (U.S. e-).

aestiv/*al, -ation* (U.S. e-).

aet. or *aetat.,* *anno aetatis suae* (of age, aged).

aether, in all meanings *use* **e-.**

aetiology (U.S. e-).

Aetna, *use* **Etna.**

A.F., Air France.

A.F.A., Associate of the Faculty of Actuaries.

A.F.A.S., Associate of the Faculty of Architects and Surveyors.

A.F.C., Air Force Cross.

aff., affirmative, affirming.

affaire/ *d'amour* (Fr. f.), love affair; *— de cœur,* affair of the heart; *— d'honneur,* duel.

affettuoso (mus.), with feeling.

affiche/*e* (Fr. f.), placard, poster; *-é,* posted up.

affidavit, abbr. **afft.**

affil/*é* (Fr.), sharp; *-ié,* affiliated.

affranchise, *not* -ize.

affreu/*x,* *fem.* **-se** (Fr.), frightful.

afft., affidavit.

Afghanistan, abbr. **Afghan.**

aficionado (Sp.), enthusiast for sport or hobby.

afield (one word).

A.F.L.–C.I.O. American Federation of Labor and Congress of Industrial Organizations.

A.F.M., Air Force Medal.

à fond/ (Fr.), thoroughly; *— de train,* at full speed;

à forfait, by contract.

a fortiori (Lat.), with stronger reason, *not* à — (ital.).

Afr., Africa, -n.

A.F.R.Ae.S., Associate Fellow of the Royal Aeronautical Society.

Africander, inferior form of **Afrikaner,** Afrikaans-speaking S. African; also S. African breed of cattle; *not* Afrikander.

Afridi, race of Cent. Asia.

Afrikaans, S. African Dutch language, abbr. **Afrik.**

Afrikander, *use* **Africander** *or* **Afrikaner.**

Afrikaner, *not* -kander.

afternoon, abbr. **aft.,** *or* **p.m.**

afterthought (one word).

afterwards (U.S. **afterward**).

A.F.V., armoured fighting vehicle.

Ag, *argentum* (silver) (no point).

A.G., Accountant-General, Adjutant-General, Agent-General (of Colonies), Air Gunner, Attorney-General.

A.G. (Ger.), *Aktiengesellschaft* (joint-stock company).

Agadah, *use* **Haggadah.**

agape, love-feast, divine love; *pron.* ag'-a-pē.

agate line (U.S.), measure of advertising space, $\frac{1}{14}$ in. deep and one column wide.

à gauche (Fr.), to the left.

ageing (U.S. **agi-**).

agend/um, a thing to be done; *pl.* **-a** (not ital.).

à genoux (Fr.), kneeling.

agent, abbr. **agt.**

Agent-General, abbr. **A.G.**

agent provocateur (Fr.) (ital.).

ages (typ.), to be printed in figures; but 'he died in his fortieth year', and, in literary contexts, 'a man of forty'.

aggrandize, *not* -ise.

aggression, in Fr. f. *agression.*

agitato (mus.), hurried.

agitat/or, *not* -er.

aglet, metal tag, *not* ai-.

agneau (Fr. m.), lamb.

agnostic/, -ism (not cap.).

agonize, *not* -ise.

agouti, S. American rodent, *not* -y, aguti.

agraffe, a clasp; in Fr. f. *agrafe.*

agreeable, in Fr. *agréable.*

agréments (Fr. m.), comforts, (mus.) grace-notes.

agric., agricultur/e, -al, -ist.

agriculturist, *not* -alist.

agrimony (bot.).

agronomy, rural economy.

A.G.S.M., Associate of the Guildhall School of Music.

agt., agent.

Ag^to, Agosto (Sp.), August.

Agulhas, Cape (S. Africa), *not* L'A-.

A.H., *anno Hegirae,* the Muhammadan era (s.caps.). *See* **hegira.**

ah, when it stands alone, takes a mark of exclamation (!). When it forms part of a sentence, it is usually followed by a comma, the ! being placed at the end of the sentence: as 'Ah, no, it cannot be!'

aha, exclam. of surprise. *See* **ha ha.**

à haute voix (Fr.), aloud.

ahimsa (Hind.), non-violence.

a.h.l., *ad hunc locum* (on this passage).

Ahmad/abad, -nagar, India, *not* Ahmed-, Amed-.

A.H.M.I., Association of Headmistresses, Incorporated. *See also* **I.A.H.M.**

Ahriman, Zoroastrian spirit of evil.

a.h.v., *ad hanc vocem* (at this word).

A.I., American Institute, Anthropological Institute, artificial insemination.

A.I.A., Associate of the Institute of Actuaries.

A.I.A.A., Architect Member of the Incorporated Association of Architects and Surveyors.

A.I.A.C., Associate of the Institute of Company Accountants.

A.I.A.S., Surveyor Member of the Incorporated Association of Architects and Surveyors.

A.I.B., Associate of the Institute of Bankers.

A.I.C., Associate of the Institute of Chemistry, *now* **A.R.I.C.**

A.I.C.S., Associate of the Institute of Chartered Shipbrokers.

A.I.D., Army Intelligence Department.

A.I.(D.), artificial insemination (donor).

Aida, opera by Verdi, 1871 (no diaeresis).

aide (Fr. m.), assistant; (f.) help.

aide-de-camp, abbr. **A.D.C.;** *pl.* **aides-** — **-** —.

aide-mémoire (Fr. m.), aid to memory; *pl.* **aides-** —.

aiglet, *use* **aglet.**

aigre/-doux (Fr.), *fem.* — **-douce,** sour-sweet.

aigrette, a spray, *not* ei-, -et (*see also* **egret**).

Ailesbury (**Marquess** *of*) (*see also* **Ayl-**).

A.I.Loco.E., Associate of the Institute of Locomotive Engineers.

aimable (Fr.), amiable.

A.I.Mech.E., Associate of the Institution of Mechanical Engineers.

A.I.Min.E., Associate of the Institution of Mining Engineers.

A.I.M.M., Associate of the Institute of Mining and Metallurgy.

A.I.M.T.A., Associate of the Institute of Municipal Treasurers and Accountants.

ain/é (Fr.), *fem.* **-ée,** elder, senior; opposed to *puîné, fem.* **puînée,** or *cadet/, -te,* younger.

A.Inst.P., Associate of the Institute of Physics.

A.I.Q.S., Associate of the Institute of Quantity Surveyors.

air-blast (hyphen).

airborne (one word).

Air Commodore, abbr. **Air Cdre.** *See also* **Commodore.**

air-condition (verb, hyphen).

aircraft, sing. and pl. (one word).

aircraftman, *not* aircrafts-man.

Aireborough, Yorks.

Airedale, Yorks., and terrier.

Air Force, *see* **Army.**

Air Gunner, abbr. **A.G.**

airline, airmail, (U.S.) **airplane** (no hyphens).

Air Ministry, *see* **M.o.D.**

air noble (Fr. m.), air of distinction

Air (**Point of**), N. Wales. *See also* **Ayre.**

air raid (two words).

air-to-air (adj., hyphen).

A.I.S.A., Associate of the Incorporated Secretaries Association.

ait, *use* **eyot,** except in proper names with Ait.

aitch-bone (hyphen), *not* H-, edge-.

Aix-la-Chapelle (hyphens, *pron.* āks), *properly* **Aachen.**

Aix-les-Bains (hyphens).

Ajaccio, Corsica.

à jamais (Fr.), for ever.

Ajax, *pl.* **Ajaxes.**

ajutage, *use* **adj-.**

A.K.C., Associate of King's College (London).

Akestes, *use* **Acestes.**

akimbo (one word).

Akkra, Ghana, *use* **Accra.**

Aktiengesellschaft (Ger. f.), joint-stock company; abbr. *A.G.*

Al, aluminium (no point).

a.l. (Fr.), *après livraison,* after delivery (of goods).

A.L., autograph letter.

A.L.A., Associate of the Library Association.

Ala., Alabama (off. abbr.).

à la/ belle étoile (Fr.), in the open air; —— **bonne heure!** well and good; —— **campagne,** in the country.

à la carte (a meal) that must be ordered from a list of available dishes (not ital.). *See* **table d'hôte.**

Aladdin, *not* Alladin.

à la/française (Fr.), in the French style (not cap.); —— **grecque,** in the Greek style (not cap.); —— **hauteur de,** on a level with; —— **lettre,** literally; —— **main,** at hand, ready; —— **mode,** in fashion; **à/l'anglaise,** in the English style (not cap.); —— **l'antique,** in the antique style; **à la parisienne,** in the Parisian style (not cap.).

alarm, *not* alarum except, obsolescent, in alarum-clock, -bell, alarums and excursions.

à la russe, in the Russian style (not cap.).

Alas., Alaska.

alas, when it stands alone, takes a mark of exclamation (!). When it forms part of a sentence, it is usually followed by a comma, the ! being placed at the end of the sentence: as, 'Alas, it is true!'

Alb., Albanian.

Alba., Alberta. *Also* **Alta.**

Alban., formerly signature of Bp. of St. Albans (full point).

albatross, *not* -os.

albin/o, *pl.* **-os,** *fem.* **-ess; -ism,** *not* -oism.

Albrighton, Salop.

album/, scrapbook; *pl.* **-s.**

album/en, natural white of egg; **-in,** its chief constituent; *adj.* **-inous.**

Albuquerque, New Mexico, U.S.

Albury, Surrey.

Alcaeus of Mytilene, Greek lyric poet.

Alcaics (cap.), metre.

alcalde (Sp.), magistrate, mayor.

alcatras, large water-bird, as pelican, gannet, albatross.

Alcatraz, U.S. prison, San Francisco Bay, Calif.

alcayde (Sp. *alcaide*), governor, gaoler.

alcázar (Sp.), palace, fortress, bazaar.

Alcestis, *not* Alk-.

Alcibiades, *not* Alk-.

A.L.C.M., Associate of the London College of Music.

Alcoran, *use* **Koran.**

Alcyone (myth.), *not* Hal-.

Aldborough, Norfolk, Yorks.

Aldbrough, Yorks.

Aldbury, Herts.

Aldeburgh, Suffolk.

Alderbury, Wilts.

Alderman, abbr. **Ald.**

Aldermaston, Berks.

Alderney, Channel Isles.

Aldine (adj.), printed by **Manutius,** q.v., who introduced italic type.

Aldis lamp, a hand lamp for signalling.

Aldsworth, Gloucester.

Aldus Manutius, printer, *see* **Manutius.**

Aldworth, Berks.

Alecto (myth.), one of the Furies.

Alectryon (myth.), *pron.* a-lek'trĭ-ōn.

alehouse (one word).

Alençon lace (ç).

à l'espagnole (Fr.), in Spanish fashion (not cap.).

Aleutian Islands, Bering Sea.

Alex., Alexand/er, -ria.

Alexandrian (cap.), of Egyptian Alexandria.

Alexandrine (cap.), metre.

à l'extérieur (Fr.), on the outside.

Alford, Aberdeen, Lincs.

Alfred, abbr. **A.,** or **Alf.**

alfresco (Eng. adj. and adv.) (one word).

Alfreton, Derbys.

Alg., Algernon, Algiers.

alg/a (bot.), pl. **-ae** (not ital.).

algebra, abbr. **alg.** See also **mathematics.**

algology (bot.).

Algonquin (Canada).

alguazil (Sp.), a constable.

Alhambra, Moorish palace at Granada; adj. **alhambresque.**

alia (Lat.), other things.

alias/ (sb.), pl. **-es;** also adv.

alibi/ (sb.), pl. **-s.**

alienator, not -er.

alieni appetens (Lat.), greedy of another's possessions.

Aligarh, Uttar Pradesh, India.

Alighieri, family name of Dante.

align/, -ment, usual, but **aline/, -ment** permissible.

alii (Lat.), other people.

alimentative/, -ness, not alimentive, -ness.

aline/, -ment, see **align.**

alinéa (Fr. m.), paragraph.

à l'intérieur (Fr.), indoors.

Alipore, W. Bengal, distinct from next.

Alipur, W. Bengal and W. Pakistan.

aliquid (Lat.), something, somewhat.

Alitalia, Aerolinee Italiane Internazionali.

ali/us (Lat.), another person; pl. **-i.**

Aliwal, E. Punjab, India, also S. Africa.

alkali/, pl. **-s.**

alkalize, not -ise.

Alkestis, use **Alc-.**

Alkoran, use **Koran.**

Alladin, use **Aladdin.**

Allahabad, Uttar Pradesh, India.

Allah il Allah, corruption of Arab. *la ilaha ill'Allah,* There is no God but God. Muslim prayer and war-cry.

Allahu akbar (Arab.), God is most great.

Allan-a-Dale, minstrel hero.

allargando (mus.), broad, spread out.

alla Tedesca (It.), in the German style.

alla ventura (It.), at a venture.

allée (Fr. f.), alley, avenue.

Allegany, Pennsylvania.

allegement, obs. for **allegation.**

Allegheny, mountains and river, U.S.; but **Allegany,** Pittsburgh, Pa.

allegro (mus.), brisk, merry.

alleluia, Lat. form (also liturgical) for Heb. (and biblical) **hallelujah.**

Allendale, Northumb.

Allen (George) & Unwin, Ltd., publishers.

Allen (W. H.) & Co., Ltd., publishers.

allerg/y, -ic, sensitiveness to certain foods, pollens, etc.

alleviator, not -er.

allez-vous-en! (Fr.), begone! (two hyphens).

All Fools' Day (caps., no hyphen).

allg., allgm., allgemein (Ger.), general (adj.).

All-Hallows, All Saints' Day, 1 Nov. (caps., hyphen).

Allhallows, Kent (one word).

allineation, not alin-.

Allingham (Margery), 1904–66, English novelist.

allons! (Fr.), let us go, come!

allot/, -table, -ted, -ting.

all' ottava (mus.), an octave higher than written; abbr. *all' ott.*

all right, not alright, all-right.

all round ('all round the Wrekin'), prep.

all-round ('an all-round man'), adj.

All/ Saints' Day, 1 Nov.;
— **Souls College,** Oxford
(no apos.); — **Souls' Day,**
2 Nov.; — **Souls' Eve,**
1 Nov. (caps., no hyphens).

allspice (one word).

all together (in a body); *but*
altogether (entirely).

alluvi/um, *pl.* **-a.**

Alma Mater, fostering
mother, one's school or
university.

almanac, *but* '**Oxford**', *also*
'**Whitaker's**', **Almanack.**

Alma Tadema (Sir
Lawrence), 1836–1912,
painter.

Almighty (the) (cap.).

Almondbury, Yorks., *pron.*
ām′bu-rĭ.

Almonsbury, Glos.

Alnmouth, Northumb.

Alnwick, Northumb., *pron.*
ăn′ĭk. *See also* **Anwick.**

A.L.O.E., A Lady of
England (Charlotte M.
Tucker, 1821–93).

alouette (Fr. f.), lark (bird).

à l'outrance should be *à*
outrance, to the bitter end.

aloyau (Fr. m.), sirloin of
beef.

Alpes-Maritimes, dép.
France; abbr. **A.-M.**

Alphaeus, Apostle James's
father.

Alpheus, classical Greek
river.

Alresford, Essex, *pron.*
Ailsford; Hants, *pron.*
Awlsford.

A.L.S., Associate of the
Linnean Society; autograph
letter signed.

Alsace-Lorraine.

Alsirat (Arab.), bridge to
paradise.

alt., alternative, altitude.

Alt., Altesse (Highness).

Alta., Alberta, Canada. *Also*
Alba.

Altenburg, Sachsen-
Altenburg; *but* **Ungarisch-**

Altenburg, *properly*
Magyaróvár, Hungary.

alter/ ego (Lat.), one's
second self; — *idem,*
another self.

Altesse (Fr. f.), Highness;
abbr. *Alt.*

Altezza (It.), Highness.

Althing, the Icelandic
parliament.

Althorpe, Lincs.

Althorp Library and **Park**
(Northants.), *pron.* Awltrop.

altitude, abbr. **alt.**

alto/ (mus.), *pl.* **-s;** abbr. **A.**

alto relievo/, high relief;
pl. **-s;** anglicized version of
It. *alto rilievo.*

aluminium, symbol **Al** (no
point); U.S. **aluminum,**
abbr. **alum.**

alumn/us, *pl.* **-i,** *fem.* **-a,** *pl.*
-ae; abbr. **alum.**

Am, americium (no point).

A.M., Air Ministry, Albert
Medal, *Artium Magister*
(Master of Arts); *Ave Maria*
(Hail, Mary!) (caps.).

A.-M., dép. France, Alpes-
Maritimes.

A.M., *anno mundi* (in the year
of the world) (s.caps.).

a.m., *ante meridiem* (before
noon) (lower case).

A.M.A., Assistant Masters'
Association, officially
I.A.A.M.; American
Medical Association.

amah, child's nurse (in Far
East).

Amalek, *not* -ech, -eck.

amant/ (Fr.), a lover; *pl.* **-s;**
fem. **-e,** *pl.* **-es.**

amantium irae (Lat.),
lovers' quarrels.

amanuens/is, *pl.* **-es.**

amari aliquid (Lat.),
something bitter.

amateur, abbr. **A.**

a maximis ad minima
(Lat.), from the greatest to
the smallest.

Ambala, India, *not* Umballa.

ambergris, waxy substance used in perfumery.

ambiance, French spelling of **ambience** (q.v.), used in English esp. of accessory details in a work of art.

ambidextrous.

ambienc/e, the surroundings (*not -y*). *See* **ambiance.**

ambivalen/t, -ce.

amblyopia, impaired vision.

Amboina, Indon., *properly* **Ambon,** *not* Amboyna.

amboyna (wood).

A.M.D.G., *ad majorem Dei gloriam* (Lat.), for the greater glory of God.

âme/ damnée (Fr.), a 'cat's paw', devoted adherent; — *de boue,* a base, ungenerous spirit.

Amednagar, Bombay, *use* **Ahmad-.**

Ameer, *use* **Amir** for Arabic, **Emir** for Turkish and Indian titles.

amende honorable (Fr. f.), honourable reparation.

a mensa et toro (Lat.), from bed and board, a legal separation, *not — — — thoro.*

âme perdue (Fr.), a desperate character.

Amer., American.

Americanize, *not -ise.*

American joint (bind.), deep groove between board and spine.

America's Cup, the, yachting trophy.

americium (chem.), symbol **Am** (no point).

Amerindian, American Indian.

à merveille (Fr.), perfectly, wonderfully.

A.M.G., Allied Military Government (of Occupied Territory) (Second World War).

amicus curiae (Lat.), a friend of the Court, a disinterested adviser.

Amir, Arab. title, *not* Ameer. *See also* **Emir.**

Ammal (Ind.), suffix used to indicate that a name belongs to a woman, e.g. Dr. E. K. Janaki Ammal.

Ammergau, Bavaria.

amoeb/a, *pl.* **-ae** (not ital.).

à moitié (Fr.), half.

amok, *use* **amuck.**

amor/ patriae (Lat.), love of one's country; — *sceleratus habendi,* accursed love of possessing.

amour propre (Fr.), self-respect, proper pride.

Ampère (A. M.), 1775–1836, French electrician (accent).

ampere, elec. unit (no accent), abbr. **A** (sing. and pl.) *or* **amp** (no point).

ampersand = &, may be used in names of firms as Smith & Co., but not at the beginning or end of lines. In general *use* **and.** For &c. *use* **etc.**

amphetamine (med.).

amphibian, (zool.) member of the Amphibia; vehicle adapted for land and water.

amphor/a, a jar; *pl.* **-ae.**

ampoule, glass container for hypodermic dose.

ampulla, two-handled flask, Roman or religious; *pl.* **-ae.**

Amritsar, India, *not* Umritsur.

amt., amount.

amuck, *not* -ock, -ok.

Amundsen (Roald), 1872–1928, Norwegian explorer; S. Pole, 1911.

Amur, Siberia, *not* -oor.

amygdalin/, *not* -e.

an, *not* **a,** before all words beginning with a vowel (not having the *sound* of w or y), or silent *h*: an heir, an honorarium, an hour/, -glass. *See also* **'a,** *not* **an'.**

A.N., Anglo-Norman.

ana/, sayings, collective pl.;
  or sing. with pl. **-s.**
anabaptize, *not* -ise.
anacoluth/on (gram.), *pl.*
  -a, *not* -outhon, -koluthon,
  -koluthon.
Anacreon/, Greek poet; **-tic,**
  adj. and metre; abbr.
  Anacr.
anaemi/a, -c.
anaerob/e, -ic.
anaesthetize, *not* -ise.
anal., analog/y, -ous,
  analys/e, -er, -is, analytic, -al.
analogous, abbr. **anal.**
analogy, abbr. **anal.**
analys/e, -er, -is, *pl.* **-es;**
  abbr. **anal.** (U.S. **-yze**).
analyst.
analytic/, -al; abbr. **anal.**
Anam, *use* **Annam.**
anamorphos/is, *pl.* **-es.**
anapaest, foot of three
  syllables ($\cup \cup -$) (U.S. **-pest**).
anastatic, (printing) from
  reliefs on zinc plates.
anastomos/is, communication by cross-connections;
  pl. **-es; -ist.**
anat., anatom/y, -ical.
anatase, a mineral, *not*
  anastase.
anathema/, a curse, pl. **-s;**
  -tize.
anatomize, dissect, *not* -ise.
anatom/y, -ical, -ist; abbr.
  anat.
anatta (bot.), orange-red dye,
  not ann-, arn-, -o.
ancest/or, *fem.* **-ress,** *not* -rix.
anchor/ite, hermit, *not* -et;
  adj. **-etic.**
anchylosis, *use* ank-.
ancienne noblesse (Fr. f.),
  the old nobility (creations
  before 1789).
ancien régime (Fr. m.), the
  old order of things.
ancient, abbr. **anc.**
Ancient Mariner (*Rime of
  the*), by S. T. Coleridge,
  1798.
Ancient Order of Druids,

abbr. **A.O.D.;** — —
  Foresters, **A.O.F.,** — —
  Hibernians, **A.O.H.**
ancle, *use* **ankle.**
and (gram.). Where *and* joins
  two or more subjects in the
  singular number the verb
  must be in the pl., e.g. Jack
  and Jill *are* going. Where
  and joins two single words
  the comma is generally
  omitted. Where *and* joins the
  last two words of a list,
  practice varies, but O.U.P.
  inserts a comma; e.g. black,
  white, and green.
and, *see also* **ampersand.**
andante (mus.), moving
  easily, steadily.
Andersen (Hans Christian),
  1805–75, Danish story-teller.
Andrea del Sarto, 1486–
  1531, Italian painter.
Andria, play by Terence.
Androcles, *not* -kles.
anele, anoint, *not* annele.
aneurysm, *not* -ism.
Angeles (Victoria de los),
  b. 1923, Spanish soprano.
Angelico (Fra), 1387–1455,
  Italian painter.
anglais/ (Fr.), *fem.* **-e,**
  English (not cap.); *but*
  Anglais/, -e, Englishman,
  Englishwoman.
angle, the sign $\angle$; angle
  between the two lines $\wedge$;
  right angle $\llcorner$; two right
  angles $\perp$.
angle brackets $\langle \rangle$.
Anglesey, Wales, *not* -ea.
Anglesey (Marquess of).
anglice, in English (no accent);
  abbr. *angl.*
anglicize, *not* -ise (not cap.).
Anglo/-French, abbr. **A.F.;**
  — **-Norman,** abbr. **A.N.;**
  — **-Saxon,** abbr. **A.S.**
Angst (Ger. f.), fear, anxiety.
Ångström (A. J.), 1814–74,
  Swedish physicist.
ångström, a unit of
  measurement, 10^{-10} m.

anguis in herba (Lat.), snake in the grass.

aniline, source of dyes. Also adj.

anility, dotage.

animalcule/, *pl.* **-s,** *not* **-ae.**

animalcul/um, *pl.* **-a.**

animé (Fr., mus.), animated.

anion (elec.), ion carrying negative charge of electricity.

ankle, *not* anc-.

ankylosis, fusion of bones, *not* anch-.

ann., annals, *anni* (years), *anno,* annual.

anna/, *pl.* **-s,** formerly 16 to rupee, now replaced by decimal coinage (Ind. and Pak.).

annales (Fr. pl. f.), annals; abbr. *ann.*

annals, abbr. **ann.**

Annam, *not* Anam, formerly kingdom within Fr. Indo-China, now merged in Vietnam.

Ann Arbor, Mich., U.S.

Anne of Geierstein, by Sir W. Scott, 1829.

Anne (Queen), 1702–14, b. 1665.

Anne (Saint).

annex, verb; **annexe,** noun (U.S. **annex**).

anno/ (Lat.), in the year, abbr. *ann.;* — *aetatis suae,* aged, abbr. *aet.,* or *aetat.;* — *Domini* (cap. *D*), abbr. **A.D.** (s.caps.), to be placed *before* the figures; — *mundi,* in the year of the world, abbr. **A.M.** (s.caps);

annos vixit (Lat.), he, *or* she, lived so many years; abbr. *a.v.*

annotat/ed, -or, *not* -er; abbr. **annot.**

annual, abbr. **ann.**

annul/ar, ring-like; **-ate, -ated, -et, -oid.**

ann/us (Lat.), year; *pl.* **-i.**

anonymous, abbr. **anon.**

Anouilh (Jean), b. 1910, French dramatist.

anschluss, union (cap. A in Ger.).

answer, abbr. **ans.**

Ant., Anthony, Antigua.

ant., antonym.

Antaeus.

antagonize, *not* -ise.

Antarctic/, -a.

ante (not ital.), stake in card game.

ante/ (Lat.), before; — *bellum,* before the war. (U.S. not ital., before the Civil War.)

antechamber, *not* anti-.

ante diem (Lat.), before the day; abbr. *a.d.*

antediluvian.

antefix/ (arch.), *pl.* **-es.**

ante/ litem motam (Lat.), before litigation commenced; — *lucem,* before the light.

antemeridian (one word).

ante meridiem (Lat.), before noon; abbr. **a.m.**

antenatal (one word).

antenn/a (zool.), *pl.* **-ae.** [(U.S.) radio, *pl.* **-as.**]

ante-room (hyphen).

Anthony, anglicized from Lat. Antonius. (N.B. *Antony and Cleopatra.*)

anthropolog/y, -ical; abbr. **anthrop.**

anthropomorphize, *not* -ise.

anthropophag/us (noun), cannibal; *pl.* **-i;** adj. **-ous.**

Antichrist (cap.), *but* **antichristian.**

anticline (geol.).

anti-freeze (hyphen).

Antigua, abbr. **Ant.**

anti-hero, principal character lacking traditional heroic qualities.

antilogarithm (one word), abbr. **antilog** (no point).

antimony, symbol **Sb** (no point).

antinomy, conflict of authority.

antipathize, *not* -ise.

antiq., antiquar/y, -ian.

antiqs., antiquities.

Antiqua (Ger. typ. f.), roman type (cap.).

antique paper, a moderately bulky, opaque book paper with roughish surface.

antisabbatarian.

anti-Semite (hyphen, one cap.).

antistrophe, stanza corresponding to the strophe in Greek dramatic chorus.

antistrophon, a retort.

antitetanus (adj., one word).

antithes/is, *pl.* **-es.**

antithesize, *not* -ise.

antitoxin (one word).

antitype, *not* ante-; that which corresponds to the type.

antonym, a word of opposite meaning; abbr. **ant.**

antrycide (against tsetse fly), *not* -tri-.

Anvers, Fr. for **Antwerp.**

Anwick, Lincs. *See also* **Alnwick.**

anybody, any person.

any body, any group of persons.

any/how, -one, -thing, -where (one word).

any one (person, thing).

Anzac, Australian and New Zealand Army Corps (First World War).

Anzeige/ (Ger. f.), notice, advertisement; *pl.* **-n.**

A.N.Z.U.S., Pact between Australia, New Zealand, and United States.

A.O., Accountant Officer, Army Order.

A.O.C.-in-C., Air Officer Commanding-in-Chief.

A.O.D., Army Ordnance Department, Ancient Order of Druids.

A.O.F., Ancient Order of Foresters.

A.O.H., Ancient Order of Hibernians.

aorist, abbr. **aor.**

aort/a (anat.), *pl.* **-ae.**

août (Fr. m.), August (not cap.).

à outrance (Fr.), to the bitter end, *not* a l'outrance.

A.P., Associated Press.

a.p., above proof, author's proof.

Ap., Apostle.

Apache, (U.S.) Indian tribe; **apache,** Paris hooligan.

apanage, *not* app-.

à part (Fr.), apart.

apart from, (U.S.) aside from.

apartheid (Afrik.), segregation.

apartments, in Fr. m. *appartement.*

ap/e, -ed, -ing, -ish.

Apennines, Italy (three *n's*), *properly* **Appennini.**

aperçu (Fr. m.), outline (ç).

à peu de frais (Fr.), at small cost; *à peu près,* nearly.

apex/, *pl.* **-es;** adj. **apical.**

aphaeretic, removing a sound from the beginning of a word.

aphid/, *pl.* **-s.**

aphi/s, *pl.* **-des.**

aphorize, *not* -ise.

aphthong, a mute letter.

à pied (Fr.), on foot.

à plaisir (Fr.), at pleasure.

aplanatic (optics), without (spherical) error.

aplomb, self-possession.

Apocalypse, abbr. **Apoc.**

Apocrypha (cap. A); abbr. **Apocr.** (for abbrs. of books see under names); adj. **apocryphal.**

apo/dictic, clearly established; *also* **-deictic.**

apogee (astr.), abbr. **apog.**

Apollinaris (**water**), mineral water from Ahr Valley, Germany.

Apollin/arius (*sometimes* **-aris**), Christian heretic *c.* 310–*c.* 390; **-arianism.**

Apollo/, Greek god;
— **Belvedere**, statue in
Vatican.

Apollonius Rhodius, Greek
poet, *c.* 200 B.C.

Apollos, Acts 18: 24,
follower of St. Paul.

Apollyon, the Devil.

apologize, *not* -ise.

apophthegm, pithy maxim.

apostasy, *not* -cy.

apostatize, *not* -ise.

a posteriori, (reasoning)
from effects to causes.

Apostle, abbr. **Ap.**, *pl.* **App.**

Apostles' Creed (caps.).

Apostroph/ (Ger. m.),
apostrophe; *pl.* -**e** (cap.).

apostrophe, *see* **possessive
case, punctuation VIII,
quotations.**

apostrophize, *not* -ise.

**apothecaries' weight,
signs:** ℔ minim; ℈ scruple;
ℨ drachm; ℥ ounce; lb.
pound. Quantities in lower-
case letters: if quantity ends
with *i*, final *i* becomes *j*, as
vij = 7.

apothegm, *use* **apophthegm.**

apotheos/is, *pl.* -**es.**

apotropaic, resisting ill
luck.

App., Apostles.

app., appendix.

appal/, -**led**, -**ling.**

Appalachian Mts., E. North
America.

appanage, *use* **apa-.**

apparatus, *pl.* **apparatuses,**
not i- (a useful synonym,
'appliances').

apparatus criticus, variant
readings; abbr. **app. crit.**

apparel/, -**led**, -**ling.**

apparitor, officer of
ecclesiastical court, *not* -er.

appartement (Fr. m.), flat,
apartments.

app. crit., apparatus criticus.

appeasement, *not* -sment.

append/ix, abbr. **app.**; *pl.*
-**ices**, zool. and general,

abbr. **apps.**; general pl.
-ixes now rare.

appetize, *not* -ise.

applejack, a liquor (U.S.).

appliqué, Eng. noun and
verb; past partic.
appliquéd.

appliqu/é (Fr.), *fem.* -**ée,**
appliquéd.

applique (Fr. f.), ornamental
accessories.

appoggiatura (mus.), type
of grace-note, leaning note.

appreciator, *not* -er.

apprentice, abbr. **appr.**

apprise (to inform).

apprize (to value).

appro., approbation.

approver, one who turns
Queen's evidence.

approximat/e, -**ely**, -**ion;**
abbr. **approx.**

appurts., appurtenances.

A.P.R.C., *anno post Romam
conditam* (in the year after
the building of Rome in 753
B.C.) (s.caps.); *but use* **A.U.C.**

après/ (Fr.), after; —**?** what
next? — *coup*, after the
event; — *livraison*, after
delivery (of goods), abbr.
a.l.; — -*midi*, afternoon
(hyphen); — *moi* (*or* **nous**)
le déluge, after me (*or* us)
the deluge.

April, abbr. **Apr.**; in
Fr. *avril* (not cap.).

a prima vista (It.), at first
sight.

a/primo (Lat.), from the
first; — *principio*, from
the beginning; — *priori*,
deductively, *not* à (ital.).

apropos (of); *à propos de
bottes* (Fr.), beside the
mark.

A.P.S., Associate of the
Pharmaceutical Society.

apse/, semicircular recess,
esp. in church; *pl.* -**s.**

apsi/s, in an orbit, point of
greatest or least distance
from central body; *pl.* -**des.**

apud (Lat.), according to, in the work, or works, of.

aq., *aqua* (water); — **bull.,** boiling water.

A.Q.C., Associate of Queen's College (London).

aq. dist., distilled water.

aquarium/, *pl.* **-s.**

aquatint (typ.), intaglio technique with a fine grain effect.

à quatre mains (Fr. mus.), for two performers.

aque/duct, *not* aqua-; **-ous.**

aquil/egia, -ine.

Ar, argon (no point).

a/r, all risks.

Ⱥ, in numismatics = silver (Lat. *argentum*).

A.R., *anno regni* (in the year of the reign) (s.caps.).

A.R.A., Associate of the Royal Academy, London.

Arabi/a, -an, -c; abbr. **Arab.**

Arabian Nights' Entertainments (The).

arabic numerals, figures used in ordinary computation, as, 1, 2, 3 (not cap.).

arach., arachnology.

A.R.A.D., Associate of the Royal Academy of Dancing.

araeostyle (arch.).

Aragon, *not* Arr-.

A.R.A.M., Associate of the Royal Academy of Music.

Aramaic, Semitic language; abbr. **Aram.**

Aranda, Spain, *not* -anta, -unta.

Aran, Island of, Donegal. *See also* **Arran.**

Aran Islands, Galway Bay, Eire. *See also* **Arran.**

A.R.B.A., Associate of the Royal (Society of) British Artists.

arbiter elegantiae (Lat.), a judge of taste.

arbitr/ament, *not* -ement.

arbitrator, legal or official word for **arbiter.**

arbor, spindle, axis.

arboret/um (bot.), tree-garden; *pl.* **-a.**

arboriculture, abbr. **arbor.**

arbor vitae, evergreen.

arbour, bower (U.S. **arbor**).

A.R.B.S., Associate of the Royal (Society of) British Sculptors.

arc, sign ⌒.

A.R.C.A., Associate of the Royal College of Art.

Arcades ambo (Lat.), two with like tastes.

Arc de Triomphe, Paris.

arc-en-ciel (Fr. m.), rainbow; *pl.* **arcs-** — -.

arch., archaic, -ism, archery, archipelago, architect, -ural, -ure.

archaeolog/y, -ical; abbr. **archaeol.**

archangel (one word).

Archbishop, abbr. **Abp.**

Archd., Archdeacon, Archduke.

archetype, *not* archi-.

archidiaconal, *not* archide-.

archiepiscopal.

Archimed/ean, *not* -ian.

archipelago/, *pl.* **-s;** abbr. **arch.**

architect/, -ural, -ure; abbr. **arch.**

arcing (elec.), *not* arck-.

A.R.C.M., Associate of the Royal College of Music.

A.R.C.O., Associate of the Royal College of Organists.

A.R.C.S., Associate of the Royal College of Science.

Arctic Circle (two caps.); **Arctic regions** (one cap.); **arctic** (not cap.), cold, (U.S. noun, warm overshoe).

Ardleigh, near Colchester.

Ardley, near Bicester (Oxon.).

A.R.E., Associate of the Royal Society of Painter-Etchers and Engravers.

areaway, (U.S.) passage to basement door (one word).

à reculons (Fr.), backwards.

aren't (typ.), to be close up.
areol/a, a small area; *pl.* **-ae** (not ital.).
Arequipa, Peru.
arête, mountain ridge.
à rez-de-chaussée (Fr., hyphens), level with the ground. *See also* **au rez-de-chaussée**.
argel, a shrub, *not* -hel.
argent (her.), silver.
argent comptant (Fr. m.), ready money.
Argentina, the country, *or* **Argentine Republic,** abbr. **Arg. Rep.**
Argentine (adj.); *also* (noun) the inhabitant. *See also* **Argentinian**.
Argentinian (adj.); *also* (noun) the inhabitant; tending to replace **Argentine**; *not* -ean.
argentum, silver, symbol, (chem.) **Ag,** (numismatics) **Æ** (no point).
argon, symbol **Ar,** *formerly* **A** (no point).
argot, slang (not ital.).
arguable, *not* -eable.
argumentum ad/ crumenam (Lat.), argument to the purse; — — *hoc,* — for this (purpose); — — *hominem,* — to the man's interests; — — *ignorantiam,* — based on the adversary's ignorance; — — *invidiam,* — to men's hatreds or prejudices; — — *rem,* — to the purpose; — — *verecundiam,* appeal to modesty; *argumentum baculinum,* or — *ad baculum,* argument of the stick, club-law.
Argyle, Minnesota, U.S.
Argyll/ and Sutherland Highlanders; — **and the Isles (Bp. of);** — **(Duke of)**.
Argyllshire, abbr. **Argyl.**
A.R.H.A., Associate of the Royal Hibernian Academy.

Arian (theol.), a follower of Arius.
A.R.I.B.A., Associate of the Royal Institute of British Architects.
A.R.I.C., Associate of the Royal Institute of Chemistry.
A.R.I.C.S., Associate of the Royal Institution of Chartered Surveyors.
Ariège, France.
Aristotel/ean, *now normally* -ian.
arithmetic/, -al, -ian; abbr. **arith.**
Arius, Christian heretic, *c.* 250–*c.* 336.
Ariz., Arizona (off. abbr.).
Ark., Arkansas (off. abbr.).
Arlay, dép. Jura, France.
Arle, Glos.
Arles, dép. Bouches-du-Rhône, France.
arles (Sc.), an earnest.
Arm., Armenian, Armoric.
armadillo/, *pl.* **-s.**
armchair (one word).
Armenia, ancient country, now in part a Soviet Socialist Republic; adj. **Armenian** (geog., ethnic, or eccles.). *See also* **U.S.S.R.**
armes blanches (Fr.), side arms—bayonet, sabre, or sword.
armful/, *pl.* **-s.**
armhole (one word).
Arminians, followers of Arminius.
armory, heraldry.
armoury, collection of arms (U.S. **armory**).
armpit (one word).
A.R.M.S., Associate of the Royal Society of Miniature Painters.
arm's length (two words).
Army: Navy, Army, and Air Force, in toasts, etc.; the Navy, being the senior service, is placed first.

Army/ Dental Corps, *now*
**R.A.D.C.; — Hospital
Corps, A.H.C.; — Nursing
Service, A.N.S.; — Order,
A.O.; — Ordnance
Corps,** *now* **R.A.O.C.;
— — Department,
A.O.D.; — Pay Depart-
ment, A.P.D.; — Service
Corps,** *later* **R.A.S.C.,** *now*
**R.C.T.; — Veterinary
Department, A.V.D.**

**Arnold (Edward)
(Publishers), Ltd.**

Arnold (E. J.) & Son, Ltd.,
publishers.

Arnold-Forster (H. O.),
1855–1909, statesman
(hyphen).

arnotto, *use* **anatta.**

Arola, Piedmont.

Arolla, Switzerland.

Arolo, Lombardy.

aroma, *pl.* **-s.**

Aroostook War, 1842,
settled border of Maine and
New Brunswick.

A.R.P., Air Raid Precautions.

arpeggio/ (mus.), striking of
notes of chord in (usu.
upward) succession; *pl.* **-s.**

A.R.P.S., Associate of the
Royal Photographic Society.

arquebus, *better* **harq-.**

A.R.R., *anno regni Regis* or
Reginae (in the year of the
King's or Queen's reign)
(s.caps.).

arr., arranged, arriv/e, -ed,
-es, -als.

Arran, Earl of.

Arran, Isle of, Scotland.
See also **Aran.**

arrectis auribus (Lat.),
with ears erect.

arrêt (Fr.), decree.

arrière/-garde (Fr. f.),
rearguard; **— -pensée,**
a mental reservation, *pl.* **-s.**

arriv/e, -ed, -es, -als; abbr.
arr.

arrondissement (Fr. m.),
division of department.

arrow-head (noun, hyphen).

arrowhead (adj., one word).

Arrows of the Chace, by
Ruskin, *not* Chase.

A.R.S.A., Associate of the
Royal Scottish Academy,
ditto Royal Society of Arts.

arsenic, symbol **As** (no
point).

ars est celare artem (Lat.),
the art is to conceal art.

A.R.S.L., Associate of the
Royal Society of Literature.

A.R.S.M., Associate of the
Royal School of Mines.

A.R.S.S., *Antiquariorum
Regiae Societatis Socius,* Fellow
of the Royal Society of
Antiquaries.

A.R.S.W., Associate of the
Royal Scottish Society of
Painting in Water Colours.

art., article, artificial,
artillery, artist.

artefact, *not* arti-.

arteriosclerosis, hardening
of the arteries (one word).

arthropod/, member of
Arthropoda, animals with
jointed body and limbs; *pl.* **-s.**

artichaut (Fr. m.), artichoke.

article, abbr. **art.**

article de fond (Fr. m.),
newspaper leading article.

articles of roup (Sc. law),
conditions of sale (by
auction).

articles (titles of), when
cited, to be roman quoted.

artificial, abbr. **art.**

artillery, abbr. **A.** *or* **arty.**

artisan, *not* -zan.

artist, one who practises one
of the fine arts, esp. painting;
one who makes his craft a
fine art.

artiste (either sex), professional singer, dancer, or
other performer.

art paper, a high-quality
coated paper used for
illustrations.

Arundel, Sussex.

Arundell of Wardour (Baron), title now extinct.

Arunta, *use* **Aranda**.

Arva, Cavan, *not* Arvagh.

A.R.W.S., Associate of the Royal Society of Painters in Water Colours.

Aryan, Indo-European, *not* -ian.

A.S. *or* **AS**, Anglo-Saxon.

As., Asia, -n, -tic.

As, arsenic (no point).

A.S.A., Amateur Swimming Association.

asafoetida (med.), ill-smelling gum resin; *not* the many variants.

Asante, mod. form of **Ashanti**, q.v.

a.s.a.p., as soon as possible.

Asbjörnsen (P. C.), 1812–85, Norwegian writer.

ascendan/ce, -cy, -t, *not* -ence.

ascender (typ.), top part of letters such as b, d, f, h, k, l.

Ascension Day (caps., two words).

ascetic, austere.

ascititious, *use* adsci-.

Asclepiad, metre, *not* Ask-.

a/s de (Fr.), aux soins de, c/o.

A.S.D.I.C., Allied Submarine Detection Investigation Committee; used for a form of hydrophone; *now usually written* **Asdic**.

A.S.E., Amalgamated Society of Engineers.

as follows: (*use* colon only, *not* :—).

Asgard, the heaven of Norse mythology.

Ashant/i, Ghana; *not* -ee. *also* **Asante**.

Ashby de la Zouch, Leics. (no hyphens).

Ashkenazim, *pl.*, Polish-German Jews, as distinct from Sephardim.

Ashkhabad, cap. of Turkmenistan, U.S.S.R.

ashlar (arch.), *not* -er.

Ashmolean Museum, Oxford.

ash-pit (hyphen).

Ashtar/oth, -eth, Bib. and Sem., *otherwise use* **Astarte**.

Ashton-under-Lyne, Lancs. (hyphens), *not* -Lyme.

Ash Wednesday, first day of Lent (two words).

Asian (adj. and noun), (native) of Asia; *pref. to* **Asiatic**, which now tends to be pejorative.

asinine, like an ass, *not* ass-.

Asir ('the inaccessible'), *see* **Saudi Arabia**.

A.S.L.E. & F., *now usually* **A.S.L.E.F.** *or* **Aslef**, Associated Society of Locomotive Engineers and Firemen.

A.S.L.I.B., *now* **Aslib**, Association of Special Libraries and Information Bureaux.

Asnières, Paris suburb; *pron.* ahn′ĭ-ār.

Asola, Lombardy; *pron.* as′ŏ-lă.

Asolo, Venetia; *pron.* as′ŏ-lō.

asp, a poisonous serpent.

asper, Greek rough breathing (′).

asperge (Fr. f.), asparagus.

asperges (noun sing.), sprinkling with blessed water.

asphalt, *not* -e.

asphodel, immortal flower in Elysium.

asphyxia, interruption of breathing.

aspic, a poisonous serpent, the great lavender, a savoury jelly, a piece of light ordnance.

A.S.R.S., Amalgamated Society of Railway Servants (*now* **N.U.R.**).

assafoetida, *use* asa-.

assagai, spear of S. African tribesman, *now usually* **assegai**.

assai (mus.), very.

assailant, in Fr. m.

   assaillant.

assassin.

assault-at-arms, in fencing; *not* -of-.

assegai, *now usual for* **assagai.**

Assemblies, National and Federal. In addition to titles in English (Parliament, Assembly, Senate, etc.) in English-speaking countries and translations of foreign titles (National Assembly for Assemblée Nationale, etc.), the following titles are correct for particular countries:

Austria—Bundesrat and Nationalrat.

Denmark—Folketing.

Finland—Eduskunta.

Germany, Federal Republic of—Bundesrat (Upper House) and Bundestag (Lower House).

Germany, Democratic Republic of—Volkskammer [not recognized by Western countries].

Iceland—Althing.

India—Rajya Sabha (Council of States) and Lok Sabha (House of the People).

Ireland, Republic of—Oireachtas (Parliament), comprising Seanad Éireann (Senate) and Dáil Éireann (House of Representatives).

Israel—Knesset.

Japan—Kokkai (Parliament, comprising two houses).

Netherlands—Staten Generaal, comprising Eerste Kamer (First Chamber) and Tweede Kamer (Second Chamber).

Norway—Storting, comprising Lagting (Upper Council) and Odelsting (Lower Council).

Spain—Cortes.

Sweden—Rikstag (or Diet).

Switzerland—Nationalrat/ Conseil National and Ständerat/Conseil des États.

Assembly (Church of Scotland) (cap. A), *properly* **General Assembly** (also in other Presbyterian Churches). *See also* **Church Assembly.**

assent/er, one who assents; **-or,** one who subscribes to a nomination paper.

assert/er, one who asserts; **-or,** an advocate.

assess/able, -or.

assez bien (Fr.), fairly well.

assiettes/ (Fr. cook. pl. f.), plates; — *volantes,* small entrées.

assign/ee, one to whom a right or property is assigned; **-or,** one who assigns.

Assiniboine, Canada, *not* Assinn-. Assiniboia superseded as name of province by Saskatchewan and Alberta.

assistant, abbr. asst.

assizer, officer with oversight of weights and measures; *not* -ser, -sor, -zor.

assizes (law), *pl.* form usual.

assoc., associat/e, -ion.

asst., assistant.

assuager, *not* -or.

Assuan, use **Aswan.**

assurance, 'the present usage is to differentiate life *assurance,* and fire and marine *insurance*' (*O.E.D.*).

Assyr., Assyrian.

assythment (Sc. law), (action for) damages.

a-starboard (hyphen).

Astarte, Syrophoenician goddess; *not* Ashtar/oth -eth.

astatine, symbol **At** (no point).

Asterabad, Persia.

asterisk, *see* **reference marks.**

Asti, Italian red wine.

A.S.T.M.S., Association of Scientific, Technical, and Managerial Staffs.

astr., astronom/y, -er.

astrakhan, lambskin from **Astrakhan,** U.S.S.R.

astrol., astrolog/y, -er.

Astronomer Royal (caps., no hyphen).

astronomy, abbr. **astr.;**
— **planetary signs:**
Sun, ☉; Moon, new, ●;
Moon, first quarter, ☽;
Moon, full, ○; Moon, last quarter, ☾; Mercury, ☿;
Venus, ♀; Earth, ⊕; Mars, ♂; Jupiter, ♃; Saturn, ♄;
Uranus, ♅; Neptune, ♆;
asteroids in order of discovery, ①, ②, ③, etc.;
fixed star, ✶, or ✳;
conjunction, ☌; opposition, ☍; ascending node, ☊;
descending node, ☋.
— **zodiacal signs:**
Aries, ♈; Taurus, ♉;
Gemini, ♊; Cancer, ♋;
Leo, ♌; Virgo, ♍; Libra, ♎; Scorpio, ♏; Sagittarius, ♐; Capricornus, ♑;
Aquarius, ♒; Pisces, ♓.

Asturias, Spain, not to be preceded by 'the'.

Asunción, Paraguay.

A.S.V.A., Associate of the Incorporated Society of Valuers and Auctioneers.

A.S.W., Amalgamated Society of Woodworkers.

Aswan, Egypt; *not* the many variations.

asymptote, line approaching but not meeting a curve.

asyndeton, omission of conjunction.

A.T. (Ger.), *Altes Testament* (the Old —).

At (no point), astatine.

at., atomic.

A.T.A.C., Air Transport Advisory Council.

Atahualpa, the last Inca.

Atalanta (Gk. myth.).

atar, *use* **attar.**

A.T.C., Air Traffic Control, Air Training Control.

Atchin, Sumatra, Indonesia, *use* **Ach-.**

A.T.C.L., Associate of Trinity College (of Music), London.

atelier, studio (not ital.).

a tempo (mus.), in time; denotes that after alteration in time, first or previous time must be resumed.

Athabasca, Canada, *not* -ka.

Atheling, *not* Aeth-.

Athenaeum, London club.

Athol, Canada, New Zealand.

Atholl (**Duke of**).

Atl., Atlantic.

atlas (arch.), male caryatid; *pl.* **atlantes.**

atmosphere, gaseous envelope around the earth, consists of **troposphere** and **stratosphere,** qq.v.

atoll, ring-shaped coral reef surrounding lagoon.

atonable, *not* -eable.

à tort et à travers (Fr.), at random.

à tout/ prendre (Fr.), on the whole; —— *prix,* at any price, at all costs.

atra cura (Lat.), black care.

à travers (Fr.), across.

atri/um, hall of Roman house; *pl.* **-ums, -a.**

Atropos, one of the Three Fates.

A.T.S., Auxiliary Territorial Service (*superseded by* **W.R.A.C.**).

ats. (law), at the suit of.

attaché/, *pl.* **-s** (not ital.).

attar (as of roses), *not* atar, otto, ottar.

Att.-Gen., Attorney-General.

Attic salt, delicate wit (cap. A).

attitudinize, *not* -ise.

Attlee (Clement Richard, Earl), 1885–1967, British politician, Prime Minister 1945–51.

attorn (law), to transfer.

attorney, abbr. **atty.**

Attorney-General, abbr. **A.-G.** *or* **Att.-Gen.**

attractor, *not* -er.

A.T.V., Associated Television.

Atwood's machine (physics), *not* Att-.

at. wt., atomic weight.

Au, *aurum* (gold) (no point).

auberge (Fr. f.), an inn; **aubergiste** (m. or f.), inn-keeper.

aubergine, fruit of egg-plant.

Aubigné, dép. Deux-Sèvres.

Aubigny, dép. Nord.

aubr/ietia, dwarf perennial, *not* -etia.

A.U.C., *anno urbis conditae* (in the year from the building of the city [Rome] in 753 B.C.) (s.caps.); also *ab urbe condita*, from the foundation of the city.

Auchinleck (Field-Marshal Sir Claude John Eyre), b. 1884, British soldier.

Auchnashellach, Ross., *use* Ach-.

au/ contraire (Fr.), on the contrary; — **courant de,** fully acquainted with; — **désespoir,** in despair.

Auditor-General, abbr. **Aud.-Gen.**

Audubon (John James), 1785–1851, American ornithologist.

A.U.E.W., Amalgamated Union of Engineering Workers.

au fait (Fr.), thoroughly conversant with.

Aufklärung (Ger.), enlightenment, esp. the eighteenth-century intellectual movement.

Auflage/ (Ger. f.), edition,

impression; *pl.* **-n** (cap.); abbr. **Aufl.; unveränderte** —, reprint; **verbesserte und vermehrte** —, revised and enlarged edition.

au fond (Fr.), at the bottom.

auf wiedersehen (Ger.), till we meet again.

Aug., August.

aug., augmentative.

Augean (stables), filthy (cap.).

auger, carpenter's boring tool.

aught, anything. *See also* nau-.

au/ grand sérieux (Fr.), in all seriousness; — **gratin,** browned with bread-crumbs.

augur, Roman soothsayer.

August, abbr. **Aug.**

au jus (Fr.), in gravy.

auk, diving bird, *not* awk.

'Auld Lang Syne' (not ital.).

Auld Reekie, Old Smoky, that is, Edinburgh.

Aumale (duc d').

Aumerle, Duke of (in Shakespeare's *Richard II*).

au/ mieux (Fr.), very intimate; — **naturel,** in its natural state.

aunty, *pref. to* -ie.

au/ pair (Fr.), at par, on mutual terms; — **pair girl** (not ital.); — **pied de la lettre,** literally; — **pis aller,** should the worst come to the worst; — **prix coûtant,** at cost price.

Aurar, *pl.* of **Eyrir**, q.v.

aurea mediocritas (Lat.), the golden mean.

aureole, a saint's halo.

au/ reste (Fr.), besides; — **revoir,** till we meet again; — **rez-de-chaussée,** on the ground floor (*see à rez-de-chaussée*).

auror/a austral/is, *pl.* **-ae -es**; — **boreal/is,** *pl.* **-ae, -es.**

aurum, gold, symbol (chem.) **Au,** (numismatics) **A/** (no point).

Aus., Austria, -n.
Auschwitz, German
concentration-camp in
Second World War.
au sérieux (Fr.), seriously.
Ausgabe (Ger. f.), edition;
abbr. *Ausg.* (cap.); *see
compounds* **Buch-, Pracht-,
Volks-.**
Austen (Jane), 1775–1817,
author of *Pride and Prejudice,*
etc.
Austin (Alfred), 1835–1913,
Poet Laureate 1896–1913.
**Austral/ia, -ian, -asia,
-asian;** abbr. **Austral.**
**Australian Capital
Territory,** abbr. **A.C.T.**
Austria, abbr. **Aus.**
Austria-Hungary (*but*
Austro-Hungarian); in
Ger. **Österreich-Ungarn.**
autarchy, absolute
sovereignty.
autarky, self-sufficiency.
Auteuil, Paris suburb.
auth., authentic, author/,
-ess, -ity, -ized.
authorities at the end of
quotations, or in notes:
(1) Name of author in roman.
(2) Name of book in italic,
and if one of a series, the
series may be in quotation
marks or in roman if likely
to be confused with the book.
(3) Title of article roman
in quotation marks, name
of journal in italic.

Act and scene	III. iv
Act, scene, and line	III. iii. 45
Book	iii
Book and line	iii. 25
Book, chapter, section, and paragraph	II. iii, § 3, ¶ 4
Canto	xvi
Chapter	xiv
Chapter and verse	2 : 34
(in older works	ii. 34)
Chapter, section, and paragraph	vii, § 3, ¶ 4

Line	l. 384
Number and page	ii. 34
Page	p. 213
Paragraph	¶ 68
Part and chapter	ii. 3
Part, book, and chapter	II. iv. 12
Part, canto, and stanza	II. iv. 12
Section	§ 5
Stanza	st. 18
Volume and chapter	IV. vi
Volume and page	iii. 32
Volume, part, section, and paragraph	II. i, § 2, ¶ 6

authorize, *not* -ise.
Authorized Version (of
Bible) (caps.); abbr. **A.V.**
autis/m, morbid absorption
in imaginative activity, to
the exclusion of contact with
reality; adj. **-tic.**
auto, do not use as abbr. for
automobile, noun.
autobahn, German arterial
road (not cap., not ital. in
anglicized form).
autochthon/, a son of the
soil; *pl.* **-s;** adj. **-ous.**
autocracy, absolute
government.
auto/-da-fé (Port.), *pl. autos-
da-fé;* (Sp.) — *de fe;* 'act
of the faith', burning of
heretic by Inquisition.
autogyro, *not* -giro.
autolithography (typ.),
printing by lithography from
stones or plates prepared
by the artist personally.
automaton, *pl.* **-s** (but
automata when used
collectively).
automobil/e (adj.),
uncommon for **car** (noun),
even in U.S. now; **-ist,** *use*
motorist.
autonomy, self-government.
autonym, a book published
under author's real name.
autore (It.), author; abbr.
aut.

autostrada, Italian arterial road.

autres temps, autres mœurs (Fr.), other times, other manners.

autumn (not cap.).

Auvergne (Fr.), *not* The —.

Auvers, Seine-et-Oise, France.

Auverse, Maine-et-Loire, France.

aux abois (Fr.), at bay, in a fix.

auxiliary, abbr. **aux.** *or* **auxil.**

Auxiliary Forces (caps.).

A/, in numismatics = gold (Lat. *aurum*) (no point).

A.V., Authorized Version (of Bible).

a/v, ad valorem.

a.v., *annos vixit* (he, *or* she, lived so many years).

av., average.

ava, Polynesian intoxicant, use **kava.**

avant/-courier, in Fr. m. **-courrier** or **-cour/eur,** *fem.* **-euse,** a forerunner; — **-garde** (f.), the advanced guard; — **-propos** (m.), preface, *pl.* same (hyphens).

av. C. (It.), *avanti Cristo* (B.C.).

avdp., avoirdupois.

ave atque vale (Lat.), hail and farewell.

Ave Maria, (Hail, Mary!); abbr. **A.M.**

aventurine, brownish glass, *not* -in, *not* avant-.

Avenue, abbr. **Ave.**

average, abbr. **av.**

Averroës, 1126–98, Muslim philosopher, *not* -oes.

averse *to,* not *from.*

avertible, *not* -able.

avertissement (Fr. m.), notice, warning.

aviculture, rearing of birds.

avid, greedy.

Avignon, dép. Vaucluse.

a vinculo matrimonii (Lat.), full divorce.

avis au lecteur (Fr.), notice to the reader.

avizandum (Sc. law), judge's consideration of case in private.

A.V.M., Air Vice-Marshal.

avocat (Fr.), a lawyer.

avocet, a bird, *not* -set.

Avogadro's Hypothesis, *not* Avro-.

avoirdupois, abbr. **avdp.**

à/ volonté (Fr.), at pleasure, at will; — **votre santé!** (here's) to your health!

Avon, new county, proposed 1971.

avril (Fr. m., not cap.), April.

avvocato del diavolo (It.), devil's advocate.

aweing, *not* awi-.

awesome, *not* aws-

awhile (adv.), *but* for a while.

A.W.O.L., absent without official leave.

ax., axiom.

axe, usual (*but* ax *O.E.D.*).

axe (Fr. m.), axis.

ay/, *pron.* ī, yes: 'Ay, ay, sir'; *pl.* **-es:** 'The ayes have it.'

ayah, Indian nurse-maid.

Aycliffe, Co. Durham, 'new town', 1947.

aye, *pron.* ā, ever: 'For ever and for aye.'

Aylesbury, Bucks. *See also* **Ail-.**

Ayr, Scotland.

Ayre (Point of), Isle of Man.

az., azure.

Azaña, the 'Popular Front' in the Spanish Civil War.

Azerbaijan/, a Soviet Socialist Republic, *see* **U.S.S.R.; -ian,** the language.

Azov (Sea of), *not* -off, -of.

Azrael (Muslim), the angel of death.

Aztec, one of a people dominant in Mexico before the Spanish conquest; adj. **Aztec/, -ian.**

azyme, Jewish Passover cake.

B

B, (chem.) boron, (chess) bishop, the second in a series.

B., Bachelor, Baron, Basso, Bay, (pencils) black, Blessed (*Beat/us,-a*), British, all proper names with this initial.

b (compass), by.

b., base, book, born, (cricket) bowled, (cricket) byes, (naut.) blue sky.

B.A., Bachelor of Arts, Booksellers Association, British Academy, — Airways (combining B.E.A. and B.O.A.C., 1973), — America, — Association.

Ba (chem.), barium (no point).

B.A.A., British Airports Authority, — Astronomical Authority.

baas (Afrik.), master, boss.

Bab. (bot.), Babington (C. C.).

Babcock & Wilcox, engineers.

Babington (C. C.), 1808–95, botanist; abbr. **Bab.**; — (**W.**), 1756–1833, mineralogist.

babingtonite, an iron ore, after William Babington.

babiroussa, a wild hog, *not* baby-, -russa.

babu, Indian title, *not* baboo.

B.A.C., British Aircraft Corporation, Ltd.

baccalaureate, university degree of bachelor.

baccarat, a card game; in Fr. *baccara* (m.).

Bacchanalia, *pl.*, festival of Bacchus.

Bacchant/, male or female follower of Bacchus; **-e,** female only.

bacci/ferous, -form, -vorous, berry-bearing, -shaped, -eating.

Bach/, German musical family, more than fifty in number in seven generations, of whom the greatest was — (**Johann Sebastian**), 1685–1750 (of the fifth generation), composer of keyboard, orchestral, and choral music; also important were his father's cousin,—(**Johann Cristoph**), 1642–1703, composer; and, of J. S. B.'s twenty children, — (**Wilhelm Friedemann**), 1710–84; — (**Karl Philipp Emanuel,** usu. referred to as **C.P.E.**), 1714–85, developer of sonata and symphony form; — (**Johann Cristoph Friedrich**), 1732–95; — (**Johann Christian**), 1735–82, 'the English Bach'.

Bacharach, small Rhineland town (wine-growing).

Bachelier ès/ lettres (Fr.), Bachelor of Letters, abbr. *B. ès L.;* — — *sciences,* ditto Science, *B. ès S.* (no hyphens).

Bachelor/, abbr. **B.;** — **of Agriculture, B.Agr.** (U.S.); — **Architecture, B.Arch.;** — **Arts, B.A.;** — **Canon and Civil Law, B.U.J.;** — **Civil Engineering, B.C.E.;** — **Civil Law, B.C.L.;** — **Commerce, B.Com.;** — **Dental Surgery, B.D.S.** *or* **B.Ch.D.;** — **Divinity, B.D.;** — **Education, B.Ed.;** — **Engineering, B.E.,** *or* **B.Eng.,** *or* **B.A.I. Dub.** (Dublin); — **Law, B.L.;** — **Laws, B.LL.;** — **Letters, B.Litt.,** *or* **Litt.B.,** in Fr. *B. ès L.;* — **Medicine, B.M.,** *or* **M.B.** (Cambridge, T.C.D.);

Bachelor (*cont.*):
— **Metallurgy**, B.Met.;
— **Mining Engineering**,
B.M.E.; — **Music**,
B.Mus., *or* Mus. Bac.; —
Obstetrics, B.A.O.;
— **Philosophy**, B.Phil.; —
Science, B.Sc., in Fr. *B. ès
S.*; — **Surgery**, B.C., B.Ch.,
B.S., *or* Ch.B.; — **Techni-
cal Science**, B.Sc.Tech.;
— **Theology**, B.Th.

bacill/us, *pl.* **-i** (not ital.).

back (typ.), *see* **margins**.

Backhuysen (**Ludolf**), 1631–
1708, Dutch painter, *not*
Bakhuisen.

backing up (typ.), printing
on the second side.

backveld (S. Afr.), outlying
country districts.

backwoodsman (one word).

Bacon (**Sir Francis**) (often
incorrectly Lord), 1561–
1626, Baron Verulam and
Viscount St. Albans.

Baconian, pertaining to
Roger Bacon, died *c.* 1292; or
to Francis Bacon; or to the
theory that Francis Bacon
wrote Shakespeare's plays.

bacshish, *use* **baksheesh**.

bacteri/um, microscopic
organism; *pl.* **-a**.

bade, past tense of bid, *not*
bad.

Baden-Baden, Germany
(hyphen).

**Baden-Powell, Robert,
Lord**, 1857–1941, founder of
Boy Scouts, 1908 (hyphen).

Baedeker (**Karl**), 1801–59,
guide-book publisher.

Baffin Bay, NE. America, *not*
-ns, -n's.

Bagehot (**Walter**), 1826–77,
pron. băj'ŭt.

baggage, in Fr. m. *bagage*.

Baghdad (U.S. **Bagd-**).

Bagnères/ de Bigorre, dép.
Hautes-Pyrénées; — **de
Luchon**, dép. Haute-
Garonne.

bagnio, bathing-house,
Turkish prison, brothel.

Bagnoles, dép. Orne.

Bagnols, dép. Gard.

bagpip/e (*not* -s), **-er** (one
word).

B.Agr. (U.S.), Bachelor of
Agriculture.

Bahrain, islands, Arabia.

Baiae, Naples.

B.A.I. Dub., Bachelor of Engineering, Univ. of Dublin.

baignoire (Fr. f.), theatre
box at stalls level.

bailee, one to whom goods
are entrusted for a purpose.

bailer (naut.), one who bails
water out, scoop used for
bailing; (cricket) a ball
which hits the bails. *See also*
bailor, bale.

bailey, outer wall of castle;
Old Bailey, London's
Central Criminal Court.

bailie (Sc.), an alderman;
bailiery, jurisdiction of a
bailie, *not* -iary.

bailiwick, office or jurisdiction of a bailiff.

Baillie (**Joanna**), 1762–1851,
Sc. poetess.

bailor (law), one who delivers
goods. *See also* **bailer.**

Baily's/ Magazine; —
Directory.

bain-marie (Fr. m.), double
saucepan; *pl.* *bains-*.

Baireuth, Bav., *use* Bay-.

Bairut, Syria, *use* Beirut.

baksheesh (Arab., Turk.),
a gratuity, *not* the many
variations.

bal., balance.

Balaclava, *not* -klava.

balalaika, Russian stringed
instrument.

balanceable, *not* -cable.

balas, a ruby, *not* -ais, ballas.

Balbriggan, Co. Dublin;
also knitted cotton goods.

baldric, sword-belt, *not* baw-,
-ick.

bale/, **-s**, abbr. **bl.**, **bls.**

bale (naut.), as verb generally preferred to *bail*; — **out**, (air) to escape from aircraft by parachute. *See also* **bailer**.

Balfour/, Lord, of Burleigh; —, **Lord, of Inchrye;** —, **Earl of.** (Three distinct titles.)

Baliol, an Anglo-Norman family, *not* the Oxford College, Balliol.

balk (verb).

Balkan Mts., Bulgaria.

Balkhan Mts., Transcaspia.

Bal/laarat, Victoria, *use* **-larat**.

ballade, medieval French poem, also its imitation.

Ballantine (James), 1808–77, artist and poet; — **(William)**, 1812–86, serjeant-at-law.

Ballantyne (James), 1772–1833; and — **(John)**, 1774–1821, Sir W. Scott's printers and publishers; — **Press**, founded 1796, named after Sir W. Scott's printers; — **(R. M.)**, 1825–94, writer for boys.

Ballarat, Victoria, *not* -aarat.

ballet; *ballet/ d'action* (Fr. m.), ballet combining action and dancing; — *divertissement*, ballet entertainment.

Balliol College, Oxford. *See also* **Bali-**.

ballistics (two *l*'s).

ballon d'essai (Fr. m.), a 'feeler' of any kind.

ballot/, -ed, -ing.

ballot (Fr. m.), a small bale.

ballroom (one word).

Ballsbridge, Dublin (one word).

bal paré (Fr. m.), fancy-dress ball.

Baluchi, a native of Baluchistan, *not* Be-, Bi-.

baluster, upright supporting a rail, commonly of stone and outdoors, the whole structure being a

balustrade. *See* **banister.**

Balzac (Honoré de), 1799–1850, French writer; — **(J. L. G.)**, 1596–1654, French writer.

banal, commonplace; *banal* (Fr.), *pl.* **banaux**, *fem.* **-ale**, *pl.* **-ales**.

banalité (Fr. f.), a commonplace.

Banco Regis (Lat.), on the King's Bench.

Bancus/ Communium Placitorum (Lat.), Court of Common Pleas; — *Reginae*, Queen's Bench; — *Superior*, King's Bench, abbr. *Banc. Sup.*

Band (Ger. m.), a volume, *pl.* *Bände*; abbr. **Bd.**, *pl.* **Bde.**

bandanna, a handkerchief, *not* -ana.

B. & F.B.S., British and Foreign Bible Society.

bandit/, *pl.* **-s.**

bandoleer, a belt for cartridges, *not* -olier, -alier.

bandolero, Spanish brigand.

bang, Indian hemp, *use* **bh-**.

Bangalore, Mysore, India.

Bangkok, Thailand, *not* Bankok.

Bangladesh, 'Land of the Bengalis', *formerly* E. Pakistan; independent 1972.

banister, upright supporting a rail, commonly of wood, indoors, on staircase, the whole structure being **banisters** (*pl.*). *See* **baluster.**

banjo/, *pl.* **-s.**

bank, abbr. **bk.**

banker envelope, one with the entry on the long side.

banking, abbr. **bkg.**

bank-note (hyphen).

bank paper, a thin, strong paper.

banlieue (Fr. f.), precinct, suburb.

banneret (law), a knight made on the field of battle.

bannerette, small banner.

banns, *not* bans.

banquet/, -ed, -ing.

banquette, a raised way behind firing-rampart.

Bantu, designating a group of Central, E., and S. African native peoples and languages.

B.A.O., Bachelor of Obstetrics.

B.A.O.R., British Army of the Rhine.

b. à p. (Fr.), *billets à payer* (bills payable).

bap., baptized.

Baptist, abbr. **Bapt.**

baptistery, *not* -try.

baptize, *not* -ise.

b. à r. (Fr.), *billets à recevoir* (bills receivable).

Bar, called to the (cap.);
bar, unit of barometric pressure.

bar., barley-corn, barometer.

Barbados, *not* -oes, abbr. **Barb.**

barbarize, *not* -ise.

Barbary, W. Africa.

barbecue (U.S.), large entertainment with whole-roasting.

barberry, the shrub *Berberis,* *not* ber-, -ery.

barbette, gun platform.

Barbirolli (**Sir John**), 1899–1970, English conductor.

barb/u (Fr.), *fem.* *-ue,* bearded.

barbue (Fr. f.), brill, *also* dab.

barcarole, Venetian gondolier's song: Fr. *barcarolle.*

B.Arch., Bachelor of Architecture.

Barclays Bank, Ltd. (no apos.).

Bareilly, Uttar Pradesh, India, *not* -eli.

Barents Sea, north of Norway and U.S.S.R., *not* -'s, -'z.

bargain/er, a haggler; **-or** (law), the seller.

Bar Harbor, Maine, U.S.

Baring-Gould (**Revd. S.**), 1834–1924 (hyphen).

baritone (mus.), *not* bary-.

barium, symbol **Ba** (no point).

bark, vessel with fore and main masts square-rigged and fore-and-aft mizen, *also* **barque.**

Barkston Ash, Yorks.

barley-corn (hyphen), *but* (**Sir**) **John Barleycorn;** abbr. **bar.**

Barmecide, one who offers illusory benefits, *not* -acide.

Barmston, Yorks.

Barnaby Bright, St. Barnabas' Day, 11 June; longest day, old style.

Barnard (**Dr. Christiaan**), S. African surgeon. *See* **Blaiberg.**

baro/graph, a recording barometer; **-gram,** the record; **-logy,** science of weight; **-meter,** abbr. **bar.**

Baron, cap. with English name; l.c. foreign (but in Ger. cap.); abbr. **B.**

baron/ (Fr.), *fem.* **-ne.**

baron and feme (law), husband and wife regarded as one.

Baronet/, abbr. **Bt.; -age,** Baronets collectively, book about them; **-cy,** patent or rank of Baronet.

baroque, exuberant arch. style of seventeenth and eighteenth centuries (not ital., not cap.).

barouche, four-wheeled carriage, *not* baru-.

barque, *see* **bark.**

barquentine, three-masted vessel with foremast only square rigged, *not* -antine, barke-.

barr., barrister.

barracuda, large W. Indian fish.

barrage, a dam; gunfire.

barrator, malicious litigant, *not* -ater, -etor.

barratry, vexatious litigation; (marine law) master's or crew's fraud or negligence.

Barrault (Jean-Louis), b. 1910, French actor, director, producer.

barrel/, -s, abbr. **bl., bls.**

barrel/led, -ling (U.S. **-ed, -ing**).

barrico/, a small cask; *pl.* **-es.**

Barrie (Sir James Matthew), 1860–1937, Sc. novelist and playwright.

barrister, abbr. **barr.**

Barrow in Furness (no hyphens).

bar sinister, *properly* **baton sinister.**

Bart., Baronet, *use* **Bt.**

Barthélemy-Saint-Hilaire (Jules), 1805–95, French statesman, Orientalist.

Bartholomew Day, 24 Aug. (caps., two words, for London local terminology but **St. Bartholomew's Day** for the massacre, 1572).

Bartolommeo (Fra), 1475–1517, Italian painter.

Bartolozzi (Francesco), 1727–1813, Italian engraver.

Bart's, St. Bartholomew's Hospital, London.

Baruch (Apocr.), not abbreviated.

bar/uche, *use* **-ouche.**

barytone, *use* **bari-** except for the Greek accent.

basan, bark-tanned sheepskin, *not* baz-. *See* **basil.**

bas bleu (Fr. m.), a 'bluestocking'.

base, abbr. **b.**

baseball, U.S. national game played by eighteen persons (nine on each side).

bashaw, *use* **pasha.**

bashi-bazouk (hyphen), Turkish mercenary.

Bashkirtseff (Marie K.), *properly* **Marya Bashkirtseva,** 1860–84, Russian diarist.

Basic English (two caps.), 'debabelized' language proposed by C. K. Ogden, 1929.

basil, aromatic herb; *also* corruption of **basan;** *not* baz-.

Basildon, Essex, 'new town', 1949.

basin, a circular vessel, *not* -on.

basinet, light steel headpiece, *not* bass-.

bas/is, *pl.* **-es.**

Baskerville (John), 1706–75, typefounder and printer.

basket/, -s, abbr. **bkt., -s.**

Basle, Switz.; in Fr. **Bâle;** in Ger. **Basel.**

bas-relief, *not* bass-.

bass, a fish, *not* -e.

bassinet, cradle, perambulator, *not* bas-, -ette, berceaunette.

basso/ (mus.), abbr. ***B.***; — *profundo* (It. mus.), lowest male voice; — *-rilievo* (It.), bas-relief, *pl.* *-i -i,* anglicized to **basso -relievo,** *pl.* **-os.**

bastaard (S. Afr.), person of mixed white and coloured parentage, whether legitimate or not.

bastardize, *not* -ise.

bastard size, a non-standard size.

Bastien-Lepage (Jules), 1848–84, French painter (hyphen).

Bastille (Fr. f.), Paris prison.

bastille, a fortified tower, *not* -ile.

bastinado/, *not* basto-; *pl.* **-s.**

Basuto/, -land, S. Africa. *See* **Lesotho.**

bataille rangée (Fr. f.), a pitched battle.

bateau/ (Fr. m.), a boat, *not* batt-; *pl.* **-x.**

Bath: & Well: sig. of Bp. of Bath and Wells (two colons).

Bath/brick, — bun, — chair, — chap (*not* chop), **— note,** folded writing paper 8 × 7 inches, **— Oliver, — stone** (cap. B).

baton, music conductor's stick; in Fr. m. *baton.*

battalion, abbr. **battn.** *or* **bn.**; in Fr. m. *bataillon.*

battels, provisions, etc., at Oxford University.

batter (typ.), a damaged letter.

batterie de cuisine (Fr. f.), a set of cooking utensils.

battery, abbr. **batt.** *or* **bty.**

battle, in Fr. f. *bataille.*

battledore, *not* -door.

battle/field, -ship (one word).

battre/ la campagne (Fr.), to beat about the bush; — *le pavé*, to loaf about.

battue, shooting (not ital.).

Batum, Georgia, U.S.S.R., *not* -oum.

Baudelaire (Charles), 1821–67, French poet, *not* Beau-.

baulk, of timber (U.S. **balk**).

Bavaria/, -n, abbr. **Bav.**; in Ger. **Bayern.**

bawbee (Sc.), halfpenny, *not* bau-.

Bay, when with name cap.; abbr. **B.**

bayadère, Hindu dancing girl.

Bayard (Pierre de Terrail, Chevalier de), 1475–1524, 'The Knight without fear and without reproach'.

bayonet/, -ed, -ing.

bayou (*pron.* by-you), tributary creek.

Bayreuth, Bavaria, *not* Bai- (*see also* **Beirut**).

Bays, the Queen's Bays Regiment.

bazaar, in Fr. m. *bazar.*

bazan, *use* **bas-.**

bazil, sheepskin, *use* **bas-.**

BB (pencils), double black.

BBB (pencils), treble black.

B.B.C., British Broadcasting Corporation. **BBC** is now usual, esp. as adj.

B.C., Bachelor of Surgery, Board of Control, British Columbia (Canada).

B.C., before Christ (s.caps.), year to precede, as 41 B.C.: the reverse of A.D., as A.D. 1900.

B.C.A., Bureau of Current Affairs.

B.Ch., B.Chir., Bachelor of Surgery.

B.Ch.D., *or* **B.D.S.,** Bachelor of Dental Surgery.

B.C.E., Bachelor of Civil Engineering; before Christian Era (*see* **A.C.E.**).

B.C.F., British Cycling Federation.

b.c.g., bacillus of Calmette and Guérin (anti-T.B. inoculation).

B.C.L., Bachelor of Civil Law.

B.C.M.S., Bible Churchmen's Missionary Society.

B.Com., B.Comm., B.Com.Sc., Bachelor of Commerce.

B.C.P., Book of Common Prayer.

B.C.S., Bengal Civil Service.

B.D., Bachelor of Divinity.

Bd., (Ger.) *Band* (a volume).

bd., board, bond, bound.

B.D.A., British Dental Association.

Bde., (Ger.) *Bände* (volumes).

Bde Maj., Brigade Major.

bdg., binding.

B.D.L., British Drama League.

bdl., bdls., bundle, -s.

Bdr., Bombardier.

B.D.S., Bachelor of Dental Surgery, Bomb Disposal Squad.

bds., (bound in) boards.

B.E., B.Eng., Bachelor of Engineering.

Be (chem.), beryllium (no point).

b.e., bill of exchange.

B.E.A., British Esperanto Association; — European Airways (*see* **B.A.**).

beach-la-mar, jargon English of W. Pacific.

bear (Stock Exchange), speculator for a fall.

beard (typ.), the space between the foot of the letter and the bottom edge of the type.

béarnaise (Fr. cook.), rich white sauce.

bearskin, military cap (one word).

beastings, *use* bee-.

beasts of the chase (law), buck, doe, fox, marten, roe; ditto **forest** (law), boar, hare, hart, hind, wolf; ditto **warren** (law), cony and hare; ditto of **venery** (law) are 'beasts of the forest'.

beatae memoriae (Lat.), of blessed memory; abbr. **B.M.**

Beata/ Maria, or — *Virgo* (Lat.), the Blessed Virgin; abbr. **B.M.,** *or* **B.V.** *See also* **B.M.V., B.V.M.**

Beatles, the, pop-group, *fl.* late 1960s.

beatnik (U.S.), cultural, sartorial, and tonsorial non-conformist, mid-twentieth century.

beau (*pl.* **beaux**), not ital.

Beaufort scale, of wind force (one cap.); *for details see under* **wind.**

beau-fils (Fr. m.), son-in-law; without hyphen, beautiful son.

beau idéal, model of excellence (not ital.).

beauidealize, *not* -ise (one word).

Beaujolais, a burgundy.

Beaulieu, Hants, *pron.* bew-lē

beau-monde, the fashionable world.

Beaune, a burgundy.

beau/ rôle (Fr. m.), a fine part; — *sabreur,* dashing cavalryman.

beaux-arts (Fr. pl. m.), fine arts.

beaux/ esprits (Fr. pl. m.), wits, *sing.* **bel esprit;** — *yeux,* good looks.

becafico, *use* becc-.

bécarre (Fr. mus. m.), the natural sign ♮.

bécasse (Fr. f.), a woodcock, a stupid woman.

bécassine (Fr. f.), a snipe.

beccafico/, *pl.* **-s,** small edible Italian bird.

bechamel (Fr. cook.), white sauce named after Béchamel, steward of Louis XIV.

bêche-de-mer, sea-slug, a Chinese delicacy.

Bechstein (F. W. K.), 1826–1900, German pianoforte maker; — **(J. M.),** 1757–1822, German naturalist.

Bechuana/, -land, S. African, *pron.* betsh-. *See* **Botswana.**

Becket (à), *see* à **Becket.**

Becquerel, French family of physicists: — **(A. C.),** 1788–1878, father of — **(A. E.),** 1820–91, father of — **(A. H.),** 1852–1908, discoverer of radioactive — **rays.**

bed (typ.), the part of the press on which the forme lies.

B.Ed., Bachelor of Education.

bedaw/een, -i, -in, *use* bedouin.

Beddgelert, Caernarvon, *not* Beth-.

bedeguar, mosslike excrescence on roses.

bedel, Oxford official form of beadle; at Cambridge, **bedell.**

Bedfordshire, abbr. **Beds.**

bedouin/, a desert Arab, *not* the many variations; *pl.* as sing.

bed/owy, use **-ouin.**

bed/room, -sore (one word).

bed/uin, use **-ouin.**

beehive (one word).

beer firkin, abbr. **b.f.**

beerhouse (law), where beer is sold to be drunk *on* or *off* the premises.

beershop (law), where beer is sold to be drunk *off* the premises.

Bees (St.), public school (no apos.).

beestings, first milk from a mammal, *not* bea-, bie-.

bees-wax (noun), **beeswax** (verb).

Beethoven (Ludwig van, *not* von), 1770–1827, German composer; divide Beethoven; *pron.* bāt′-ho-vn.

beetling beating of clothes with a beetle.

B.E.F., British Expeditionary Force.

befall, *not* -al.

Beggar's Opera, not -s'.

beghard, lay brother, orig. Flemish, thirteenth century.

beglerbeg, high Ottoman governor, (cap. as title).

beguine, lay sister, *see* **beghard;** a Latin American dance.

behemoth, biblical animal (book of Job), thought to be the hippopotamus.

behoof (noun), benefit.

behove (verb), to be incumbent on (U.S. **-oove**).

Behring Isle, Sea, and **Strait,** use **Bering** —.

beif., beiflgd. (Ger.), *beifolgend,* [sent] herewith.

beignet (Fr. m.), a fritter.

Beinn Bhuidhe, near Inveraray; Sound of Mull; *not* Ben Bui.

Beirut, Lebanon, *not* Ba-, Bai-. *See also* **Bayreuth.**

bel air (Fr. m.), good deportment.

Belalp, Switz. (one word).

Bel and the Dragon (Apocr.), abbrev. **Bel & Dr.**

beldam, a hag, *not* -e.

bel/ esprit (Fr. m.), a brilliant wit, *pl.* **beaux esprits;** — *étage,* the first floor, *not* belle —.

Belgique (Fr. f.), Belgium; *belge,* Belgian (not cap., unless used as a noun).

Belg/ium, -ian, -ic, abbr. **Belg.**

believable, *not* -eable.

belladonna (bot.), deadly nightshade (one word).

belle (not ital.).

belle/ amie (Fr. f.), female friend; — *assemblée,* fashionable gathering; — *-de-jour,* convolvulus; — *-de-nuit* (bot.), marvel of Peru; — *-fille,* daughter-in-law, stepdaughter; without hyphen, beautiful girl.

Belle-Île-en-Mer, dép. Morbihan (hyphens).

Belle Isle (Straits of), between Newfoundland and Labrador.

Belleisle, Fermanagh.

belle/-mère (Fr. f.), mother-in-law, stepmother; without hyphen, beautiful mother; — *mort,* natural death; — *passion,* the tender passion.

belles-lettres, literature, is *plural* (hyphen).

Bell Island, off NE. coast of Newfoundland.

Bell Rock, North Sea. *See* **Inchcape Rock.**

Bel/oochee, -uchi, use **Baluchi.**

Belorussia, White Russia, a Soviet Socialist Republic. *See* **U.S.S.R.**

belvedere (It.), a raised building, *not* belvi-; *pron.* bel-ve-dēr' (not ital.).

Belvedere, Kent, Eng.; California, U.S.

Belvidere, Ill., U.S.

Belvoir, castle, Leics., *pron.* Beaver.

B.E.M. British Empire Medal.

bench-mark (hyphen).

Ben Day (typ.), mechanical method for producing shading and stippling effects.

bene decessit (Lat.), he died naturally.

Benedic (liturg.), canticle from Psalm 103.

Benedicite, the 'Song of the Three Children', from Apocr., as canticle.

benedicite! bless you!

Benedick, confirmed bachelor newly married, *not* -ict (from Shakespeare's *Much Ado about Nothing*).

Benedictus, the Canticle of Zaccharias (Luke 1: 68 ff.), or a choral passage in the Mass, beginning *Benedictus qui venit* (Matt. 21: 9)

bene/ esse (Lat.), well-being; — *exeat*, certificate of good character.

benefactor, *not* -er.

benefit/, -ed, -ing.

Benelux, Belgium, the Netherlands, Luxemburg.

bene/ merenti (Lat.), to the well-deserving; — *meritus*, having well deserved, *pl.* — *meriti.*

Beneš (Eduard), president of Czechoslovakia, 1935–8.

Benet, English form of the name Benedict; used of St. Benedict and institutions bearing his name, e.g. St. Benet's Church, — — Hall.

Benét (Stephen Vincent), 1898–1943, and — (**William Rose**), 1886–1950, American poets.

bene vale (Lat.), farewell, abbr. *b.v.*; — *vobis!* prosperity to you!

ben ficcato (It.), well established.

B.Eng., Bachelor of Engineering.

Bengali/, person born in, language of, (adj.) of, Bengal, *not* -ee, *pl.* **-s**; abbr. **Beng.**

Benghazi, Libya, *not* -gasi.

Pen/ Lawers, Perth; — **Macdhui,** Aberdeen.

Bennet, John, *c.* 1600, English madrigalist; family name of Earl of Tankerville.

benth/al, ocean depths exceeding 6,000 feet; **-os,** the flora and fauna of the sea-bottom, as opp. to **plankton.**

Bentham (G.), 1800–84, bot.; abbr. **Benth;** — (**Jeremy**), 1748–1832, English pol. philosopher.

ben trovato (It.), well invented.

Ben/ Venue, — Vrackie, Perth (two words).

ben venuto (It.), welcome.

Ben Vorlich, Dunbarton and Perth.

benzedrine (med.), inhalant or nerve stimulant, *not* -in.

benzene, a spirit obtained from coal-tar.

benzine, a spirit obtained from petroleum.

benzoin, aromatic resin of Japanese tree.

benzol, crude benzene, *not* -ole.

benzoline, benzine.

Beowulf, Anglo-Saxon epic.

bequeather, a testator.

berberry, *use* **bar-.**

berceau (Fr. m.), cradle.

berceaunette, *use* **bassinet.**

berceuse, a cradle song.

Berg/ (Ger. m.), a mountain; *pl.* **-e** (cap.).

berg (Afr.), a mountain.

Bergamask, native of
Bergamo, Lombardy;
bergamask, rustic dance
attributed to them.

bergamot, tree of citrus
family; type of pear, *not*
burg-.

Bergerac, French town;
wine made there; —
(Savinien Cyrano de),
1619–55, French writer.

berhyme (one word).

beriberi, tropical disease,
not -ria (one word).

Bering Isle, Sea, and **Strait,**
not Beh-, ings.

Berk. (bot.), Berkeley.

Berkeley, Calif., U.S.

berkelium, symbol **Bk** (no
point).

Berkhamsted, Herts.

Berks., Berkshire.

Bernard (Claude), 1813–78,
French physiologist.

Bernardine, Cistercian,
from St. Bernard of Clairvaux,
1091–1153.

Berne, Swiss canton and
town; — **Convention** (1886
and later modifications)
deals with copyright (*see*
**Universal Copyright
Convention**); in Ger. **Bern.**

Berners (Dame Juliana),
wrote *Boke of St. Albans,* first
ed. 1486.

Bernhardt (Rosine, *called*
'**Sarah'**), 1845–1923, actress.

Bern/oulli, family of Swiss
mathematicians, *not* -illi.

bernouse, use **burnous,**
Arab cloak.

bersaglier/e (It.), a rifleman;
pl. **-i.**

berth (naut.), *not* bi-.

Berthelot (P. E. M.), 1827–
1907, French chemist.

Berthollet (Count C. L.),
1748–1822, French chemist.

beryllium, symbol **Be** (no
point).

Berzelius (J. J., baron),
1779–1848, Swedish chemist.

B.E.S.A., British Engineering
Standards Association.

B. ès A., now **B. ès L.**

Besa, 7.92 mm. machine-gun.

Besançon, dép. Doubs.

bes-antler, use **bez-antler.**

B. ès L. (Fr.), *Bachelier ès
lettres* (Bachelor of Letters).

beso/ las manos (Sp.), 'I
kiss the hands' (frequently
said or written); — **los pies,**
'I kiss the feet'.

B. ès S., *Bachelier ès sciences*
(no hyphens).

Bessarabia, district in
Moldavia and Ukraine, ceded
by Romania to U.S.S.R.,
1940.

Bessbrook, Co. Armagh.

Bessemer process, *in* steel
mfr. (one cap.).

Besses o' th' Barn, village
near Manchester

bestialize, *not* -ise.

betatron, apparatus for
accelerating electrons.

bête (Fr.), stupid.

betel, leaf of betel-pepper,
chewed in East

betel-nut, misnomer for
areca-nut, chewed with betel.

Betelgeu/se (astr.), red star in
Orion, *not* -x.

bête noire (Fr. f.), one's pet
aversion, *not* — noir.

bethel, Nonconformist chapel
(*not* cap.).

bêtise (Fr. f.), stupidity.

Betjeman (Sir John), b.
1906, English poet and writer
on architecture; appointed
Poet Laureate 1972.

betony (bot.), *not* bett-.

B.E.T.R.O., British Export
Trade Research Organization.

better, one who bets, *not* -or.

Bettws-y-coed, Caernarvon
(hyphens).

bevel/, -led, -ling (U.S. **-ed,
-ing**).

Beverley, Yorks.

Beverly, Mass., U.S.

Beverly Hills, Calif., U.S.

bevy, proper word for a company of ladies, larks, maidens, quails, or roes.

Bexleyheath, Kent (one word).

bey (Turk.), a governor, **beylik,** jurisdiction of a bey, *not* -ic.

Beyrout, *use* **Beirut** (U.S. **Beyrouth**).

bez. (Ger.), *bezüglich* (with reference to).

bezant, gold coin first struck at Byzantium, *not* by-.

bez-antler, *or* **bay-,** of deer's horn, *not* bes-, bis-.

bezw. bzw. (Ger.), *beziehungsweise* (respectively, relatively, in the circumstances, or).

b.f., bloody fool, brought forward, (typ.) bold face.

B.F.B.S., British and Foreign Bible Society.

B.F.I., British Film Institute.

B.F.M.P., British Federation of Master Printers.

Bhagavadgita, philosophical dialogue in the Hindu epic *Mahabharata.*

B'ham, Birmingham.

bhang, Indian hemp, *not* ba-.

bheesty, bhisti, Indian water-carrier, *not* -ie.

b.h.p., brake horse power.

Bhutan, protectorate of Rep. of India since 1949.

B.Hy. Durh., Bachelor of Public Health, Univ. of Durham.

Bi (chem.), bismuth (no point).

B.I.A.E., British Institute of Adult Education.

Biafra, portion of Nigeria, seceded 1967–70.

biannual, half-yearly, *but* **biennial,** two-yearly.

bias/, -ed, -ing.

Bib., Bible, Biblical.

bibl., *bibliotheca* (library).

Bible, abbr. **Bib.** (cap., *but* three bibles = three copies of the Bible). *See also* **authorities, quotations.**

Biblia Pauperum, 'books of the poor', block books (caps.).

biblical (not cap.), abbr. **Bib.**

bibliograaf (Dutch), bibliographer; Ger. m. *Bibliograph;* Fr. m. *bibliographe.*

bibliograph/er, -ic, -ical, -y; abbr. **bibliog.**

bibliopeg/y, bookbinding as a fine art; **-ist.**

biblio/theca (Lat.), a library; *-thécaire* (Fr. m.), a librarian; *-thèque* (Fr. f.), a library.

Bibliothek/ (Ger. f.), a library; *-ar* (m.), a librarian (caps.).

bicameral, with two legis-lative chambers.

Bickleigh, Devon.

Bickley, Cheshire, Kent.

bidet, raised narrow wash-bowl that can be bestridden, *not* -ette.

bien/ aim/é (Fr.), *fem.* -ée, well-beloved; — *chauss/é, fem.* -ée, well-shod; — *entendu,* of course; — *gant/é, fem.* -ée, well-gloved.

biennial, two-yearly, (bot.) ②, *but* **biannual,** half-yearly.

biennium, a two-year period.

bienséance (Fr. f.), propriety.

bière (Fr. f.), beer, bier.

biestings, *use* bee-.

B.I.F., British Industries Fair.

biff/é (Fr.), *fem.* -ée, cancelled.

Bigelow (E. B.), 1814–79, American inventor and industrialist; — **(John),** 1817–1911, American journalist and diplomat.

Biglow Papers (*The*), anti-slavery poems, 1848 and 1857–61, by James Russell Lowell.

bigot/, -ed.

bijou/, a 'gem'; *pl.* **-x.**

Bilbao, Spain.

bilberry, *not* bill-.

bilbo/, Spanish sword or rapier; *pl.* **-s.**
bilboes, *pl.,* fetters.
Bilderdijk (Willem), 1756–1831, Dutch poet, philologist.
bile-duct (hyphen).
Bill (parliamentary) (cap.).
billa vera (law), a true bill.
billet/, -ed, -ing.
billet-doux (Fr. m.), a love letter; *pl.* **billets-doux** (hyphens).
billiards, in Fr. m. *billard.*
billion (Eng., Ger.), a million millions; (Fr., U.S.), a thousand millions.
bill of/ exchange, abbr. **b.e.;** — — **lading,** abbr. **B/L.** (printed six to a sheet on folio post); — — **sale,** abbr. **b.s.**
biltong (Afrik.), sun-dried meat.
Biluchi, *use* **Bal-.**
B.I.M., British Institute of Management.
bimetall/ic, -ism, -ist.
bimillenary, a period of 2,000 years.
bi-monthly, avoid as ambiguous.
bindery, a bookbinder's establishment (esp. U.S.).
binnacle (naut.), a compass-stand.
binocle, a field-glass.
binocular/ (adj.), for two eyes; **-s** (pl. noun), field or opera glasses.
Binstead, I. of Wight.
Binsted, Alton, Hants.
Binyon (Laurence), 1869–1943, poet.
biograph/er, -ic, -ical, -y; abbr. **biog.**
biolog/y, -ical; abbr. **biol.**
Bipont/, -ine, books printed at Bipontium (Zweibrücken), Bavaria.
bird-cage (hyphen).
bird's-eye view (one hyphen).
Birmingham, abbr. **B'ham;** Small Arms, **B.S.A.**

Birnam, Perth, immortalized in *Macbeth.*
Birstall, Leicester, Yorks.
birth (naut.), *use* **be-.**
birth/-control, -rate (hyphens).
birthplace, abbr. **bpl.**
birthright (one word).
B.I.S., Bank of International Settlements.
bis (Fr., It., Lat.), twice.
bis., bissextile.
Biscayan, abbr. **Bisc.,** pertaining to Biscay, Spain; Basque.
bis dat qui cito dat (Lat.), he gives twice who gives quickly.
B.I.S.F., British Iron and Steel Federation.
Bishop, abbr. **Bp.;** (chess) **B** (no point).
Bishopbriggs, Lanarkshire.
Bishop *in partibus infidelium*, R.C. bishop taking title from ancient see situated 'in territory of unbelievers', now termed 'Titular Bishop'.
Bishop's Castle, Salop (apos.).
bishop's length (painting), canvas 58 × 94 in., half canvas 45 × 56 in.
Bishop's Lydeard, Somerset (apos.).
Bishop's Stortford, Herts. (apos.).
Bishopsteignton, Devon (one word).
Bishopston, Glos., Glam.
Bishopstone, Bucks., Hereford, Sussex, Wilts.
Bishop's Waltham, Hants (apos.).
Bishopthorpe, residence of Abp. of York (one word).
Bishopton, Renfrewshire.
bisk, a rich soup (not ital.) (U.S. **bisque**).
Bismarck (Karl O. E. L., Fürst von), 1815–98, German statesman, *not* -ark.

bismillah (Arab.), 'in the name of God', *not* biz-.

bismuth, symbol **Bi** (no point).

bisque, in tennis, croquet, golf; *also* unglazed white porcelain (not ital.).

bissextile (noun and adj.), Latin leap-year, abbr. **bis.**

bistoury, surgeon's scalpel.

bit (U.S.), 12½ cents.

bitts (naut., pl.), pair of posts on deck for fastening cables, etc.

bitumin/ize, -ous.

bivouac/, -ked, -king.

bi-weekly, avoid as ambiguous. Cf. **semi-w.**

bizarre (not ital.).

Bizet (**Georges**), 1838–75, French composer.

Björnson (**Björnstjerne**), 1832–1910, Norwegian writer.

bk., bank, book.

bkg., banking.

bkt., bkts., basket, -s.

B.L., Bachelor of Law, breech-load/er, -ing.

B/L, bill of lading.

bl., bls., bale, -s, barrel, -s.

Bl., Ger. *Blatt,* newspaper.

B.L.A., British Liberation Army (*later* **B.A.O.R.,** q.v.).

Blackfoot (N. Amer. Indian), *pl.* **Blackfeet.**

Black Friars, Leics.

Blackfriars, London.

Black Friday, 11 May 1866.

black game (two words), black grouse: *male,* **blackcock** (one word), *fem.,* **grey-hen** (hyphen).

black letter (typ.), general term for gothic or Old English.

black Maria, prison van (two words, one cap.).

Blackmoor, Hants.

Blackmore, Essex; — (**R. D.**), 1825–1900, writer.

blackout (noun, one word); **black out** (verb, two words).

Blackrock, Brecon, Cork, Co. Dublin, Louth.

Blackrod, Lancs.

Black Rod, abbr. for 'Gentleman Usher of the Black Rod'.

blacks (typ.), when spaces print.

blackshirt/, a Fascist; **-ed** (one word).

blaeberry, Sc. for **bil-.**

Blaenau Ffestiniog, Merioneth (no hyphen).

blague/ (Fr. f.), humbug; *-ur* (m.), hoaxer.

Blaiberg (**Philip**), 1909–69, S. African, lived for 18 months after heart-transplant operation by Dr. Christiaan Barnard.

Blairadam, Kinross (one word).

Blair Atholl, Perth (caps., no hyphen).

Blairgowrie, Perth (one word).

Blairs College, Aberdeen (no apos.).

blameable, *see* **-able.**

blanchaille (Fr. f.), whitebait.

blanchisseuse (Fr. f.), laundress.

blancmange (cook.) (one word, not ital.); Fr. *blanc-manger.*

Bland, Mrs., *see* **Nesbit.**

blanket/, -ed, -ing.

Blantyre Works, Lanark, a village (two words, caps.).

blas/é, surfeited with enjoyment (not ital.); *fem.* **-ée.**

Blatherwycke, Northants., *not* -wyck, -wick.

bldg., bldgs., building, -s.

bled, bleed (typ.), an illustration going to the trimmed edge.

bleed (bookbinding), to overcut the margins and mutilate the printing.

blesbok (Afrik.), an antelope, *not* -buck.

blind/blocking, *or*
— **tooling** (bookbinding),
impression by hot tools only.
blind ¶, paragraph mark,
with closed loop.
B.Lit., Bachelor of Literature.
B.Litt., *Baccalaureus Literarum*
(Bachelor of Letters).
Blitzkrieg (Ger. m.), violent
attack; Eng. abbr. **blitz** (no
point).
blk. (typ.), black, block, -s.
B.LL., Bachelor of Laws.
bloc (Fr.), combination of
nations or parties.
Bloch (**Ernest**), 1880–1959,
Swiss-American composer.
block (typ.), letterpress
printing plate for an
illustration.
blocking (bookbinding),
impressing lettering or a
design into the case of a
book; **blind** —, without foil
or colour; **gold** —, with
gold foil.
Block (**Maurice**), 1816–1901,
French economist.
blond, fair-complexioned;
fem. blonde (not ital.).
**blood/-pressure, -stream,
-supply** (hyphens).
blottesque, painting with
blotted touches (not ital.).
Blount, *pron.* Blunt.
blowup (noun), an enlarged
picture (one word).
blow up (verb), to enlarge
(two words).
blowzy, coarse-looking, *not*
blou-, -sy.
B.L.R., breech-loading rifle.
B.L.S. (U.S.), Bureau of
Labor Statistics.
Blubberhouses, Yorks. (one
word).
Blücher (**G. L. von**), 1742–
1819, German Field-
Marshal.
bluebell (one word).
Blue book, U.K. governmental report (cap., two
words).

blueing (U.S. **blui-**).
blueish, *use* **bluish.**
bluejacket, R.N. sailor (one
word).
blueprint (one word).
blue-printing, a photog.
process (hyphen).
bluey.
bluing, *use* **blueing.**
bluish, *not* blue-.
Blundellsands, Lancs. (one
word).
blurb, eulogy or résumé of
book, printed on jacket.
Blut und Eisen (Ger.),
blood and iron.
Blyth (surname), *pron.* Bly.
Blyth Bridge, Peebles.
Blythebridge, Staffs.
B.M., Bachelor of Medicine;
Beata Maria (the Blessed
Virgin), *beatae memoriae* (of
blessed memory); (Survey)
bench-mark; British
Museum.
b.m., *bene merenti* (to the
well-deserving).
B.M.A., British Medical
Association.
B.M.E., Bachelor of Mining
Engineering.
B.M.J., *British Medical
Journal.*
B.Met., Bachelor of
Metallurgy.
B.M.R., basal metabolic
rate.
B.Mus., Bachelor of Music.
B.M.V., *Beata Maria Virgo*
(Blessed Virgin Mary).
bn., battalion.
B.N.B., British National
Bibliography.
B.N.C., Brasenose College,
Oxford.
B.N.O.C., British National
Opera Company.
b.o., branch office, broker's
order, buyer's option.
B.O., body odour.
B.O.A., British Optical
Association, — Olympic
Association.

Boabdil, last Moorish king of
Granada, 1482–92; d. *c.* 1533.
B.O.A.C., British Overseas
Airways Corporation (*see*
B.A.).
Boanerges, *sing.* or *pl.*, loud
preacher(s).
board-foot, carp. measure
of 1 in. by 1 ft. sq.
Board of Trade, abbr.
B. of T., absorbed in
**Department of Trade and
Industry,** 1970.
board-school, before 1902,
managed by a school-board
acc. to Educ. Act of 1870.
boatswain, *pron.* bō′sn;
abbr. **bos'n** (no point).
bobolink, N. American
songbird.
bob-white, American quail.
bocasin, a fine buckram.
Boccaccio (Giovanni),
1313–75, Italian writer
(four *c*'s).
Bodicote, Oxon.
Bodleian Library.
Bodoni (Giambattista),
1740–1813, Italian printer.
body (typ.), the measurement
from front to back of the
shank of a piece of type; in
the Anglo-American system
12 pt. = 0·166 in. *See*
Didot.
bodyguard (one word).
body-weight (hyphen).
Boerhaave (Herman),
1668–1738, Dutch naturalist.
Boëthius (Anicius), A.D.
470–525, Roman statesman
and philosopher.
bœuf (Fr. m.), beef.
B. of T., Board of Trade, q.v.
bogey, Colonel Bogey, in
golf.
bogie, a truck.
Bogotá, Colombia, S. America.
bog/y, ghost, *not* -ey; *pl.* **-ies.**
Bohemian (noun or adj.),
socially unconventional
(person); **bohemianism**
(not cap.).

Bohun, *pron.* Boon.
boiler-room (hyphen).
boiling-point (hyphen), abbr.
b.p.
Bokhara, river, N.S.W.,
Australia. See **Bukhara** for
the town in Uzbekistan.
bolas/, a lasso with two balls;
pl. **-es.**
bold-face type, as this;
indicated in MS. by wavy
underline; abbr. **b.f.**
bolero/, Spanish dance,
woman's short jacket;
pl. **-s.**
bolivar, the Venezuelan
monetary unit.
Bolivia/, -n, abbr. **Bol.**
Bologna, Italy; adj.
Bolognese.
bolometer, radiation
measurer.
Bolshevik, advocate of
proletarian dictatorship by
soviets; member of majority
group of Russian Social
Democratic Party, later the
Communist Party, opp. to
Menshevik
bolts (bind.), folds before
they are trimmed off.
Boltzmann constant (phys.),
k (no point).
bolus/, large pill; *pl.* **-es.**
Bombardier, cap. when
defining rank; abbr. **Bdr.**
bombasine, a fabric, *not*
-bazeen, -bazine, -bycine
(U.S. **-bazine**).
bona (law), goods.
bon-accord (Sc.), goodwill.
bonae notae (Lat.),
meritorious.
bona/ fide (Lat.), genuinely;
— **fides,** good faith (no
accent); *bona mobilia,*
movable goods.
bonanza (U.S.), good luck.
Bonaparte, *not* Buonaparte,
Corsican family.
bona/ peritura (Lat.),
perishable goods; —
vacantia, unclaimed goods.

bon-bon, a kind of sweet, a Christmas cracker; **bonbonnière,** a box for sweets.

bon camarade (Fr. m.), good comrade; *fem.* **bonne** —.

bon-chrétien, a pear; *pl.* **bons-chrétiens.**

bon/ compagnon (Fr. m.), pleasant companion; — *courage,* good courage.

bond, abbr. **bd.**

bon de poste (Fr.), postal order.

bondholder (one word).

bon diable (Fr. m.), good-natured fellow.

bond paper, a hard, strong paper.

bon enfant (Fr. m.), good fellow.

Bo'ness, Linlithgow, apostrophe, being originally Borrowstounness. *See also* **Bowness.**

bon/ goût (Fr. m.), good taste; — *gré, mal gré,* whether one will or not.

Bonheur (Rosa), 1822–99, French painter.

bonhomie (Fr. f.), good nature.

bonhomme (Fr. m.), a pleasant fellow, a friar.

Bonhomme (Jacques), the French peasant.

bonjour (Fr. m.), good day (one word).

bon jour, bonne œuvre (Fr.), 'the better the day, the better the deed'.

bon/ marché (Fr.), a cheap shop, cheap; — *mot,* a witticism, *pl.* **bons mots** (two words).

bonne (Fr. f.), a nursemaid.

bonne-bouche, a dainty morsel, *pl.* **bonnes-bouches;** *bonne/ compagnie* (Fr.), well-bred society; — *foi,* good faith; — *fortune,* success, *pl.* **bonnes**

fortunes; — *grâce,* gracefulness, *pl.* **bonnes grâces.**

bonnement (Fr.), frankly.

bonne mine (Fr. f.), pleasant look.

bonnet/, -ed, -ing.

bonnet rouge (Fr. m.), Republican's cap.

Bononia, Lat. for Bologna, Italy.

bons à vue (Fr. m.), bills, etc., at sight.

bontebok (Afrik.), pied antelope, *not* -buck.

bon ton (Fr. m.), good style.

bonum/ omen (Lat.), a good omen; — *publicum,* the public good, abbr. *b.p.*

bon vivant/, one fond of luxurious living (no hyphen, not ital.); *pl.* **-s.** The fem., **bonne vivante,** is not in French usage.

bon viveur, a luxurious liver;

bon voyage! (Fr.), a pleasant journey!

Booerhave, *use* **Boerhaave.**

book/, -s, abbr. **bk., bks.**

bookbinding (one word).

book-keeping (hyphen).

booklet (typ.), usually an inset, saddle-stitched piece of printing, with limp cover.

book-plate (hyphen).

books (cited titles of), in italic.

book sizes (typ.): the following are the standard untrimmed book sizes in mm., 4to and 8vo: **metric crown,** 252×192, 192× 126; **metric large crown,** 264×204, 204×132; **metric demy,** 282×222, 222×141; **metric royal,** 318×240, 240×159; **A4,** 305×215; **A5,** 215×152·5. For the former standard book sizes *see* **crown, demy, foolscap, imperial, medium, pott, royal, small royal.**

books of Scripture (typ.), not to be italic, nor quoted; for abbrs. *see* separate titles.

Booksellers Association, abbr. **B.A.**

book trim (bind.): standard trim is 3 mm. off head, foredge, and tail margins.

bookwork, *see* **preliminary matter.**

Boone (Daniel), 1735–1820, American explorer and colonizer.

Boötes (astr.), the constellation; *pron.* bo-ō′tēz.

booze, to drink, *not* -se, bouse, -ze, bowze.

B.O.P., *Boy's Own Paper.*

bor., borough.

Borak, Al, the winged horse on which Muhammad, in a vision, ascended to heaven.

bordar, a villein.

Bordeaux, a claret or any wine of Bordeaux (in Fr. m. *not* cap.).

Bordeaux mixture, of lime and copper sulphate, to kill fungus and insect parasites on plants.

border (typ.), an ornament.

bordereau (Fr. m.), a memorandum, docket.

Boreas (Gr. myth.), god of the north wind.

borecole, kale.

Borghese, Italian family, *pron.* bor-gā′zĕ.

Borgia (Cesare), 1476–1507; — **(Lucrezia),** 1480–1519.

born, abbr. **b.**

Borodin (A.P.), 1834–87, Russian composer and chemist.

boron, symbol **B** (no point).

borough, abbr. **bor.**

bortsch, Russian ragout.

borzoi/, Russian wolf-hound; *pl.* **-s.**

Bosanquet (Bernard), 1848–1923, English philosopher.

bosbok, *see* **bushbuck.**

bos'n, contr. of **boatswain.**

Bosna Serai, Turkish for

Sarajevo, Bosnia, once in Turkey, now in Yugoslavia.

Bosphorus, *use* **Bosporus.**

Bossuet (J. B.), 1627–1704, French bishop, writer.

Boswellize, to write laudatory biography (cap.).

bot/, -fly, *not* -tt.

Botallack, Cornish mine.

botanize, *not* -ise.

botan/y, -ical, -ist, abbr. **bot.;** genera, species, and varieties to be ital.; all other divisions roman:

Rosaceae (order or family); *Rosa* (genus), but genera in popular use in roman, as Geranium, Lobelias (pl.); *Rosa damascena* (species).

Specific and infraspecific epithets, even when derived from names of persons, should be l.c.: *Lilium wardii, Camellia × williamsii,* not *Wardii, Williamsii.* Also l.c. are names of flowers used non-technically, as geranium, lobelia.

Signs in general use: dioecious, ♂♀; doubtful, ?; female, ♀; hermaphrodite, ♀; hybrid, ×; male, ♂; monoecious, ♂-♀ (not common); number indefinite, ∞; personally verified, |; polygamous, ♂♀♂ (not common); section (of a genus), §.

bothy (Sc.), hut, *not* -ie.

Botswana, S. African independent republic 1966, *formerly* Bechuanaland.

Botticelli (Sandro), 1447–1515, Florentine painter.

Boucicault (Dion), 1822–90, Irish dramatist; *pron.* boo′-si-kō.

boudoir (not ital.).

bouffant/ (Fr.), *fem.* **-e,** puffed out, as a dress.

bougainvillaea, trop. plant with rosy bracts.

Bouguereau (W. A.), 1825–1905, French painter.

bouillabaisse, thick fish soup (not ital.).

bouilli (Fr. m.), stewed meat (not ital.).

bouill/ie (Fr. f.), infant food; *-on* (m.), broth, a flounce; *-onné,* puffed, flounced.

boul., boulevard.

boule, a French game akin to bowls (not ital.).

boule, *usually spelt* **buhl,** q.v.

Boulē, legislative council in ancient Greece.

boulevard/ (Fr. m.), abbr. **boul.; -ier,** a 'man about town'.

boulevers/é (Fr.), overturned; *-ement* (m.), a violent inversion.

Boulogne, Haute Garonne and Pas de Calais, France.

bounceable, *not* -cable.

bouncy, *not* bouncey.

bound, abbr. **bd.**

bouquet.

bouquetin, the ibex.

bouquinist, second-hand bookseller; in Fr. m. *bouquiniste.*

bourgeois/ (Fr.), *fem.* **-e,** one of the middle-class; **-ie,** the middle-class (not ital.).

bourgeois (typ.), old name for a size of type, about 9 pt.; *pron.* berjo'yce.

Bourn, Cambs.

Bourne, Lincs., Surrey.

bourne, a limit, *not* -n.

Bournemouth.

Bournville.

bourse, foreign money-market, esp. Paris.

boursier (Fr.), stockbroker.

bouse (naut.), to haul, *not* -wse.

boutique, small shop (often within a shop) for individual clothes and accessories.

boutonnière (Fr. f.), a button-hole.

bouts-rimés, rhymed endings.

bowdlerize, to expurgate, from Dr. T. Bowdler (not cap.).

bowie, long knife (U.S.). from Col. Bowie (*not* cap.).

bowled (cricket), abbr. **b.**

Bowness, Cumb., Westmorland. *See also* **Bo'ness.**

box/, -es, abbr. **bx., bxs.**

box-office (hyphen).

boycott, to exclude from society or business, from Capt. Boycott (*not* cap.).

Boy's Own Paper, abbr. *B.O.P.*

bozza (It.), printer's proof.

B.P., British Petroleum; — Public; — Pharmacopoeia.

Bp., Bishop.

b.p., below proof, bill of parcels, bills payable, boiling-point, *bonum publicum* (the public good).

b.p.f. (Fr.), *bon pour francs,* value in francs.

B.Phil., Bachelor of Philosophy.

bpl., birthplace.

B.P.O.E. (U.S.), Benevolent and Protective Order of Elks.

B.Q., *Bene quiescat* (may he, *or* she, repose well!).

B.Q.M.S., Battery Quartermaster-Sergeant.

B.R., Book of Reference, British Rail, Railways.

Br., British, (bot.) R. Brown.

Br (chem.), bromine (no point).

br., brig.

b.r., bills receivable.

'Brabançonne (La)', Belgian national anthem.

brace (typ.), *see* **punctuation XIV** (⌒).

brackets (typ.) square [ ], angle ⟨ ⟩; not the parentheses or round form ( ). *See* **punctuation XI.**

braggadocio, empty boasting (not ital.).

Brahe (Tycho), 1546–1601, Danish astronomer.

Brahma, supreme Hindu god (not ital.).

brahma, brahmaputra, domestic fowl (not cap.).

Brahmah (lock) (cap.).

Brahman/ (Hind.), one of the highest caste; *pl.* **-s.**

Brahmaputra, Indian river.

brahminee (adj.), pertaining to the highest caste.

Brahmoism, reformed theistic Hinduism.

brail, to haul up.

braille, signs composed of raised dots, replacing letters for the blind.

braise (cook.), *not* -ze (*see also* **braze**).

brake, for wheel, a large vehicle, etc., *not* break.

Br. Am., British America.

bran/, -ny.

Brandes (**Georg M. H.**), 1842–1927, Danish writer.

brand-new, *not* bran-.

Brandywine, battle, 1777, of American War of Independence.

brant-goose, *use* **brent-.**

Brantôme (**P. de B.**), 1540–1614, French writer.

Brasilia, new cap. of Brazil, 1960.

brass (bind.), die for blocking book-cases; *pl.* **-es.**

brassard, badge worn on arm.

brasserie, beer-garden, licensed restaurant; *brasserie* (Fr. f.), *also* brewery.

brassière, woman's undergarment supporting breasts.

brassy (Sc.), the wrasse fish, a golf club, *not* -ie.

bratticing, (arch.) open carved work; (coal-mining) wooden shaft-lining or screen.

Brauneberger, a white wine.

Braunschweig, Ger. for **Brunswick.**

brav/a! (It.), 'well done!' to a woman; *-o!* to a man;

brav/o (noun), a cry of 'well done!'; *pl.* **-os.**

bravo/, a desperado; *pl.* **-es.**

braze, to solder, *not* -ise, -ize. See also **braise.**

brazier, worker in brass, pan for holding lighted coal, *not* -sier.

Brazil/, -ian, abbr. **Braz.**

Brazzaville, cap. of Congo, q.v., Cent. Africa.

B.R.C.S., British Red Cross Society.

break/ (*see* **brake**); (typ.) the division into a fresh paragraph; — **-line,** last one of a paragraph: never to begin page, and should have more than five letters, except in narrow measures.

breakdown (noun), a collapse, analysis of statistics (one word).

Breakspear (**Nicholas**), Pope Adrian IV from 1154 to 1159, *not* -eare.

breakthrough (noun, one word).

breakup (noun, one word).

breathalyser, device for testing amount of alcohol in the breath, *not* -iser, -izer.

b.rec., bills receivable.

breccia, rock composed of angular fragments, *not* -cchia.

Brechin, Angus.

breeches-buoy, life-saving apparatus (hyphen).

breech-load/er, -ing, abbr. **B.L.;** — **-ing rifle, B.L.R.**

bren-gun, light machine-gun (hyphen, not cap.).

brent-goose, *not* bra-.

Brescia, Lombardy, Italy.

Breslau, Ger. for **Wroclaw** (Poland).

Bretagne, Fr. for **Brittany; Grande —,** Great Britain.

Breton, (inhabitant) of Brittany, abbr. **Bret.**

Bretton Woods, New Hampshire, U.S. (U.N. Monetary Conf., 1944).

Breughel, *use* **Brueghel.**

brev., brevet, -ed.

breve, a curved mark (◡) to indicate a short vowel or syllable.

brevet d'invention (Fr. m.), a patent.

breveté s.g.d.g. (Fr.), patented without government guarantee (*sans garantie du gouvernement*).

breviary, book containing R.C. daily service.

brevier (typ.), old name for a size of type, about 8 pt.

briar, *use* **-er.**

Briarean, many-handed, like **Briareus,** of Greek myth., *not* -ian.

bribable, *not* -eable.

bric-à-brac, curiosities in furniture and furnishings (hyphens, accent).

Bridge End, Lincs.

Bridgend, Angus, Argyl., Banff, Cornwall, Donegal, Glam., Inner Hebr., Perth.

Bridge of Allan, Stirling.

Bridgeport, Ala., Calif., Conn., Nebr., Penn., Tex. (U.S.).

Bridges Creek, E. Virg. (U.S.), bpl. of George Washington.

Bridges (Robert Seymore), 1844–1930, Poet Laureate 1913–30.

Bridgeton, Glasgow; New Jersey, U.S.

Bridgetown, Som., Staffs., Wexford, Barbados, N.S. (Canada), W. Austr.

Bridgewater, N.S. (Canada).

Bridgnorth, Salop.

Bridgwater, Somerset, *not* Bridge-.

bridoon, a bridle, *not* bra-.

brier/, — -root, — -rose, *not* briar-, brere.

brig (naut.), abbr. **br.**

Brig., brigad/e, -ier.

Brillat-Savarin (A.), 1755–1826, French gastronomist.

brilliant (typ.), old name for a size of type, about 3½ pt.

bring up (typ.), to underlay or overlay.

Brinvilliers (Marie, marquise de), 1630–76, French poisoner.

Bri-Nylon, trade mark (caps., hyphen).

brio (mus.), fire, life, vigour.

brioche (Fr. f.), a bun, a blunder.

briquette, block of compressed coal-dust, *not* -et.

brisling, Norwegian sprat, *not* brist-.

Bristol-board, cardboard used by artists.

Brit./, Britain, Britann/ia, -icus, -ica, British; — **Mus.,** British Museum.

British/, abbr. **Brit.;** — **Academy, B.A.;** — **America, Br. Am.;** — **Columbia, B.C.;** — **Museum, Brit. Mus., B.M.;** — **Rail, Railways, B.R.**

britschka, acceptable form for **bryczka,** q.v.

Britt. (on coins), Britanniarum, 'of the Britains'.

Brittany, in Fr. **Bretagne.**

Britten (Edward Benjamin), O.M., C.H., British composer, b. 1913.

B.R.M., British Racing Motors.

bro., bros., brother, -s.

Broad-Churchman (caps., hyphen).

Broad Haven, Pembs., Mayo.

Broad Oak, Dorset, Hereford, Sussex.

Broadoak, Cornwall, Salop.

Brobdingnag, land of giants in *Gulliver's Travels*, *not* -dignag.

broccoli, a hardy cauliflower, It. *pl.*, but Eng. *sing.* or *pl.*

brochure, a booklet or leaflet.

Broke, surname; *pron.* Brŏŏk.

bromine, symbol **Br** (no point).

bronch/i, *pl.,* the main forks of the windpipe (*sing.* **-us**); **-ia,** *pl.,* ramifications of the above, bronchioles.

bronco/, Mexican horse, *not* -cho/; *pl.* **-s.**

Brontë (Anne), 1820–49 ('Acton Bell'); — **(Charlotte),** 1816–55 ('Currer Bell'); — **(Emily),** 1818–48 ('Ellis Bell'), English writers.

Bronx (the), borough in New York City.

bronzing (typ.), printing in yellow and then dusting with bronze powder to imitate gold.

brooch, a dress-fastening, *not* -ach.

Brooke, Norfolk; — **(Lord);** — **(Rupert),** 1887–1915, poet.

Brookline, Mass., U.S.

Brooklyn, New York.

Brooks's Club, London, *not* -es's.

broomstick (one word).

brother/, abbr. **b.** *or* **bro.,** *pl.* **-s, brethren,** abbr. **bros.;** — **-german,** 'whole' brother; — **-in-law** (hyphens).

brougham, one-horse or electric closed carriage (not cap.).

brouhaha (Fr. m.), a commotion.

Brown (Ford Madox), 1821–93, painter; — **(Robert),** 1773–1858, botanist; abbr. **Br.**

Browne (Hablot Knight), 1815–82, English artist, pseud. Phiz, illustrated Dickens; — **(Sir Thomas),** 1605–82, physician and author.

Brown-Séquard (C. E.), 1817–94, British physiologist.

browse, to eat, read for enjoyment, *not* -ze.

B.R.S., British Road Services.

Bruch (Ger. m.), a break, (arith.) fraction.

Brueghel (Pieter), *c.* 1520–69, Flemish painter, *not* Breu-.

Brummagem, abbr. **Brum.,** derog. form of Birmingham; adj. tawdry.

Brummell (G. B., 'Beau'), 1778–1840.

Brunei, NW. Borneo.

Brunhild (Norse myth.).

Brünhilde, Wagnerian heroine.

Brunonian, noun, an alumnus of Brown University, U.S.; adj., of the system of medicine of Dr. John Brown of Edinburgh, 1736–88.

Brunswick, normal Eng. for **Braunschweig,** Germany.

Brussels, cap. of Belgium, in Flem. **Brussel,** in Fr. **Bruxelles.**

Brussels sprouts (cap., no apos.).

brutalize, *not* -ise.

Bruxelles, Fr. for **Brussels.**

bryczka, a Polish carriage (the Polish spelling; Eng. has various spellings, all beginning **bri-**).

Bryn Mawr College, Philadelphia, U.S.

Brynmawr, Brecs.

bryology, study of mosses; abbr. **bryol.**

Brython, Welsh for Briton.

B.S., Bachelor of Surgery; Blessed Sacrament.

b.s., balance sheet, bill of sale.

B.S.A., Birmingham Small Arms, British School at Athens.

B.Sc., Bachelor of Science; **B.Sc. (Econ.),** ditto in faculty of Economics; **B.Sc. (Eng.),** ditto Engineering, Glas.; **B.Sc. Tech.,** Bachelor of Technical Science.

b.s.g.d.g., see **breveté**.

B.S.I., British Standards Institution. A complete list of British Standards is in BS Yearbook. Standards in fields relevant to this dictionary are BS 1219 (Proof correction and copy preparation), BS 1991, Part I (1967) (Letter symbols, signs, abbreviations), BS 2961 (Typeface nomenclature), BS 3763 (SI units).

B.S.I.U., British Society for International Understanding.

B.S.R., British School at Rome.

B.S.S., British Sailors' Society.

B.S.T., British Summer Time (before 1968 and from 1972); — Standard Time (1968–71) (both 1 hr. ahead of G.M.T.).

Bt., Baronet, *not* Bart.

B.T.C., British Transport Commission.

B.Th., Bachelor of Theology.

B.T.U. (*or* **B.Th.U.**), British Thermal Unit.

bty., battery.

B.U., Brown University, Rhode Island, U.S.; Baptist Union.

bu., bushel(s).

buccaneer, piratical adventurer of seventeenth century, *not* -ier.

Buccleuch (**Duke of**), *not* -gh; *pron.* bŭ-kloo´.

Bucellas, white wine from B., near Lisbon.

Buch (Ger. n.), book; *pl.* *Bücher*.

Bucharest, *properly* **Bucuresti,** *not* Buka-.

Buchausgabe, edition of a book.

Buckinghamshire, abbr. **Bucks.**

Bucknall, Lincs., Staffs.

Bucknell, Oxon., Salop; also American university at Lewisburg, Pa.

buckram, coarse fabric, (bind.) a good quality cloth.

Budapest, Hungary, *not* -pesth (one word). Collective name for two towns, Buda and Pest.

Buddha (Skt.), Gautama Sākyasinha, died 543 B.C.

Buddh/ism, -ist; (typ.) if necessary divide at stroke; abbr. **Budd.**

budgerigar, a parakeet.

budgeted, *not* -etted.

buen/as noches (Sp.), good-night; *-as tardes,* good-afternoon; *-os dias,* good-day, good-morning.

Buenos/ Aires, cap. of Argentine Rep.; also in Panama. *Use* — **Ayres** in titles of Arg. railway companies.

buffalo/, *pl.* **-es.**

buffer State (cap. S only).

buffet/, -ed, -ing.

Buffon (**G. L. L.**), 1707–88, French naturalist.

buhl (adj.), German form of **boule,** from **Boule** (**André**), cabinet-maker to Louis XIV.

building, abbr. **bldg.,** *pl.* **bldgs.**

B.U.J. (*Baccalaureus utriusque juris*), Bachelor of Canon and Civil Law.

Bukarest, *use* **Buch-.**

Bukhara, town, Uzbekistan, U.S.S.R., *not* Bo-. *See* **Bokhara.**

buksheesh, *use* bak-.

bul., bulletin.

bulbul (Pers.), 'the nightingale of the East'.

Bulgaria/, -n, abbr. **Bulg.**

bull (Stock Exchange), a speculator for the rise.

bulletin (not ital.); abbr. **bul.**

bull's-eye, centre of target (apos. and hyphen).

bulrush, *not* bull-.

bulwark, defence, *not* bull-, -work.

Bulwer (Sir Henry; in full, **William Henry Lytton Earle),** later **Lord Dalling,** 1801–72, English diplomat.

Bulwer-Lytton (Edward George Earle Lytton), first **Lord Lytton,** 1803–73, English novelist.

Bulwer-Lytton (Edward Robert), first **Earl of Lytton,** 1831–91, son of above, English poet and diplomat, pseud. **Owen Meredith.**

bumkin (naut.), projection from bows or stern of ship.

bumpkin, countryman.

buncombe, more correct form, *but use* **bunkum.**

Bundesanstalt, German off. institution since 1945. *See* **Reichsanstalt.**

Bundesrat (Ger.), federal council, *not* -rath.

bundle/, -s, abbr. **bdl/., -s.**

Bunker Hill, Mass., battle of American War of Independence, 1775, actually fought at neighbouring Breed's Hill, *not* er's.

bun/kum, accepted, though incorrect, for **-combe.**

Buonaparte, *use* **Bona-.**

buona sera (It.), good-evening; *buon giorno,* good-day.

buoyan/t, -cy.

B.U.P., British United Press.

bur, clinging seed-vessel or catkin. *See* **burr.**

burden, *not* -then.

Burdett-Coutts (A. G., Baroness), 1814–1906, English philanthropist.

bureau/, *pl.* **-x** (not ital.); **-cracy.**

Bureau Veritas, maritime underwriters' association at Brussels (two caps.).

burg., burgess, burgomaster.

burgamot, *use* ber-.

burgaudine, mother of pearl, *not* -andine.

burgeois, *see* **bourgeois** (typ.).

burgess, abbr. **burg.**

burgh (Sc.), a town possessing a charter, *not* borough.

burgomaster (one word); abbr. **burg.**

burgrave, a governor, *not* burgg-.

burgundy, a wine.

burial-service (hyphen, no caps.).

burl, a lump in cloth.

burl., burlesque.

Burlington House, London, headquarters of Royal Academy, British Association, and other artistic and learned bodies.

Burm/a, *not* -ah; **-an,** native of Burma, *pl.* **-ans.**

Burmah Oil Co., *not* Burma.

Burne-Jones (Sir Edward), 1833–98, painter (hyphen).

burnous, Arab cloak, *not* -e, bernouse.

Burntisland, Fife (one word).

burnt sienna, orange-red pigment, *not* — siena.

burr, a rough edge, rough sounding of letter *r.* *See* **bur.**

burro (Sp.), donkey.

Burroughs (John), 1837–1921, American naturalist and poet.

bursar, treasurer of a college, *not* -er.

burthen, *use* **burden.**

Burundi, sovereign state of Cent. Africa, 1962.

Bury St. Edmunds (no apos., no hyphen).

bus, omnibus, *not* 'bus, *pl.* **buses** (U.S. *pl.* **buses** or **busses**).

bushbuck (S. Afr.), antelope, *properly* **bosbok.**

bushel, 2,218 cubic inches; in U.S. 2,150·4; abbr. **bu** (*sing.* and *pl.*).

Bushey, Herts., *not* -hy.
bushido, code of the samurai or Japanese mil. caste.
Bushy House, contains part of National Physical Laboratory, q.v.
Bushy Park, Middlesex.
bustard, long-legged running-bird. *See* **buzzard.**
busybody, *not* busi-.
busyness, state of being busy, distinct from **business.**
Butte, Montana, U.S.
buttermilk (one word).
buyer's option, abbr. **b.o.**
Buys-Ballot (C. H. D.), 1817–90, Dutch meteorologist.
buzzard, large bird of prey. *See* **bustard.**
B.V., *Beata Virgo* (the Blessed Virgin); pseudonym of James Thomson, q.v.
b.v., bene vale (farewell).
B.V.M., *Beata Virgo Maria,* the Blessed Virgin Mary.
B.W.I., British West Indies, *now* **W.I.;** — Workmen's Institute.
bx., bxs., box, -es.
by- (as prefix) is tending to form one word with the following noun, but a hyphen is still frequently found, as in eleven words given below.
by and by (no hyphens).
by-blow, side-blow, bastard (hyphen).
bye/, -s (cricket), abbr. **b.**
bye-bye, a nursery good-bye (hyphen).
by-election (hyphen).
bygone (one word).
by-lane (hyphen).
by-law, *not* bye-.
by-line (U.S.), line giving name of writer of article, etc.
byname, a sobriquet (one word).
bypass (one word).
bypath (one word).
by-play (hyphen).
by-plot, by-product, *not* bye-.
by-road (hyphen).
bystander (one word).
by-street (hyphen); *but* Masefield's '*The Widow in the Bye Street*'.
by the by (no hyphens).
by-way (hyphen).
byword (one word).
byzant, *use* be-.

C

C (no point), carbon, *centum* (a hundred), the third in a series.

C., Cape, Catholic, Celsius (but no point in scientific work), centigrade (but no point in scientific work), century, Chancery, chief, Church, Command paper (q.v.), (mus.) common time, congress(ional), Conservative, consul, contralto, Council, counter-tenor, Court, and all proper names with this initial.

C (ital. cap., no point), coulomb (elec.), symbol for capacitance.

©, copyright.

c (no point), one hundredth as prefix.

c., cent, -s, centime, chapter, city, colt, conductor, constable, copeck, cubic, (cricket) caught, (naut.) cloudy.

c., circa, about.

Ɔ (inverted C), 500.

C.A., Central Africa, Central America, M. Inst. Chartered Accountants of Scotland, Chief Accountant, Church Army, Civil Aviation, commercial agent, Confederate Army, Controller of Accounts.

C/A, capital account, commercial account, credit account, current account.

Ca (chem.), calcium (no point).

ca., cases, cathode.

ca., abbr. of *circa,* use *c.*

çà (Fr.), here.

Caaba, *use* **Kaaba.**

caaing-whale, *use* **ca'ing-whale.**

C.A.B., Citizens' Advice Bureau, (U.S.) Civil Aeronautics Board.

cabal, secret faction.

cabbala, Heb. tradition, *not* k-, cabala, -alla.

Cabul, *use* **Kabul.**

C.A.C., Central Advisory Committee, County Agricultural Committee.

ca' canny (Sc.), go easily!

cacao, trop. American tree from whose seeds cocoa and chocolate are made. *See* **coco.**

cache-poussière (Fr. m.), dust-coat, dust-cloak.

cachet, (in general) a packet.

cachet, distinctive mark, capsule containing medicine.

cachou, lozenge to sweeten smoker's breath, *not* cashew.

cachucha, lively Spanish dance.

cacique, W. Indian and S. American chief, political boss, *not* caz-.

cacodemon, an evil spirit, *not* -daemon.

cacoethes/ (Gr.), an evil habit; — *loquendi* (Lat.), an itch for speaking; — *scribendi* (Lat.), ditto for writing.

cact/us (bot.), *pl.* **-i.**

caddie, golf-attendant.

caddis/, May-fly larva, *not* -ice; — **-worm.**

caddy, tea-box.

cadeau/ (Fr. m.), a gift; *pl.* **-x.**

cadi, Oriental judge, *not* k-; *properly* qàdhi.

Cadmean, of Cadmus of Thebes, *not* -ian; — **victory,** a ruinous one.

cadmium, symbol **Cd** (no point).

cadre, nucleus of mil. officers, *not* ital.

caduce/us, the rod of Hermes; *pl.* **-i.**

caducous (bot.), tending to fall.

C.A.E.C., County Agricultural Executive Committee.

Caedmon, d. 670, English poet, *not* Ce-.

Caermarthen, *use* **Car-.**

Caernarvon, *not* Car-; abbr. **Caern.**

caerulean, *use* **ce-.**

Caesar/, -ean, *not* -ian.

Caesarea Philippi, in ancient Palestine.

caesium, symbol **Cs** (no point).

caesura, division of a metrical line, *not* ce-.

café (Fr. m.), coffee-house (**é,** not ital.).

café/ au lait (Fr.), coffee and milk; — **noir,** strong coffee without milk.

caffè (It.), coffee-house (**è**).

Caffre, *use* **Kaffir.**

caftan, long-sleeved Turkish or Persian garment, *not* k-.

cagey, shrewd, *not* -gy.

cahier (Fr. m.), a paper book, sheets of MS., exercise-book.

Caiaphas, Jewish high priest, Luke 3: 2.

caiman, *use* **cay-.**

Cainan, grandson of Seth. *See also* **Canaan.**

Caine (Sir Thomas Henry Hall), 1853–1931, English novelist.

cainozoic (geol.), tertiary, *not* caeno-, ceno-, kaino-.

caïque, Bosporan skiff, Levantine sailing ship (diaeresis).

'Ça ira', 'That's the thing!', French revolutionary song.

caisson, ammunition chest, dock pontoon, *not* cassoon; *pron.* kăsŏōn'.

Caius (*properly* **Gonville and Caius**) **College,** Cambridge, *pron.* kēz; abbr. **Cai.**

cajolery, coaxing (one *l*).

cajuput, aromatic oil, *not* caja-, caje-.

caky, *not* -ey.

Cal. (California), *use* **Calif.**

cal (no point), calorie.

cal., calendar.

cal. (mus.), *calando*.

calamanco, a woollen stuff, *not* **cali-, calli-.**

calamary, the squid.

calamus, a reed, a pen.

calando (mus.), tone and rate diminished; abbr. **cal.**

calcareous, chalky, *not* -ious.

calcedony, *use* **chal-.**

calceolaria, slipper-like flower, *not* calci-.

calcium, symbol **Ca** (no point).

calculator, *not* -er.

calculer (Fr. typ.), to 'cast off' MS.

calcul/us, stony concretion in the body, *pl.* **-i,** adj. **-ous;** a system of computation, *pl.* **-uses,** adj. **-ar.**

Caldecott (Randolph), 1846–86, English artist and illustrator.

Calderón de la Barca (Pedro), 1600–81, Spanish dramatist.

caldron, *use* **caul-.**

calendae, calends, *use* **k-.**

calendar, an almanac, *not* k-; abbr. **cal.**

calend/er, to make smooth (cloth, paper, etc.); a machine that does this; **-rer,** a man who does this.

calender (Pers., Turk.), a dervish, *not* k-.

calends, the first day of a Latin month; the **Greek —,** a time that never comes; *not* k-.

calf, abbr. **cf.**

'Caliban upon Setebos', by R. Browning.

calib/re, size of bore of tube (U.S. **-er**).

Caliburn, King Arthur's sword, *not* cala-, cale-.

calico/, *pl.* **-es.**

California, off. abbr. **Calif.**

Californium (chem.), symbol **Cf** (no point).

caligraphy, *use* **calli-.**

calimanco, *use* cala-.

calipers, *use* **callipers.**

caliph/, Muhammadan chief civil and religious ruler; **-ate;** *not* ka-, -if.

calisaya, cinchona bark.

calisthenics, *use* **call-.**

cal/ix (physiol. and biol.), cup-like cavity or organ; *pl.* **-ices.**

calk, *use* **caulk.**

Callander, Perth.

Callendar (Prof. H. L.), 1863–1930, British physicist and stenographer.

calligraphy, *not* cali-.

Calliope, Greek muse of eloquence and epic poetry; **calliope,** steam-organ on roundabout.

callipers (*pl.*), compasses for measuring inside or outside diameters of objects (U.S. **cali-**).

Callirrhoe, wife of Alcmaeon; *pron.* kăl-i-rō′ē.

callisthenics, beauty exercises (U.S. **cali-**).

call/us, thick skin; *pl.* **-uses;** adj. **-ous.**

Calmann-Lévy, publishers, Paris.

calorescence, change of heat rays to light rays (badly formed word).

calori/e, unit of heat, abbr. **cal** (no point); **-meter,** heat measurer; **-motor,** voltaic battery.

calotte, skull-cap (R.C. clergy).

Caltech, California Institute of Technology.

caltrop (mil.), horse-maiming

iron ball with spikes, *not* -throp, -trap.

calumniator, *not* -er.

Calvé (Emma), 1866–1942, French operatic soprano.

Calverleigh, N. Devon.

Calverley, Leeds, and Tunbridge Wells; — **(C. S.),** 1831–84, writer.

calves-foot jelly, *not* f's, ves', -feet.

Calypso, sea-nymph in the *Odyssey*; **calypso** (not cap.), W. Indian negro song, usu. about current affairs.

caly/x (bot.), whorl of leaves forming outer case of bud; *pl.* **-ces.**

camaraderie, good-fellowship.

Camb., Cambridge.

camblet, *use* **camlet.**

Cambodia, Indo-China, sovereign state 1953, *not* Kam-, -oja; Fr. **Cambodge.**

Cambrai (Fr.), *not* -ray.

cambrai, machine-made lace.

cambric, fine white linen; *pron.* kā-.

Cambridge/, abbr. **Camb., Cantab.;** — **University, C.U.;** — **University Press, C.U.P.**

Cambridgeshire, abbr. **Cambs.**

camellia, flowering shrub, *not* -elia.

camelopard, giraffe.

camelot, *use* **camlet.**

Camembert, a French cheese.

cameo/, striated stone carved in relief; *pl.* **-s.** *See* **intaglio.**

camera/, *pl.* **-s;** — **obscura,** *not* — oscura.

Camera Stellata, the Star Chamber.

Cameroon Republic, Cent. Africa, independent state 1960.

camlet, a woollen stuff, *not* -blet, -elot.

Cammaerts (Émile), 1878–1953, Belgian poet.

Camoens (Luis de), 1524–80, Portuguese poet, *not* Camö-.

camomile, medicinal plant, *not* cha-.

Camorra, Neapolitan secret society, practising violence and extortion. *See* **Mafia.**

camouflage, disguise (noun or verb).

Campagna di Roma, the plain round Rome.

campanile/, bell-tower, usu. detached; *pl.* **-s.**

Campbell-Bannerman (Sir H.), 1836–1908, statesman (hyphen).

Campbeltown, Argyl.

Campeche Bay, City, *or* **State,** Mexico, *not* -peachy.

camp/o (It.), open ground, *pl.* **-i;** *campo santo* (It., Sp.), a cemetery.

Campus Martius, field of Mars, anc. Rome.

Can., Canada.

can., canon, canto, cantoris.

Canaan, son of Ham (*see also* **Cainan**).

Canada, abbr. **Can.**

cañada (Sp.), a gorge.

Canadian River, Okl., U.S.

canaille (Fr. f.), the rabble.

Canaker, *use* **Kanaka.**

Canaletto (Antonio), 1697–1768, Italian painter.

canalize, *not* -ise.

canapé/, caviare, anchovies, etc., on fried bread or toast; *pl.* **-s.**

canard (Fr. m.), an absurd story, a duck; *canard sauvage,* wild-duck.

canasta, a card-game.

canaster, a tobacco, *not* k-, -ister.

cancan, high-kicking Parisian dance (one word).

cancel (typ.), deleted matter, a reprint correcting error (the signature sometimes preceded by *).

cancel/, -led, -ler, -ling, -ment.

cancelled figures, *see* **figures (cancelled).**

Candahar, *use* **K-.**

candela, standard unit of light intensity; abbr. **cd.**

candelabr/um, a candle-stand; *pl.* **-a.**

Candide, by Voltaire.

Candiote, native of Candia, *more usually* **Cretan.**

c. and l.c. (typ.), capital(s) and lower case.

Candlemas Day, 2 Feb.

candlepower (one word).

canephor/os (arch.), sculptured youth or maiden with basket on head; *pl.* **-i.**

caneton (Fr. m.), duckling.

canister, small metal box, *not* -aster.

cannabis, Indian hemp, *not* cana- (not cap., except for the bot. genus).

Cannes, S. France; *pron.* kăn.

Canning (George), 1770–1827, statesman; — **(C. J., Earl),** 1812–62, statesman.

cannon/, -ade; in Fr. m. *canon/, -nade.*

cannon (billiards), U.S. **carom.**

cannon/-ball, -bone, -clock, -fodder (hyphens).

canoe/, -ing.

canon, abbr. **can.**

canon (typ.), old name for a size of type, about 44 pt.

cañon (Sp.), a gorge; *pron.* kă′nyon.

canonize, *not* -ise.

'Canon's Yeoman's Tale', by Chaucer.

Canosa, Apulia, Italy.

Canossa, Emilia, Italy, scene of penance of Emperor Henry IV before Pope Gregory VII, 1077; hence **to go to —,** 'to eat humble pie'.

Canova (Antonio), 1757–1822, Italian sculptor.

Canrobert (F. C.), 1809–95, Marshal of France.

canst (no apos.).

Cant., Canterbury, Canticles.

can't (typ.), to be set close up.

cantabile (mus.), in a singing, graceful style.

Cantabrigian, of Cambridge, *not* -dgian.

Cantabrigiensis, of Cambridge University; abbr. **Cantab.**

cantaloup, a musk-melon, *not* cante-, -loupe.

cantatrice (It. and Fr.), professional woman singer.

Canterbury, abbr. **Cant.**

Canterbury bell, flower (one cap.).

canticle, a hymn; abbr. **cant.**

Canticum Canticorum, 'The Song of Songs', *also* **Canticles**, abbr. **Cant.**, same as **Song of Solomon.**

cantilever, a form of bridge, *not* canta-, -liver.

cantini/er, *fem.* *-ère*, a canteen-keeper.

Cantire, Argyl., *use* **Kintyre.**

canto/, a song; *pl.* **-s**, abbr. **can.**

cantonment, mil. quarters; *pron.* kan-tōōn′-ment.

cantoris of the precentor, that is on north side of choir; abbr. **can.**

Cantor Lectures (Royal College of Physicians, *and* Society of Arts).

Cantuar., *Cantuarius*, *Cantuariensis* (of Canterbury).

Cantuar: signature of Abp. of Canterbury (colon).

Cantuarian, of Canterbury.

Canute, accepted variant of **Cnut**, 995–1035, king of Norway, Denmark, and England.

canvas/, coarse linen; **-ed, -es.**

canvass/, to solicit votes; **-ed, -es.**

canyon (U.S.), a gorge.

caoutchouc, india-rubber.

cap., capital letter, *capitulum* (a small head, or knob), foolscap.

cap., caput (head), chapter.

cap-à-pie, from head to foot (accent, hyphens, not ital.).

Cape/, cap. when with name, abbr. **C.;** — **Breton**, Nova Scotia, *not* Briton, Britton, Britun, abbr. **C.B.;** — **of Good Hope**, abbr. **C.G.H.;** — **Province** (of S. Africa), abbr. **C.P.**

capercailzie, wood-grouse, *not* -caillie, -cailye.

Cape Town, S. Africa (two words).

Cape Verde Islands, off W. Africa, *not* — Verd, — de Verd.

Cap Haitien, town in Haiti.

capias, writ of arrest.

capibara, *use* capy-.

capitalize, *not* -ise.

capitalization. When in doubt use lower case. Initial capitals for:

Abstract qualities personified: O Fame!

Acts of Parliament (titles of).

Adjectives derived from proper names, as Gargantuan, Homeric, but not those which by use have become common, as morocco leather.

Architectural periods: the Renaissance.

Associations, as Charity Organization Society.

Bible, and synonyms.

Botany, all divisions higher than species, that is, genera, families, orders, classes. *See also* **botany.**

Churches, as Methodist Church.

Compass point abbreviations, N., N. b E., NNE., NE. b N., etc.

capitalization (*cont.*):
  Compound titles, as
    Assistant Adjutant-General,
    Chief Justice, Ex-President,
    Major-General, Vice-
    President.
  Days, as Christmas Day,
    Lady Day, Monday, New
    Year's Day.
  Deity (**the Christian**),
    synonyms, as Almighty,
    Christ, *Dominus*, Father,
    God, Jehovah, Lord, the
    Deity, the Holy Trinity; but
    not pronouns except at
    author's request.
  Emphasis—as a means of.
  Festivals, as Easter, Whit-
    suntide.
  German substantives,
    but not adjectives derived
    from proper names, or
    denoting a class; also
    personal pronouns of the
    second person.
  Government (**the**).
  **Historic names and
    phrases,** as the Dark
    Ages, the Plague, etc.
  **House of Lords,
    Commons,** etc.
  Interrogation: the next
    word following a note of
    interrogation (?) should
    generally begin with a
    capital letter.
  MS., MSS., manuscript, -s
    (one point only).
  Nicknames, as the Iron
    Duke, the Admirable
    Crichton.
  O! and **Oh!** (the inter-
    jections), and **O** (vocative).
  Palaeontology, all divisions
    higher than species.
  Periods, caps., after all,
    except abbreviations.
  Poetry, generally at
    beginning of each line in
    classical English and
    French; not necessarily
    in German, Latin, or
    Greek.

  Political bodies, as
    Assembly, Senate.
  **Postal district abbre-
    viations,** as E.C.
  Proper names, including
    English Christian names,
    surnames, and names of an
    individual, family, place,
    locality, and the like,
    except initial *ff*. Verbs
    formed from them, as
    boycott, are not usually
    capped.
  PS., postscript (one point).
  Quotations, complete and
    intended to be emphatic:
    'Thou art the man'.
  Rank, when individuals are
    referred to or addressed by
    their rank, as 'the Squire
    said', 'Good evening,
    General'.
  Religious denominations,
    Nonconformist.
  **Roads, Gardens, Gates,
    Groves, Hills, Parks,
    Squares, Streets,
    Terraces,** etc., when with
    name.
  Sects, as the Primitive
    Methodists.
  Sovereign (**the**), in pro-
    clamations, all personal
    pronouns, referring to, as
    Her, Him, His, etc.
  Speeches, first letter of cited.
  State (**the**).
  **Titles, and Sub-titles, of
    books,** the important
    words only, as 'Com-
    promise', 'I Forbid the
    Banns'.
  Titles of corporations,
    Board of Trade.
  **Titles of courtesy and of
    honour;** H.R.H., T.R.H.,
    President Roosevelt, His
    Grace, Sir John Smith,
    J. Smith, Esq., Mr. J.
    Smith, etc.
  Titles of distinction, as
    F.R.S., LL.D., are usu.
    put in large caps. Even

s.caps. often improve general effect.

Titles of periodicals: pictures, plays, etc.: *The Times*; 'Chill October'; *Hamlet*.

Titles of poems and songs, when formed from the first line, to be similarly capitalized, as 'I Fear no Foe', 'Where the Bee Sucks'.

Trade Association Titles: Ironfounders Engineers.

Zoology, all divisions higher than species: genera, families, orders.

capital letter, abbr. cap.

capitals (large), indicated in MS. by three lines underneath the letter; abbr. **cap.** *See also* **capitalization.**

capitals (small), USUALLY ABOUT TWO-THIRDS SIZE OF LARGE CAPS., AS THIS TYPE, indicated in MS. by two lines underneath; may be used (with initials in large caps.) in printed letters for the address, date, and signature, and for name of newspaper in paper itself. They are not used in German or Greek. Abbr. **s.cap.,** *pl.* **s.caps.; even s.caps.,** ditto without large initials.

Capitol, temple of Jupiter on Capitoline Hill, anc. Rome; Congress building, Washington D.C., U.S.

capitulary, collection of ordinances or laws.

capitulum (bot., anat.), small head, knob; abbr. **cap.**

câpres (Fr. pl. f.), capers.

capriccio/ (mus.), fanciful work; adj. *-so.*

caps. and smalls (typ.), to set in small capitals with the initial letters in large capitals; abbr. **c. and s.c.**

capsize, *not* -ise.

Captain, abbr. **Capt.**

caption (typ.), the heading of a chapter, section, page, or illustration (used mostly in America).

Captivity (the) of the Jews (cap. C).

caput/ (Lat.), head; abbr. *cap.*; — *mortuum*, residue after distillation.

capybara (Braz.), largest living rodent, *not* capi-.

Car., Carolus (Charles).

car., carat.

carabineer, soldier with carbine, *not* carb-, -ier.

Caracci, family of painters, 1550–1619, *not* Carr-.

Caractacus, accepted form of **Caratacus,** *fl.* A.D. 50, king of Silures, anc. Britain.

carafe, water-bottle, *not* -ff, -ffe.

caramba! (Sp.), wonderful! how strange!

carat, a weight, *not* caract, carrat, karat; abbr. **K.,** *or* **car.** (U.S. **k.**).

caratch, use *kharaj.*

Caravaggio (M. A. A.), 1569–1609, Italian painter.

caravanserai, large unfurnished inn or courtyard, used as halting-place for caravans, *not* -sary, -sery, -sera. *See* **khan.**

caraway, plant with aromatic fruits ('seeds'), *not* carra-.

carbineer, *use* **carabineer.**

carbon, symbol **C** (no point).

carbonize, *not* -ise.

carburett/ed, -or (U.S. one t).

carcass/, *not* -ase; *pl.* -es.

carcinom/a, a cancer; *pl.* -ata.

card., cardinal.

cardamom, aromatic capsules of ginger plants, *not* -on.

carefree (one word).

carême (Fr. m.), Lent.

care of, abbr. **c/o.**

Care Sunday (Sc.), fifth in Lent.

caret, insertion mark (∧).

car/ex, sedge; *pl.* **-ices.**

Carew (Richard), 1555–1620, English poet; — **(Thomas),** 1595–1639 (?), English poet and courtier.

Carey (Henry), 1690(?)–1743, English poet and composer; — **(Henry Charles),** 1793–1879, American economist, son of next; — **(Mathew,** one t), 1760–1839, American publicist; — **Street,** London, syn. with the Bankruptcy Court.

cargo/, *pl.* **-es.**

Caribbean Sea, W. Indies, *not* Carr-.

Cariboo Mountains, Brit. Columbia.

caribou, N. American reindeer, *not* -boo.

Caribou Highway, Brit. Columbia.

Caribou Mountain, Idaho, U.S.

carillon, chime of bells.

cariole, *use* **carr-.**

Carisbrooke, I.W.

carità (It. art), representation of maternal love.

Carleton (William), 1794–1869, Irish novelist.

Carlile/ (Richard), 1790–1843, English reformer and politician; — **(Revd. Preb. W.),** 1847–1942, founder of Church Army. *See also* **Carlisle, Carlyle.**

Carling Sunday, Care Sunday, fifth in Lent, *not* -lin.

Carliol, signature of Bishop of Carlisle.

Carlisle, Cumberland; — **(Earl of).** *See also* **Carlile, Carlyle.**

Carlist, supporter of Spanish pretender Don Carlos (1788–1855).

Carlovingian, of the Frankish dynasty of Charlemagne; *also* **Carolingian;** *not* K-.

Carlsbad, Czechoslovakia, *properly* **Karlovy Vary.**

Carlsruhe, Germany, *not* K-.

Carlton Club, London.

Carlyle (Thomas), 1795–1881, writer. *See also* **Carlile, Carlisle.**

Carlylean, *not* -eian, -ian.

Carmagnola, Piedmont.

'Carmagnole', French revolutionary song and dance.

Carmarthen, *not* Caer-; abbr. **Carm.**

Carnarvon, *use* **Caer-.**

Carnatic, Madras, India, *not* K-.

'Carnaval de Venise, le' (mus.), popular type of air and variations, early nineteenth century.

Carnegie (Andrew), 1837–1910, American millionaire and philanthropist.

carnelian, *use* **cor-.**

carn/ival, in Fr. m. *carnaval,* in Ger. n. *Carneval.*

Carnoustie, Angus.

carol/, -ler, -ling.

Carolingian, *not* K-. *See* **Carlovingian.**

Carolus, Charles; abbr. **Car.**

carousal, *pron.* ca-rowz'-al, a feast.

carousel, *pron.* ca-roo-zel', a tilting match with side-shows; (U.S.) a roundabout. *See* **Carrousel.**

Carpathian Mts., E. Europe, *not* K-.

carpe diem (Lat.), enjoy the day.

carpet/, -ed, -ing.

carp/us, the wrist; *pl.* **-i.**

Carracci, *use* **Caracci.**

carrageen, Irish moss; *not* — moss, -gheen; from Carragheen, near Waterford.

Carrara, N. Italy, source of marble.

carrat, *use* **carat.**

carraway, *use* **cara-.**

carrelet (Fr. cook. m.), flounder.

Carribbean, *use* **Cari-.**

Carrigtohill, Cork (one word).

carriole, a carriage, *not* cariole.

Carroll, Lewis (Charles Lutwidge Dodgson), 1832–98, author.

carrot, in Fr. f. *carotte.*

Carrousel (place du), Paris, from Fr. *carrousel* (m.), a tilting-match.

Carrutherstown, Dumfries (one word).

carte (fencing), *not* quarte.

carte blanche (Fr. f.), full discretion (ital.); abbr. *c.bl.*

cartel, a challenge, manufacturers' union, *not* ch-.

Carte (Richard D'Oyly), 1844–1901, *use* **D'Oyly Carte.**

Carter, Paterson & Co., former carriers, London.

cartography, map-drawing, *not* ch-.

cartouche (arch.), scroll ornament, (archaeol.) enclosing line on ancient Egyptian monuments, *not* -ch-.

Cartouche (L. D.), 1693–1721, French Dick Turpin.

cartridge paper, a firm, strong paper.

carvel-built (naut.), with smooth planking.

Cary (H. F.), 1772–1844, English translator of Dante; — **(Joyce),** 1888–1957, English novelist (male); — **(Lucius),** Lord Falkland, 1610–43; — **(Alice),** 1820–71, **(Phoebe),** 1824–71, American sisters, poets.

caryatid/, female figure as a column; *pl.* **-es.**

C.A.S., Chief of the Air Staff.

Casa Grande, prehistoric ruin in Arizona, U.S.

'Casa Guidi Windows', by Mrs. Browning.

Casanova de Seingalt (Giovanni Giacomo), 1725–1803, Italian adventurer.

Casas Grandes, Mexican village with famous ruins.

Casaubon (Isaac), 1559–1614, French scholar and theologian.

case (typ.); **upper** —, capitals; **lower** —, small letters.

casein, milk protein, *not* -ine.

cases, abbr. **ca.**

cash, former Chinese coin, perforated for stringing, one-thousandth of a tael.

cashew, trop. American tree with edible nuts.

Cashmer/, -e, *use* **Kashmir.**

cashmere, soft wool fabric, *not* -meer, cachemere, -ire. *See also* **cassimere.**

Casimir-Perier (J. P. P.), 1847–1907, French Pres. 1894–5 (no accent).

casino/, *pl.* **-s** (not ital.).

cask/, -s, abbr. **ck.**

Caslon (William), 1692–1766, typefounder.

Caslon type, an 'old-face' type as cut by W. Caslon.

cassareep, a W. Indian condiment, *not* cassi-, -reepe.

Cassation (Cour de) (f.), highest court of appeal in France.

cassava, the manioc, *not* cas-, -ave.

Cassel, Germany, *use* **K-.**

cassimere, twilled woollen cloth, *not* casi-, karsimer, kerseymere. *See also* **cashmere.**

Cassiopeia (astr.), a constellation.

cassiopeium, symbol **Cp** (no point), *now* **lutetium.**

Cassivellaunus, *fl.* 50 B.C., British prince.

cassoon, an ammunition chest; *use* **caisson.**

cast, actors in a play.

caste, hereditary class.

Castellammare, Campagna and Sicily, Italy.

Castelnuovo-Tedesco (Mario), 1895–1968, Italian composer.

caster, one who casts (*see also* **-or**); (typ.) a casting machine.

Castil/e, N. Spain, *not* -ille; **-ian.**

cast iron (noun); **cast-iron** (adj.).

Castle Cary, Somerset.

Castlecary, Stirling, Donegal.

Castlerea, N. Ireland; *pron.* -ray.

Castlereagh (Robert S., Viscount), 1769–1822, British statesman; *pron.* -ray.

Castleton, Derby.

Castletown, I. of Man.

cast off (typ.), to estimate amount of printed matter MS. would make.

castor, a beaver (hence **castor oil**) or its fur; a small wheel for furniture; a small pot with perforated lid (hence **castor sugar**). *See also* **-er.**

Castor and Pollux, stars, also patrons of sailors.

casual, incidental, not regular. *See also* **causal.**

casus/ belli (Lat.), the cause of war; — *foederis,* case stipulated by treaty; — *omissus,* case unprovided for by statute.

C.A.T., computer-assisted typesetting.

cat., catalogue, cataplasm, catechism.

catachthonian, subterranean.

cataclasm, violent disruption.

cataclysm/, deluge; **-ist,** *not* -atist.

Catalan, of Catalonia; abbr. **Cat.**

catalogu/e, abbr. **cat.; -ed, -er, -ing, -ize** (U.S. **catalog**).

catalogue raisonné (Fr. m.), an explanatory catalogue.

catal/yst, a substance facilitating chem. change; **-yse,** *not* -ize (U.S. **-yze**); **-ysis; -ytic.**

catamaran, a raft; *also* two-hulled boat.

cataplasm, poultice; abbr. **cat.**

catarrh, inflammation of mucous membrane.

catarrhine, a section of the monkeys, *not* -arhine.

Catch (Jack), *use* **Ke-.**

catchline (typ.), a line containing catchword(s), signature letter, etc.

catchpole, a sheriff's officer, *not* -poll.

catchup, (U.S.) a sauce, *see* **ketchup;** *not* catsup, katsup, ketsup.

catchword (typ.), the first word of next page printed at bottom of preceding page.

catechism, teaching by question and answer; abbr. **cat.**

catechiz/e, -er, -ing.

catechu, an astringent, *not* cascheu, caschu.

catechumen, convert under instruction before baptism.

categorize, to classify.

caten/a, a chain; *pl.* **-ae.**

cater-cousin, a good friend.

caters (campan., *pl.*), changes on nine bells.

Cath., Catherine, Catholic.

cath., cathedral.

Catharine, Kansas, New York, Pennsylvania.

Cathay, poetical for China, *not* K-.

cathedral, when with name cap., as Ely Cathedral; abbr. **cath.**

Catherine, abbr. **Cath.**; **St. —**, hence **— pear** and **—-wheel**; **— I** and **II**, empresses of Russia; **— of Aragon**, **— Howard**, **— Parr**, first, fifth, and sixth wives of Henry VIII of England; **— de Medici**, 1519–89, Queen of France.

cathism/a, section of Greek Psalter; *pl.* **-ata**.

cathod/e, negative electrode; abbr. **ca.**; **-ic**, **-ograph**; *not* k-.

Catholic, abbr. **C.**, *or* **Cath.**

catholicize, *not* -ise.

Catilin/a, -e (Lucius Sergius), 108–62 B.C., Roman conspirator, *not* Cata-.

cation (elec.), ion carrying positive charge of electricity, *not* k-.

cat-o'-nine-tails (hyphens).

cat's-cradle, a children's game, *not* cratch-, scratch-.

Catskill Mountains, New York.

cat's-paw, person used as tool, (naut.) a light air, *not* catspaw.

catsup, *use* ketchup.

Cattegat, *use* Dan. **Kattegat** (Swed. **Kattegatt**).

Cattleya, an orchid genus.

Catullus (Caius Valerius), 87–54 (?) B.C., Roman poet.

Cauchy (A. L.), 1789–1857, French mathematician.

caucus (U.S.), political meeting.

Caudillo, Spanish 'leader', title assumed by Gen. Franco after Spanish Civil War.

caught (cricket), abbr. **c.**

cauldron, *not* cal-.

caulk, to make watertight, *not* calk.

caus., causa/tion, -tive.

causa/ causans (Lat.), a primary cause; *— causata*, a secondary cause; *— mali*, a cause of mischief; *vera —*, a true cause.

causal, having to do with a cause. *See also* **casual**.

causa/tion, -tive, abbr. **caus.**

cause célèbre (Fr. f.), famous law case.

causerie, chat, usu. as informal essay (not ital.).

causeur (Fr. m.), a conversationalist, tattler.

causeuse (Fr. f.), a small sofa.

cauterize, *not* -ise.

cautery/ (actual), by hot iron; **electric —**, by platinum wire; **potential —**, by caustics.

cautionnement (Fr. m.), bail.

cav., cavalry.

cava, *use* k-.

Cavagnari (Sir Pierre Louis Napoleon), 1841–79, British (by naturalization) mil. administrator.

Cavalcaselle (G. B.), 1820–97, Italian writer on art.

Cavalleria Rusticana (Rustic Gallantry), opera by Mascagni, 1890; *pron.* ka-val-ā-rē′ă —.

cavalry, abbr. **cav.**

cavass, *use* k-.

caveat, a formal warning (not ital.).

caveat/ actor (Lat.), let the doer beware; *— emptor*, ditto buyer; *— viator*, ditto traveller.

cave canem (Lat.), beware of the dog.

cavesson, a nose-band for horses, *not* -zon.

caviare, pickled sturgeon-roe, *not* -iar, -ier.

cavil/, to make trifling objections, **-led, -ler, -ling.**

cavo-riliev/o (It.), hollow relief; *pl.* **— -i**.

Cavour (Count Camillo), 1810–61, Italian statesman.

Cawnpore, usual form in English history of the now correct **Kanpur**.

Caxton (William), 1422–91, first English printer.

Cayenne, capital of Fr. Guiana.

cayman/, American alligator, *not* cai-, kai-; *pl.* **-s.**

Cayman Islands, W. Indies.

cayuse (U.S. and Canada), an Indian pony.

cazique, *use* **cacique.**

C.B., Cape Breton, Cavalry Brigade, Chief Baron, Common Bench, Companion of the Bath, (naval) Confidential Book, Confined to Barracks; County Borough.

Cb (chem.), columbium (no point).

C.B.A., Council for British Archaeology.

C.B.C., Canadian Broadcasting Company.

C.B.E., Commander (of the Order) of the British Empire.

C.B.E.L., Cambridge Bibliography of English Literature.

C.B.I., Confederation of British Industry.

c.bl., carte blanche.

C.B.S., Columbia Broadcasting System, Confraternity of the Blessed Sacrament.

C.C., Caius College, Chess Club, Circuit Court, City Council, -lor, Civil Court, Common Councilman, Consular Corps, County Clerk, — Commissioner, — Council, -lor, — Court, Cricket Club, Curate-in-Charge, Cycling Club.

CC, 200.

cc (no points), cubic centimetre (in engines, etc.).

c.c., *compte courant* (account current), contra credit.

cc., *capita* (chapters).

C.C.C. Corpus Christi College.

CCC, 300.

CCCC, *or* **CD,** 400.

C.C.F., Combined Cadet Force.

C.C.P., Code of Civil Procedure, Court of Common Pleas.

C.Cr.P., Code of Criminal Procedure.

C.C.S., Casualty Clearing Station, Ceylon Civil Service.

CD, 400.

Cd (chem.), cadmium (no point).

cd, candela (no point).

C.D., Civil Defence.

Cd., Cmd. (old series), **Cmnd.** (new series), Command paper, q.v. (with number following).

c.d., cum dividend (with dividend).

C.D.A., College Diploma in Agriculture.

C.D. Acts, Contagious Diseases Acts.

C.D.C., Commonwealth Development Corporation (Colonial till 1963).

C.D.H., College Diploma in Horticulture.

Cdr., Commander.

Cdre., Commodore (naval).

c.d.v., carte-de-visite.

C.E., Chief Engineer, Civil Engineer, Christian Era (*see* **A.C.E.**).

Ce (chem.), cerium (no point).

C.E.A., Central Electricity Authority.

cedar, a tree.

ceder, one who cedes.

cedilla c (typ.), the ç.

Cedron (*or* **Ki-**), Palestine, **Ke-** in N.E.B.; Arabic **Wadi en Nar.**

C.E.G.B., Central Electricity Generating Board.

cel., celebrated.

celanese, an ̈artificial silk (trade-name).

cela/ va sans dire (Fr.), needless to say; — *viendra,* that will come.

celebrated, abbr. **cel.**

celebrator, *not* -er.

célèbre (Fr.), famous.

céleri (Fr. m.), celery.

celiac, *use* **coeliac.**

célibataire (Fr. m. or f.), a bachelor or spinster.

cellar, *not* -er.

Cellini (Benvenuto), 1500–71, Italian goldsmith and sculptor.

cellist (mus.), a violoncello player.

cell/o, violoncello; *pl.* **-i.**

cellophane, transparent wrapping material.

Cels., Celsius (temperature scale same as centigrade).

Celt/, -ic, -icism, *not* K-; abbr. **Celt.**

C.E.M.A., Council for the Encouragement of Music and the Arts (*now* **A.C.G.B.**).

cembalist, harpsichord player, orchestral piano-player.

C.E.M.S., Church of England Men's Society.

cenobite, *use* **coen-.**

cenogamy, *use* **coe-.**

cenozoic, *use* **caino-.**

censer, incense vessel.

censor, Roman magistrate.

censor morum (Lat.), a regulator of morals.

cent., central, century.

cent/, -s, American coin; abbr. **c., ct.,** *or* **cts.**

cental, corn measure of 100 lb.; *pl.* **-s**; abbr. **ctl.**

centauromachy, centaurs fighting.

centenarian, one who is a hundred years old.

centen/ary, -nial.

centering, framing for an arch, *not* -reing. *See also* **centre.**

centibar, one-hundredth of a bar (q.v.).

centigrade (not cap.); abbr. **C.**

centigramme, off. B.S.I. spelling; abbr. **cg** (no point).

centilitre, abbr. **cl** (no point).

centime/, one-hundredth of French franc; *pl.* **-s**; abbr. **c.** *or* **cts.**

centimetre, 0·394 inch, *not* -er; abbr. *s.* and *pl.* **cm** (no point).

centner, German weight, about 1 cwt.; in Ger. *Zentner.*

cent/o, writing composed of scraps from various authors; *pl.* **-os.**

central, abbr. **cent.**

centralize, *not* -ise.

Central Provinces (India), *now* **Madhya Pradesh.**

centr/e, -ed, -ing (U.S. **center,** etc.). *See also* **centering.**

centre-notes (typ.), those between columns.

cents, abbr. **c.,** *or* **cts.**

centum, a hundred; abbr. **C,** *or* **cent.**

centumvir/, Roman commissioner; *pl.* **-i.**

centurion, one who commands a hundred, *not* -ian.

century (typ.), spell out in bookwork; abbr. **C.,** *or* **cent.** *See also* **nineteenth century.**

cephalic, of the head, *not* k-.

ceramic, etc., *not* k-; abbr. **ceram.**

Cerberus, three-headed dog at gate of Hades (Greek myth.).

cerebell/um, the hinder brain; *pl.* **-a.**

cerebr/um, the brain proper; *pl.* **-a.**

cere/cloths, -ments, grave-clothes, orig. dipped in wax; *pron.* sēr-.

cerge, *use* **cie-.**

ceriph (typ.), *use* **serif.**

cerise (Fr. f.), cherry.

cerise, a colour.

cerium, symbol **Ce** (no point).

cert., certificate, certify.

certiorari, a writ removing a case to a higher court (not ital.).

cerulean, blue, *not* cae-, coe-.

Cervantes Saavedra (**Miguel de**), 1547–1616, author of *Don Quixote*.

Cesarean, *use* **Cae-**.

Cesarevitch, Tsar's eldest son, *use* **Tsarevich**.

Cesarewitch, horse-race.

cesser (law), the coming to an end.

c'est/-à-dire (Fr.), that is to say; — *à vous à parler*, it is your turn to speak; — *à vous de parler*, it is your duty to speak; — *bien ça*, that's just it; — *la guerre*, it's according to the customs of war; — *le premier pas qui coûte*, it is the first step that is difficult.

Cestr., signature of Bishop of Chester (full point).

Cestrian, of Chester.

c'est/ selon (Fr.), that depends on circumstances; — *tout dire*, that's saying everything.

cestui que/ trust (law), a beneficiary, *pl.* cestuis — — (*not* trustent); — — vie, he on whose life land is held, *pl.* cestuis — —.

c'est une autre chose (Fr.), that's another matter.

cestus, (Aphrodite's) girdle, *not* -os; anc. Roman boxing-glove(s), *not* cae-.

cesura, *use* cae-.

cetera/ desiderantur or — desunt (Lat.), the rest are wanting.

ceteris paribus (Lat.), other things being equal; abbr. *cet. par.*

Cetinje, Yugoslavia, formerly cap. of Montenegro, *not* Cett-, Zet-, ingé.

C.E.T.S., Church of England Temperance Society.

C.E.U., Christian Endeavour Union.

C.E.W.C., Council for Education in World Citizenship.

Ceylon, republic within Commonwealth, 1972, officially Sri Lanka (Ceylon); adj. **Ceylonese**.

Cézanne (**Paul**), 1839–1905, French artist.

C.F., Chaplain to the Forces.

Cf, californium (no point).

c.f., carried forward.

cf., calf, *confer* (compare).

c.f.i., cost, freight, and insurance.

C.G., Captain-General, Captain of the Guard, coast-guard, Coldstream Guards, Commissary-General, Consul-General.

cg, centigramme(no point).

c.g., centre of gravity.

C.G.H., Cape of Good Hope.

C.G.M., Conspicuous Gallantry Medal.

CGPM, *Conférence Générale des Poids et des Mésures*, General Conference of Weights and Measures.

C.G.S., Chief of the General Staff.

c.g.s., centimetre-gramme-second system.

C.G.T. (*Confédération Générale du Travail*), General Federation of Labour.

C.H., clearing-house, Companion of Honour, court-house, custom-house.

Ch., chaplain, Chin/a, -ese, Church, and proper names with this beginning, (Lat.) *Chirurgiae* (of surgery).

ch., chapter, chief, child/, -ren, chirurgeon, (mus.) choir organ.

Chablis, a white burgundy.

chaconne, dance.

chacun son goût (*à*) (Fr.), everyone to his taste.

Chad, Cent. Africa, independent rep. 1960; **Lake Chad**, in Sudan, *not* Tchad.

chadar (Ind.), *use* **chuddar**.

Chagall (**Marc**), b. 1887, Russian painter.

chairman (m. and f.), abbr. **C.**, *or* **chn.**

chaise-longue/, a couch, day-bed; *pl.* **-s.**

chal, a gipsy; *fem.* **chai.**

chalaz/**a** (biol.), string attached to yolk of egg; *pl.* **-ae.**

chalcedony, a form of quartz, *not* calce-, chalci-; *pron.* kal-.

Chald/**ea**, Babylonia (*not* -aea); **-aic, -aism** (*not* -ism), **-ean, -ee**; abbr. **Chald.**

chalet, a Swiss cottage, *not* châ- (not ital.).

Chaliapin (**Feodor Ivanovich**), 1873–1938, Russian bass singer.

Challemel-Lacour (**P.A.**), 1827–96, French statesman.

chamb., chamberlain (cap. as a title of office).

Chambers's Encyclopaedia.

Chambertin, a red burgundy.

chambre/ *à coucher* (Fr. f.), bedroom, *pl.* **chambres** — —; — *d'ami*, spare bedroom.

chameleon, lizard of changeable colour, *not* chamae-.

chamfer, to bevel.

chamois-leather, *not* shammy- —.

chamomile, *use* cam-.

Chamonix, dép. Haute-Savoie, *not* -ouni, -ounix, -ouny.

champagne, a sparkling wine.

champaign, a flat open country.

Champassac, former French principality, now part of Laos.

champerty, an illegal agreement, *not* -arty.

champignon (Fr. m.), a mushroom, *not* -pinion.

Champlain, Lake, between N.Y. and Vt., U.S.

Champlain (**Samuel de**), 1570–1635, French founder of Quebec, Can.

champlevé, an enamel.

Champollion (**J. F.**), 1791–1831, French Egyptologist.

Champs-Élysées, Paris.

chancellery, *not* -ory.

Chancellor, abbr. **C.**, *or* **Chanc.**

chance-medley (law), a form of homicide (hyphen).

Chancery, abbr. **C.**

chandelier, branched hanging support for lights.

change/**able, -ability.**

change-over (noun, hyphen).

channel/, **-led, -ling.**

chanson/ (Fr. f.), a song; **-nette**, a little song.

chant/, singing; **-er**, of bagpipe, *not* chau-.

Chantilly, dép. Oise.

Chantrey/ (**Sir F.**), 1781–1841, sculptor; — **Fund**, Royal Academy of Arts, London.

chantry, endowed chapel.

chanty, *use* **shanty.**

chap., a skin-crack, *not* chop.

chap., chaplain, chapter.

chaparejos (*pl.*), cowboy's leather riding-breeches, *not* -ajos.

chapeau/ (Fr. m.), a hat, *pl.* **-x**; *chapeaux bas!* hats off! *chapeau-bras*, three-cornered hat carried under arm; *chapeau rouge*, red hat of a cardinal.

chapel (typ.), an association of workers in a printing-office.

Chapel-en-le-Frith, Derbys. (hyphens).

chapelle ardente (Fr. f.), a chapel lighted for a lying-in-state (no hyphen).

Chapel Royal, *pl.* **Chapels —.**

chaperon, *not* -one, -onne.

Chap.-Gen., Chaplain-General.

chaplain, abbr. **chap.**

Chappell (William), 1809–88, music publisher.

chapter/, -s, abbr. **c., ch.,** *or* **chap.**

chapter-headings (typ.), type a matter of taste; no general rule can be stated.

char/, -red, -ring.

char-à-banc/ *or* (completely anglicized) **charabanc/,** a motor-coach; anglicized *pl.* **-s.** In Fr., *char-à-bancs, pl. chars-à-bancs.*

characteriz/e, *not* -ise; **-able, -ation, -er.**

charbon (Fr. m.), coal, *also* anthrax.

chargé, *more fully* **chargé d'affaires** (not ital.).

charisma, spiritual power of person or office.

Charity Organisation Society, off., *not* organiz-; abbr. **C.O.S.** *Now* **F.W.A.,** q.v.

charivari (Fr. m.), a mock serenade; *London Charivari* (*The*), *Punch.*

Charlemagne, 744–814, king of the Franks from 768.

Charles, abbr. **C.,** *or* **Chas.**

Charleston, Ill., S. Car. (source of the dance), W. Virg. (U.S.).

Charlestown, Boston (U.S.).

Charlottenburg, Berlin.

charlotte russe (cook.), custard or cream enclosed in sponge-cake (not ital.).

Charon (class. myth.), the ferryman; *pron.* kār′ŏn.

charpoy, Indian bedstead.

chartel, *use* **car-.**

Chartered Accountant, abbr. **C.A.**

charter-party, written evidence of agreement, esp. naut. (hyphen).

charter-plane (hyphen).

Charters Towers, Queensland, Australia (no apos.).

chartography, *use* **ca-.**

chart paper, machine-made from best rags.

chartreuse, a liqueur first made at Carthusian monastery near Grenoble.

Chartreux, a Carthusian monk.

Charybdis, personified whirlpool in St. of Messina.

Chas., Charles.

chase (typ.), metal frame holding composed type.

Chasles/ (Michel), 1793–1880, French mathematician; **— (Philarète),** 1798–1873, French lit. critic.

chasse/ (Fr. f.), a liqueur glassful, hunt; **— -marée,** coasting or fishing vessel.

chassé (Fr. m.), dance step.

châsse (Fr. f.), a shrine.

chasseu/r (Fr.), a huntsman; *fem.* **-se.**

chassis, window sash, a framework as of motor-car (not ital.).

chastis/e, *not* -ize; **-ement, -ing.**

château/ (Fr. m.), a castle; *pl.* **-x** (not ital.).

Chateaubriand (François René, Vicomte de), 1768–1848, French writer and statesman (no accent).

Châteaubriant, dép. Loire-Inférieure.

Châteaubriant (Fr. cook.), fillet of beef, cut thick and grilled.

Châteaudun, dép. Eure-et-Loir.

Châteauguay, Quebec.

Château-Lafite, a claret.

châteaux en Espagne (Fr.), 'castles in the air'.

châtelain/, lord of the manor; *fem.* **-e.**

Chattanooga, Tenn., U.S., battle in American Civil War.

Chatto & Windus, Ltd., publishers.

Chaucer (Geoffrey), 1340–1400, English poet.

chauffeu/r, motor-car driver, *fem.* **-se.**

chaunt/, -er, *use* **chant.**

chaussée (Fr. f.), a causeway, the ground level.

chaussures (Fr. f.), boots, shoes, etc.

Chautauqua, New York State, celebrated resort.

Chauvin (Fr.), French equivalent of Jingo, q.v.

Ch.B., *Chirurgiae Baccalaureus* (Bachelor of Surgery).

Ch. Ch., Christ Church, Oxford.

Chebyshev (P. L.), 1821–94, Russian mathematician.

check, to stop. *See also* **cheque.**

checkers (U.S.), draughts (*see also* **chequer**).

Cheddar cheese, *not* -er.

cheeper, partridge- or grouse-chick.

Cheeryble Brothers, in *Nicholas Nickleby.*

cheetah, hunting leopard, *not* chet-.

chef/ (Fr. m.), a cook; *chef de cuisine,* head cook; — *d'orchestre,* leader of the orchestra; — *-d'œuvre,* a masterpiece, *pl.* **chefs- —.**

cheir-, except for next, *use* **chir-.**

Cheiroptera, the bats, not **Chir-.**

Chekhov (Anton Pavlovich), 1861–1904, Russian playwright and story-writer, *not* the many variants.

C.H.E.L., *Cambridge History of English Literature.*

chem/ical, -ist, *not* chy-; abbr. **chem.**

chemin de fer (Fr. m.), railway; a form of baccarat.

chemistry (typ.), caps. for initial letters of symbols, no point at end. Names of chemical compounds to be in roman, not caps. Some prefixes are ital. or s.caps.; abbr. **chem.**

cheque, a written order (U.S. check).

chequer, (noun) pattern of squares; (verb) to variegate, interrupt; **Chequers,** Prime Minister's official country house in **Bucks.**

Cherbourg, dép. Manche.

cherchez la femme (Fr.), look for the woman.

chère amie (Fr. f.), a sweetheart (*è*).

chér/i (Fr.), *fem.* **-ie,** darling (*é*).

Cherokee, N. American Indian.

Chersonese, name applied to various peninsulas.

Chertkov (Vladimir Grigorevich), 1854–1936, Russian writer.

cherub/, *pl.* **-s, -im.**

Cherubini (Maria Luigi), 1760–1842, Italian operatic composer.

Cherwell, Oxford river; *pron.* Char-.

che sarà sarà (It.), what will be, will be.

Cheshire, abbr. **Ches.**

Chesil Beach, Dorset.

chess (masters of): Alekhine, Anderssen, Blackburne, Botvinnik, Bronstein, Capablanca, Chigorin, Euwe, Fischer, Janowski, Lasker, Morphy, Philidor, Pillsbury, Reshevsky, Réti, Rubinstein, Schlechter, Spassky, Staunton, Steinitz, Tarrasch, Zukertort.

Chesse (*The Game and Playe of*), the second book printed by Caxton.

Chester-le-Street, Durham (hyphens).

chestnut, *not* chesnut.

chetah, *use* chee-.

Chetniks, guerrilla forces raised in Yugoslavia during Second World War by Gen. Mikhailovitch.

cheval (Fr. m.), a horse, *pl. chevaux; cheval/ de bataille,* a favourite subject; — *de frise* (mil.), obstacle to cavalry advance, *usually in the pl. chevaux de frise; cheval de retour,* ticket-of-leave man.

chevalet (mus.), the bridge of a stringed instrument.

cheval-glass, tall mirror on frame.

Chevalier/(Albert), 1861–1923, English music-hall artiste; — **(Maurice),** 1888–1972, French entertainer.

chevalier d'industrie (Fr. m.), a swindler.

Chevallier (Gabriel), 1895–1969, French novelist.

cheville, violin peg, stop-gap word in sentence or verse.

chevrette, goatskin for gloves.

chevreuil (Fr. m.), roebuck, venison.

Chevreul (M. E.), 1786–1889, French chemist.

Cheyenne, Wyoming, U.S.; *also* an Indian tribe.

Cheyne Walk, Chelsea; *pron.* tshā′-nĭ.

Chi., Chicago.

Chiang Kai-shek, Nationalist Chinese statesman, b. 1887; *not* Kai-Shek.

Chianti, Italian wine.

chiaroscuro, light and shade, *not* chiaro-oscuro.

chibouk, anglicized form of **chibuq,** a Turkish pipe.

chic, 'style' (not ital.).

Chicago, Ill., U.S.; abbr. **Chi.;** *pron.* shĭ-kah′-go.

Chichele, Oxford professor-ship; *pron.* -ĕlĭ, *not* -eel.

Chichen Itzá, Mexico, site of antiquities.

chick (Anglo-Ind.), bamboo screen-blind.

Chickahoming (battles of the), in SE. Virginia, American Civil War.

Chickamauga (battle of), 1863, N. Georgia.

chicory, *not* chiccory.

chief, abbr. **C.,** *or* **ch.; Chief/ Accountant, C.A.;** — **Baron, C.B.;** — **Justice** (caps., no hyphen), abbr. **C.J.;** — **of General Staff,** abbr. **C.G.S.**

chield (Sc.), a young man, *not* chiel.

chiffon, dress fabric or ornaments.

chiffonier, a sideboard, *not* -nnier (not ital.).

chiffonn/ier (Fr.), *fem.* -*ière*, rag collector (ital.).

chiffre (Fr. m.), figure, numeral, monogram.

chignon, a coil of hair.

chigoe, W. Indian parasite, *not* jigger.

Chihli, Gulf of, China, *not* Pechihli.

child/, -**ren,** -**ren's,** abbr. **ch.**

Childe Harold's Pilgrimage, by Byron, 1811–17.

Childermas, 28 Dec.

childlike (one word).

Chile, S. America, *not* Chili; **Chilean.**

Chilianwala, W. Pakistan, *not* Chilianwallah, Killian-wala.

chilli/, red, or Guinea, pepper, *not* chile, chili, chilly; *pl.* -**es.**

chimaera (biol.), an organism with cells of two or more genetically distinct types. *See* **chimera.**

Chimborazo, Ecuador.

chimer, bishop's upper robe, *not* -ere.

chimera, a creation of the

imagination, *not* -aera; *pron.* kǐ-mē′ra. *See* **chimaera**.

Chin/a, -ese, abbr. **Chin.**

chincapin, dwarf chestnut, *not* -kapin, -quapin.

chinchona, *use* **cin-**.

Chindits, British glider-borne troops in Burma in Second World War.

chiné (Fr.), variegated (of stuffs).

Chinese/, abbr. **Ch.,** *or* **Chin.;** — **Classics,** the sacred books.

chinoiserie, Chinese decorative objects.

chipmuck *or* **chipmunk,** a N. American ground-squirrel.

Chipping Campden, Glos.

chi-rho, monogram of *XP,* first letters of Greek 'Christos'.

chiromancy, palmistry, *not* cheir-.

Chiron, the centaur, *not* Cheir-; *pron.* kī-.

chiropodist, one who treats hands and feet, *not* cheir-, -pedist.

chiropract/ic (*sing.*), removal of nerve interference by manipulation of spinal column; **-or,** one who does this.

Chiroptera, *use* **Cheir-**.

chirosophy, palmistry, *not* cheir-.

chirrup/, -ed, -ing.

chirurgiae (Lat.), of surgery; abbr. **Ch.**

chit, chitty (Anglo-Ind.), a letter.

Chittagong, Bangladesh.

chlorine, symbol **Cl** (no point).

chlorodyne, medicine containing chloroform, *not* -ine.

chlorophyll (bot.), green colouring matter of plants, *not* -il, -yl.

Ch.M., *Chirurgiae Magister* (Master of Surgery).

chn., chairman.

choc., chocolate.

chock-full, *not* choke-.

Choctaw, N. American Indians, *not* Chacatos, Chactaws, Chakta.

choir, part of a church, *or* singers, *not* quire.

choke-full, *use* **chock-**.

cholera morbus, acute gastro-enteritis.

cholesterol, fatty alcohol found in parts of the body, *not* -in.

Cholmeley, Cholmondeley, Chomley, *all pron.* chumlǐ.

chop, *see* **chap.**

Chopin (Frédéric François), 1810–49, Polish composer.

'Chops of the Channel', west entrance to English Channel.

choreograph/er, -y, arrange/r, -ment of ballet.

chorography, description of districts (intermediate between geography and topography).

chorus/, *pl.* **-es; -ed.**

chose (law), a thing.

Chose (Monsieur) (Fr.), Mr. So-and-so.

chota hazri (Anglo-Ind.), early breakfast.

Chota Nagpur, Bihar, India.

chou/ (Fr. cook. m.), cabbage, puff (pastry), a dress rosette; — *-fleur,* cauliflower (hyphen), *pl.* *choux-fleurs; choux de Bruxelles,* Brussels sprouts; *chou marin,* sea-kale.

Chou en-Lai, Communist Chinese politician, b. 1898.

Chr., Christ, Christian, Chronicles.

Chr. Coll. Cam., Christ's College, Cambridge.

Christ Church, Oxford, abbr. **Ch. Ch.**

Christchurch, Hants, *and* N.Z.

Christ-cross-row, the alphabet, *not* criss — —.

Christe eleïson, 'Christ, have mercy'.

Christian/, -ity (cap.).

Christiania, former name of **Oslo,** capital of Denmark.

Christiania, a type of turn in skiing; abbr. **Christy** (no point).

christianize, *not* -ise (cap. in historical uses).

Christie, Manson, & Woods, auctioneers, London, ('Christie's').

Christmas Day (caps.); **Old — —,** 6 January.

Christoff (Boris), b. 1919. Bulgarian bass singer.

Christ's College, Cambridge; abbr. **Chr. Coll. Cam.**

Christy-minstrels, coloured entertainers, with bones, banjos, etc. (after George Christy, of New York).

chromatosphere (astr.), *use* **chromosphere.**

chromium, symbol **Cr** (no point).

chromo/ (typ.), (no point), abbr. of **chromolithograph,** picture printed in colours from stone; *pl.* **-s.**

chromolithography (one word).

chromo paper, one with a special smooth coating.

chromosphere, gaseous envelope of sun.

chron., chronolog/y, -ical, ically.

Chronicles, First, Second Book of, abbr. **1 Chr., 2 Chr.**

chrysal/is, *pl.* **-ises.**

Chrysaor, son of Neptune.

Chryseis, daughter of Chryses, a Trojan priest.

Chrysler Building, New York.

chrysoprase, green chalcedony, *not* -phrase.

Chrysostom (St. John), 347–407.

chthonian, pertaining to the lower world of Greek mythology.

chudder (Anglo-Ind.), female overgarment, *not* the many variations (not ital.).

Chur, Switzerland; in Fr. **Coire.**

Church, initial cap. when referring to a body of people, as the Methodist Church; lower case for building; abbr. **C.,** *or* **Ch.**

Church Assembly (*properly* National Assembly of the Church of England), set up 1920, absorbed in General Synod, 1970.

Church Commissioners, *formerly* Ecclesiastical Commissioners and Queen Anne's Bounty.

Churchill (Sir Winston Leonard Spencer), 1874–1965, British statesman; **— (Winston),** 1871–1947, American writer.

churchwarden (one word).

chute, slide, etc.; *pron.* sh-.

chutney, condiment, *not* -nee, -ny.

chymist, *use* che-.

C.I., Channel Islands, Chief Inspector, — Instructor, (Imperial Order of the) Crown of India (ladies).

C.I.A., (U.S.) Central Intelligence Agency.

Cibber (Colley), 1671–1757, Poet Laureate 1730–57.

cicad/a, the tree cricket, *not* cig-, -ala; *pl.* **-ae** (biol.), **-as** (general) (U.S. **locust).**

cical/a (It.), the grasshopper; *pl.* **-e.**

cicatrice/, scar; *pl.* **-s.**

cicatri/x (in surgery), scar; *pl.* **-ces.**

cicatrize, *not* -ise.

Cicero (Marcus Tullius,

'Tully'), 106–43 B.C., Roman orator; abbr. **Cic.**

ciceron/e, a guide, *pl.* **-i;** *pron.* chich-er-ō′-nĕ.

Cicestr., signature of Bp. of Chichester (full point).

cicisbe/o, a married woman's gallant; *pl.* **-i.**

C.I.D., Committee for Imperial Defence, Criminal Investigation Department.

Cik Campeador, the, 1040–99, Spanish warrior.

cider, *not* cy-.

ci-devant, formerly (not ital.).

C.I.E., Companion (Order) of the Indian Empire.

Cie (Fr.), *compagnie* (company) (no point).

cierge, large candle, *not* cer-, ser-.

c.i.f., cost, insurance, freight.

c.i.f.c., cost, insurance, freight, and commission.

cigala, *use* cicada *or* cicala.

ci-gît (Fr.), here lies.

C.I.G.S., Chief (of the). Imperial General Staff.

C.I.I., Chartered Insurance Institute.

cili/um, a hair-like appendage; *pl.* **-a.**

cill, *use* sill.

Cimabue (G.), 1240–1300, Italian painter; *pron.* tshēm-aboo-ĕ.

cim/eter, *use* scimitar.

cim/ex, bed-bug; *pl.* **-ices.**

Cimmerian, intensely dark (cap.); *pron.* kim-.

C.-in-C., Commander-in-Chief.

cinchona bark, source of quinine, *not* chin-.

Cincinnati, Ohio (U.S.).

cinema(tograph), accepted form of k-.

cinerari/a, plant with ash-coloured foliage; *pl.* **-as.**

cinerari/um, niche for urn with ashes of deceased; *pl.* **-a.**

Cingalese, *use* **Sinhalese.** *But see* **Ceylon.**

cingul/um, a girdle or zone; *pl.* **-a.**

cinquecento, 1500–99, and Renaissance art of that century.

Cinque Ports, Hastings, New Romney, Hythe, Dover, and Sandwich, plus Winchelsea and Rye.

C.I.O. (U.S.), Congress of Industrial Organizations.

cipher, *not* cy-.

cipolin (one *l*), anglicized form of It. *cipollino,* veined white and green marble.

Cipriani (Giambattista), R.A., 1727–85, Italian painter and engraver.

C.I.R., Commission for Industrial Relations.

circ., circiter (about).

circa (Lat. prep.), about; in Eng. used mainly with dates and quantities; abbr. *c.*

Circean, of Circe, *not* -aean.

circiter (Lat. adv.), about, approximately; abbr. *circ.*

circle, sign ○; **arc of circle,** ⌒.

Circuit Court, abbr. **C.C.**

circuit edges (binding), covers turned over to protect the leaves.

circulariz/e, to issue circulars, *not* -ise; **-ing.**

circum (Lat.), about; in Eng. used as prefix meaning around.

circumcise, *not* -ize.

circumflex (typ.), the accent, *â, ê, î, ô, û.*

circumflexion, *not* -flect-.

circumstance: mere situation is expressed by 'in the circumstances', action affected is performed 'under the circumstances' (*O.E.D.*).

Cirencester, Glos., obsolescent *pron.* Sis′-iter.

cirque, natural amphitheatre (not ital.).

cirrhosis, a liver disease.
cirrus, a curl-like tuft.
cisalpine, on the Roman side of the Alps (not cap. except in Cisalpine Gaul).
ciseau/ (Fr. m.), chisel; *pl.* *-x,* scissors.
cisel/eur (Fr. m.), a metal-chaser; *-ure* (f.), art of chasing.
cispontine, on the north side of the Thames. *See* **transpontine.**
cist (archaeol.), tomb covered with stone slabs. *See* **cyst.**
cit., citation, cited, citizen.
citations, *see* **authorities,** *also* **quotations.**
cities/ (typ.), names of, not to be abbreviated if avoidable; — **of Refuge:** *east of Jordan,* Bezer, Ramoth, Golan; *west of Jordan,* Hebron, Shechem, Kedesh.
citizen, abbr. **cit.**
cito (Lat.), quickly.
citoyen/ (Fr.), *fem.* *-ne,* citizen.
citrine (noun and adj.), lemon-colour(ed).
cittadin/o (It.), a citizen, *pl.* *-i;* *fem.* *-a,* *pl.* *-e.*
city, abbr. **c.; City Editor,** the supervisor of financial matters; (N. Amer.) editor of local news. *See also* **cities.**
ciudad (Sp.), city, *not* cui-.
Ciudad Trujillo, recent name for Santo Domingo, cap. of Dominican Republic.
civ., civil, -ian.
civics, the science of citizenship.
Civil/ Court, abbr. **C.C.;** — **Engineer,** abbr. **C.E.**
civiliz/e, *not* -ise; **-able.**
Civil/ Servants, — Service (caps.), abbr. **C.S.**
C.J., Chief Justice.
ck., cask, -s.
Cl, chlorine (no point).
cl, centilitre (no point).
cl., class, clause, cloth.

Clackmannan, Scotland (three *n*'s); abbr. **Cla.**
Clairaut (A. C.), 1713–65, French mathematician, *not* -ault.
claire-cole, *use* clear-.
clairvoyant/, *fem.* **-e** (not ital.).
clam/, to clog, smear; **-miness, -my.**
clamjamphrie (Sc.), rubbish, *also* a mob, *not* the many variations.
clang, quality of musical sound; in Ger. *Klang.*
clang/our, *not* -or (except in U.S.).
clans/man, *pl.* **-men.**
Claparède (Jean Louis), 1832–70, Swiss naturalist.
claptrap, empty words (one word).
claque, hired applauders (not ital.).
claquer, hired applauder; in Fr. m. *claqueur.*
clar., (mus.) clarinet; (typ.) clarendon.
clarabella (mus.), an organ stop, *not* clari-.
Clarenceux, the second King-of-Arms, *not* -cieux.
clarendon (typ.), a thickened modern type, abbr. **clar.**
Clarendon Press, the original printing house of the University Press at Oxford; hence the imprint on learned books of the O.U.P. printed there or elsewhere.
claret, originally a light-red, now (in Britain) a dark-red wine of Bordeaux.
Claretie (Arsène-Arnaud, *called* Jules), 1840–1913, French historian and lit. critic.
clarinet/, -tist, *not* -ionet; abbr. **clar.**
Clarissa Harlowe, by Samuel Richardson.
class, abbr. **cl.**
class., classic, -al, classi-fication.

classes (bot., zool.), (typ.) to have capital initials.

Claude Lorrain, 1600–82, French painter, *not* -aine.

clause so-and-so (typ.), to have lower-case *c*; of paragraphs thus, (1), (2), (3); abbr. **cl.**

Clausewitz (Karl von), 1780–1831, Prussian mil. writer.

clav/is, a key; *pl.* *-es*.

C.L.B., Church Lads' Brigade.

cld., cleared (goods or shipping), coloured.

clean (typ.), said of proofs or revises with few errors, or pulled after matter has been corrected.

clear-cole, a coating of size, *not* claire-.

clear days, time to be reckoned exclusive of the first and last.

cleared (goods or shipping), abbr. **cld.**

clearstory, *use* clere-.

clef (mus.), 𝄢 bass, 𝄡 or 𝄡 tenor, 𝄞 treble.

cleistogam/ic, -ous (bot.), permanently closed and self-fertilizing, *not* k-.

Clemenceau (Georges E. B.), 1841–1929, French politician, *not* Clé-.

Clemens (S. L.), 1835–1910 ('Mark Twain'), American writer.

clench (to) the fist or fingers, grasp firmly, fix, settle. *See also* clinch.

clepsydra/, a time measurer, *not* k-; *pl.* *-s*.

cleptomania, *use* k-.

clerestory, a special upper row of windows, *not* clear-; *pron.* klēr-.

clerk, abbr. **clk.**

Clerke (Agnes M.), 1842–1907, English astronomer.

Clerk-Maxwell (James), 1831–79, *use* **Maxwell (James Clerk)**.

Clerk/ of Parliaments (caps.); — **of the Peace**, abbr. **C.P.**; — **of the Privy Council**, abbr. **C.P.C.**

Clermont-Ferrand, France (hyphen).

Cleveland, new name proposed for Teesside (q.v.), 1972.

clevis, U-shaped iron at end of beam for attaching tackle, *not* cliv/es, -ies.

clew, ball of thread; (naut., verb or noun) (to draw up) lower corner of sail, *not* clue.

cl. gt. (bookbinding), cloth gilt.

cliché (typ.), a block; a hackneyed phrase.

clicker (typ.), a supervisor in the composing rooms.

Clicquot (Veuve), a brand of champagne.

clientele, clients collectively (no accent, not ital.).

climacteric (noun or adj.), (pertaining to) a critical period; **grand —**, the age of 63.

climactic, pertaining to a climax.

climatic, pertaining to climate.

clinch (to), a nail, to make fast a rope in a special way, to make firm and sure—as an argument. *See also* clench.

clin d'œil (Fr. m.), a wink.

clinic, *not* clinique.

Clinker (Humphry, *not* -ey), by Smollett.

clinometer, instrument for measuring slopes, *not* k-.

Clio (Gr.), muse of history, *pron.* klī'-ō

cliqu/e, -ism, -y, *not* -eism, -ey (not ital.).

clish-ma-claver (Sc.), gossip (hyphens).

Clitheroe, Lancs.

clitor/is (anat.), female organ; *pl.* **-ides.**

clk., clerk.

Cloaca Maxima, sewer of anc. Rome (caps.).

cloche (hort.), bell-glass *or* glass cover; woman's close-fitting hat (not ital.).

cloff, an allowance on commodities, *not* clough.

cloisonné, enamel (not ital.).

close (typ.), the second member of any pair, as ']); *pron.* klōz.

close up (typ.), to push together, to remove spacing-out leads; **close matter,** unleaded, or thinly spaced.

closure, a stopping, esp. of debate in Parliament; Fr. f. *clôture.*

Clos Vougeot, a burgundy.

clot-bur (bot.), burdock, *not* clote-, cloth-.

clote (bot.), burdock and similar burry plants, *not* — -bur.

cloth/, abbr. **cl.;** — **of Bruges,** gold brocade.

Clotho (Gk. myth.), the Fate that spins the thread of life.

clotted cream, *not* clouted cream.

clôture (Fr. f.), closure.

clouds, general meanings: **cirrus,** curling fibres; **cumulus,** rounded masses on horizontal base; **nimbus,** rain-clouds; **stratus,** horizontal sheet. General order, from highest to lowest: **cirrus, cirro-stratus, cirro-cumulus, cumulo-nimbus, alto-stratus, alto-cumulus, cumulus, strato-cumulus, nimbo-stratus, stratus.** (U.S. **cirrostratus,** etc.)

cloudy (naut.), abbr. **c.**

clough, a ravine.

clove-hitch, a knot (hyphen).

clubbable, sociable.

clue, information to be followed up, *not* clew (except in U.S.).

Cluniac, (monk or nun) of branch of Benedictine order stemming from Cluny, France.

Clwyd, river, N. Wales. *Also* new Welsh county comprising Flintshire and part of Denbighshire, proposed in 1971.

Clydebank, Dunbarton, a town.

clypeiform, clypeate, buckler-shaped.

Clytemnestra, wife of Agamemnon, *not* Clytae-.

C.M., Certified Master or Mistress, *Chirurgiae Magister* (Master of Surgery), (mus.) common metre, Corresponding Member.

c.m., *causa mortis* (by reason of death).

cm, centimetre(s) (no point).

Cm, curium (no point).

C.M.B., coastal motor-boat.

Cmd., Command paper (old series).

cmdg., commanding.

Cmdr., Commodore (naval).

C.M.F., Central Mediterranean Force.

C.M.G., Companion of (the Order of) St. Michael and St. George.

Cmnd., Command paper (new series), with number following.

C.M.P., Corps of Military Police.

C.M.S., Church Missionary Society.

C.N.D., Campaign for Nuclear Disarmament.

Cnossus, Crete, *use* **Knossos.**

Cnut, more correct than **Canute,** *not* Knut.

C.O., Colonial Office, Commanding Officer, Commonwealth office, Conscientious Objector, Criminal Office, Crown Office.

Co, cobalt (no point).
Co., Colon, Company, county.
c/o, care of.
coad., coadjutor.
coagul/um, a clot; *pl.* **-a.**
Coalbrookdale, Salop.
coalfield (one word).
coalmouse (ornith.),
  the coal titmouse, *not*
  cole-.
coal-pit (hyphen).
Coalville, Leics.
coast-guard, the body of
  men (hyphen), abbr. **C.G.;**
  coastguardsman, the
  individual (one word).
coaxial (one word).
cobalt, symbol **Co** (no point).
Cobbe (Frances Power),
  1822–1904, British social
  writer.
coble, boat, *not* cobble.
Coblenz, *not* -tz, K-.
COBOL (Common Business
  Oriented Language),
  a computer-programming
  language; caps. or s.caps.
cobra de capello, Indian
  snake, *not* da, di.
Coburg, Iowa, U.S.; **Saxe-**
  —, Germany, *not* -ourg, -urgh.
coca, Bolivian shrub, source
  of cocaine.
Coca Cola, pop. abbr. **Coke**
  (no point), carbonated soft
  drink from cola nut and
  cacao leaf (trade-names).
cocaine, *not* -ain; pop. abbr.
  coke (no point).
cocco (bot.), Jamaica plant
  tuber, *not* cocoa, coco.
coch., cochl., cochlear,
  a spoonful; — **amp., mag.,**
  med., parv., table/spoon-
  ful, large —, dessert —,
  tea —. Superseded by doses
  in ml.
Cochin-China, formerly
  part of Fr. Indo-China,
  now of S. Vietnam
  (hyphen).
cochle/a, the ear passage; *pl.*
  -ae.

cochon de lait (Fr. m.),
  sucking pig.
Cockaigne, London, *not*
  Cocagne, Cockayne.
cockatiel, small crested
  Australian parrot, *not* -teel.
cockatoo/, large crested
  Australian parrot; *pl.* **-s.**
cockatrice, fabulous serpent.
Cockburn, *pron.* Cō′-burn.
Cockcroft (Sir John), 1897–
  1967, British nuclear
  scientist.
Cocker (Edward), 1631–75,
  reputed author of *Arithmetic*;
  'according to Cocker',
  accurate.
cockie-leekie, *use* **cocky-**
  leeky.
cockney, native of cent.
  London (not cap.).
cockscomb, a plant. *See*
  coxcomb.
cockswain, *use* **coxswain.**
cocky-leeky (Sc.), hotch-
  potch, a soup, *not* cockie-
  leeky, cock-a-leeky.
Cocles (Horatius), Roman
  who 'kept the bridge'; *pron.*
  kŏk′-lēz.
coco, trop. palm-tree bearing
  the **coconut** (correct form)
  or **cokernut** (commercial
  usage). *See* **cacao.**
Cocos Islands (Keeling
  Islands), Bay of Bengal.
cocotte (Fr. f.), a prostitute.
Cocytus, a river in Hades.
C.O.D., cash, *or* collect, on
  delivery.
C.O.D., Concise Oxford
  Dictionary.
cod., codex.
coddl/e, pamper, parboil;
  -ing.
Code Napoléon (Fr. m.),
  civil code promulgated
  1804–11.
cod/ex, ancient MS., abbr.
  cod.; *pl.* **-ices,** abbr. **codd.**
cod-fish (hyphen).
codling, small cod, elongated
  apple.

Cody (William Frederick),
1846–1917, 'Buffalo Bill',
American showman.

coeducation (one word).

coefficient (one word).

*Coelebs in Search of a
Wife*, by Hannah More.

Coelenterata, a zool. sub-
kingdom (not ital.); *pron.*
sĕ-lent′-.

coeliac, abdominal, *not* ce-;
pron. see′.

coenobite, member of
monastic community, *not*
cen-; *pron.* sēn-.

coenogamy, community of
wives, *not* ce-; *pron.* see′-.

coerulean, *use* ce-.

coetaneous, of the same age,
not coae-; *pron.* kō′-it-.

coeternal (one word); *pron.*
kō′-it-.

Cœur de Lion, Richard I of
England (no hyphens).

coeval, of the same age (one
word); *pron.* kō-ē′-val.

coexist (one word).

coextensive (one word).

C. of E., Church of England.

coffer-dam, a watertight
enclosure.

cognate, abbr. **cog.**

cognati (law), relations by
mother's side.

cognit/um, any object of
cognition; *pl.* **-a.**

cogniz/e, to become conscious
of, *not* -ise; **-able, -ance,
-ant.**

cognoscent/e (It.), a
connoisseur; *pron.* kŏ-nyō-
shĕn′tā; *pl.* **-i.**

cognovit (actionem) (law),
an acknowledgement that
the action is just.

coheir/, -ess (one word).

C.O.I., Central Office of
Information.

C.O.I.D., Council of
Industrial Design.

coiff/eur (Fr. m.), hairdresser;
-ure (f.), head-dress, hair-
style.

coke (no point), pop. abbr.
for **cocaine.**

Coke (no point), pop. abbr.
for **Coca Cola.**

Coke/, *pron.* Cŏŏk; — **(Sir
Edward)**, 1552–1634, Lord
Chief Justice of England.

Coire, Grisons, Switz.; *use*
Chur.

coits, *use* **quoits.**

Col., Colonel, Colossians.

col., colonial, column.

colander, a strainer, *not*
colla-, culle-.

colcannon, an Irish dish, *not*
cale-, culle-.

Cold Harbor, E. Virginia,
scene of three Civil War
battles.

Coldharbour, Herts.,
Surrey.

Coldstream/, Berwick,
a town; — **Guards**, *not* The
Coldstreams, abbr. **C.G.**

cold war, the (not caps.).

Coleoptera (biol.), the beetles.

cole-pixy, *use* **colt-pixie.**

Colerain, N. Carolina.

Coleraine, Londonderry.

Coleridge (Hartley), 1796–
1849, English minor poet
and critic, son of next; —
(Samuel Taylor), 1772–
1834, English poet and
critic; — **(Sara**, *not* -ah),
1802–52, English writer.

Coleridge-Taylor (Samuel),
1875–1912, English
composer.

coleslaw, U.S. salad of
chopped cabbage.

colic/, -ky.

Coligny (Gaspard de),
1517–72, French Huguenot
leader.

Colin/ Clout, pastoral name
in Spenser's poems; —
Tampon, nickname of a
Swiss (*see also* **Colyn**).

Coliseum, London theatre.
See also **Coloss-.**

coll., colleague, collection,
collector, college.

collaborateur (Fr. m.) (ital.).

collaborator (not ital.).

colla/ parte or *— voce* (mus.), adapt to principal part or voice; abbr. *col. p.*, or *col. vo.*

collage, art composition with components pasted on to a surface; *pron.* -ăhzh′.

coll' arco (mus.), with the bow.

collat., collateral, -ly.

collat/e, (bind.) to check after gathering sections, (typ.) to put the sheets of a book in right sequence, to compare critically; **-or**, *not* -er.

colleague, abbr. **coll.**

collect., collectively.

collectable, *not* -ible.

collectanea, collected notes.

collect/ion, -or, abbr. **coll.**

collections, an Oxford college examination.

colleen (Anglo-Irish), a girl.

college, abbr. **coll.**

Collège de France (m.).

College of Justice (Sc.), supreme civil courts.

collegi/um, an ecclesiastical body uncontrolled by the State; *pl.* **-a.**

col legno (mus.), with the wood of the bow.

collie, a dog, *not* -y.

Collinge axle (mech.), *not* Collins.

Collins, a letter of thanks for hospitality (from the Jane Austen character).

Collins (William), Sons & Co., Ltd., publishers.

collogue, to talk confidentially.

collop, a piece of meat.

colloq., colloquial, -ly, -ism.

colloqui/um, talk; *pl.* **-a.**

colloqu/y, talk; *pl.* **-ies.**

collotype (typ.), a planographic process used mainly

for the finest reproduction work.

Colo., Colorado, U.S.

Colombia (Republic of), S. America. *See also* **Colu-.**

Colombo, cap. of Ceylon, *not* Colu-.

Colon, Cent. Amer.; abbr. **Co.** *See also* **Columbus.**

colon, in Fr. m. *deux points*, in Ger. m. *Doppelpunkt*, or n. *Kolon*. *See* **punctuation** IV.

Colonel/, abbr. **Col.**; *—* **Bogey** (golf), the imaginary player.

colonial, abbr. **col.**

Colonial Office, abbr. **C.O.**, merged, 1966, with the Commonwealth Relations Office to form the **Commonwealth Office**, q.v.

coloniz/e, *not* -ise; **-able, -ation.**

colonnade, row of columns.

colophon (typ.), an inscription at the end of a book, giving the sort of details now usually found on the title-page.

Colorado, off. abbr. **Colo.**

coloration, *not* colour-.

Colosseum, Rome. *See also* **Colis-.**

Colossians, abbr. **Col.**

Colossus of Rhodes.

Coloured/ (S. Afr.), of Asian or mixed ancestry (adj.); **-s**, Cape Coloured people (cap.).

colourist, *not* colorist (U.S. **color-.**

Colour-Sergeant, *not* -jeant; abbr. **Col.-Sgt., Col.-Sergt.**

Colour (Trooping the), *not* Colours.

col. p. (mus.), *colla parte*. (adapt to principal part).

colporteur, hawker of books, esp. bibles (not ital.).

Colquhoun, *pron.* ko-hoon.

Colston's Day, Bristol, 13 Nov.

colt, abbr. **c**.

colter, *use* **cou-**.

colt-pixie, a mischievous fairy, *not* cole-pixy.

columbari/um, a dovecot, place for cremation urns; *pl.* **-a**.

Columbia, District of, U.S., abbr. **D.C.** *See also* **Colo-**.

Columbia, British, Canada.

columbium, symbol **Cb** (no point), *now called* **niobium**.

Columbus (Christopher), 1436–1506; in Sp. **Cristóbal Colon**.

column, abbr. **col**.

colure (astr.), each of two great circles of the celestial sphere.

Colvile (Sir H. E.), 1852–1907, made Uganda a British protectorate, 1893.

Colville of Culross (Viscount).

col. vo. (mus.), *colla voce* (adapt to principal voice).

'Colyn Cloute', by John Skelton (*see also* **Colin**).

Com., Commander, Communist.

com., comedy, comic, commission, -er, committee, common, -er, -ly, commun/e, -ity, communicat/e, -ed, -ion.

com/a (med.), stupor; *pl.* **-as**.

com/a (astr.), nebulous envelope round head of comet, (bot.) tuft of hair; *pl.* **-ae**.

comb., combin/e, -ed, -ing.

combat/, -ed, -ing, -ive.

Combermere (Viscount).

combin/e, -ed, -ing, abbr. **comb**.

Comd., Comdr., Commander.

Comdt., Commandant.

come-at-able, accessible (hyphens).

Comédie Française, La, off. name of Le Théâtre Français (caps.).

comédien/ (Fr.), actor; *fem.* **-ne**.

comedy, abbr. **com**.

comendador (Sp.), a knight commander.

come/ prima (It. mus.), as at first; — *sopra*, as above, abbr. *co. sa.*

comfit/, sweetmeat; **-ure** (obs.), a preserve; *not* con-.

comfrey (bot.), ditch plant, *not* cum-, *but pron.* kum′-.

comic, abbr. **com**.

Comintern, the Communist (Third) International, 1919–43, *not* Kom-.

comitadji, band of irregulars (in the Balkans).

comitatus, a retinue, a county or shire; *pl.* same.

Comitia, a meeting of the Senate of Dublin University; — *Aestivalia*, ditto in summer; — *Hiemalia*, ditto in winter; — *Vernalia*, ditto in spring.

comity of nations, international courtesy.

Comm. (naval), Commodore.

comm., commentary, commerce, commonwealth.

comma/, *pl.* **-s**. *See* **punctuation II; scratch comma.**

Commandant (accent on last syll.); abbr. **Comdt**.

commandeer, to seize for mil. service.

Commander/, abbr. **Cdr**. (Admiralty), **Com.**, **Comd.**, **Comdr.**; — **-in-Chief** (hyphens), abbr. **C.-in-C.**

commanding, abbr. **cmdg.**; **Commanding Officer**, abbr. **C.O.**

commanditaire (Fr. m.), a sleeping partner.

commandite (Fr. f.), limited liability (company).

commando/ (S. Afr.), a mil. raiding force; (Brit. army, Second World War), a unit of shock troops; *pl.* **-s**.

Command paper, abbr. **C.** (1870–99) or **Cd.** (1900–18) or **Cmd.** (1919–56) (old series); **Cmnd.** (1956–   ) (new series), followed by number.

comme ci, comme ça (Fr.), indifferently, so-so.

commedia dell' arte, Italian Renaissance comedy, mainly improvised by guild of professional actors.

comme il faut (Fr.), as it should be.

Commemoration, at Oxford, annual ceremony in memory of founders and benefactors.

Commencement, ceremonial conferring of university degrees, as at Cambridge; (U.S.) a Speech-day.

commendam, ecclesiastical benefice held *in commendam,* i.e. without duties.

commentary, abbr. **comm.**

commentator, writer of expository treatise; eye-witness describing a ceremony or sporting event; *not* -er.

commerce, abbr. **comm.**

Commissary-General (hyphen); abbr. **C.G.**

commission/, -er, abbr. **com.**

commissionaire, uniformed door-attendant (not ital.); in Fr. m., *commissionnaire,* less specific in meaning.

commit/, -table (*not* -ible), **-ted, -ting.**

committee, representative group from a larger body (coll. sing., with sing. verb); abbr. **com.** *See also* **committor.**

committ/er, one who commits; **-or** (law), a judge who commits a lunatic to the care of a person who is called the **committee,** *pron.* committee'.

Commodore (naval), abbr.

Cdre., Cmdr. *See also* **Air Commodore.**

common/, -er, -ly, abbr. **com.**

Common Bench, abbr. **C.B.**

common metre (mus.), abbr. **C.** or **C.M.**

commonplace (adj.) (one word).

Common Pleas, abbr. **C.P.**

common-sense (adj.) (hyphen).

common sense, adj. with noun (no hyphen).

Common Serjeant, *not* -geant; abbr. **C.S.,** or **Com.-Serj.**

Common Version (of the Bible); abbr. **C.V.** or **Com. Ver.**

commonwealth (not cap.); abbr. **comm.**

Commonwealth (Australian), abbr. **Cwlth** (no point).

Commonwealth Office, formed 1966 by merging Colonial Office with Commonwealth Relations Office. Combined, 1968, with the Foreign Office to form the Foreign and Commonwealth Office.

commorient (law), dying together, as by shipwreck.

commune, small territorial division (France and elsewhere); abbr. **com.**

commune bonum (Lat.), a benefit to all.

communibus annis (Lat.), in average years.

communicat/e, -ed, -ion, abbr. **com.**

communi consensu (Lat.), by common consent.

communiqué, an official report.

Communist, abbr. **Com.;** — **Party,** abbr. **C.P.**

communize, to make common; *not* -ise.

commutator, apparatus for reversing electric current.

commuter, one who lives in a suburb and works in the town.

comp., comparative, comparison, compil/e, -ed, -er, -ation, compos/er, -ition, -itor, compound, -ed.

compagnie (Fr. f.), company; abbr. *Cie* (no point).

compagnon (Fr. typ. m.), a journeyman; — *de voyage,* travelling companion.

Companies Act (no apos.).

Companion of the Bath, abbr. **C.B.**

companionship (typ.), a group of compositors working together; abbr. **'ship.**

company, abbr. **Co.,** (mil.) **Coy.** *See also* **compagnie.**

comparative, abbr. **comp.**

compare one thing *with* another (to note agreement or difference); — one thing *to* another (which it is believed to resemble); abbr. **cf.** (*confer*), *or* **cp.**

comparison, abbr. **comp.**

compass (typ.), the points, when printed in full, to be hyphened without caps., as north-by-east, north-north-east, north-east-by-north. Abbreviations to be caps. with full point after the last letter, as N., N. b E., NNE., NE. b N., NE.

competit/or, *fem.* **-ress.**

Compiègne, dép. Oise.

compil/e, -ed, -er, -ation, abbr. **comp.**

complacent, self-satisfied.

complainant, abbr. **complt.**

complaisant, obliging.

Compleat Angler, by Izaak Walton, 1653.

complement, to make complete, a completion.

completori/um, compline; *pl.* **-a.**

complexion, *not* -ction.

compliment, praise, flattery.

compline, last service of the day (R.C.C.) (modern and now accepted form of **complin**).

complt., complainant.

'Complutensian Polyglot', 1514–17, the earliest complete polyglot Bible, publ. at Complutum (Alcalá) in Spain.

compo, a bankrupt's composition; a mortar of cement (no point).

compos/er, -ition, -itor, abbr. **comp.**

compositeur (Fr. m.), compos/er, -itor.

compos mentis (Lat.), in one's right mind.

compote (Fr. f.), stewed fruit.

compound/, -ed, abbr. **comp.**

compound ranks *or* **titles,** each word to have cap., as Assistant Adjutant-General, Vice-President.

compris/e, *not* -ize; **-ed, -ing.**

compromise, *not* -ize.

compte/ (Fr. m.), an account; — *rendu,* official report, *pl.* *comptes rendus.*

'Comptes Rendus', reports of the French Academy (caps.).

comptoir (Fr. m.), commercial agency, also shop counter.

Compton-Burnett (Ivy), 1884–1969, English novelist (hyphen).

comptroller, erroneous spelling of **controller.**

Comptroller-General of the Patent Office (caps., hyphen).

computer, calculating and data-processing machine; **Computer Science, Institute of,** London Univ.

computerize, *not* -ise.

Com.-Serj., Common Serjeant, *not* -geant.

Comt/e (Auguste), 1798–1857, French philosopher; **-ian, -ism, -ist.**

comte (Fr.), Count; *fem.* *comtesse* (not cap.).

Con., Consul.

con/, to direct a ship's course, to examine, *not* -nn, -un; **-ning.**

con., conclusion, conics, conversation.

con., conjux (consort), *contra* (against, in opposition to).

con amore (It.), with affection.

con brio (mus.), with spirit.

conc., concentrat/ed, -ion.

Conceição, name of many places in Portugal and Brazil.

concensus, *use* **conse-.**

Concepcion, name of many Cent. and S. American places (but not in Brazil).

Concert/, -meister, -stück (Ger. mus.), *now* **Konzert/** (cap.).

Concertgebouw Orchestra, Amsterdam.

concerto/, *pl.* **-s**; abbr. **cto.**

concessionnaire (Fr. m.), holder of a concession, usu. of a monopoly from a foreign government (two *n*'s, not ital.).

conch/, a shell; *pron.* kongk; *pl.* **-s.**

conch., conchology.

concierg/e (Fr. m. or f.), house-porter, -portress; **-erie** (f., no accent), porter's lodge.

conclusion, abbr. **con.**

concordance, index of words or phrases in book or author.

concordat, an agreement (not ital.).

concours (Fr. m.), a competition.

concur/, -red, -ring.

conde (Sp.), a count, *not* -dee.

Condé, Louis II de Bourbon, Prince de ('The Great'), 1621–86, French general.

condensed type, a narrow typeface.

condottier/e (It.), a captain of mercenaries; *pl.* **-i.**

conductor, *not* -er; abbr. **c.**

con espressione (mus.), with expression, *not ex-*; abbr. *con esp.*

coney, *use* **cony.**

conf., conference.

confection/ery (noun), **-ary** (adj.).

Confederacy (U.S. hist.), the league of seceding states in the Civil War.

Confederate Army, abbr. **C.A.**

confer (Lat.), compare; abbr. **cf.**

conference, abbr. **conf.**

conférence (Fr. f.), lecture.

confer/, -red, -ring, -rable, -rer, *but* **-ee, -ence.**

Confessio Amantis, by Gower, 1393.

confett/i (It.), bits of coloured paper, etc.; **-o,** a sweetmeat (not ital.).

confidant/, a trusted friend, *fem.* **-e;** in Fr. *confident/,* *fem.* **-e.**

confiture, *use* **com-.**

confiture (Fr. f.), jam.

confrère (Fr. m.), colleague (not ital.).

Confucius, Chinese sage, 551–478 B.C.

cong., congregation, -al, -alist, -ist, congress, -ional.

congé/ (Fr. m.), leave; — *d'accorder,* leave to agree; — *d'aller,* ditto depart; — *d'appel,* ditto appeal; — *d'élire,* ditto elect, *not* — *de lire.*

Congo, Democratic Republic of, Cent. Africa, indep. 1960, *formerly* Belgian

Congo (*cont.*):
Congo; commonly referred to as **Congo** (**Kinshasa**); since 1972 **Republic of Zaire**, q.v.

Congo, Republic of, Cent. Africa, indep. 1960, *formerly* Fr. Middle Congo. commonly referred to as **Congo** (**Brazzaville**).

congou, a black tea, *not* -o, kongo.

congregation/, -al, -alist, -ist, abbr. **cong.**

Congress, India, the political party; U.S., the legislative body (cap.); spell out number, as fifty-fourth, *not* 54th.

congress/, -ional, abbr. **C.,** *or* **cong.**

conics, geometry of the cone and its sections; abbr. **con.**

conjugation, inflexions of a verb; abbr. **conj.**

conjunction, connection; abbr. **conj.**; (astr.) proximity of two heavenly bodies, sign ☌.

conjunctiv/a, mucous membrane between eyelid and eyeball; *pl.* **-ae** (not ital.).

conjurer, a magician.

conjuror, one bound by oath.

Conn., Connecticut, U.S.

Conna, Cork.

Connah's Quay, Flints.

connect/er, one who connects; **-or,** that which connects.

Connecticut, U.S.; abbr. **Conn.**

connection, *not* connexion.

connivance, tacit assent, *not* -ence.

connoisseur, well-informed judge in matters of taste (not ital.).

conoscente, use **cogno-.**

conquistador/ (Sp.), a conqueror, esp. of Mexico and Peru; *pl.* **-es.**

Conrad (**Joseph**), 1857–1924, Polish-English novelist (not K-).

cons., consonant, constable, constitution, -al.

conscience' sake, etc.

conscientious objector, abbr. **C.O.** *or* (First World War) **conchy** (no point).

con. sec., conic sections.

consenescence, general decay.

consensus, *not* -census.

conservat/oire (Fr. m.); *-orio* (It., Port., Sp.); *Konservatorium* (Ger. noun, cap.).

consol., consolidated,

console, (arch.) bracket; key-desk of an organ; cabinet for radio(gram), etc.

Consolidated Funds, abbr. **Consols** (no point).

consommé/ (Fr. m.), clear soup; — *de tête de veau,* mock-turtle soup.

consonant, abbr. **cons.**

consonantize, to make consonantal; *not* -ise.

conspectus (Lat.), a general view (not ital.).

constable, abbr. **c.** *or* **cons.**

Constans, Roman emperor 337–50.

Constans, mythical King of Britain.

Constant (**Benjamin**; in full, **Henri Benjamin Constant de Rebecque**), 1767–1830, French/Swiss political novelist; — (**Benjamin Jean Joseph**), 1845–1902, French painter.

Constantino/ple, in Turk. **Istanbul; -politan.**

Constitution of a country (cap. C).

constitution/, -al, abbr. **cons.**

construction, abbr. **constr.**

Consuelo, by George Sand, 1842.

Consul, abbr. **C.,** *or* **Con.;** Lat. *pl.* **consules,** abbr. **coss.**

Consul-General, abbr. **C.G.**

Consumer Council, *not* -ers', dissolved 1970.

consummate (verb), *pron.* kon′-sŭm-āt, to perfect or complete; (adj.), *pron.* con-sŭm′-it, perfect, complete.

consummatum est (Lat.), it is finished.

cont., containing, contents, continent, continue, -d.

contadin/o, Italian peasant, *pl.* -i; *fem.* -a, *pl.* -e.

contagi/um, contagious matter; *pl.* -a.

containing, abbr. **cont.**

contaki/on (Gr. Ch.), a sort of short prose hymn; *pl.* -a.

contango (Stock Exchange), charge for carrying over.

contemptible, *not* -able.

contents, abbr. **cont.**

conterminous, with a common end or boundary, *not* cot-.

Contes Drolatiques, 1832-7. by Balzac.

Continent/ (the) (cap.); — **of Europe,** etc. (not cap.); abbr. **cont.**

continu/e, -ed, abbr. **cont.**

continu/um (philos.), a continuous quantity; *pl.* -a.

cont-line (naut.), spiral space between rope strands, space between stowed casks.

contr., contract, -ed, -ion, -s, contrary.

contra (Lat.), against; abbr. **con.**

contrabandista (Sp.), a smuggler.

contract/, -ed, -ion, -s, abbr. **contr.**

contracting-out (hyphen).

contractions, *see* **abbreviations.**

contractor, *not* -er.

contracts for Government

(typ.), copy to be strictly followed.

contrafagotto (mus.), the double bassoon (one word).

contrainte par corps (Fr. law), arrest for debt.

contra jus gentium (Lat.), against the law of nations.

contralt/o (mus.), lowest female voice; *pl.* -os, It. *pl.* -i; abbr. **C.**

contra/ mundum (Lat.), against the world; — *pacem* (law), against the peace.

contrariwise.

contrary, abbr. **contr.**

contrat/ aléatoire (Fr. law), conditional contract; — *de vente,* contract of sale.

Contrat social (Le), by J.-J. Rousseau, 1762.

contrat synallogmatique (Fr. law), reciprocal contract.

contraviolin/o (It. mus.), the double-bass; *pl.* -i.

contre-dance, *use* **country-dance.**

contretemps, a hitch (not ital.).

contributor, *not* -er.

control/, -led, -ling.

contrôlé (Fr.), hall-marked, registered.

controller, *not* comp-.

Controller-General, *but* **Comptroller-General of Patent Office.**

Controller of Accounts, abbr. **C.A.**

conundrum/, riddle; *pl.* -s.

convector, apparatus for heating by **convection.**

convener, one who calls a meeting.

convent/, -ion, -ional, abbr. **conv.**

conventionalize, *not* -ise.

conversation (typ.), every new speech to begin new par.; abbr. **con.**

conversazione/, a meeting for learned conversation; *pl.* -s.

converter, *not* -or.

convey/er, (person) *not* -or; (thing) **-or** is acceptable alternative, esp. in **conveyor belt.**

Convocation, a provincial synod of the Church of England; a legislative assembly of certain universities.

convolvulus/, flower; *pl.* **-es.**

cony/, a rabbit, *not* coney, *pl.* **conies;** — **-garth,** a rabbit-warren.

Cooch Behar, India, *not* Kuch-.

cooee, Australian bush call, *not* -ey, -hee, -ie.

cookie (Sc. and U.S.), a small cake, *not* -ey, -y.

coolie (Ind., Ch.), native hired labourer, *not* -y.

Coomassie, W. Africa, *use* **Kumasi.**

Cooninxloo (G. van), 1544–1600, Flemish painter.

Cooper (James Fenimore, one *n*), 1789–1851, American novelist.

co-operat/e, -ive (hyphen), *but* **uncooperative** (no hyphen).

Co-operative Society (hyphen).

Coopers Hill Engineering College (no apostrophe or hyphen).

co-opt (hyphen).

co-ordinate (hyphen); *but* **uncoordinated.**

Cop., Copernican.

cop., copper, copulative.

copaiba (med.), **a** balsam from a S. American tree, *not* -va.

coparcen/ary (law), joint heirship to an undivided property, *not* -ery; **-er,** joint heir ditto.

C.O.P.E.C., Conference on Politics, Economics, and Citizenship.

copeck, Russ. **kopeika,** a hundredth of a rouble, *not* -ec, -ek, ko-; abbr. **c.**

Copenhagen, in Dan. **København.**

Copernican, abbr. **Cop.**

'Cophetua and Penelophon' (the beggar maid).

copia verborum (Lat.), a full vocabulary.

copier, *not* copyer.

copper, abbr. **cop.;** symbol **Cu** (*cuprum*) (no point).

copperas, ferrous sulphate, green vitriol.

copperize, to impregnate with copper, *not* -ise.

copro- (in compounds), dung-, *not* k-.

Copt., Coptic, language of Christian descendants of anc. Egyptians.

copul/a (gram., logic, anat., mus.), that which connects; *pl.* **-ae.**

copulative, abbr. **cop.**

copy (typ.), matter to be reproduced in type. *See* **manuscript.**

copy-book (hyphen).

copyholder (typ.), a proof-reader's assistant.

Copyright notice, the symbol ©, date of issue, and name of copyright claimant must appear on the verso of the title-page in every book claiming copyright protection sold in U.S. *See also* **Universal Copyright Convention, Press (freedom of the).**

coq/ (Fr. m.), cock; — *de bruyère,* black game.

coque (Fr. f.), egg-shell.

Coquelin (B. C.), 1841–1909; — **(E. A. H.),** 1848–1909; — **(Jean),** 1865–1944, French actors.

coquet/, *fem.* **-te,** a flirt; **-ry, -ting, -tish.**

coquille (Fr. typ. f.), a misprint.

Cor., Epistle to the Corinthians (N.T.), Cornelia, Cornelius, Coroner.

cor., corpus, (mus.) cornet, horn.

coram/ (Lat.), in presence of; — *judice* (law), before a judge; — *nobis,* before us; — *paribus,* before one's equals; — *populo,* before the people.

Coran, *use* **Koran.**

cor anglais, tenor oboe.

Corday (Charlotte), 1768–93, French revolutionist.

cordelier, Franciscan friar, wearing knotted waist-cord.

cordillera/ (Sp.), a mountain chain; *pl.* **-s.**

cordite, an explosive.

Cordoba, Spain, *not* -va; in Sp. **Córdoba.**

cordoba, monetary unit of Nicaragua.

cordon bleu (Fr. m.), blue ribbon, a first-rate cook.

cordon sanitaire (Fr. m.), sanitary cordon (of men), to prevent spread of contagious disease.

cordwain, Spanish leather.

Corea/, **-n,** *use* **K-.**

co-respondent, in divorce cases (hyphen).

corf, coal-miner's basket, tub, or trolley; lobster-cage; *pl.* **corves.**

Corfe Castle, Dorset, castle and village.

Corflambo, the giant in *Faerie Queene.*

Corinthians, First, Second, Epistle to the, abbr. 1 Cor., 2 Cor.

Corliss (steam) engine.

Corn., Cornish, Cornwall.

corncrake, bird (one word).

corne/a, the eyeball covering; *pl.* **-ae.**

Corneille (Pierre), 1606–84, French dramatist.

Cornel/ia, -ius, abbr. **Cor.**

cornelian, red quartz, *not* carnelian, -ion.

cornemuse, French bagpipe.

cornet (mus.), abbr. **cor.**

cornfield (one word).

cornflour, finely ground maize.

cornflower, blue-flowered plant.

Corniche (La), coast road from Nice to Genoa; in It. **La Cornice.**

Cornish/, abbr. **Corn.;** — **gillyflower,** a variety of apple.

Corn Laws (caps.).

corn/o (It. mus.), a horn, *pl.* **-i; corno inglese,** tenor oboe.

cornu/ (anat.), hornlike process; *pl.* **-a.**

Cornubia, Cornwall.

cornucopia/, horn of plenty; *pl.* **-s;** adj. **-n.**

Cornwall, abbr. **Corn.;** in Fr. f. **Cornouailles.**

coroll., corollary, inference.

corolla/ (bot.), *pl.* **-s.**

coron/a (arch., bot., astr.), *pl.* **-ae.**

Coroner, abbr. **Cor.**

coronis, mark of contraction (crasis, ') in Greek.

Corot (J. B. C.), 1796–1875, French painter.

Corporal, abbr. **Corp., Cpl.**

corpor/al, of the human body; **-eal,** physical, mortal, opp. to spiritual.

corporealize, to materialize, *not* -ise.

corposant, St. Elmo's fire, *not* cour-.

corps, *sing.* and *pl.*

corps/ *d'armée,* army corps; — *de ballet,* company of ballet-dancers; — *de bataille,* central part of an army; — *de bâti-ment, or* — *de logis,* the main building; — *d'élite,* a picked body; — *des lettres* (typ.), the body of

corps (cont.):
the type; — *diplomatique*,
diplomatic body; —
dramatique, dramatic
body; — *législatif*,
representative assembly; —
volant, flying corps.

corp/us, the body; *pl.* **-ora**,
abbr. **cor.**

Corpus Christi, festival of
the Eucharist, on the
Thursday after Trinity
Sunday.

Corpus Christi College,
abbr. **C.C.C.**

corpus delicti (Sc. law), the
essential facts of the crime
charged.

corp/us vil/e, worthless
substance; *pl.* **-ora -ia**.

corr., correct/ion, -ive, -or;
correspond, -ence; corrupt,
-ed.

corral (noun *or* verb), pen
(for) cattle (two *r*'s).

correcteur (Fr. typ. m.),
corrector of the press.

correct/ion, -ive, -or, abbr.
corr.

correction of proofs, *see*
proof correction marks.

Correctors of the Press,
see **press.**

Correctur, use *Korrektur*.

Correggio (A. A.), 1494–
1534, Italian painter.

corregidor (Sp.), a magistrate.

correlate, bring into relation.

correlative, abbr. **correl.**

correspond/, -ence, -ent,
in Fr. *correspond/re,*
-ance, -ant, fem. -ante; **-ing**
abbr. **corr.**

Corresponding Member,
abbr. **C.M.,** *or* Corr. Mem.

Corrèze, dép. France.

corrida de toros (Sp.),
a bull-fight.

corrigend/um, thing to be
corrected; *pl.* **-a.**

Corr./ Mem., Corresponding
Member; — **Sec.,** Corresponding Secretary.

corroboree, Australian
aboriginal dance, *not* -bery,
-borie, -bory.

corrupt/, -ed, -ion, abbr.
corr.

corrupter, *not* -or.

corselet (Fr. dress. m.),
a **corslet,** q.v.

corset, close-fitting inner
bodice.

Corsica, abbr. **Cors.;** in Fr.
f. **Corse.**

corslet, (armour) cuirass;
combined waistband and
brassière; *not* -elet.

corso (It.), (horse-)race,
street for same.

Corstorphine, suburb of
Edinburgh.

cort., cortex.

cortège (funeral) procession.

Cortes, the legislative house
of Spain; *pron.* kor′tĕz.

Cortés (Hernando), 1485–
1547, conqueror of Mexico.

cort/ex, bark; *pl.* **-ices,**
abbr. **cort.**

Corunna, in Sp. **Coruña.**

corvée (Fr. f.), feudal forced
labour, drudgery.

corvette, a small frigate.

corybant/, a Phrygian
priest; *pl.* **-es** (not ital.).

Corycian nymphs, the
Muses.

coryphae/us, a chorus leader,
not -eus; *pl.* **-i.**

coryphée (Fr. m.), chief
ballet-dancer.

C.O.S., Charity Organisation
Society (*now* **F.W.A.,** q.v.),
Chief of Staff.

cos (math.), cosine (no point).

co. sa. (mus.), *come sopra,* as
above.

cosec (math.), cosecant (no
point).

cosey, use **cosy.**

cosh (math.), hyperbolic
cosine (no point).

cosh/ar, -er (Heb.), use
kosher.

cosher/ (Ir.), to live at free

quarters on dependants;
-ing, -y.
Cosi fan tutte ('All women are like that'), opera by Mozart, 1790.
cosine (no hyphen), abbr. **cos** (no point).
cosmogony, cosmography, abbr. **cosmog.**
coss., *consules* (consuls).
cosseted, pampered, *not* -etted.
Coster (Laurens Jans-zoons), according to the Dutch, invented printing about 1440.
cosy, *not* -sey, -zey (U.S. **-zy**).
cotangent (no hyphen), abbr. **cot** (no point).
cote (Fr. f.), market quotation, figure, mark, share.
côte (Fr. f.), hillside, shore.
côté (Fr. m.), side.
Côte d'Azur, eastern Mediterranean coast of France.
Côte-d'Or, dép. France.
côtelette (Fr. f.), a cutlet.
coterie, a 'set' of persons (not ital.).
coterminous, *use* cont-.
Côte-rôtie (Fr. f.), a red wine.
côtes de bœuf (Fr. f.), ribs of beef.
Côtes-du-Nord, dép. Fr.
cotillion, a dance; in Fr. m. *cotillon.*
cottar, peasant, *not* -er.
Cottar's Saturday Night, by Burns, 1786.
cotter, pin, wedge, etc.
Cottian Alps, Savoy and Piedmont.
cotton/, in Fr. m. *coton;* — **-tail** (hyphen), American rabbit; — **wool** (two words), raw cotton.
Cottonian Library, in British Museum.
cottonize, to make cotton-like, *not* -ise.

coudé (astr.), telescope bent at an angle.
Couéism, psychotherapy by auto-suggestion (Emile Coué, 1862–1926).
couldn't, to be set close up.
couldst (no apos.).
coulé (mus.), a slur.
coulée, a lava-flow; (U.S. and Can.) a ravine.
couleur/ (Fr. f.), colour; — *de rose,* roseate (figurative).
coulisses (*pl.*), the wings in a theatre.
couloir, a gully.
Coulomb (C. A. de), 1736–1806, French physicist; **coulomb** (elec.), unit of charge, abbr. **C** (cap., no point).
coulter, a plough blade, *not* col-.
council/, assembly; **-lor,** member of a council.
counsel/, advice, barrister; **-led, -ling; -lor,** one who counsels.
Count, abbr. **Ct.**
count-down (hyphen).
counter (typ.), space wholly or mainly enclosed by strokes of letter.
counterbalance (one word).
counter-carte (fencing), *not* -quarte (hyphen).
counter/-cheer, — **-claim** (hyphens).
counter-clockwise, contrary to a clock hand's motion.
counter-tenor (mus.), abbr. **C.**
Counties palatine, Cheshire and Lancs. (cap. C only).
countrif/y, -ied, *not* country-.
country-dance, *not* contre-dance, contra-danse.
countryside (one word).
county, abbr. **Co.**
County Council/, -lor, abbr. **C.C.**
County court (one cap.); abbr. **C.C.**
coup (Fr. m.), a stroke.

Coupar Angus, Perth (no hyphen), *not* Cupar —.

coup/ d'aile (Fr. m.), flap (of the wings), a flight of imagination; — *d'archet* (mus.), a stroke of the bow; — *de chapeau,* salute with the hat; — *d'éclat,* a sensational stroke; — *d'essai,* first attempt; — *d'état,* sudden stroke of State policy; — *de fouet* (fencing), a 'beat'; — *de grâce,* a finishing stroke; — *de main,* sudden attack to gain a position; — *de maître,* a master-stroke; — *d'œil,* a glance, wink; — *de pied,* a kick; — *de poing,* blow with the fist; — *de soleil,* sun-stroke; — *de théâtre,* sudden sensational act; —*de vent,* a gale; — *de vin,* sip of wine.

coupé, a covered motor-car for two (accent, not ital.).

coupee, in dancing, a salute to partner.

couper (Sc.), a dealer.

Couperin (François), 1688–1733, French composer.

Couperus (Louis), 1863–1923, Dutch novelist.

coup manqué (Fr. m.), a failure.

Cour de Cassation, supreme French tribunal.

courge/ (Fr. f.), gourd; — *à la moelle,* vegetable marrow.

courgette, small marrow (*not* ital.).

courier, travelling attendant, in Fr. m. *courrier.*

Court, abbr. **C.,** *or* **Ct.**

Courtauld Institute of Art, London.

Courtelle, trade-name.

Courtenay, fam. name of Earl of Devon. *See also* **Courtney.**

courtesan, a court-mistress, **court-house,** abbr. **C.H.**

court martial (noun, two words), *pl.* **courts** —; **court-martial** (verb, hyphen).

Courtney (Leonard Henry, Baron), 1832–1918, British politician.

Court of/ Common Pleas, abbr. **C.C.P.;** — — **Guestling,** of Cinque Ports; — — **Lode-manage,** ditto; — — **Probate,** abbr. **C.P.;** — — **St. James's** (apos.); — — **Session,** abbr. **C.S.**

Courtrai, Belgium, *not* -ay.

Courts of Justice (caps.).

couscous, NW. African dish of granulated flour steamed over broth. *See also* **cuscus.**

cousin-german, *not* -aine, -ane; *pl.* **cousins-.**

Cousins of the Sovereign (law), British dukes, marquesses and earls.

coûte que coûte (Fr.), at any cost, *not* — qui —.

Coutts & Co., bankers.

couturière (Fr. f.), a dress-maker.

couvade, 'man child-bed' (not Fr.).

couveuse (Fr. f.), apparatus for preserving infants prematurely born, incubator.

Covenanter (Sc. hist.).

covenantor (law).

Coverley (Sir Roger de).

Cowling, Yorks.

Cowlinge, Suffolk.

Cowper (William), 1731–1800, poet; *pron.* koo'per.

cowrie, the shell, *not* -ry. In Africa, before 1930, 250 equal about £1; in Siam 90,000 about £1. *See also* **kauri.**

coxcomb, a fop. *See* **cockscomb.**

coxswain (naut.), *not* cocks-; *pron.* kŏk'sn, abbr. **cox** (no point).

Coy., company (army).

coyote, N. American prairie wolf; *pron.* ko-yō′-tĭ (or, W. Amer., kī-yōt′).

coypu, S. American aquatic rodent, source of nutria fur, *not* -ou.

cozey, cozy (U.S.), *use* **cosy.**

C.P., Cape Province (of S. Africa), Carriage Paid, Central Provinces, *now* Madhya Pradesh (India), Chief Patriarch, Civil Power, — Procedure, Clarendon Press, Clerk of the Peace, Code of Procedure, College of Preceptors, Common Pleas, Common Prayer, Com-munist Party, *Congregatio Passionis* (Passionist Fathers), Court of Probate.

Cp, cassiopeium, q.v.

cp., compare.

c.p., candlepower.

C.P.C., Clerk of the Privy Council.

Cpl., Corporal.

C.P.O., Chief Petty Officer.

C.P.R., Canadian Pacific Railway.

C.P.R.E., Council for the Preservation of Rural England.

C.P.S., *Custos Privati Sigilli* (Keeper of the Privy Seal).

C.P.S.U., Communist Party of the Soviet Union.

C.R., Central Railway, *Carolina Regina* (Queen Caroline), *Carolus Rex* (King Charles), *Civis Romanus* (a Roman citizen), Community of the Resurrection, *Custos Rotulorum* (Keeper of the Rolls), notice of delivery paid (international abbr. for telegraphing).

Cr., credit, -or, Crown.

Cr, chromium (no point).

cr., created.

Crabb (George), 1778–1854, English philologist.

Crabbe (George), 1754–1832, English poet.

crabe (Fr. m.), crab.

cracklin, kind of china-ware, crazed in the kiln as an ornament.

Cracow, acceptable anglicized spelling of **Kraków,** Poland.

Craigton, Glasgow.

Crane (Hart), 1899–1932, American poet; — **(Stephen),** 1871–1900, American novelist and poet.

crane's-bill, the geraniums, *not* cranesbill.

craniol., craniology.

craniom., craniometry.

crani/um, skull; *pl.* **-a.**

Crapaud (Johnny), nick-name for a Frenchman.

crap/e, gauze-like fabric, usu. black, for mourning; adj. **-y** (*see also* **crêpe**).

crassa negligentia (law), criminal negligence.

crawfish, *use* **crayfish.**

Crawford and Balcarres (Earl of).

Crawford (Francis Marion), 1854–1909, American novelist.

crayfish, freshwater crustacean, *not* crawfish (except U.S.).

cream/-laid, a writing paper with wire marks; — **-wove,** ditto without.

created, abbr. **cr.**

Creation (the) (cap.).

crèche, a public nursery.

Crécy (battle of), *not* Cressy, Créci.

credit/, -or, abbr. **Cr.**

crédit/ foncier (Fr. m.), loan society on real estate; — *mobilier,* ditto on personal estate.

creese, a Malay dagger, *not* kr-, -ease, -is.

Crefeld, Germany, *use* **Krefeld.**

Creighton (Mandell), 1843–1901, Bp. and hist.; *pron.* krī′-tn.

crematori/um, *pl.* **-a**.

crème de la crème (Fr. f.), the very best, *not* cre-.

Cremona, any violin made there (cap.).

Cremonese, of Cremona.

crenate (bot.), notched (of leaves).

crenellate(d) (mil.), furnish(ed) with battlements.

crenulate (bot.), finely notched.

Creole (strict use, usu. cap.), pure-blooded descendant of French, Spanish, Portuguese settlers in W. Indies, Louisiana, Mauritius, Africa, and E. Indies; (loose use, not cap.) a Negro born in America; a Creole-Negro half-breed speaking a Spanish or French dialect.

crêpe (Fr. m.), crapy fabric other than black crape; — **de Chine**, raw silk crêpe; — **lisse**, smooth crêpe.

crêpe (Fr. f.), a pancake.

crêpé (Fr.), frizzled.

crépon (Fr. m.), cluster of curls, hair-pad.

crescendo (mus.), growing in force; abbr. *cres.*, *cresc.*, <.

crescendo/ (noun, non-tech.), gradually increasing noise; *pl.* **-s** (not ital.).

cresson (Fr. m.), cress, watercress.

cretaceous, chalky, *not* -ious.

Cretan, of Crete.

cretin, type of mental defective; in Fr. *crétin*.

cretonne, a cotton cloth.

Creusot (Le), dép. Saône-et-Loire, *not* -zot.

crevasse, large fissure, esp. in the ice of a glacier, and (U.S.) in the bank of a river.

crève-cœur (Fr. m.), heart-break; *pl. unchanged*.

crevette (Fr. f.), prawn.

crevice, small fissure.

Crichton (James), 1560–91, Scottish scholar and soldier, 'the Admirable —.'

cricket/, -er, -ing.

crim. con. (law), criminal conversation, adultery.

crimen/ falsi (law), forgery; — *laesae majestatis*, treason.

crime passionnel (Fr. m.), crime caused by sexual passion (two *n*'s).

Criminal Office, abbr. **C.O.**

Crimplene, trade mark.

cring/e, -ing.

crinkum-crankum, intricate, crooked, *not* -cum, -cum.

cris/is, *pl.* **-es**.

criss-cross, *see* **Christ-**.

crit., critic/al, -ized.

criteri/on, standard of judgement; *pl.* **-a**.

criticaster, a petty critic.

criticize, *not* -ise.

critique, a review (not ital.).

Critique of Pure Reason, in German *Kritik der reinen Vernunft*, by Kant, 1781.

C.R.O., Commonwealth Relations Office.

Croat, a native of Croatia; *pron.* krō′-ăt; Serbo-Croatian **hrvat**.

crochet/, hooked-needle work; *pron.* krō′shă; **-ed, -ing**.

Crockford, the 'Who's Who' of the clergy, from 1858.

Crockford's, London club.

crocus/, *pl.* **-es**.

Croesus, rich king of Lydia.

Croix de Guerre, French decoration.

Croix des Evadés, Belgian decoration (1944).

Cro-Magnon (anthrop.), of a prehistoric race, remains found at —, dép. Dordogne, France.

cromesquis (Fr. cook. pl.), *see* **kromesky**.

Crookes (Sir William), 1832–1919, English physicist.

Crookes's tubes (phys.).

Croonian Lecture, of Royal Society.

croquet, game (not ital.).

croquette (Fr. f.), rissole (*not* ital.).

crore (Ind.), ten millions, point thus 1,00,00,000. *See* **lakh**.

crosier, Bp.'s or Abp.'s staff, *not* -zier.

cross (typ.), in proof corrections, a faulty letter.

Cross-bench (Parl.) (cap. C only, hyphen).

cross-bill (law), a promissory note given in exchange; a bill brought by defendant against plaintiff in a Chancery suit (hyphen).

crossbill, a passerine bird.

crossette (arch.), a ledge, *not* crose-.

Crossgates, Fife.

Cross Gates, Yorks.

Crosshill, Ayr, Renfrew.

Cross Hill, Workington, Cumberland.

Crosskeys, Antrim, Cavan.

Cross Keys, Monmouth.

crosslet (her.), small cross, *not* croslet.

cross, Maltese ✠; Latin ✝; Greek +; tau cross, of St. Anthony, ⊤. *See also* **crux** *and* **ecclesiastical signs**.

cross-section (hyphen).

crotchet/, a note (music), a whim; **-ed, -ing, -y**.

croupier, gaming-table attendant.

croûton (Fr. m.), a bit of crust, or toast.

Crowland, Lincs., *not* Croy-.

Crown (the) (cap. C); abbr. **Cr.**

crown, former standard size of paper, 15 × 20 in.; — 4to, 10 × 7½ in.; — 8vo, 7½ × 5 in. (untrimmed); basis for size of metric crown, 768 × 1008 mm. *See* **book sizes**.

Crowner's quest, dialectal for **Coroner's inquest** (cap. C only).

Crown Office, abbr. **C.O.**

crozier, *use* **cros-**.

C.R.P., *Calendarium Rotulorum Patentium* (Calendar of the Patent Rolls).

C.R.R., Curia Regis Roll.

C.R.T., cathode ray tube, *or* **c.r.t.**

cru (wine), growth (no accent).

Crucifixion (the) (cap. C).

Cruft's Dog Show, *not* s'.

Cruikshank (George), 1792–1878, English caricaturist.

cruse, a jar, *not* cruise.

Cruso, N. Carolina.

Crusoe (*Robinson*), by Defoe, 1719.

crux, of an argument; *pl.* **cruces** (not ital.).

crux/ (astr.), the Southern cross; — *ansata*, the cross with a handle, ☥ ; — *commissa*, the tau cross, ⊤ ; — *decussata*, cross of St. Andrew, or St. Patrick, × ; — *stellata*, the cross with arms ending in stars. *See also* **cross**.

cryogenics, the study of low-temperature refrigeration.

cryptogam (bot.), any member of the Cryptogamia, flowerless plants.

cryptogram, anything written in code.

crypton (chem.), *use* **k-**.

cryptonym, a private name.

crystal, crystallography.

crystalliz/e, *not* -ise; **-ed, -ing**.

C.S., Civil Service, Clerk to the Signet, Common Serjeant, Court of Session, *Custos Sigilli* (keeper of the seal).

Cs, caesium (no point).

C.S.A., Confederate States Army, ditto of America.

Csar, etc., *use* **Ts-.**

csárdás, Hungarian dance, *not* cz-.

C.S.C., Conspicuous Service Cross, Civil Service Commission.

C.S.C.A., Civil Service Clerical Association.

C.S.I., Companion of the (Order of the) Star of India.

C.S.I.R., Commonwealth Council for Scientific and Industrial Research. *See next.*

C.S.I.R.O., Commonwealth Scientific and Industrial Research Organization, *formerly* C.S.I.R.

C.S.M., Company Sergeant-Major.

C.S.N., Confederate States Navy.

C.S.S.A., Civil Service Supply Association.

C.T., Certificated Teacher.

Ct., Count, Court.

ct., cent.

C.T.C., Cyclists' Touring Club.

ctl., cental, -s.

cto. (mus.), concerto.

cts., centimes, cents.

C.U., Cambridge University.

Cu, *cuprum* (copper).

cu., cubic.

cubic, abbr. **c., cu.,** *or* **cub.**

cubicul/um, cubicle or dormitory; *pl.* **-a.**

C.U.D.S., Cambridge University Dramatic Society.

Cufic, pertaining to Cufa, near Babylon, and to the alphabet used on coins, etc., found there, *not* K-, -phic.

cui bono? (Lat.), who gains by it?

cuidad, erron. *for* **ciudad.**

Cuillins, mountains in Skye.

cuisine, cookery (not ital.).

cujus/, of which, abbr. *cuj.*; *-libet* (one word), of any, abbr. *cujusl.* Modern texts of classical Latin use *cuius,* etc.

culch, oyster spawn, *not* cultch.

cul-de/-four (arch.), spherical vault, *pl.* **culs-de-four;** — — *-lampe,* tail-piece, *pl.* **culs-de-lampe; cul-de-sac,** a blind alley, a trap, *pl.* **culs-de-sac.**

cul/ex, a gnat; *pl.* **-ices.**

Cullen (Countee), 1903-46, American Negro poet; — **(William),** 1710-90, Scottish physician.

cullender, *use* **colan-.**

Cullinan, famous diamond.

culpa/ (law), a fault; — *lata,* gross neglect; — *levis,* excusable neglect. *See* **mea culpa.**

Culpeper, Virginia, U.S., from governor — **(Thomas, Lord),** 1578-1662.

C.U.M., Cambridge University Mission.

cum (Lat.), with (not ital.).

Cumaean, of Cumae, near Naples.

Cumb., Cumberland.

Cumbernauld, Dumbartonshire, 'new town', 1956.

Cumbria, new name for a revised Cumberland and Westmorland, proposed 1971.

cum dividend, with dividend; abbr. **c.d.**

cum grano salis (Lat.), with a grain of salt.

cumin, oil of, *not* cummin.

cummerbund, a waistbelt, *not* ka-, ku-, -band.

cum multis aliis (Lat.), with many others.

cum. pref., cumulative preference.

cumshaw (Ch.), a gratuity, *not* ku-.

cumul/us (meteor.), a cloud form; *pl.* **-i**; abbr. **k.**

cuneiform, wedge-shaped, *not* cuni-, cune-.

Cunninghame Graham (**R. B.**), 1852–1936, British writer.

C.U.P., Cambridge University Press.

Cupar/, Fife; — **Angus,** Perth, *use* **Coupar Angus.**

cur., currency, current.

curaçao, liqueur, *not* -oa.

curare, a drug, *not* -a, -i.

curb, for verb, and curb of bridle; *also* U.S. for **kerb.**

curbstone, *use* kerb-.

curé, French priest; *petit —,* French curate.

Curia/, the papal court (cap.); — *advisare vult,* the court desires to consider; abbr. *c.a.v.*

curio/, an object of art; *pl.* **-s** (not ital.).

curiosa felicitas, studied felicity (as in the poetry of Horace).

curios/o, a curio admirer; *pl.* **-i.**

curium (chem.), symbol **Cm** (no point).

curlicue, a fantastic curl, *not* -eque, -ycue.

currach, a coracle, *not* -agh.

Curragh, The, Co. Kildare.

curren/t, -cy, abbr. **cur.;** **electric current,** symbol *I* (ital., no point).

currente calamo (Lat.), easily, fluently.

curricul/um, course of study, *pl.* **-a;** — *vitae,* summary of a career.

Currie, Midlothian.

Curry, Sligo.

curry (cook.), in Fr. m. *kari, or à l'indienne.*

Cursivschrift, use K-.

curt., abbr. of 'current', the Scotch equivalent of English 'instant'.

curtain-raiser (theat.), Fr. *lever de rideau.*

Curtiss (**Glenn H.**), 1824–92, American pioneer aviator.

curtsy/, *not* -sey; **-ing.**

Curwen (**John**), 1816–80, pioneer of Tonic Sol-fa.

cuscus/, a marsupial; — -grass, of India. *See also* **couscous.**

cushat, cushie-doo (Sc.), the ring-dove.

cushla machree (Ir.), my heart's delight.

cuspidor, (U.S.) a spittoon (not ital.).

custodia legis (Lat.), in the custody of the law.

custom-house (hyphen); abbr. **C.H.**

cust/os, a custodian, *pl.* **-odes;** *custos/ brevium;* keeper of the briefs; — *morum,* guardian of morals; *Custos/ Privati Sigilli,* Keeper of the Privy Seal, abbr. **C.P.S.;** — *Regni,* a regent; — *Rotulorum,* Keeper of the Rolls, abbr. **C.R.;** — *Sigilli,* ditto Seal, abbr. **C.S.**

cut and dried (adj., no hyphens).

Cutch, India, *use* K-.

cutch, catechu, extract of Indian plants, *not* k-.

cutch, tough paper sheets used by gold-beaters, *not* k-.

cute, smart, *not* 'cute.

cut edges, *see* **edges.**

cutis/ (anat.), skin; — *anserina,* skin roughened by cold; goose-flesh.

cuts (typ.), illustrations.

cutt/y (Sc.), anything short, *pl.* **-ies.**

Cutty Sark, 'short shirt', famous clipper, now in dry dock at Greenwich.

cutty stool, stool of repentance.

cuvée (Fr. f.), a vatful, or sort, of wine (not ital.).

Cuyp, Dutch artists, *not* K-.

c.v.d., cash against documents.

C.V.O., Commander (of the Royal) Victorian Order.

Cwlth (no point), Commonwealth (Australian).

Cwmbran, Mon., 'new town', 1949.

c.w.o., cash with order.

C.W.S., Co-operative Wholesale Society.

cwt, hundredweight (no point).

cybernetics, study of communication processes in animals and machines.

cyc., cycloped/ia, -ic.

Cycle of the Saros (astr.), 6,585½ days.

cycloped/ia, -ic; abbr. **cyc.**

Cyclop/s, a giant with one eye; *pl.* **-es;** adj. **-ean.**

cyclotron, apparatus for accelerating particles, used in nuclear disintegration, artificial radioactivity, etc.

cyder, *use* **cider.**

Cyllaros, the horse of Castor and Pollux.

Cym., Cymric.

cyma (arch.), a moulding of the cornice.

cymbalist, a cymbal-player. *See* **cembalist.**

cymbiform, boat-shaped, *not* cymbae-.

Cymmrodorion (Honourable Society of) (two *m*'s).

Cymric, Welsh, *not* K-.

Cymru, Wales.

Cymry, the Welsh nation.

C.Y.M.S., Catholic Young Men's Society.

Cynewulf, eighth century, Anglo-Saxon poet.

cynocephalus, a dog-headed creature.

Cynthia, the moon.

Cynthius, Apollo,

cypher, *use* **cipher.**

cy près (law), as near as possible to a testator's intentions.

Cyprian, of Cyprus.

Cypriot, inhabitant or language of Cyprus.

Cyprus, independent rep. 1960.

Cyrenaic, pertaining to Cyrene or its school of philosophy.

Cyrillic, pertaining to the alphabet used by Slavonic peoples of the Eastern Church (two *l*'s).

cyst/ (biol.), sac; **-ic;** *not* ci-.

Cytherean, pertaining to Aphrodite, *not* -ian.

C.Z., Canal Zone (Panama).

Czar/ of Russia, **-evich, -evna, -ina,** *use* **Tsar/.**

Czech, native or language of Bohemia.

Czechoslovak, *not* -ian, pertaining to **Czechoslovakia.**

Czerny (Karl), 1791–1857, Austrian composer; *pron.* tsher'nĭ.

D

D, 500, (chem.) deuterium (= heavy hydrogen), the fourth in a series.

D., Deputy, democrat, Duke, (Lat.) *Deus* (God), *Dominus* (Lord), all proper names with this initial.

Ð ð, A.S. and Icelandic letter, *pron.* dh (as th in *then*); *eth, see* **eth.**

d., date, daughter, day, dead, degree, desert/ed, -er, died, dime, diopter, dose, (Fr.) *douane* (customs), *droite* (the right hand), (It.) *destra* (right), (Lat.) *decretum* (a decree), denarii (pence), denarius (penny), (naut.) drizzling.

d' (typ.), as prefix to an unanglicized proper name should, in accordance with continental practice, be lower case and *not* cap., as d'Arsonval. Signatures to be copied.

ɔ (typ.), *deleatur* (delete).

D.A., deposit account, (U.S.) District Attorney.

Da., Danish; **d.a.** *or* **d/a,** days after acceptance.

D.A.B., *Dictionary of American Biography.*

da/ ballo (It. mus.), dance style; — *capo,* or — *capo al fine,* repeat to the word *fine;* — *capo dal segno,* repeat from the sign **𝄋,** abbr. **D.C.;** — *capella,* or — *chiesa,* church style.

Dachau, Nazi concentration camp, 1933–45.

dachshund, badger-dog.

dacoit, Indian robber, *not* dak-, dec-.

dactyl/, foot of three syllables (– ∪ ∪), **-ic.**

daddy-long-legs, the crane-fly (hyphens).

dado/, wooden skirting; *pl.* **-s.**

D.A.E., Director of Army Education.

Daedalus, builder of the Cretan labyrinth.

daemon (Gk. myth.), supernatural being, in-dwelling spirit, *not* demon.

daffadowndilly, a daffodil, *not* daffi-, daffo-, daffy- (one word).

dagger (†), (typ.), the second reference mark (first in math. works), coming after the asterisk. In Eng. before, in Ger. after, a person's name, signifies 'dead' or 'died'.

daggle-tail, *use* **draggle-.**

dago/, Spaniard, Portuguese, *or* Italian (derogatory); *pl.* **-s.**

Dagonet, Sir, King Arthur's fool.

Daguerre (L. G. M.), 1789–1851, French pioneer of photography.

daguerreotype (not cap.).

D.A.H., disordered action of the heart.

Dáil Eireann, Lower House of Irish Parliament.

d'ailleurs (Fr.), besides.

daimio/, Japanese noble; *pl.* **-s.**

Daimler motor-car.

dais, small platform, *not* daïs.

dakoit, *use* **dac-.**

Dakota (North and South), off. abbr. **N. Dak., S. Dak.**

Dalai Lama, the Grand Lama of Tibet.

Dalzell, fam. name of Earl of Carnwath.

Dalziel, *pron.* dē-ĕl.

damageable, *not* -gable.

Damara/, **-land**, SW. Africa.
damascen/e, **-er**, orna-
ment(er) in metal, *not* -keen,
-kin.
Dame aux Camélias (*La*),
play by Dumas fils.
dame/ de compagnie (Fr.),
lady's paid companion; —
d'honneur, maid of
honour; — *du palais*, lady-
in-waiting; — *quéteuse*,
one who collects for the poor.
Damien de Veuster
(**Joseph**), 1840–89, Belgian
priest to leper colony in
Hawaiian Islands, 'Father
Damien'.
damnosa haereditas (Lat.),
a legacy involving loss.
damnum absque injuria
(Lat.), damage without
wrong.
Damon and Pythias (Gk.
myth.), model friends.
Dan., Daniel, Book of Daniel.
Dan/aë, mother of Perseus,
also asteroid; **-aea**, fern
genus; **-aïd**, dau. of
Danaüs; **-aüs**, son of Belus.
Dandie Dinmont, breed
of Scottish terrier, from
Andrew Dinmont, farmer
in *Guy Mannering*.
dandruff, scurf, *not* -riff.
Danegeld, land-tax, *not* -lt.
Daniel (**Book of**), abbr. **Dan.**
Daniell's battery (elec.),
usu. called a **Daniell cell**.
Danish/, abbr. **Da.**; —
alphabet (typ.), the special
letters are *å*, *æ*, and *ø*,
which follow at end of the
alphabet. Printing generally
in roman characters.
danke schön (Ger.), many
thanks.
Dannebrog, Danish national
standard, *also* order of
knighthood, *not* Dane-.
d'Annunzio (**Gabriele**),
1864–1938, Italian writer.
danse macabre (Fr. f.),
dance of death.

danseuse, a female dancer
(not ital.).
Dant/e Alighieri, 1265–1321,
Italian poet; **-ean**, **-esque**,
-ist (caps.).
Danubian Principalities,
Moldavia and Walachia
(*now* part of Romania).
Danzig, Baltic free port.
daou, *use* **dhow**.
D.A.R., Daughters of the
American Revolution.
D'Aranyi (**Jelly**), 1895–
1966, Hung.-Brit. violinist.
d'Arblay (**Mme**), 1752–
1840, the English novelist
Fanny Burney.
Darby and Joan, devoted
old married couple.
d'Arc (**Jeanne**), Joan of Arc,
1412–31; *properly* **Darc**.
daren't, to be close up.
dare say (two words).
Dar es Salaam, cap. of
Tanzania (no hyphens).
Darjeeling, *not* Darji-.
Dark Ages (**the**) (caps.).
Darwen, Lancs., *not* Over —.
Darwin (**Charles Robert**),
1809–82, author of *Origin of
Species*; — (**Erasmus**),
1731–1802, English
physician and poet, grandfather of Charles.
das (Ger.), the (*neut. sing.
nominative and accusative*); *also*
that. *See das heisst*.
dash, *see* **punctuation** XII.
das/ heisst (Ger.), that is to
say, abbr. *d.h.*; — *ist*, that
is, abbr. *d.i.*
dass (Ger.), that
(conjunction).
dat., dative.
dat/a, sing. **-um** (not ital.).
datable, capable of being
dated, *not* -eable.
date, abbr. **d.** The order is
day, month, year, as 5 June
1903; in Fr. 5 juin 1903; in
Ger. 5. Juni 1903. Names
of days and months generally
in full, but may be abbrevi-

ated in footnotes. All-figure
form in Britain 5. 6. 1903;
in U.S. 6. 5. 1903 (month
first); international dating
system, usable in Britain
from 1971, is year, month,
day, e.g. 71. 04. 20. No
comma in four-figure years,
but 10,000 B.C., etc. For
periods use least number of
figures, as 1904–7, 1920–1,
1926–8; *but* 1890–1905,
1913–15, and always in full
in display matter.
dative, indirect object; abbr.
dat.
Daudet (Alphonse), 1840–
97, French novelist; —
(Léon), 1867–1942, French
writer and politician.
daughter, abbr. **d.,** *or* **dau.**
d'aujourd'hui en huit (Fr.),
this day week.
d'Aumale (duc).
Daumier (Honoré), 1808–
79, French painter.
Dauntsey's School, Devizes.
dauphin, eldest son of King
of France, 1349–1830;
dauphiness, his wife, in Fr.
dauphine.
Dauphiné, SE. France.
Dav., David.
Davies (Sir H. W.), 1870–
1941, musician; — **(W. H.),**
1871–1940, poet.
da Vinci (Leonardo),
1452–1519, Italian painter,
etc.; *pron.* vĭn´tshĭ.
Davis (Jefferson), 1808–89,
Pres. Conf. States.
Davy (Sir Humphry), *not*
-ey, -ey, 1778–1829, English
chemist, inventor of Davy
lamp.
Davy Jones's locker, the
sea-bed.
Dawley, Salop, 'new town'.
day, abbr. **d.;** (typ.), of the
week, and of fasts, feasts,
festivals, holidays, to have
initial caps. Abbr., when
necessary, **Sun., Mon.,**

**Tue., Wed., Thur., Fri.,
Sat.**
Dayak, *use* **Dyak.**
daybook (one word); abbr.
d.b.
daylight (one word).
days after/ date, abbr.
d.d.; — — **sight, d.s.**
day's date, abbr. **d.d.;** —
journey (Heb.), 16·95
miles; — **sight,** abbr. **d.s.**
day-time (hyphen).
Dayton, Ohio, U.S.
Daytona Beach, Florida,
U.S.
D.B., Domesday Book.
dB, decibel (no point).
d.b., daybook.
D.B.E., Dame Commander
of the (Order of the) British
Empire.
dbl., double.
d.c., direct current (elect.).
DC, 600.
D.C., deputy-consul, District
of Columbia (U.S.), (mus.)
da capo (from the beginning).
d.C. (It.), *dopo Cristo* (A.D.).
D.Ch., Doctor of Surgery.
D.C.L., Doctor of Civil Law.
D.C.M., Distinguished
Conduct Medal.
D.C.M.G., Dame Com-
mander of (the Order of) St.
Michael and St. George.
D.C.V.O., Dame Com-
mander of the Royal
Victorian Order.
D.D., *Divinitatis Doctor*
(Doctor of Divinity).
D.d., *Deo dedit* (gave to God).
d.d., days after date, day's
date, *dono dedit* (he gave as
a gift).
dd., delivered.
D-Day, 6 June 1944.
D.D.A., Dangerous Drugs
Act.
D.D.D., *dat, dicat, dedicat* (he
gives, devotes, and dedi-
cates); *dono dedit dedicavit* (he
gave and consecrated as a
gift).

D.D.S., Doctor of Dental. Surgery.

D.D.T., dichloro-diphenyl-trichloro-ethane (an insecticide.)

de, prefix to a proper name, in accordance with continental practice, should *not* have initial cap., as de Candolle; except when anglicized, as De Vinne. Signatures to be copied.

deaconate, *use* diac-.

dead, abbr. **d.** *See also* **dagger.**

Dead Letter Office, *now* **Returned** ditto; **dead/ reckoning** (naut.), abbr. **D.R.;** — **reprint** (typ.), an absolute facsimile; — **weight,** abbr. **d.w.**

Dean of Faculty (Sc.), (*not* of the), president of the Faculty of Advocates; abbr. **D.F.**

Dear Sir, in printed letter full stop (even s.caps., comma, no dash).

deasil (Sc.), righthandwise, as the hands of a clock, opp. to withershins; *not* the many variants.

death/-bed, -rate (hyphens).

deb., debenture.

deb (no point), abbr., esp. U.S., of **débutante.**

débâcle, a downfall.

debarkation, disembarkation.

debatable, *not* -eable.

debauchee, a libertine, in Fr. *débauché,* fem. *-ée.*

debenture/, abbr. **deb.;** — -holder (hyphen).

debonair, gaily elegant, *not* -aire; in Fr. *débonnaire.*

de bonne/ grâce (Fr.), willingly; — — *part,* or *source,* on good authority.

déboutonn/é (Fr.), fem. *-ée,* careless.

Debrett (*Peerage*).

debris, ruins (no accent); in Fr. m. *débris.*

debtor, abbr. **Dr.**

début/, -ant, fem. *-ante* (not ital.). *See* **deb.**

de but en blanc (Fr.), bluntly, abruptly.

Dec., December.

dec., deceased, declaration, declension, declination, decorative.

dec. (mus.), *decrescendo.*

déc. (Fr.), *décéd/é,* fem. *-ée* (deceased), *décembre* (not cap.) (December).

Decalogue, the Ten Commandments (U.S. **decalog**).

Decameron (*The*), by Boccaccio, 1352.

Decan, India, *use* **Decc-.**

de Candolle (A. L. P.), 1806–93, Swiss botanist, abbr. **DC,** son of — **(A. P.),** 1778–1851, Swiss botanist.

decani, dean's or south side of a choir (north side in Durham Cathedral), opp. to **cantoris.**

decanter, bottle to hold decanted liquor.

Deccan, India, *not* Decan.

deceased, abbr. **dec.**

décéd/é (Fr.), fem. *-ée,* deceased; abbr. *déc.*

December, abbr. **Dec.;** in Fr. m. *décembre,* abbr. *déc.* (not cap.), *also* X^bre.

décence (Fr. f.), comeliness, decency.

decenni/um, a decade; *pl.* **-a.**

decentralize, *not* -ise.

decern (Sc. law), to judge. *See also* **discern.**

decibar, one-tenth of a bar, q.v.

decibel, unit for comparing intensity of noises; abbr. **dB** (no point).

Decies (Baron), *pron.* dē'shēz.

decigramme, off. B.S.I. spelling, *not* -am.

decimal currency (British,

as from 15 February 1971).
For amounts less than a
pound express as (new)
pence: 54p (roman, no
point); for amounts of one
pound or more express as
pounds and decimal fractions
of a pound: £54, £54·65,
£54·07 (omitting p); the
(new) halfpenny should be
expressed as a fraction:
£54·07½.

decimal fractions, no
decimal can be plural, or
take verb in pl., however
many figures it contains;
(typ.) print in figures. The
decimal point should be
centred, as 1·5, not on the
line.

decimalize, *not* -ise. But
Decimal Currency Board
used -ise, -isation.

decimator, one who deci-
mates, takes every tenth part
or man, *not* -er.

decimetre, one-tenth of
a metre, 3·937 in., *not* -er
(except U.S.); in Fr. m.
décimètre.

decimo-octavo (typ.), 18mo
(not ital.). *See also* **sexto-
decimo.**

deckle edge, ragged edge
of hand-made paper, *not* -el.

declar/ation, -ed, abbr. dec.

déclaration de faillite (Fr.
f.), adjudication in
bankruptcy.

**Declaration of Indepen-
dence,** U.S., 4 July 1776.

déclass/é (Fr.), *fem.* **-ée,** one
who has fallen to an inferior
status.

declension (gram.), system
of case-endings; abbr. **dec.**

declination (astr.), angular
distance from the celestial
equator; abbr. **dec.**

decoit, *use* **dac-.**

decollate, to behead;
Decollation of St. John, 29
August.

décollet/é, *fem.* **-ée** (Fr.),
with low-necked dress.

decolour, to render
colourless (U.S. **decolor,** to
render colorless).

decolorize, *not* -ise.

décor, stage scenery and
fittings.

decorat/e, -or.

Decoration Day, U.S., 30
May.

decorative, abbr. **dec.**

décor/é (Fr.), *fem.* **-ée,**
wearing an order of merit.

decorum, propriety of
conduct.

décousu/ (Fr.), *fem.* **-e,**
unsewed, disconnected (of
style).

decree nisi (law), the first
stage in the dissolution of
marriage.

decrepit, decayed, *not* -id.

decrescendo (mus.),
decreasing in loudness; abbr.
dec., *or* **decres.**

decret/um (Lat.), a decree;
pl. **-a**; abbr. **d.**

dedans (real tennis) (not ital.).

de die in diem (Lat.), from
day to day, continuously;
abbr. **de d. in d.**

dédit (Fr. m.), penalty for
breach of contract,
retraction.

deducible, able to be
inferred, *not* -eable.

deductible, able to be
subtracted, *not* -able.

deemster, a judge (Isle of
Man).

def., defendant, deferred
(shares), defined, definite,
definition.

de facto (Lat.), in actual
fact.

defecat/e, -or, *not* defae-.

défectueux (Fr. typ.),
spoiled.

defectus sanguinis (law),
failure of issue.

defence, *not* -se (except U.S.).

defendant, abbr. **def.**

défense/ d'afficher (Fr.), stick no bills; — **d'entrer,** no admittance; — **de fumer,** no smoking.

defensible, *not* -ceable, -sable.

defensor fidei (Lat.), Defender of the Faith; abbr. **D.F.**

defer/, -ence, -red, -rer, -ring.

deferred (shares), abbr. **def.**

de fide (Lat.), authentic, to be believed as part of the (Christian) faith.

definable, *not* -eable.

defin/ed, -ite, -ition; abbr. **def.**

definit/um (Lat.), a thing defined; *pl.* **-a.**

deflate, to remove air.

defle/ct, to bend downwards; **-xion,** correct, *but* **-ction** is increasingly common, and usual in U.S.

Defoe (Daniel), 1661–1731, English writer, *not* de Foe.

deg., degree(s).

dégag/é (Fr. m.), *fem.* **-ée,** unconstrained.

Degas (E. H. G.), 1834–1917, French painter (no accent).

de Gaulle (General Charles A. J. M.), 1890–1970, French President 1944–5, 1959–69.

degauss/ -ing, anti-magnetic-mine device or method.

dégoût (Fr. m.), disgust.

degree, 1/360th part of circle; sign °; — **of latitude,** 69 statute or 60 geog. miles; abbr. **d.** *or* **deg.**

degrees of/ inclination (typ.), to be in words, as 'an angle of forty-five degrees', except in scientific and technical work; — — **temperature,** to be in figures, as 70°F (no point). *See also* **titles of honour.**

de/ haut en bas (Fr.), contemptuously; — **haute lutte,** with a high hand.

Deïaneira, wife of Hercules; *also* an asteroid.

de-ice (hyphen).

Dei/ gratia, by the grace of God; abbr. **D.G.;** — **judicium,** the judgement of God (*see also* **Deo**).

Deity (the Christian) (typ.), synonyms to have initial caps., as Christ, *Dominus,* Father, God, Jehovah, Lord, the Deity; pronouns to have lower case unless caps. requested by author, *but always* who, whom.

déjeuner/ (Fr. m.), breakfast *or* lunch; **petit** —, coffee and rolls on rising; — **à la fourchette,** meat breakfast, early lunch.

de jure (Lat.), by right.

Dekker (Thomas), *c.* 1570–1640, English dramatist, *not* Deck-.

Del., Delaware (off. abbr.).

del., delegate.

del., *delineavit* (he, *or* she, drew it).

Delacroix (Eugène, 1799)–1863, French painter.

De la Mare (Walter), 1873–1953, English poet.

de la Ramée (Louise), pen-name 'Ouida'.

Delaware, off. abbr. **Del.**

De La Warr (Earl).

dele (typ.), delete.

deleatur (Lat.), let it be deleted; abbr. **ɟ.**

delegate, abbr. **del.**

delenda (Lat.), things to be deleted.

delf, glazed earthenware made at Delft (*formerly* Delf) in Holland.

delicatesse, delicacy (not ital.); in Fr. f. **délicatesse.**

delicatessen, (Germanic pl. of above), prepared foods, shop or department selling same.

delineavit (Lat.), he, *or* she, drew it; abbr. **del.**

delirium/, disordered state of mind, with hallucinations, *pl.* **-s;** — **tremens,** delirium with trembling induced by heavy drinking, abbr. **d.t.**

De L'Isle (William Philip Sidney, Viscount).

délit (Fr. m.), transgression.

delivered, abbr. **dd.**

deliverer, *not* -or.

Della-Cruscan (noun and adj.), (member) of Florentine *Accademia della Crusca*, sifters of language, sixteenth century; or of English poetical group in Florence, eighteenth century.

Della-Robbia, an enamelled terra-cotta invented by Luca della Robbia. *See* **Robbia.**

de luxe (Fr.), luxurious.

dem (Ger.), to *or* for the (*m. and n. sing., dative*).

demagog/ue, -ic, (of) a leader of the people (U.S. **demagog**).

dem/ain, *use* **-esne.**

de mal en pis (Fr.), from bad to worse.

demarcate, to mark the limits of, *not* -kate.

demarch, chief officer of anc. Attic deme; modern Greek mayor.

démarche (Fr. f.), political procedure.

demean, to lower in dignity.

demeanour, bearing towards another.

démenti (Fr. m.), contradiction.

dementia, mental enfeeblement (not ital.).

demesne, a landed estate, *not* -ain.

demigod (one word).

demi/-monde (Fr. f.), prostitutes (ital., hyphen); — **-saison,** spring or autumn fabric.

demise, death; to bequeath, *not* -ize.

demi-tasse (Fr. f.), small cup.

demobilize, to discharge from the army; abbr. **demob** (no point).

democrat/, -ic, abbr. (U.S.) **D.**

democratize, *not* -ise.

Democrit/us, Greek philosopher; adj. **-ean.**

démod/é (Fr.), *fem.* **-ée,** out of fashion.

demoiselle, young lady (not ital.).

Demoivre (A.), 1667–1754, French mathematician (one word).

demon., demonstrative.

demonetize, to divest of value as currency, *not* -ise.

demon/ic, -ize, *not* dae.

demoralize, *not* -ise.

de mortuis nil nisi bonum or *bene* (Lat.), speak nothing but good of the dead.

demos, the people (not ital.).

dempster, *use* **deem-.**

demurrage, undue detention of ship, railway wagon, etc.; compensation for same.

demurrer (law), plea that opponent's facts, though true, do not support his case.

demy, a scholar at Magdalen Coll., Oxford; *pron.* dĕ-mī'; *pl.* **demies.**

demy, *pron.* dĕ-mī', former standard size of paper, $17\frac{1}{2} \times 22\frac{1}{2}$ in.; — 4to, $11\frac{1}{4} \times 8\frac{3}{4}$ in.; — 8vo, $8\frac{3}{4} \times 5\frac{5}{8}$ in. (untrimmed); basis for size of metric demy, 888×1128 mm. *See* **book sizes.**

den (Ger.), the (*m. sing., accusative*); to the (*pl., dative*).

Den., Denmark.

denar, *use* **dinar.**

denar/ius (Lat.), penny; *pl.* **-ii,** pence; abbr. **d.**

denationalize, *not* -ise.

D.Eng., Doctor of Engineering.

5

dengue, *not* — fever, denga, -gey.

Denholm, Roxburgh.

Denholme, Yorks.

denier, one-twelfth of French sou; unit of silk, rayon, nylon yarn weight.

denim, twilled cotton fabric for overalls, etc.

Denmark, abbr. **Den.** *See also* **Assemblies.**

dénouement, an unravelling (accent, not ital.).

denounce, give notice to terminate (treaty).

de nouveau (Fr.), afresh.

de novo (Lat.), afresh.

dent., dent/al, -ist, -istry.

dentelle (Fr. f.), lace-work.

dentil, one of the tooth-like blocks under the bed-moulding of a cornice, *not* -el, -ile.

den/y, -ial, -ier.

deodand, personal chattel that has caused death.

deodar, E. Indian cedar.

deodoriz/e, *not* -ise; **-er.**

Deo/ favente (Lat.), with God's favour; — *gratias,* thanks to God; — *volente,* God willing, abbr. **D.V.** (*see also* **Dei**).

dep., departs, deposed, deputy.

dép. (Fr.), *département* (shire), *députe* (deputy).

D.E.P., Department of Employment and Productivity.

département (Fr. m.), shire; abbr. **dép.**

department, abbr. **dept.**

departmentalize, *not* -ise.

Department of Education and Science, combining the two Ministries in 1964.

Department of Health and Social Security, combining the two Ministries in 1968.

Department of Trade and Industry, 1970, combined most of functions of Board of Trade and Ministry of Technology; abbr. **D.T.I.**

dépêche (Fr. f.), message, dispatch.

dependable, *not* -ible.

depend/ant (noun), **-ence, -ent** (adj.).

depilatory, hair removing, or remover.

de pis en pis (Fr.), from bad to worse.

de plano (law), clearly.

deponent, abbr. **dpt.**

deposed, abbr. **dep.**

depositary, a person.

depository, a place.

depot, in Fr. m. *dépôt.*

depressible, *not* -able.

de profundis (Lat.), out of the depths.

de proprio motu (Lat.), spontaneously.

dept., department.

députe, a member of the lower French Chamber.

deputy, abbr. **dep.**

De Quincey (Thomas), 1785–1859, English essayist.

der (Ger.), the (*m. sing. nominative*); of *or* to *or* for the (*f. sing., genitive and dative*).

der., deriv/ation, -ative, -ed.

dérang/é (Fr.), out of order; **-ement,** confusion.

derby (U.S.), a bowler-hat; *pron.* der'-bi.

Derbyshire, abbr. **Derby.**

de règle (Fr.), in order.

de rigueur (Fr.), according to etiquette.

derisible, laughable, *not* -able.

derisory, derisive, scoffing.

deriv/ation, -ative, -ed; abbr. **der.**

derm, the true skin; *also* **derm/a, -is.**

dernier/ (Fr.), last; — *cri,* the very latest; — *ressort,* a last resource.

derring-do, daring action, *not* — doe.

der Tag (Ger.), the day.

D.E.S., Department of Education and Science.

des (Fr.), of the (*pl.*).

dès (Fr.), since.

des (Ger.), of the (*m. and n. sing., genitive*).

désagrément/ (Fr. m.), unpleasantness; *pl. -s.*

Descartes (René), 1596–1650, French mathematician and philosopher; adj. **Cartesian.**

descend/ant (noun), person or thing descended; **-ent** (adj.), descending.

descender (typ.), lower part of letters such as g, j, p, g, y.

desert, a wilderness; to abandon. *See also* **dessert.**

desert/ed, -er, abbr. **d.**

déshabillé (Fr. m.), undress, dishabille.

desiccate, to dry, *not* dessicate.

desiderat/um, something desired; *pl.* **-a** (not ital.).

desipere in loco (Lat.), to play the fool on occasion.

desirable, *not* -eable.

Des Moines, Iowa, U.S.

désœuvr/é (Fr.), *fem.* **-ée,** unoccupied; **-ement** (m.), lack of occupation.

désorient/é (Fr.), *fem.* **-ée,** confused as to direction.

despatch, *use* **dis-.**

desperado/, a desperate man; *pl.* **-es** (not ital.).

despise, *not* dis-.

despotize, to act the despot, *not* -ise.

dessert, a dinner course. *See also* **desert.**

dessertspoonful/, *pl.* **-s,** two drams (one word). *See* **coch.**

dessous/ (Fr.), below, under; *— des cartes*, a secret.

dessus (Fr.), on, upon, (mus.) soprano.

destra/ (It.), right-hand side, abbr. **d.**; *— mano,* the right hand, abbr. **D.M.**

destructor, a refuse-burning furnace, *not* -er.

desuetude, disuse; in Fr. f. *désuétude.*

desunt/ *cetera* (Lat.), the rest are wanting; *— multa,* many things are wanting.

Detaille (J. B. É.), 1848–1912, French painter (no accent).

detector (person or thing), *not* -er.

de te fabula narratur (Lat.), of thee is the story told.

detent, a catch (mechanical).

détente (Fr.), cessation of strained relations between states.

détenu/ (Fr.), *fem.* **-e,** one detained in custody.

deterrent, *not* -ant.

detonat/e, -or.

detour, a circuitous way; in Fr. m. *détour.*

detract/or, *fem.* **-ress.**

detritus, debris (not ital.).

de trop (Fr.), not wanted; superfluous.

Deus/ (Lat.), God, abbr. **D.**; *— avertat!* God forbid! *— det,* God grant; *— ex machina,* 'a god from a machine', from Greek theatre where one was shown at an elevation to solve humanly insoluble problems; *— misereatur,* God be merciful.

deuterium (chem.), symbol **D** (no point); *— oxide,* heavy water.

Deuteronomy, abbr. **Deut.**

Deutsch (André), Ltd., publishers.

Deutsche Mark (W. Ger. currency), usu. written and spoken **Deutschmark** *or* **D-Mark,** abbr. **DM.**

Deutschland, Deutsches Reich, Germany.

de Valera (Éamon), b. 1882, Prime Minister of Éire,

de Valera (*cont.*):
1937–48, 1951–4, 1957–9,
President, 1959–.

develop/, -ment, *not* -pe.

devest, *see* **divest.**

deviat/e, -or, *not* -er.

devil (typ.), cap. for Devil
of the Bible, not cap. when
an expletive.

deviling, a young devil.

devilling, working as a hack.

devilry, *not* -try.

devil's advocate, official at
papal court who proposed
objections to a canonization.

Devil's Island, penal
settlement, Fr. Guiana.

De Vinne (Theodore Low),
1828–1914, American printer.

devis/e, *not* -ize; **-er,** one
who devises (non-legal).

devis/ee, -or, one who is
bequeathed (bequeaths)
real estate.

devitalize, to render lifeless,
not -ise.

devoir, an act of civility (not
ital.).

Devonshire, abbr. **Devon.**

De Vries (Hugo), 1848–
1935, Dutch botanist.

**De Wet (Christian
Rudolph),** 1854–1922,
Boer general and statesman.

Dewey (George), 1837–
1917, American admiral; —
(John), 1859–1952,
American philosopher; —
(Melvil), 1851–1931,
American librarian; —
(Thomas Edmund), 1902–,
American politician.

dexter (her.), the shield-
bearer's right, the observer's
left, opp. **sinister.**

dexterous, the usual form,
though **dextrous** is correct.

D.F., *defensor fidei* (Defender
of the Faith), Dean of
Faculty, (*or* **D/F**)
direction-find/er, -ing.

D.F.C., Distinguished Flying
Cross.

D.F.M., Distinguished Flying
Medal.

dft., draft.

D.G., *Dei gratia* (by the grace
of God), *Deo gratias* (thanks
to God), (Ger.) *durch Güte*
(by favour of Mr.), Director-
General, Dragoon Guards.

dg, decigramme (no point).

D.H., De Havilland.

d.h. (Ger.), *das heisst* (that is
to say).

dhobi, Indian washerman.

dhooly, *use* **doolie.**

dhoti, nether garment of
male Hindu, *not* -ee, -ootie.

dhow, an Arab vessel
(accepted mis-spelling of
dow), *not* daou, daw.

Dhuleep, *use* **Du-.**

dhurrie, Indian cotton
fabric, *not* durrie.

Di (chem.), didymium, q.v.
(no point).

d.i. (Ger.), *das ist* (that is).

diablerie, devilry, *not* -ry
(not ital.).

diachylon, a plaster, *not*
-um, -culum.

diaconate, office of deacon,
not de-.

diacritical, *see* **accents.**

diaeresis (typ.), *not* die-.

**Diaghilev (Sergei Pavlo-
vich),** 1872–1929, Russian
ballet impresario.

diagnos/is, *pl.* **-es.**

dialect/, -al, -ic, -ical;
abbr. **dial.**

diallage (rhet.), *pron.*
dī-al′-a-jĕ, figure of speech
in which various arguments
are brought to bear on one
point.

diallage (mineral.), *pron.*
dī′-al-ĕj, a brown, grey, or
green mineral similar to
augite.

dialling (U.S. **dialing**).

dialogue, conversation in
drama, novels, etc., not
necessarily between two
persons only (U.S. **dialog**).

dialyse (chem.), to separate by filtration through a membrane, *not* -ize.

dialys/is, *pl.* **-es.**

diameter, abbr. **diam.**

diamond (typ.), old name for a size of type, about 4½ pt.

diapason normal (mus.), French standard pitch. C = 517.

diarchy, rule by two authorities, *not* dy-.

diarrhoea, *not* œ.

diaspora, a dispersal; (cap.) the dispersed Jews after the Babylonian captivity or of the apostolic age; *pron.* dī-ăsp′-or-ah.

diatessaron, a harmony of the four gospels (not cap.); *pron.* dī-a-těs′-a-rŏn.

diathes/is, a habit of body, *pl.* **-es;** *pron.* dī-ath′-ě-sĭs.

D.I.C., Diploma of Imperial College, London.

dichotomize, to divide into two parts, *not* -ise.

Dickens House, London, headquarters of the Dickens Fellowship (no apos.).

dicker (U.S.), barter, haggle.

dickey, false shirt front.

Dicksee (Sir Frank), 1853–1928, painter, P.R.A. 1924–8.

dicky, rear seat (usu. folding type).

dict., dictator, dictionary.

dictaphone, *not* dicto-.

dictionnaire (Fr. m., two *n*'s), dictionary.

dict/um, a saying; *pl.* **-a.**

didactyl, two-fingered, *not* -le.

didn't (typ.), to be close up.

Didot (typ.), continental system for type measurement; 12 pt. Didot = 4·512 mm. *See* **body.**

didst (no apos.).

didymium, symbol **Di** (no point), obsolete name for a supposed element, found to be a mixture of neodymium and praseodymium.

die (Ger.), the (*f. sing., and m., f.,* and *n. pl.,* *nominative and accusative*).

diecious, *use* dioe-.

died, abbr. **d.** *See* also **dagger.**

dieresis, *use* diae-.

dies (Lat.), day.

diesel, compression ignition engine.

dies/fausti (Lat.), auspicious days; — *infausti*, inauspicious days; — *irae*, day of wrath.

dies/is (typ.), the double dagger ‡; *pl.* **-es.**

dies/juridicus (Lat.), a day on which courts sit; — *nefasti*, blank days; — *non* (law), a day when no business is done.

die-stamping (typ.), intaglio process leaving raised impression.

dietitian, *not* -cian.

Dieu et mon droit, God and my right (English royal motto).

Die Wacht am Rhein (Ger.), the Watch on the Rhine, famous German patriotic song.

differ/, -ence, abbr. **diff.**

differenti/a, a distinguishing mark; *pl.* **-ae.**

digester, person or instrument, *not* -or.

digestible, *not* -able.

digraph, two letters representing one sound, as *ph* in *digraph*. See **diphthongs**, and *Hart's Rules*, p. 58.

dike, *not* dyke.

dil., dilute.

dilapidat/e, -ed, -ion, *not* de-.

dilatable, *not* -eable.

dilatation, expansion, 'more correct than dilation' (*O.E.D.*).

dilator, muscle that expands, incorrectly formed but more common than **dilatator.**

dilemma/, position involving choice between two unsatisfactory lines of argument or action; *pl.* **-s.**

dilettant/e (It.), a lover of or dabbler in the fine arts; *pl.* **-i.**

diligence, a stage-coach (not ital.).

diluvi/um (geol.), aqueous deposit; *pl.* **-a** (not ital.).

dim., *dimidium* (one half), diminutive.

dime (U.S.), ten cents; abbr. **d.**

diminuendo (It. mus.), getting softer; abbr. *dim.*

DIN, Deutsche Industrie Normal, international paper size system: $A_0 = 841 \times 1,189$ mm, $A_1 = \frac{1}{2} A_0$, $A_2 = \frac{1}{2} A_1$, etc. *See* **book sizes.**

Dinan, dép. Côtes-du-Nord.

Dinant, Belgium.

dinar, Byzantine gold coin (denarius); unit of currency, Iraq, S. Yemen, and Yugoslavia.

Dinard, Brittany.

diner, U.S. restaurant in style of dining-car.

dîner/ (Fr.), to dine, (m.) dinner; — *par cœur,* to go dinnerless.

dingbats (U.S. typ.), small ornaments used in jobbing work.

ding-dong (hyphen).

dinghy, small boat, *not* -gey, -gy.

dingo/, Australian native dog; *pl.* **-es.**

dining-room (hyphen).

dioces/e, -an; abbr. **dioc.**

dioecious (bot.), *not* die-.

Diogenes, Cynic philosopher, 412–323 B.C.

Diogenes Laertius, biographer of philosophers, about A.D. 200.

dionym, a binomial name, as *Homo sapiens.*

Dionysia (noun pl.), orgiastic and dramatic festival(s) of Dionysus.

Dionysius, 430–367 B.C., tyrant of Syracuse.

Dionysus, Greek god Bacchus.

diopter, lens measure, in Lat. **dioptra;** abbr. **d.**

Dioscuri (the), Castor and Pollux.

diphtheria, *not* dipth-.

diphthongs (typ.), *Æ, æ, Œ, œ,* for *single sounds,* are employed in French, Icelandic, Old-English, and Scandinavian words, instead of the separate letters ae, oe. ae and oe should be used in Latin and Greek words. Generally no ligatures are used in U.S. *See also* **German.**

diplomat, U.S. for **diplomatist,** which it is displacing in Britain; abbr. **dipl.**

diplomate, one holding a diploma; in Fr. *diplômé.*

Diplomatic, Lecturership in, *not* Diplomatics.

dipsomania/, -c.

Directoire, French Directorate of 1795–9; adj., of the dress or furniture of the period (cap.).

directress, female director.

directrix (geom.).

Dirichlet series (maths.).

dirigible.

dirndl, Alpine peasant bodice and full skirt.

dis., discipline, discount, (typ.) distribute.

dis aliter visum (Lat.), the gods have thought otherwise.

disassemble, take (machine) apart. *See* **dissemble.**

disassociate, *use* **dissociate.**

disburden, *not* -then.

disbursement, *not* -sment.

disc, now accepted for **disk,** esp. in compds., disc-harrow, disc-jockey, slipped disc.

disc., discover/ed, -er; discount.

discern/, to see; **-ible.** *See also* **decern.**

disciplinary, *not* -ery.

discipline, abbr. **dis.**

discipular, disciple-like.

discobol/us, a discus-thrower, *not* -ulus; *pl.* *-i* (*not* cap.). The Discobolus (cap.), the lost statue by Myron, of which discoboli are copies.

discoloration, *not* discolour-.

discolour/, **-ed, -ment,** *not* discolor (except U.S.).

discomfit/, **-ed, -ing,** to thwart; noun, **-ure.**

discomfort, noun, lack of ease; verb to make uneasy.

disconnection.

discothèque, small hall used for dancing to recorded music; the equipment used in such a room.

discount, abbr. **dis.**

discover/ed, -er; abbr. **disc.**

discreet, judicious.

discrete, separate.

disenfranchise, *use* **disfranchise.**

disenthral/, *not* -enthrall, -inthral, -inthrall; **-led, -ment.**

disenthrone, *use* **dethrone.**

diseu/r, -se, artist entertaining with mono-logues.

disfavour, *not* -vor (except U.S.).

disfranchise, *not* -ize.

disguise/e, -er.

dishabille, untidy dress.

dishevelled, with hair or dress in disorder, *not* -eled (except U.S.).

disinterested, impartial (not the same as uninterested).

disjecta membra (Lat.), scattered remains, *but* 'disjecti membra poetae' (Horace).

disk, correct spelling, *but see* **disc.**

dislodgement.

dismissible, *not* -able.

disorganiz/e, -er, *not* -ise.

dispatch/, -er, *not* des-.

dispensable, *not* -ible.

dispensary, abbr. **disp.**

Disraeli (Benjamin), 1804–81, Earl of Beaconsfield.

d'Israeli (Isaac), 1766–1848, writer, father of the foregoing.

disseis/e, to dispossess wrongfully, *not* -ze; **-ee, -in, -or, -oress.**

disseminat/e, to scatter abroad; **-or.**

Dissenter (cap.).

dissertation, abbr. **diss.**

dissociate, to separate, *not* disassociate.

dissoluble, *not* -uable.

dissolvable, *not* -ible.

dissyllable, *use* disy-.

dist., distance, distinguish, -ed, district.

distension, state of being stretched, *not* -tion.

distich/, couplet; *pl.* **-s.**

distil, *not* -ill; *but* **distillation.**

distinction (titles of) (typ.), as F.R.S., LL.D., are usually put in large caps. Even s.caps. often improve general effect.

distingu/é (Fr.), *fem.* *-ée,* distinguished.

distinguish/, -ed; abbr. **dist.**

distrait/, *fem.* **-e,** absent-minded (not ital.).

distributary, one of the streams of a river delta.

distribute (typ.), to put type back into case, or to melt down type; abbr. **dis.**

distributor, he who *or* that which distributes.

district, abbr. **dist.**

District/Attorney (U.S.), abbr. **D.A.;** — **Court,** — **of Columbia,** abbr. **D.C.;** — **Railway, D.R.;** — **Registry, D.R.**

disyllab/le, -ic, -ize, of two syllables, *not* diss-; Fr. m. *dissyllabe.*

ditheism, belief in two gods, *not* dy-.

dithyramb, wild hymn of Bacchic revellers, *not* dythi-.

ditto, abbr. **do.**

dittogram (typ.), a letter repeated by mistake.

div., divide, -d, dividend, divine, division, divisor, Fr. *divers* (diverse).

divers, sundry; **diverse,** different.

diverticul/um, a by-way, esp. of the intestines; *pl.* **-a.**

divertiment/o (It.), a kind of ballet, *pl.* **-i;** also (Fr.) *divertissement.*

divest, *not* de- (except in law, as *devest out of*).

divid/e, -ed, -end, division, divisor; abbr. **div.;** sign for divide ÷.

divide et impera (Lat.), divide and rule.

Divina Commedia, La, 1300–18, by Dante, *not* Come-.

Divine (typ.), when used directly of the Deity, cap. D; abbr. **div.**

Divine Spirit, as title of Deity (caps.).

Divis (Ger. typ. noun), the hyphen.

divisi (mus.), in several parts.

divisim (Lat.), separately.

division of words; as a rule, divide a word after a vowel, taking over the consonant. In present participles take over -ing, as sound-ing, divid-ing; but trick-ling, chuck-ling, and similar words.

Generally, whenever two consonants come together, divide between them, as splen-dour, depen-dant. Terminations such as -cian, -sion, -tion should not be divided when forming one sound, as Gre-cian, ascen-sion, subtrac-tion.

Avoid divisions which might confuse: re-cover (*recover*), leg-ends (*le-gends*), reap-pear (*re-appear*), ex-acting (*exact-ing*).

American printers divide strictly according to pronunciation. For a fuller treatment and for word-division in foreign languages see *Hart's Rules.*

divisor (math.), a factor.

divorc/é (Fr.), *fem.* **-ée,** a divorced person; Eng. **divorcee** is common gender.

Dixie, or — **Land,** the Southern States, U.S.

D.I.Y., do it yourself.

Djakarta, Indonesia, *not* Jak-.

djinn, use j-.

dl, decilitre(s) (no point).

D.L., Deputy-Lieutenant.

D.L.I., Durham Light Infantry.

D.Lit., Doctor of Literature; *but* **D.Litt.** (Aberdeen), **Litt.D.,** Doctor of Letters.

D.L.M. (mus.), double long metre.

d. l. M. (Ger.), *des laufenden Monats,* of the current month.

D.L.O., Dead Letter Office, *now* **Returned** — —.

DM., Deutsche Mark (W. Ger. currency).

D.M., Deputy Master, Doctor of Medicine (Oxford), (Fr.) *Docteur en Médecine* (Doctor of Medicine), (It. mus.) *destra mano* (the right hand).

dm, decimetre(s) (no point).

D.M.I., Director of Military Intelligence.

D.Mus., Doctor of Music.

D.N., *Dominus noster* (our Lord).

DNA, deoxyribonucleic acid (no points).

D.N.B., *Dictionary of National Biography.*

Dnepr River, White Russia–Ukraine; *properly* **Dnepr** (Russ.), **Dnipro** (Ukr.); *not* Dnieper.

Dnestr River, Ukraine–Romania; *properly* **Dnister** (Ukr.), **Dnestr** (Russ.), **Nistrul** (Rom.); *not* Dniester.

D.N.I., Director of Naval Intelligence.

D-notice official request ('denial') to newspaper not to publish item.

do., ditto, the same.

doat, *use* **dote.**

doc., documents.

Docent (Ger.), a university teacher, now **Doz-.**

doch-an-doris (Sc.), a parting-cup.

docket/, -ed, -ing.

dockyard (one word).

Doctor/, abbr. **D.,** *or* **Dr.;** — of Civil Law, **D.C.L.;** — **Dental Surgery, D.D.S.;** — **Divinity, D.D.;** — **Engineering, D.Eng.;** — **Letters, D.Litt.** (Aberdeen), **Litt.D.;** — **Literature, D.Lit.;** — **Medicine** (Oxford), **D.M.;** — **Music, D.Mus.,** *or* **Mus.Doc.;** — **Philosophy, Ph.D.,** *or* **D.Ph.** *or* **D.Phil.** (Oxford); — **Science, D.Sc.;** — **University of Paris, Dr. Univ. Par.**

Doctors' Commons, London, where marriage licences were formerly issued by the Bishop of London's Registry (apos.).

doctrinaire, an unpractical theorist; theoretical and unpractical (not ital.).

documentary (noun), factual report or film.

documents (typ.), to be an exact reprint; abbr. **doc.**

dodecaphonic (mus.), of the twelve-note scale.

dodo/, extinct flightless bird; *pl.* **-s.**

dogana (It. f.), custom-house.

dogate, office of doge, *not* -eate (not ital.).

dog-days, 3 July–11 August (hyphen).

doge, chief magistrate of Venice (not ital.).

doggerel, unpoetic verse, *not* -grel.

Doggett's Coat and Badge, trophies of Thames Watermen's championship.

dog-Latin, barbarous Latin (hyphen).

dogma/, authoritative doctrine; *pl.* **-s.**

dogmatize, *not* -ise.

dogsbody (naut. slang), pease-pudding; junior officer, general drudge.

Dohnányi (E. von), 1877–1960, Hungarian composer.

doily, a napkin, *not* -ey, doyley, -ly, d'oyley, -ie.

dol., dollar.

dolce/ far niente (It.), delightful idleness; — **maniera,** — manners; — -**piccante,** bitter-sweet; — **vita,** sweet life.

doleful, *not* -ll.

dollar/, abbr. **d.,** *or* **dol.;** — **mark** (typ.), $, to be *before,* and close up to, the figures, as $50. Various dollars differentiated as $A (Australian), $HK (Hong Kong), $US, etc.

Dollfuss (Engelbert), 1892–1934, Austrian politician, Chancellor 1932–4.

dolman, Turkish robe, hussar's jacket, woman's mantle.

dolmen, prehistoric stone table.

dolorous, doleful, *but* **dolour** (U.S. **dolor**).

D.O.M., *Deo optimo maximo* (To God the best and greatest); *Dominus omnium magister* (God the Master, or Lord, of all).

Dom (Ger.), cathedral; (Russ.) house; (Port.) title of nobility; *also* title of certain monks, as Dom Gasquet; *not* Don.

dom., domestic, dominion.

Domenichino, real name **Domenico Zampieri,** 1581–1641, Italian painter.

'Domesday Book', *not* Dooms-; abbr. **D.B.**

domestic, abbr. **dom.**

Domine dirige nos (Lat.), O Lord, direct us (motto of the City of London).

Dominica, one of the Windward Islands, W. Indies.

dominica/ ad palmas, or *in palmis,* Palm Sunday; — *de Passione,* Passion —; — *dies,* Sunday; — *in albis* (*deponendis*), Low —.

Dominican Republic, W. Indies, *otherwise* **Santo Domingo,** the eastern portion of the island of Haiti.

dominie (old Sc.), teacher, preacher; (current locally) headmaster.

dominion, abbr. **dom.**

Dominion Day, Canada, 1 July.

domino/, cloak, mask, piece in game; *pl.* **-es.**

Dominus/ (Lat.), Lord; abbr. **D.;** — *noster,* our Lord, **D.N.**

Domus Procerum (law), the House of Lords; abbr. **D.P.,** *or* **Dom. Proc.**

Donegal, Ireland.

Donegall (**Marquess of**).

Donizetti (**Gaetano**), 1797–1848, Italian composer.

donna (It.), a lady (ital.).

Donne (**John**), 1573–1631, English poet.

don't, to be close up.

doolie (Ind.), a litter, palanquin, *not* dhooley, -lie, -ly, dooly.

Doolittle (**Hilda**), *see* H. D.

'Doomsday Book', *use* **Domesday** —.

dop (Afrik.), brandy, tot.

dopo Cristo (It.), A.D.; abbr. **d.C.**

Doppelpunkt (Ger. m.), the colon.

doppio (*movimento*) (It.), double (speed).

Doppler effect (phys.), apparent change of frequency when source of vibrations is approaching or receding, from **Doppler** (**Christian**), 1803–53, Austrian physicist; *not* ö.

Dor., Doric.

D.O.R.A., 'Dora', Defence of the Realm Act, 1914.

Doré (**P. Gustave**), 1833–83, French painter and engraver.

dormeuse (Fr. f.), a settee, nightcap, travelling sleeping carriage.

dormouse, *not* door-.

dormy (golf), as many up as there are holes to play, *not* -ie.

Dorneywood, Bucks., country house used as off. residence by any Minister designated by the Prime Minister.

dorp (Afrik.), village, country town.

d'Orsay (**A. G. G., count**), 1801–52, 'the last dandy'.

Dorset, *not* Dorsetshire.

dory, John Dory, fish, *not* -ey.

dos-à-dos (Fr.), back to back, a sofa made for sitting so.

dosage (med.), *not* -eage.

dose (med.), abbr. **d.**

dossier, papers referring to some matter (not ital.).

Dostoevsky (Fëdor M.), 1821–81, Russian novelist.

dot/e, to show great love, *not* doat; -age.

Douai, dép. Nord, *not* -y; **Douai School,** but **Douay Bible.**

douane (Fr. f.), customs; abbr. **d.**

double (typ.), a word, etc., erroneously repeated.

double (paper), to calculate a double paper size, double the smaller of the two basic dimensions.

doubl/é (Fr.), *fem.* -ée, lined (of clothes).

double-barrelled (hyphen), *not* -eled (except U.S.).

double-bass (mus.) (hyphen).

Double Crown Club, for distinguished British typographers and printers.

double entendre, word or phrase of two meanings, one of them usu. indecent (obs. Fr., now anglicized; the mod. Fr. is *double entente* (*un mot à*)).

double pica (typ.), old name for a size of type, about 22 pt.

doublure (Fr. typ. f.), ornamental lining to a book-cover.

doucement (Fr. mus.), sweetly.

douceur (Fr. f.), a gratuity.

douche, jet of water directed at the body (not ital.).

dough, mass of flour kneaded but not baked. *See* **duff.**

doughboy (U.S.), a dumpling, an American infantryman (one word).

Doukhobors, *use* **Duk-.**

Dounreay, Caithness, atomic research station.

douse, to drench with water (*see also* **dowse**).

douzaine (Fr. f.), dozen; abbr. *dzne.*

dovecot, *not* -cote.

dow, *use* **dhow.**

dowager, a widow with a dower; abbr. **dow.**

dower, widow's life-interest in her husband's property.

Down, Ireland.

Downe (Viscount).

down/fall, -stairs (one word).

dowry, portion brought by a bride to her husband.

dowse, to use a divining rod (*see also* **douse**).

doyen, the senior member of a society (not ital.).

d'oyl/ey, -ie, *use* **doily.**

D'Oyly Carte (Richard) 1844–1901, theatrical impresario.

doze, to sleep.

dozen/, -s, abbr. **doz.**

Dozent (Ger. m.), a university teacher, *not now* Doc- (cap.).

D.P., displaced person (refugee); (law) *Domus Procerum* (the House of Lords).

D.P.A.S., Discharged Prisoners' Aid Society.

D.P.H., Department of Public Health, Diploma in ditto.

D.Ph., Doctor of Philosophy, *usually* **Ph.D.**

D.Phil., Doctor of Philosophy (Oxford, Sussex, York).

D.P.P., Director of Public Prosecutions.

D.R. (naut.), dead reckoning, dispatch rider, District Railway, — Registry, (Ger.) *Deutsches Reich* (German Empire).

Dr., debtor, doctor, driver.

dr., drachma (a dram), dram, -s, drawer.

drachm, *use* **dram,** except for apothecaries' weight.

drachma/, a dram, various coins; *pl.* -s, abbr. **dr.**

draft, a deduction in weighing, a mil. party, a money order, a rough sketch; to draw off, to sketch; abbr. **dft.** *See also* **draught.**

draftsman, one who drafts documents. *See also* **draughtsman.**

dragée, a sweetmeat enclosing drug or nut or fruit.

draggle-tail, a slut, *not* daggle-.

dragoman/, Arabic interpreter; *pl.* -s, *not* -men.

dragonnade, French persecution of Protestants in 1681, *not* -onade, -oonade.

Dragoon Guards, abbr. **D.G.;** these are not 'Guardsmen'.

dram, sixty grains, one teaspoonful, sixty minims, *not* drachm; *pl.* -s, abbr. **dr.,** sign ℨ. *see* **coch.**

dramat/ic, -ist, abbr. **dram.**

dramatis personae, (list of) characters in a play, abbr. **dram. pers.**

dramatize, *not* -ise.

Drang nach Osten (Ger.), desire for expansion eastwards.

draught, act of drawing, a take of fish, 20 lb of eels, act of drinking, a dose, a vessel's depth in water, a current of air, liquor 'on draught'. *See also* **draft.**

draughtsman, one who makes drawings, plans, etc. *See also* **draftsman.**

drawback, in tech. meaning of excise duty remitted, abbr. **dbk.**

drawer, abbr. **dr.**

drawing-room (hyphen).

draw-on cover (bind.), limp cover fixed to back of book.

dreadnought, thick cloth, battleship, *not* -naught.

Dred Scott, U.S. law case.

Dreibund (*der*), the Triple Alliance of Germany, Austria-Hungary, and Italy, 1882–1915.

Dreiser (**Theodore**), 1871–1945, American novelist.

DRGM, Deutsches Reichs-Gebrauchs-Muster (German Protection of Patents).

driblet, a trickle, *not* dribb-.

dri/er, -est, -ly; *also* **drier,** he who or that which dries; but **dry/ish, -ness.**

drip/-dry, -proof (hyphens).

drivell/ed, -er, -ing (two *ll*'s, except U.S.).

drive out (typ.), to set matter with wide word spacing.

drizzling (naut.), abbr. **d.**

droit (Fr. m.), moral and legal right.

droite (Fr. f.), the right hand; abbr. **d.**

Drontheim, *use* **Trondheim.**

dropped heads (typ.), the first pages of chapters, etc., beginning lower than others.

droshky (Russ. *properly* *drozhki*), a four-wheeled vehicle, *not* -sky.

drought/, -y, aridity, *not* drouth.

D.R.P., Deutsches Reichspatent (German patent).

Dr. Univ. Par., Doctor of the University of Paris.

drunkenness (three *n*'s).

Druse, one of a Syrian sect, *not* Druz, -e.

Dr. u. Vrl. (Ger.), *Druck und Verlag* = Publisher, printed and published (by).

Dryasdust (one word), a dull pedant (character in prefaces of Scott's novels).

dry goods (U.S.), textiles.

dry-point, etching needle, the work produced by it (hyphen).

D.S. (mus.), *dal segno* (It.), from the sign.

d.s., day's sight, days after sight.

Ds., *dominus*; at Cambridge, a graduate.

D.S.C., Distinguished Service Cross.

D.Sc., Doctor of Science.

D.S.I.R., Department of Scientific and Industrial Research. Became part of Ministry of Technology, 1964, and of Department of Trade and Industry, 1970.

D.S.M., Distinguished Service medal; (mus.) double short metre.

D.S.O., Distinguished Service Order.

d.s.p., *decessit sine prole* (died without issue).

d.t., delirium tremens.

D.Ter., Dakota Territory (U.S.), *now* N. and S. Dakota.

D.T.I., Department of Trade and Industry.

Du., Dutch.

du, as prefix to a proper name, in accordance with continental practice, should *not* have initial cap., as du Châtelet, except when anglicized. Signatures to be copied.

Dual Monarchy (caps.).

dub., *dubitans* (doubting), *dubius* (dubious).

du Barry (**Jeanne Bécu**), 1746–93, favourite of Louis XV of France.

Dublin, abbr. **Dubl.**

Dubois-Raymond (**Emil**), 1818–96, German physiologist, *not* du Bois.

duc (Fr.), Duke (not cap.).

duces tecum, a subpoena.

du Chaillu (**Paul Belloni**), 1837–1904, French-American explorer in Africa.

ductus (med.), a duct; *pl. same.*

duell/er, -ing (two *l*'s, except U.S.).

duello (It.), a duel.

duenna, Spanish chaperon (not ital.).

duff, a pudding boiled in a bag, esp. **plum- —**. *See* **dough.**

duffel/, coarse woollen cloth; **— bag, — coat** (no hyphens) (U.S. **duffle**).

Duguesclin (**Bernard**), 1314–80, Constable of France.

duiker (Afrik.), a small antelope, *not* duy-.

Duke, abbr. **D.**; in Fr. *duc* (not cap.).

Dukhobors, Russian sect, *not* Douk-.

Duleep Singh, *not* Dhuleep, Dulip.

dullness, *not* dulness.

Dulong and Petit (**law of**) (physics).

Dumas (**Davy de la Pailleterie —, Alexandre**), 1803–70, French writer; **—** (fils, **Alexandre**), his son, 1824–95, also writer; **—** (**J. B.**), 1800–84, chemist.

Du Maurier (**George L. P. B.**), 1834–96, English artist and author.

Dumbarton, county town of Dunbarton, q.v.

Dumbarton Oaks, estate in Washington, D.C., at which **— —** Conference was held, 1944.

dumb-bell (hyphen).

dumbfound/, -ed, -er, *not* dumf.

dum sola (law), while unmarried.

Dunbarton, county. *See also*
  Dumbarton.
Dunblane, Perth, *not* Dum-.
dun cow (Devon), a ray fish.
Dunelm., signature of Bp.
  of Durham (full point).
dungaree, coarse calico; *pl.*
  overalls made of it; *not*
  -eree(s).
duniwassal (Sc.), a Highland gentleman, *not* dunni-.
Dunkirk, dép. Nord; in Fr.
  Dunkerque.
Dunnottar Castle, Kin-
  cardine (two *n*'s and *t*'s).
Duns Scotus (Johannes),
  1265 or 1274–1308,
  metaphysician.
duodecimo/ (typ.), *see*
  twelvemo.
duologue, (stage) conversation between two (U.S.
  -log).
duplex/ apartment (U.S.),
  one on two floors; — **house**
  (U.S.), one for two families.
duplication of points, *see*
  punctuation XV.
Du Pont, family of American
  industrialists.
Duquesne/ (Abraham,
  marquis), 1610–88, French
  admiral; —, **Fort,** French
  fort, 1754, renamed Fort
  Pitt (Pittsburgh, Pa.), 1758,
  on its capture by the English.
Dürer (Albrecht), 1471–
  1528, German painter;
  Dureresque, his style.
duress, constraint, *not* -e.
Durham, abbr. **Dur.**
durrie, *use* **dhurrie.**
Dussek (Jan Ladislav),
  1760–1812, Bohemian
  composer.
Düsseldorf, Germany.
dust-bowl, area denuded
  of vegetation by drought
  (hyphen); esp. **Dust Bowl**
  (caps., no hyphen), the
  region along the western
  edge of the Great Plains,
  U.S.

Dutch/, abbr. **Du.;** —
  alphabet (typ.), same as
  English but *q* and *x* only in
  borrowed foreign words.
  Accented letters are often
  used in stressed syllables.
  Marked letters *ë* and *ö*,
  diaeresis. *ch* must never be
  separated; for *y* use *ij*.
duumvir/, one of a pair
  of Roman officials; Eng.
  pl. **-s.**
dux/ (Lat.), a leader, *pl.*
  duces; — *gregis,* leader
  of the flock.
D.V., *Deo volente* (God willing).
Dvořák (Antonin), 1841–
  1904, Czech composer.
d.v.p., *decessit vita patris*
  (died during his, *or* her,
  father's lifetime).
Dvr. (mil.), Driver.
D.V.S., Doctor of Veterinary
  Science (*or* Surgery).
d.w., deadweight.
dwarf/, *pl.* **-s.**
dwt., pennyweight, -s, 24
  troy grains, *not* pwt.
Dy (chem.), dysprosium (no
  point).
Dyak, of Borneo.
dyarchy, *use* **diarchy.**
dyeing (cloth, etc.).
Dyfed, new Welsh county,
  proposed in White Paper
  of Feb. 1971, comprising
  Cardiganshire, Carmarthenshire, and Pembrokeshire.
dygogram (naut.), abbr.
  for dynamo-gonio-gram,
  a force-and-angle diagram
  showing a magnetic devia-
  tion curve.
dying (not living).
dyke, *use* **dike.**
Dymoke (F. S.), 1862–
  1946, English Sovereign's
  Champion, *not* Di-, Dimock,
  Dymock.
dynamics, science of matter
  and motion (sing.); abbr. **dyn.**
dynamo/, *pl.* **-s.**
dyotheism, *use* **ditheism.**

dys-, prefix meaning
difficult or defective;
distinguish it from dis-,
meaning apart.
dysentery.
dyslexia, word-blindness.
dyspepsia, chronic
indigestion, *not* dis-.

dysprosium (chem.),
symbol **Dy** (no point).
dziggetai, Mongolian wild
ass, *not* the many variants.
dzne. (Fr.), *douzaine* (dozen).
D-Zug (Ger. m.), *Durch-
gangszug* (an express corridor-
train).

E

E, the fifth in a series.

E., Earl, Earth (astr.), east, Egyptian (in £E), English, second-class merchant ship at Lloyd's, (naval) engineering, all proper names with this initial.

e, eccentricity of ellipse, (dyn.) coefficient of elasticity, (elec.) electromotive force of cell.

e, or ε (math.), base of Napierian logarithms.

e (It.), (Port.), and.

é (Port.), is.

è (It.), is.

è (e grave accent), to be used for the last syllable of past tenses and participles when that otherwise mute syllable is to be separately pronounced, as, 'Hence, loathèd melancholy!'

E.A. (naval), Electrical Artificer.

each (gram.) must be followed by verb and pronoun in sing., as 'each person *knows his* own property'; abbr. **ea.**

E.A.E.C., European Atomic Energy Commission (*also* **Euratom**).

eagre, tidal wave, *not* -er.

E.A.M., (Greek) National Liberation Front, Second World War.

E. & O. E., errors and omissions excepted.

Earl, abbr. **E.**

earlier, correlative of *later*.

Earls Court, London (no apos.).

ear-ring (hyphen).

Earth (the), cap. only in astr., abbr. **E.,** sign ⊕.

east, abbr. **E.** *See also* **compass.**

East End, London (caps.).

Easter Day, first Sunday after the calendar full moon on, or next after, 21 March.

East Kilbride, Lanarkshire, 'new town'.

East Riding, *see* **Humberside.**

easy chair (two words).

easygoing (adj., one word).

eau/-de-Cologne, — -de-vie (hyphens); — **forte,** nitric acid, *also* an etching; — **-fortiste,** an etcher; — **sucrée,** sugar and water (not ital.).

E.B., *Encyclopaedia Britannica.*

Ebbw Vale, Mon., a town.

Eblis, chief of fallen angels in Muslim myth., *not* I-.

ebonize, *not* -ise.

Ebor., *Eboracum* (York), *Eboracensis,* signature of Abp. of York (full point).

E. b S., east-by-south.

E.B.U., European Broadcasting Union.

eburnean, like ivory, *not* -ian.

E.C., Education(al) Committee, Electricity Council (*see* **C.E.G.B.**), Engineer Captain, Episcopal Church, Established Church, Eastern-Central London, Executive Committee.

E.C.A., Economic Cooperation Administration, *now* M.S.A.

écart (Fr. m.), error.

écarté, a game of cards.

Ecce/ Homo, 'Behold the Man'; — **signum,** here is the proof.

Ecclefechan, Dumfriesshire, birthplace of Carlyle, 4 Dec. 1795.

Ecclesiastes, abbr.
Eccles.

ecclesiastical/, abbr.
eccles.; — signs: Greek
cross ✠ used in R.C. service
books to notify 'make the
sign of the cross', also before
signatures of certain Church
dignitaries; Latin cross †;
St. Andrew's cross ✕; in
service books: ℞ response,
℣ versicle, ✱ words to be
intoned.

Ecclesiasticus, abbr.
Ecclus.

échalote (Fr. f.), a shallot,
not esch-.

Echegaray (José), 1832–
1910, Spanish dramatist.

echelon (mil.), a troop
formation (not ital., no
accent).

echo/, *pl.* **-es,** *not* -os.

éclair, small pastry filled
with cream.

éclaircissement (Fr. m.),
explanation.

éclat, renown (not ital.).

eclectic, borrowing freely
from various sources.

eclogue, a pastoral poem.

ecology, the study of
organisms in their
environment, *not* oe-; abbr.
ecol.

Economist, (The) (cap. *T*).

economize, *not* -ise.

econom/y, -ical, -ics, -ist,
abbr. **econ.**

écossais/ (Fr.), *fem.* **-e,**
Scottish (not cap.); *also*
écossaise, a dance.

ecraseur, surgical instrument
(no accent).

écrevisse (Fr. f.), crayfish.

ecru, unbleached linen
colour (no accent, not
ital.).

E.C.S.C., European Coal
and Steel Community.

ecstasy, rapture, *not* ex-, -cy.

E.C.T., electro-convulsant
therapy.

E.C.U., English Church
Union.

Ecuador, *not* Eq-; abbr.
Ecua.

ecumenic/, -al, belonging to
the entire Christian Church,
not oec- except in special
uses.

eczema, a skin inflammation.

Ed., editor.

ed., edited, editor.

E.D.C., European Defence
Community.

ed. cit., the edition cited.

*E.D.D., English Dialect
Dictionary.*

Edda/, a collection of
Icelandic legends; *pl.* **-s;
The Elder —,** a collection
of poems, eleventh century
and earlier; **The Younger
—,** thirteenth-century
stories, prosody, and
commentary.

Eddy (Mary Baker), 1821–
1910, founder of Christian
Science.

Eddystone Lighthouse.

edelweiss, Alpine plant.

edema/, -tous, use oed-.

Edgbaston, Birmingham,
not Edge-.

edge-tool, *not* edged —, but
'with edged tools' (fig.
sense).

edgeways, *not* -y, -wise.

Edgeworth (Prof. F. Y.),
1845–1926, English
economist; — **(Maria),**
1767–1849, English
novelist.

Edgware Road.

edidit (Lat.), he, *or* she,
edited.

edile, *use* aedile.

Edinburgh, abbr. **Edin.**

Edison (Thomas Alva),
1847–1931, American
inventor.

édit/é, fem. **-ée, par** (Fr.),
published by.

éditeur (Fr. m.), a publisher
not editor.

edition, the state of a book (also the copies, or any one copy, so printed) at its first publication, and after each revision, enlargement, abridgement, or change of format (2nd, 3rd, etc./ revised/enlarged/abridged/ paperback, etc., edition); *not* any reprint containing no substantial alteration (*see* **impression**); abbrev. **edn.;** in trade practice **1/e, 2/e,** etc. = 1st, 2nd, etc., ed. *See also* **title-pages.**

édition de luxe, a sumptuous edition (ital.).

editio/ princeps, a first printed edition; *pl.* *-nes principes.*

editor, abbr. **ed.,** *pl.* **eds.** *or* **edd.;** in Fr. m. *directeur, rédacteur en chef,* or *gérant.*

Edm. and Ipswich, signature of former Bishops of St. Edmundsbury and Ipswich. *See also* **St. Edm. and Ipswich.**

edn., edition.

E.D.S., English Dialect Society.

educationist (U.S. **-alist**).

Eduskunta, Parliament of Finland.

Edward, abbr. **E., Ed., Edw.**

E.E., Early English, errors excepted, (Ger.) *Euer Ehrwürden* (your Reverence).

ee (Sc.), eye; *pl.* **een.**

E.E. & M.P., Envoy Extraordinary and Minister Plenipotentiary.

E.E.C., European Economic Community (the Common Market).

eerie, weird, *not* -y.

E.E.T.S., Early English Text Society.

effect/er, one who effects; **-or** (biol.), an organ that effects a response to a stimulus.

Effendi, Turkish title of respect, *not* -dee.

effluvi/um, vapour from decaying matter; *pl.* **-a.**

effluxion, that which flows out, *not* -ction.

E.F.T.A., European Free Trade Association.

e.g., *exempli gratia* (for example) (l.c., not ital., preceded by comma). Use 'for example' rather than e.g.

égarement/ (Fr. m.), error, bewilderment; *pl.* **-s.**

ego/, the self which is conscious and thinks; *pl.* **-s.**

egotize, to act egotistically, *not* -ise.

egret, the lesser white heron (*see also* **aigrette**).

Egypt/, -ian, abbr. **Egy.,** *see* **United Arab Republic.**

egyptian (typ.), a type face with thick stems and slab serifs.

Egyptian pound, abbr. **£E.**

Egyptolog/ist, -y, abbr. **Egyptol.** (cap.).

eh, when exclamation, to be followed by exclamation point; when question, by note of interrogation.

Ehrenburg (Ilya Grigorevich), 1891–1967, Russian writer.

-ei-, in words the pronunciation of which does not imply the spelling: ceiling, conceit, conceive, counterfeit, cuneiform, deceit, deceive, deign, eider, eidograph, eight, eighth (etc.), eirenicon, either, feign, feint, foreign, forfeit, freight, heifer, heigh-ho, height, heinous, heir, -ess, inveigh, inveigle, kaleidoscope, leisure, meiosis, neigh, -bour, -bourhood, neither, non-pareil, obeisance, perceive, plebeian, receipt, receive, reign, reindeer,

-ei- (*cont.*):
reins, Seidlitz, *seigneur*, seize, skein, sleight, sovereign, surfeit, their, veil, vein, weigh, -t, weir, weird. *See also* -ie.

E.I.C., East India Company.

eidol/on, a phantom; *pl.* **-a.**

Eifel Mountains, Germany.

Eiffel/ (A. G.), 1832–1923, French engineer; — **Tower,** Paris.

eighteenmo (typ.), decimo-octavo, abbr. **18mo** (no point).

Eighteenth Amendment to the Constitution of the U.S., 1920, introducing prohibition of intoxicating liquor; repealed by Twenty-first Amendment, 1933.

eigret/, -te, *use* **aigrette.** *See also* **egret.**

eikon, *use* **icon.**

Eikon Basilike, pamphlet reputedly by Charles I, more probably by John Gauden, 1605–52, bishop and writer; another, written by Titus Oates, ded. to William III and attacking James II.

einfach (Ger. mus.), simple.

Einstein (Albert), 1877–1955, German physicist (naturalized American 1940).

einsteinium (chem.), symbol **Es** (no point).

Eire, in Erse (q.v.) means 'Ireland'; off. name of the Republic of Ireland (or 'the Irish Republic'), i.e. the 26 counties, formerly Irish Free State.

eirenicon, a peace proposal, *not* ir-.

Eisenhower (Dwight David), 1890–1969, President U.S.A., 1953–61; American general, Supreme Commander of Allied Expeditionary Force in Second World War.

Eisteddfod/, a congress of bards; *pron.* īs-tĕdh'-vod; *pl.* **-au.**

either (gram.), correctly used for only one of two, must be followed by verb and pronoun in sing., as 'either *is* to be taken'. Correlative *or*, not *nor*.

ejector, he who, that which, ejects, *not* -er.

ejusdem/ (Lat.), of the same, abbr. **ejusd.**; — *generis,* of the same kind.

El (Heb.), God.

el (Sp. m.), the.

él (Sp.), he.

Elagabalus, 204–22, emperor of Rome 218–22, *not* Elio-, Helio-.

El-Al, Israel Airlines, Ltd.

élan, dash, spirit (ital.).

E.L.A.S., Greek guerrilla organization in Second World War, National Popular Liberation Army.

Elbrus (Mount), Caucasus, *not* -ruz, -urz.

Elburz, mts., Iran, *not* -bruz.

elchee, anglicized version of *elchi,* Turkish ambassador.

Elder Brethren of Trinity House (caps.).

El Dorado, the golden land (two words, not ital.).

elec., electricity, electrical, electuary.

elector, *not* -er.

Electra complex, exaggerated attachment of daughter to father, the fem. analogue of **Oedipus complex.**

electress, *not* -toress.

electro/ (no point), abbr. of **electrotype**; *pl.* **-s.**

electrocute, to put to death by electricity, *not* -icute.

electrolyse, to break up by electric means, *not* -yze.

electrometer, electricity measurer (one word).

electromotive, producing electricity (one word).

electromotor, an electric motor (one word).

electrotype, duplicate printing plate made by copper electrolysis (one word); abbr. **electro** (no point).

electuary, a sweetened medicine; abbr. **elec.**

eleemosynary, charitable.

élégant/ (Fr.), a fashionable man; *fem.* **-e.**

eleg/y, funeral song, pensive poem; adj. **-iac; -ist,** writer of elegy, *not* -iast. *See* **elogy** *and* **eulogy.**

elementary, abbr. **elem.**

elements (chemical), no point after symbols. *See also* under each name.

elench/us (logic), a refutation; *pl.* **-i;** adj. **elenctic,** *not* -chtic.

elephant, old name for a size of paper 20 × 27 in.

elephanta, a violent storm, *not* -er (not ital.).

Elephantiné, Egypt, famed for archaeological yields.

elevator, *not* -er.

Elgin Marbles, to British Museum from Acropolis, Athens, 1805–12, by Earl of Elgin; *pron.* g hard.

El Giza, Egypt, site of the pyramids, *not* Ghizeh, Gizeh.

Elien, signature of Bishop of Ely.

eligible, *not* -able.

Eliogabalus, *use* Ela-.

Eliot, fam. name of Earl of St. Germans; — **(George),** 1819–90, pen-name of Mary Ann, or Marian, Evans, English novelist; — **(Thomas Stearns),** 1888–1965, American (naturalized British) poet.

Élisabethville, *now* **Lubumbashi,** Republic of Zaïre (former Congolese Republic).

elision (typ.), suppression of letters or syllables in such contractions as e'en, there'll, I'd, you've, it's (it is), William's (William is, has). In Eng. and Fr. set close up. In It. set close up where the apostrophe follows a consonant (e.g. dall'aver, senz'altro). In Gr., Lat., Sp. to be spaced. *See also* **ellipsis.**

élite, the chosen ones (not ital.).

elixir, alchemist's preparation to change metals into gold or to prolong life indefinitely.

Elizabeth, abbr. **Eliz.**

Ellice Islands, Pacific Ocean.

Elliot, fam. name of Earl of Minto.

ellips/is, the omission of words; *pl.* **-es;** (typ.) three points (not asterisks) separated by normal space of line are sufficient. When three points are used at the end of an incomplete sentence a fourth point should not be added; normal space before the first point. Where the sentence is complete, the closing point is set close up, followed by the three points for omission. See *Hart's Rules* for rules in foreign languages. *See also* **elision.**

Ellis Island, New York harbour.

éloge (Fr. m.), an oration of praise; anglicized as **elog/e** (no accent).

elogy; elogi/um, *pl.* **-a; eloge** (*see above*); (funeral) oration of praise. *See also* **elegy** *and* **eulogy.**

Elohim (Heb.), the Deity.

eloin (law), to abscond, *not* -gn.

E. long., east longitude.

El Paso, Texas, *not* -ss-.

El Salvador, rep. of Cent. America, cap. San Salvador.

Elsass-Lothringen, *use*
Alsace-Lorraine.

Elsinore, Eng. for Dan.
Helsingør.

elucidator, one who makes
clear, *not* -er.

elusive, difficult to grasp,
mentally or physically. *See*
illusory.

elver, a young eel.

Elysée palace, Paris.

Elysium (Gk. myth.), abode
of dead heroes (cap., *not*
ital.).

elytr/on, hard wing-case of
beetle; *pl.* **-a** (not ital.).

E.M., Earl Marshal, Edward
Medal, *Equitum Magister*
(Master of the Horse).

Em., Emmanuel, Emily,
Emma.

em (typ.), the square of the
body of any size of type;
also the standard unit of
typographic measurement,
equal to 12 pt., 4·2 mm.,
the 'pica' em.

E.M.A., European Monetary
Agreement.

embalmment, preservation
of dead body by aromatic
drugs (three *m*'s);
embalming is the more
usual noun.

embank/, -ment, *not* im-, en-.

embargo, temporary ban
on trade; *pl.* **-es.**

embarkation, *not* -cation.

embarras/ (Fr. noun); —
de richesses, a superfluity
of good things; — *du
choix,* difficulty of choosing,
not de.

embarrass (verb).

embassy, *not* am-.

embathe, *not* im-.

embed/, -ded, -ding, *not*
im-.

embezzlement, fraudulent
appropriation of money, *not*
-lment.

embitter, to make hostile,
not im-.

emblaz/e, -onry, *not* im-.

**embod/y, -ied, -ier,
-iment,** *not* im-.

embolden, *not* im-.

embonpoint, plumpness
(not ital.).

embosom, to receive into
one's affections, *not* im-.

emboss, to raise in relief,
not im-.

embouchement, a river-
mouth (not ital.).

embouchure (mus.),
mouthpiece, shaping of the
mouth (not ital.).

embower, to shelter with
trees, *not* im-.

embrangle, to entangle,
confuse, *not* im-.

embrasure, door or window
recess, widening inwards, *not*
-zure.

embroglio, *use* **im-.**

embroil, to confuse, involve
in hostility, *not* im-.

embrue, *use* **im-.**

embryo/, *pl.* **-s.**

embryology, abbr.
embryol.

embue, *use* **im-.**

em dash (typ.), a long dash
(—). See **punctuation** XII.

emend, to remove errors.

emerald (typ.), old name for
a size of type, about 6½ pt.

emerit/us, honourably
retired; *pl.* **-i.**

emerods, *use*
haemorrhoids.

Emerson (**Ralph Waldo**),
1803–82, American poet,
essayist, and philosopher.

emeu (bird), *use* **emu.**

émeute (Fr. f.), insurrec-
tion.

e.m.f., electromotive force.

E.M.I., Electrical and
Musical Industries (Ltd.).

émigr/é (Fr.), *fem.* **-ée,** an
emigrant, esp. French
royalist,

Emir, in Turk. and Indian
titles, *not* Amir, Ameer.

Emmanuel/ College, Cambridge; — (**I–III**), Kings of Italy, *properly* **Emanuele.**

Emmental cheese, Swiss, *not* -thal.

Emp., Emperor, Empress.

empaestic, connected with embossing, *not* -estic.

empair, *use* **im-.**

empale, *use* **im-.**

empanel/, to enrol, *not* im-; **-led, -ling** (U.S. **-ed, -ing**).

empassioned, *use* **im-.**

Emperor, abbr. **Emp.**

emphas/is, *pl.* **-es.**

emphasize, *not* -ise.

employ/é (Fr.), *fem.* **-ée;** *pl.* **-és,** *fem.* **-ées** (not ital.), *use* **employee/s** (m. and f., no accent).

empori/um, centre of commerce, large shop; *pl.* **-a** (U.S. **-ums**).

empress/é (Fr.), *fem.* **-ée,** keen, eager.

empressement (Fr. m.), eagerness, good offices, attention.

emprise (archaic), chivalrous enterprise, *not* -ize.

emptor, a purchaser.

empyema, pus in a cavity, esp. of a lung.

empyre/an, the highest heaven; adj. **-al.**

empyreum/a, the 'burnt' smell of organic matter; *not* -ruma; *pl.* **-ata.**

em rule (typ.), a long dash (—). *See* **punctuation** XII.

emu, Australian running bird, *not* emeu.

emulator, rival, *not* -er.

en (typ.), half the width of an em.

E.N.A., English Newspaper Association.

enactor, *not* -er.

enamel/led, -ler (U.S. **-ed, -er**).

enamorato, *use* **in-.**

enamoured, inspired with love (U.S. **-ored**).

en/ arrière (Fr.), behind; — *attendant,* meanwhile; — *avant,* forward; — *bloc,* in the mass; — *bon français,* without mincing matters.

enc., enclos/ed, -ure.

Encaenia, Commemoration at Oxford, *not* -cenia (not ital.).

encage, *not* in-.

encase (U.S. **in-**).

enceinte, pregnant, a fortified enclosure (not ital.).

enchase, to put in a setting, engrave, *not* in-.

enchiridi/on, handbook or manual; *pl.* **-a** (not ital.).

en clair (Fr.), in ordinary language (not in cipher).

enclasp, *not* in-.

enclave, territory surrounded by foreign dominions.

enclose, *not* in- (*but* Inclosure Acts).

encomium/, a eulogy; *pl.* **-s** (not ital.).

encore, again (not ital.).

encroach, to intrude usurpingly, *not* in-.

encrust, *not* in-.

encumber, to hamper, burden, *not* in-.

encycloped/ia, -iac, -iacal, -ial, -ian, -ic, -ical, -ism, -ist, -ize; abbr. **ency.**

Encyclopaedia Britannica, abbr. **E.B., Ency. Brit.**

en dash (typ.), a short dash as in '1914–18', 'the Fischer–Spassky match'; contrast hyphen. *See* **punctuation** XII.

endemic, regularly found in a specified place, opp. to **epidemic.**

endemn/ify, -ity, *use* **in-.**

endent/, -ure, *use* **in-.**

en/ dernier ressort (Fr.), as a last resource; — *déshabillé,* in undress; — *deux mots,* to cut a long story short.

end leaves, *see* **endpapers.**

endorse, to write on the back of, *not* in-.

endpapers (bind.), the sheets at the beginning and end of a book, half of each pasted to inside of cover, half forming fly-leaf.

endue, to clothe, *not* in-.

endur/e, -able, -ed, -er, -ing, *not* in-.

endways, *not* -wise.

Endymion, Greek legend, and Keats's poem; *also* Disraeli's last novel.

ENE., east-north-east. *See also* **compass.**

E.N.E.A., European Nuclear Energy Agency.

en échelle (Fr.), ladder-like.

enema/, (syringe for making) injection into rectum; *pl.* **-s** (not ital.).

energize, *not* -ise.

en famille (Fr.), with one's family.

enfant/ gâté (Fr. m.), spoilt child; *— prodigue* (*l'*), the prodigal son.

enfants perdus (mil.), forlorn hope.

enfeoff, to give a fief to, *not* -fief.

en fête (Fr.), in festivity.

enfin (Fr.), finally (one word).

enfold (U.S. **in-**).

enforce/, -able, *not* in-.

en français, in French.

en Français, as a Frenchman.

enfranchis/e, -able, -ement, -ing, *not* -ize.

Eng., England, English.

eng., engineer, -ing, engrav/ed, -er, -ing.

Engadine, Switzerland; in Ger. **Engadin.**

en garçon (Fr.), as a bachelor.

Engels (Friedrich), 1820–95, German socialist, associate of Karl Marx.

engineer/, -ing, abbr. **E.,** *or* **eng.**

engine-room (hyphen).

Engl/and, -ish, abbr. **Eng.**

English (typ.), old name for a size of type, about 14 pt.

engraft, *not* in-.

engrain, to dye in the raw state, *not* in-. *But see* **ingrain.**

en grande/ tenue, or *— — toilette* (Fr.), in full dress; *en grand seigneur,* magnificently.

engross, to buy wholesale, copy in a large hand, *not* in-.

engulf, *not* in-, -gulph.

enigma/, riddle; *pl.* **-s.**

enisle, to isolate, *not* in-.

enjambment, in verse, the continuation of sense beyond the end of a line; Fr. m. *enjambement.*

en masse (Fr.), in a body.

enmesh, to entangle, *not* emm-, imm-.

Enniskillen, Ireland; — **(Earl of),** *but* **Inniskilling Dragoons** and **Fusiliers.**

ennui, boredom (not ital.).

ennuy/é, *fem.* **-ée,** bored (not ital.).

enoculate, *use* in-.

en/ passant (Fr.), by the way, in passing; *— pension,* as a boarder; *— petit,* on a small scale; *— plein jour,* in broad daylight; *— prince,* in princely style; *— prise* (chess), in a position to be taken.

enquête (Fr. f.), inquiry, *not* inquest.

enquire, to ask, is tending to supersede **inquire,** which is correct.

enquiry, a question, is becoming the general word, **inquiry** being reserved for an official investigation.

en/ rapport (Fr.), in sympathy; *— règle,* as it should be, in order; *— résumé,* to sum up; *— revanche,* in revenge.

enrol/, -ment, *not* enroll-; *but* **-led, -ler, -ling** (U.S. **-ed, -er, -ing**).

en route (Fr.), on the way.

en rule (typ.), a short dash (–). *See* **punctuation** XII.

ens, an entity; Lat. *pl.* **entia.**

E.N.S.A., *also* **Ensa** (no point), Entertainments National Service Association.

Enschedé-en-Zonen, printing house at Haarlem.

ensconce, to protect with an earthwork, *not* ins-, es-.

ensemble, general effect (not ital.).

ensheath, *not* -the.

ensilage, storage of green fodder in pits or silos.

ensnare/, -ment, *not* in-.

en somme (Fr.), in short.

ensuing, *not* -eing.

en suite (Fr.), to match.

ensuite (one word) (Fr.), after, following.

ensure, to make safe. *See also* **assurance, insurance.**

enswathe, to wrap, *not* in-.

E.N.T., ear, nose, and throat.

entailed estate, settled on a series of heirs, *not* in-.

entente/ (Fr. f.), meaning; *— cordiale,* cordial understanding, (caps.) that between England and France, 1904 onwards; *—, un mot à double,* a word or phrase with two meanings, *pl.* *mots à double entente. See* **double entendre.**

enterpret, *use* in-.

enterprise, *not* -ize.

entêt/é (Fr.), *fem.* *-ée,* infatuated, obstinate.

enthral/, -led, -ler, -ling, -ment.

entomology, the study of insects; *abbr.* **entom.**

entourage, surroundings, attendants (not ital.).

en-tout-cas (Fr.), umbrella-cum-parasol, type of hard tennis-court.

entozo/on, internal parasite; *pl.* **-a** (not ital.).

entr'acte/ (performance in) the interval between two acts; *pl.* **-s.**

en train (Fr.), in progress.

entrain, to board a train, to put aboard a train.

entrain (Fr. m.), heartiness.

entrap/, -ped, -ping, *not* in-.

entreat, to beseech, *not* in-.

entrechat, a jump in which a dancer strikes his heels together several times (not ital.).

entrecôte (Fr. m. cook.), the 'undercut'.

entrée, a made dish, right of admission (not ital.).

entremets, side dishes (not ital.).

entrench, *not* in-.

entre nous (Fr.), confidentially.

entrepôt, a market (not ital.).

entrepreneur, person in control of business enterprise, a contractor (not ital.).

entresol, a storey between ground-floor and first-floor (not ital.).

entrust, *not* in-.

Ent. Sta. Hall, Entered at Stationers' Hall.

entwine, *not* in-.

entwist, *not* in-.

enunciat/e, -or.

enure, *use* inure.

enveigle, *use* in-.

envelop/ (verb), **-ed, -ment.**

envelope (noun).

en vérité (Fr.), in truth.

Env. Extr., Envoy Extraordinary.

enwrap/, -ped, -ping, *not* in-.

enwreathe, *not* -in.

enzyme (chem.), protein with catalytic properties.

E.O., Education Officer.
Eocene (geol.) (cap., not ital.).
e.o.d., every other day.
Eolian, etc., *use* Aeo-.
eon, *use* aeon.
e.o.o.e. (Fr.), *erreur ou omission exceptée* (error or omission excepted).
Eōthen ('from the east'), by Kinglake, 1844.
E.P., electroplate.
e.p. (chess), *en passant.*
Ep., Epistle.
epact, age of the moon on 1 Jan.
epaulet, shoulder-piece, *not* -ette.
E.P.D., Excess Profits Duty.
E.P.D.A., Emergency Powers Defence Act.
épée, sword used in fencing.
epergne, table ornament to hold flowers or fruit (not ital., no accent).
éperlans (Fr. m.), smelts.
Épernay, French white wine.
Eph., Ephesians, Ephraim.
ephah, Hebrew measure, *not* epha.
ephedrine, an alkaloid used as cardiac depressive or for asthma, *not* -in.
ephemer/a, *same as* -on; *pl.* -ae (not ital.).
ephemer/is, a calendar; *pl.* -ides.
ephemer/on, insect that lives for a day; *pl.* -a (not ital.).
Ephesians, abbr. Eph.
ephod, Jewish priestly vestment.
ephphatha (Aram.), 'Be opened.'
épice (Fr. f.), spice.
epicene, sexless (contemptuous).
epicentr/e, -um, point over centre of earthquake.
epicure/, one who indulges in a refined way in the pleasures of the table; adj. -an.

Epicurean, a philosopher who identifies pleasure with virtue, following the Greek **Epicurus,** 342–270 B.C.
epideictic, adapted for display, *not* -ktic.
epidemic, (disease) breaking out locally and lasting only for a time.
epidermis, the outer skin or cuticle.
epilogue, concluding part of a lit. work (U.S. **epilog**).
épinards (Fr. m. pl., cook.), spinach.
epiornis, *use* aepy-.
epiphany, the manifestation of a god; (cap.) 6 Jan., the manifestation of Christ to the 'wise men'.
epiphyte, a plant that lives on the surface of another.
episcopal, belonging to bishops, with **episc.**; (cap.) title of churches in Scotland and U.S.A.
epithalami/um, a nuptial song; *pl.* -a.
epitomize, to shorten, summarize, *not* -ise.
epizo/on (zool.), an animal that lives on the surface of another; *pl.* -a.
e pluribus unum (Lat.), many made one (motto of U.S.).
E.P.N.S., electroplated nickel silver.
eppur si muove (It.), and yet it does move (Galileo, after his recantation).
épreuve/ (Fr. typ. f.), a proof.
Epstein (Jacob), 1880–1959, English sculptor.
E.P.T., Excess Profits Tax.
E.P.U., Empire Press Union, European Payments Union.
épuis/é (Fr.), *fem.* -ée, exhausted; (typ.) out of print.
eq., equal.
Equador, *use* Ecu-.

equal/ *to* (no longer *with*);
-led, -ling (U.S. **-ed, -ing**).
equaliz/e, -ation, *not* -ise.
equal mark (typ.), = (a
space before and after).
equanimity, evenness of
mind or temper.
Equator/, -ial, abbr. **Eq.**
equerry, off. attendant on
royal personage, *not* -ery.
equestri/an, horseman;
fem. **-enne.**
equiangular, sign ⩳.
equilateral, sign ⩵.
equinoctial, *not* -xial.
equinox/, period of year
when night and day are
equal; *pl.* **-es.**
equivalent, abbr. **equiv.**
equivocator, user of
misleading words, *not* -er.
equivoque, a quibble (not
ital.).
Er (chem.), erbium (no
point).
E.R., East Riding, *Edwardus
Rex* (King Edward),
Elizabetha Regina (Queen
Elizabeth).
E.R.A. (naval), Engine-room
Artificer.
Eragny Press, of L. Pissaro.
eraser, he who, *or* that
which, rubs out, *not* -or.
Erasmus (Desiderius),
1466–1536, Dutch scholar.
Erato (Gr.), the lyric muse.
erbium, symbol **Er** (no
point).
Erckmann–Chatrian, two
French writers collaborating
from 1848 to 1870.
Erdgeist (Ger. myth.), an
earth-spirit.
erector, he who, *or* that
which, erects, *not* -er.
erethism (path.), excitement,
not ery-.
E. R. et I., *Edwardus Rex et
Imperator* (Edward King and
Emperor).
erf (Afrik.), plot of ground;
pl. **erven.**

erg, unit of work (not ital.).
ergo (Lat.), therefore (ital.).
Erie, one of the Great
Lakes (U.S. and Canada).
Erin go bragh (Ir.), Erin
for ever.
Eriny/s (Gk. myth.), one of
the three Furies, Eumenides,
or avenging deities; *pl.* **-es.**
Eris, Greek goddess of
discord.
Ernie, device for selecting
weekly and monthly winners
in National Premium Bonds
(Electronic Random Number
Indicator Equipment).
Eros, Greek god of love.
E.R.P., European Recovery
Programme.
erpetolog/y, -ist, *use* h-.
errat/um, error in writing
or printing; *pl.* **-a** (not ital.).
erroneous, wrong, *not* -ious.
ersatz (Ger.), substitute.
Erse, the Irish Gaelic
language.
erstens (Ger.), in the first
place; *erstgeboren,* first-
born.
E.R.U., English Rugby
Union.
erven, *see* **erf.**
erysipelas, a skin disease,
St. Anthony's fire, *not* -us.
erythism, *use* ere-.
Erzerum, Turkish Armenia,
not -oum, -om.
Es (chem.), einsteinium (no
point).
E.S. (paper), engine-sized.
esc. (Fr.), *escompte,* discount.
escalade, to mount and
enter by a ladder.
escalat/e, -ion, to rise
steadily and inevitably, like
an escalator.
escallop, shell-fish, *use*
scallop.
escalope (Fr. f.), collop,
slice of meat.
escargot (Fr. m.), edible snail.
escarp/, -ment, a steep
slope, *not* -pe.

eschalot, use **shallot.**

escheator, official who watches over forfeited property, *not* -er.

eschscholtzia, a yellow-flowered plant.

Escorial, Spain, *not* Escu-.

escritoire, *not* -oir (not ital.).

Esculap/ius, -ian, use **Ae-.**

escutcheon, plate for key-hole, etc., *not* scut-.

Esdras, in the Apocrypha, First, Second, Book of, abbr. **1, 2 Esd.**

ESE., east-south-east. *See also* **compass.**

Eskimo/, *not* Esquimau; *pl.* **-s.**

esophag/us, -eal, use **oes-.**

esp., especially.

ESP, extra-sensory perception.

espagnol/, -e (Fr.), Spanish.

espagnolette, french-window fastening.

espalier, a lattice-work, a trained fruit-tree (not ital.).

especially, abbr. **esp.**

Esperanto, an artificial universal language, invented by L. L. Zamenhof, 1887.

espièglerie, roguishness (not ital.).

espionage, spying (not ital.).

espressivo (It. mus.), with expression, *not* ex-.

espresso, apparatus for making coffee under pressure (not ital.).

esprit/ (Fr. m.), genius, wit; — *de corps,* respect for a society, by its members; —*fort,* a strong-minded person, *pl.* **esprits forts** (ital.).

Esquimalt, Vancouver Island, *not* -ault; *pron.* eskwĭ'-mawlt.

Esquimau, use **Eskimo.**

Esquire, abbr. **Esq.;** J. Smith, **jun., Esq.,** *not* Esq., jun.

esquisse (Fr. f.), a sketch.

E.S.R.O., European Space Research Organisation (*not* -zation).

ess, name of the letter *s*; *pl.* **esses.**

ess., essences.

essays (typ.), cited titles to be roman quoted; caps. as in title.

Essouan, use **Aswan.**

E.S.T. (U.S.), Eastern Standard Time.

established, abbr. **est.**

Established Church (caps.); abbr. **E.C.**

Establishment (the), (the values held by) the established sector of society (cap.).

estamin, a woollen fabric, *not* ét-.

estaminet (Fr. m.), a café.

estanci/a (Sp.-Amer.), cattle farm; *-ero,* its keeper.

Estate/s of the Realm, the Parliament of Scotland before union with England in 1707; — **s, the Three,** Lords Spiritual (clergy), Lords Temporal, Commons; —, **the Third,** French bourgeoisie before the Revolution; —, **the Fourth,** the Press.

*est*da (Sp.) *estimada,* esteemed (letter, favour).

Esther (O.T.), not to be abbr.

esthet/e, -ic, use **aes-.**

estimator, *not* -er.

estiv/al, -ation, use **aes-.**

Estonia, *not* Esth-, a Soviet Socialist Republic. *See* **U.S.S.R.**

estoppel (law), a conclusive admission, *not* -ple, -pal.

E.S.U., English-Speaking Union.

e.s.u., electrostatic unit(s).

E.T., English translation.

E.T.A., estimated time of arrival.

étage (Fr. m.), floor; *étagère* (f.), a set of shelves.

et alibi (Lat.), and else-where; abbr. *et al.*

et alii (Lat.), and others; abbr. *et al.*, *not* et als.

etat-major (Fr. m.), a staff of military officers.

E.T.C., Eastern Telegraph Co.

et cetera (not ital.), abbr. **etc.**, *or* **&c.**; (typ.) abbreviate in bookwork to 'etc.'; no comma between 'etc. etc.'

etceteras, extras, sundries (one word).

Eternal City (the), Rome.

eth, *pron.* ĕdh, the Anglo-Saxon and Icel., Đ, ð (distinguish from 'thorn', þ, þ). (U.S. *pref. sp.* **edh**.)

ether, medium filling all space, *not* ae-.

ethereal/, **-ity**, **-ly**, *not* -ial.

ethics, the science of morals.

Ethiopia, modern name of Abyssinia.

ethn/ic, concerning races; **-ology**, **-ological**, abbr. **ethnol.**

et hoc genus omne (Lat.), and all this kind of thing.

ethology, the study of character formation or animal behaviour.

etiology, *use* ae-.

etiquette, conventions of courtesy (not ital.).

Etna, Sicily, *not* Ae-.

et sequen/s, and the following, abbr. *et seq.* or *et sq.*; *pl.* **-tes**, **-tia**, abbr. *et sqq.*

E.T.U., Electrical Trades Union.

étude/ (Fr. f.), a study; — *de concert* (mus.), concert study.

étui, case for small articles, *not* etwee (not ital.).

etymolog/y, the study of derivations; **-ical**, **-ically**, **-ist**; abbr. **etym.**

etymon, a root-word.

Eu (chem.), europium (no point).

E.U., Evangelical Union.

eucalypt/us (bot.), *pl.* **-i**.

euchre, a card game, *not* eucre.

Euclid/, Athenian geometer, *c.* 300 B.C.; his treatise (cap.); adj. **-ean** (cap.).

eudemon, a good angel.

Euer (Ger. m.), your; abbr. *Ew.*

Eugène, French Christian name (è).

Eugénie (Empress), wife of Napoleon III (é).

eulogium/, eulogy; *pl.* **-s.**

eulogize, *not* -ise.

eulogy (**a**, *not* **an**), spoken or written praise. *See* **elegy, elogy**

Eumenides (Gk. myth.), the avenging Furies: Alecto, Tisiphone, and Megaera; (ital.) play by Aeschylus.

euphem/ism (**a**, *not* **an**), a mild term for something unpleasant; **-istic(al)**; abbr. **euphem.**

euphemize, *not* -ise.

euphonize, *not* -ise.

euphony (**a**, *not* **an**), agreeable sound.

euphorbia (bot.), spurge.

euphor/ia, a feeling of well-being; **-ic.**

Euphues, a prose romance in affected style, 1579, by John Lyly (1554–1606); hence **euphuism**.

Euratom, *see* **E.A.E.C.**

Eure-et-Loir, Fr. dép.; *not* Loire; not to be confused with Fr. dép. **Eure**.

Eureka, I have found [it]! *not* Heu- (not ital.). *See also* **heuristic.**

Europe, abbr. **Eur.**

European (**a**, *not* **an**); abbr. **Eur.**

europeanize, *not* -ise.

europium, symbol Eu (no point).

Euterpe (Gr.), muse of Music.

euthanasia, peaceful death, mercy killing.

Evangelical Union, abbr. **E.U.**

evangelize, to inform about the Gospel, *not* -ise.

evaporimeter, instrument to measure evaporation, *not* -ometer.

evening, abbr. **evng.**

even pages (typ.), the left-hand, or verso, pages.

even s.caps. (typ.), s.caps. without cap. initials.

everglades (U.S.), tracts of low swampy ground; (cap.) a large area like this in Florida.

every must be followed by verb and pronoun in sing., as 'every bird *tries* to protect *its* young'.

every/body, -day (adj.), **-one, -thing, -way** (adverb), **-where** (one word).

evviva (It.), shout of applause.

ewe, female sheep (**a**, *not* an).

ewer, jug (**a**, *not* an).

Ewigkeit (Ger. f.), eternity.

E.W.O., Essential Works Order.

ex (Lat.), out of (not ital.).

ex., examined, example, exchange, excursion, executed, executive.

exactor, one who exacts, *not* -er.

exaggeration, in Fr. f. *exagér-*.

exalter, one who exalts, *not* -or.

examination/, abbr. **exam.;** — **paper,** the questions (U.S. — **questions**); — **script,** the answers (U.S. — **papers**).

examined, abbr. **ex.**

examplar, erron. for **exemplar.**

example, abbr. **ex.,** *pl.* **exx.;** in Fr. m. *exemple.*

exanimate, lifeless, depressed.

ex animo (Lat.), from the mind, earnestly.

exasperate, to irritate, *not* -irate.

Exc., Excellency.

exc., excellent, except, -ed, -ion, *excudit* (he, *or* she, engraved it).

Excalibur, King Arthur's sword, *not* -bar, -bour (not ital.). *See* **Caliburn.**

ex cathedra (Lat.), from the Pope's, professor's chair, with authority.

excavator, *not* -er.

excellence/, superiority; *pl.* **-s,** *not* -cies.

Excellenc/y, *pl.* **-ies** (persons), abbr. **Exc.**

excellent, abbr. **exc.**

except/, -ed, -ion, abbr. **exc.**

exceptionable, open to criticism.

exceptional, out of the ordinary.

excerpt, an extract.

exchange, abbr. **ex.,** *or* **exch.; Stock —** (caps.), abbr. **St. Ex., S/E.**

exchangeable, *not* -gable.

exchequer, abbr. **exch.**

excisable, liable to excise duty, *not* -eable.

excitability, *not* -ibility.

exciter, one who, *or* that which, excites, (elec.) auxiliary machine supplying current for another, *not* -or.

excitor (anat.), a nerve stimulating part of the body, *not* -er.

exclamat/ion, -ory, abbr. **excl.,** *or* **exclam.**

exclamation point (!), *see* **punctuation VII.**

ex/ commodo (Lat.), conveniently; — *concesso*, from what has been granted.

excreta, *pl.*, excreted matter (not ital.).

excudit (Lat.), he, *or* she, engraved it; abbr. *exc.*

ex curia (Lat.), out of court, not -*â*.

excursion, abbr. **ex.**

excursus/, a digression; *pl.* **-es** (not ital.).

ex dividend, without next dividend; abbr. **ex div.**, *or* **x.d.**

exeat/, 'let him depart', a formal leave of temporary absence; *pl.* **-s** (not ital.). See **exit** *and* **exit.**

execut/ed, -ive, abbr. **ex.**

execut/er, one who executes; **-or** (law), abbr. **exor.**; *fem.* **-rix**, abbr. **exrx.**, *pl.* **-rices.**

exeges/is, explanation; *pl.* **-es** (not ital.).

exemplaire (Fr. m.), a specimen, a copy; in Ger. noun *Exemplar.*

exemplar, pattern, *not* exa-.

exemple (Fr. m.), example.

exempli gratia (Lat.), for example; abbr. **e.g.**, *or* **ex. gr.** (l.c., not ital., comma before).

exempl/um (Lat.), a copy; *pl.* **-a.**

exequatur/, an off. recognition by a foreign government of a consul or other agent; *pl.* **-s** (not ital.).

exequies, *pl.*, funeral ceremony (not ital.).

exercise, *not* -ize.

Exeter, in Lat. *Exonia*, abbr. **Exon.**

exeunt omnes (Lat. stage direction), they all leave.

ex. gr., *see* **exempli gratia.**

ex gratia (Lat.), voluntary.

exhibitor, *not* -er.

exhilarat/e, to enliven; **-ing, -ion.**

exigeant/ (Fr.), *fem.* **-e**, exacting (no accent).

exigency, urgency.

exigent, urgent.

exiguous, small, scanty.

ex interest, without next interest; abbr. **ex int.**, *or* **x.i.**

existence, *not* -ance.

existentialism, the philosophy that values can only be created by living, not by thinking.

exit/, a way out; *pl.* **-s.**

exit (Lat. stage direction), he or she goes out; *pl.* **exeunt**, they go out (ital.). See **exeat** *and* **exit.**

ex lege (Lat.), arising from law.

ex-libris (*sing.* and *pl.*), 'from the library of', a book-plate (not ital.); abbr. **ex lib.**

ex necessitate (Lat.), necessarily.

ex new, without the right to new shares; abbr. **ex n.**, *or* **x.n.**

ex nihilo nihil fit (Lat.), out of nothing, nothing comes.

exodi/um, conclusion of a drama, a farce following it; *pl.* **-a**; anglicized as **exode.** See **exordium.**

exodus, a departure, esp. of a body of people; (cap., O.T.), departure of Israelites from Egypt, biblical book, abbr. **Exod.**

ex officio (Lat.), by virtue of one's official position.

exon, officer of the Yeoman of the Guard.

Exon., signature of Bp. of Exeter (full point).

exor., executor.

exorcize, to expel an evil spirit from, *not* -ise.

exordium/, introductory part of a discourse; *pl.* **-s.** See **exodium.**

exp., export, -ation, -ed, express.

expanded type (typ.), a type with unusually wide face.

ex parte (Lat.), one-sided(ly).

ex pede Herculem (Lat.), judge from the sample.

expendable, able to be sacrificed for some end.

expense, *not* -ce.

experimenter, *not* -or.

expertise, expert knowledge.

experto crede! (Lat.), believe one who has tried it!

explanation, abbr. **expl.**

export/, -ation, -ed, abbr. **exp.**

exposé, explanation, exposure (not ital.).

expositor, one who expounds, *not* -er.

ex post facto (Lat.), after the fact.

expostulator, one who remonstrates, *not* -er.

Ex-President (caps.).

express, abbr. **exp.**

expressible, *not* -able.

expressivo (mus.), with expression, *use es-.*

exrx., executrix.

ext., extension, external, -ly, extinct, extra, extract.

extasy, extatic, *use* ecs-.

ex tempore (Lat.) (adverb), without preparation (ital.).

extempore (adj.), unprepared (not ital.).

extemporize, *not* -ise.

extender, *not* -or.

extendible, *not* -able.

extensible, *not* -able.

extension, abbr. **ext.**

extensor, a muscle, *not* -er.

extent (typ.), the number of pages in a book.

external/, -ly, abbr. **ext.**

externalize, *not* -ise.

externat (Fr. m.), a day school.

externe, non-resident hospital physician, day-pupil.

extinct, abbr. **ext.**

extirpator, one who destroys completely, *not* -er.

extol/, -led, -ler, -ling.

extra, extract, abbr. **ext.**

extractable, *not* -ible.

extractor, *not* -er.

extracts, *see* **authorities, quotations.**

extramural, outside the scope of ordinary teaching (one word); *but*
Extra-Mural Studies (of Universities).

extraneous, brought in from outside, *not* -ious.

extra-sensory perception, abbr. **ESP.**

extravaganza, a fantastic composition (not ital.).

ex usu (Lat.), by use.

exuviae, cast coverings of animals.

ex-voto/, an offering made in pursuance of a vow; *pl.* **-s** (not ital.).

exx., examples.

Exzellenz (Ger. f.), Excellency; abbr. ***Exz.,*** *not* Exc-.

Eyck, Van (Hubert), 1366–1426, and — **(Jan),** 1385–1440, Flemish painters.

eyeball (one word).

eyebath (one word).

eyebrow (one word).

eyeful (one word), *not* -full.

eyeglass (one word).

eyeing (U.S., eying).

eye/lash, -lid (one word).

eye-muscles (hyphen).

eye/piece (optics), **-sight, -sore, -witness** (one word).

eyot (U.S. ait), islet (*not* ait except in proper names with Ait).

Eyre & Spottiswoode (Publishers), Ltd.

eyrie, common spelling of **aerie.**

Eyrir, coin of Iceland, one-hundredth of Krona; *pl.* **Aurar.**

Ezekiel, abbr. **Ezek.**

Ezra, not to be abbr.

F

F (elec.), farad, fluorine, (photog.) focal length, (pencils) fine, (on timepiece regulator) fast, the sixth in a series. *See* **Fahrenheit.**

F., fair, Fellow, felon, (naut.) fog, formula, -ae, Friday, all proper names with this initial except ff. *See* **Fahrenheit.**

f., farthing, fathom, feminine, filly, following, franc, free, from, furlong.

f (mus.), *forte* (loud).

f. (Lat.), *fortasse* (perhaps).

Fa., Florida, *use* **Fla.**

F.A., Football Association; Fédération Aéronautique.

f.a.a., free of all average.

Faber & Faber, Ltd., publishers.

fabliau/, a metrical tale; *pl.* **-x.**

fac., facsimile.

façade, front face of a building (not ital.).

F.A.C.C.A., Fellow of the Association of Certified and Corporate Accountants.

face (typ.), the printing surface of type; a type design.

facet/, one side of a cut gem; **-ed, -ing,** *not* -tt-.

facetiae, humorous anecdotes (not ital.).

facia, tablet over shop front, with occupier's name; dash-board of a motor car (also spelt **fascia**). *See* **fascia.**

facies (nat. hist.), general aspect (ital.).

facile princeps (Lat.), easily best.

facilis descensus Averni (*not* Averno) (Lat.), easy is the descent to Avernus.

façon de parler (Fr.), mere form of words.

facsimile/, exact copy (one word, not ital.); *pl.* **-s;** abbr. **fac.**

facta, non verba (Lat.), deeds, not words.

factious, motivated by party spirit.

factitious, not natural.

factotum/, servant who attends to everything; *pl.* **-s** (not ital.).

factum est (Lat.), it is done.

facul/a, bright solar spot; *pl.* **-ae;** *not* fac-.

faec/es, *pl.,* excrement; adj. **-al** (U.S. **fec-**).

Faerie Queene, The, by Spenser, 1590–6.

Faeroe Isles, Danish, in N. Atlantic, *use* **The Faeroes.**

fag-end (hyphen).

faggot, bundle of sticks (U.S. **fagot**).

Fahrenheit, temperature scale; abbr. **F.** *or* **Fahr.,** *but* no point if used in scientific work.

F.A.I., Fellow of the Auctioneers' Institute; superseded by **F.R.I.C.S.,** q.v., in 1970.

F.A.I.A., Fellow of the Association of International Accountants.

faience, glazed pottery, *not* faï-, fay-.

fainéant, idle, idler (not ital.).

faint ruled (paper), *use* **feint.**

fair, abbr. **F.**

fair-and-square (hyphens).

fair copy, transcript free from corrections; abbr. **f. co.**

faire/ *des frais* (Fr.), to make efforts to please; — *ses frais,* to cover one's

faire (*cont.*):
expenses; — *école,* to found
a school (of art, etc.); —
une école, to make a
blunder; — *feu,* to fire
guns, etc.; — *du feu,* to
light a fire; — *son paquet,*
to pack up and go; — *un
paquet,* to make a parcel;
— *suivre,* to forward, abbr.
F.S.

fair play (two words).

fairway, *not* fare- (one word).

faisan (Fr. m.), pheasant.

fait accompli (*un*) (Fr.
m.), an accomplished fact.

faithful/, -ly.

Faizabad, Uttar Pradesh
(India), *use* **Fyz-**.

faker, one who fakes.

fakir, Muslim or Hindu
religious mendicant, *not* the
many variants.

Falang/e (-ist), Fascist
party (member) in Spain.

falderal, song refrain, *not*
fal de rol, folderol.

faldetta, Maltese hooded
cape (not ital.).

faldstool, *not* fold- (one
word).

Falernian, wine of ancient
Campania.

Falkland Islands,
S. Atlantic.

Falk Laws, 1874–5,
German anti-Catholic laws
introduced by politician
Adalbert Falk.

Falla (Manuel de), 1876–
1946, Spanish composer.

fal-lal, finery, *not* fallol.

fallible, liable to err, *not*
-able.

**Fallodon (Sir Edward, Visc.
Grey of),** 1862–1933, English
statesman, *not* -en.

fall-out (noun), from nuclear
explosion (hyphen).

F.A.L.P.A., Fellow of the
Incorporated Society of
Auctioneers and Landed
Property Agents.

falsa lectio (Lat.), a false
reading; abbr. *f.l.*

falucca, *use* **felucca**

falutin, *use* **highfalutin**
(one word).

F.A.M., Free and Accepted
Masons.

fam., familiar, family.

familiarize, *not* -ise.

family, abbr. **fam.** *See also*
botany, zoology.

fandango/ (Sp.), a dance or
its music; *pl.* **-es** (not ital.).

Faneuil Hall, historic
building, Boston, Mass., U.S.

fanfare (mus.), a flourish.

fanfaronade, brag, *not*
-nnade, -farronade.

fantasia (mus.), a free
composition (not ital.).

fantasmagoria, an inco-
herent series of fantasms.

fantast, a dreamer, *not* ph-.

fantasy, *not* ph-.

Fantin-Latour (Henri),
1836–1904, French painter.

fantoccini (It.), marionettes.

fantom, *use* ph-.

F.A.N.Y., First Aid Nursing
Yeomanry.

F.A.O., Food and Agriculture
Organization (of U.N.).

F.A.P., First Aid Post.

f.a.q., free alongside quay.

faqu/eer, -ir, *use* **fakir.**

far., farriery, farthing.

farad/ (elec.), unit of
capacitance; abbr. **F** (no
point); **-ic current** (med.),
not -aic.

Faraday (Michael), 1791–
1867, chemist.

faradization, application of
med. elec.; *not* faradais-.

farce (Fr. f.), force-meat.

farceu/r (Fr.), *fem.* **-se,**
a joker.

fareway, *use* **fair-**.

farewell (one word).

far-fetched (hyphen).

farinaceous, starchy, *not*
-ious.

Faringdon, Berks., *not* Farr-.

farm/house, -stead, -yard (one word).

Farne Islands, N. Sea, *not* Farn, Fearne, Ferne.

far niente (It.), doing nothing; *dolce* — —, q.v.

farouche, sullen from shyness (not ital.).

Farquhar (George), 1678–1707, Irish dramatist.

farrago, a hotch-potch, *not* fara-.

Farrar (F. W., Dean), 1831–1903, English divine and writer.

farriery, horse-shoeing; abbr. **far.**

farther, *see* **further.**

farthing, abbr. **f.,** *or* **far.**

F.A.S., Fellow of the Anthropological Society; ditto Antiquarian Society.

f.a.s., free alongside ship.

fasces (*pl.*), a bundle of rods, the symbol of power (ital.).

fasci/a (arch.), long flat surface under eaves or cornice; *pl.* **-ae.** *See* **facia.**

fascicle, fascicule, fascicul/us (*pl.* **-i**), a bundle, bunch; one part of a book published by instalments.

Fascism, Fascist.

Fastens/ -een, -eve, -even (Sc.), Shrove Tuesday, *not* Feastings-.

fata Morgana, mirage seen in Str. of Messina (ital.).

fat face type, one with thick stems and fine hairlines.

Fates (the Three), Atropos, Clotho, and Lachesis.

Father (relig.), abbr. **Fr.**

father of the chapel, a shop steward in a printing office.

fathom, abbr. **f.,** *or* **fm.**

fatigable, *not* -guable.

fatstock (one word).

faubourg (Fr. m.), a suburb, cap. F when with name (not ital.).

faucet (chiefly U.S.), tap.

Faucit (Helen), Lady Martin, 1820–98, actress.

Faulkland, in *The Rivals,* by Sheridan.

Faulkner (William), 1897–1962, American novelist.

fault-finding (hyphen).

faun/, a Roman rural deity; *pl.* **-s.**

fauna/ (*coll. sing.*), the animals of a region or epoch; *pl.* **-s.**

fausse tortue (Fr. f.), mock-turtle.

faute de mieux (Fr.), for want of better.

fauteuil/, armchair; *pl.* **-s** (not ital.).

faux/ (Fr. m.), a forgery; (f.) a scythe; **—** *jour* (astr.), false light; **—** *pas* (Fr. m.), a blunder (two words).

favete linguis (Lat.), be silent.

favour/, -able, -ite (U.S. **favor-**).

Fawkes (Guy), 1570–1606, conspirator.

fawn, young deer, its colour.

fayence, *use* **faience.**

F.B., Fenian Brotherhood, Fishery Board, Free Baptist.

F.B.A., Fellow of the British Academy, *not* F.R.B.A.

F.B.A.A., Fellow of the British Association of Accountants and Auditors.

F.B.C.S., Fellow of the British Computer Society.

F.B.H.I., Fellow of the British Horological Institute.

F.B.I., (U.S.) Federal Bureau of Investigation, Federation of British Industries (now merged in **C.B.I.**).

F.B.I.M., Fellow of the British Institute of Management; *formerly* F.I.I.A.

F.B.O.A., Fellow of the British Optical Association.

F.B.S., Fellow of the Botanical Society.

F.C., Football Club, Free Church (of Scotland).

F.C.A., Fellow (of the Institute of) Chartered Accountants in England and Wales (or Ireland) (off.).

F.C.C.S., Fellow of Corporation of (Certified) Secretaries.

F.C.G.I., Fellow of the City and Guilds of London Institute.

F.C.I.A., Fellow of the Corporation of Insurance Agents.

F.C.I.B., Fellow of the Corporation of Insurance Brokers.

F.C.I.I., Fellow of the Chartered Insurance Institute.

F.C.I.S., Fellow of the Chartered Institute of Secretaries.

F.C.O., Foreign and Commonwealth Office.

f. co., fair copy.

F.C.P., Fellow of the College of Preceptors.

fcp., foolscap.

F.C.R.A., Fellow of the Corporation of Registered Accountants.

F.C.S., Fellow of the Chemical Society.

F.C.S.P., Fellow of the Chartered Society of Physiotherapy.

F.C.S.T., Fellow of the College of Speech Therapists.

F.C.T., Federal Capital Territory (of Australia), *now* **A.C.T.,** q.v.

F.C.W.A., Fellow of the Institute of Cost and Work Accountants.

F.D., *fidei defensor* (Defender of the Faith).

Fe, *ferrum* (iron) (no point).

Fearne Isles, use **Farne —.**

fearnought, a woollen cloth, *not* -naught.

feasible, practicable, *not* -able.

Feastings-, see **Fastens-.**

featherfew, use **fever-.**

featherweight paper, light but bulky book paper.

February, abbr. **Feb.**

fecal, feces, use **fae-.**

fecerunt (Lat.), they made it; abbr. ***ff.***

fecial, use **fetial.**

fecit (Lat.), he, *or* she, made it; abbr. *fec.*

federal associations, see **Assemblies.**

Federalist, abbr. **Fed.**

federalize, *not* -ise.

feedback, return of part of output to input (one word).

feeoff/, -ee, use **feo-.**

feet, use only for two feet and over, *not* for one and a half foot, etc.; abbr. **ft** (no point), sign **′.**

feff/, -ment, use **feoff.**

Fehmgericht (Ger.), use *Femgericht,* q.v.

Feilding, fam. name of Earl of Denbigh. *See also* **Fie-.**

feint, to pretend.

feint ruled (paper), *not* faint.

F.E.I.S., Fellow of the Educational Institute of Scotland.

feldspar, use **felspar.**

feliciter (Lat.), happily.

fellah/, Egyptian peasant; *pl.* **-in,** *not* -s, -een. *See also* **Fulahs.**

fellmonger, hide-dealer.

felloe, wheel rim, *not* felly.

Fellow, abbr. **F.;** in Lat., *socius;* or, in the Royal Society, *sodalis.*

fellow citizen (two words).

fell/y, use **-oe.**

felo de se (Anglo-Lat.), suicide; *pl. felos de se.*

felon, one who commits a grave crime; abbr. **F.**

fel/spar, a rock-forming mineral; adj. **-spathic;** *not* feld-, which is correct but in disuse.

felucca, small Mediterranean vessel, *not* the many variants.

fem., feminine.

female (bot., zool.), sign ♀.

feme/ (law), wife, *not* femme; — **covert,** married woman (no hyphen); — **-sole,** unmarried woman (hyphen). *See also* **femme.**

Femgericht/ (Ger.), *pl.* **-e,** medieval German tribunal, anglicized as **Vehmgericht,** q.v.

feminine, abbr. **f.,** *or* **fem.**

feminize, to make feminine, *not* -ise.

femme/ **de chambre** (Fr. f.), chambermaid, *pl. femmes* — — ; — **galante,** a prostitute; — *incomprise,* an unappreciated woman; — *savante,* learned woman. *See also* **feme.**

fem/ur, thigh bone, *pl.* **-ora** (not ital.); **-oral.**

fencible, able to be fenced; (hist., noun) soldier liable only for home service; *not* -able.

fencing, abbr. **fenc.**

Fénelon (François de S. de la M.), 1651–1715, French ecclesiastic and writer, *not* Féné-.

fenestr/a (anat.), a small hole in a bone; *pl.* **-ae** (not ital.).

Fenian, adj., belonging to the legendary *fíanna* or to the modern Fenians, a league of Irish in U.S., 1858, to overthrow Brit. govt. in Ireland; noun, a member of this.

fenugreek, leguminous plant, *not* foenu-.

feoff/, a fief; **-ee,** a person invested with it; **-or,** he who grants it; *not* feeoff, feff.

F.E.R.A., (U.S.) Federal Emergency Relief Administration.

ferae naturae (law), adj., wild (of animals), lit. of a wild nature.

Ferd., Ferdinand.

Ferdausi, Persian poet, *use* **Fir-.**

fer-de-lance, venomous snake (trop. Amer.).

Feringhee, in the Orient, a European, esp. a Portuguese; *not* the many variants.

Fermanagh County, N. Ireland, abbr. **Ferm.**

fermium (chem.), symbol **Fm** (no point).

Fernando de Noronha, Brazilian penal colony in S. Atlantic.

Fernando Po, island in Bay of Biafra, Span. Guinea.

Ferne Islands, *use* **Farne** —.

Ferrara (Andrea), sword-smith, sixteenth century.

Ferrari (Paolo), 1822–89, Italian dramatist.

Ferrero (Guglielmo), 1871–1942, Italian historian.

ferret/, **-ed, -er, -ing.**

ferrule, metal cap on end of stick (two *r*'s). *See* **ferule.**

ferrum (iron.), symbol **Fe** (no point).

fertilize, *not* -ise.

ferule, a cane or rod for punishment (one *r*). *See* **ferrule.**

fervour (U.S. -or).

F.E.S., Fellow of the Entomological Society, ditto Ethnological Society.

Fescennine, relating to anc. Etruscan festivals, scurrilous.

fesse (her.), *not* fess.

festa (It.), a festival.

festina lente (Lat.), hasten slowly.

fêt/e, entertainment, **-ed** (not ital.); *fête-champêtre,* outdoor entertainment; *Fête-Dieu,* feast of Corpus Christi, *pl. Fêtes-* — (ital., hyphen).

fetial, ambassadorial, *not* fec-.

fetid, ill-smelling, *not* foe-.
fetish/, inanimate object worshipped by savages, *not* -ich, -iche; **-eer, -ism, -ist** (not ital.).
fetor, bad smell, *not* foe-.
fetus, *use* foe-.
feu/ (Sc.), ground-rent, *pl.* **-s.**
feu/ (Fr.), late, deceased; *fem.* **-e.**
Feuchtwanger (Lion), 1874–1958, German novelist.
feud., feudal.
feudalize, to make feudal.
feu/ d'artifice (Fr. m.), firework, *pl. feux* —; *— de joie,* a salute, *pl. feux* — —.
feu-duty (hyphen).
Feuermann (Emanuel), 1902–42, Austrian cellist.
feuille (Fr. typ. f.), a sheet.
Feuillet (Octave), 1821–90, French novelist and playwright.
feuillet/ (Fr. typ. m.), a leaf; *— blanc,* blank leaf.
feuilletage (Fr. cook. m.), puff-pastry.
feuilleton (Fr. m.), light literature; in Fr. a continuous story printed at the bottom of a newspaper page (not ital.).
feverfew (bot.), *Chrysanthemum Parthenium, not* feather-, fetter-foe.
fez/, a cap; *pl.* **-es** (not ital.).
F.F., *Felicissimi Fratres* (Most Fortunate Brothers), (naut.) thick fog.
F.f. (Ger.), *Fortsetzung folgt* (to be continued).
ff., folios, following (*pl.*, preferred to *et seqq.*).
ff (typ.), as initials for proper name, *not* Ff.
ff (mus.), *fortissimo* (very loud).
ff., fecerunt, q.v.
F.F.A., Fellow of the Faculty of Actuaries (Scotland).

F.F.A.S., Fellow of the Faculty of Architects and Surveyors.
fff (mus.), *fortississimo* (as loud as possible).
F.F.Hom., Fellow of the Faculty of Homoeopathy.
F.F.P.S., Fellow of the Faculty of Physicians and Surgeons.
F.F.R., Fellow of the Faculty of Radiologists.
F.G., Fire Guard, Foot-guards.
f.g.a., free of general average.
F.G.O., Fellow of the Guild of Organists.
F.G.S., Fellow of the Geological Society.
F.H., fire-hydrant.
F.H.A., Fellow of the Institute of Hospital Administrators.
F.H.S., Fellow of the Heraldry Society.
F.I.A., Fellow of the Institute of Actuaries.
F.I.A.A., Fellow Architect Member of the Incorporated Association of Architects and Surveyors.
F.I.A.C., Fellow of the Institute of Company Accountants.
fiacre (Fr. m.), a four-wheeled cab.
F.I.A.I., Fellow of the Institute of Industrial and Commercial Accountants.
fianc/é, *fem.* **-ée,** one betrothed (not ital.).
fianna, the militia of Finn and other legendary Irish kings; **Fianna/,** *pl.,* the Fenians; **— Eireann,** the Fenians of Ireland; **— Fáil,** the Irish Republican party.
F.I.Arb., Fellow of the Institute of Arbitrators.
F.I.A.S., Fellow Surveyor Member of the Incorporated Association of Architects and Surveyors.

fiasco/, a failure; *pl.* **-s**.

fiat, formal authorization (not ital.).

Fiat, Fabbrica Italiana Automobile Torino (It. motor car, company, and factory).

fiat/ justitia (Lat.), let justice be done; *— lux*, let there be light.

F.I.B., Fellow of the Institute of Bankers.

F.I.Biol., Fellow of the Institute of Biology.

fibre (U.S. **fiber**).

fibrin, blood protein appearing as network of fibres, *not* -ine.

F.I.C., Fellow of the Institute of Chemistry, *now* **F.R.I.C.**

fichu, woman's neckerchief (not ital.).

F.I.C.S., Fellow of the Institute of Chartered Shipbrokers.

fict., fictilis (Lat.), made of pottery, fictile.

fic/tion, -titious, abbr. **fict.**

F.I.D., Fellow of the Institute of Directors.

fidalgo (Port.), a noble.

Fidei Defensor, Defender of the Faith; abbr. *F.D.*, or *Fid. Def.*

fides Punica (Lat.), Punic faith, bad faith.

fidget/, -ed, -ily, -ing, -y (one *t* only).

F.I.D.O., Fog Investigation Dispersal Operation.

fi donc! (Fr.), for shame! fie!

fidus Achates (Lat.), a trusty friend.

Fielding (Henry), 1707–54, novelist. *See also* **Fei-**.

Field-Marshal (hyphen, caps.); abbr. **F.M.**

Field Officer (no hyphen); abbr. **F.O.**

Fiennes, *pron.* fīnz.

fieri facias (Lat.), 'see that

it is done', a writ; abbr. *fi. fa.*

fiesta (Sp.), festivity, holiday (ital.).

F.I.F.S.T., Fellow of the Institute of Food Science and Technology.

fift/y, -ieth, symbol L.

Fig., figure.

fig., figurative, -ly, figure.

figurant/ (Fr. m.), a member of the ballet chorus, *pl.* **-s**; *fem.* **-e**, *pl.* **-es**. *Also* (It. m. *or* f.) **figurant/e**, *pl.* **i**.

figures, to be used for: **ages**, but 'he died in his eightieth year'; **book-work**, rarely, and only those over 100, but in statistical details figures are used more freely; **dates**, days and years regularly, months for brevity; **degrees**, of heat; **distances; dollars**, omit the ciphers for cents when there are none, as e.g. $100, *not* $100.00; **narrow measure** (works of); **numbers** with vulgar or decimal fractions; **races**, distance and time; **scores**, of games and matches; **specific gravity; statistics; time of day** when followed by a.m. or p.m.; **votes; weights;** not to be combined with words, for one amount: use all figures, or spell all out; commas to separate each three consecutive figures from the right when four or more, except in math. work and pagination; in scientific work thin spaces are used instead of commas: 1 234 567 *not* 1,234,567; in pagination, dates, etc., use the least number of figures possible: 42–5, 161–4, 1961–8, 1960–1, 1966/7 (but this does not apply to

figures (*cont.*):
the numbers 10–19, which
represent single words, so
10–11, 16–18, 210–11,
1801–1900); number
of a house in road or
street, etc., not to be
followed by comma as it
does not make the meaning
clearer.

**figures, spell out for:
accuracy** — when
important; **book-work**
generally, always under 100,
except in statistical matters
or in weights and measures,
and such-like; **beginning of
sentences; degrees of**
inclination; **indefinite
amounts,** as two or three
miles; **legal work,** *always*;
street names (numerical),
as First Street, Fifth
Avenue; **one-and-twenty,**
etc. (hyphens). *See also*
fractions.

figures/ (arabic), 1, 2, 3,
etc.; **— and plates,**
references to be 'Plate II, Fig.
4'; caps. on the plate to be
s.caps. in the text; **—
(cancelled),** 2, 9, etc.,
indicate figures cancelled,
but which are to be printed;
— (dotted), 1, 2, 3, may
indicate repeating decimals;
— (roman numerals), i,
ii, iii, etc., to be used for
folios of preliminary
matter (no point after), not
to be used for date on
title-page. *See also*
**authorities, decimal
currency, lakh, numerals.**

F.I.H., Fellow of the
Institute of Hygiene.

F.I.H.E., Fellow of the
Institute of Health
Education.

F.I.I.A., Fellow of the
Institute of Industrial
Administration, *now*
F.B.I.M., q.v.

F.I.Inst., Fellow of the
Imperial Institute.

F.I.J., *use* **F.J.I.**

Fildes (Sir Luke), 1844–
1927, English painter.

filemot, a yellowish-brown,
'dead leaf' colour, *not*
filamort, filmot, phil-.

filet (Fr. cook. m.), fillet.

filibeg (Sc.), kilt, *not* the
many variants.

filibuster, one who obstructs
public business by a long
speech, the speech, *not* fill-.

filigree/, ornamental
metallic lacework, *not* fila-,
file-; **— letter** (typ.), an
initial with filigree
background.

Filipin/as, Sp. for
Philippine Islands; -o(s),
native(s) of the islands.

fille de/ chambre (Fr. f.),
chambermaid, *pl.* *filles —
—;* **— —** *joie,* a prostitute.

fillet/, in Fr. m. *filet;* **-ed,
-ing.**

fillibeg, *use* **fili-.**

fillip/, a stimulus; **-ed, -ing.**

fillipeen, game of forfeits;
use **philippina.**

filmot, *use* **filemot.**

filmsetting (typ.), setting
type photographically.

filoselle, floss silk (not
ital.).

fils (Fr. m.), son, as Dumas
fils (not ital.).

filucca, *use* **felucca.**

F.I.M.T.A., Fellow of the
Institute of Municipal
Treasurers and
Accountants.

F.I.N., Fellow of the
Institute of Navigation.

fin., ad finem (Lat.),
towards the end.

Fin., Finland, Finnish.

finable, liable to a fine.

finale, conclusion (not ital.).

F.Inc.S.T., Fellow of the
Incorporated Society of
Shorthand Teachers.

fin de siècle (Fr.), end of the (nineteenth) century, decadent.

fine-paper edition, abbr. **F.P.**

finesse, subtlety (not ital.).

finger-end, *pl.* **finger-ends.**

finicking, fastidious, *not* finikin.

finis, the end (not ital.).

Finistère, dép. France.

Finisterre (Cape), Spain.

finnan haddock, smoked haddock (two words), *not* the many variants.

Finnegans Wake, novel by James Joyce (no apos.).

Finnish/, abbr. **Fin.; — language** (typ.), is set in ordinary roman characters.

Finno-Karelia, a Soviet Socialist Republic. *See* **U.S.S.R.**

Fin. Sec., Financial Secretary.

F.Inst.P., Fellow of the Institute of Physics.

F.I.O., Fellow of the Institute of Ophthalmic Opticians.

F.I.O.B., Fellow of the Institute of Builders.

F.I.O.P., Fellow of the Institute of Printing.

fiord (Norw.), arm of the sea, *properly* **fjord** (not ital.).

F.I.P.A., Fellow of the Institute of Practitioners in Advertising.

F.I.Q.S., Fellow of the Institute of Quantity Surveyors.

fir., firkin, -s.

Firdausi, 930(?)–1020, Persian poet, *not* Ferdausi, Firdousi, Firdusi.

fire/-arms, — -escape, — -fly, — -hydrant (abbr. **F.H.**); **— -place, — -plug** (abbr. **F.P.**), **— -proof** (hyphens).

Firenze (It.), Florence.

fireside (one word).

firkin/, small cask; *pl.* **-s;** abbr. **fir.**

firman/, an edict, *pl.* **-s.**

firn, névé, granular snow not yet compressed into ice at head of glacier (not ital.).

first-born (hyphen).

first-fruit/, -s (hyphen).

first proof (typ.), the first impression taken, and corrected by the 'copy'.

first-rate (hyphen).

First World War, 1914–18, *not* World War I.

firth, an estuary, *not* fri-.

F.I.S., Fellow of the Institute of Statisticians.

F.I.S.A., Fellow of the Incorporated Secretaries Association.

Fischer-Dieskau (Dietrich), b. 1925, German baritone.

F.I.S.T., Fellow of the Institute of Science Technology.

fist (typ.), the ☞.

fisticuffs, *not* fisty-.

fistul/a, opening of internal organ to the exterior or to another organ, *pl.* **-ae,** (not ital.).

fitchew, a polecat.

FitzGerald (Edward), 1809–83, poet and translator (one word), cap. G.

Fitzgerald/ (Francis Scott), 1898–1940, American novelist; **—** contraction (sci.); lower-case *g.*

Fitzwilliam/College, — Museum, Cambridge.

fivefold (one word).

fixed star, sign ✳ or ✶.

fizgig, flirtatious girl, small firework, *not* fis-, fizz-.

fizz, a sound, *not* fiz.

F.J.I., Fellow of the Institute of Journalists, *not* F.I.J.

fjord, Norw. for **fiord.**

Fl., Flanders, Flemish.

F.L. (naval), Flag
Lieutenant.

fl., florin, fluid, (Aus.)
Gulden.

fl., flores (flowers), *floruit*
(flourished).

f.l., falsa lectio (a false
reading).

Fla., Florida (off. abbr.).

F.L.A., Fellow of the Library
Association.

flabbergast, to dumbfound,
not flaba-, flaber-.

flabell/um (eccles. and bot.),
a fan; *pl.* **-a.**

flageolet, (mus.) straight
flute, (bot.) kidney-bean,
not -elet (not ital.).

flagon, large wine bottle.

flagrante/ bello (Lat.),
during hostilities; — *delicto,*
in the very act.

flag/ship, -staff (one word).

flair, faculty for nosing out
(not ital.).

flambeau/, a torch; *pl.* **-x**
(not ital.).

flamboyant, showy (not
ital.).

flamenco, type of gipsy
song or dance from
Andalusia (not ital.).

flamingo/, trop. bird;
pl. **-s.**

Flamsteed (John), first
English Astronomer Royal
(1675–1719), *not* -stead.

flanconade (fenc.), a thrust
in the side, *not* -nnade.

Flanders, abbr. **Fl.**

flân/erie (Fr. f.), lounging;
-eur, *fem.* **-euse,** an idler.

flannelette, cotton imitation
of flannel, *not* -llette.

flannelled, *not* -eled (except
U.S.).

F.L.A.S., Fellow of the
Land Agents' Society;
qualification superseded by
F.R.I.C.S., q.v., in 1970.

flash/back, -point (one
word).

flat/ impression *or* — **pull**

(typ.), a proof without
makeready.

Flaubert (Gustave), 1821–
80, French novelist.

flautist, *not* flut-.

flavour/, -ed, -ing, -less,
but **flavorous; (U.S.**
flavor/, etc.).

flèche (Fr. f.), an arrow;

flèche (arch., not ital.),
a slender spire.

flection, *use* flexion.

Fleming, a native of
Flanders.

Fleming (Sir Alexander),
1881–1955, English
bacteriologist, discovered
penicillin.

flesher (Sc.), a butcher.

fletcher, a maker of arrows.

fleur-de-lis, heraldic lily,
not — lys, *nor* flower-de-
luce; *pl.* **fleurs-de-lis** (not
ital.).

fleuret (bind.), flower-shaped
ornament.

fleuret (Fr. m.), a fencing-
foil.

fleuron (Fr. typ. m.), a type
ornament.

Flexiback (bind.), method
by which linen replaces
double lining in the
back.

flexible, *not* -able.

flexion (U.S. -ction).

F.L.G.A., Fellow of the
Local Government
Association.

Flg/Off., F.O., Flying Officer.

flibbertigibbet, frivolous
person.

Fliegende Holländer (Der)
(The Flying Dutchman),
opera by Wagner, 1843.

flier, *use* flyer.

F.L.N., *Front de Libération
Nationale,* Algeria.

floatage, *not* flot-.

floatation, *use* flotation.

floccul/us (Lat.), a small
tuft, (anat.) a small lobe in
the cerebellum; *pl.* **-i.**

Floirac, a claret.

flong (typ.), material used for making the mould for stereotyping.

Flood (**the**) (cap.).

flor., floruit (flourished).

flora/ (bot.), (list of) plants of an epoch or region; *pl.* **-s** (not ital.).

floreat (Lat.), may he, she, it flourish.

flores (Lat.), flowers; abbr. *fl.*

florescent, flowering.

floriat/e, -ed, florally decorated, *not* -eate.

Florida, off. abbr. **Fla.**

florin, abbr. **fl.**

floruit (Lat.), flourished; abbr. *fl.*, or *flor.*

FLOSY, Front for the Liberation of Occupied South Yemen. *See also* **N.L.F.**

flotation, illogical but accepted form of **floatation.**

flotsam and jetsam (naut.), floating wreckage and goods thrown overboard (and now cast ashore).

flourished, abbr. **fl.**

flowers (typ.), type ornaments.

F.L.S., Fellow of the Linnean Society (off. spelling), *not* Linnae-.

Flt. Lt., Flight Lieutenant.

Flt. Sgt., Flight Sergeant.

fluent (math. typ.), the sign of integration *∫*.

fluffing (typ.), release of paper fluff or dust during printing.

Flügel (**J. G.**), 1788–1855, German lexicographer.

flugelman, *use* fugle-.

fluid, abbr. **fl.**

fluky, *not* -ey.

flummox, to confound, *not* -ix, -ux.

flunkey/, liveried servant (now contemptuous); *pl.* **-s.**

fluoresce/, -nce, -nt, be luminous, etc.

fluorine, *not* -in; symbol **F** (no point).

fluoroscope, instrument for X-ray examination, with fluorescent screen.

flush (typ.), set to margin of column or page. *See* **full out.**

Flustr/a, a seaweed; *pl.* **-ae** (not ital.).

flutist, *use* **flautist.**

fluty, flute-like, *not* -ey.

fluxions (math.), *not* -ctions.

flyer (U.S. **flier**).

fly/leaf (typ.), a blank leaf at the beginning or end of a book, also blank leaf of a circular; **-sheet,** a two- or four-page tract (one word).

flywheel (one word)

F.M., field magnet, Field-Marshal, Foreign Mission, frequency modulation.

Fm (chem.), fermium (no point).

fm., fathom.

F.M.D., foot-and-mouth disease.

F.M.S., Fellow of the Medical Society.

f.n., *or* **fn.,** footnote.

F.O., Field Officer, (naval) Flag Officer, (R.A.F.) Flying Officer (*also* **Flg/Off**), Foreign Office, (mus.) full organ.

fo., folio.

f.o.b., free on board, *not* caps.

F.O.C., father of the chapel, q.v.

focalize, *not* -ise.

fo'c'sle, *also* **forecastle.**

focus/, *pl.* **-es,** (sci.) **foci.**

focus/ed, -es, -ing, *not* -uss-.

Foerster (**Friedrich Wilhelm**), 1869–1966, German philosopher and polit. writer.

foetid, *use* fe-.

foetor, *use* fe-.

foet/us, fully developed embryo in womb; **-al, -ation, -icide;** *not* fet- (except U.S.).

fog (naut.), abbr. **F.; thick —,** abbr. **F.F.**

foggy, misty.

fog/y, one with antiquated notions, *not* -ey, -ie; *pl.* **-ies.**

Föhn, Alpine south wind.

foie (Fr. m.), liver.

Fokine (Michel), 1880–1942, Russian-American choreographer.

fol., following.

fold, used as suffix close up (e.g. threefold).

folderol, *use* **falderal.**

foldstool, *use* **fald-.**

foliaceous, leaf-like, *not* -ious.

foliate, number folios consecutively.

Folies Bergère (ital.).

folio (typ.), a sheet of MS. or copy; the act of numbering; a page number; a book based on two leaves, four pages, to the basic sheet; *pl.* **-s;** abbr. **fo.**

foli/um (Lat.), a leaf; *pl.* **-a.**

folk-dance (hyphen).

Folketing, Danish Parliament; *not* -thing.

folklor/e, -ism, -ist, -istic (no hyphen).

folk-song (hyphen).

follic/le (bot.), small sac, *not* -cule; *but* **-ular, -ulated.**

following, abbr. **f.,** *or* **fol.**

fonda (Sp.), an inn.

fondant, a sweetmeat (not ital.).

fondue (Fr. cook. f.), melted cheese, eggs, etc., *not* fondu (ital.).

fons et origo (Lat.), source and origin.

font (Amer. typ.), Eng. **fount.**

Fontainebleau, dép. Seine-et-Marne.

Fonteyn (Dame Margot), b. 1919, English prima ballerina, m. Dr. Roberto Emilio de Arias (of Panama).

foodstuff (one word).

foolscap, former standard size of paper, $17 \times 13\frac{1}{2}$ in.; — 4to, $8\frac{1}{2} \times 6\frac{3}{4}$ in.; — 8vo, $6\frac{3}{4} \times 4\frac{1}{4}$ in. (untrimmed). *See* **book sizes.**

foot, in metric system 30·48 centimetres; *pl.* **feet,** one and a half *foot,* etc., *not* feet until two are reached; abbr. **ft** (no point), sign ′.

foot-and-mouth disease (hyphens), abbr. **F.M.D.**

football (one word).

Foot-guards (in order of precedence), the Grenadier, Coldstream, Scots, Irish, Welsh Guards (hyphen); abbr. **F.G.**

foot/hills, -hold (one word).

foothook (naut.), *use* **futtock.**

footlights (one word).

foot-loose (hyphen).

footnotes, in MS. should be written either at the bottom of the folio or on a separate sheet, with reference figures for identification; (typ.) all references in text to be by superior figures outside the punctuation mark or quote (except in specified instances); separate footnotes from text with a space. In math. works use † ‡, etc., to avoid confusion. *See also* **reference marks.**

foot/sore, -stool (one word).

for., foreign, forestry.

f.o.r., free on rail, *not* caps.

foram/en (anat., bot.), an orifice; *pl.* **-ina.**

forasmuch (one word).

foray, a raid, *not* forr-.

forbade, *not* -bad.

for/bear, to abstain; **-bore, -borne.**

Forbes-Robertson (Sir Johnston), 1853–1937, English actor.

force majeure (Fr. f.), circumstances beyond one's control.

forcemeat, meat finely chopped and seasoned, *not* forced- (one word).

forceps, surgical pincers; *pl. same.*

forcible, *not* -eable.

Ford (Ford Madox), orig. surname **Hueffer**, 1873–1939, English writer.

forearm, noun and verb (one word).

forebear, ancestor, *also spelt* **forbear**.

forecast.

forecastle, *also* **fo'c'sle.**

foreclose.

foredge (bind.), the edge of a book opposite the binding, *not* fore- (*see also* **margins**).

fore-edge (hyphen in non-technical uses).

fore-end, *not* forend.

Forefathers' Day (U.S.), anniversary of landing of the Pilgrims at Plymouth, Mass., 21 Dec. 1620, usu. celebrated on 22 Dec.

forefinger (one word).

foregather, use **forg-**.

forego, to go before (**foregone** conclusion, the **foregoing** facts); **forgo**, to abstain from, relinquish, etc.

forehead.

foreign, abbr. **for.**

Foreign and Commonwealth Office, formed, 1968, from the two separate Offices; abbr. **F.C.O.**

Foreign/ Mission, abbr. **F.M.;** — **Office** (caps.), abbr. **F.O.**, combined, 1968, with the Commonwealth Office.

forel, vellum-like covering for books, *not* forr-.

foreleg (one word).

fore-run (hyphen), *but* **forerunner.**

fore/said, -see, -shorten, -sight, -stall, *not* for- (one word).

Forester (Cecil Scott), 1899–1966, English novelist.

foretell, *not* fort-, fortel.

for ever, for one's lifetime, for eternity (two words); **forever**, continually (one word).

forewarn, *not* for- (one word).

forfeit.

forfend, avert, *not* fore-.

forgather, *not* fore-.

forget-me-not (bot.).

forgett/able, -ing.

forgivable, *not* -eable.

forgo, to abstain from, relinquish, etc.; **forego**, to go before.

formalin, a germicide or preservative, *not* -ine.

forma pauperis (in) (Lat.), as a pauper.

format (typ.), the size and layout for a book (not ital.).

forme (typ.), a body of type secured in the frame called a chase, *not* form.

former, correlative of *latter.*

formul/a, *pl.* **-as**, (scient.) **-ae** (not ital.); abbr. **F.**

fornent (Sc.), facing, *not* -nst.

forray, use **foray.**

forsaid, *use* fore-.

Fors Clavigera, by Ruskin.

Forster (John), 1812–76, English biographer; — **(E. M.)**, 1879–1970, English novelist.

forsw/ear, -ore, -orn.

Fort, cap. F when with name, as Fort Southwick, Tilbury Fort; abbr. **Ft.**

fort., fortification, fortified.

forte, person's strong point (not ital.).

forte/ (mus.), strong and loud, abbr. *f*; — *-piano*, loud, then immediately soft, abbr. *fp*; — *-possibile*, as loud as possible.

fortell, use fore-.

fortissimo, very loud; abbr. *ff*.

fortississimo, as loud as possible; abbr. *fff*.

fortiter in re (Lat.), bravely in action. *See suaviter in modo.*

Fortsetzung/ folgt (Ger.), to be continued, abbr. *F.f.*: — *und Schluss folgen* (Ger.), to be continued and concluded, abbr. *F.u.S.f.*

forty-eightmo (typ.), a book based on forty-eight leaves, ninety-six pages, to the basic sheet; abbr. **48mo** (no point).

forzando (mus.), forced; abbr. *fz. See sforzando.*

f.o.s., free on station, *not* caps.

foss/a (anat.), a cavity; *pl.* **-ae.**

fosse, a ditch, *not* foss.

fossilize, *not* -ise.

Foster (Birket), 1825–99, English painter; — **(John),** 1770–1843, English essayist (*see also* **Forster**); — **(Stephen Collins),** 1826–64, American song writer; — **(Sir Harry Hylton-),** *see* **Hylton-Foster.**

f.o.t., free on truck, free of tax.

Foucault (John Bernard Léon), 1819–68, French physicist.

Foulahs, use Fulahs.

foulard, a fabric (not ital.).

foully.

foul proof (typ.), a proof-reader's marked proof, as opposed to the corrected (or clean) proof which succeeds it.

foumart, a polecat, *not* foul-.

foundry, *not* -ery; — **proof,** final proof from type which has been prepared for plating.

fount (typ.), a complete set of type of one particular face and size; in Amer. font.

Fouqué (Friedrich, Baron de la Motte), 1777–1843, German poet and dramatist.

Fouquet (Jean), 1416–80, French painter; — **(Nicolas),** 1615–80, French statesman; *not* Foucq-.

four-colour process (typ.), printing in yellow, magenta, cyan, and black to give a complete colour reproduction.

fourfold (one word).

Fourier (François Marie Charles), 1772–1837, French socialist, hence **Fourier/ism, -ist, -ite;** — **(Jean Baptiste Joseph),** 1768–1850, French mathematician and physicist, hence **Fourier series.**

four-poster, four-post bed.

Fourth of July, U.S. Independence Day (caps.).

Fourth of June, George III's birthday. Eton's great day.

Fowler (F. G.), 1870–1918, English lexicographer; — **(H. W.),** 1858–1933, English lexicographer, author of *Modern English Usage* and joint-author, with brother F. G., of *The King's English.*

Fox (Charles James), 1749–1806, English politician; — **(George),** 1624–91, English preacher, founder of Society of Friends (Quakers).

Foxe (John), 1516–87, martyrologist.

foxed paper, stained with yellowish-brown spots.

foxhound (one word).

foyer, theatre lounge (not ital.).

F.P., Fine Paper (the best edition of a work); fire-plug; (Scot.) former pupil(s).

f.p., freezing-point.

fp (mus.), *forte-piano*, loud, then soft.

F.P.A., Foreign Press Association, Franklin P. Adams (Amer. humorist).

f.p.a., free of particular average.

F.Ph.S., Fellow of the Philosophical Society of England.

F.Phy.S., Fellow of the Physical Society.

F.P.S., Fellow of the Pharmaceutical Society of Great Britain.

F.R., *Forum Romanum* (the Roman Forum).

Fr (chem.), francium (no point).

Fr., Father, France, French, Friar, Friday; (Ger.) Frau (Mrs., wife); (It.) *Fratelli* (Brothers).

fr., fragment, franc, from, (Ger.) *frei* (free).

fra (It.), brother, friar (no point).

fracas, noisy quarrel; *pl. same* (not ital.).

fractionize, *not* -ise.

fractions (typ.), spell out simple fractions in textual matter, e.g. one-half, two-thirds, three-quarters; hyphenate compounded numeral in compound fractions such as nine thirty-seconds, forty-seven sixty-fourths; in statistical matter use one-piece fractions where available ($\frac{1}{2}$, $\frac{2}{3}$, $\frac{3}{4}$, etc.), but if these are not available use **split fractions,** i.e. those with dividing line attached to denominators and the numerator justified above it, e.g. nineteen hundredths, $\frac{19}{100}$. *See also* **figures.**

fractions, decimal (typ.), centred point, not on the line.

F.R.A.D., Fellow of the Royal Academy of Dancing.

F.R.Ag.Ss., Fellow of the Royal Agricultural Societies.

F.R.A.I., Fellow of the Royal Anthropological Institute.

frais (Fr. m. pl.), cost, expenses; (adj.) fresh.

Fraktur (typ.), German name for German style of black letter, as Fraftur

F.R.A.M., Fellow of the Royal Academy of Music.

framable, *not* -eable.

framboise (Fr. f.), raspberry.

franc (Fr. m.), coin (not ital.); abbr. **f.** *or* **fr.,** *pl.* **f.** *or* **frs.,** to be put *after* the figures, as 10 f. 50 c., or 10.50 fr.

française (*à la*) (Fr.), in the French style, *not* cap. F.

France, abbr. **Fr.**

franchise, the right to vote, *not* -ize.

francium (chem.), symbol **Fr** (no point).

Franck (César), 1822–90, Belgian-born French organist and composer.

Franco (Francisco, General), 1892– , Spanish head of state 1939– .

franc-tireur (Fr. m.), an irregular sharp-shooter; *pl.* ***francs-tireurs.***

frangipane, an almond paste, cream, or cake (from its inventor Frangipani).

frangipani, W. Indian red jasmine, and the perfume of it.

Frankenstein (in Mary Shelley's novel), the maker of the monster which destroyed him, *not* the monster.

Frankfort, Ind. and Ky. (U.S.).

Frankfurt/-on-Main, — -on-Oder, Germany; Ger. **Frankfurt/am Main, am Oder** (no hyphens).

frankfurter, American small smoked sausage, of German origin.

Frankfurter Zeitung, German newspaper, *not* Frankfor-, -für-.

Franz Josef Land, Arctic Ocean (U.S.S.R.).

frappant (Fr.), striking, affecting.

frappé (Fr.), iced.

F.R.A.S., Fellow of the Royal Astronomical Society, ditto Asiatic Society; note **F.R.Ae.S.,** ditto Aeronautical Society,

Fraser, family name of Barons Lovat and Saltoun. *See also* **Frazer.**

Fraser River, Brit. Columbia.

Fraser's Magazine.

frat/e (It.), a friar; *pl. -i.*

fraternize, *not* -ise.

Frau (Ger. f.), Mrs., wife, *not* Frau; *pron.* frow; abbr. **Fr.;** *pl.* **Frauen.**

Fräulein (Ger. n.), Miss, unmarried lady, *pron.* froi'-:līn; *pl. same;* abbr. **Frl.**

Frazer (Sir James George), 1854–1941, English anthropologist. *See also* **Fraser.**

F.R.B.S., Fellow of the Royal Botanic Society; Fellow of the Royal Society of British Sculptors.

F.R.C.G.P., Fellow of the Royal College of General Practitioners.

F.R.C.M., Fellow of the Royal College of Music.

F.R.C.O., Fellow of the Royal College of Organists.

F.R.C.O.G., Fellow of the Royal College of Obstetricians and Gynaecologists.

F.R.C.P., Fellow of the Royal College of Physicians, London.

F.R.C.Path., Fellow of the Royal College of Pathologists.

F.R.C.S., Fellow of the Royal College of Surgeons, England.

F.R.C.V.S., Fellow of the Royal College of Veterinary Surgeons, London.

Freacadan Dubh (Gael.), Black Watch (regiment).

F.R.Econ.Soc., Fellow of the Royal Economic Society.

Fred., Frederic, Frederick. When it is the full name, or a diminutive of familiarity, it takes no point.

Frédérick, stage name of A. L. P. Lemaître, q.v.

Frederictown, New Brunswick, Canada, *not* -ck-.

free/ of all average, abbr. **f.a.a.;** — **general average, f.g.a.;** — **particular average, f.p.a.;** — **alongside ship, f.a.s.;** — **on board, f.o.b.;** — **on rail, f.o.r.;** — **on station, f.o.s.**

freedman, an emancipated slave; **freeman,** one to whom the freedom of a city has been given.

free/-thinker, — -thought (hyphens).

free will, the power of self-determination (two words); **freewill** (adj., one word).

freeze, to convert to ice. *See also* **frieze.**

freezing-point, abbr. **f.p.**

frei (Ger.), free; abbr. *fr.*

Freiberg, Saxony, Germany.

Freiburg/ im Breisgau, Baden, Germany; Ger. abbr. — **i.B.**

Freiburg, Switzerland, *use* **Fribourg.**

Freiherr, Ger. title; abbr. *Frhr.*

Freischütz (Der), opera by Weber, 1819.

freize, erron. for **frieze.**

Fremantle, W. Australia, *not* Free-.

French, abbr. **Fr.;** (typ.), alphabet as English. There are strict rules for capitalization, division of words, and spacing, etc. The following must suffice here, but reference to *Hart's Rules* is strongly recommended. Division of words is according to spoken syllables, rarely etymology: single consonant goes with following vowel, including consonant+*r* or +*l*; take over *gn* (e.g. *sei-gneur*); doubled consonants may be divided. No caps. for adjectives of nationality, the first pers. pronoun, days of week, months, names of cardinal points, names indicating rank, as *anglais, je, lundi, mars, le nord, le duc.* **Accents: acute** (´) used only over *e*; when two *e*'s come together the first always has acute accent, as *née*; **grave** (ˋ) used over *a, e, u*; **circumflex** (^) used over any vowel. **Cedilla c** (ç) used only before *a, o, u.* **Diaeresis** as in Eng.; the digraph *æ* is not to be separated (e.g. *Œuvre, cœur*). **Quotation marks** are usu. *guillemets* (« »), though rules are more commonly used in conversational passages.

french chalk (*not* cap.).

French groove (bind.), extra space between board and spine.

frenchified, French-like (not cap.).

french polish/, -er, — windows (two words, not cap.).

frenetic, *use* ph-.

frenum, *use* **frae-.**

frenzy, *not* ph-.

freq., frequent, -ly, -ative.

frère (Fr. m.), brother, friar.

fresco/, water-colour done on damp plaster; *pl.* **-es** (not ital.).

freshwater, adjective (one word), noun (two words).

Fresnel (Augustin Jean), 1788–1827, French physicist.

Freud (Sigmund), 1856– 1939, Austrian neurologist and founder of psycho-analysis; adj. **Freudian.**

F.R.G.S., Fellow of the Royal Geographical Society.

F.R.Hist.Soc., Fellow of the Royal Historical Society.

Frhr. (Ger.), *Freiherr* (a title).

F.R.H.S., Fellow of the Royal Horticultural Society.

Fri., Friday.

friar's balsam, tincture of benzoin, *not* s'.

F.R.I.B.A., Fellow of the Royal Institute of British Architects (*pl.* **FF.**).

F.R.I.C., Fellow of the Royal Institute of Chemistry.

F.R.I.C.S., Fellow of the Royal Institution of Chartered Surveyors.

Fribourg, Switzerland, *not* Frei-.

fricandeau/, braised and larded fillet of veal; *pl.* **-x** (not ital.).

fricassee, a white stew (not ital., no accent).

Friday, abbr. **F.,** or **Fri.;** (astr.) sign ♀.

frier, one who fries, *use* **fryer.**

frier (typ.), light patch of inking.

Friesian, breed of cattle, *not* Fris-.

frieze, cloth, also part below cornice, *not* frei-.

F.R.I.P.H.H., Fellow of the Royal Institute of Public Health and Hygiene.

frip/ier (Fr.), *fem.* **-ière,** dealer in **-erie** (f.), old clothes and furniture.

frippery, tawdry finery.

Fris., Frisia (Friesland, in Netherlands), Frisian. *See* **Friesian.**

fris/ette, curls on forehead, *not* friz-; **-eur,** hairdresser; **-ure,** mode of hairdressing.

frit/ (Fr. cook.), *fem.* **-e,** fried.

frizz, to roughen, curl, *not* friz.

Frl. (Oer.), Fräulein (Miss).

F.R.M.C.S., Fellow of the Royal Medical and Chirurgical Society.

F.R.Met.S., Fellow of the Royal Meteorological Society.

F.R.M.S., Fellow of the Royal Microscopical Society.

F.R.N.S., Fellow of the Royal Numismatic Society.

F.R.N.S.A., Fellow of the Royal Navy School of Architects.

fro (no point).

Froebel (**Friedrich W. A.**), 1782–1852, German educationist, founder of kindergarten system.

frolic/, -ked, -king.

fromage (Fr. m.), cheese.

Fronde, French rebel party during minority of Louis XIV.

Frontignac, a muscat grape or wine (not ital.).

frontispiece (typ.), illus. facing title-page (one word).

Froude (**James A.**), 1818–94, English historian.

Froufrou, comedy by Meilhac and Halévy.

frou-frou, a rustling of dress (not ital.).

frowsty, musty, stuffy.

frowzy, unkempt, slatternly.

F.R.P.S., Fellow of the Royal Photographic Society.

F.R.S., Fellow of the Royal Society, in Lat. **S.R.S.** (*Societatis Regiae Sodalis*).

frs., francs.

F.R.S.A., Fellow of the Royal Society of Arts.

F.R.S.H., Fellow of the Royal Society for the Promotion of Health, *formerly* **F.R.San.I.,** Fellow of the Royal Sanitary Institute.

F.R.S.L., Fellow of the Royal Society of Literature.

F.R.S.M., Fellow of the Royal Society of Medicine.

F.R.S.T., Fellow of the Royal Society of Teachers.

frumenty, boiled wheat with milk, sugar, etc., *not* the many variations.

frust/um (geom.), lower portion of intersected cone or pyramid; *pl.* **-a;** *not* -rum.

F.R.V.A., Fellow of the Incorporated Association of Rating and Valuation Officers.

fryer, one who fries, *not* frier.

F.S. (Fr.), *faire suivre* (to be forwarded).

F.S.A., Fellow of the Society of Antiquaries.

F.S.A.A., Fellow of the Society of Incorporated Accountants and Auditors.

F.S.E., Fellow of the Society of Engineers.

F.S.I., Fellow of the Surveyors' Institution.

F.S.S., Fellow of the Royal Statistical Society.

F.S.S.U., Federated Superannuation Scheme for Universities.

F.S.V.A., Fellow of the Incorporated Society of Valuers and Auctioneers.

Ft., fort.

ft., feint (paper), flat, fortified.

ft (no point), foot, feet.

F.T.C.D., Fellow of Trinity College, Dublin.

F.T.C.L., Fellow of Trinity College (of Music), London.

F.T.I., Fellow of the Textile Institute.

fuchsia (bot.) (not ital.).

fuc/us (Lat.), a seaweed; *pl.* **-i.**

Fuehrer (Ger.), *use* **Führer.**

fuelled, *not* -eled.

fugleman, leader in mil. exercises, *not* flugel-, flugle-, fugal-, fugel-.

fug/ue (mus.) (not ital.); adj. **-al.**

Führer, leader, title assumed by Hitler in Nazi Germany.

Fujiyama, mt., Japan, *properly* **Fujisan,** *not* Fusi-.

Fulahs, Sudanese, *not* Felláh, Fellani, Feulhs, Foulahs, Fulbe. *See also* **fellah.**

fulcr/um, point of purchase for lever; *pl.* **-a** (not ital.).

fulfil/, -led, -ling, -ment.

fulgor, splendour, *not* -gour.

full-bound (bind.), completely cased in the same material (hyphen).

fullness, *not* fulness.

full out (typ.), set to margin of column or page.

full point (typ.), the **full stop** or **period.** *See* **punctuation V.**

fulmar, a petrel.

fulsome, excessive and cloying, *not* full-.

fumatory, a place for smoking. *See also* **fumi-.**

fumigator, *not* -er.

fumitory (bot.), a plant. *See also* **fuma-.**

function (math.), abbr. F (no point).

fung/us, *pl.* **-i; fungous** (adj.) (not ital.).

funny-bone (humerus) (hyphen).

fuoco (mus.), fire, passion.

fur., furlong.

für (Ger.) for; abbr. **f.**

furbelow, a flounce, *not* -llow.

furfur/, dandruff; adj. **-aceous.**

furlong, eighth of mile; abbr. **f.,** *or* **fur.**

furmenty, *use* fru-.

Furness (Christopher, Baron), 1852–1912, shipping magnate; — **(Horace H.),** 1833–1912, American Shakespearian scholar; — **(Horace H.)** 1865–1930, son of above, also a Shakespearian scholar.

Furniss (Harry), 1854–1925, caricaturist.

furniture (typ.), spacing material.

Furnivall (Frederick J.), 1825–1910, English philologist.

furor (Lat.), rage (ital.).

furore (It.), enthusiastic admiration (not ital.).

furry, fur-like.

Fürst von Bismarck, *see* **Bismarck.**

further, use as the comparative of far (*not* **farther**).

Furtwängler (Wilhelm), 1886–1954, German conductor.

fusain, artists' fine charcoal crayon.

fus/e, -ee, fuselage, *not* fuz-.

F.u.S.f. (Ger.), *Fortsetzung und Schluss folgen* (to be continued and concluded).

fusible, *not* -able.

fusil, musket, *not* -zil.

fusilier, *not* -leer.

fusillade, *not* -ilade.

Fusiyama, mt., Japan, *use* **Fujiyama.**

fut., future.

futhorc, runic alphabet, *not* -ark, -ork.

futtock (naut.), one of ship's middle timbers, *not* foot-hook, -oak.

fuz/e, -ee, -il, *use* **fus-.**

f.v., *folio verso* (on the back of the page).

fv^{da} (Sp.), *favorecida* (esteemed).

F.W.A., Factories and Workshops Act, Family Welfare Association.

F.W.B., Free Will Baptists.

fylfot, the swastika, *not* fil-.

Fyzabad, Uttar Pradesh (India), *not* Faizabad.

F.Z.S., Fellow of the Zoological Society.

G

G, the seventh in a series.

G., Grand, Gulf, (naval) gunnery, all proper names with this initial.

g., guinea, -s, (Fr.), *gauche* (left), *gros/, -se* (big), (naut.) gloomy.

g (no point), gramme(s), (dyn.) local gravitational acceleration. *See also* **gn.**

G.A., General Assembly (Sc. Ch.).

Ga., Gallic, Georgia, U.S. (off.).

Ga (chem.), gallium (no point).

gabbro/ (geol.), an igneous rock; *pl.* **-s.**

gaberdine, a loose cloak, *not* gaba-.

Gaboon, W. Africa, indep. rep. 1960.

Gaboriau (Émile), 1835–73, French novelist.

gaby, a simpleton, *not* -ey, gabbey, gawby.

Gadarene swine.

Gaddi, family of Florentine painters, 1259–1396.

Gadhel/, a Gael of the Irish, Highland Scottish, Manx branch; adj. **-ic.**

Gaditanian, of Cadiz, SW. Spain.

gadolinium, symbol **Gd** (no point).

Gadshill, Charles Dickens's residence 1860–70 (one word).

Gaekwar, title of prince of Baroda, India, *not* Gaik-.

Gaelic/, abbr. **Gael.;** — alphabet, same as English, but no *j, k, q, v, w, x, y, z.*

Gagarin (Yuri Alekseyevich), 1934–68, Russian cosmonaut, first to orbit earth, 1961.

gage, a, *or* to, pledge. *See also* **gauge.**

gage d'amour (Fr. m.), love-token.

gaieté de cœur (Fr. f.), light-heartedness (*not* gaîté).

gaiety, *not* gay-.

Gaikwar (title), *use* **Gaek-.**

gaillardia (bot.), a plant.

gaily, *not* gayly.

Gairdner (James), 1828– 1912, English historian; — (Sir W. T.), 1824–1907, English physician. *See also* **Gard.**

gairfish, *use* garfish.

gairfowl, *use* gare-fowl.

Gair Loch, Dunbarton, *use* Gare —.

Gairloch, Ross and Cromarty, *not* Gare-.

Gal., Galatians.

gal., gallon, -s.

gala/, festive occasion; *pl.* **-s** (not ital.).

galantine, white meat served cold in jelly, *not* gall-.

Galantuomo (Il Re), King Victor Emmanuel I of Italy.

galanty show, a shadow pantomime, *not* -tee, gallantee, -ty.

Galatea (Acis and).

Galati, Romania, *not* -acz, -atch, -atz.

Galatia, Asia Minor.

galavant, *use* galli-.

gale (met.), wind moving 40–70 miles per hour.

galena, lead ore, *not* -aena.

galera (Sp. typ.), a galley.

galère (Fr. f.), galley (ship); *qu'allait-il faire dans cette* —? (how did he get into this scrape?).

Galilean, of Galilee, or of Galileo.

Galileo [Galilei], 1564–1642, Italian astronomer and mathematician; in Fr. *Galilée,* It. *Galilei.*

galingale, a sedge with medicinal root, *not* gala-.

galiot, a vessel, *use* **gall-.**

galipot, a resin. *See also* **gall-.**

gallanty show, *use* gala-.

gallaway, *see* **gallo-.**

gall-bladder (hyphen).

Galle (Point de), Ceylon.

gallery, in Fr. *galerie,* f.

Galles (Fr. f. sing.), Wales; adj. *gallois/, fem. -e.*

galley/ (typ.), a flat oblong tray for holding composed type; — **proofs,** those supplied in 'slips' about 18 in. long (i.e. impressions taken from type on galleys). *See* **proof.**

Gallic, of Gaul, French; abbr. **Ga.**

gallice (Lat.), in French.

gallicize, to make Gallic or French, *not* -ise.

Galli-Curci (Amelita), 1889–1963, Italian soprano.

galligaskins, *pl.,* breeches, *not* -in.

gallimaufry, a medley.

Gallio, a typical sceptic (Acts 18: 7).

galliot (U.S. **gali-**), Dutch cargo-boat.

Gallipoli, S. Italy, Turkey.

gallipot, a small jar. *See also* **gal-.**

gallium, symbol **Ga** (no point).

gallivant, to gad about, *not* gala-, gali-.

gallon/, -s, abbr. **gal.**

galloon, a dress trimming.

gallop/, a horse's movement; **-ed, -er, -ing.** *See also* **galop.**

Gallop (Dr. George), founded American Institute of Public Opinion, 1936.

gallopade, Hungarian dance, *not* galop-, gallopp-.

Gallovidian, of Galloway.

Galloway, SW. Scot.

galloway, a horse, *also* breed of cattle, *not* galla-.

gallows, treated as sing.

galoot, an awkward fellow, *not* gall-, geel-.

galop, a dance. *See also* **gallop.**

galore, in abundance.

galosh/, an overshoe, *not* -oche, -oeshoe, -oshe, goloshe; **-ed;** in boot-trade **golosh.**

galumph, to gallop triumphantly.

galv., galvan/ic, -ism.

Galvani (Luigi), 1737–98, discoverer of galvanism.

galvanize, *not* -ise.

Galway, W. Ireland.

Galwegian, of Galloway.

Gama (Vasco da), 1467–1524, Portuguese navigator, first round Africa to India.

Gambia, W. Africa, independent, 1965.

gambier, a gum, *not* -beer, -bir.

gambit, chess opening in which pawn or piece is risked to obtain attacking position.

gamboge, yellow pigment, *not* -booze.

gambol/, to frisk; **-led, -ling** (U.S. **-ed, -ing**).

gamekeeper (one word).

gamin/, a street arab, f. **-e** (not ital.).

gammon, a cured ham, *not* gamon.

gamy, having the flavour or scent of game left till high, *not* -ey.

Gand, Fr. for **Ghent,** Belgium.

Gandhi, Mohandas (Mahatma Gandhi), 1869–1948, Indian nationalist leader.

Gandhi (Mrs. Indira), *b.* 1917, Prime Minister of India 1966– , daughter of Pandit Nehru, not related to preceding.

gangli/on, a knot on a nerve; *pl.* **-a.**

gangue, rock or earth in which ore is found; *pron.* gang.

gangway (one word).

ganister, a hard stone, *not* gann-.

gantlet, *use* **gaun-.**

gantry, platform to carry travelling crane, etc.

Ganymede (Gr. myth.), cupbearer to the gods.

gaol/, -er, *preferred to* **jail/, -er.** *See also* **goal.**

Garamond (Claude), 1496–1561, French letter-cutter.

Garay (János), 1812–53, Hungarian poet.

Garcilaso de la Vega, 1503–36, Spanish poet; — — ('the Inca'), 1540–1616, Spanish historian.

garçon (Fr. m.), bachelor, boy, waiter (ital.).

Garde nationale (Fr.), national guard (l.c. *n*).

gardenia (bot.), an ornamental shrub (not ital.).

Gardens, abbr. **Gdns.**

Gardiner (Samuel Rawson), 1829–1902, historian; — (**Stephen**), 1483–1555, Bp. of Winchester. *See also* **Gair-.**

Gardner (E. A.), 1862–1939, archaeologist; — (**Percy**), 1846–1937, archaeologist. *See also* **Gair-.**

gardyloo, 'beware slops' (Edinburgh).

gare (Fr. f.), railway station.

gare-fowl, the great auk, *not* gair-, gar- (hyphen).

Gare Loch, Dunbarton, *not* Gair —.

Gareloch, Ross and Cromarty, *use* **Gair-.**

garfish, similar to pike, *not* gair-, gare-.

gargantuan, enormous (not cap.).

gargoyle (arch.), grotesque spout, *not* -ile, -oil.

Garhwal, Uttar Pradesh, India.

gari, *use* **gharry.**

garish, gaudy, *not* gair-.

garlic, *but* **garlicky.**

garnet, red precious stone.

Garnet (Henry), 1555–1606, of the Gunpowder Plot.

Garnett (Dr. Richard), 1835–1906, English author and librarian.

garn/i (Fr.), *fem.* **-ie,** furnished.

garron, small horse, Irish or Scottish, *not* -an.

garrott/e, to throttle; **-er,** *not* -ote, garotte.

Garter King-of-Arms, herald, *not* -at-.

gas (U.S. colloq.), gasoline (Eng. petrol).

gasconade, boasting, to boast, *not* gasconn-.

gaselier, gas chandelier, *not* gasa-, gaso-.

gaseous.

Gaskell (Mrs. Elizabeth Cleghorn), 1810–65, English novelist.

gasogene, *use* **gazo-.**

Gaspé, peninsula (Quebec prov.).

gast/eropod (U.S. **-ropod**), any member of the **Gast/eropoda** (U.S. **-ropoda**), mollusc class (not ital.).

Gast/haus (Ger. n.), an inn; *pl.* **-häuser** (cap.).

Gast/hof (Ger. m.), an hotel; *pl.* **-höfe** (cap.).

gastronome, a judge of good eating (not ital.).

gât/é (Fr.), *fem.* **-ée,** spoiled.

gâteau (Fr. m.), a cake.

gate/-keeper, — **-post** (hyphens).

gateway (one word).

gather (bind.), to collect the printed and folded sections in sequence.

GATT, General Agreement on Tariffs and Trade.

gauch/e, awkward; **-erie,** awkwardness (not ital.).

gauche (Fr.), left; abbr. **g.** (ital.).

gaucho/, a mounted herdsman, native of the pampas, *not* gua-; *pl.* **-s.**

Gaudichaud (C.), 1789–1864, botanist; abbr. **Gaud.**

gaudy, college-students' merry-making; (adj.) showy.

gauffer, *use* goffer.

gaug/e, a measure; **-ing,** *not* guage. *See also* **gage.**

Gauguin (Paul), 1848–1903, French painter.

Gaul, anc. France; adj. **Gallic,** (Fr.) *gaulois/,* fem. **-e.**

gauntlet/, a long glove, *not* gant-; **-ed.**

gauntr/ee, -y, *use* gantry.

gaur, Indian ox (not ital.).

Gauss (J. Karl Friedrich), 1777–1855, German mathematician and physicist.

Gauss constant (astron.), *k.* (with point).

Gautama Buddha, founder of Buddhism.

gauzy, *not* -ey.

gavel, a president's mallet.

gavotte, a dance or music.

gawby, *use* gaby.

Gay-Lussac (Joseph Louis), 1778–1850, French chemist and physicist.

gaz., gazett/e, -ed, -eer.

gazebo/, summer-house, belvedere; *pl.* **-s.**

gazel, *use* ghazal.

gazelle, antelope, *not* -el.

gazett/e, -ed, -eer, abbr. **gaz.**

gazogene, aerated-water apparatus, *not* -en, gasogene (not ital.).

gazump, to raise proposed purchase price before completion.

G.B., Great Britain.

G.B.E., Knight *or* Dame Grand Cross of Brit. Empire.

G.B. & I., Great Britain and Ireland.

gbr. (German), *gebräuchlich* (usual).

G.B.S. (George Bernard Shaw, 1856–1950), Irish-born British dramatist and critic.

G.C., George Cross.

G.C.A., Ground Controlled Approach (radar).

G.C.B., Knight Grand Cross of the Bath.

G.C.C., Gonville and Caius College, Cambridge.

g.c.d. (U.S.), greatest common divisor.

G.C.E., General Certificate of Education.

G.C.F., *or* **g.c.f.** (math.), greatest common factor.

G.C.I., Ground Controlled Interception (radar).

G.C.L.H., Grand Cross of the Legion of Honour.

G.C.M., general court martial.

G.C.M., *or* **g.c.m.** (math.), greatest common measure.

G.C.M.G., Knight Grand Cross of St. Michael and St. George.

G.C.S.I., Knight Grand Commander of the Star of India.

G.C.V.O., Knight Grand Cross of the Royal Victorian Order.

G.D., Grand Duchess, — Duchy, — Duke.

Gd (chem.), gadolinium (no point).

Gdns., Gardens.

Gdsm., Guardsman.

Ge (chem.), germanium (no point).

g.e. (binding), gilt edges.

gear-box, -change, -lever (hyphens).

gearshift, (U.S., one word).

gear-wheel (hyphen).

geb. (Ger.), *geboren* (born), *gebunden* (bound).

gecko/, a house-lizard; *pl.* **-s.**

gee/-ho, — **-up,** call to horses, *not* je-.

geezer (slang), a quaint elderly person. *See also* **geyser.**

Geiger counter (in full, **Geiger-Müller counter**), instrument for detecting radioactivity.

Geisenheimer, a white Rhine wine.

geisha, Japanese dancing-girl; *pl. same; pron.* gā′-sha.

Geissler (Heinrich), 1814–79, German physicist, inventor of — vacuum tube. *See also* **Giesler.**

gelatine (U.S. **-in**).

gelatinize, *not* -ise.

Geld (Ger. n.), money (cap.).

Gelderland, E. Netherlands, *not* Guel-.

gelder rose, *use* gue- —.

gelée (Fr. f.), frost, jelly.

Gelée (Claude), *see* **Lorrain.**

Gelert, faithful dog of Welsh legend.

Gellert (Christian F.), 1715–69, German poet.

Gelsemium/ (bot.), *not* inum; *pl.* **-s.**

gem (typ.), old name for a size of type, about $3\frac{1}{2}$ pt.

gemel, finger-ring, hinge, etc., *not* gemew, gimbal, gimmal, gimmer.

Gemini (astr.), Castor and Pollux, symbol Ⅱ (not ital.).

gemm/a, a bud; *pl.* **-ae.**

gemsbok, S. African antelope, *not* -buck.

gemütlich (Ger.), leisurely, comfortably.

Gen., General, Genesis, Geneva.

gen., gender, genera, general, -ly, generic, genitive, genus.

gendarme/ (Fr. m.), *pl.* **-s.**

gendarmery, in Fr. f. *gendarmerie,* body of soldiers used as police.

gender, abbr. **gen.**

gên/e (Fr. f.), constraint; *-é, fem.* **-ée,** constrained.

gene/, the carrying unit of a cell, the unit of heredity; *pl.* **-s.**

genealogy, family's pedigree, *not* -ology.

genera, *see* **genus.**

General, abbr. **Gen.**

General Assembly (Sc. Ch.), abbr. **G.A.**

general election (not caps.).

generalia, general principles.

Generalissimo, supreme commander.

generalize, *not* -ise.

generator, *not* -er.

Genesis, abbr. **Gen.**

genes/is, *pl.* **-es.**

genet, kind of civet-cat. *See also* **jennet.**

Geneva, Switzerland, in Fr. **Genève,** Ger. **Genf;** adj. **Genevan; Genevese** (sing. and pl.), native(s) of —, in Fr. *genevois/, fem.* **-e**(**s**).

Geneviève (Sainte), patron of Paris.

Genghis Khan, 1162–1227, Mongol conqueror of N. China and Iran.

gen/ie, a spirit in Muslim myth., *pl.* **-ii;** *also written* **jinnee,** *pl.* **jinn.**

genitive, abbr. **gen.** *or* **genit.**

genius/, (person of) consummate intellectual power; *pl.* **-es** (genii is pl. of genie).

genius loci (Lat.), the pervading spirit of a place.

Gennesaret (Sea of), *not* -eth.

Genoa, Italy; in Fr. **Gênes,** It. **Genova;** adj. **Geno/ese,** *not* -vese.

genocide, deliberate extermination of a race.

genre (art), a painting of the ordinary scenes of life (not ital.).

gens (Lat.), a clan; *pl. gentes*.

Gens de Lettres (*Société des*), French society of authors.

Gensfleisch, *see* Gutenberg.

gent., gentle/man, -men.

genteel, fashionable, snobbishly refined.

Gentle's green, a colour.

gentil/ (Fr.), *fem. -le,* gentle; *pron.* zhahn·tē.

Gentile, anyone not a Jew (cap.).

gentilhomme (Fr. m.), nobleman, gentleman; *pl. gentilshommes*.

gentleman/-at-arms; — -at-large (hyphens); **— of the Chapel Royal,** a lay singer there (no hyphen).

Gentleman's Magazine, (*not* -en's).

genuflexion, a bending of the knee (U.S. **-ction**).

genus, *pl.* **genera,** abbr. **gen.** *See also* **botany, zoology,** etc.

Geo., George.

geod., geode/sy (large-scale earth measurement), -tic.

Geoffroy Saint-Hilaire (Étienne), 1772–1844, French zoologist, *not* -frey (one hyphen only).

geog., geograph/er, -ical, -y.

Geoghegan, *pron.* gā′gan.

geographical qualifiers, used before nouns, as common everyday terms, usually have lower-case initials, as chinese white, indian ink, roman type. *But* Brussels sprouts, London pride.

geol., geolog/ical, -ist, -y.

geologize, *not* -ise.

geology, names of formations to have caps., as Old Red

Sandstone. *See also* **botany, capitalization, italic, zoology.**

geom., geome/ter, -trical, -try.

geometry, *see* **mathematics.**

Georg, Ger. for George.

Georgia, U.S.; abbr. **Ga.**

Georgia, a Soviet Socialist Republic. *See* **U.S.S.R.**

Georgium sidus (astr.), old name for Uranus.

Ger., German, Germany.

ger., gerund, -ial.

geranium/ (bot.), *pl.* **-s** (not ital.).

Gerard (John), 1545–1612, English botanist, *not* -arde.

Géricault (Jean Louis A. T.), 1791–1824, French painter.

gerkin, *use* ghe-.

German, abbr. **Ger.;** (typ.) same letters as English. There are elaborate rules for capitalization, division of words, compounding, etc. The following must here suffice. The German character is '*Fraktur*', the Roman '*Antiqua*'. Fraktur has no small caps. or italics, emphasis being given by interspacing each letter. *Ae, Oe, Ue,* except in some proper names, are now always rendered *Ä, Ö, Ü.* The ligatures *æ, œ,* are not generally used. *t* is now used for *th* in all but proper names and foreign words, as *Tal,* not *Thal, Rat,* not *Rath.* The plural of many words is formed by changing *a, o, u,* to *ä, ö, ü,* as *Vater* (father), *Väter* (fathers). Division of words is by sound, but prefixed nouns, prepositions, etc., remain intact, as *Erb/recht, hin/aus, ent/erben*; also suffixes beginning with a consonant, as *-chen, -keit, -lein, -ling,*

-nis. ALL NOUNS AND WORDS USED AS SUCH HAVE CAPITAL INITIALS. So also the personal pronouns of the second person, *Ihren, Ihr, Sie* (to you, your, you), and adjectives from names of places and persons, as *Leipziger Messe, Kantische Philosophie*; but adjectives of countries l.c., as *russische Sprache, deutsche Industrie.*
In roman type ß is generally rendered ß. Quotation marks are two straight commas before and two turned at end, „and", or as in French. Spacing (thin spaces) is to be observed in abbreviations (e.g. **d. h., z. B.**) and also before and after metal rules. Reference to *Hart's Rules* and Duden, *Rechtschreibung*, is recommended.

german (cousin-).

germane to, relevant.

germanium, symbol **Ge** (no point).

germanize, *not* -ise.

Germany, abbr. **Ger.**

Gérôme (Jean Léon), 1824–1904, French painter.

gerrymander, to manipulate unfairly, *not* je-.

Ges. (Ger.), *Gesellschaft* (a company or society) (cap.).

Gesellschaft (Ger. f.), a company or society (cap.), abbr. ***Ges.***

gest. (Ger.), *gestorben,* deceased.

***Gestalt*/** (Ger. f.), the whole as more than the sum of its parts; *pl. -en*; also used as adj. to describe philosophy or psychology based on this.

Gestapo, German secret police (under Hitler).

Gesta Romanorum (Lat.), medieval collection of anecdotes.

gesticulator, one who moves

his hands and arms in talking, *not* -er.

gestorben (Ger.), deceased; abbr. ***gest.***, sign †.

get-at-able (hyphens).

Gettysburg (battle of), Pennsylvania, 1863.

Geulinex (Arnold), 1625–69, Dutch philosopher.

Gewandhaus (Ger. n.), Clothworkers' Hall, concert-hall in Leipzig.

gewgaw (one word), gaudy plaything.

geyser, hot spring (not ital.); Icelandic *properly* ***geysir***, *pron.* gā·sĭr. *See also* **geezer.**

G.F.S., Girls' Friendly Society.

G.G., Girl Guides, Grenadier Guards.

Gg, gigagramme (gramme × 10⁹).

g.gr., a great gross, or 144 dozen.

Ghana, *formerly* Gold Coast Colony, independent 1957, republic 1960; adj. and subst. **Ghanaian.**

gharry, a vehicle in India.

ghat (Anglo-Ind.), mountain pass, steps to a river, *not* ghât, ghát, ghaut.

ghazal, Persian and Arabic poetic metre, *not* ga-, -zel, -sel, -zul.

Gheel, Belgian commune long celebrated for its treatment of the mentally ill.

Ghent, Belgium, in Fr. **Gand,** Fl. and Ger. **Gent.**

gherkin, a small cucumber, *not* ge-, gi-, gu-.

ghetto/, Jewish quarter; *pl.* **-s** (not ital.).

ghiaour, *use* **gi-.**

Ghibelline, one of the Emperor's faction in medieval Italian states, opp. to **Guelph**; *not* -in, Gib-, Guib-.

Ghiberti (Lorenzo), 1378–1455, Italian sculptor, painter, goldsmith.

ghillie, *use* gi-.

Ghirlandaio (Domenico), 1449–94, Italian painter.

Ghizeh, *use* **Giza**.

Ghoorkas, *use* **Gurkhas**.

ghoul, an evil spirit, *not* -ool, -oule, -owl; *pron.* gool.

G.H.Q., General Headquarters.

G.I. (U.S.), Government Issue, (colloq.) serviceman.

Giacometti (Alberto), 1901–66, Swiss sculptor, painter, poet.

giallo antico (It.), a rich-yellow marble.

Giant's Causeway, Antrim, *not* -ts'.

giaour, Turk. for infidel, *properly* **gyawur**, *not* ghiaour, giaur; *pron.* jowr.

Gib., Gibraltar.

gibber, to chatter, *not* j-.

gibbet/, -ed, -ing.

Gibbon (Edward), 1737–94, English historian.

Gibbons (Grinling), 1648–1720, English carver; — **(Orlando)**, 1583–1675, English composer.

gibbo/us, hump-backed, doubly convex like the moon between half and full; **-sity.**

gib/e, to sneer; **-er, -ing.** *See also* **gybe, jib.**

Gibeline, *use* **Ghibelline**.

gibelotte (Fr. f.), rabbit stew.

gibier (Fr. m.), game, wild-fowl.

giblets, *pl.*, internal eatable parts of fowl; *adj.* **giblet.**

Gibraltar, abbr. **Gib.**

gibus, opera hat (not ital.).

Gielgud (Sir (Arthur) John), b. 1904, English actor and producer.

Giesler, a champagne. *See also* **Geissler.**

Giessen, university city, Germany.

gigot (cook.), leg of mutton, (dress.), leg-of-mutton sleeve; *not* j-.

Gil Blas, picaresque satire by Le Sage, 1715.

gild, *use* **guild.**

Gilead, mountainous district east of R. Jordan.

Gill (Eric), 1882–1940, type designer.

Gillette (King Camp), 1855–1932, American inventor of safety-razor; —**(William)**, 1857–1937, American actor and writer.

gillie (Sc.), attendant on Highland chief or sportsman, *not* gh-, -y.

Gillott (Joseph), 1799–1873, steel pen-maker and art patron; *pron.* j-.

Gillray (James), 1757–1815, English caricaturist.

gillyflower, clove-scented flower, *not* jilli-.

gilt, abbr. **gt.**

gimcrack, trumpery, *not* jim-.

gimlet, a tool, *not* gimb-.

gimmick (U.S.), a contrivance, device.

gimp, a trimming, a fishing line, *not* gui-, gy-.

ginger/ ale, — beer (two words).

ginglym/us (anat.), a hinge-like joint such as the elbow, *pl.* **-i;** *adj.* **-oid.**

ginn, *use* j-.

Gioconda (La), *see* **Mona Lisa.**

Giorgione (Giorgio Barbarelli da Castelfranco), 1478–1510, Italian painter.

Giotto di Bondone, 1266–1337, Italian painter and architect; *adj.* **Giottesque.**

gipsy, *no longer* gyp-.

girandole, a firework (not ital.).

girasol, a fire-opal, *not* -ole.

Giraudoux (Jean), 1882–1944, French novelist and playwright.

girkin, *use* ghe-.

Giro, a Post Office system of money transference, *not* Gy-.

Girond/e, dép. SW. France; **-ist**, French moderate republican, 1791–3.

gitan/o (Sp.), *fem.* **-a**, a gipsy.

gite, a stopping-place; in Fr. m. *gîte*.

giuoco piano (It.), quiet play (a chess opening).

gives (fetters), *use* gy-.

Giza, site of pyramids, Egypt, *not* Ghiz-, -eh.

Gizeh, *use* Giza.

G.J.C., Grand Junction Canal.

Gk., Greek.

Gl (chem.), glucinum (no point), *now* beryllium.

glace (Fr. cook. f.), ice.

glacé (Fr.), glazed.

glacier (not ital.).

gladiol/us (bot.), *pl.* **-i**.

Gladstonian, *not* -ean.

Glam., Glamorganshire. *See also* **Mid Glamorgan, South Glamorgan, West Glamorgan.**

Glamis, Scotland, *pron.* glahmz.

glam/our, *but* -orous.

glaserian fissure (anat.), *not* glass-.

Glasse (Mrs. Hannah), wrote *The Art of Cookery* in 1747, *not* Glass.

glassful, *pl.* **glassfuls**.

glass-house (colloq.), mil. prison.

Glaswegian, of Glasgow.

Glauber (Johann Rudolf), 1604–68, German chemist; **—'s salt**, a cathartic (apos.).

glaucoma, an eye-disease.

glaucous, greenish; (bot.) covered with bloom.

glazer, a polisher.

glazier, a window-glass fitter.

Glazunov (Alexander), 1865–1936, Russian composer.

G.L.C., Greater London Council.

Gleep, Graphite Low Energy Experimental Pile, the first British atomic pile.

Glenalmond, Perth.

Glencoe, Argyll.

Glenealy, Wicklow.

Gleneely, Donegal.

glengarry, a Scotch cap.

Glenlivet, a whisky, *not* -at, -it (one word).

Glenrothes, Fife, 'new town', 1948.

glissade, a slide down a steep slope (not ital.).

glissando (mus.), slurred, in a gliding manner.

glockenspiel/, orchestral percussion instrument, *pl.* **-s**; Ger. *Glockenspiel/*, *pl.* *-e*.

Gloria/ (liturgy), *pl.* **-s**, abbr. *gl.*

'Gloria/in excelsis', **'— Patri'**, hymns.

Gloria Tibi, glory to Thee (cap. *T*).

Glos., Gloucestershire.

gloss, a superficial lustre.

gloss, a marginal note; (Fr. f.), *glose*.

gloss., glossary, a collection of glosses, dictionary of specialized words.

Gloucestershire, abbr. **Glos.**

glower, to gaze angrily, *not* glour.

glow-worm (hyphen).

gloxinia (bot.), a flower; *pl.* **-s** (not ital.).

glucinum (chem.), symbol Gl, *now* beryllium, symbol Be (no point).

Gluck (Christoph W. von), 1714–87, German composer, *not* Glü-.

glu/e, -ey, -ing.

glut/en, nitrogenous part of wheat-flour, *not* -in; *but* **-inize, -inous.**

glycerine (U.S. **-in**).

G.M., George Medal, Grand Master.

gm., gramme, *use* **g** (no point).

gm², grammes per square metre, metric method for measuring weight of paper.

G.m.b.H., Gmbh (Ger.), *Gesellschaft mit beschränkter Haftung*, limited liability company.

G.M.C., General Medical Council.

G-man (U.S. colloq.), special (police) agent of the F.B.I.

G.M.K.P., Grand Master of the Knights of St. Patrick.

G.M.M.G., Grand Master (of the Order of) St. Michael and St. George.

G.M.T., Greenwich Mean Time.

gn (dyn.), standard acceleration, 981 cm/s², formerly printed **g**, 32 ft./sec./sec.

gnar, to snarl, *not* gnarl, gnarr, knar.

G.N.C., General Nursing Council.

gneiss (geol.), a laminated rock; *pron.* nīs (not ital.).

gnome, *pron.* nō′-mē, a pithy saying; adj. **gnomic.** *See also* **nomic.**

gnosiology, philosophy of cognition, *not* -eology.

gnos/is, knowledge of spiritual mysteries; **-tic,** having spiritual knowledge; **-ticism** (cap. G), an eclectic philosophy of the redemption of the spirit from matter through knowledge.

G.N.P., gross national product.

Gnr. (mil.), gunner.

gnu/, antelope; *pl.* **-s.**

G.O., general order, great (*or* grand) organ.

goal, the objective at games. *See also* **gaol.**

goatee, chin-tuft like a goat's beard.

goat/herd, -skin, -sucker (bird) (no hyphens).

goaty, goat-like.

gobang, Oriental board-game.

Gobbo (Launcelot), in *Merchant of Venice.*

Gobelin tapestry, *not* -ins.

gobe-mouches (Fr. m. sing. and pl.), a credulous person.

Gobi, desert in Mongolia and E. Turkistan.

goby, a fish (not ital.).

G.O.C., General Officer Commanding.

godchild (one word).

god-daughter (hyphen).

godfather (one word).

God-fearing (hyphen, cap.).

Godhead (one word, cap.).

Godlee (Sir Rickman J.), 1849–1925, English surgeon.

godless, one word.

Godley (Arthur), *see* **Kilbracken.**

godmother (one word).

godown, warehouse in parts of Asia, esp. India.

godparent (one word).

God's acre, a burial-ground (apos., one cap.).

god/send, -sent (one word).

godson (one word).

God-speed (cap., hyphen).

godwit, a marsh bird.

Goebbels (Joseph Paul), 1897–1945?, German minister of propaganda, 1933–45, *not* Gö-.

Goering (Hermann), 1893–1945, German field-marshal, *not* Gö-.

Goethe (Johann Wolfgang von), 1749–1832, German poet and playwright, *not* Gö-, Gœ-.

gofer, a thin batter-cake, *not* gau-, -pher, -fre.

goi (Heb.), a Gentile; *pl.* *goim.*

Goidel, a member of Gadhelic races, a Gael.

Golconda, a rich source of wealth (from a ruined city near Hyderabad).

gold (chem.), symbol **Au** (no point).

Golders Green, NW. London (no apos.).

gold-field (hyphen).

Goliath, Philistine giant, *not* -iah.

Gollancz (Sir Israel), 1864–1930, English writer; — **(Sir Victor),** 1893–1967, British publisher and writer.

golosh, boot-trade spelling of **galosh.**

G.O.M., Grand Old Man (W. E. Gladstone).

Gomorr/ah (O.T.); **-ha** (N.T.), but **-ah** in N.E.B.

gondola/, *pl.* **-s** (not ital.).

Gonds, a tribe of cent. India, *not* Gh-.

Gongo, tributary of the Congo.

Góngora y Argote (Luis de), 1561–1627, Spanish poet.

Gonville, *see* **Caius.**

good-bye (hyphen).

good-day (salutation) (hyphen).

Good Friday (caps., two words).

good humour (two words); **good-humoured** (hyphen).

good nature (two words); **good-natured** (hyphen).

good-night (salutation) (hyphen).

Good/ Samaritan, — **Templar** (caps.).

goodwill, of a business, etc. (one word).

Goorkhas, *use* **Gur-.**

goosey, dim. of goose, *not* -sie, -sy.

G.O.P., Grand Old Party (Republican party in U.S.).

gopher, a kind of wood, (U.S.) name for various burrowing animals, *not* goff-.

Gordian knot, tied by Gordius, cut by Alexander the Great.

Gordonstoun School, Elgin, Morayshire.

Gorgonzola, a cheese.

Gorky (Maxim), 1868–1936, pen-name of A. M. Pyeshkov, Russian writer.

gormand, *use* **gour.**

gormandize, to eat greedily, *not* gour-.

Görres (Johann Joseph von), 1776–1848, German Catholic writer.

gors/e, furze; adj. **-y.**

gorsedd, meeting of Welsh bards and druids.

Goschen (Viscount).

Göschen (G. J.), 1752–1828, German publisher, grandfather of the first Viscount Goschen (1831–1907).

Goshen, a land of plenty.

Gospodin (Russ.), Lord, Mr.; *fem.* *Gospoja.* [In modern Russian *tovarish* (comrade) is off. use.]

Goss (Sir John), 1800–80, composer.

Gosse (Sir Edmund), 1849–1928, writer; — **(P. H.),** 1810–88, naturalist.

gossip/, -ed, -er, -ing, -y (one *p*).

gossoon (Anglo-Ir.), a youth.

Gotham (wise men of), i.e. fools; — (U.S. colloq.), New York City.

Gothic, architecture, etc. (cap.); abbr. **Goth.**

Gothic (typ.), title used for a particular style of sans serif face, and for black letter (cap.).

Götterdämmerung
(Twilight of the Gods), opera
by Wagner, 1876.

Göttingen University,
State of Lower Saxony.

gouache, a method of
water-colour painting; *pron.*
guash.

Gouda, a Dutch cheese.

gouge, a concave chisel.

goujon (Fr. m.), gudgeon
fish.

gouk, *use* **gowk.**

gour, Indian ox, *use* **gaur.**

gourmand, a glutton, *but*
gormandize.

gourmet, an epicure.

goût (Fr. m.), taste.

Goutte d'or, a white
Burgundy wine.

gouvern/eur (Fr.), governor;
fem. **-ante.**

gov., govern/or, -ment.

Government, meaning the
State (cap.); abbr. **Govt.**

Governor-General, abbr.
Gov.-Gen.

Gowers (Sir Ernest),
1880–1966, English civil
servant, author of *Plain
Words,* reviser of Fowler's
Modern English Usage.

gowk, a fool, *not* gouk.

**Goya y Lucientes
(Francisco José de),**
1746–1828, Spanish painter.

G.P., general practitioner,
Graduate in Pharmacy,
Gloria Patri (glory be to the
Father).

Gp/Capt (no points) (R.A.F.),
Group Captain.

G.P.D.S.T., Girls' Public
Day School Trust.

G.P.I., general paralysis of
the insane.

G.P.M. (Freemasonry),
Grand Past Master.

G.P.O., General Post Office.

G.P.U., *see* **O.G.P.U.**

G.R., *Georgius, or Gulielmus,
Rex* (King George, or
William).

Gr., Grand, (bot.) Asa
Gray, (entom.) J. L. K.
Gravenhorst, Greece,
Grecian, Greek.

gr., grain, -s.

Graal, *use* **Grail.**

**Gracchus (Caius
Sempronius,** 153–121 B.C.,
and **Tiberius Sempronius,**
163–133 B.C.), the Gracchi,
Roman reformers.

grace-note (mus.), e.g. an
appoggiatura (hyphen).

gradatim (Lat.), step by step.

gradus ad Parnassum
(Lat.), step(s) to Parnassus;
Lat. or Gk. poetical
dictionary; any series of
graded exercises.

Graeae (Gr. myth.), three
sisters who guarded the
abode of the Gorgons.

Graec/ism, a Greek
characteristic; **-ize, -ophil**
(U.S. **Gre-**).

Graf (Ger.), a count; *fem.*
Gräfin (cap.).

graffit/o, scribbling, usu.
on an ancient wall; *pl.* **-i.**
See also **sgraffito.**

Grahame (Kenneth),
1859–1932, English author.

Graian Alps, Savoy.

Grail (the Holy), in
medieval legend, the platter
used by Christ at the Last
Supper, and by Joseph of
Arimathea to catch Christ's
blood, *not* Graal, Graile.

grain, apothecaries',
avoirdupois, or troy weight,
all the same, being 0·0648
gramme; abbr. **gr.**

Grainger (Percy Aldridge),
1882–1961, Australian-born
American composer.

gralloch, deer's entrails, to
disembowel a deer, *not* -ock.

gram, *see* **gramme.**

gram., gramm/ar, -arian,
-atical.

graminivorous, feeding on
grass, *not* gramen-.

gramm/ar, -arian, -atical, abbr. **gram.**

gramme, 0·001 of the standard kilogramme (U.S. **gram**); abbr. **g** (no point).

Grammont, E. Flanders, Belgium.

Gramont (Philibert, comte de), 1621–1707, French courtier, adventurer, and soldier, *not* Gramm-.

gramophone, *not* grama-, grammo-. Superseded by **record-player.**

granadilla, one of the passion-flowers, *not* gren- (not ital.).

Gran Chaco (El), region in Bolivia, Paraguay, and Argentina, S. America.

Grand, abbr. **G.**

grandam, grandmother, old woman, *not* -dame.

Grand Canyon, Arizona, U.S.

grandchild (one word).

Grand Coulee Dam, Washington, U.S.

granddaughter (one word).

Grand/ Duchess, — Duchy, — Duke (two words, both caps. if used as a title); abbr. **G.D.**

grande/ tenue, or — toilette (Fr.), full dress.

grandeur naturelle (Fr. f.), life-size.

grandfather (one word).

grand jury (not caps.).

Grand Master (caps.), abbr. **G.M.**

grand'messe (Fr. f.), high mass.

Grand Monarque (le), Louis XIV.

grand monde (le) (Fr.), the Court and nobility.

grandmother (one word).

grand/nephew, — -niece (hyphens).

Grand Old Party (U.S.), the Republican party; abbr. **G.O.P.**

grandparent (one word).

Grand Rapids, town, Michigan, U.S.

grand signior, one of high rank; caps. the Sultan of Turkey; in Fr. *grand seigneur*; It. *gran signore*; Sp. *gran señor*.

grandson (one word), abbr. **g.s.**

grangerize, to illustrate a book by cutting title-plates and illustrations from other books, *not* -ise (not cap.).

grannom, angler's fly, *not* granam.

Granta (The), a Cambridge periodical.

Grant Duff (Sir M. E.), 1829–1906 (no hyphen).

granter, one who grants.

Granth, the Sikh scriptures, *not* Grunth.

grantor (law), one who makes a grant.

Granville-Barker (Harley), 1877–1946, English playwright, producer, and actor.

graphology, study of character from handwriting, *not* graphio-.

gras (Fr.), *fem. grasse*, fat. See also **gros.**

Grasmere, Westmorland.

grass/ (typ.), casual work; **— hand,** one casually employed.

Grasse, France, dép. Alpes-Maritimes.

gratia Dei (Lat.), by the grace of God.

gratin, see au gratin.

gratis, for nothing, free (not ital.).

Grattan (Henry), 1746–1820, Irish statesman and orator.

Gratz, Austria, *use* **Graz.**

Grätz, Czechoslovakia, *use* **Hradec.**

Grätz, Poland, *use* **Grodzisk.**

grauwacke, *use* **grey-**.

gravam/en, chief ground of complaint; *pl.* **-ina**.

grave (mus.), slow, solemn.

grave accent (ˋ).

gravel/led, covered with gravel, puzzled (U.S. **-ed**).

Graves, a Bordeaux white wine.

Graves's disease, exophthalmic goitre (apos.).

gravestone (one word).

graveyard (one word).

Gravis (Ger. m.), grave accent (cap.).

gravure (typ.), intaglio printing process (from **photogravure**).

gray, *use* **grey**.

Gray (Asa), 1810–88, bot., abbr. **Gr.**; — (**Thomas**), 1716–71, English poet. *See also* **Grey**.

grayling, a fish, *not* grey-.

Gray's Inn, London.

Graz, cap. of Styria, Austria, *not* Gratz.

grazier, one who pastures cattle, *not* -zer.

G.R.C.M., Graduate of the Royal College of Music.

greasy, *not* -ey.

Great Britain, abbr. **G.B.**

Greater Manchester, *see* **South-East Lancashire and North-East Cheshire.**

great gross, 144 dozen; abbr. **g.gr.**

Great Powers (the) (caps.).

great primer (typ.), old name for a size of type, about 18 pt.; *pron.* prim′-er; abbr. **g.p.**

Greats, Oxford B.A. final examination for honours in Lit. Hum.

Grecian, almost entirely superseded by **Greek,** but still used as noun for a Greek scholar, a boy in the top form at Christ's Hospital, a Greek-speaking Jew of the Dispersion; as adj., — **bend,** an affected walk; — **knot,** a hair style; — **nose,** — **profile,** — **slippers**.

Grec/ism, -ize, -ophil, *use* **Grae-**.

Greco (El), a chess opening.

Greco (El), 1541–1614, Spanish painter, born in Crete, real name **Domenico Theotocopuli.**

gredalin, *use* **gride-**.

Greece, abbr. **Gr.**

Greek (typ.), classical and modern printed the same; alphabet, 17 consonants, 7 vowels, 2 breathings (asper ʽ and lenis ʼ), 3 accents (acute, grave, and circumflex), 1 apostrophe, 1 diaeresis; note of interrogation same as English semicolon; the colon or semicolon same as turned point (·); comma, exclamation point, and period, as in English. There are many detailed rules for composition (see *Hart's Rules*), but the following must suffice here: grave accent is possible only on last syllable; in diphthongs, accents or breathings are on second vowel; all vowels or diphthongs beginning a word have a breathing, and initial ρ has asper; headings set in caps. have no breathings or accents; use σ for initial or medial sigma, *s* for final; space after elision. Abbr. **Gr.** or **Gk.**

Greek alphabet: α, β, γ, δ, ε, ζ, η, θ, ι, κ, λ, μ, ν, ξ, ο, π, ρ, σ (ς), τ, υ, φ, χ, ψ, ω.

Greek calends, never; *ad Kalendas Graecas*.

Greeley (Horace), 1811–72, American journalist and politician.

Greely (Adolphus Washington), 1844–1935, American general and Arctic explorer.

Green (John Richard), 1837–83, historian. *See also* **Greene, Grein.**

greenback, U.S. bank-note.

Greene (Sir Conyngham), 1854–1934, British diplomatist; — **(Graham)**, b. 1904, English novelist; — **(Plunket)**, 1865–1936, English singer; — **(Robert)**, 1560–92, English dramatist and pamphleteer.

greengage, a plum (one word).

green laver, edible seaweed (two words).

green-room, room off-stage for actors (hyphen).

greensand, a sandstone; **Lower** and **Upper Greensand**, two strata of the Cretaceous system.

Greenwich Mean Time (caps.), abbr. **G.M.T.**

gregale, the Mediterranean NE. wind, *not* -cale, grigale (not cap.).

Gregory's Day (St.), 12 March.

Greifswald, German university town.

Grein (Jacob Thomas), 1862–1931, Dutch-British dramatic critic and manager.

Grenada, W. Indies.

grenadine, a thin silk fabric; (cook.) dish of veal or poultry fillets; a syrup made from currants or pomegranates, in Fr. *grenadin*, m.

Grenadines, chain of islands between Grenada and St. Vincent, W. Indies.

Gresham's Law, 'bad money drives out good', from Sir Thomas —, 1519–79.

G.R. et I., *Georgius Rex et Imperator*, George King and Emperor.

Grétry (André E. M.), 1741–1813, French composer.

Grévy (F. P. J.), 1807–91, French President, 1879–87.

grey (U.S. **gray**).

Grey (Lady Jane), 1537–54 proclaimed queen of Eng., 1553, deposed, beheaded; — **of Fallodon (Viscount)**, 1862–1933, politician. *See also* **Gray.**

grey-hen, *fem.* of blackcock (hyphen).

greyhound (one word).

greyling, *use* gra-.

greywacke (geol.), a sedimentary rock, *not* gray- (not ital.).

gridelin, violet-grey, *not* grida-, greda-, -ine.

Grieg (Edvard Hagerup), *not* Edward, 1843–1907, Norwegian composer.

griffin, a fabulous animal, *not* -on, gryphon.

griffon, the European vulture; a French breed of dog.

grigale, *use* gre-.

grill, to broil.

grille, grating (not ital.).

grillé/, -e (Fr. cook.), broiled.

grimalkin, a cat.

Grimm (Jakob), 1785–1863, — **(Wilhelm)**, 1786–1859, German philologists, collectors of fairy-tales; **Grimm's Law**, deals with consonantal changes in Germanic languages.

Grimond (Rt. Hon. Joseph), b. 1913, English Liberal politician.

grimy, begrimed, *not* -ey.

Grindelwald, Switz., *not* Grindle-.

gringo/ (Sp. Amer.), a foreigner, esp. English-speaking (derogatory); *pl.* -s (not ital.).

grippe (*la*), Fr. for influenza, *also* **the grip,** *not* the grippe.

Griqua/, half-breed of Cape Dutch and Hottentot parents; **-land,** in S. Africa.

grisaille, a method of decorative painting (not ital.).

Griselda, a model of patience, *not* -ilda.

grisette (Fr. f.), a working girl.

grisly, terrible, *not* grizz-.

Gris-Nez (**Cap**), Pas-de-Calais (hyphen).

Grizel, a proverbial meek wife.

grizzly bear, *not* gris- —.

gro., gross.

Grodzisk, Poland, *not* Grätz.

grogram, coarse fabric (not ital.).

groin, the fold between belly and thigh; (arch.) line of intersection of two vaults. *See also* **groyne.**

Grolier de Servières (**Jean**), 1479–1565, French bibliophile. (Hence **Grolier Club,** for American bibliophiles.)

gros/ (Fr.), *fem.* **-se,** big, abbr. *g.*; *une grosse femme,* a stout woman; *une femme grosse,* a pregnant woman. *See also* **gras.**

grosbeak, the hawfinch.

gros bleu (Fr. m.), dark blue.

groschen (m.), old German small silver coin; *pl.* same.

groseille/(Fr. f.), currant (*— à grappes*); gooseberry (*— à maquereau*).

gross (144) is *sing.* and *pl.*; abbr. **gro.**

Grosseteste (**Robert**), 1175–1253, Bp. of Lincoln.

Grote (**George**), 1794–1871, English historian.

grotesque (typ.), nineteenth-century sans serif typeface; abbr. **grot.**

grotesquerie, *not* -ery (not ital.).

Grotius (**Hugo**), 1583–1645, Dutch jurist and statesman (latinized form of De Groot).

grotto/, *pl.* **-es.**

ground floor (U.S. **first floor**), noun (two words); **ground-floor,** adj. (hyphen).

ground level, noun (two words); **ground-level,** adj. (hyphen).

ground-rent (hyphen).

groundwork (one word).

grovel/, **-led, -ler, -ling** (U.S. **-ed, -er, -ing**).

Grove's Dictionary of Music and Musicians.

groyn/e, a breakwater; **-ing.** *See also* **groin.**

G.R.S.M., Graduate of the Royal Schools of Music (the Royal Academy and the Royal College).

G.R.T., gross registered tonnage.

Grub Street, London, former haunt of literary hacks, *now* Milton Street.

grummet (naut.), a rope ring (U.S. **gro-**).

Grundtvig (**Nikolai**), 1783–1872, Danish poet; — (**Sven**), 1824–83, Danish philologist.

Grundy (**Mrs.**), in Thos. Morton's *Speed the Plough,* 1798, type of conventional propriety.

Grunth, the Sikh scriptures; *use* **Granth.**

Gruyère (Fr. m.), a French-Swiss cheese.

Gruyères, Switzerland.

Gryphius (**Sebastian**), 1493–1556, German-born French printer, *not* Gryptinus.

gryphon, *use* **griffin.**

grysbok (Afrik.), an
antelope, *not* -buck.

G.S., General/Secretary, —
Service (mil.), — Staff.

g.s., grandson.

G.S.A., Girl Scouts of
America.

G.S.M., Guildhall School
of Music.

G.S.O., General Staff
Officer.

G.S.P. (naval), Good
Service Pension.

G.T., Good Templar.

g.t. (binding), gilt top.

gt., gilt, great, gutta.

guacho (error), *use* **gaucho.**

Guadalupe/, Spain; —
Hidalgo, Mexico; — **Mts.,**
Texas and New Mexico.

Guadeloupe, W. Indies.

guage (error), *see* **gau-.**

guaiacum (bot.), trop.
American tree; resin
obtained from it.

Guaira (**La**), Venezuela, *not*
Guayra.

Guam, Marianas Islands,
not Guaham, Guajam.

guana, a lizard, shortened
from **iguana.**

guano, fertilizer from sea-
birds' excrement.

guarant/ee (more general
word than guaranty, which
it is displacing), *verb,* to
secure against loss or
damage; *noun,* security
against loss or damage;
maker's or vendor's
warranty of goods made or
sold; person to whom a
guaranty is given (correl. of
next); **-or,** one who gives
a guaranty; **-y,** *noun only*
(legal and commercial), the
act of giving a security,
something given as a
security.

guards (binding), strips of
paper or cloth inserted in
the backs of books for plates,

or additional leaves, to be
pasted on.

guard-ship (hyphen).

Guareschi (**Giovanni**),
1908–68, Italian novelist.

Guarnieri, violin makers,
not -neri.

Guatemala, Cent. America.

Guayaquil, Ecuador.

Guayra, *use* **La Guaira.**

guazzo (It.), same as
gouache.

Guelderland, *use* **Geld-.**

guelder rose, *not* gelder —
(not ital.).

Guelph, one of the Pope's
faction in medieval Italian
states, opp. to **Ghibelline,**
not Guelf.

Guenevere, Defence of, by
W. Morris. *See* **Guinevere.**

guerdon, a reward.

guère (*ne* . . .) (Fr.), hardly.

Guernsey, a Channel
Island.

guernsey, a heavy knitted
woollen upper garment, as
worn by seamen.

guerre (Fr. f.), war.

guerrilla/(loosely) a man or
body of men engaged
in — **warfare,** irregular
fighting by small bodies.

guess-work (hyphen).

Guevara de la Serna
(**Ernesto, 'Che'**), 1928–69,
Cuban revolutionary leader,
killed in Bolivia.

Guglielmo, It. for **William.**

Guiana (**British**), *now*
Guyana.

Guibelline, *use* **Ghi-.**

guichet, ticket-office window.

guide-book (hyphen).

Guido, It. for **Guy.**

Guilbert (**Yvette**), 1869–
1944, French *diseuse.*

guild, an association, *not*
gild.

Guildford, Surrey, *not*
Guilf-.

guild-hall, *not* gi- (hyphen);
but **the Guildhall,** London.

Guilford (Earl of).

guillemets (Fr. typ. m.), Fr. quotation marks « ».

guillemot, a sea-bird.

guilloche, architectural ornament (not ital.).

guillotine, a beheading apparatus, a paper-cutting machine, a device for terminating parliamentary debates.

guimp, *use* **gimp.**

Guinea, *formerly* Fr. W. Africa, independent 1958.

Guinea (New), E. Indies.

guinea/, 21/-, £1·05, *pl.* **-s;** abbr. **g.**

guinea-pig, a small S. American rodent, a fainéant company-director, the subject of an experiment (hyphen).

Guinevere, wife of King Arthur. *See* **Guenevere.**

Guiranwala, W. Pakistan.

Gujarat, area in India. *See* **Gujrat.**

Gujrat, town in W. Pakistan.

gulden, Dutch silver florin; *also* med. German coin and Austrian unit of account.

gules (her.), red.

Gulf/ cap. when with name, as Gulf of Corinth, Persian Gulf; abbr. **G.;** — **Stream** (no hyphen).

Gulielmus, Lat. for **William.**

gullible, easily cheated, *not* -able.

Gulliver's Travels, by Swift, 1726.

gully, a channel, *not* -ey.

gumbo, kind of soup.

gun., gunnery.

gunboat (one word).

Gundamuk, Afghanistan, *use* **Gandamak.**

Gungl (Josef), 1810–89, Hungarian composer.

gun-lock (hyphen).

gunman (one word), armed thug.

gunnery (naval), abbr. **G.,** *or* **gun.**

gunny, sacking.

gunpowder (one word).

gunshot (one word).

Gunter's chain, a surveyor's, 66 ft long.

Gunther, character in the *Nibelungenlied* (no umlaut).

gunwale, upper edge of ship's side, *not* gunnel; *pron.* gun'l.

gup (Anglo-Ind.), gossip (not ital.).

Gurkhas, Nepalese soldiers in Indian or British service, *not* Ghoor-, Goor-.

gurkin, *use* **gher-.**

gurnard, a fish, *not* -net.

guru, religious teacher, esp. Sikh, *not* Gooroo.

Gutenberg *or* **Gensfleisch (Johann),** 1397–1468, German inventor (so generally assumed) of movable metal types.

gutt/a, a drop, abbr. **gt.;** *pl.* **-ae,** abbr. **gtt.**

gutta-percha, hard rubber-like substance (hyphen, not ital.).

gutter (typ.), space between imposed pages of type allowing for two foredge margins.

guttural, connected with the throat.

g.u.v. (Ger.), *gerecht und vollkommen* (correct and complete).

Guyana, NE. South America, *formerly* Brit. Guiana, independent 1966.

Guyot (Yves), 1843–1928, French economist.

Guy's Hospital, London (apos.).

Guzerat, India, *use* **Gujarat.**

Gwalia, Sons of, a mining company.

Gwalior, India.

Gwent, new Welsh County,

proposed 1971, including
Newport and parts of
Breconshire and
Monmouthshire.

G.W.R., Great Western
Railway (prior to
nationalization).

Gwyn (Nell), 1650–87,
English actress, mistress of
Charles II.

Gwynedd, new Welsh
county, proposed 1971,
comprising Anglesey,
Caernarvonshire, Merioneth,
part of Denbighshire.

Gwynn (Stephen), 1864–
1950, English writer.

gybe (naut.), change course
(U.S. **jibe**). *See also* **gibe,
jib.**

gymkhana, an athletic

display, a pony club
competition, *not* -kana (not
ital.).

gymnasium/, *pl.* **-s** (not
ital.); abbr. **gym.**

gymnot/us, the electric eel;
pl. **-i** (not ital.).

gymp, *use* **gimp.**

gynaeceum, (Gk. and
Rom.) women's apartments
in a house; (bot.) female
organ of flower, *not* gynoe-,
-ium.

gynaecology, study of
women's diseases (U.S.
gynec-); abbr. **gyn.**

gypsum, hydrous sulphate
of lime.

gypsy, correct by derivation
(Egyptian), *but use* **gipsy.**

gyves, fetters, *not* gi-.

H

H, henry (unit of inductance), (chem.) hydrogen, (lead pencils) hard, (former motion-picture certificate) horrific, (mus.) B natural in German system, the eighth in a series.

H., harbour, hydrant, all proper names with this initial.

H., Heft (Ger.), number, part.

h, hour, -s (in scientific work).

h., hardness, height, husband, (naut.) hail.

h, Planck's constant, q.v.

ha, hectare (no point), 10,000 square metres ($10^4 m^2$).

H.A., Historical Association, Horse Artillery.

h.a., hoc anno (this year), *hujus anni* (this year's).

Haag, den, Dutch for Hook (of Holland).

Haakon, name of seven Norwegian kings.

H. A. & M., Hymns Ancient and Modern.

haar, a raw sea-mist (E. coast of England and Scotland).

Haarlem, Netherlands. *See also* **Har-.**

hab., habitat.

Habakkuk (O.T.), abbr. **Hab.**

Habana, Sp. for **Havana.**

habanera, a Cuban Negro dance.

habeas corpus, writ to produce a person before court; abbr. **hab. corp.**

Habeas Corpus Act (caps., not ital.).

habendum (law), part of a deed.

habet (Lat.), 'he's had it'. *See* **hoc habet.**

habile, skilful, able, *not* -ille (not ital.).

habitat, normal abode of animal or plant (not ital.); abbr. **hab.**

habitu/é (Fr.), *fem. -ée,* a frequenter (ital.).

Habsburg (House of), Austrian Imp. family, *not* Hap-.

H.A.C., Honourable Artillery Company.

Hachette et Cie, publishers, Paris and London.

hachis (Fr. cook. m.), minced meat, hash.

hachisch, *use* **hashish.**

hachure, line used in map hill-shading.

hacienda (Sp.), large estate with mansion.

Hackenschmidt (George), 1877–1968, Estonian-born British wrestler.

Hackluyt, *use* **Hak-.**

hackney/, to make trite; **-ed.**

hac lege (Lat.), with this proviso.

Hades (Gr. myth.), abode of the dead (cap.).

hadji, a Muslim who has made the pilgrimage (*hadj*) to Mecca (not ital.); **hajji** is strictly correct, but not in common use.

Hadramaut, S. Arabia, *not* Hadhra-.

hadst (no apostrophe).

haema-, haemo-, the prefix meaning blood (U.S. **hema-, hemo-**).

haemorrh/age, -oids (U.S. **hemo-**).

hafiz (Arab., Pers.), a Muslim who knows the Koran by heart.

Háfiz, d. A.D. 1388, Persian poet, actual name **Shams ud-din Mohammed.**

hafnium, symbol **Hf** (no point).

Hag., Haggai.

hagberry, the bird-cherry (U.S. **hack-**).

Haggadah, legendary part of the Talmud, *not* Agadah, Hagada, -ah.

Haggai (O.T.), abbr. **Hag.**

haggard, wild-looking, like an untamed hawk, in Fr. *hagard.*

haggis, Sc. dish, *not* -ess, -ies.

Hague (Cap de La), NW. France.

Hague (The), cap. of Netherlands; in Dutch 's Gravenhage; (caps.).

ha ha, laughter (two words).

ha-ha, a sunk fence, *not* aha, haw-haw (not ital.).

Haidarabad, *use* Hyder-.

haik, an Arab garment, *not* -ck.

Haile Selassie, b. 1892, Emperor of Ethiopia.

Haileybury College, Herts.

hail-fellow-well-met (adj.), friendly (three hyphens).

hail/stone, -storm (one word).

hair/breadth, -brush (one word).

hair-do, coiffure (hyphen).

hair/dresser, -dressing (one word).

hair's breadth (two words).

hair-space (typ.), very thin space used for letter-spacing (hyphen).

hair-stroke (typ.), a fine serif (hyphen).

Haiti, W. Indies, *not* Hayti; east part, **Santo Domingo.**

hajji, *see* hadji.

hakenkreuz, the swastika.

hakim, pron. ha-kēm', Oriental medical man, *not* -keem.

hakim, pron. ha'-kēm, Oriental ruler.

Hakluyt (Richard), 1553–1616, English historian and geographer; — **Society;** *not* Hack-.

halberd/, combined spear and battle-axe, *not* -ert; **-ier.**

hale, to drag, *not* hail.

Halevi (Judah), *c.* 1085–1140, Spanish-Jewish philosopher and poet.

Halévy (Jacques François F. É.), 1799–1862, French composer; — **(Joseph)** 1827–1917, French traveller; — **(Ludovic),** 1834–1908, French playwright and novelist.

half, *see also* **fractions.**

half/ a dozen, — an hour, — an inch (no hyphens).

half-and-half (hyphens).

half/-binding (bind.), when the spine and corners are bound in a different material from the sides (hyphen); — **-bound** (hyphen).

half/-caste, a half-breed, *not* -cast (not ital.); — **-crown;** — **-dime** (U.S.), five cents (not ital.); — **-dozen;** — **-holiday;** — **-hour;** — **-inch;** — **-mast;** — **-minute;** — **-moon;** — **-past;** — **-pay,** abbr. **H.P.** *or* **h.p.** (hyphens).

halfpenny (one word).

halfpennyworth (one word), abbr. **ha'p'orth.**

half/-price, — -sovereign *or* **h.p.** (hyphens).

half-title (typ.), the short title before the full title.

halftone (typ.), technique whereby the various tones are represented by varying sizes of minute dots.

half/-way, — -wit (hyphens).

half-year/, -ly (hyphens).

Haliburton (Thomas C.), 1796–1865, Canadian-born British writer; pen-name Sam Slick.

halibut, a fish, *not* hol-.

halieutic, of fishing.

hallabaloo, *use* **hulla-.**

Hallé/ (Sir Charles), 1819–95, German-born Mancunian pianist and conductor, founded — **Orchestra** 1857; — **(Lady),** 1839–1911, violinist (**Mme Norman-Neruda**).

Halle an der Saale, Saxony, Germany; abbr. **Halle a/S.**

hallelujah, *formerly preferred to* **alleluia** (which is in H. A. & M.), 'praise Jehovah', a song of praise, *not* -luiah;

'Hallelujah Chorus' (Handel).

Halles (Les), Paris, the central market until 1968.

Halley (Edmond, *not* -und), 1656–1742, English astronomer.

halliard, *use* **halyard.**

Halliwell-Phillips (James O.), 1820–89, English Shakespearian scholar.

hallmark, mark used at Goldsmiths' Hall and by Govt. assay officials for marking standard of gold and silver.

Hallow/e'en, 31 Oct.; **-mas** (one word), 1 Nov., All Saints' Day.

hall/ux, the great toe; *pl.* **-uces.**

halm, stalk or stem, *use* **haulm.**

halo/, ring of light round moon, head, etc.; *pl.* **-es.**

Hals (Franz), 1580 (or 84)–1666, Dutch painter.

halyard (naut.), a rope for elevating, *not* halli-, hauly-.

hamadryad/, a wood-nymph, serpent, or baboon; *pl.* **-s,** Lat. *pl.* **-es.**

Hambleden, Bucks.; — **(Viscount).**

Hambledon, Hants, Surrey.

Hambleton, Lancs., Rutland, Yorks.

Hambros Bank, Ltd. (no apos.)

Hamburg/, city in Germany, a fowl, a grape; **-er** (not cap.), Ger.–U.S. large sausage, or chopped steak in a roll.

'Hamelin (Pied Piper of)', by R. Browning.

hammal, an Oriental porter, *not* hummaul.

hammam, Turkish bath, *not* hummum, -aum.

Hammarskjöld (Dag), 1905–62, Sec.-Gen. of U.N. 1953–62.

Hammergafferstein (Hans), pen-name of Henry W. Longfellow.

Hampden (John), 1594–1643, English patriot and statesman.

Hampe-Allgaier, a chess opening.

Hampshire, abbr. **Hants** (no point).

Hampton Court, Middlesex.

hamster, rodent from Syria.

hand (typ.), ☞, called **fist.**

hand/bell, -bill, -book (one word).

Handbuch (Ger.), manual (cap.).

h. & c., hot and cold (water).

Handel (George Frederick), 1685–1759, German composer of oratorio and Italian opera, resident in England; in Ger. **Händel.**

Handelsblatt (Ger. n.), trade journal (cap.).

handful/, *not* -ll; *pl.* **-s.**

handicap/, -per, -ping.

handiwork, *not* handy-.

handkerchief, abbr. **hdkf.**

hand-made (hyphen).

handmaid/, -en (one word).

Handschrift (Ger. f.), MS., *not* Manuskript; abbr. **Hs.** (cap.).

handsel/, earnest-money; **-ling**, *not* hans-.

handwriting (one word).

handy-man (hyphen).

handywork, *use* **handi-**.

hangar, a shed.

hanged, past tense or partic., used of capital punishment; in other senses use **hung**.

hanger, one who, or that which, hangs; *also* a sword, a wood.

hanging/ paragraph *or* **indent** (typ.), short paragraph or listed items (as in bibliographies) set with second and following lines indented under first line (as here).

Hanover, in Ger. **Hannover**.

Hans/ (Du., Ger.), Jack; **— Niemand**, 'Mr. Nobody'.

hansel, *use* **hand-**.

hansom, a two-wheeled cab.

Hants (no point), Hampshire.

hapax legomenon (Gr.), a word found once only.

haphazard (one word).

ha'p'orth, a halfpennyworth.

happy-go-lucky (hyphens).

happy hunting-ground (one hyphen).

Hapsburg, Imperial House of Austria, *use* **Hab-**.

hara-kiri (Jap.), suicide, *not* hari-kari, hurry-curry.

haram, *use* **-em**.

harangu/e, to address like an orator; **-ed**.

harass, *not* harr-.

harbour (U.S. **-or**), abbr. H.

hard (pencils), abbr. H (no point).

hard/-a-lee, **— -a-port**, **— -a-starboard**, **— -a-weather** (two hyphens each).

hardi/hood, **-ness**, *not* hardy-.

hardline (adj.), unyielding (one word).

hardness (mineral.), abbr. **h.**

hards, coarse flax, *not* hur-.

Hardt Mountains, Bavarian Palatinate. *See also* **Harz —.**

hardwood (one word), *but* **hard-wooded**.

hard-working (hyphen).

harebell (bot.), *not* hair- (one word).

hare/-brain, **— -lip**, *not* hair- (hyphens).

harem (Arab.), the women's part of a house, *not* -am, -eem, -im (not ital.).

hareng/ (Fr. m.), herring; **— *pec***, salted herring.

Harewood, *pron.* har-.

Hargraves (Edmund Hammond), 1816–91, discoverer of the Australian gold-fields.

Hargreaves (James), 1720–78, English weaver, inventor of the spinning-jenny.

haricot/ (Fr. cook. m.), haricot, a ragout usu. of mutton and beans; **—*de mouton***, Irish stew; **—*s blancs***, kidney beans; **—*s d'Espagne***, scarlet runners; **—*s verts***, French beans.

haridan, *use* **harridan**.

harier, *use* **harrier**.

hari-kari, *use* *hara-kiri*.

Häring (Georg Wilhelm Heinrich), 1798–1871, German writer; pen-name Willibald Alexis.

Haringey, Greater London borough, 1965, *not* -ay.

Harington (Sir John), 1561–1612, English poet and pamphleteer.

hark, listen, *not* hea-.

harken, *use* **hear-**.

harl, a fibre, *not* -le.

Harlech, Merioneth, *not* -ck.

Harleian, of Harley.

Harlem, New York, U.S.

Harlesden, Middlesex.

Harleston, Norfolk.

Harlestone, Northants.

Harlow (Jean), 1911–37, American film-actress.

Harlow, Essex, 'new town', 1947.

Harlowe (*Clarissa*), by Richardson, 1748.

harmattan, W. African land-wind.

harmonize, *not* -ise.

Harper's Bazaar, American magazine of fashion, founded 1857; also the English version, founded 1929.

Harpers Ferry, West Virginia, U.S. (no apos.).

Harper's Magazine, American monthly magazine, founded 1850.

harquebus/, a portable gun, *not* -ss; arquebus; **-ier.**

Harraden (**Beatrice**), 1864–1936, English writer.

harridan, a haggard old woman, *not* hari-.

harrier, one who harries, a hound for hunting hare, a hawk, a cross-country runner, *not* harier.

Harrington (**Earl** *of*). *See also* **Hari-.**

Harrogate, Yorks., *not* Harrow-.

Hart (**Horace**), Printer to the University of Oxford 1883–1915.

hartal, closing of Indian shops as political gesture.

Harte (**Francis Bret**), 1836–1902, American novelist and story-writer.

hartebeest, S. African antelope, *not* hartb-, -bees.

Hartlepool, Co. Durham, *pron.* hart-le-pool.

hartshorn, ammonia (one word).

Hart's Rules for Compositors and Readers, 37th edition, completely revised, 1967, reprinted with corrections, 1970.

Hartzenbusch (**Juan Eugenio**), 1806–80, Spanish dramatist.

Hartz Mountains, *use* **Harz** —. *See also* **Hardt.**

harum-scarum, reckless (hyphen), *not* harem-scarem.

Harun ar- Rashid, 763–809, a caliph of Baghdad, hero of the *Arabian Nights* (**al- Rashid** *now more usual*).

Harvard University, abbr. H.U., at Cambridge, Mass., U.S.

Harv/ey (**William**), 1578–1657, English physician, discovered blood circulation; **-eian,** *not* -eyan.

Harz Mountains, NW. Germany, *not* Hartz —. *See also* **Hardt.**

has-been (**a**), one that has been (hyphen); *pl.* **has-beens.**

Hase (**Karl August von**), 1800–90, German Protestant theologian.

hashish, hemp smoked or chewed as drug, *not* hach-, hasch-, -eesh, -isch.

Haslar Hospital (Naval), Hants.

Haslemere, Surrey. *See also* **Haz-.**

hassagai, *use* **assagai.**

Hasse (**Johann Adolph**), 1699–1783, German composer.

Hassler (**Hans Leo**), 1564–1612, German composer.

hatband (one word).

hatchway (one word).

hâte (Fr. f.), haste.

Hatshepsut, queen of Egypt, 1501–1481 B.C.

hatti/, short form of — *-humayun or* — *-sherif,* Turkish edict made irrevocable by Sultan's mark.

hauler, one who *or* that which hauls.

haulier, a man employed in hauling something, esp. coal in a mine, goods by road.

haulm (bot.), a stalk or stem, *not* halm.

Hauptmann (Gerhart),
1862–1946, German poet
and dramatist; — **(Moritz),**
1792–1868, German
composer.

Hausa, of Cent. Sudan, *not*
-ssa, Housa.

Hausfrau, Germanic
housewife.

Hausmann (J. F. L.), 1782–
1859, German metallurgist,
hence **hausmannite.**

haussier (Fr. m.),
speculator for a rise, a 'bull'.

Haussmann (G. E., baron),
1809–91, Paris architect.

haussmannize, to open out
and rebuild.

haut/bois, -boy (mus.), *use*
oboe.

haute/ bourgeoisie (Fr. f.),
upper middle-class; —
couture, elegance inspired
by the high-fashion houses;
— *école,* advanced horsemanship; — *nouveauté,*
latest fashion.

Hautes-Alpes, dép. SE.
France (hyphen).

Haute-Saône, dép. E.
France (hyphen), *pron.* sōn.

Hautes-Pyrénées, dép. SW.
France (hyphen).

haut et bon (Fr.), great and
good.

hauteur, haughty demeanour
(not ital.).

Haute-Vienne, dép. Cent.
France (hyphen). *See also*
Vienne.

haute volée (Fr. f.), the
upper ten.

haut-goût (Fr. m.), high
flavour.

Haut-Rhin, dép. NE.
France (hyphen).

Havana, Cuba, *not* -ah,
-annah; in Sp. **Habana.**

Havas, a French news agency.

haver (Sc.), to talk nonsense
(*not* to vacillate).

Haverfordwest, Pembrokeshire.

Havergal (Francis Ridley),
1836–79, English hymn-
writer.

haversack, bag for carrying
food, *not* -sac.

havoc, *not* -ck.

Havre, France, *use* **Le
Havre.**

Hawai/i, one of the Hawaiian
Islands, formerly Sandwich
Islands; **-ian.**

Haweis (Hugh Reginald),
1838–1901, English
clergyman and musicologist.

haw-haw, *use* **ha-ha.**

Haw-haw (Lord), nickname
of William Joyce, American-
born German propagandist
in Second World War, exec.
1946.

hawk's-bill, a turtle (U.S.
hawkbill).

hawse (naut.), a part in the
bows of a ship.

hawthorn (one word).

Hawthorne (Julian), 1846–
1934, American writer; —
(Nathaniel), 1804–64,
American novelist.

hay, a country dance, *not*
hey (but *Sheperd's Hey,* by
P. A. Grainger).

Haydn (Joseph), 1732–
1809, Austrian composer;
— **(Joseph),** d. 1856,
compiled *Dictionary of Dates.*

**Haydon (Benjamin
Robert),** 1786–1846,
English painter.

hay fever (two words).

hay/maker, -rick, -stack
(one word).

Hayti, *use* **Haiti.**

hazel/-hen, — **-nut**
(hyphens).

Hazlemere, Bucks. *See also*
Has-.

Hazlitt (William), 1778–
1830, English essayist; —
(William Carew), 1834–
1913, English bibliographer.

hazy, indistinct, *not* -ey.

HB (pencils), hard and black.

H.B.C., Hudson's Bay Company.

H.B.M., Her, *or* His, Britannic Majesty.

H-bomb, hydrogen bomb (no point, hyphen).

H.C., habitual criminal, Heralds' College, High Church, Holy Communion, Home Counties, (Fr.) *hors concours* (not competing), House of Commons, House of Correction.

h.c., *honoris causa.*

H.C.F. *or* **h.c.f.** (math.), highest common factor.

H.C.M., His, *or* Her, Catholic Majesty.

H.C.S., Home Civil Service.

hdkf., handkerchief.

hdqrs., headquarters.

H.E., His Eminence, — Excellency; high explosive.

h.e., horizontal equivalent.

He, helium (no point).

head (typ.), the blank space at the top of a page. *See also* **margins.**

headache (one word).

headachy, *not* -ey.

headband (binding), sewn ornament at head, and tail, of spine of bound book.

head/-dress, — **-gear** (hyphens).

headings (typ.), should be graded to show relative importance of different headings, with numbered or lettered subheads in the same weight throughout the work.

Headless Cross, Worcs.

headlight (one word).

headlines *or* **running titles** (typ.), at head of pages; various combinations can be adopted, including book, part, section, or chapter title, subhead, or summary of page content, shortened if necessary to keep it to a single line; in bookwork

chapter title generally most suitable on both recto and verso, dividing long titles across opening; pagination, q.v., may be included in outer corners.

headman, a chief (one word).

head/master, -mistress, as general term (one word).

Head Master, official title at certain schools (two words).

head-note, summary at head of chapter or page, (mus.) a tone produced in the head register (hyphen).

head-on (hyphen).

head-phone(s) (hyphen).

headpiece (one word).

headquarters (one word); abbr. **H.Q.,** *or* **hdqrs.**

head-rest, support for the head (hyphen).

head-sail, one before the fore-mast (hyphen).

head/-sea, — **-shake** (hyphens).

headship, position of chief (one word).

headsman, executioner (one word).

headstock (mech.), device to support the end of a member (one word).

head/stone, -strong, -way (one word).

head-word (typ.), a word forming a heading (hyphen).

head-work (hyphen).

healthful, *not* -ull.

Heap, *see* **Heep.**

hear, hear!, interjection in speeches, *not* here, here.

hearken, *not* har-.

Hearn (Lafcadio), 1850–1904, American author.

heart/ache, -beat (one word).

heart-break/, -er, -ing, heart-broken (hyphens).

heartburn (one word).

heart-disease (hyphen).

heartfelt (one word).

hearthstone (one word).

heart-rending (hyphen).

heart's-ease, a pansy (apos., hyphen).

heart/sick, -sore (one word).

heart/-strings, —— -whole (hyphens).

heathenize, *not* -ise.

heather mixture, fabric of mixed hues (two words).

heave ho! (two words).

Heaven, cap. when equivalent to the Deity; l.c. when a place, as 'heaven is our home'.

heaven/-born, —— -sent (hyphens).

Heaviside layer, layer of the atmosphere that reflects wireless waves, *not* Heavy-.

heavy-weight (boxing) (hyphen).

Heb., Hebrew, Epistle to the Hebrews (N.T.).

hebdomad/, a group of seven, a week, *not* -ade; adj. **-al.**

hebraize, to make Hebrew, *not* -ise, -aicize.

Hebrew (typ.), 22 letters (all consonants) and many accents, points (representing vowel sounds), etc. The consonants have numerical values, the first ten being 1 to 10, the next nine 20 to 100, the remaining three 200, 300, 400. Numbers 11, 12, etc., are 10+1, 10+2, etc., but 15 is 9+6, and 16 is 9+7, because 10+5 and 10+6 resemble the name of the Deity, Yahweh. There is the ordinary square fount, and the 'rabbinical'. It is read from right to left: hence if any passage is divided, the right-hand words must go in the first line, and the left-hand in the second. Set with the nick downwards. Abbr. **Heb.**

Hebridean, *not* -ian.

Hecat/e, a Greek goddess; adj. **-aean.**

hecatomb, sacrifice of many (lit. 100) oxen.

Heckmondwike, Yorks.

Hecla, mt., Hebrides, *not* Hek-. *See also* **Hekla.**

hecto-, prefix meaning 100; **hectogramme** (**hg**), 100 grammes; **hectolitre** (**hl**), 100 litres; **hectometre** (**hm**), 100 metres.

Hedda Gabler, play by Ibsen, 1890.

hedgerow (one word).

hedgrah, use **hegira.**

hee-haw, a, *or* to, bray, *not* he-, hiu-.

Heep (**Uriah**), in *David Copperfield, not* Heap.

Heer (Ger. n.), army (cap.).

Hegel/ (**Georg,** *not* -e, **W. F.**), 1770–1831, German philosopher; adj. **-ian.**

hegira, the flight of Muhammad from Mecca to Medina, 16 July, A.D. 662, from which the Muslim era is reckoned (Ar. **hijrah**); *not hedgrah,* heijira (not ital.). The calendar follows a 355-day lunar cycle, and it is difficult to equate A.D. and A.H. dates.

H.E.I.C., Honourable East India Company.

Heidelberg, German university town.

Heidsieck, a champagne.

heighday, *use* hey-.

heigh-ho, an audible sigh, *not* hey-.

height to paper (typ.), height of type, 2·33 cm.

heil (Ger.), hail!

Heiland (*der*) (Ger.), the Saviour (cap.).

heilig (Ger.), holy; abbr. *hl.*

Heilige Schrift (Ger. f.), Holy Scripture (caps.); abbr. *Hl.S.*

Heimskringla, 'the round world', a history of Norse kings by Snorri Sturluson, 1178–1241.

Heimweh (Ger. n.), home-sickness.

Heine/ (Heinrich, *but signed* Henri), 1797–1856, German poet; adj. **-ian.**

Heinemann (William), Ltd., publishers.

heinous, odiously wicked, *pron.* hān-.

Heinrich, Ger. for Henry.

Heinz, Ger. for Harry.

heir (an, *not* a).

heir apparent, legal heir, whoever may subsequently be born (two words); abbr. heir app.

heirloom (an, *not* a) (one word).

heir presumptive, legal heir if no nearer relative should be born (two words); abbr. heir pres.

Heisenberg (Werner Karl), b. 1901, German physicist, associated with principle of uncertainty.

Hejaz, 'the boundary'. *See* Saudi Arabia.

hejira, *use* hegira.

Hekla, volcano, Iceland, *not* Hec-. *See also* Hecla.

Hel., Helvetia (Switz.).

Hel (Norse myth.), originally, the abode of the dead; later, the abode of the damned, opp. Valhalla; later still, the goddess of the dead (*also* Hela).

hélas! (Fr.), alas! (*s* sounded).

Heldentenor (Ger. m.), 'hero-tenor', with robust operatic voice.

Helensburgh, Dunbarton, *not* -borough.

Helicon (Gr. myth.), mountain range in Boeotia, home of the Muses, site of fountains Aganippe and Hippocrene.

Heliogabalus, *use* Elag-.

heliogravure, a gravure process (not ital.).

helium, symbol He (no point).

hel/ix, a spiral curve like the thread of a screw; *pl.* -ices.

hell (not cap.); in Ger. f. *Hölle.*

hell (Ger.), clear, bright.

Helle (Gr. myth.), sister of Phrixus, fell from the golden ram into strait afterwards named Hellespont (the Dardanelles).

Hellen (Gr. myth.), son of Deucalion and Pyrrha, progenitor of the Greek race.

Hellen/e, a Greek; *pl.* -es, *pron.* hel'ēnz; adj. -ic (cap.).

Hellenist, one skilled in Greek; one who has adopted Greek ways, esp. a Jew of the Dispersion.

Hellenistic, of the Greek language and culture of the period after Alexander the Great.

hellenize, to make Greek, *not* -ise (cap. in hist. and cultural usage).

helmsman, one who steers (one word).

Héloïse, 1101–64, and Abélard, *not* El-.

helpmate, *not* -meet (one word).

helter-skelter (hyphen).

Helvellyn, mountain, Cumberland–Westmorland.

Hely-Hutchinson, Irish name (hyphen).

hema-, prefix, *use* hae-.

Hemel Hempstead, Herts. (two words).

Hemingway (Ernest), 1898–1961, American novelist.

hemistich (prosody), half a line; *pron.* -stik.

hemo-, prefix, *use* hae-.

hempseed (one word).

hem-stitch (hyphen).

hence/forth, -forward (one word).

hendiadys, one idea expressed by two words joined by a conjunction, as 'by might and main'.

henna/, Oriental shrub, leaves used for dyeing nails and hair; **-ed.**

henpeck/, -ed (one word).

Henri, Fr. for **Henry.**

henry, *pl.* **henrys,** international unit of inductance; abbr. **H** (no point).

Henry, abbr. **Hy** (no point).

Henry (O.), *nom de plume* of William Sidney Porter (1867–1910), American author.

Henschel (Sir George, Isidor Georg), 1850–1934, German-born English musician.

Henslow (John Stevens), 1796–1861, English botanist and geologist.

Henslowe (Philip), d. 1616, English theatrical manager, wrote 'Diary'.

Hepplewhite, eighteenth-century style of furniture, from George —, d. 1786, *not* Heppel-.

her., heraldry.

her. (Lat.), *heres* (heir).

Heracl/es, hero in Greek myth. (*not* Herak-); *adj.* **-ean,** *not* -ian. *See also* **Hercules, herculean.**

heraldry, abbr. **her.**

Heralds' College, abbr. **H.C.** (apos.).

herb/, -al (a, *not* an).

herbaceous, *not* -ious.

herbari/um, a collection of dried plants; *pl.* **-a** (not ital.).

Herbart (Johann Friedrich), 1776–1841, German philosopher and educationist.

Hercegovina, Yugoslavia.

Herculaneum, Roman town overwhelmed by Vesuvius, A.D. 79, *not* -ium.

herculean, very big and strong (**a,** *not* an), not cap. unless referring to Hercules, as 'Herculean labours'.

Hercules, the Greek hero **Heracles.**

herd-book (hyphen).

here/about, -s, -after, -by, in, -of, -on, -out (one word).

here/s (Lat.), heir; *pl.* **-des,** abbr. *her.*

here/to, -tofore, -under, -upon, -with (one word).

Hergesheimer (Joseph), 1880–1954, American novelist.

Heriot-Watt University, Edinburgh, 1966.

heritrix, an heiress, *not* -tress, here-.

Her Majesty (caps.), abbr. **H.M.**

hermeneutics, the science of interpretation, treated as sing.

hernia/, a rupture; *pl.* **-s.**

hero/ (a, *not* an); *pl.* **-es;** *adj.* **-ic.**

heroin, a drug, *not* -ine.

heronry, heron breeding-place, *not* heronery.

herpes, a skin disease; *herpes zoster,* shingles.

herpetolog/y, study of reptiles; **-ist.**

Herr/ (Ger. m.), Mr., Sir, *pl.* **-en; -in,** lady, mistress, *pl.* **-innen.**

Herr (der), the Lord (cap.).

Herre (Dan.), **herre** (Sw.), Mr., Sir.

Herrenvolk (Ger. n.), master race, (in Nazi ideology) the German people.

Herrgott (Ger.), Lord God.

herring-bone, a stitch (hyphen).

Herrnhuter, one of the sect of the Moravians (not ital.).

Her Royal Highness, abbr. **H.R.H.**

hers (no apostrophe).

Herschel (**Caroline Lucretia**), 1750–1848, German-born English astronomer; — (**Sir John Frederick William**), 1792–1871, English astronomer, son of — (**Sir William,** orig. **Friedrich Wilhelm**), 1738–1822, German-born English astronomer.

Herschell (**Baron**), 1837–99, Lord Chancellor.

Herstmonceux, Sussex, site of Royal Observatory, *not* Hurst-.

Herts., Hertfordshire.

Hertz (**Heinrich**), 1857–94, German physicist, discoverer of **Hertzian waves,** used in radio-communication.

Hertz, the unit of frequency; abbr. **Hz** (no point).

Hertzog (**J. B. M.**), 1866–1942, S. African statesman, *not* Herzog.

Herz (Ger. n.), heart (cap.).

Herzegovina, *use* Herce-.

Herzog/ (Ger. m.), duke, *pl.* *-e*; *-in* (f.), duchess; *-tum* (n.), duchy, *not* -thum (caps.).

Hesperis, a genus of plants.

Hesperus, evening star.

Hesse, German state, in Ger. **Hessen; Hessian,** inhabitant of Hesse, in Ger. **Hess**/**e,** *f.* **-in.**

hessian, a coarse cloth.

het (Du. n.), the; abbr. *'t,* as van't Hoff.

hetaer/**a** (Gr.), a courtesan, *pl.* *-ae*; *-ism, not* -tair-, -tar-.

heterogeneous, dissimilar.

heteroousian, believing Father and Son to be of unlike substance, *not* heterou-. *See* **homoiousian, homoousian.**

heu (Lat.), Alas!

Heureka, *use* **Eu-.**

heureusement (Fr.), happily.

heuristic, inciting to find out (an educational method). *See also* **Eureka.**

hex-, Gr. prefix for six; in Lat. **sex-.**

hey, a dance, *use* **hay.**

heyday, prosperity, *not* heigh- (one word).

heyduck, Hungarian of an ennobled mil. class (Hung. *hajdu, pl. hajduk*).

Heyerdahl (**Thor**), b. 1914, Norwegian ethnologist (*Kon-Tiki* expedition, 1947).

hey presto, conjuror's exclamation (two words).

HF (of lead in pencils), hard firm.

H.F., Home Fleet, — Forces.

Hf, hafnium (no point).

h.f., high frequency.

H.F.R.A., Honorary Fellow of the Royal Academy.

H.G., His, *or* Her, Grace, Home Guard, Horse Guards, High German.

Hg, *hydrargyrum* (mercury) (no point).

H.G.D.H., His, *or* Her, Grand Ducal Highness.

H.H., His, *or* Her, Highness; His Holiness (the Pope).

HH (pencils), harder than H.

hhd., hogshead, -s.

HHH (pencils), very hard.

H.I., Hawaiian Islands, *hic iacet* (here lies).

hiatus/, *pl.* **-es** (not ital.).

Hiawatha, American-Indian hero of Longfellow's poem.

hibernate, to spend the winter in torpor or in a warm climate, *not* hy-.

hibernize, *not* -ise.

hic, speech interruption, representing drunken hiccup.

hic (Lat.), this, here.

hiccup, *not* -cough, -kup.

hic et ubique (Lat.), here and everywhere.

Hichens (Robert S.), 1864–1950, English novelist.

hic iacet (*or jacet*) (Lat.), here lies; —— *sepultus*, here lies buried; abbr. **H.I.S.** *or* **H.J.S.**

hidalgo/, Spanish gentleman by birth; *pl.* **-s.**

hide-and-seek, a game (hyphens).

hieing, *not* hy-.

hier (Ger.), here; *Hier spricht man Deutsch*, German spoken here.

hieroglyph/, sacred character used in picture-writing; **-ic(s)**, **-ist**, **-ize** (*not* -ise).

hi-fi, high fidelity (no points).

higgledy-piggledy, haphazard, in confusion.

High Church (hyphen when adj.); **High-Churchman** (hyphen, caps.).

highfalutin (U.S.), bombast(ic), *not* -en, -n', -ng, hifalutin.

high-fidelity (radio), reproducing sound faithfully; abbr. **hi-fi** (no points).

high/-flown, —— **-flyer** (U.S. **-flier**) (hyphens).

highjacker, *use* **hijacker**.

highlight (one word).

high pressure, abbr. **H.P.**

high priest, abbr. **H.P.** (two words).

high/ road; —— **seas (the)**, outside territorial waters (two words).

high-water mark (one hyphen).

highwayman (one word).

H.I.H., His, *or* Her, Imperial Highness.

hijacker, (U.S.) armed person who preys on bootleggers; one who illegally takes control of lorry or aircraft; *not* high-.

Hijra/, **-h**, *use* **hegira**.

Hil., Hilary.

Hilary, a session of the High Court of Justice, a term of Oxford and Dublin universities; from **St. Hilary** of Poitiers, d. *c.* 367, festival 13 Jan.

hill, when with name to have cap., as Box Hill.

Hillary (Sir Edmund), b. 1919, N.Z. apiarist and mountaineer, climbed Everest 1953.

Hillingdon, Middlesex.

Hillington, Norfolk.

hill/side, **-top** (one word).

H.I.M., His, *or* Her, Imperial Majesty.

Himachal Pradesh, Indian state.

Himalaya *or* **the Himalayas**, India.

hinc/ (Lat.), hence; —— *illae lacrimae*, hence those tears.

Hinckley, Leics., *not* Hink-.

Hind., Hindu, -stan, -stani.

Hindi, a language of N. India, *not* -dee (not ital.).

hind leg (two words).

hindmost, *not* hinder-.

Hindoo, *use* **Hindu**.

hind quarters (two words).

hindrance, *not* -erance.

hindsight, being wise after the event (one word).

Hindu/, *not* -doo, abbr. **Hind.** (not ital.); **-ism**, **-ize.**

Hindu Kush, mountains, Afghanistan.

Hindustan, abbr. **Hind.**

Hindustani, Urdu, the Indian lingua franca; abbr. **Hind.**

hing/e, **-ing.**

Hinshelwood (Sir Cyril Norman), 1897–1967, British chemist.

hinterland, the 'back country' (not ital.).

hip/-bone, —— **-joint** (hyphens).

Hippocrat/es, *fl.* 400 B.C., Greek 'Father of Medicine'; **-ic.**

Hippocrene, fountain of the Muses on Mt. Helicon.

hippogriff, a fabulous monster, *not* -gryph (not ital.).

hippopotamus/, *pl.* **-es.**

hirdy-girdy (Sc.), in disorder. *See also* **hurdy-gurdy.**

hireable, obtainable for hire (U.S. **hira-**).

hire-purchase (hyphen), abbr. **H.P.** *or* **h.p.**

Hiroshima, Japanese city.

hirsel (Sc.) (noun), crowd; flock of sheep.

hirsle (Sc.) (v.i.), to slide, move in sitting position.

hirsute, hairy, *not* her-.

H.I.S., *hic iacet sepultus* (here lies buried).

His/ Eminence, abbr. **H.E.; — Excellency, H.E.; — Majesty, H.M.** (caps., not ital.).

his non obstantibus (Lat.), nevertheless.

hispanicize, to render Spanish, *not* -ise.

His, *or* **Her, Royal Highness** (caps.), abbr. **H.R.H.**

hist., histor/ian, -ic, -ical.

Historicus, pen-name of George Grote, also of Sir W. Vernon Harcourt.

history (a, *not* an); notable epochs or events to have caps., as the Julian Era, the Middle Ages, the Peace of Utrecht.

Hitchin, Herts., *not* -en.

Hiuen Tsang, seventh-century Chinese traveller.

H.J., *hic iacet* (here lies).

H.J.S., *hic iacet sepultus* (here lies buried).

H.K., House of Keys, Isle of Man.

H.L., House of Lords.

hl, hectolitre (no point).

hl. (Ger.), *heilig* (holy).

H.L.I., Highland Light Infantry, now incorp. into Royal Highland Fusiliers.

Hl.S. (Ger.), *Heilige Schrift* (Holy Scripture).

H.M., Her, *or* His, Majesty; Home Mission.

hm, hectometre (no point).

h.m., *hoc mense* (in this month), *huius mensis* (this month's).

H.M.A., Headmasters' Association.

H.M.C., Her, *or* His, Majesty's Customs; Headmasters' Conference.

H.M.I., Her, *or* His, Majesty's Inspector.

H.M.O.W., Her, *or* His, Majesty's Office of Works, now **M.P.B.W.**

H.M.P., *hoc monumentum posuit* (he, or she, erected this monument).

H.M.S., Her, *or* His, Majesty's Service, *or* Ship.

H.M.S.O., Her, *or* His, Majesty's Stationery Office.

H.M.T., Her, *or* His, Majesty's Trawler.

H.O., Home Office.

Ho, holmium (no point).

ho., house.

hoar-frost (hyphen); U.S., one word.

hoarhound, use hore-.

Hobbema (Meindert), 1638–1709, Dutch painter.

Hobbes (Thomas), 1588–1679, English philosopher.

hobbledehoy, raw youth, *not* the many variations.

hobby-horse (hyphen).

hob-nob (hyphen).

hobo/ (U.S.), a tramp; *pl.* **-es.**

Hoboken, N.J., U.S.

hoboy (mus.), use oboe.

hoc/ age (Lat.), attend! **— anno,** in this year, abbr. **h.a.; — genus omne,** all this class; **— habet,** a palpable hit! (of gladiators).

hochepot (Fr. cook. m.), hotchpotch, stew, ragout.

Hocking (Joseph), 1855–1937; — **(Silas K.),** 1850–1935; British novelists.

hoc/ loco (Lat.), in this place; — *mense,* in this month, abbr. **h.m.;** — *monumentum posuit,* he, *or* she, erected this monument, abbr. **H.M.P.;** — *quaere,* look for this, **h.q.;** — *sensu,* in this sense, **h.s.;** — *tempore,* at this time, **h.t.;** — *titulo,* in, *or* under, this title, **h.t.**

hocus/, to hoax, drug; **-sed, -sing** (U.S. **-ed, -ing**).

hocus-pocus, jugglery, deception (hyphen).

hodge-podge, a medley. *See also* **hotch-.**

hodie (Lat.), today.

hodmandod, a snail.

hodograph (math.), a curve.

hodomet/er, distance measurer; **-ry** (U.S. **od-**).

Hoe, Plymouth; *pron.* hō.

Hoe, American printers: **Robert,** 1784–1833, his son **Richard March,** 1812–86, and grandson **Robert,** 1839–1909.

hoeing, *not* hoing.

Hofer (Andreas), 1767–1810, Tirolese patriot.

Hoffmann (Daniel), 1576–1601, German theologian; — **(Ernst Theodor Amadeus,** orig. **Wilhelm),** 1776–1822, German writer and composer, source of Offenbach's *Tales of Hoffmann*; — **(Frederic),** 1660–1742, German chemist. *See also* **Hof-.**

Hoffnung (Ger. f.), hope (cap.).

Hoffnung (Gerard), 1925–59, English humorous artist and musician.

Hofmann (August Wilhelm von), 1818–92, German chemist; — **(Josef Casimir),** 1876–1957, Polish pianist and composer; — **(J. C. K. von),** 1810–77, German theologian. *See also* **Hoff-.**

Hofmannsthal (Hugo von), 1874–1929, Austrian poet, librettist of Richard Strauss.

hogg, yearling sheep; **hogget** also in use.

Hogmanay (Sc.), the last day of the year.

hogshead/, -s, abbr. **hhd.**

Hogue (La), France, dép. La Manche.

Hohenzollern (House of), Prussian Imperial family.

hoiden, *use* hoy-.

hoing, *use* hoe-.

hoi polloi (*not* the — —) (Gr.), the masses, *not* oi —.

hokey-pokey, ice-cream, *not* hoky-poky (hyphen).

hokum, stage business used for cheap effect.

Holbein (Hans), German painters: 'the Elder', 1465–1524; 'the Younger', 1497–1543.

Holbrooke (Joseph Charles), 1878–1958, English composer.

hold-up (noun), detention by force with view to robbery (hyphen).

hole-and-corner, secret (hyphens).

holey, having holes.

Holi, Hindu religious festival.

holibut, *use* halibut.

holily, sacredly.

Holinshed (Raphael), d. 1580, English chronicler, *not* -ings, -head.

holland, a linen (not cap.).

hollandais/ (Fr.), *fem.* **-e,** Dutch; abbr. **holl.** (not cap.).

Hollands, Dutch gin.

Hölle (Ger. f.), hell.

hollow (bind.), paper reinforcement of spine of case.

hollyhock, a plant.

Hollywood, Los Angeles, Calif., U.S.

Holman-Hunt (William), 1827–1910, English painter (hyphen).

Holmes McDougall, Ltd., publishers.

holmium, symbol **Ho** (no point).

holocaust, whole burnt-offering, wholesale sacrifice or destruction.

Holofernes, Assyrian general (-ph- in N.E.B.); a pedantic teacher (Shakespeare: *Love's Labour's Lost*).

holograph, a document wholly in the handwriting of the person from whom it proceeds.

Holtei (Karl Eduard von), 1798–1880, German poet and actor.

Hölty (Ludwig Heinrich C.), 1748–76, German poet.

holus-bolus, all at once (hyphen).

Holy Communion (caps.), abbr. **H.C.**

Holy Cross Day (three words, caps.), Holy-rood Day, feast of the Exaltation, 14 Sept.

Holy/ Ghost; — Land (two words, caps.).

Holyoake (George Jacob), 1817–1906, English writer and agitator; — **(Rt. Hon. Sir Keith Jacka, G.C.M.G., C.H.),** b. 1904, Prime Minister of New Zealand, 1960–72.

holy of holies, inner chamber of the Jewish tabernacle (not caps.).

Holy Roman Empire (caps.), abbr. **H.R.E.**

Holy-rood Day (one

hyphen, two caps.). *See* **Holy Cross Day.**

Holyroodhouse, Palace of, Edinburgh.

Holy Saturday, one before Easter (caps.).

Holy Spirit, as Deity (caps.).

holystone (naut.), (to scour decks with) soft sandstone (one word).

Holy Thursday, Ascension Day in English Church; but Thursday in Holy Week, or Maundy Thursday, in Roman Church.

Holy Week, one before Easter (two words, caps.).

Holywood, Co. Down, N. Ireland.

homage, public acknowledgement of allegiance, in Fr. *hommage* (m.).

homard (Fr. m.), lobster.

hombre (Sp.), man.

Home, surname, *pron.* Hūm.

home-brewed (hyphen).

Home Counties (the), Essex, Herts., Kent, Middlesex, Surrey (sometimes includes Berks., Bucks., Sussex); abbr. **H.C.**

home-guard, member of a volunteer force for home defence (hyphen); **Home Guard** (two words, caps.), (member of) British citizen army formed in 1940.

homely, familiar, unpretentious, (U.S.) ugly.

home-made (hyphen).

homeopathy, *use* homoeo-.

Home/ Rule, — Ruler (two words, caps.); abbr. **H.R.**

homesick/, -ness (one word).

homespun (one word).

homing, *not* -eing.

hominy (U.S.), ground maize.

Hommage/ d'auteur, — de l'auteur (Fr.), with the author's compliments; — *d'éditeur, — de l'éditeur,* ditto publisher's, *not* editor's.

homme/ *d'affaires* (Fr.), business man, *not* — des —; — *de bien*, a respectable man; — *de cour*, a courtier; — *de lettres*, author; — *de paille*, man of straw; — *d'épée*, a mil. man; — *de robe*, lawyer; — *d'esprit*, man of wit; — *d'état*, statesman; — *de tête*, man of resource; — *du monde*, man of fashion.

hom/o (Lat.), human being; *pl.* **-ines**.

homoeopathy, treatment of diseases by minute doses of drugs that excite similar symptoms (U.S. **homeo-**).

homogeneous, consisting of parts all of the same kind.

homogenize, to make (milk) homogeneous, *not* -ise.

homogenous, similar through common descent.

homoiousian, believing Father and Son to be of like substance (not ital.). *See* **heteroousian**, **homoousian**.

homonym, a word of like spelling but different meaning, *not* -me.

homoousian, believing Father and Son to be of the same substance, *not* homou- (not ital.). *See* **heteroousian**, **homoiousian**.

homophones, words spelt differently but pronounced alike.

Homo sapiens (biol.), the species man.

homy, home-like, *not* -ey.

Hon., Honourable (son of a peer), Honorary.

hon. (Fr.), *honoré* (honoured).

Honble., Honourable (former Indian title).

Honegger (Arthur), 1892–1955, Swiss-French composer.

honest (**an**, *not* a).

honey-bee (hyphen).

honeycomb (one word).

honeydew, a sticky substance, a tobacco (one word).

honeyed, sweet, *not* -ied.

honey/moon, -suckle (one word).

Hong Kong (S. coast of China; no hyphen).

Honi soit qui mal y pense, shamed be he who thinks evil of it (motto of the Order of the Garter).

honnête homme (Fr. m.), a worthy man; *homme honnête*, a polite man.

honoraires (Fr. pl. m.), fee, salary.

Honorar (Ger. n.), honorarium (cap.).

honorarium/ (**an**, *not* a), voluntary fee for professional services; *pl.* **-s** (not ital.).

honorary secretary, abbr. **Hon. Sec.**

honoré/ (Fr.), *fem.* **-e**, honoured; abbr. *hon.*

honorific, doing honour.

honoris/ causa, or — *gratia* (Lat.), for the sake of honour.

honour (**an**, *not* a), U.S. **-or.**

honourable (**an**, *not* a); abbr. for son of peer, **Hon.**, for Indian title, **Honble.**

Hon. Sec., honorary secretary.

hoodwink (one word).

hoof/, usual *pl.* **-s**, *not* -ves.

Hooghly, India, *not* Hugli.

Hook./ (bot.), **Sir William J. Hooker**, 1785–1865, English botanist; — **fil.** (bot.), **Sir Joseph D. Hooker**, 1817–1911, English botanist, son of Sir William.

Hook (Theodore Edward), 1788–1841, English humorist. *See also* **Hooke**.

hookah, Oriental pipe, *not* hook/a, -er, hoqqa, houka, hukah (not ital.).

hook and eye (no hyphen).

Hooke (Robert), 1635–1703, English physicist. *See also* **Hook**.

Hooker, English botanists, see **Hook**.

hooping-cough, use wh-.

hoopoe, S. European bird; *pron.* hoo'poo.

hope (**a**, *not* an).

Hopi/, American-Indian, *pl.* **-s**, *not* -ki, -qui.

Hopkins (Gerard Manley), 1844–89, English poet; — (**Johns**, *not* John) University, U.S. (no apos.).

hop-o'-my-thumb, a pygmy (hyphens).

hop-picker (hyphen).

Hoppner (John), 1758–1810, English painter.

hopscotch, children's game (one word).

hor., horizon.

hor/a (Lat.), hour, *pl.* -ae; *horae/ canonicae*, hours for prayer; — *subsecivae*, leisure hours.

Horatius Cocles, who kept the Sublician Bridge; *pron.* kŏk'lēz.

horde, a wandering tribe, *not* hoard.

horehound, a plant (juice used for coughs), *not* hoar-.

horizon, abbr. **hor.**

horn (English), one of the oboes, usu. called **cor anglais**; — (**French**), one of the trumpet class.

hornblende, a mineral, *not* -d.

hornpipe, a dance (one word).

horologe, a timepiece (not ital.).

horology, abbr. **horol.**

horresco referens (Lat.), I shudder to mention it.

hors/ (Fr.), beyond, out of; — *concours*, not for competition (*not* de); — *de combat*, disabled; — *de la loi*, outlaw; — *de pair*,

without an equal; *hors d'œuvre* (cook., *sing.* and *pl.*), appetizer(s).

Horse Artillery (caps.), abbr. **H.A.**

horseback (one word).

horse/-chestnut, *not* -chesnut; — **-coper**, *not* -couper; — **-flesh**; — **-fly** (hyphens).

Horse Guards, abbr. **H.G.** (two words, caps.).

horsehair (one word).

horse/-marines, an imaginary corps; — **-play**, rough behaviour (hyphens).

horsepower (abbr. **hp**), unit of power (7.46×10^2 watts).

horse-race (hyphen), *but* **Horserace** (one word) **Totalisator Board**, and **Horserace Betting Levy Board**.

horse-radish (hyphen).

horseshoe (one word).

Horseshoe Fall, Niagara; **Horse Shoe Falls**, Guyana.

horse-tail, Turkish standard; a plant (hyphen).

horsewhip (one word).

hors ligne (Fr.), exceptional.

'Horst Wessel Song', song of the German Nazi party, named from the writer of the words.

horsy, horse-like, *not* -ey.

hort., horticulture.

hortus siccus, collection of dried plants.

Hos., Hosea.

Hosanna/, a shout of praise, 'save, we pray', *not* -ah (not ital.); — **Sunday**, Palm Sunday.

hospital (**a**, *not* an), abbr. **hosp.**

hospitaller, one of a charitable brotherhood (U.S. **-aler**).

hostel/, -ry.

hostler, see **ostler**.

hotbed (one word).

hotchpot (law), commixture of property to secure equable distribution (one word).

hotchpotch (cook.) (one word). *See also* **hodge-**.

hôte (Fr. m.), innkeeper, host; *also* guest.

hotel (**name of**), when cited, if ambiguous, to be roman quoted, as 'The Farmhouse'.

Hôtel des Invalides, Paris, founded 1670 as hospital for disabled soldiers, contains Napoleon's tomb (caps.).

hôtel/ de ville (Fr. m.), town hall; — *-Dieu* (*l'*), chief hospital of a town (one cap.); — *garni,* — *meublé,* furnished lodgings.

hotelier, hotel-keeper (not ital., no accent).

hot-house (hort.) (hyphen).

Houdan, breed of fowls.

Houdin (**J. E. Robert-**), 1805–71, French conjuror.

Houdini (**Harry**), real name **Ehrich Weiss,** 1874–1926, American escapologist.

Houdon (**Jean-Antoine**), 1741–1828, French sculptor.

Houghton-le-Spring, Co. Durham (hyphens).

hour/ (**an**, *not* a); abbr. **hr., hrs.,** but **h** (no point, same in pl.) in scientific work; — **-glass** (**an**, *not* a) (hyphen).

houri/, a nymph of the Muslim paradise; *pl.* **-s.**

Housa, African race, *use* **Hausa.**

house, number of, in a street, should have no comma after, as 6 Fleet Street; abbr. **ho.**

House (**the**), the Stock Exchange, Christ Church (Oxford), the House of Commons, (in past usage) the work-house.

house/-agent, — **-boat** (hyphens).

housebote (law), tenant's right to wood to repair his house (one word).

housebreaker (one word).

house/-flag, distinguishing flag of a shipping company; — **-fly** (hyphens).

house/holder, -keeper, -maid (one word).

house/-painter, — **-physician,** abbr. **H.P.;** — **-surgeon,** abbr. **H.S.** (hyphens).

housewife (one word).

Housman (**Alfred Edward**), 1859–1936, English scholar and poet; — (**Laurence**), 1867–1959, English writer and artist, brother of preceding.

Houssaye (**Arsène**), 1815–96, French novelist and poet; — (**Henri**), 1848–1911, French historian, son of preceding.

Houyhnhnm, one of a race of horses with noble human characteristics (*Gulliver's Travels*), *pron.* hwĭn'ĭm; contrasted with **Yahoo,** q.v.

hovell/er, uncertificated boatman doing casual coasting work; his boat; **-ing** (two *l*'s).

howbeit (one word).

howdah, elephant-seat, *not* -a, houda, -ah, -ar.

how-do-you-do, *or* **how-d'ye-do** (hyphens).

howitzer, a cannon.

hoyden, tomboy, *not* hoi-.

H.P., half-pay (*also* **h.p.**), high pressure (*also* **h.p.**), high priest, hire-purchase (*also* **h.p.**), house-physician, Houses of Parliament.

hp, horsepower (no point).

H.Q., Headquarters.

h.q., *hoc quaere* (look this up).

H.R., Home Rule, -r, House of Representatives.

hr., hrs., hour, -s (non-technical use).

Hradec, Czechoslovakia, *not* Grätz.

Hrdlicka (Aleš), 1869–1943, American anthropologist, born in Bohemia.

H.R.E., Holy Roman Empire.

H.R.H., Her, *or* His, Royal Highness.

H.R.I.P. (Lat.), *hic requiescit in pace* (here rests in peace).

H.S., *hic sepultus* (or *situs*) (here is buried), *hoc sensu* (in this sense), house-surgeon.

HS, symbol for sesterce, Roman coin equivalent to ¼ of a denarius (no point).

Hs. (Ger.), *Handschrift* (manuscript).

H.S.C., Higher School Certificate, *now* G.C.E., A-level.

H.S.E., *hic sepultus* (or *situs*) *est* (here lies buried).

H.S.H., His, *or* Her, Serene Highness.

H.S.M., His, *or* Her, Serene Majesty.

H.S.S., *Historicae Societatis Socius* (Fellow of the Historical Society).

h.t., *hoc tempore* (at this time), *hoc titulo* (in, *or* under, this title); (elec.) high tension.

ht. wkt. (cricket), hit wicket.

H.U., Harvard University.

hubble-bubble, Oriental pipe (hyphen, not ital.).

Huberman (Bronislaw), 1882–1947, Polish violinist.

hubris/ (Gr. drama), insolent pride that invites disaster, *not* hy- (not ital.); adj. **-tic.**

huckaback, rough-surfaced linen fabric, *not* hugga-.

Hucknall Torkard, Notts., where Byron is buried.

Hudson Bay, N. America, *but* **Hudson's Bay Company.**

hue and cry (no hyphen).

Hueffer, later **Ford (F. M.),** q.v.

hugger-mugger, secret(ly) (hyphen, **not ital.**).

Hughenden, Bucks., *not* -don.

Hugli, *use* **Hooghly.**

Hugo (Victor Marie), 1802–85, French poet, novelist, playwright.

Huguenot (hist.), a French protestant, *not* -onot.

huis clos (à) (Fr.), with closed doors, *in camera.*

huissier (Fr. m.), bailiff, doorkeeper.

huîtres (Fr. f.), oysters.

huius anni (Lat.), of this year; abbr. **h.a.**

hullabaloo, uproar (*not* the many variants).

Hullah (John Pyke), 1812–84, English musician.

Hulsean Lectures, Cambridge.

Humaniora (Lat.), the humanities; abbr. **Hum.** *See also* **Lit Hum.**

humanize, *not* -ise.

Humberside, new county, proposed 1971, including East Riding of Yorkshire, Hull, Grimsby, Scunthorpe, and other parts of Lincolnshire.

humble (a, *not* an).

humble-bee (hyphen).

humble pie (to eat), *not* umbel (two words).

Humboldt (Friedrich H. A., Baron von), 1769–1859, German naturalist; —— **(Karl W., Baron von),** 1767–1835, German philologist, statesman, and poet.

humdrum, commonplace (one word).

Humean, of David Hume, 1711–76, Scottish historian and philosopher, *not* -ian.

humerus, upper-arm bone (not ital.).

hummel/ (Sc.), of cattle, hornless; of grain, awnless; verb, to remove barley awns; **-led, -ler.**

humming-bird (hyphen).

hummum, Turkish bath; *use* **hammam**.

humoresque, a musical caprice, *not* humour-.

humor/ist, -ize, *not* -ise.

humorous/, -ly, -ness.

humour/, -some (capricious), (U.S. **humor/**).

humpback (one word).

Humperdinck (**Engelbert**), 1854–1921, German composer; — (—), b. 1936, English pop singer, real name Dorsey (Arthur George).

Humphrey (**Duke of Gloucester**), 1391–1447, son of Henry IV of England, Protector during minority of Henry VI.

Humphrey's Clock (*Master*), by Dickens, 1840.

Humphry (*not* -ey) *Clinker*, by Smollett, 1771.

humpty-dumpty (hyphen), a short, squat person (from **Humpty-dumpty** in nursery-rhyme).

hum/us, vegetable mould; adj. **-ous**.

hunchback (one word).

hundert (Ger.), hundred.

hundred/, symbol **C**; **-weight/, -s** (one word), abbr. **cwt** (no point).

Hundred Years War, between England and France, 1337–1453 (no apos.).

Hung., Hungar/y, -ian.

Hungary, abbr. **Hung.**; in Fr. **Hongrie**, in Ger. **Ungarn**, in Hung. (Magyar) **Magyarország**.

Hunstanton, Norfolk.

Hunter's Inn, N. Devon (apos.).

Hunter's Quay, Argyl. (apos.).

Huntingdonshire/, abbr. **Hunts.**

Huntington, Yorks.; — **Library**, San Marino, California.

Huntley, Glos.

Huntly/, Aberdeen; — (**Marquess of**), *not* -ey.

Hunyadi János, Hungarian mineral water.

Hunyady (**János C.**), 1387–1456, Hungarian general of Romanian descent, *not* -adi.

hurds, *use* **hards**.

hurdy-gurdy (mus.), *not* hirdy-girdy, q.v.

hurly-burly, commotion, *not* hi- bi-.

hurrah, *not* -ay.

hurry-scurry, pell-mell, *not* -sk-.

Hurstmonceux, Sussex, *use* Herst-.

Hurstpierpoint, Sussex (one word).

husband, abbr. **h.**

Husbands Bosworth, Rugby (no apos.).

Huss (**John**), 1369–1415, Bohemian religious reformer, in Ger. **Hus** (**Johann**).

hussy, pert girl, *not* -zzy.

Huygens (**Christian**), 1629–95, Dutch mathematician and astronomer, *not* -ghens; *pron.* hī'gĕnz.

Huysmans (**Joris Karl**), 1848–1907, French novelist.

huzza, a hurrah.

huzzy, *use* **hussy**.

Hwang Ho (riv. China), *not* Hoangho.

H.W.M., high-water mark.

Hy, Henry (man's name) (no point).

hyacinth (bot.).

Hyacinthe (**Père**), Charles Jean Marie Loyson, 1827–1912, French priest.

hyaena, *use* **hyena**.

hybernate, *use* **hi-**.

hybridize, etc., *not* -ise.

hyd., hydrostatics.
Hyderabad, Deccan, India; Sind, Pakistan; *not* Haidar-, Hydar-.
hydrangea, a shrub, *not* -ia.
hydro/, an abbr. of hydropathic establishment (no point), *pl.* **-s.**
hydro/carbon, -dynamics (one word).
hydrogen, symbol H (no point).
hydrolysis, decomposition of water.
hydrophobia, aversion to water, rabies (not ital.).
hydroplane, kind of motor-boat (one word).
hydrostatics, abbr. **hyd.**
hydrotherap/eutics, -y (one word).
hyena, *not* hyae-.
Hyères, dép. Var, France.
Hygeia, (Gr.) goddess of health, *not* -gea, -giea, -gieia (the older Gr. spelling); adj. **hygeian,** healthy.
hygiene, science of health.
hying, *use* **hie-.**
Hylton-Foster (Sir Harry), 1905–65, Speaker of the House of Commons 1959–65.
hymen/ (anat.), virginal membrane (not ital.); adj. **-al.**
Hymen (Gr. and Rom. myth.), god of marriage; adj. **hymeneal.**
hymn-book (hyphen).
hyp., hypothesis, hypothetical.

hyperaem/ia, excess of blood; adj. **-ic** (U.S. **-emia**); *not* -haemia.
hyperbola, a curve.
hyperbole, exaggeration.
hypercritical, excessively critical.
hyphen/ize, *not* -ise; *but use* **-ate.**
hyphens, *see* **punctuation** XIII.
hypnotize, *not* -ise.
hypochondria, morbid anxiety about health, *not* -condria.
hypocrisy, pretence.
hypocrite (a, *not* an), a pretender.
hypocritical, pretend/ed, -ing.
hyperderm/a, an underlying tissue; *pl.* **-ata.**
hypotenuse (geom.), *not* hypoth-.
hypothecate, to mortgage.
hypothes/is (an, *not* a), provisional explanation; *pl.* **-es;** abbr. **hyp.**
hypothesize, to assume, *not* -ise, -tize.
hysterectomy (surg.), removal of the womb.
hysteresis (phys.), a lagging of variation in effect behind variation in cause.
hysteron proteron (Gr.), the reverse of natural order, the cart before the horse.
hysterotomy (surg.), cutting into the womb.
Hz, Hertz, SI unit of frequency (no point).

I

I, iodine, (roman numeral) one (no point), the ninth in a series.

I (ital. cap.), symbol for electric current.

I., island, -s, all proper names with this initial, *imperator* (emperor), *imperatrix* (empress), (Ger.) *Ihr* (your), etc.

i., *id* (that).

ι (Gr.), iota (no dot).

I (it is), *see* **it is I.**

Ia., Iowa.

I.A., Incorporated Accountant, Indian Army, infected area.

I.A.A.F., International Amateur Athletic Federation.

I.A.A.M., Incorporated Association of Assistant Masters, usu. called **A.M.A.**

I.A.H.M., Incorporated Association of Headmasters. *See* **A.H.M.I.**

I.A.M., Institute of Advanced Motorists.

iamb/us, foot of two syllables (⏑ –); *pl.* **-i; -ic, -ics.**

-iana (suffixed to a name), writings by or (now usu.) anecdotes about or objects connected with a person, as Shakespeariana, Victoriana.

I.A.T.A., International Air Transport Association.

I.B., Intelligence Branch.

I.B.A., Independent Broadcasting Authority (from 1972).

Iberian, pertaining to Spanish peninsula.

ibex/, mountain-goat; *pl.* **-es.**

ibidem (Lat.), in the same place, abbr. **ib.,** *or* **ibid.** (not ital., not cap.). *See also* **idem.**

ibis/, wading bird; *pl.* **-es.**

Iblis, *use* **E-.**

I.B.R.D., International Bank for Reconstruction and Development.

Ibsen (Henrik), 1828–1906, Norwegian writer.

I.C., *Iesus Christus* (Jesus Christ); inferiority complex; Intelligence Corps.

i/c, in charge.

I.C.A., Institute of Contemporary Arts.

I.C.A.N., International Commission for Air Navigation.

I.C.A.O., International Civil Aviation Organization.

Icarian, of Icarus, *not* -ean.

I.C.B.M., inter-continental ballistic missile.

I.C.E., Institution of Civil Engineers.

Ice., Iceland, -ic.

ice-cream (hyphen).

Icelandic (typ.), roman now used, but with many special characters.

ich (Ger.), I (cap. only at beginning of sentence).

Ich dien (Ger.), I serve (motto of the Princes of Wales).

I.Chem.E., Institution of Chemical Engineers.

ichneumon, fly *and* weasel.

ichthyology, study of fishes; abbr. **ichth.**

ichthyosaur/us, extinct marine animal; *pl.* **-i.**

Ichthys (Gr. 'fish', early Christian symbol), initial letters of *Iesous Christos Theou Uios Soter* (Jesus Christ, God's Son, Saviour).

Ici on parle français, French spoken here (l.c. *f*).

Icknield Street *or* **Way.**

I.C.N., *In Christi nomine* (in Christ's name).

icon/, an illustration or portrait, esp. religious; *pl.* **-s; -ic;** *not* ik-, eik- (not ital.). *See also* **eikon.**

icon., iconograph/y, -ic.

I.C.S., Indian Civil Service.

I.C.T., *Iesu Christo Tutore* (Jesus Christ being our protector).

I.C.U., International Code Use (signals).

i.c.w., interrupted continuous wave.

I.D. (mil.), Intelligence Department.

id (Lat.), that; abbr. **i.**

id., *idem* (the same).

I'd, I had, *or* I would; (typ.) to be close up.

id (in Freudian psychology), not cap.

I.D.A., International Development Association (U.N.).

Idaho, off. not abbr.

I.D.B. (S. Afr.), illicit diamond buy/er, -ing.

I.D.C., Imperial Defence College.

idealize, *not* -ise.

idealogical, *see* **ideo-.**

idée fixe (Fr. f.), fixed idea.

idem/ (Lat.), the same, *or* as mentioned before; abbr. **id.,** *pl.* same, used generally to avoid repetition of author's name in footnotes or bibliographical matter (*see also* **ibidem**); — **quod,** the same as, abbr. *i.q.*

Identikit (picture), composite drawing of face used in police work (cap.).

ideograph, a character, not a word, symbolizing an idea, *not* idea-.

ideolog/y, study of ideas, a way of thinking; **-ical, -ist;** *not* ideal-.

ides (noun, pl.), in Roman calendar the fifteenth day of March, May, July, October, the thirteenth of other months.

id est (Lat.), that is; abbr. **i.e.** (abbr. not ital., no caps., comma before).

id genus omne (Lat.), all of that kind.

idiocy, *not* -tcy.

idiosyncra/sy, a peculiarity of temperament, *not* -cy; **-tic.**

idl/ing, -y, *not* -eing, -ey.

I.D.N., *In Dei nomine* (in God's name).

idolater, *not* -or.

idolize, *not* -ise.

idol/um, -on, a false mental image; *pl.* **-a.**

Idumaea, *not* -ea.

idyll, a work of art depicting innocence or rusticity (U.S. **idyl**).

-ie-, in words, the pronunciation of which does not imply the spelling: achieve, adieu, aggrieve, Aries, befriend, belie, belief, believe, besiege, bier, bombardier, brief, brigadier, calefacient, cashier, cavalier, chandelier, chief, chiffonier, coefficient, collie, coterie, eyrie, fief, field, fieldfare, fiend, fierce, flies, friend, frieze, gaselier, grenadier, grief, griev/e, -ance, -ous, handkerchief, hygienic, lief, liege, lieu, lieutenant, mien, mischief, mischievous, niece, piece, -meal, pier, pierce, prairie, priest, relie/f, -ve, reprieve, retrieve, reverie, review, rilievo, shield, shriek, siege, sieve, species, thief, thieve, tier, tierce, tiercel, view, -less, wield, yield, and in the pl. of nouns, comparative of adverbs, and past part. of verbs ending in y (*not* -ey), as fancies, speedier, hurried. *See also* **-ei-.**

I.E., (Order of the) Indian Empire, Indo-European.

i.e., *id est* (that is) (not ital., no caps., comma before).

I.E.E., Institution of Electrical Engineers.

I.E.R.E., Institution of Electronic and Radio Engineers.

Iesu (Lat.), Jesus (vocative).

I.F.C., International Finance Corporation (U.N.).

I.F.S., Irish Free State.

I.F.T.U., International Federation of Trade Unions (*now* World ditto).

I.G., Indo-Germanic, (mil.) Inspector-General.

I.Gas.E., Institution of Gas Engineers.

igloo/, Eskimo snow-hut; *pl.* **-s.**

ign., *ignotus* (unknown).

igneous, of *or* like *or* produced by fire, *not* -ious.

ignis fatuus (Lat.), will-o'-the-wisp; *pl.* **ignes fatui.**

ignitable, *not* -ible.

ignoramus/, an ignorant person; *pl.* **-es.**

ignoratio elenchi (Lat.), refuting a proposition differing from that one professes to be refuting.

ignotum per ignotius (Lat.), the unknown by means of the more unknown, *not* ignotus.

ignotus (Lat.), unknown; abbr. **ign.**

i.h., *iacet hic* (here lies).

IHC *or* **I.H.C.,** same as **IHS,** C being a form of **Gr.** cap. S.

ihm (Ger.), to him.

Ihnen (Ger.), to you (in address) (cap.); to them (not cap.).

Ihr (Ger.), your (cap.).

ihr (Ger.), to her, her, their (not cap.).

IHS *or* **I.H.S.,** abbr. of Gr. *Iesous* (H being Gr. cap. E); later interpreted as Lat. *Iesus Hominum Salvator* (Jesus Men's Saviour); *In Hoc Signo* (*vinces*), in this sign

(thou shalt conquer); *In Hac* (*Cruce*) *Salus*, in this (cross) is salvation.

I.H.V.E., Institution of Heating and Ventilation Engineers.

II (roman numeral), two (no point).

I.I.A., Institute of Industrial Administration.

III (roman numeral), three (no point).

IIII, *use* **IV,** except sometimes on clock-face.

i.J., *im Jahre* (in the year).

ij (med.), two. In Dutch now used instead of **y.**

i.J.d.W. (Ger.), *im Jahre der Welt* (in the year of the world).

I.K.H. (Ger.), *Ihre königliche Hoheit* (Her Royal Highness).

ikon, *use* **icon.**

il (Fr.), he *or* it; (It., m. sing.), the.

I.L.E.A., Inner London Education Authority.

Île de France (Fr. prov.).

ilex/, the holm-oak; *pl.* **-es.**

Iliad, of Homer (ital., not quoted).

Ilichpur, India, *use* **Ellich-.**

ilk (of that), of the same name as ancestral estate.

Ill., off. abbr. Illinois.

ill., *illustrissimus* (most distinguished).

I'll, I shall or will; (typ.) to be close up.

ill-advised/, -ly (hyphens).

Ille-et-Vilaine, dép. France.

illegalize, *not* -ise.

illegitimatize, *not* -ise.

ill health (two words).

Illinois, off. abbr. **Ill.**

ill nature (two words); **ill-natured** (hyphen).

illuminati (noun, pl.), the enlightened ones (cap.), a name of various sects, esp. German, freethinkers of late eighteenth century.

illusory, of more apparent than real value. *See* **elusive.**

illustrat/ed, -ion, abbr. **illus.**

illustrations, references to be as 'Pl. II, Fig. 4'.

illustrator, *not* -er.

ill will (two words).

il n'y a pas de quoi (Fr.), don't mention it.

I.L.O., International Labour Organization, ditto Office (at Geneva).

I.L.P., Independent Labour Party.

'Il Penseroso', poem by Milton.

I.L.S., Incorporated Law Society.

I.L.T.F., International Lawn Tennis Federation. *But see* **tennis.**

I'm, I am; (typ.) to be close up.

imagines maiorum (Lat.), ancestors' portraits.

imag/o, winged insect; *pl.* **-ines** (not ital.).

imam, Muslim priest, *not* -âm, -aum.

I.Mar.E., Institute of Marine Engineers.

imbroglio/, a tangle; *pl.* **-s;** *not* em- (not ital.).

imbrue, to stain, dye, *not* em-.

imbue, to saturate, inspire (with feelings), *not* em-.

I.M.C.O., Inter-governmental Maritime Consultative Organization.

I.Mech.E., Institution of Mechanical Engineers.

I.M.F., International Monetary Fund.

I.Min.E., Institution of Mining Engineers.

im Jahre (Ger.), in the year; abbr. *i.J.*

I.M.M., Institution of Mining and Metallurgy.

immanent, inherent. *See also* **immi-.**

immediately.

immesh, *use* en-.

imminent, coming on soon. *See also* **imma-.**

immobiliz/e, *not* -ise; **-ation.**

immortalize, *not* -ise.

immortelle, an everlasting flower (not ital.).

Immortels (Les), the members of the French Academy.

immov/able, -ability, -ableness, -ably.

immunize, to render immune from contagion, *not* -ise.

imp., imperative, imperial, impersonal, import/ed, -er, imprimatur.

imp., (Fr.) *imprimeur* (printer); (Lat.) *imperator* (emperor).

I.M.P., Institute of Management in Printing.

impair, *not* em-.

impale, *not* em-.

impa/nel, -nnel, *use* **em-panel.**

impassable, not to be passed.

impasse, a blind alley (not ital.).

impassible, insensible.

impassioned, emotionally stirred, *not* em-.

impasto, the thick laying on of colour.

impayable (Fr.), invaluable, priceless.

impedance (elec.), hindrance.

impedimenta (noun, pl.), (mil.) baggage.

impel/, -led, -ling.

imperative, (mood) expressing command; abbr. **imp.**

imperat/or (Lat.), *fem.* **-rix,** absolute ruler; abbr. **I.**

imperf., imperfect, (stamps) imperforate.

imperial, abbr. **imp.**

imperial, former standard

size of paper, 22 × 30 in.; —
4to, 15 × 11 in.; — 8vo,
11 × 7½ in. (untrimmed).
See **book sizes.**
imperil/, -led, -ling (U.S.
-ed, -ing).
imperium in imperio
(Lat.), an empire within an
empire.
impermeable, impervious.
impersonal, abbr. **imp.**
impetus/, momentum,
incentive; *pl.* **-es.**
imphee, a sugar cane, *not*
-fe, -phie (not ital.).
impi, Zulu regiment.
imping/e, to make an
impact (on); **-ing.**
import/ed, -er, abbr. **imp.**
impose (typ.), to arrange
pages of type in a 'forme'
so that they will read
consecutively when the
printed sheet is folded.
impostor, *not* -er.
impostume (archaic), an
abscess, *not* -thume.
impresa (It.), an under-
taking.
impresario/, manager of
operatic or other cultural
undertakings (one *s*, not
ital.); *pl.* **-s.**
impressa (It.), an imprint.
impression (typ.), product
from one cycle of a printing
machine; complete reprinting
of an unaltered edition;
indentation in paper by a
printing surface; pressure
exerted between printing and
impression surfaces.
imprimatur, official licence
to print, sanction; abbr.
imp. (not ital.).
imprim/er (Fr.), to print;
-erie (f.), printing office;
-eur (m.), printer.
imprimi potest (Lat.),
formula giving imprimatur
(ital.).
imprimis (Lat.), in the first
place, *not* in primis (ital.).

imprint, a book must show
the name and address of the
printer; name and address
of printer and publisher
must appear on *all* parliamentary and municipal
election work. —
(publisher's), the name of
the publisher, place of
publication, and date, usu.
printed at the foot of the
title-page. *See also* **title-
pages.**
impromptu/, *pl.* **-s** (not
ital.).
improvis/e, to extemporize;
-ator, one who composes as
he performs, or speaks
without preparation; **-er,** in
general, one who improvises.
I.Mun.E., Institution of
Municipal Engineers.
In (chem.), indium (no point).
in., inch, **-es,** (q.v.).
in (Ger), in, into.
I.N.A., Institution of Naval
Architects, *now* **R.I.N.A.**
in/ abstracto (Lat.), in the
abstract; — *actu,* in
reality; — *aeternum,* for
ever; — *alio loco,* in
another place.
inadverten/t, (of people)
negligent, (of actions)
unintentional; **-ce.**
inamorat/o, *fem.* **-a,** a lover
(not ital.); in It.
innamorat/o, -a.
in articulo mortis (Lat.),
at the moment of death.
inasmuch (one word).
Inauguration Day (of U.S.
President), 20 Jan.; before
1937, 4 Mar.
in banco (Lat.), before a
quorum of judges.
Inbegriff (Ger. m.), epitome,
embodiment (cap.).
Inc. (U.S.), Incorporated.
Inca, one of the royal race
of Peru, *not* Y-.
in caelo quies (Lat.), in
heaven (is) rest, *not* coe-.

incage, *use* **en-.**

in| camera (Lat.), not in open court; — *capite,* holding direct from the Crown.

incase (vb.), *use* **en-.**

in| cathedra (Lat.), in the chair of office; — *cautelam,* for a warning.

incavo (It.), the incised part of an intaglio.

inch/, in metric system 25·4 millimetres; *pl.* **-es,** abbr. **in.,** sign ". Not now to be used in scientific work.

inchase, *use* **en-.**

Inchcape Rock *or* **Bell Rock** (two words).

inchmeal, little by little.

in Christi nomine (Lat.), in Christ's name; abbr. **I.C.N.**

incipit| (Lat.), (here) begins; *-ur,* it is begun.

incise, to cut into, engrave, *not* -ize.

incl., including, inclusive.

inclasp, *use* **en-.**

incloister, *use* **en-.**

inclose, etc., *see* **en-.**

including, abbr. **incl.**

'In Coena Domini', celebrated papal bull.

Incogniti, cricket club.

incognit/o (noun or adj.), (a man) with name concealed or disguised; *pl.* **-i;** *fem.* **-a,** *pl.* **-e;** *also* adv.; abbr. **incog.** (not italic).

income tax (two words).

in| commendam (Lat.), temporarily holding a vacant benefice; — *concreto,* in the concrete.

incommunicado, without means of communication (not ital.); in Sp. *incomunicado.*

inconnu| (Fr.), *fem.* **-e,** unknown.

incor., incorporated.

incorrigible, *not* -able.

increas/ed, -ing, abbr. **incr.**

incredible, *not* -able.

incroach, *use* **en-.**

incrust, *use* **en-.**

incubous (bot.), having the upper leaf-margin overlapping the leaf above.

incub/us, person or thing that oppresses like a nightmare; *pl.* **-uses** (*preferred*) *or* **i.**

incumber, etc., *use* **en-.**

incunabul/a, sing. **-um,** the earliest examples of any art; (bibliog.) books printed before 1501.

incur/, to bring on oneself; **-red, -ring, -rable.**

in curia (Lat.), in open court.

incu/s (anat.), a bone in the ear; *pl.* **-des.**

in custodia legis (Lat.), in legal custody.

Ind, poetical for India (no point).

Ind., India, -n; off. abbr. for Indiana, U.S.

ind., independent, index, indication.

I.N.D., *in nomine Dei* (in the name of God).

in das (Ger. n.), into the; abbr. *ins.*

indeclinable (gram.), having no inflexions; abbr. **indecl.**

indefatigabl/e, tireless; **-y.**

indefeasible, that cannot be forfeited, *not* -able.

indefensible, that cannot be defended, *not* -able.

indefinite, abbr. **indef.**

indelible, that cannot be blotted out, *not* -able, -eble.

indemni/fy, to protect against harm or loss; **-ty;** *not* en-.

indent (typ.), to begin a line, or lines, with a blank space.

indention (**hanging** *or* **reverse**) (typ.), *see* **hanging paragraph.**

indenture, sealed agreement, esp. one binding apprentice to master, *not* en-.

independ/ence, -ent, abbr.
  ind.
Independence Day, U.S.,
  4 July.
**Independent Order of Odd
  Fellows,** *not* Oddfellows.
in deposito (Lat.), in
  deposit.
index/, *pl.* **-es,** abbr. **ind.**
  For general instructions for
  setting indexes *see Hart's
  Rules,* pp. 18–22.
ind/ex (sci. and math.), *pl.*
  -ices.
'Index/ Expurgatorius'
  (Lat.), index of the passages
  to be expunged; **'——
  Librorum/ Expurgan-
  dorum'** (R.C.C.), a list of
  books which might be read
  only in expurgated editions;
  '—— Prohibitorum'
  (R.C.C.), a list of books
  which the Church forbade to
  be read.
index/ rerum (Lat.), an
  index of things; ——
  verborum, ditto of words.
India/, -n, abbr. **Ind.**
India/man, a large ship in
  the Indian trade; *pl.* **-men.**
india matting.
Indiana (U.S.), off. abbr.
  Ind.
Indianapolis, U.S.
indian/ corn, —— ink, *not*
  india —— (not cap.).
Indian summer (U.S. and
  Canada), period of warm
  weather in late autumn or
  early winter.
Indian Territory, U.S., off.
  abbr. **Ind.T.**
India paper, thin book
  paper, *not* -ian (no hyphen);
  Oxford —— ——, very thin,
  strong bible paper made only
  for the O.U.P.
indiarubber (U.S. **India
  rubber**).
indication, abbr. **ind.**
indicative (gram.), abbr.
  indic.

ind/ices (sci. and math.), *not*
  -exes; *sing.* **-ex.**
indict/, to accuse by legal
  process; **-er,** *not* -or.
indiction (later Rom. Emp.),
  cycle of years for
  administrative and dating
  purposes.
indigestible, *not* -able.
indiscreet, injudicious.
indiscrete, not divided into
  distinct parts.
in disparte (It.), aside.
indispensable, *not* -ible.
indite, to put into written
  words.
indium, symbol **In** (no
  point).
individualize, *not* -ise.
individu/um (Lat.), the
  indivisible; *pl.* **-a.**
Indo-China (U.S.,
  Indochina), former
  collective name for
  the countries of the
  south-eastern peninsula
  of Asia.
Indo-European, abbr. **I.E.,**
  or **Indo-Eur.**
Indo-German/, -ic, abbr.
  I.G., *or* **Indo-Ger.**
Indonesia, independent
  1950, *formerly* Dutch East
  Indies, with W. New Guinea
  added 1962; abbr. **Indon.**
indoor/, -s (one word).
indorse, etc., *use* **en-.**
Indostan, *use* **Hindu-.**
indraught, a drawing in,
  not -aft.
Ind.T., off. abbr. for Indian
  Territory, U.S.
in dubio (Lat.), in doubt.
indubitably.
induction, *not* -xion.
indu/e, -re, *use* **en-.**
inédit/, *fem.* **-e** (Fr.), unpublished.
inedita (Lat.), unpublished
  compositions.
ineffaceable.
ineligible, *not* -able.
inept, absurd.

inertia (not ital.), *but vis inertiae.*

in/ esse (Lat.), actually existing; — ***excelsis,*** in the highest (degree); — ***extenso,*** in full; — ***extremis,*** at the point of death.

in f., in fine (finally).

inf., infantry, infinitive.

inf., infra (below).

infallibilist, a believer in the Pope's infallibility, *not* -blist.

Infanta, dau. of King and Queen of Spain; **Infante,** younger son of ditto.

infantry, abbr. **inf.**

infected area, abbr. **I.A.**

infer/, to draw a conclusion; **-red, -ring.**

inferable, *not* -rr-, -ible.

inferiority complex, abbr. **I.C.**

inferiors (typ.), small characters set at bottom of ordinary characters, as in maths. and chem., $_1$, $_2$, $_a$, $_b$.

inferno, a scene of horror; (cap and ital.) the first part of Dante's *Divina Commedia,* describing his journey through Hell.

in fieri (Lat.), in course of completion.

infima species (Lat.), the lowest species in a genus; *pl. infimae —.*

infin., infinitive.

in fine, finally; abbr. **in f.** (not ital.).

infinitive, abbr. **inf.,** *or* **infin.**

in flagrante delicto (Lat.), in the very act of committing the offence.

inflatable, *not* -eable.

inflator, one who or that which inflates (U.S. **-er**).

inflexible.

inflexion, modulation of voice, gram. termination (U.S. **-ction**).

infold, etc., use **en-.**

inforce, etc., use **en-.**

in forma pauperis (Lat.), as a pauper.

in foro/ conscientiae (Lat.), in the court of conscience; — — ***domestico,*** in a domestic, not foreign, court; — — ***seculari,*** in a secular court.

infra/ (Lat.), below, abbr. *inf.;* — ***dignitatem,*** undignified, abbr. *infra dig.*

infra-red (hyphen).

infula, the ribbons of a bishop's mitre.

infuser, one who or that which steeps something in a liquid, *not* -or.

infusible, that cannot be melted.

infusoria (obs., biol.) (noun, pl.), class of protozoa found in infusions of decaying matter.

in futuro (Lat.), in, *or* for, the future.

Ingelow (**Jean**), 1820–97, English poetess and author.

in genere (Lat.), in kind.

ingenious, inventive.

ingénue (Fr. f.), an artless girl.

ingenuity, inventiveness.

ingenuous, free-born, free from guile.

ingesta (noun, pl.), materials taken into the body (not ital.).

ingle-nook, chimney corner (hyphen).

Ingoldsby Legends, by R. H. Barham, 1840.

ingraft, ingrain (verb), use **en-.**

ingrain/ (adj.), dyed in the yarn; **-ed** (adj., less specific), deeply rooted, inveterate.

in gremio legis (Lat.), in the lap of the law.

in/gross, -gulf, *use* **en-.**

inhabitant, abbr. **inhab.**

in hac parte (Lat.), on this part.

in/ hoc (Lat.), in this respect; — *hoc salus,* safety in this; — *infinitum,* for ever.

I.N.I., *in nomine Iesu* (in the name of Jesus).

in initio, in the beginning, abbr. *in init.;* — *integrum,* entire; — *invidiam,* to excite prejudice; — *invitum,* compulsory.

Inishfail, poet. for Ireland, *not* Inn-.

inisle, *use* **en-.**

init., initio (Lat.), in the beginning.

initial/, -led, -ling.

initial letter (typ.), large letter used at beginning of chapter.

Initial Teaching Alphabet (caps.), abbr. **i t a** (spaced l.c., no points).

in iure (Lat.), in law (sometimes spelt *in j-*).

iniuri/a (Lat.), a wrong; *pl.* **-ae.**

Inkerman, Crimea, *not* -ann.

ink/pot, -stand (one word).

in/ limine (Lat.), at the outset, abbr. *in lim.;* — *loco,* in place of; — *loco citato,* in the place cited, abbr. **loc. cit.;** — *loco parentis,* in the position of parent; — *medias res,* into the midst of affairs; — *medio,* in the middle; — *medio tutissimus ibis,* the middle course is safest; — *memoriam,* to the memory (of).

innamorat/o, fem. **-a,** mod. It. spelling of **inam-.**

inner (typ.), the side of a sheet containing the second page.

Innes (Cosmo), 1798–1874, Scottish historian; —

(James Dickson), 1887–1914, British painter; — **(Michael),** pseud. of John Innes Mackintosh Stewart, b. 1906, British novelist; — **(Thomas),** 1662–1744, Scottish historian.

Inness (George), 1825–94, American painter.

innings (U.S. **inning**), portion of game played by one side; *pl. same.*

Innisfail, *use* **Inishfail.**

Inniskilling/ Dragoons, — Fusiliers. *See also* **E-.**

innkeeper (one word).

Innocents' Day, 28 Dec. (caps.).

innoculate, *use* **ino-.**

innocuous, harmless.

in/ nomine (Lat.), in the name (of a person); —*notis* (Lat.), in the notes.

innovation, a novelty (two *n*'s).

innoxious, harmless.

inns (names of), when cited, if ambiguous, to be roman quoted, as 'The Farmhouse'.

Inns of Court (the), Inner Temple, Middle Temple, Lincoln's Inn, Gray's Inn.

in/ nubibus (Lat.), in the clouds; — *nuce,* in a nutshell.

innuendo/, an injurious insinuation, *pl.* **-es,** *not* inu- (not ital.).

Innuit, an Eskimo of Alaska. *See* **Yuit.**

inoculate, to inject an immunizing serum into, *not* en-, inn-.

in/ pace (Lat.), in peace; — *pari materia,* in an analogous case; — *partibus infidelium,* in the regions of unbelievers, abbr. **i.p.i.** *or* **in partibus.**

in-patient (of a hospital), (hyphen).

in/ perpetuum (Lat.), for ever; — *persona*, in person; — *pontificalibus*, in pontifical vestments; — *posse*, potentially; — *posterum*, for the future; — *potentia*, potentially; — *praesenti*, now; — *praesentia*, for the present; — *primis, use* imprimis; — *principio*, in the beginning, abbr. **in pr.**; — *propria causa*, in his, *or* her, own suit; — *propria persona*, in his, *or* her, own person; — *puris naturalibus*, naked.

inquire, correct, but being superseded by **enquire.**

inquiry, an off. investigation. *See also* **enquiry.**

in/ re (Lat.), in the matter of; — *rem* (law), relating to a matter; — *rerum natura*, in the nature of things.

I.N.R.I., *Iesus Nazarenus, Rex Iudaeorum* (Jesus of Nazareth, King of the Jews).

inroad (one word).

inroll, *use* **enrol.**

I.N.S. (U.S.), International News Service.

ins., insurance.

in saecula saeculorum (Lat.), for ever and ever.

insconce, *use* **en-.**

in se (Lat.), in itself, in themselves.

Insecta (zool.), (Lat. pl.) insects, *not* -ae.

inset (typ.), to insert as an inset; an extra page or set of pages inserted in a proof, or book; an advertisement on a separate leaf inserted in a magazine; one folded sheet laid inside another.

inset/, -ted, -ting.

insh'allah, [if] God [is] willing (Arab.).

insignia, badges of office, is pl. (not ital.).

insisten/ce, -t, *not* -ance, -ant.

in situ (Lat.), in position.

insnare, *use* **en-.**

in so far (three words).

insomnia, sleeplessness.

insoucian/ce, lack of concern; **-t,** unconcerned (not ital.).

Inspector, abbr. **Insp.**

Inspector-General, abbr. **I.G.,** *or* **Insp.-Gen.**

I.N.S.T., *in nomine Sanctae Trinitatis* (in the name of the Holy Trinity).

inst., instant, institut/e, -es, -ion.

Inst. Act., Institute of Actuaries.

install (two *l*'s).

instalment (one *l*).

instant, of this month, abbr. **inst.**

instantaneous, taking no appreciable time.

instanter, at once (jocular) (not ital.).

instar omnium (Lat.), worth all the rest.

in statu/ pupillari (Lat.), in a condition of pupillage; — — *quo* (*ante, prius, or nunc*), in the same state (as formerly or now).

Inst.F., Institute of Fuel.

instil/, to inculcate gradually; **-led, -ling.**

Institut de France, the association of the five French Academies.

Institut Français du Royaume-Uni, the French Institute, London.

Institute, *see* separate entries beginning **I.** *or* **Inst.** (Institute of), **F.I.** (Fellow of the Institute of), **R.I.** (Royal Institute of).

Institution, *see* separate entries beginning **I.** (Institution of), **F.I.** (Fellow of the Institution of), **R.I.** (Royal Institution of).

institutor, *not* -er.

instructor, *not* -er.

instrument/, -al, abbr. **instr.**

insurance, the present usage is to differentiate life *assurance,* and fire and marine *insurance;* abbr. **ins.**

inswathe, *use* en-.

int., interest, interior, interjection, interpreter.

int. (Fr.), *intérêt* (interest).

intaglio/, incised design; *pl.* **-s** (not ital.). *See* **cameo.**

intaglio (typ.), a printing process based on an etched or incised plate, as **gravure,** q.v.

integration (sign of), ∫.

intelligentsia (coll. noun), the intellectual part of the population, *not* -zia.

Intelsat, International Consortium for Satellite Telecommunications.

in tenebris (Lat.), in darkness, in doubt.

intens., intensive, intensative.

inter/, to bury; **-red, -ring.**

inter/ (Lat.), between; — *alia,* among other things; — *alios,* among other persons.

intercom, internal telephone system (no point).

interest, abbr. **int.;** in Fr. m. *intérêt.*

interim, noun, the meanwhile; adj., temporary (not ital.).

interior, abbr. **int.**

interjection, abbr. **int.,** *or* **interj.**

interlea/f, an extra leaf, usu. blank, inserted between the regular leaves of a book; *pl.* **interleaves; -ve,** to insert such a leaf.

interlinear matter (typ.), small type between lines of larger. *See also* **quotations.**

intermarr/iage, -y (one word).

intermedi/um, an inter-

vening agent; *pl.* **-a** (not ital.).

intermit/, to stop for a time; **-ted, -tent, -ting.**

International, the first, association of working classes of all countries (Marxist, 1862–73); —, **the second** (French, 1889–); —, **the third** (Russian communist, 1919–43), in Fr. **Internationale,** also called the **Comintern.**

Internationale, The, French Socialistic hymn.

internationalize, *not* -ise.

inter nos (Lat.), between ourselves.

interoceanic (one word).

interpellate, demand explanations.

Interpol, the International Criminal Police Commission.

interpolate, make insertions.

interpret, *not* en-.

interpretative, *not* interpretive.

interpreter, abbr. **int.**

interregn/um, period between one ruler and another; *pl.* **-ums,** now displacing **-a.**

interrog., interrog/ation, -ative, -atively.

interrogation point (?), abbr. **inter.** *See* **punctuation** VI.

in terrorem (Lat.), as a warning.

interrupter, *not* -or.

inter/ se (Lat.), among, *or* between, themselves; — *vivos,* from one living person to another.

Intertype, a composing machine that casts lines of type.

in testimonium (Lat.), in witness.

inthra/l, -ll, *use* enthral.

intitule, etc., *not* en-, *but* **entitle.**

intonaco (It.), plaster surface for fresco painting, *not* -ico.

in toto (Lat.), entirely.

intra/ (Lat.), within; — *muros*, privately.

intrans., intransitive.

in trans., *in transitu* (on the way).

intransigent (adj.), irreconcilable; in Fr. *intransigeant* (m. and adj.) (no accent).

in transitu (Lat.), on the way; abbr. *in trans.*

intrap, *use* en-.

intravenous, within a vein (one word).

intra vires (Lat.), within one's powers.

intreat, *use* en-.

intrench, *use* en-.

intrigant/ (Fr.), *fem.* -e, intriguer (ital.).

introduction, abbr. **introd.** *See also* **preliminary matter.**

intrust, *use* en-.

intussusception (physiol.), taking in of foreign matter by living organism, withdrawal of one portion of tube into another (double *s*).

intwine, intwist, *use* en-.

inuendo, *use* inn-.

inure, to accustom, *not* en-.

in/ *usu* (Lat.), in use; — *utero*, in the womb; — *utroque iure*, under both laws (canon and civil). ¶

inv., *invenit* (designed it).

inv., invert/ed, -or, invoice.

in vacuo (Lat.), in empty space.

Invalides (Hôtel des), Paris. *See* **Hôtel.**

inveigle, to entice, *not* en-.

invenit (Lat.), designed it; abbr. *inv.*

invented, abbr. **inv.**

inventor, *not* -er; abbr. **inv.**

in ventre (Lat.), in the womb.

Inveraray, Argyl., *not* -ry.

inverness, man's sleeveless coat with removable cape (not cap.).

Inverness-shire (hyphen).

Invertebrata (coll. noun), all animals other than vertebrates.

inverted commas, *see* **quotation marks.**

Inverurie, Aberdeen.

investor, *not* -er.

in vino veritas (Lat.), a drunken man speaks the truth.

in vitro (Lat.), in the test-tube.

in vivo (Lat.), in the living organism.

invoice, abbr. **inv.**

involucre (anat., bot.), a covering, envelope (not ital.).

inweave, *not* en-.

inwrap, inwreathe, *use* en-.

I/O, Inspecting Order.

io (Gr., Lat.), exclamation of triumph (ital.).

I.O.D.E., Imperial Order of Daughters of the Empire (Canada).

iodine, symbol **I** (no point).

I.O.F., Independent Order of Foresters.

I.O.G.T., International Order of Good Templars.

I.O.M., Indian Order of Merit.

I.o.M., Isle of Man (*also* **I.O.M.**).

Ion., Ionic.

ionize, to convert into ions, *not* -ise.

I.O.O.F., Independent Order of Odd Fellows.

I.O.P., Institute of Painter. in Oil Colours.

I.O.R., Independent Order of Rechabites.

iota, the Gr. *i* (ι, no dot).

IOU, I owe you (no points).

I.O.W., Isle of Wight (*better* **I.W.**).

Iowa, not to be abbr.

I.P., input primary.
I.P.A., International Phonetic Association.
I.P.C.S., Institution of Professional Civil Servants.
I.P.D. (Sc. law), *in praesentia Dominorum* (in the presence of the Lords [of Session]).
ipecacuanha (bot., med.), a purgative.
i.p.i., *in partibus infidelium* (in the regions of unbelievers).
I.P.I., International Press Institute.
I.Prod.E., Institution of Production Engineers.
ipse dixit (Lat.), he himself has said it.
ipsissima verba (Lat.), the very words.
ipso/ facto (Lat.), by the fact itself; — *iure,* by the law itself.
I.Q., intelligence quotient.
i.q., *idem quod* (the same as).
Iquique, Chile; *pron.* ēkēkĕ.
I.R., Inland Revenue.
Ir, iridium (no point).
Ir., Irish.
I.R.A., Irish Republican Army.
irade (Turk.), a written decree signed by the Sultan himself.
Iran/, *formerly* Persia; **-ian, -ic,** abbr. **Iran.**
Iraq, *formerly* Turkish Mesopotamia, *not* Irak.
Irawadi, use **Irrawaddy.**
I.R.B., Irish Republican Brotherhood.
I.R.B.M., intermediate range ballistic missile.
I.R.C., International Red Cross.
Ireland, abbr. **Ire.**
Irena, Ireland personified.
irenicon, use **ei-.**
iridescen/ce, play of rainbow colours; **-t.**
iridium, symbol **Ir** (no point).
iris/ (anat., bot.), *pl.* **-es.**

Irish, abbr. **Ir.**
Irishism, *not* Iricism.
Irkutsk, E. Siberia, *not* Irkoo-, Irkou-.
irlandaise (*à l'*) (Fr.), in the Irish style (l.c. *i*).
I.R.O., International Refugee Organization; Inland Revenue Office.
iron, symbol **Fe** (no point).
ironclad (one word).
iron-mould (U.S. **-mold**) (hyphen).
ironwork (one word).
Iroquois, American Indians.
Irrawaddy, river in Burma, *not* Irawadi.
irreconcilable, *not* -eable, -iable.
Irredentist, one who (re)claims regions for his country on grounds of language, esp. Italian.
irrefragable, unanswerable, *not* -ible.
irreg., irregular, -ly.
irrelevant, not to the point.
irrepairable, of things broken.
irreparable, of losses.
irresistibl/e, -y, *not* -abl/e, -y.
Irvine, Ayrshire, 'new town', 1966.
I.S., input secondary, Irish Society.
Isa., Isaiah.
Isaian, of the prophet Isaiah, *not* Isaiahian.
I.S.B.N., International Standard Book Number.
I.S.C., Imperial Service College (Windsor), now combined with Haileybury.
-ise, the following end in -ise, *not* -ize: advertise, affranchise, apprise (to inform), chastise, circumcise, comprise, compromise, demise, despise, devise, disfranchise, disguise, emprise, enfranchise, enterprise, excise, exercise,

-ise (*cont.*):
franchise, improvise, incise, merchandise, premise (vb.), prise (to force open), reprise, seise (law), supervise, surmise, surprise, televise. *See also* **-ize, -yse.**

Iseult, Tristram's lady-love, *not* the many variants.

Isfahan, city in Iran, *not* Isp-.

isl., island, -s, isle, -s.

Islam, lit. 'surrender (to God)', the Muslim religion. *See also* **Muslim.**

island/, -s, abbr. **I.,** *or* **isl.;** (typ.) when with name to have cap., as Cape Verde Islands, Isle of Man. In Fr. f. **île.**

I'sland, Ice. for Iceland.

Island (Ger. and Dan. n.), Iceland; **Isländer,** an Icelander.

Islay, Argyl., *not* Isla.

isle/, -s, abbr. **I.,** *or* **isl.**

Isle of/ Man, abbr. **I.o.M.,** *or* **I.O.M.;** — **Wight,** abbr. **I.O.W.,** *or* **I.W.**

Isleworth, W. London; *pron.* **i′zel-.**

I.S.M., Imperial Service Medal; Incorporated Society of Musicians.

isn't, is not; to be close up.

I.S.O., (Companion of the) Imperial Service Order.

ISO, International Standards Organization.

isobar (meteor.), *not* -are (not ital.).

Isocrates, 436–338 B.C., Athenian orator.

isola (It.), island.

Iso/ld, -lt, -lte, -ulde, *use* **Iseult.**

isosceles (geom.), of a triangle, having two sides equal.

isotope, a form of an element differing from other forms in the nuclear mass of its atoms.

isotron, a device for separating isotopes by accelerating ions.

Ispahan, *use* **Isfahan.**

Israel/i (noun and adj.), (a citizen) of the modern state of Israel, est. 1948; **-ite** (noun), one of the Jewish people, adjs. **-itic, -itish.**

Istanbul, Turk. for Constantinople.

isth., isthmus.

I.Struct.E., Institution of Structural Engineers.

It., Italian, Italy.

I.T., Indian Territory, N. Amer. (off. abbr. **Ind.T.**).

I.T.A., Independent Television Authority. *See* **I.B.A.**

i t a (spaced l.c., no points), Initial Teaching Alphabet.

ital., italic.

Italian (typ.), same alphabet as Eng., omitting $k, w, x, y.$ Punctuation nearly as Fr. Letter j is obsolete in mod. It. except in names. There are two accents, grave ' and acute '; any vowel may have either. In general, plural of nouns is formed by changing the final o or e into i; fem. nouns ending in a change it to e. The apostrophe is frequently used at the end of a word. After an apostrophe following a vowel put the normal spacing of the line (this may, when necessary, end a line); but no space after an apostrophe following a consonant (this may not end a line); e.g. *a′ nemici, de′ libri,* but *dell′amico, l′onda.* In dividing words letters *ch* and *gn* must not be separated; correct division of words like *dell′amico* is *del-* and *l′amico.* For more detail see *Hart's Rules.* Abbr. **It.**

italic (typ.), *a style of type, as this,* indicated in MS. by a single underline. Use italic in English for foreign words and phrases not naturalized; for words or letters mentioned by name, as the letter *a*; for titles of books, very long poems, plays, films, operas, works of art, newspapers, and periodicals; and as a method of emphasizing or distinguishing. There is no italic in German, Greek, or Bernard Shaw's plays, letters being interspaced instead. Abbr. **ital.** *See also* **botany,** *Economist* (*The*), **quotation marks,** *Times* (*The*), **zoology,** the many words and phrases in this dictionary where a preference for italic or roman is indicated, and a fuller treatment in *Hart's Rules*.

italice, in Italian.

italicize, to print in italic type, *not* -ise.

italienne (*a l'*) (Fr.), in Italian style (l.c. *i*).

Italiot, of the ancient Greek colonies in S. Italy, *not* -ote.

Italy, abbr. **It.;** in Fr. f. *Italie*; in Ger. n. *Italien*; in It. *Italia*.

I.T.C., Infantry Training Centre.

item, a separate thing.

item (Lat.), also, likewise.

itemize, to give item by item, *not* -ise.

itin., itinerary.

it is I, it is me, latter used in speech, but should not be printed, except as a colloquialism.

I.T.O., International Trade Organization.

its, poss. pronoun (no apos.).

it's, it is; (typ.) no space before apos. *See also* **punctuation VIII.**

I.T.U., International Telecommunications Union.

ITV, Independent Television (no points).

I.U., international unit.

I.U.L.A., International Union of Local Authorities.

Ivanovich (**Ivan**), nickname for a Russian, as in Eng. John Bull.

I've, I have; to be close up.

ivied, clothed with ivy, *not* ivyed.

Ivory Coast, W. Africa, independent 1960.

ivy, *pl.* **ivies.**

Ivybridge, Devon (one word).

I.W., Isle of Wight.

I.W.E., Institution of Water Engineers.

I.W.G.C., Imperial War Graves Commission.

Iwo Jima, island in N. Pacific, taken by U.S. Marines, 1945.

I.W.T.(D.), Inland Water Transport (Department).

I.W.W., Industrial Workers of the World (U.S.).

I.X., *Iesus Christus* (Jesus Christ).

Izaak (*not* Isaac) **Walton,** 1593–1683, English author.

-ize, the normal suffix added to the stems of nouns in -ism (criticize), -ization (civilize), -izer (appetize), -y (agonize), or to a complete noun (canalize). Many common examples are given in this book. *See also* **-ise, -yse.**

I Zingari, cricket club.

J

J (phys. elec.), joule, Joule's mechanical equivalent of heat; it is not used in the numeration of series; *pron.* in Fr., Port., Rom. zh, in Sp. h, in Ger. and most other languages y.

J., judge, *judex* (judge), (after judge's name) Justice, all proper names with this initial; (Ger.) *Jahr* (year).

j (med. prescriptions), one; (math.) square root of minus one.

j. (Fr.), *journal* (newspaper).

J.A., Judge Advocate (no hyphen).

Jabalpur, *use* Jubbulpore.

jabot, ornamental frill on woman's bodice *or* (hist.) man's shirt-front.

Jac., Jacobus (James).

jacana, small tropical wading bird, *not* jaç-, jass-.

jacconet, *use* jaco-.

jackanapes (noun, sing.), a pert fellow (one word).

Jack and Gill, correct, but popularly **Jill**.

jackaroo (Austral. slang), a newcomer (usu. from England).

jackass, a male ass.

jack-in-the-box (hyphens).

Jack Ketch, the hangman, *not* — Ca-, — Ki-.

Jackson (Andrew), 1767–1845, American President 1829–37; — **(Thomas Jonathan, 'Stonewall')**, 1824–63, American Confederate general at first battle of Bull Run, 1861.

Jacob/ean, of the reign of James I of England; of St. James the Less. *See also* **-ian**.

Jacobi (Karl Gustav Jacob), 1804–51, German

mathematician, hence (in math.) **Jacob/ian**. *See also* **-ean**.

Jacobin, a French Dominican monk; a member of a French revolutionary society which met, 1793–9, in a Jacobin convent; **jacobin**, a hooded pigeon; *not* -ine.

Jacobite, an adherent of James II of England after his abdication in 1688, or of his line.

Jacobus, Lat. for **James**; abbr. **Jac.**

jacobus, a gold coin of James I.

jaconet, a medium cotton cloth, *not* jacc-.

Jacq. (bot.), abbr. for J. F. Jacquin, 1766–1839, *or* N. J. Jacquin, 1727–1817, French botanists.

Jacquard (Joseph Marie), 1752–1824, French weaver; hence — **loom**.

Jacquemart (Jules), 1837–80, French etcher.

Jacquerie, the French peasant revolt of 1358.

Jacques Bonhomme, good fellow James, popular name for French peasant.

jacta est alea (Lat.), the die is cast.

jactation, boasting.

jactitation, (law) false pretence of marriage; (path.) restless tossing of the body.

j'adoube (Fr.), 'I adjust', said by a chess-player touching, but not moving, a piece.

Jaeger, a woollen clothing material from which vegetable fibres are excluded.

Jäger (Ger. m.), huntsman, rifleman; anglicized as **yager.**

jag/gernaut, -anath, *use* **juggernaut.**

jaghire, Indian land tenure, *not* -gheer, -geer, -gir.

Jahn (Friedrich Ludwig), 1778–1852, German pedagogue known as 'Turnvater' ('father of gymnastics').

Jahr (Ger. n.), year, *pl.* **-e,** abbr. **J.** (*not* Jä-); **-buch,** n. year-book; **-esbericht,** m. annual report (caps.).

jährlich (Ger. adj.), annual.

Jahveh, *use* **Yahweh,** q.v.

jail/, -er, *use* **gaol/, -er.**

Jaipur, Rajasthan, India, *not* Jeypore.

Jakarta, Indonesia, *use* **Djakarta.**

Jakob, Ger. for **Jacob, James;** *pron.* yah-.

Jakutsk, Siberia, *use* **Yakutsk.**

Jalalabad, Afghanistan; and Uttar Pradesh, India, *not* Jela-.

Jalandhar, *use* **Jullundur.**

jalopy, a dilapidated motor car, *not* -ppy.

jalousie, external window shutter.

jam/, to pack tightly, *not* jamb; **-med, -ming.** *See also* **jamb.**

Jam., Jamaica.

Jamaica, independent 1962; abbr. **Jam.**

jamb, a side post, as of a door. *See also* **jam.**

jambon/ (Fr. cook. m.), a ham; **-neau,** small ham.

jamboree, rally of boy scouts.

James, abbr. **J.,** *or* **Jas.**

Jamesone (George), 1588–1644, Scottish painter.

Jameson Raid, S. Africa, 1895–6, from **Sir Leander Starr —,** 1853–1917.

James's Day (St.), 25 July (caps., apos.).

jamidar, *use* **jema-.**

Jamieson (John), 1759–1838, Scottish lexicographer. *See also* **James-.**

jam satis (Lat.), enough by this time.

Jan., January.

Janáček (Leoš), 1854–1928, Czechoslovak composer.

jane, a fabric, *use* **jean.**

Janeite, an ardent admirer of Jane Austen.

janizary, Turkish soldier, *not* -issary.

Jan Mayen, Arctic island (Norwegian).

Jansen/ (Cornelius), 1585–1638, R. C. Bishop of Ypres; **-ist,** one who believes, with Jansen, that the natural human will is perverse.

Janssen (Cornelius), 1590–1665, Dutch painter; —— (**Johannes**), 1829–91, German historian; —— (**Pierre Jules César**), 1824–1907, French astronomer.

Janssens (Abraham), 1569–1631, Dutch painter.

janty, *use* **jaunty.**

January, abbr. **Jan.**

Janus, Roman god of doors.

janvier (Fr. m.), January; abbr. *janv.* (not cap.).

Jap/, a Japanese; *pl.* **-s** (no point).

Japan, abbr. **Jap.;** native name **Nippon.**

japan/, to lacquer with a hard varnish; **-ned, -ner, -ning.**

Japanese/, abbr. **Jap.;** —— **paper,** hand-made in Japan with vellum surface. Used for proofs of etchings and engravings.

Japheth, third son of Noah, *not* -et.

Jaques, in *As You Like It*; *pron.* jā′kwĕz.
jar/, -red, -ring.
Jardin des Plantes, Paris, bot. and zool. gardens.
jardinière (Fr. f.), ornamental flower-pot.
jargon, debased language; a kind of zircon; *not* -oon.
jargonelle, a pear, *not* -el (not ital.).
jarl, old Danish chieftain, *not* y-; *pron.* yarl.
Järnefelt (Edvard Armas), 1869–1958, Finnish composer.
Jaroslav, Russ., *use* **Yaroslavl;** Pol., *use* **Jaroslaw.**
jarrah, Australian mahogany gum-tree.
jarvey/, hackney-coachman, driver of Irish car, *not* -vie, -vy; *pl.* -s.
Jarvie (Bailie Nicol), in *Rob Roy.*
Jas., James.
Jasmin (Jaques), 1798–1864, Gascon poet.
jasmine (bot.), *not* -in, jessamine, -in.
jaspé, mottled, veined, of materials and floor-coverings (not ital.).
Jaunpur, Uttar Pradesh, India.
jaunty, sprightly, *not* jan-.
Jav., Javanese.
javelle water, a bleacher, *not* -el (not cap.).
jaw-bone (hyphen).
J.C., Jesus Christ, Julius Caesar, Juris-consultus (jurisconsult), Justice Clerk.
J.-C. (Fr.), *Jésus-Christ* (hyphen).
J.C.D., *Juris Civilis Doctor* (Doctor of Civil Law).
J.C.R., Junior Common Room, — Combination Room.
J.D., Junior Deacon, — Dean, *Jurum Doctor* (Doctor of Laws).

je (Fr.), I, not cap. except at beginning of sentence.
Jeaffreson (John Cordy), 1831–1901, English historical writer.
jean/, a twilled cotton, *not* jane; *pl.* -s, informal trousers of same.
Jeanne d'Arc (Fr.), Joan of Arc.
Jean Potage, nickname for a Frenchman.
Jeddah, *use* **Jidda.**
Jeejeebhoy (Sir Jamsetjee), 1783–1859, Indian philanthropist.
Jefferies (Richard), 1848-87, English naturalist.
Jefferson (Thomas), 1743–1826, third President of U.S.
Jefferys (Thomas), *fl.* 1732–71, English cartographer.
Jeffrey (Francis, Lord), 1773–1850, Scottish jurist and literary critic.
Jeffreys (George, Baron), 1648–89, the infamous judge.
jehad, *use* **jihad.**
Jehlam, *use* **Jhelum.**
Jehovah, traditional form of **Yahweh,** q.v.
jejune, uninteresting (not ital.).
Jekyll (Dr.) and Mr. Hyde (**Strange Case of**), by R. L. Stevenson.
Jelalabad, Jellalabad, *use* **Jala-.**
jellify, to convert into jelly *not* -yfy.
jelly-fish (hyphen).
Jemappes (battle of), Belgium, French victory over Austrians, 1792, *not* Jemm-.
jemimas, elastic-sided boots (not cap.).
je ne sais/ quoi (Fr.), an indescribable something; — — — *trop,* I don't exactly know.

Jenisesi, *use* **Yeniseisk;**
Jenissei, *use* **Yenisei.**

**Jenkin (Henry Charles
Fleeming),** 1833–85, British
engineer and physicist.

Jenkins's Ear, incident
which precipitated War
with Spain, 1739.

jennet, a Spanish horse, *not*
genit, gennet, -tt. *See also*
genet.

jeopardize, to endanger, *not*
-ise.

Jephthah, judge of Israel.

jequirity, Indian shrub with
ornamental and medicinal
seeds, *not* -erity.

Jer., Jeremiah.

jeremiad, a lamentation,
not -de.

Jerez, Spain, *not* Xeres.

jerfalcon, *use* ger-.

jeroboam, wine-bottle
containing 10–12 quarts.

Jérôme Bonaparte, 1784–
1860, bro. of Napoleon I.

jerry-builder, builder of
unsubstantial houses
(hyphen).

jerrymander, *use* g-.

jersey, a knitted fabric,
a garment of same (not cap.).

Jervaulx Abbey, Yorks.

Jervis, *pron.* jar′vis.

Jes., Jesus.

**Jespersen (Jens Otto
Harry),** 1860–1943, Danish
philologist, *not* -son.

jessamin/, -e, *use* **jasmine.**

Jessop (Gilbert Laird),
1874–1955, English cricketer.

Jessopp (Revd. Augustus),
1824–1914, English essayist
and antiquary.

Jesuits (Order of), *Societas
Jesu* (Society of Jesus); abbr.
S.J.

Jesus, abbr. **J.,** *or* **Jes.**

jet-black (hyphen).

jetsam (naut.), goods
thrown overboard, *not* -som,
-some, -son. *See also*
jettison.

jettison (naut.), the act of
throwing goods overboard.
See also **jetsam.**

jetzt (Ger.), now.

jeu/ (Fr. m.), game, *pl.* **-x;**
— *de mains,* horse-play;
— *de mots,* play upon
words; — *de paume,*
real tennis (-court); *Musée
du — de Paume* (caps.),
Paris, exhib. of impressionist
paintings; — *d'esprit,*
a witty trifle; — *de scène,*
or — *de théâtre,* claptrap.

jeune fille (Fr.), a girl.

jeune premier (Fr.),
a stage lover; *fem.* —
première.

jeunesse dorée (Fr. f.),
gilded youth.

jewel/, -led, -ler, -lery
(U.S. **-ed, -er, -ry**).

Jew's harp, small lyre-
shaped instrument played
against the teeth (U.S.
jew's-harp),

Jeypore, Orissa, India, *not*
Jaipur.

Jhelum, W. Punjab,
Pakistan, *not* Jehlam.

Jhind, Punjab, *use* **Jind.**

JHS, *use* **IHS,** q.v.

jib, of a horse, *also* a sail, *not*
jibb. *See also* **gibe, gybe.**

jibber, to chatter, *use* g-.

jibe, *see* **gibe, gybe, jib.**

jiblet, *use* g-.

J.I.C., Joint Industrial
Council.

Jidda, Arabia, *not* Jeddah.

jiffy, a short time, *not* -ey.

jig, a standard factory pattern.

jigger, W. Indian insect, *use*
chigoe.

jigot, *see* **gigot.**

jigsaw (one word).

jihad, a holy war
(Muslim), *not* je-.

jilliflower, *use* gilly-.

jimcrack, *use* g-.

Jim Crow (U.S. colloq.),
a Negro; as adj.,
hyphenated.

Jind, P.E.P.S.U., India, *not* Jh-.

Jingo/, a blatant patriot; *pl.* -es.

jinnee, a spirit in Muslim myth., *not* djinn, ginn; *pl.* **jinn,** often used as sing.

jinricksha, two-wheeled, man-drawn carriage, *not* the many variants.

jiu-jitsu, *use* ju-jitsu.

JJ., justices.

Jno., John, but should not be used, except in exact reprints of documents, etc.

joannes, *use* johan-.

jobbing work (typ.), minor pieces of printing.

jobmaster, livery-stable keeper (one word).

'Jock o' Hazeldean', by Sir W. Scott.

jodel, *use* y-.

Jodhpur, Rajasthan, India.

jodhpurs, long riding-breeches.

joe (*also* **joey**), a fourpenny-bit (from Joseph Hume, M.P., 1836), a threepenny-bit; a shortened form of **johannes** (no point).

johannes, a gold coin of John V of Portugal, *not* joa-; abbr. **joe** (no point).

Johannesburg, S. Africa.

Johannine, of the apostle John, *not* Johannean.

Johannisberg, Hesse, Germany.

Johannisberger, Rhine wine, *not* -berg (not ital.).

Johannisfest (Ger.), St. John's (Midsummer) Day.

John, abbr. **J.** *See also* **Jno.**

John Dory, a fish, *not* — -ey.

John Hancock (U.S.), a person's autograph.

Johnian, (member) of St. John's College, Cambridge.

Johnny Crapaud, nickname for a Frenchman.

John o' Groat's House, Caithness.

Johns Hopkins University, U.S., *not* John — — (no apos.).

Johnson (**Samuel**), 1709–84, English prose-writer and lexicographer. *See also* **Jonson.**

Johnsonese, a stilted style, *not* Jon-.

John the Baptist (caps.).

Johore, *see* **Malaya, Federation of.**

joie de vivre (Fr.), joy of life (no hyphens).

joint/ capital, — stock, etc., *but* hyphen usual when used as adjective.

Jókai (**Maurus**), 1825–94, Hungarian novelist.

Jon., Jonathan.

jongleur, a wandering minstrel (not ital.).

jonquil, a narcissus (not ital.); in Fr. f. *jonquille.*

Jonson (**Benjamin—'Ben'**), 1572–1637, English dramatist. *See also* **Johnson.**

Jordaens (**Jakob**), 1593–1678, Dutch painter.

Jordan, a united kingdom from 1950.

Jorrocks's Jaunts, by R. S. Surtees.

jorum, a large drinking vessel or its contents, *not* -am.

Jos., Joseph.

Joseph, Flavius Josephus, 37–96, Jewish historian.

Josephine (**the Empress**), Marie Josèphe-Rose Tascher de la Pagerie, widow of Visc. Beauharnais, m. Napoleon I 1796, divorced 1809.

Josh., Joshua (O.T.).

jostl/e, to push; **-er, -ing,** *not* ju-.

jot/, -ted, -ting.

joule (phys.), SI unit of energy (symbol **J**).

jour., journal, journey.

jour/ (Fr. m.), day, abbr. *jr.;* — *de fête,* a festival; — *de*

jour/ (*cont.*):
l'an, New Year's Day; —
des morts, All Souls' Day,
2 Nov.; — *gras,* flesh-day;
— *maigre,* fish-day;
(*ouvrage*) *à* —, open work;
au —, by daylight.
journal, abbr. **jour.**
journ/al (Fr. m.), *pl. -aux,*
newspaper, abbr. *j.;*
journal intime, a private
diary.
Journal Officiel, the French
equivalent of *London Gazette.*
journey, abbr. **jour.**
journeyman (typ.),
a compositor, printer, or
bookbinder who has
completed his apprenticeship.
joust, knightly combat; **just**
is correct but in disuse.
jowl, the jaw, *not* jole.
J.P., Justice of the Peace.
J.R., *Jacobus Rex* (King
James).
jr., junior, *use* **jun.** (U.S. **Jr.**).
jr. (Fr.), *jour* (day).
J.T.C., Junior Training
Corps (in schools).
Juan, Sp. for **John.**
Jubbulpore, Madhya
Pradesh, India, *not*
Jabalpur.
J.U.D., *Juris utriusque Doctor*
(Doctor of both civil and
canon law).
jud., judicial.
Judaean, of Judaea, *not*
Judean.
judaize, to make Jewish,
not -ise.
Judg., Judges (O.T.).
Judge/, abbr. **J.;** —
Advocate/ (no hyphen),
abbr. **J.A.;** — — -**General**
(one hyphen), abbr. **J.A.G.**
(caps.).
judgement, *but* **judgment**
in legal works.
Judges (O.T.), abbr. **Judg.**
judicial, abbr. **jud.**
judo, modern form of
ju-jitsu.

jug/, -**ged, -ging, -ful.**
juge/ de paix (Fr. m.),
justice of the peace; —
d'instruction, examining
magistrate.
Juggernaut, incarnation of
Vishnu, carried in car
beneath whose wheels
devotees were said to
sacrifice themselves; *not* the
many variants.
Jugoslavia, *use* **Yugoslavia.**
jugular vein (in the neck).
juillet (Fr. m.), July (not
cap.).
juin (Fr. m.), June (not
cap.).
ju-jitsu, Japanese wrestling.
See **judo.**
julep, a medicated drink;
American drink of spirits,
sugar, ice, and mint, *not*
-ap, -eb.
Julian/, 'the Apostate'
Roman emperor, 331–63;
— **Alps,** Italy–Yugoslavia.
Julien (**Saint-**), a claret
(hyphen).
julienne (Fr. f.), a clear soup
containing vegetables in
strips, *also* a pear.
Jullundur, E. Punjab,
India, *not* Jalandhar.
July, not to be abbreviated.
jumbal, a sweet cake, *not*
-ble (not ital.).
jumelles (Fr. f. pl.), opera-
glass.
Jun., Junius.
jun., junior.
junction, abbr. **junc.**
June, not to be abbreviated.
junior, abbr. **jun.,** *not* jnr.,
jr., junr. (U.S. **Jr.**);
J. Smith, jun., Esq., *not* Esq.,
jun.
Junker (Ger. m.), a young
squire or noble (cap.).
junket/, -**ed, -ing.**
Jun. Opt., Junior Optime
(Cambr. Univ.).
junta (It., Sp.), an assembly
(not ital.).

Junto, the Whig chiefs in reigns of William and Anne.

junto, a club or assembly (not ital.).

jupe (Fr. dress f.); **jupon** (m.), a skirt or petticoat.

Jurassic (adj.), a geol. period (cap., not ital.).

jure/ divino (Lat.), by divine right; — *humano,* by human law.

jurisp., jurisprudence.

Juris utriusque Doctor (Lat.), Doctor of both civil and canon law; abbr. **J.U.D.**

jus (Fr. cook. m.), gravy.

jus (Lat.), law; — *canonicum,* canon law; — *civile,* civil —; — *divinum,* divine —; — *gentium,* law of nations; — *gladii,* the right of the sword.

jusjurandum (Lat.), an oath; *pl. jurajuranda.*

jus/ mariti (Lat.), right of husband to wife's property; — *naturae,* law of nature.

jus relictae (Lat.), right of the widow.

Jussieu (Adrien de), 1797–1853, French botanist, abbr. **Juss.,** son of — **(Antoine Laurent de),** 1748–1836, French botanist.

Just., Justinian.

just, a knightly combat; *use* **joust.**

juste milieu (Fr. m.), the golden mean.

Justice, a judge; abbr. **J.,** *pl.* **JJ.**

Justice-Clerk (Lord), second highest Scottish judge (caps.); abbr. **J.C.**

Justice-General (Lord), highest Scottish judge (caps.).

Justice of the Peace, abbr. **J.P.**

justiciar/, -y, a judge, *not* -er, -itiar (not ital.).

Justiciary (High Court of), supreme Scottish criminal court.

justify (typ.), to space out a line of type; to adjust types of differing bodies so that they range.

Justinian, 483–565, Roman emperor of the East, codified Roman law; abbr. **Just.**

just/itiar, *use* -iciar.

justle, *use* jos-.

justo/ tempore (Lat.), at the right time; — *titulo,* lawfully.

jut/, -ted, -ting.

Juvenal (Decimus Junius Juvenalis), *c.* 60–140, Roman poet.

juvenescen/ce, -t, becoming a young man instead of an infant.

j'y suis, j'y reste (Fr.), here I am, here I stay.

K

K (chem.) *kalium* (potassium), Kelvin (temperature scale), (chess) king (no point); the tenth in a series.

K., (assaying) carat, king(s), Kirkel (Mozart op. no.), all proper names with this initial.

k, prefix meaning 1000 (kilo-).

k., (meteor.) cumulus, (U.S.) carat.

k, (phys.) Boltzmann constant, (astron.) Gauss constant.

K2, the second highest mountain in the world, in Karakoram Mts.

Kaaba, the most sacred shrine at Mecca, properly *al-Ka'bah*; not Caaba.

kaan, *use* **khan.**

kaava, *use* **kava.**

kabbala, *use* **c-.**

Kabul, Afghan., *not* C-.

kadi, use **cadi.**

Kaffir, S. African Bantu.

kaffir-boom (Afrik.), a tree, *not* -boom tree.

Kaffraria, S. Africa.

Kafir, native of Kafiristan.

Kafka (Franz), 1883–1924, Czechoslovak poet and novelist.

kaftan, *use* **c-.**

kail, *see* **kale.**

kaiman, *use* **cay-.**

kainozoic, *use* **c-.**

Kaisar-i-Hind (Anglo-Ind.) (the Caesar of India), former Indian title of English monarch; *not* Q-.

Kaiser (Ger. m.), emperor (cap., not ital.).

kakemono (Jap.), a wall-picture.

Kal., kalendae.

kale/, the cabbage genus; — **-yard,** a cabbage garden,

kail-yaird only in strict Scots.

kaleidoscop/e, -ic, (an optical toy) producing a changing variety of colours and shapes.

kalendae (Lat.), the kalends (first day of the month), abbr. *kal.*

kalendar, *use* **c-.**

Kalevala, national epic of Finland, *not* -wala.

kali/f, -ph, *use* **caliph.**

kalium (Lat.), potassium; symbol **K** (no point).

kalmia (bot.), American evergreen shrub, *not* c-.

Kalmuck, member or language of Mongolian race, *not* -muk, C-.

kamarband, *use* **cummer-band.**

Kamboja, *use* **Cambodia.**

Kamchatka, E. Siberia, *not* Kams-, -mtchatka, -mtschatka.

Kamerad (Ger.), comrade (word used by soldier surrendering).

Kamerun, *use* **Cameroons.**

kamsin, *use* **kh-.**

Kan., Kansas, U.S.

kanaka, a South Sea Islander; esp. an indentured labourer.

Kanar/a, district of W. India; adj. **-ese.**

kanaster, a tobacco, *use* **c-.**

Kanchenjunga, *use* **Kinchin-.**

Kandahar, Afghanistan, *not* C-.

Kanpur, Uttar Pradesh, India, correct modern form of the more usual **Cawnpore.**

Kans/as, off. abbr. **Kan.;** adj. **-an.**

Kant (Immanuel), 1724–1804, German philosopher.

kaolin, a fine white clay.

kapellmeister, director of orchestra or choir (not cap., not ital.).

Kapurthala, E. Punjab, India.

kaput (slang), broken, ruined (not ital.), from Ger. *kaputt*.

Karachi, W. Pakistan, *not* Kurrachee.

Karafuto, southern portion of Sakhalin Island, E. Asia.

Karaite, a member of Jewish sect which interprets scriptures literally.

Karajan (Herbert Von), b. 1908, Austrian conductor.

Karakoram Mts., Kashmir, *not* -um.

karat (U.S.), in Eng. use **carat**.

karate, the Japanese art of delivering blows with the side of the hand, fingers, and feet; **Karateka**, an expert in this.

kari/ (Fr. cook.), curry (not cap.); — *à l'indienne*, Indian curry. *See also* **karri, kauri**.

Karlovingian, *use* C-.

Karlsbad, Czechoslovakia, *use* trad. Eng. **Carlsbad** or mod. Czech. **Karlovy Vary**.

Karls/krona (Sweden), **-ruhe** (W. Germany), etc., *not* C-.

karma (Budd.), destiny (not ital.).

Karnatak, *use* **Kanara**.

Karnatic, *use* C-.

Karoo, high pastoral plateau in S. Africa, *not* Karr-.

Karpathian Mts., *use* C-.

karri, Australian blue gum-tree, *not* kari. *See also* **kari, kauri**.

Karroo, *use* **Karoo**.

Kartoum, *use* **Khartoum**.

Kashmir, NW. India, *not* C-.

Kassel, Germany, *not* C-.

Kathay, *use* C-.

Kathiawar, *now* Saurashtra, Bombay, *not* Kattywar.

kathode, *use* c-.

kation, *use* c-.

Katmandu, cap. of Nepal.

ka-tou, *use* **kotow**.

katsup, *use* **ketchup**.

Kattegat (Dan.), **Kattegatt** (Sw.), the strait between Denmark and Sweden, *not* C-.

Kauffman (Angelica), 1741–1807, English painter.

Kaufman (George S.), 1889–1961, American playwright.

Kaufmann (C. von), 1818–82, Russian general.

kauri, N. Zealand coniferous tree, etc., *not* cowdi, -ri, -ry, kourie, kowrie (not ital.). *See also* **cowrie, kari, karri**.

kava, Polynesian intoxicant, *not* ava, cava, kaava, kawa.

kavass, Turkish armed attendant, *not* the many variants.

kayak/, Eskimo canoe, *not* -iak, -jak, -yack, kiak, kyack; **-er, -ing**.

Kaye-Smith (Sheila), 1889–1955, English novelist (hyphen).

Kay-Shuttleworth (Sir James Phillips), 1804–77, English politician and educationist (hyphen).

Kazakhstan, a Soviet Socialist Republic. *See* U.S.S.R.

Kazan, E. Russia, *not* Kas-.

KB (chess), king's bishop (no points).

K.B., King's Bench, Knight Bachelor, Knight of the Bath.

K.B.E., Knight (Commander) of the British Empire.

kc, kilocycle. *See also* **kc/s.**

K.C., King's College, — Counsel.

K.C.B., Knight Commander of the Bath.

K.C.L., King's College, London.

K.C.M.G., Knight Commander of (the Order of) St. Michael and St. George.

kc/s, *better* **kHz,** q.v.

Kčs, the Koruna, unit of Czechoslovak currency; *pl.* same.

K.C.V.O., Knight Commander of the Royal Victorian Order.

K.E., kinetic energy.

Keats House, Hampstead (no apos.).

Keb. Coll., Keble College, Oxford.

keblah, use kiblah.

Kedah, *see* **Malaya, Federation of.**

keddah, *use* **kheda.**

kedgeree (cook.), a dish of rice, fish, etc., *not* the many variations (not ital.).

Kedron, *see* **Ki-** *or* **Ce-.**

keelhaul, naval punishment (one word).

keelson, *use* **kelson.**

keepsake (one word).

keep standing (typ.), keep type stored in page form after first printing for possible reprint.

keffiyeh, Bedouin Arab head-dress, *not* the many variations.

Kelantan, *see* **Malaya, Federation of.**

kell/eck, -ick (naut.), *use* **killick.**

Kellner/ (Ger.), *fem.* **-in,** waiter (cap.).

Kellogg Pact, Paris, 1928, fifteen leading nations renounced war.

Kelly's Directories.

Kelmscott Press, 1890–8, founded by W. Morris.

kelpie, a water-spirit, *not* -y.

kelson (naut.), inboard keel (U.S. **keel-**).

Kelt/, -ic, -icism, *use* **C-.**

kelter (prov. and U.S., **kilter**), good condition.

kelvin, sci. unit of temperature. *See* **Thompson.**

Kempis (Thomas à), 1379–1471, German monk, reputed author of *Imitatio Christi.*

Kenia, *use* **-ya.**

Kenmare, Kerry.

Kenmore, Perth.

kennel/, -led, -ling (U.S. **-ed, -ing**).

Kenney (James), 1780–1849, Irish dramatist.

Kenny (Elizabeth), 1884–1952, Australian nurse who developed treatment for poliomyelitis.

Kents Bank, Lancs. (no apos.).

Kentucky, off. abbr. **Ky.**

Kenwigs (Morleena), in *Nicholas Nickleby.*

Kenya, E. Africa, independent 1963, *not* -ia.

kephalic/, -al, *use* **c-.**

kepi (no accent, not ital.), anglicized form of Fr. *képi,* mil. cap.

Kepler (Johann), 1571–1630, German astronomer, *not* Kepp-.

Ker, surname; *pron.* kar.

keramic, etc., *use* **c-.**

kerb/, -stone (U.S. **curb/**).

Kerch, Crimea, *not* Kertch.

Kerguelen Island, Indian Ocean.

kermis (Du.), a fair or entertainment, *not* -ess, kirmess. *See also* **kumis.**

kerned (typ.), said of a type which has any part of the face projecting beyond the body.

kernel/, seed within a hard shell; **-led, -ly.**

kerosene (U.S. and Canada), paraffin.
kerrie, *see* **knobkerrie**.
kerseymere, a twilled cloth.
Kertch, *use* **Kerch**.
ketch (naut.), a two-masted vessel.
Ketch (**Jack**), the hangman, *not* Ca-, Ki-.
ketchup, a sauce (U.S. **catchup**).
kettle-drum (hyphen).
Keuper (geol.), uppermost division of the Trias.
key, a wharf, *use* **quay**.
keyboard (mus., etc.) (one word).
key-bugle (hyphen).
key/hole, -note (one word).
Keys (**House of**), Isle of Man (caps.); abbr. **H.K.**
keystone (one word).
Key West, Florida (two words).
keyword (one word).
K.G., Knight of the (Order of the) Garter.
kg, kilogramme.
K.G.B., *Komitet Gosudarstvennoi Bezopasnosti* ('secret state security of Russia').
Kgs. (1, 2), Kings, First, Second Book of (O.T.).
Khaibar Oasis, Saudi Arabia.
Khaiber Pass, *use* **Khyber**.
khaki.
khal/eefate, -ifat, *use* **caliphate**.
khalif/, -a, *use* **caliph**.
khamsin, Egyptian hot wind, *not* ka-, -seen.
khan, Eastern inn in a town or village. *See* **caravanserai**.
kharaj (Turk.), tax on Christians, *not* -ach, -age.
Khartoum, cap. of Sudan, *not* -tum.
Khayyám (**Omar,**) 1050?–1122, Persian poet.
kheda, Indian enclosure to catch elephants, *not* keddah.

khediv/e, a viceroy of Egypt between 1867 and 1914; **-a**, his wife; **-ate**, his office; adj. **-al**.
khidmutgar (Ind.), a male waiter (*not* the many variants).
khoja, a professor in a Muslim college.
Khrushchev (**Nikita**), 1894–1970, Soviet politician.
Khyber Pass, NW. Frontier Province, W. Pakistan, *not* Khaiber.
kHz, 1000 Hertz (no point, cap. H).
kiak, *use* **kayak**.
kibbutz/, Israeli communal agricultural settlement, *pl.* **-im; -nik**, a member of same.
kibitzer, intrusive onlooker at cards, etc.
kiblah, the point to which Muslims turn in prayer, *not* ke-.
kick-off (foot.) (hyphen).
kickshaw, a trifle (one word).
kidmutgar, *use* **khid-**.
kidnap/, -ped, -per, -ping, *not* -aped, etc.
kidney bean (two words).
Kidron (*or* Ce-), Palestine, **Ke-** in N.E.B.; Arabic, **Wadi en Nar**.
Kieff, Ukraine, *use* **Kiev**.
kierie, *see* **knobkerrie**.
Kierkegaard (**Søren Aaby**), 1813–55, Danish philosopher.
Kieseritzki gambit, chess opening, *not* Keis-.
Kiev, Ukraine, *not* -eff.
K.i.H. (*or* **K.I.H.**), Kaiser-i-Hind medal.
kil., kilderkin, liquid measure of 18 gallons.
Kilauea, volcano in Hawaii, *not* -aua.
Kilbracken (**Baron**) (Sir Arthur Godley, of the India Office), 1847–1932.

Kilimanjaro, mt., E. Africa (one word, divide Kilimanjaro).

kill (typ.), to cancel a line.

Killala, Mayo, *also* Bp. of.

Killaloe, Clare, *also* Bp. of.

Killaloo, Londonderry.

Killea, Donegal.

Killeagh, Cork.

Killen, Ross-shire.

Killianwala, *use* **Chilianwala.**

killick, a stone used as anchor, *not* -ock, kelleck, -ick.

Killiecrankie, Perth.

Killin, Perth.

Killylea, Armagh.

Killyleigh, Down.

'Kilmansegg (Miss)', by T. Hood, 1828, *not* -eg.

kilo-, prefix meaning 1000.

kilo/, shortened form of kilogramme or kilometre (no point); *pl.* **-s.**

kilocycle, abbr. **kc,** *but use* **kHz** for **kc/s.**

kilogramme, SI unit of mass; abbr. **kg** (no point).

kilometre, 1000 metres; abbr. **km** (no point).

kilowatt, 1000 watts; abbr. **kW** (no point).

kilter, good condition; *use* **ke-.**

Kimeridgian (geol.), an Upper Jurassic clay found at Kimeridge, Dorset (cap.).

kimono (Jap.), kind of gown.

Kimric, Welsh, *use* **Cym-.**

Kin., Kinross-shire.

kinaesthesis, the sense of muscular effort, *not* kine-, -ia.

Kincardine(shire), abbr. **Kinc.**

Kincardine-O'Neil, Aberdeen (hyphen, three caps.).

Kinchinjunga, mt. in Himalayas, *not* Kanchen-.

kindergarten/, a school for young children (not ital., not cap.); **-er,** its teacher.

kinematograph, *use* **c-.**

King/, -s, abbr. **K.;** (typ.) print as Edward VII, *or* the Seventh, *not* the VII; — **Charles's spaniel** (two caps.).

kingd., kingdom.

kingfisher (one word).

King-of-Arms, *not* — -at- — (hyphens).

Kings, First, Second Book of (O.T.), abbr. **Kgs.** (1, 2).

Kingsale (Baron). *See also* **Kinsale.**

King's Bench, abbr. **K.B.** (apos.).

King's College, abbr. **K.C.,** — **Counsel, K.C.;** — **County** *now* **Offaly;** — **Cross,** London.

king's evil, scrofula (apos.).

King's/ Langley, Herts.; — **Lynn,** Norfolk (apos.).

Kingsteignton, Devon (one word).

Kingston, Jamaica, New York, Ontario.

Kingstone, Hereford, Somerset.

Kingston/ upon Hull; — **upon Thames** (no hyphens).

Kingstown, Dublin, off. Dun Laoghaire.

Kington, Hereford.

Kinloss (Baroness).

Kinnoull (Earl of).

Kinross (Baron).

Kinross-shire (hyphen).

Kinsale, Co. Cork. *See also* **Kingsale.**

Kinshasa, cap. of Zaïre, q.v.; *formerly* Léopoldville.

Kintyre, Argyl., *not* Cantire.

kiosk, light outdoor structure (not ital.).

Kioto, Japan, *use* **Kyoto.**

Kirghizia, a Soviet Socialist Republic. *See* **U.S.S.R.**

Kirkaldy, testing experts.

Kirkcaldy, Fife.

Kirkcudbright, Sc. Stewartry, *pron.* kirk-oo′-brī, abbr. **Kirkc.**

kirk-session, the lowest Presbyterian court (hyphen).

Kirschwasser, a cherry liqueur, *not* kirschen-.

kismet (Turk.), fate, *not* -at, -ut.

kistvaen, chest-shaped burial chamber, *not* c-.

kit-cat, a portrait 36 × 28 in., like those painted, *temp.* James II, of the Whig politicians of the Kit-cat Club.

kitchen-garden/, -er, -ing; kitchen-maid (hyphens).

kitmutgar, use khid-.

Kit's Coty House, Aylesford, Kent, a dolmen, *not* — Coity —, — Cotty —.

kiwi (N. Zealand), the apteryx, *not* kivi, kiwi-kiwi.

K.K.K., Ku-Klux-Klan.

KKt, (chess) king's knight; **KKtP,** king's knight's pawn (no points).

kleistogamous, use c-.

Klemperer (Otto), b. 1885, German conductor.

klepsydra, use c-.

kleptomania, irresistible tendency to theft, *not* c-.

klieg light, arc light used in making motion pictures.

klinometer, use c-.

Klischograph (typ.), electronic scanning machine.

K.L.M., Royal Dutch Air Lines (Koninklijke-Luchtvaart-Maatschappij N.V.).

Klondike, Yukon, Canada, *not* -yke.

Klopstock (Friedrich Gottlieb), 1724–1803, German poet.

km, kilometre.

K.Mess., King's Messenger.

knee-cap, the patella (hyphen).

kneel/, -ed (*or* **knelt**), **-ing.**

Kneipp's (Father), water-cure.

knick-knack (hyphen), *not* nicknack.

knight, abbr. **K., Knt., Kt.,** (chess) **Kt** *or* **N** (no point). *See also* **K.B., K.B.E., K.C.B., K.G., K.P., K.T.**

Knightbridge, Cambridge professorship, *not* Knights-.

knight-errant, *pl.* **knights-errant** (hyphen).

Knightsbridge, London.

Knights/Hospitallers, charitable military brotherhood (otherwise — **of St. John,** — **of Rhodes,** — **of Malta**), maintaining hospital for pilgrims in Jerusalem from middle of eleventh century.

knit/, -ted, -ting.

knitting-needle (hyphen).

knobby, knob-shaped.

knobkerrie (S. Africa), short stick with knobbed head, *not* -kerry, -kiri; from Afrik. **knopkierie.**

knock/-about (theat.); — **-down,** adj.; — **-knee/, -d;** — **-out** (hyphens).

Knole, Kent.

Knollys, *pron.* nōlz.

knopkierie, use **knobkerrie.**

Knossos, Crete, *not* Cnossos, Ga-.

knot/, -ted, -ting.

know-how (hyphen).

Knowl, Yorks.

Knowle, Glos., War.

knowledgeable.

knur/, a knot; — **and spell,** a game, *not* n-, -rr.

knurl, a small projection, *not* nurl.

Knut, use **Cnut.**

K.O. *or* **k.o.,** knock-out (boxing).

koala, Australian arboreal marsupial.

København, Dan. for **Copenhagen.**

Koch (Ludwig), b. 1881, German-born, English domiciled musician and recorder of bird-song.

Kock (Charles Paul de), 1794–1871, French novelist.

Kodaikanal Observatory, Madras, India.

Kodaly (Zoltan), 1882–1967, Hungarian composer.

koedoe, *use* **koodoo**.

Koenig & Bauer, inventors of early cylinder printing machine,' 1814.

Koestler (Arthur), b. 1905, Hungarian novelist.

Koh-i-noor diamond, *not* núr, -nûr (hyphens).

kohlrabi, a turnip-cabbage (one word).

Köln, off. **Cöln**, Ger. for **Cologne**.

komitaji, *use* **comitadji**.

Königgrätz, Czechoslovakia; in Czech. **Hradec Králové**.

Königsberg, *now* **Kaliningrad**, U.S.S.R. (*formerly* E. Prussia).

Konzert/meister (Ger. m.), leader of orchestra; *-stück* (n.), concert-piece.

koodoo, a S. African antelope; in Afrik. **koedoe**.

kookaburra, the laughing jackass, an Australian bird.

koomiss, *use* **kumis**.

Koords, *use* **Kurds**.

kopek, *use* c-.

koppie (Afrik.), hill, *not* -pje, -pjie, -ppje.

koprolit/e, -h, *use* c-.

Koran, Muslim sacred book, from Ar. **Qur'ān**.

Korea/, independent 1948; adj. **-n**, *not* C-.

K.O.R.R., King's Own Royal Regiment.

K.O.S.B., King's Own Scottish Borderers.

Kosciusko (Thaddeus), 1746–1817, Polish patriot; in Pol. **Kościuszko (Tadeusz)**.

kosher, (of food), prepared according to the Jewish law, *not* coshar, -er, koscher.

kotow/ (U.S. **kowtow**), a Chinese obeisance; **-ing, -ism**.

Kotzebue (August Friedrich F. von), 1761–1819, German dramatist.

koumiss, *use* **kumis**.

Koussevitsky (Serge Alexandrovich), 1874–1951, Russian conductor.

kowrie, *use* **kauri**.

kow-tow, *use* **kotow**.

K.O.Y.L.I., King's Own Yorkshire Light Infantry.

KP (chess), king's pawn (no points).

K.P., Knight of (the Order of) St. Patrick.

KR (chess), king's rook (no points).

K.R., King's Regiment; — Regulations.

Kr, krypton (no point).

kr., kreuzer, krone.

kraal (Afrik.), enclosure; native village.

Krafft-Ebing (Richard von, Baron), 1840–1902, German psychiatrist.

Kraft *or* **Krafft (Adam)**, *c.* 1455–1509, German sculptor.

Krakatoa (Mount), Straits of Sunda, *not* -au.

Kraków, Polish for **Cracow**.

krans (Afrik.), cliff, *not* krantz.

Krapotkine (Prince), *use* **Kropotkin**.

kreese, *use* c-.

Krefeld, Germany, *not* C-.

Kremer (Gerhard), *see* **Mercator**.

Kremlin, the, Moscow citadel, used for the Russian government.

kremlin, any Russian citadel (not cap.).

9

kreosote, use c-.
kreuzer, Austrian and old German copper coin; abbr. **kr.**
Kriegsspiel (Ger. n.), the war game.
kris, use **creese**.
kromesky, Russian dish of minced chicken fried in bacon; in Fr. *cromesqui*.
Krone/, silver coin, Austrian (*pl.* **-n**), Danish (*pl.* **-r**), Norwegian (*pl.* **-r**), Swedish (**Kron/a**, *pl.* **-or**), and Icelandic (**Kron/a**, *pl.* **-ur**), all abbr. **Kr.** Czechoslovak **Koruna**, abbr. **Kčs** (*sing.* and *pl.*).
Kroo, W. African negro, *not* -ou, -u (not ital.).
Kropotkin (Prince Peter Alexeivich), 1842–1921, Russian geographer, revolutionist and author, *not* Kra-, -ine.
KRP (chess), king's rook's pawn (no points).
K.R.R., King's Royal Rifles.
K.R.R.C., King's Royal Rifle Corps.
Kru, use **Kroo**.
krypton, *not* c-; symbol **Kr** (no point).
K.S., King's Scholar; (typ.) keep standing.
Kshatriya, the warrior caste of the Hindus (cap., not ital.).
K.S.L.I., King's Shropshire Light Infantry.
K.T., Knight of the (Order of the) Thistle, — Templar.
Kt (chess), knight (no point).
Kt., knight.
Kt. Bach., Knight Bachelor.
κτλ. (Gr.), *kai ta loipa* (and the rest, *or* etc.).
Kuala Lumpur, cap. of Malaysia (and of Selangor).
Kublai Khan, 1214–94, first Mongol Emperor of China.

'Kubla Khan', poem by Coleridge.
Kuch Behar, *use* Coo- —.
kudos (Gr.), renown (not ital.).
kudu, use **koodoo**.
Kufic, form of Arabic, *use* C-.
Ku-Klux-Klan, U.S. secret society (not ital.); abbr. **K.K.K.**
kukri (Ind.), a curved knife, *not* the many variants.
kulak, Russian peasant proprietor.
Kultur (Ger.), culture.
Kulturkampf (Ger.), the war of culture (between Bismarck's government and the Catholic Church, c. 1872–87).
Kumasi, Ghana, *not* Coo-, -assi.
kumis, a preparation of mares' milk (U.S. **kumiss**).
Kümmel, a liqueur.
kummerbund, use **cummerbund**.
Kunstlied (Ger.), art-song.
Kuomintang, the Chinese nationalist people's party, founded 1912.
kupfernickel (mineral.) (one *f*, not cap.).
kupfferite (mineral.) (two *f*'s).
Kurds, of Kurdistan, *not* Koo-.
kuriologic/, **-al**, use c-.
Kurrachee, use **Karachi**.
Kursaal (Ger. m.), a hall at a spa or resort (ital., cap.).
Kursiv, Kursivschrift (Ger. typ. m.), italic type.
Kutch, kutch, use C-, c-.
Kuwait, Arabia.
Kuyp, use C-.
kV (no point), kilovolt.
kvass (Russ.), rye-beer, *not* quas, quass.
kW (no point) (elec.), kilowatt.

kWh, kilowatt-hour.
Ky., Kentucky (off. abbr.).
Kymric, *use* **C-.**
Kyoto, Japan, *not* Ki-.
Kyrie eleison (eccles.),
'Lord, have mercy'; abbr.
Kyrie, *not* — eleëson.
Kyrle (John), 1637–1724,
English philanthropist, 'the
Man of Ross'.

L

L, fifty, fiftieth, learner (motor vehicle), the eleventh in a series.

L., Lady, Lake, Latin, (theat.) left (from the actor's point of view), (Lat.) *liber* (a book), Liberal, licentiate, (bot.) Linnaeus, (It.) *lir/a, -e,* (Fr.) *livre* (pound), (Lat.) *locus* (place), (U.S.) elevated railroad, all proper names with this initial.

L. *or* **£,** pound, the form **£** to be used and placed *before* figures, as £50. If *l.* ordered, to be placed *after,* as 50*l.* **£E,** Egyptian pound (100 piastres); **I£,** Israeli pound (100 agorot); **£m.,** (one) million pounds. *See also* **decimal currency.**

L (elec.), symbol for inductance.

l (no point), litre. When this may cause confusion, the word should be spelt out in full.

l., league, length, (Ger.) *lies* (read), (naut.) lightning, line, link.

Ł, ł, Polish letter, *pron.* nearly **w.**

L.A., law agent, Legislative Assembly, Library Association, Local Authority, Los Angeles.

La, lanthanum (no point).

La., Louisiana, U.S. (off. abbr.).

laager, encampment, esp. in circle of wagons; in Afrik. *laer. See also* **lager.**

Lab., Labour (party), Labrador.

lab (no point), laboratory.

label, -led, -ling (U.S. **-ed, -ing**).

labi/um, (anat.) a lip or lip-like structure; *pl.* **-a.**

Lablache (Luigi), 1794–1858, Franco-Italian operatic bass.

Labor Day (U.S.), first Monday in Sept.

lab/our, -orious.

Labour Day (Great Britain and many other countries), 1 May.

Labourers Act (caps., no apos.).

Labrador, abbr. **Lab.**

labr/um (Lat.), lip of a jug, etc.; *pl.* **-a.**

La Bruyère (Jean de), 1645–96, French writer and moralist.

labyrinth/, structure with many confusing passages; **-ian, -ic, -ine.**

L.A.C., Leading Aircraftman, Licentiate of the Apothecaries' Company, London Athletic Club.

lac, a resin.

Laccadive Islands, off Madras west coast.

Lachaise (Père), Paris cemetery (two words).

lâche (Fr.), lax, cowardly (ital.).

laches, negligence (not ital.).

Lachesis (Gr. myth.), one of the three Fates.

lachryma Christi, a sweet red wine from Mt. Vesuvius area.

lachrym/al, of tears; **-atory, -ose;** *not* lacry-; **lacri-** (U.S.) is a correct form, increasingly used in Britain.

lackadaisical, listless.

lacker, *use* **lacquer.**

lackey, a footman, *not* -quey.

Laconian, Spartan.

laconic, concise (not cap.).

L.A.C.P., London Association of Correctors of the Press.

lacquer, a varnish, *not* lacker.

lacrimal, *see* **lachry-.**

La Crosse, town, Wis., U.S.

lacrosse, ball game.

lacun/a, a missing portion, esp. in ancient MS.; *pl.* **-ae** *or* **-as** (not ital.).

lacy, lace-like, *not* -ey.

Ladies' Field, newspaper.

Ladies'/Gallery, House of Commons; — **Mile,** Hyde Park, London.

ladies'/man, — school.

Ladismith, Cape Province. *See also* **Ladysmith.**

Lady, abbr. **L.**

Lady (Our) (caps.).

ladybird (one word).

lady-cow, a ladybird (hyphen).

Lady Day/, 25 Mar. (two words, caps.); — — **in Harvest,** 15 Aug.

Lady Dedlock, in *Bleak House, not* Dead-.

lady-in-waiting (hyphens).

ladylike (one word).

Lady Margaret Hall, Oxford.

'Lady of Shalott', by Tennyson, 1832.

lady's maid, *pl.* **ladies' maids** (no hyphen).

Ladysmith, Natal. *See also* **Ladismith.**

laer (Afrik.), *use* **laager.**

laesa majestas (Lat.), lese-majesty.

Laetare Sunday, fourth in Lent.

laevo-, the prefix meaning left, *not* le- (except in U.S.).

Lafayette/(Marie Joseph, marquis de), 1757–1834, French general, aided Americans in Revolution (one word); — **College** (U.S.).

Laffitte (Jacques), 1767–1844, French statesman.

Lafite (Château-), a claret (hyphen).

Lafitte (Jean), 1780–*c.* 1826, buccaneer of unknown origin.

La Follette (Robert Marion), 1855–1925, American politician.

La Fontaine (Jean de), 1621–95, French writer.

lager beer (two words, not ital.).

lagoon, *not* -une.

Lagrange (Joseph Louis, comte), 1736–1813, French mathematician.

Lagting, Upper House of Norwegian Parliament.

La Guaira, Venezuela, *not* -yra.

LaGuardia/(Fiorello H.), 1882–1947, Mayor of New York (one word, two caps.); — **Airport,** New York, U.S.

L.A.H., Licentiate of Apothecaries' Hall, Dublin.

La Hague (Cape), NW. France.

la haute politique (Fr.), State politics.

La Haye, Fr. for **The Hague.**

La Hogue, in Fr. **La Hougue,** a roadstead, NW. France.

Lahore, W. Pakistan, *not* -or.

Laibach, Yugoslavia, Ger. for **Ljubljana.**

laicize, to secularize, *not* -ise.

laid paper, that which when held to the light shows close-set parallel lines.

l'Aiglon, son of Napoleon I.

Laïs, a Greek courtesan and beauty of fourth century B.C.

laissez/-aller (Fr.), absence of restraint; — *-faire,* let people do as they think best, let well alone!

laissez-passer (Fr. s. m.), pass, permit (for persons and things).

lait (Fr. m.), milk; *au —*, with milk.

laitance (Fr. f.), soft roe of fish.

laitue (Fr. f.), lettuce.

Lake (typ.), capital when with name, as Bala Lake, Lake Superior; abbr. **L.**

lakh/ (Anglo-Ind.), 100,000, *not* -ck, -c (not ital.); **— of rupees** (typ.), pointing above one lakh is with a comma after the number of lakhs: thus 25,87,000 is 25 lakhs 87 thousand rupees. *See* **crore.**

Lalitpur, Uttar Pradesh, India, *not* Lalat-.

'L Allegro', poem by John Milton.

L.A.M., London Academy of Music.

Lam., (O.T.) Lamentations, (bot.) Lamarck.

lama, Buddhist priest. *See also* **ll-.**

Lamarck/ (**Jean Baptiste P. A. de M.**), 1744–1829, French naturalist; **-ian;** abbr. **Lam.**

Lamarque (**comte M.**), 1770–1832, French general.

Lamartine (**Alphonse Marie Louis de**), 1790–1869, French poet.

lamasery, a lama monastery.

Lambaréné, Gabon, site of Albert Schweitzer's hospital.

lambda, the Gr. *L*, *l* (*Λ*, *λ*).

lamb's fry (cook.) (apos., two words).

lambskin (one word).

lamb's-wool (apos., hyphen).

L.A.M.D.A., London Academy of Music and Dramatic Art.

lamell/a, a thin plate; *pl.* **-ae.**

Lamentations (**Book of**), abbr. **Lam.**

lamin/a, a thin plate; *pl.* **-ae.**

Lammas, 1 Aug.

lammergeyer, the bearded vulture, *not* lae-, le-, -geier (not ital.).

lamp-black (hyphen).

lamplighter (one word).

lamp-post (hyphen).

lamproie (Fr. f.), lamprey.

Lancashire, abbr. **Lancs.**

Lance-Bombardier, abbr. **L/Bdr., L.Bdr.**

Lance-Corporal, abbr. **L.Corp., L/Cpl.**

lancewood, a tough W. Indian wood (one word).

lancinat/e, to pierce; **-ing.**

Lancing College, Sussex.

Lancs., Lancashire.

landau/, -let, a carriage (not ital.).

landdrost (S. Afr.), a district magistrate (not ital.).

landgrav/e, a German count; *fem.* **-ine.**

landgraviate, a land-grave's territory, *not* -vate.

landlocked (one word).

land-lubber (hyphen).

landmark (one word).

L. & N.W.R., London and North-Western Railway, became **L.M.S.R.** until nationalization.

Landor (**Walter Savage**), 1775–1864, English poet and prose writer.

landowner (one word).

landscape (typ.), book, page, or illustration wider than it is deep.

Land's End, Cornwall.

Landsmaal, Norwegian peasant dialect given literary form *c.* 1850, and now called **Nynorsk,** new Norse. *See* **Rigsmaal.**

lands/man, *pl.* **-men.**

Landsting, Upper House of the Danish Parliament.

Landsturm (Ger. m.), reserves of the whole nation for national defence.

L. & S.W.R., London and South-Western Railway, became **S.R.** until nationalization.

Landtag (Ger. m.), the legislative body, diet.

land-tax (hyphen).

Landwehr (Ger. f.), militia.

L. & Y.R., Lancashire and Yorkshire Railway, became part of **L.M.S.R.** until nationalization.

Lang (Andrew), 1844–1912, Scottish man of letters; — **(Cosmo Gordon),** 1864–1945, Archbp. of Canterbury.

lang., language.

Langeberg Mountains, S. Africa; in Afrik. **Langeberge.**

langouste (Fr. f.), a spiny lobster.

langsam (Ger., mus.), slowly.

langsyne, long ago (one word, not ital.); **'Auld Lang Syne'** (song) (three words).

langue/d'oc, medieval French spoken south of the Loire; — **d'oïl,** ditto north of the Loire.

Languedoc, former French province, between R. Loire and Pyrenees.

languor/, lassitude; **-ous.**

langur, an Indian monkey.

Lankester (Sir Edwin Ray), 1847–1929, English zoologist.

lanner/, a female falcon; male, **-et.**

lanolin, fat in sheep's wool, *not* -ine.

Lansdown (battle of), 1643.

Lansdowne (Marquess of).

Lanston (Tolbert), 1844–1913, inventor of the Monotype composing machine.

lantern, *not* -thorn.

lanthanum, symbol **La** (no point).

lanyard, short rope attached to something, *not* lani-.

Laocoön, Trojan priest.

Laodicean, lukewarm (of feelings).

Laos, independent 1949, *formerly* the kingdoms of Luang Prabang and Vientiane and the principality of Champassac (Fr. E. Indies).

Lao-tsze, born 605 B.C., founder of Taoism (hyphen).

Lap., Lapland. *See also* **Lapp.**

lap-dog (hyphen).

lapel/, the lap-over of a coat, *not* -elle, lappelle; **-led.**

lapereau (Fr. m.), a young rabbit.

lapilli (Lat.), pebbles.

lapin/ (Fr. m.), rabbit; — *au kari,* curried rabbit.

lapis lazuli, a rich blue stone or its colour (two words, not ital.).

Lapland, abbr. **Lap.**

Lapp, a native of Lapland, Lappish.

lappelle, *use* lapel.

lapsable, liable to lapse, *not* -ible.

lapsus/ (Lat.), a slip; — *calami,* ditto of the pen; — *linguae,* ditto tongue; — *memoriae,* ditto memory.

Laputa/, flying island in *Gulliver's Travels*; **-n,** visionary, absurd.

lar/ (Lat.), a household god; *pl.* **-es; lares and penates,** personal or household objects.

lard (Fr. m.), bacon.

lardon bacon for larding, *not* -oon.

large crown, *see* book sizes.

large-paper, special copies of a book, with large margins, etc.; also termed édition de luxe; abbr. **L.P.**

largess, a free gift, *not* -esse (*not* ital.).

largo (mus.), slow, broad.

lariat, rope for picketing animals, *not* -iette, larriet (*not* ital.).

larikin, *use* **larr-**.

larkspur (bot.) (one word).

La Rochefoucauld (François duc de), 1613–80, French writer.

Larousse, French work of reference.

larrikin, Australian street rowdy, *not* lari-.

larv/a, *pl.* -ae (not ital.).

laryn/x (anat.), *pl.* -ges; -geal, -gitis.

Lasalle (Antoine Chevalier L. C., comte de), 1775–1809, French general.

La Salle (Antoine de), *c.* 1400–60, French soldier and poet ; — **(St. Jean Baptiste de),** 1651–1719, French founder of the order of Christian Brothers; — **(René Robert Cavelier),** 1643–87, French explorer.

lascar, E. Indian sailor (not ital.).

Las Casas (Bartolomé de), 1474–1566, Spanish missionary, 'the apostle of the Indies'.

Las Cases (E. D., comte de), 1766–1842, friend of Napoleon I on St. Helena.

laser, light amplification by stimulated emission of radiation (acronym). *See also* **maser.**

lashkar, a body of Indian irregular troops (not ital.).

Las Meninas, by Velazquez, *not* -iñas.

La Spezia, NW. Italy, *not* -zzia.

Lassa, Tibet, *use* **Lhasa.**

Lassalle (Ferdinand), 1825–64, German Socialist (one word). *See also* **Lasa-.**

Lassell (William), 1799–1880, English astronomer.

lasso/, -ed, -es, -ing.

Last Supper (the) (caps.).

Lat., Latin; **lat.,** latitude.

Latakia, Syria, *not* Ladi-, -ieh, -yah.

La Tène ware (pottery).

later, correlative of *earlier.*

Lateran (St. John), church in Rome.

lath, a thin strip of wood.

lathe, machine for turning.

lathi, heavy stick carried by Indian police.

Latin, abbr. **L.,** *or* **Lat.;** (typ.) alphabet same as English without *w*. Accents and ligatures falling into disuse; most scholars do not differentiate the letter *j* from *i*, and many use *u* for *v*; V usually stands for both U and V. See *Hart's Rules,* esp. for word-division.

Latin Cross, †.

latin de cuisine (Fr.), dog-Latin.

latine (Lat.), in Latin.

Latinity, the quality of one's Latin.

latinize, to make Latin, *not* -ise (not cap., except in hist.).

latitude, abbr. **lat.**

Latour (Château-), a claret (hyphen).

latten, metal like brass (not ital.).

latter, correlative of *former.*

Latter-day Saint, a Mormon (two caps., one hyphen).

Latvia, a Soviet Socialist Republic, *see* **U.S.S.R.;** adj. **Latvian** *or* **Lettish.**

laudator temporis acti (Lat.), a praiser of past times.

laura/ (early Christianity), a group of monks' cells; *pl.* **-s.**

laurel/, -led (U.S. **-ed**).

Laurence (Friar), in *Romeo and Juliet.*

Laurentian Mts. and (geol.) rocks, near the St. Lawrence River, Canada.

Laurier (Sir Wilfrid), 1841–1919, Canadian statesman.

laurustinus, an evergreen, *not* laures-, lauris-.

Laus Deo (Lat.), Praise (be) to God.

lauwine, an avalanche, *not* law-.

laverock, a lark, *not* lavr-.

Lavoisier (Antoine Laurent), 1743–94, French chemist (one word).

law (typ.), practically no punctuation used in legal documents. Copy must be followed. Spell out all figures; **law/ agent,** abbr. **L.A.;** — **-binding,** — **-calf,** — **-sheep,** binding in smooth pale brown calf- or sheep-skin.

lawcourt (one word).

Law Courts, the (caps., no hyphen).

lawgiver (one word).

lawine, *use* **lauwine.**

lawn tennis (two words), originally an offshoot of tennis (real tennis), now called **tennis,** and played on grass and hard courts. *But see* **I.L.T.F.**

Lawrence (David Herbert), 1885–1930, English novelist; — **(Sir Thomas),** 1769–1830, English painter; — **(Thomas Edward),** 1888–1935, English archaeologist and soldier, 'Lawrence of Arabia', (from 1927) A/C Shaw; — **(St.),** Canadian river (*see also* Lau-).

lawrencium, symbol **Lr** (no point).

Laws, abbr. **LL.**

law-sheep, *see* **law.**

law-stationer (hyphen).

lawsuit (one word).

lay, untilled land, *use* **lea.**

lay-by, short 'siding' on main road (hyphen), *pl.* **lay-bys.**

layette, complete outfit for a baby (not ital.).

layout (noun, one word).

lazaretto/, a place for quarantine (not ital.); *pl.* **-s.**

lazy/-bones, — **-tongs** (hyphen).

lazzaron/e, one of a low class at Naples, *not* lazar-; *pl.* **-i.**

L.B., *Baccalaureus Literarum* (Bachelor of Letters), *Lectori benevolo* (to the kind reader), Local Board.

l.b. (cricket), leg-bye.

lb (no point), pound, pounds (weight).

L.B. & S.C.R., London, Brighton, and South Coast Railway, became part of **S.R.** until nationalization.

L.Bdr. (*or* **L/Bdr.**), Lance-Bombardier.

lbw. (cricket), leg before wicket, *not* l.b.w.

L.C., (theat.) left centre, Legislative Council, (U.S.) Library of Congress, Lord Chamberlain, — Chancellor, Lower Canada, letter of credit.

l.c., *loco citato* (in the place cited), (typ.) lower case, that is *not* caps.

L.C.B., Lord Chief Baron.

L.C.C., London County Council, -lor. *See* **G.L.C.**

L.Ch., Licentiate in Surgery.

L.C.J., Lord Chief Justice.

L.C.M. *or* **l.c.m.,** least common multiple.

L.Corp., L/Cpl., Lance-Corporal.

L.C.P., Licentiate of the College of Preceptors.

l/cr. (Fr.), *lettre de crédit* (letter of credit).

L.D., Lady Day, *Laus Deo* (praise be to God), Low

Dutch, (U.S.) Doctor of
Letters.

Ld., lord.

Ldg., (naval) Leading.

L.d'H., Légion d'Honneur.

Ldp., lordship.

L.D.S., Licentiate in Dental
Surgery.

L.D.V., Local Defence
Volunteers (later **Home
Guard**).

£E, Egyptian pound(s).

L.E.A., Local Education
Authority.

lea, untilled land, *not* lay,
lee, ley.

lead (typ.), a thin strip of
metal less than type high,
used to separate lines of
type.

lead (chem.), symbol **Pb** (no
point).

leaded/ matter, — type,
having the lines separated
by leads.

leader, *see* **leading article.**

leaderette a short editorial
paragraph, printed in the
same type as the leaders in
a newspaper.

leaders (typ.), dots used
singly or in groups to guide
the eye across the page.

leading (typ.), the action of
placing leads between lines
of type.

leading article, one of the
longer articles in a
newspaper, appearing as
the expression of editorial
opinion on any subject:
a leader.

leaf (typ.), single piece of
paper, two pages back to
back; abbr. **l.**

leaflet (typ.), minor piece of
printing, usu. 2, 4, or 6 pp.

leaf-mould (U.S. **-mold**)
(hyphen).

league, abbr. **l.**

Leamington Spa, War.,
pron. Lem-. *See also* **Lem-,
Lym-.**

lean/, -ed, *or* **-t.**

leap-frog, a game (hyphen).

leap year (two words).

learn/, -ed, *or* **-t.**

Lease-Lend, *see* **Lend-
Lease Act.**

least common multiple,
abbr. **L.C.M.** *or* **l.c.m.**

leatherette, a cloth and
paper imitation of leather.

leaves, abbr. **ll.**

Leban/on, independent
1943; adj. **-ese.**

Lebensraum (Ger.), room
for expansion.

Lebesgue/ (Henri Léon),
1875–1941, French
mathematician; — theory
of integration (math.).

Lebewohl! (Ger. n.), farewell!

L.E.C., Local Employment
Committee.

Lecocq (**Alexandre
Charles**), 1832–1918,
French composer.

Leconte de Lisle (**Charles
Marie René**), 1818–94,
French poet.

Lecoq (**Monsieur**), of Du
Boisgobey's, and Gaboriau's,
detective stories.

Le Corbusier, pseud. of
Charles Edouard
Jeanneret, b. 1887, Swiss
architect.

Lecouvrier (**Adrienne**),
1692–1730, French actress;
ital. when name of play
(1849) by E. Scribe and
E. Legouvé.

lect., lecture.

lectern, church reading-
desk, *not* -urn.

Lectori benevolo (Lat.), to
the kind reader; abbr. **L.B.**

lee, untilled land, *use* **lea.**

leeming, *use* **lemm-.**

Leeuwenhoek (**Anton van**),
1632–1723, Dutch
microscopist.

left/ (theat.) (from actor's
point of view), abbr. **L.;** —
centre, abbr. **L.C.**

Leg., legislat/ive, -ure.

leg., legal, *legit* (he, *or* she, reads), *legunt* (they read, pres. tense).

legalize, *not* -ise.

Le Gallienne (Richard), 1866–1947, English author and journalist; — **(Eva),** b. 1899, American actress, d. of above.

legato (mus.), smooth.

leg-bye (cricket), abbr. **l.b.**

legenda (Lat.), things to be read.

legerdemain, sleight of hand (not ital.).

leger line (mus.), *not* led-.

leges (Lat.), laws; abbr. *ll.*

leggiero (mus.), light, swift, delicate.

Legh, family name of Baron Newton; *pron.* lē. *See also* **Leigh.**

Leghorn, former English name for Italian port **Livorno; leghorn,** a straw plait, a breed of domestic fowl.

Légion d'honneur (la), French order of merit.

legionnaire, a member of a legion, a legionary (not ital.); in Fr. *lég-.*

legislat/ive, -ure, abbr. **Leg.**

Legislative Assembly, abbr. **L.A.** *See also* **Assemblies.**

legit (Lat.), he, *or* she, reads; abbr. **leg.**

legitimize, *not* -ise.

légumes (Fr. m. pl.), table vegetables.

legunt (Lat.), they read (pres. tense); abbr. **leg.**

Le Havre, France, *not* Havre.

Lehigh University, U.S. (one word).

Leibniz (Gottfried Wilhelm, Baron von), 1646–1716, German mathematician and philosopher, *not* -itz.

Leicester, abbr. **Leics.**

Leigh (Baron), *pron.* lē. *See also* **Legh.**

Leighton Buzzard, Beds. (no hyphen).

Leipzig, Ger., abbr. **Lpz.** *or* **Leip.**

leitmotiv (mus.), theme associated with person, situation, or sentiment, *not* -if, -ive (one word, not ital.).

Leix, Ireland, *formerly* Queen's County.

le juste milieu (Fr.), the golden mean. *See also* **milieu.**

L.E.L., pen-name of Letitia Elizabeth Landon, 1802–38.

Lely (Sir Peter), 1618–80, Dutch-English painter.

Lemaître (Antoine Louis Prosper), usu. known as **Frédérick,** 1800–76, French actor; — **(François Jules),** 1853–1914, French writer and critic.

leming, *use* **lemm-.**

Lemington, Northumb. *See also* **Lea-, Ly-.**

lemm/a, a title or theme, proposition taken for granted; *pl.* **-as** (not ital.).

lemm/a, husk of a fruit; *pl.* **-ata.**

lemming, rodent, *not* leeming, leming.

Le Moine (Sir James MacPherson), 1825–1912, Canadian ornithologist and historian.

Lemoinne (John Émile), 1815–92, French journalist.

Lemprière (John), 1765–1824, English lexicographer.

Lenclos (Ninon de), 1616–1706, a French beauty.

lending library (two words).

Lend–Lease Act, 1941, *not* Lease–Lend.

L'Enfant (Pierre Charles), 1754–1825, French architect, designed Washington, D.C.

length, abbr. **l.**

Lenin, assumed name of **Vladimir Ilich Ulianov,** 1870–1924, Russian political leader.

Leningrad, name for Petrograd, q.v., since 1924.

Lennox, family name of Duke of Richmond.

Lennoxtown, Stirling (one word).

Lenox Library, New York.

lens/, *not* lense; *pl.* **-es.**

Lent, from Ash Wednesday to Easter (cap.).

lentille/ (Fr. f.), lentil, optical lens; *-s* (pl.), freckles.

lento (mus.), slow.

Leonardo da Vinci, 1452–1519, Italian painter, sculptor, engineer.

Leoncavallo (Ruggiero), 1857–1919, Italian composer.

leonid/, a meteor; *pl.* **-es** (not ital.).

Léopoldville, Zaïre, q.v., *now* **Kinshasa.**

Lepidoptera, *pl.,* butterflies and moths (cap.).

leprechaun, Irish sprite, *not* lepra-, -awn.

Le Queux (William Tufnell), 1864–1927, English novelist and traveller.

Lermontov (Mikhail Yurevich), 1814–41, Russian poet.

Le Roy/ le veult, the royal assent to Bills in Parliament; —— *s'avisera,* ditto dissent.

Leroux (Pierre), 1798–1871, French philosopher and economist.

Lerroux (Alejandro), 1864–1949, Spanish statesman.

lès or lez (Fr. topog.), near (with names of towns).

Le Sage (Alain René), 1668–1747, French novelist and dramatist.

les convenances (Fr. f.), the proprieties.

lese-majesty, treason (hyphen, not ital.); in Fr. *lèse-majesté.*

L. ès/ L., *Licencié ès Lettres,* Licentiate in (*or* of) Letters; —— **S.,** ditto Sciences.

Lesotho, S. Africa, independent 1966, *formerly* Basutoland.

Lethe, a river in Hades.

let-in notes (typ.), those let into the text, as distinct from side-notes.

le tout ensemble (Fr.), the general effect.

letterhead (typ.), printed letter- or note-paper (one word).

letterpress (typ.), printing from type and/or blocks; text as opposed to illustrations (one word).

letterset (typ.), printing by letterpress on to a blanket and then offsetting on to the paper (one word).

letters of distinction, as F.R.S., LL.D., etc., are usually put in large caps. Even s.caps. often improve general effect.

letterspacing (typ.), shown in MS. by a stroke between letters, and # above (one word).

letters patent, formal writing conferring patent or privilege (two words).

lettre de/ cachet (Fr. f.), warrant for imprisonment, bearing the royal seal; —— *créance,* —— *crédit,* letter of credit, abbr. *l/cr.;* —— *marque,* letter of marque, q.v.; *pl.* **lettres de —.**

lettuce, *not* -ice.

leucotomy, a brain operation, *not* -k-.

leukaemia, excess of white corpuscles in blood, *not* -c-, -ch- (U.S. **-kemia**).

Leuwenhoek, *use* **Leeuwenhoek.**

Lev., Leviticus.

lev/, *pl.* **-a,** Hungarian monetary unit.

levant morocco (binding), a superior quality with prominent grain.

levee, an assembly (no accent, not ital.); U.S. river embankment.

level/, -led, -ler, -ling (U.S. **-ed, -er, -ing**).

lever de/ rideau (Fr. m.), opening piece at theatre, 'curtain-raiser'; — — *séance,* closing of a meeting.

Leveson-Gower, *pron.* loo'sn-gor.

Leviathan, book by Hobbes; **leviathan,** sea-monster.

Leviticus, abbr. **Lev.**

levo-, the prefix, *use* **laevo-,** q.v.

Lewes, Sussex.

Lewes (Charles Lee), 1740–1803, English actor; — **(George Henry),** 1817–78, English philosopher and critic. *See also* **Lewis.**

Lewis, isle in Hebrides.

Lewis (Sir G. Cornewall, *not* Cornw-), 1806–63, English statesmen and man of letters; — **(Sir George Henry),** 1833–1911, English solicitor; — **(J. F.),** 1805–76, English painter; — **(Matthew Gregory, 'Monk'),** 1775–1818, English writer of romances.

lex (Lat.), law; *pl.* *leges.*

lexicog., lexicograph/er, -y, -ical.

lexicon/, dictionary, esp. of Greek, Hebrew, Arabic; *pl.* **-s;** abbr. **lex.** (not ital.).

lex/ loci (Lat.), local custom; — *non scripta,* unwritten law; — *scripta,* statute law; — *talionis,* 'an eye for an eye'; — *terrae,* the law of the land.

ley, untilled land, *use* **lea.**

Leyd., Leyden, Netherlands; in Dutch, **Leiden.**

ley farming, grass-growing.

Leys School, Camb.; *pron.* lēz.

lez, see **lès.**

L.F. *or* **l.f.,** low frequency.

L.F.B., London Fire Brigade.

L.F.P.S., Licentiate of the Faculty of Physicians and Surgeons.

L.G., (gunpowder, leather, wheat) large grain, Life Guards.

L.G.B., Local Government Board.

L.G.O.C., London General Omnibus Co. *See* **L.P.T.B.**

L.Ger., Low German.

L.Gr., Low Greek.

L.G.U., Ladies' Golf Union.

l.h., left hand.

L.H.A., Lord High Admiral.

Lhasa, Tibet, *not* -ssa, Lassa.

L.H.C., Lord High Chancellor.

L.H.D., *Literarum Humaniorum Doctor* (lit. Doctor of the more humane letters).

L.H.T., Lord High Treasurer.

L.I., Light Infantry, Long Island (U.S.).

Li, lithium (no point).

liaison, illicit amour; joining of words; (mil.) connection, touch (and so now also in general usage).

lib./, librarian, library; — **cat.,** library catalogue.

lib., **liber** (a book).

libel/, -led, -ler, -ling, -lous (U.S. **-ed, -er, -ing, -ist, -ous).**

liber (Lat.), a book; abbr. **L.,** *or* **lib.**

Liberal/, abbr. **L.;** — **Unionist,** abbr. **L.U.** (caps., no hyphen).

liberalize, etc., *not* -ise.

Liberia, rep., W. Africa.

libr/a, pound, *pl.* *-ae;* abbr. **L.,** £**, l., lb** (no point). *See also* **L.** *or* £**.**

librair/e (Fr. m.), bookseller;
  -ie (f.), bookseller's shop.
librar/ian, -y; abbr. **lib.**
library, in Fr. f. *biblio-
  thèque.*
libretto/ (It.), words of an
  opera, etc.; *pl.* **-s** (not ital.).
libris (**ex-**) (*s.* and *pl.*), 'from
  the library of'; a book-plate
  (hyphen, not ital.).
libr/o (It.), a book; *pl.* *-i.*
Libya, N. Africa, independent
  1951, *formerly* Tripolitania,
  Cyrenaica, and Fezzan
  (Italian).
Libyan desert.
licence (noun), a permit;
  (U.S. **-se**).
licens/e (verb), to authorize;
  -ee, -er, -ing.
licensed victualler.
licentiate, abbr. **L.**
licet (Lat.), legal; it is
  allowed.
lichee, *use* **litchi.**
lichen, epiphytic veg.
  growth, *pron.* li′-ken.
Lichfield, Staffs. *See also*
  Litch-.
lich-gate, *use* **lych-.**
lichi, *use* **litchi.**
lickerish, desirous, greedy;
  but **liquorice.**
Lick Observatory,
  California.
licorice, *use* **liquor-.**
Lie (Jonas Lauritz Edemil),
  1833–1908, Norwegian
  novelist, — **(Trygve
  Halvdan),** 1896–1968,
  Sec.-Gen. of U.N. 1946–53.
Liebfraumilch, a hock; in
  Ger. *Liebfrauen-.*
**Liebig/ (Justus, Baron
  von),** 1803–73, German
  chemist; —, a beef extract
  first prepared by him (cap.).
Liechtenstein, principality
  on Upper Rhine.
Lied/ (Ger. n.), a song; *pl.*
  -er.
Lieder ohne Worte, songs
  without words.

Liège, Belgium, *not* Lié-;
  Liègeois/, -e, an inhabitant
  of Liège.
lieu, in lieu of (not ital.).
Lieutenant/, abbr. **Lt.,** *or*
  Lieut.; — **-Colonel,** abbr.
  Lt.-, *or* **Lieut.-Col.;** —
  -Commander, abbr. **Lt.-,**
  or **Lieut.-Com.;** —
  -General, abbr. **Lt.-,** *or*
  Lieut.-Gen.; — **-Governor,**
  abbr. **Lt.-,** *or* **Lieut.-Gov.**
  (hyphens).
lièvre (Fr. m.), hare.
life-assurance, U.S. —
  insurance. *See also*
  assurance.
lifeboat (one word).
life-guard (hyphen).
Life Guards, regiment of
  household cavalry (two
  words); **Life-guardsman**
  (hyphen).
lifelike (one word).
lifelong, lasting for life (one
  word). *See also* **livelong.**
life-size (hyphen).
lifetime (one word).
ligature (typ.), two or more
  letters joined together and
  forming one character or
  type, as *Æ, Œ, ffi. See also*
  diphthongs.
lightening, making less
  heavy.
lighthouse (one word).
Light Infantry, abbr. **L.I.,**
  or **Lt. Inf.**
lighting-up time (one
  hyphen).
lightning (naut.), abbr. **l.**
lightship (one word).
ligneous, of wood, woody.
Li Hung-Chang, 1823–1901,
  Chinese statesman (one
  hyphen).
-like. In formations
  intended as nonce-words, or
  not generally current, the
  hyphen should be used.
  Nouns in *-l* require the
  hyphen, e.g. eel-like.
likeable, *not* lika-.

Liliput, Liliputian, *use*
  Lilli-.

lillibullero, a seventeenth-
  century song refrain, *not* the
  many variants (not ital.).

Lilliput/, country of the
  pygmies in *Gulliver's Travels*;
  -ian.

lily of the valley (no
  hyphens).

limande (Fr. f.), the dab-fish,
  lemon sole.

limbo/, the borderland of
  Hell, a place of oblivion;
  pl. **-s** (not ital.).

limbus/ fatuorum (Lat.), a
  fool's paradise;—*infantium,*
  limbo of unbaptized
  children; — *patrum,* limbo
  of pre-Christian good men.

lime-kiln (hyphen).

limelight (one word).

limestone (one word).

Limey (U.S. slang), a
  British sailor, an Englishman.

Limited, abbr. **Ltd.**

limy, lime-like, sticky, *not*
  -ey.

lin., line/al, -ar.

linable, able to be covered
  on the inside, *not* linea-.

linage, the number of lines,
  payment by the line, *not*
  -eage.

linament, *use* lini-.

Lincoln Center, New York,
  a nexus of theatres, opera-
  house, concert-hall, etc.

Lincolnshire, abbr. **Lincs.**

Lindley (**John**), 1799–1865,
  English botanist; abbr.
  Lindl.

Lindsay (**Earl of**), family
  name Lindesay Bethune; —
  (**Sir Coutts**), 1824–1913,
  English artist; — (**Sir
  David**), 1490–1555,
  Scottish poet; — (**Nicholas
  Vachel**), 1879–1931,
  American poet.

Lindsey (**Earl of**), family
  name Bertie.

line, abbr. **l.**; *pl.* **ll.**

lineage, ancestry; *pron.*
  lin'-i-ij.

line/al, -ar, abbr. **lin.**

lineament, a feature, *not*
  lina-. *See also* **lini-.**

line block (typ.), letterpress
  block for lines and solids.

**linen/-draper, — -fold, —
  -scroll** (hyphens).

lingerie, linen articles
  collectively, women's
  underclothing (not ital.).

lingua franca, an international jargon, esp. a
  mixture of It., Fr., Gr., and
  Span. used in the Levant
  (not ital.).

liniment, an embrocation,
  not lina-. *See also* **linea-.**

lining figures (typ.), those
  that align at top and
  bottom, 1234567890.

lining paper (binding), that
  inside the cover.

link, 7·92 in.; one-hundredth
  of a chain; abbr. **l.**

Linn/aean, abbr. **Linn.;** *but*
  -ean Society, London (off.
  spelling); abbr. **L.S.**

Linnaeus (**Carolus**), 1707–
  78, Swedish naturalist; in
  Sw. **Carl von Linné**; abbr.
  L. *or* **Linn.**

Linotype, a composing
  machine that casts lines of
  type; abbr. **Lino** (no point).

linsey-woolsey, a thin
  coarse fabric of linen and
  wool; gibberish; *not* linsy-,
  -wolsey.

Linson (bind.), strong paper
  used in place of bookcloth
  (trade mark).

liny, full of lines, *not* -ey.

Lion (**Gulf of the**) *or* **Lion
  Gulf,** off Mediterranean Fr.
  coast; in Fr. **golfe du Lion,**
  not Lions, Lyon, Lyons.

Lionardo da Vinci (*use* Le-).

lionize, *not* -ise.

Lippi (**Fra Filippo**), 1412–
  69; — (**Filippino**), 1460–
  1504, Italian painters.

lipsalve (one word).

liq., liquid, liquor.

lique/faction, -fiable, -fy, *not* liqui-.

liqueur, a strong alcoholic liquor, sweetened and flavoured (not ital.).

liquid, abbr. **liq.**

liquidambar, a genus of balsam-bearing trees, *not* -er (one word, not ital.).

liquor on draught, *not* draft.

liquorice (U.S. licor-).

liquorish, desirous, greedy, *use* licker-.

lir/a, unit of Italian currency; *pl.* **-e;** abbr. **L.**

lissom, supple, *not* -e.

Liszt (Abbé Franz), 1811–86, Hungarian pianist and composer.

lit., litre, literal, -ly, literary, literature.

Litchfield, Hants, *also* Connecticut, U.S. *See also* Lich-.

litchi, Chinese fruit (-tree), also grown in Bengal, *not* the many variants (not ital.).

Lit.D., *Literarum Doctor* (Doctor of Letters) (*see also* **D.Lit., D.Litt., Litt.D.**).

lite pendente (Lat.), during the trial.

liter/al, -ally, -ary, -ature; abbr. **lit.**

literal (typ.), a literal error, in which the required character has been set up as a different character, or as a 'turn' or a 'wrong fount', or in defective type.

literalize, etc., to render literal, *not* -ise.

litera (or *littera*) *scripta manet* (Lat.), the written word remains.

literat/i, the learned as a class; *sing.* **-o,** *not* -us, litt-.

literatim (Lat.), letter for letter.

Lith., Lithuanian.

lithium, symbol **Li** (no point).

lithography (typ.), planographic printing process from smooth plate, originally a stone; abbr. **litho** (no point). *See* offset.

Lithuania, a Soviet Socialist Republic. *See* U.S.S.R.

Lit. Hum., *Literae Humaniores,* Faculty (Classics and Philosophy) at Oxford.

litigious, fond of going to law.

Litolff (Henri Charles), 1818–91, French pianist, composer, music-publisher.

litre, abbr. **l** (no point), one-thousandth of a cubic metre, 1·76 pint.

Litt.B., *Literarum Baccalaureus,* Bachelor of Literature (Letters).

Litt.D., *Literarum Doctor* (Doctor of Letters, Camb., and T.C.D.), *not* D.Lit. (Doctor of Literature). *See also* **Lit.D.**

littérateur, a literary man (not ital.).

litterati, *use* lite-.

Little-go (obs.), 'The Previous Examination' at Cambridge and T.C.D. (cap., hyphen, not ital.).

Littlehampton, Sussex (one word).

Little Peddlington, imaginary place (two *d*'s), from a satire by John Poole (1786–1872).

Littleton, family name of Baron Hatherton; — (**Sir Thomas**), 1407?–81, English jurist. *See also* Lyttelton.

littoral, a region by a coast.

Littré (M. P. E.), 1801–81, French lexicographer.

liturg., liturg/ies, -ical, -y.

liv. (Fr.), *livre* (m. book, f. pound).

liveable, *not* liva-.

livelong, intensive and emotional form of **long.** *See* **lifelong.**

Liver/politan, -pudlian, inhab. of Liverpool.

livestock (one word).

Livingston (Robert R.), 1746–1813, American statesman.

Livingston, W. Lothian, 'new town', 1962.

Livingstone (David), 1813–73, Scottish explorer and missionary.

Livorno, Italian seaport, *formerly* in Eng. **Leghorn.**

livraison (Fr. f.), a part of a work published by instalments.

livre (Fr. m.), book; (f.) pound; abbr. **L.,** *or* **liv.**

liv. st. (Fr.), *livre sterling* (pound sterling).

L.J., Lord Justice; **L.JJ.,** Lords Justices.

Ljubljana, Yugoslavia; in Ger. **Laibach.**

L.L., late-, law-, *or* Low-, Latin, Lord-Lieutenant, -s;

ll., leaves, lines, *leges* (laws).

ll in Spanish and Welsh words not to be divided.

-ll (words ending in), followed by -ful, -ly, -ness, usu. omit one *l*.

L.L.A., (*formerly*) Lady Literate in Arts (St. Andrews Univ.).

llama, S. American ruminant, *not* la-. *See also* **lama.**

Llandeilo Group, Carmarthenshire (geol.) (caps.).

Llanelli (*not now* -y).

llano(s), S. American plain(s).

LL.B. (Lat.), *Legum Baccalaureus* (Bachelor of Laws) (two points only).

LL.D., *Legum Doctor* (Doctor of Laws) (two points only).

LL.EE. (Fr. f.), *Leurs Excellences* (Their Excellencies).

LL.ÉÉ. (Fr. f.), *Leurs Éminences* (Their Eminences).

L.L.I., Lord-Lieutenant of Ireland.

LL.M., *Legum Magister* (Master of Laws).

LL.MM. (Fr.), *Leurs Majestés* (Their Majesties).

Lloyd (Norddeutscher), the North-German Lloyd Steamship Co. (two words); abbr. **N.D.L.**

Lloyd's/, the association of underwriters, *not* -s'; — **marks,** in order of merit, for wooden ships, **A1, A1** (in red), **Æ,** and **E;** for iron or steel, **100 A1, 90 A1, 80 A1.** *See also* **Loyd.**

Lloyds Bank, Ltd.

L.M., Licentiate in Midwifery; long metre (mus.).

l.M. (Ger.), *laufenden Monats* (of the current month).

£m., (one) million pounds.

L.M.B.C., Lady Margaret Boat Club (St. John's College), Camb.

L.M.D., long metre double.

L.M.H., Lady Margaret Hall (Oxford).

L.M.S., London Missionary Society.

L.M.S.(R.), London, Midland, & Scottish (Railway) (prior to nationalization).

L.M.S.S.A., Licentiate in Medicine and Surgery, Society of Apothecaries.

L.M.T. (phys.), length, mass, time.

L.N.E.R., London and North Eastern Railway (prior to nationalization).

L.N.W.R., London & North-Western Railway (prior to nationalization).

L.O., Liaison Officer.

loadstar, *use* **lodestar.**

loadstone, magnetic oxide of iron, *not* lode- (one word).

load-water-line (hyphens); abbr. **L.W.L.**

loath, averse, *not* loth.

loathe, to hate.

loathsome, *not* loth-.

Lobachevski (Nikolai Ivanovich), 1793–1856, Russian mathematician.

Lobanov-Rostovski (Alexis Borisovich, Prince), 1824–96, Russian statesman.

'Lobgesang', Mendelssohn's 'Hymn of Praise', 1840.

lobscouse, a sailor's dish.

lobworm (one word).

locale, scene of operations (erron. form, but well established).

localize, *not* -ise.

loc. cit., *loco citato* (in the place cited) (not ital.).

loch, Scottish lake, *not* -ck.

Lochalsh, Ross.

lochan, small Scottish lake.

Loch Awe, Argyll.

Lochearnhead, Perth.

Lochgilphead, Argyll.

Loch Leven, Kinross.

Lochnagar, mountain in Aberdeen (one word).

Lock/e (John), 1632–1704, English philosopher; **-ian,** *not* -ean.

lock-jaw (hyphen).

lock-out, employers' strike; *pl.* **lock-outs** (hyphen).

locksmith (one word).

lock-up (noun *or* adj., hyphen).

lock-up (typ.), exertion of pressure to hold various elements in the forme together.

loco, locomotive (no point).

loco/ (Lat.), in the place; — *citato,* ditto cited, abbr. **l.c.,** *or* **loc. cit.** (not ital.); — *laudato,* ditto cited with approval, abbr. **loc. laud.;** — *supra citato,*

ditto before cited, abbr. **l.s.c.** (not ital.).

Locofoco (U.S.), extreme section of Democratic Party, 1835.

locum/-tenency (hyphen); — **tenens,** a substitute, *pl.* — **tenentes** (not ital.).

loc/us (Lat.), a written passage, a curve, *pl.* **-i;** *locus/ citatus,* the passage quoted; — *classicus,* an authoritative passage from a standard book, *pl.* **loci** *classici;* — *communis,* a commonplace; — *delicti,* the place of a crime; — *in quo,* the place in which; — *poenitentiae,* a place of repentance; — *sigilli,* the place of the seal, abbr. **L.S.;** — *standi,* recognized position, (law) right to appear.

L.O.D., *Little Oxford Dictionary.*

lodestar, star steered by, *not* load-.

lodestone, *use* load-.

lodg/e, -eable, -ement, -ing.

lodging-house (hyphen).

loess (geol.), deposit of fine yellowish loam in certain valleys, *not* loëss, löss.

L. of C., line of communication.

Lofoten Islands, Norway, *not* -den, -ffoden.

log, logarithm (no point).

log., logic.

logan-stone, a rocking-stone, *not* loggan-, logging-.

logarithm, abbr. **log** (no point).

Logau (Friedrich von), 1604–55, German poet.

log-book (hyphen).

loge, a theatre stall (not ital.).

loggia/ (It.), a gallery; *pl.* **-s.**

logi/on, a saying of Christ not in the Gospels; *pl.* **-a** (not ital.).

logotype (typ.), several letters, or a word, cast as one type.

log-roll/, -er, -ing, mutual aid among politicians or reviewers (hyphen).

Lohengrin, German hero; (ital.) opera by Wagner.

Loire, French river, *also* dép.; **Loire-Atlantique,** dép.; **Haute-Loire,** dép.

Loir-et-Cher, French dép.

lollipop, a sweetmeat, *not* lolly-.

Lombroso (Cesare), 1836–1909, Italian criminologist.

London., sig. of Bp. of London, *not* -in. (full point).

London/, abbr. **L.,** *or* **Lond.;** — **Apprentice,** hamlet in Cornwall; — **County Council/, -lor,** abbr. **L.C.C.** *See also* **G.L.C.**

long., longitude.

longe, *use* **lu-.**

longe (Fr. cook. f.), loin.

long/eval, long-lived, *not* -aeval; **-evity.**

Longfellow (Henry Wadsworth, *not* Words-), 1807–82, American poet.

long-hand, ordinary handwriting (hyphen).

Long Island, U.S.; abbr. **L.I.**

longitude, abbr. **long.**

long/ letter (typ.), *ā, ē,* etc.; — **mark,** that placed over the long letter: the macron.

Longman Group Ltd., publishers.

Longmynd Group (geol.), Salop (caps.).

longo intervallo (Lat.), at a long interval.

long page (typ.), one having a line or lines more than its companion pages.

long primer (typ.), old name for a size of type, about 10 pt.; *pron.* prĭm-er.

long s, ſ, italic *ſ*.

Longships, lighthouse off Cornwall.

long-shore (adj., hyphen), *not* 'long-; *but* **longshoreman** (one word).

longueur, tedious passage in book, play, film, usu. pl. (ital.).

long vowel (typ.), *ā, ē,* etc.

long/ways, -wise (one word).

looking-glass (hyphen).

look/ -out, *pl.* — **-outs** (hyphen).

loophole (one word).

loosestrife (bot.) (one word).

loping, with long strides, *not* lope-.

lop-sided (hyphen).

loquitur (Lat.), he, *or* she, speaks; abbr. *loq.*

lord, abbr. **Ld.**

Lord/-Advocate of Scotland, abbr. **L.A.S.;** — **Chamberlain,** — **Chancellor,** abbr. **L.C.;** — **Chief Baron,** abbr. **L.C.B.;** — **Chief Justice,** abbr. **L.C.J.;** — **Justice,** abbr. **L.J.,** *pl.* **L.JJ.;** — **-Lieutenant,** *pl.* — **-s** (hyphen), abbr. **L.L.;** — **Mayor** (two words, caps.); — **of hosts,** — **of lords,** as Deity (one cap.); — **Privy Seal,** abbr. **L.P.S.;** — **Provost,** abbr. **L.P.**

Lord's Cricket Ground, London (apos.).

Lord's Day (caps.).

lordship, abbr. **Ldp.**

Lord's/ Prayer, — Supper, — Table (caps.).

Lorelei, siren of the Rhine, *not* -ey, Lurlei.

Lorenzo, *see* **Lourenço.**

Loreto, Colombia, Italy, Mexico, Peru.

Loretto, anglicized version of the It. **Loreto;** *also* Scottish school.

lorgnette (Fr. f.), opera-glass, or pair of eye-glasses with long handle.

loris, the Ceylon sloth, *not* lori, lory.

Lorrain (Claude) (*né Gelée*), 1600–82, French painter, *not* -aine.

Lorraine, *see* Alsace-Lorraine.

lorry, a wagon.

lory, one of the parrots.

Los Angeles, California.

löss (geol.), *use* loess.

lota, Hindu brass waterpot, *not* lotah, -oote, loto.

Lot-et-Garonne, dép. France.

loth, averse, *use* loath.

Lothario/, 'the gay', in Nicholas Rowe's *The Fair Penitent,* 1703; *pl.* -s.

Loti (Pierre), pen-name of Julien Viaud, 1850–1923, French writer.

loto, *use* lota.

lotus/, Egyptian and Asian water-lily; *pl.* -es.

lotus-eater, *not* lotos-; but 'The Lotos-Eaters' (Tennyson).

loud-speaker (hyphen).

Louisiana, U.S.; off. abbr. **La.,** *not* Lou.

Louis-Philippe, 1773–1850, French king.

Louis/-Quatorze, 1643–1715; — **-Quinze,** 1715–74; — **-Seize,** 1774–93; — **-Treize,** 1610–43 (Louis XIV, XV, XVI, XIII), art styles (hyphens).

loukoum (Gr., Turk.), national sweetmeat.

loung/e, -ing.

lour, to frown (U.S. **lower**).

Lourenço Marques, Mozambique, *not* Lorenzo —, -ez.

louver, shutter, ventilator, *not* -re.

lovable, *not* -eable.

Love's Labour's Lost, Shakespeare, 1598 (two apos.).

Low Church (two words, caps.); **Low-Churchman** (hyphen, caps.).

lower, to frown, *use* lour.

Lower California (caps.).

lower case (typ.), the case containing the small letters, hence the small letters a–z; abbr. **l.c.**

Low (Sampson), Marston, & Co., publishers.

Low Sunday, first after Easter (caps.).

low water (two words).

low-water mark (hyphen).

Loyd (Sam), 1841–1911, American chess-player. *See also* Lloyd/, 's.

Loyson (Charles), 1827–1912, 'Père Hyacinthe'.

L.P., long-playing record, Lord Provost, (paper) large post.

l.p., low pressure.

L.P.C., Lord President of the Council.

L.P.O., London Philharmonic Orchestra.

L.P.S., Lord Privy Seal.

L.P.T.B., London Passenger Transport Board (policy and financial control by Min. of Transport), defunct 1969, replaced 1970 by London Transport Executive, **L.T.E.** (policy and financial control by G.L.C.).

Lr, lawrencium (no print.)

L.R.A.M., Licentiate of the Royal Academy of Music.

L.R.C.M., Licentiate of the Royal College of Music.

L.R.C.P., Licentiate of the Royal College of Physicians.

L.R.C.S., Licentiate of the Royal College of Surgeons.

L.R.C.V.S., Licentiate of the Royal College of Veterinary Surgeons.

L.S., Leading Seaman, Linnean Society, *loco* or

L.S. (*cont.*):
locus sigilli, (in) the place of the seal.

l.s., left side.

L.S.A., Licentiate of the Society of Apothecaries.

LSD (no points), the hallucinatory drug *d*-lysergic acid diethylamide tartrate.

L.S.D., *librae, solidi, denarii* (pounds, shillings, and pence), Lightermen, Stevedores, and Dockers.

L.S.E., London School of Economics.

L.S.O., London Symphony Orchestra.

L.(&)S.W.R., London and South Western Railway (became part of **S.R.** until nationalization).

Lt., Lieutenant.

l.t., low tension.

L.T.A., Lawn Tennis Association, London Teachers' Association.

L.T. & S.R., London, Tilbury, and Southend Railway (became part of **L.M.S.** until nationalization).

L.T.C.L., Licentiate of Trinity College of Music, London.

Lt.-Col., Lieutenant-Colonel.

Lt.-Com., Lieutenant-Commander.

Ltd., Limited.

L.T.E., London Transport Executive. *See* **L.P.T.B.**

Lt.-Gen., Lieutenant-General.

L.Th., Licentiate in Theology (Durham).

Lt. Inf., Light Infantry.

L.T.M., Licentiate in Tropical Medicine.

Lu, lutetium (no point).

Luang Prabang, *see* **Laos.**

Lübeck, Germany, *not* Lue-.

Lubumbashi, Zaïre, *formerly* **Élisabethville.**

Lucan, of St. Luke, *not* Luk-.

lucarne, a dormer-window.

Lucerne, in Ger. **Luzern.**

lucerne, a plant, *not* -ern.

Lucile, by Robert Lytton, 1860, *not* -lle.

Lucknow, Uttar Pradesh, India.

lucus a non lucendo (Lat.), *approx.* inconsequent or illogical.

Ludlow (typ.), a composing machine for setting display lines.

L.U.E. (theat.), left upper entrance.

Luftwaffe, German air-force.

Luggnagg, island in *Gulliver's Travels.*

lug-sail (hyphen).

Luke (St.) (N.T.), not to be abbreviated; adj. **Lucan,** *not* Luk-.

lukewarm/, -ness, tepid(ity) (one word).

lumbar (anat.), of the loins.

lumber, to move clumsily; unused furniture, etc.

lum/en (anat.), a cavity, *pl.* *-ina;* *lumen/* (phys.), the unit of luminous flux, *pl.* *-s.*

lumpen (adj.), of the very poor social classes; hence (noun) **lumpenproletariat.**

lunation, time from one new moon to next, 29·5305887 days.

lunge, long rope for exercising horses, *not* lo-.

lunging, *not* lungeing.

lunn, *see* **sally-lunn.**

lupin, a garden plant.

lupine (adj.), of a wolf.

Lurlei, *use* **Lorelei.**

Lusiads (*The*), by Camoens, 1572.

Lusitania, Portugal.

lustr/um, a five-year period; *pl.* *-a.*

lusus naturae (Lat.), a freak of nature; *pl.* same.

lutetium symbol **Lu** (no point), *formerly* **cassiopeium.**

Luth., Lutheran.
Lutine bell, bell rung once at Lloyd's to announce the loss, twice for the arrival, of a vessel overdue.
luxe (édition de) (Fr.), a sumptuous edition (not ital.); *train de luxe,* luxurious railway train.
Luxembourg, Gardens and Palace, Paris.
Luxemburg, prov. of Belgium; *also* **Grand Duchy of** —; in Fr. **-ourg.**
Luxemburg (Rosa), 1870–1919, German socialist.
Luzern, German for **Lucerne.**
L.W.L., load-water-line.
L.W.M., low-water mark.
Lwów, *see* **Lemberg.**
LXX, the Septuagint, seventy (no points).
lycée (Fr. m.), higher secondary school.
Lyceum (the), Aristotle's school of philosophy; **lyceum/,** a college of literary studies, *pl.* **-s.**
lychee, *use* **litchi.**
lych-gate, roofed gateway of churchyard; *not* lich-.

lyddite, an explosive (two *d*'s).
lying-in, childbed (hyphen).
lyke-wake, night-watch over dead body.
Lyly (John), 1554?–1606, English author. *See* **euphuism.**
Lymington, Hants. See also **Lea-, Le-.**
lynch law, *not* -'s, Linch's (two words).
lynx/, animal of cat-tribe; *pl.* **-es.**
Lyon King-of-Arms, chief Scottish herald.
Lyonnais (Crédit), French banking corporation.
Lyons, in Fr. **Lyon.** See also **Lions.**
lysin (chem.), *not* -ine.
Lyte (Henry Francis), 1793–1847, English hymn-writer (*see also* **Maxwell-Lyte**).
Lytham St. Annes, Lancs. (no apos.).
Lyttelton, family name of Viscount Cobham (*see also* **Littleton**); — (**Humphrey Richard Adeane**), b. 1921, English jazz musician.
Lytton, *see* **Bulwer-Lytton.**

M

M, 1,000 (no point); (as prefix) mega- (1 000 000); the twelfth in a series.

M. (cricket) maiden over, Majesty, Marqu/ess, -is, Member, metronome, middle, militia, (in Peerage) minor, Monday, all proper names with this initial, (Fr.) *main* (hand), *mille* (a thousand), monsieur, (It.) *mano* (hand), *mezz/o, -a* (half), (Lat.) *magister* (master), *medicinae* (of medicine).

m, metre, (prefix) milli- (10⁻³).

M', *see* **Mac.**

m., male, married, masculine, (mech.) mass, merid/ian, -ional, mile, -s, mill, million, minute, -s, (naut.) mist, month, -s, moon, (Lat.) *meridies* (noon).

m/ (Fr.), *mois* (month).

℔, minim (drop).

µ (mu, Gr. m), (math.) modulus, (phys.) symbol for magnetic permeability, (as prefix) micro- (10⁻⁶); **µm,** micrometre, micron; **mµ,** millimicron, *use* **nm.**

M.A., *Magister Artium* (Master of Arts), Military Academy.

Ma (chem.), masurium (no point), *now* **technetium (Te).**

ma (Italian), but.

mA (elec.), milliampere (no point).

m/a (book-keeping), my account.

ma'am, *see* **madam.**

Maartens (Maarten), pen-name of Joost Marius van der Poorten-Schwartz, 1858–1915, Dutch novelist, wrote in English.

Maastricht, Holland, *not* Maes-.

Mabinogion, collection of ancient Welsh romances.

Mac (the prefix), spelling depends upon custom of the one bearing the name, and this must be followed, as: MacDonald, Macdonald, McDonald, MͨDonald, M'Donald (the turned comma is usual here, not the apos.). In alphabetical arrangement it should, however spelt, be treated as Mac.

macadamize, to cover with layers of small broken stone, each rolled in, *not* -ise; from **John L. McAdam,** 1756–1836, British engineer.

macarism, blessing, *not* mak-.

macaron/i (*not* macc-), long tubes of wheaten paste; an eighteenth-century dandy, *pl.* **-ies; -ic,** in burlesque verse, Latinized modern and modernized Latin.

MacArthur (Gen. Douglas), 1880–1964, U.S. general.

macaw, a parrot, *not* macao, maccaw.

Macc. (1, 2), Maccabees, First, Second Book of.

Maccabean, of the Maccabees, *not* bæan.

Macchiavelli, *use* **Mach-.**

MacDiarmid (Hugh), b. 1892, Scottish poet, pen-name of **Christopher Murray Grieve.**

Macdonald (Alexandre), 1765–1840, Duke of Taranto, French marshal.

MacDonald (Flora), 1722–1790, Jacobite heroine; — **(George),** 1824–1905, Scottish novelist and poet; — **(Rt. Hon. James Ramsay),** 1866–1938, British Prime Minister

Maced., Macedonian.

macédoine, mixed fruit or vegetables embedded in jelly (not ital.).

Macgillicuddy's Reeks, mountains in Kerry.

McGraw-Hill Publishing Co., Ltd.

MacGregor, family name of Rob Roy.

ma chère (Fr. f.), my dear. *See also mon/ cher.*

Machiavell/i (Niccolò), 1469–1527, Florentine statesman, playwright, writer on political opportunism, *not* Macch-; adj. **-ian** (cap. only in lit. or hist. usage); noun, **-ism,** *not* -ianism.

machina (Lat.), a machine. *See deus ex —.*

machine revise, final proof before actual printing.

mach number, ratio of speed of a body to speed of sound in surrounding atmosphere (not cap.), from **Ernst Mach,** 1836–1916, Austrian physicist.

Machpelah, burial-place of Abraham, *not* Macp-.

macintosh, a waterproof, abbr. **mac** (no point); patented by **Charles Macintosh,** 1766–1843, Scottish chemist; *not* mack-.

McKinley (William), 1843–1901, American President 1896–1901.

mackle, printing blemish.

macle, twin crystal, spot in a mineral.

MacLehose & Sons, printers, Glasgow.

MacLeish (Archibald), b. 1892, U.S. poet.

Macleod (Fiona), pseud. of **William Sharp,** 1856–1905, Scottish poet and novelist.

MacMahon (Marie Edmé P. M. de), 1808–93, Duke of Magenta, French marshal, President 1873–9.

Macmillan International, publishers, includes **Macmillan, London, Ltd.** and **Macmillan Press, Ltd.** The **Macmillan Company, New York,** which became an independent organization, is now part of **Collier-Macmillan, Inc.**

McNaghten Rules, on insanity as defence in criminal trial; *not* named from **MacNaghtan (Edward),** 1830–1913, English judge, but from the murderer of Sir Robert Peel's private secretary, 1843.

MacNeice (Louis), 1907–63, Anglo-Irish poet, critic, traveller.

Macon, Georgia, U.S.

Mâcon, dép. Saône-et-Loire; *also* a burgundy, *not* -çon.

macramé lace, a trimming of knotted thread, *not* -mi.

macrocosm, the great world. *See also* **microcosm.**

macron, the long mark over a vowel, as *ā*.

macroscopic, visible to the naked eye.

macrurous (zool.), long-tailed, *not* macrourous.

Macsycophant (Sir Pertinax), in *Man of the World,* 1781, by **Macklin (Charles),** 1699–1797, Irish actor and playwright.

macul/a (Lat.), a spot; *pl.* **-ae.**

Madagascar, off SE. coast of Africa, independent 1960 as the **Malagasy Republic.**

madam, *pl.* **-s;** colloq. abbr. **'m, ma'am** (cap. for the correct form of address to the Queen), **marm, m'm, mum.**

Madame, abbr. **Mme,** *not* Mdme; *pl.* **Mesdames,** abbr. **Mmes** (in Fr. no point after abbrs.).

Mädchen (Ger. n.), girl; *pl. same* (cap.).

Madeira, island, wine, cake.
Mademoiselle, abbr.
Mlle, *not* Mdlle;
pl. **Mesdemoiselles,** abbr.
Mlles, *not* Mdlles (in Fr.
no point after abbrs.).
madère (Fr. m.), Madeira
wine.
Madhya Pradesh (India),
formerly Central Provinces;
abbr. **M.P.**
Madonna, the Virgin Mary
(cap.).
madonna (It.), my lady,
madam (in 3rd person only,
not cap.).
madrasah (Ind.), a school
or college (not the many
variants).
Mad. Univ., Madison
University, U.S.;
Madras —.
Maecenas/, a patron of the
arts, *not* Me-; *pl.* **-es.**
maelstrom, whirlpool, *not*
mal-.
maenad/, a female follower
of Bacchus, *not* me-; *pl.* **-s.**
maestoso (mus.), majestical,
stately.
Maestricht, Holland, *use*
Maas-.
maestr/o (mus.), master,
composer, conductor; *pl.* **-i**
(not ital.).
Maeterlinck (Maurice),
1862–1949, Belgian poet,
dramatist, essayist,
philosopher.
Mafia, Sicilian secret society,
extending to U.S. *See also*
Camorra.
ma foi! (Fr.), upon my
word!
Mag., Magyar (Hungarian).
mag., magazine, magnetism.
Maga, colloq. for *Blackwood's Magazine.*
magasin de/ modes (Fr.
m.), dressmaker's shop;
— — *nouveautés,* linen-
draper's —, *not* — des —.
magazine, abbr. **mag.**

magazines (titles of) (typ.),
(when cited, to be in italic).
magdalen, a repentant
prostitute, a hospital for
such; *but* **Mary Mag-
dalene** (*pron.* mag-da-lēn).
Magdalen College, Oxford,
pron. mawd'-lin.
Magdalene College, Cambridge, *pron.* mawd'-lin.
maggot, a grub. *See also*
magot.
magilp, *use* **meg-.**
magister (Lat. m.), master,
abbr. **M.;** — *artium,*
Master of Arts, abbr.
M.A.; — *Chirurgiae,* ditto
Surgery, **M.Ch.**
magistrand, an arts student
ready for graduation, esp.
now at Aberdeen Univ.;
at St. Andrews a fourth-
year student.
magma/, a mass; *pl.* **-s.**
Magna Charta (1215).
*magna est veritas et
praevalet* (Lat.), great is
truth and it prevails; *ditto
praevalebit,* ditto will
prevail.
magnalium, alloy of
magnesium and aluminium.
magnesium, symbol **Mg**
(no point).
magnetize, *not* -ise.
magneto/, type of electric
generator; *pl.* **-s.**
magnification sign, ×
(followed by figure).
magnif/y, -ied, -ying.
magnifying glass (two
words).
magnum, a reputed two-
quart wine bottle.
magnum bonum, a large,
good variety, esp. of plums
or potatoes; *pl.* **magnum
bonums** (two words, not
ital.).
magn/um op/us (Lat.), an
author's chief work; *pl.* **-a
-era.** *See also* **opus
magnum.**

magot, ape, *also* Chinese or Japanese figure. *See also* **maggot.**

mag/us, a wise man; *pl.* **-i;** *but* **the Magi** (cap.).

Magyar, dominant race in Hungary; a Hungarian; the Finno-Ugric speech of Hungary; abbr. **Mag.**

magyar, type of blouse or of its sleeves.

Mahabharata, Indian epic (accent on third syllable).

Mahame/dan, -tan, *use* **Muhammadan,** q.v.

Mahan (Rear-Adm. Alfred Thayer), 1840–1914, American naval writer.

Mahara/ja, *not* **-jah,** Indian title; *fem.* **-ni,** *not* **-nee.**

mahatma, in esoteric Buddhism one possessing supernatural powers; (with cap.) title prefixed to exalted persons, esp. **Gandhi.**

mahaut, *use* **mahout.**

Mahican (member of) an American Indian tribe between the Hudson River and Narragansett Bay. *See* **Mohegan** *and* **Mohican.**

mah-jong, Chinese game played with tiles, *not* **-ngg** (hyphen).

mahlstick, painter's hand-rest, *use* **maul-.**

mahlstrom, *use* **mael-.**

Mahom/et, the trad. English spelling, *not* **-ed;** *but use* **Muhammad.** *See also* **Islam, Muhammadan, Muslim.**

mahout, elephant-driver, *not* **-aut.**

Mahratta, *use* **Maratha.**

Mahratti, *use* **Marathi.**

mahseer, large Indian fresh-water fish (not the many variants).

mahwa, Indian tree (not the many variants.)

Maia (Gr. myth.), mother of Apollo.

maidan (Ind., Pers.), a plain, an esplanade, *not* **-aun.**

maidenhair, a fern (one word).

maieutic, helping childbirth.

maigre day (R.C.C.), one when no flesh is eaten.

mailable (U.S.), capable of being sent by mail.

main/ (Fr. f.), a hand, *also* a quire, abbr. **M.;** — *droite,* right hand, abbr. **M.D.;** — *gauche,* left —, **M.G.**

Maine, U.S., off. abbr. **Me.**

Maine-et-Loire, dép. France (hyphens).

mainprize (law), suretyship, *not* **-ise.**

main/sail, -spring, -stay (one word).

Mainz am Rhein, German city (no hyphens).

maiolica, *use* **maj-.**

maison/ d'arrêt (Fr. f.), prison; — *de campagne,* country house; — *de santé,* private asylum; — *de ville,* guildhall.

maisonette, a small house, a flat; anglicized form of Fr. ***maisonnette.***

maison garnie, furnished house.

maître/, title of French advocate, abbr. **Mᵉ;** — *d'hôtel* (Fr. m.), house steward; *à la* — —, plainly prepared with parsley (no hyphen).

maîtresse (Fr. f.), mistress.

maiuscol/a (It. typ.), capital letter; *-etto,* small capital letter.

Maj., Major.

Majesté (Sa) (Fr. f.), His, *or* Her, Majesty, *not Son* —.

Majesty, abbr. **M.**

majolica, an Italian glazed or enamelled earthenware, *not* **maiol-;** in It. *maiolica.*

Major/, abbr. **Maj.;** — **-General** (caps., hyphen), abbr. **Maj.-Gen.**

major-domo, a house steward (hyphen); in It. *maggiordomo.*

majuscule, a capital, or upper-case, letter.

makarism, *use* maca-.

make-believe (hyphen).

makeready (typ.), preparing forme or plate on printing machine (one word).

makeshift (one word).

make-up (typ.), arrangement of matter into pages.

make-weight (hyphen).

Mal., Malachi, Malayan.

Malacca, *see* **Malaya, Federation of.**

malacology, study of molluscs; abbr. **malac.**

maladdress, awkwardness (one word, not ital.); in Fr. f. *maladresse* (ital.).

malade imaginaire (Fr. m.), imaginary invalid.

maladroit, clumsy (not ital.).

mala/ fide (Lat.), treacherously; — *fides,* bad faith; — *in se* (Lat.), acts which are intrinsically wrong.

Malagasy, native or language of Madagascar.

Malagasy Republic, *see* **Madagascar.**

malaise (Fr. m.), discomfort, uneasiness.

Malaprop (Mrs.), in *The Rivals,* by Sheridan, 1775.

malapropos, unseasonably; in Fr. *mal à propos.*

Malawi, Cent. Africa, independent state within the Commonwealth, 1964, republic 1966; *formerly* Nyasaland.

Malaya, Federation of: till 1957 consisted of nine states (Johore, Kedah, Kelantan, Negri Sembilan, Pahang, Perak, Perlis, Selangor, Trengganu) and the two British settlements of Penang and Malacca; adj. **Malayan,** abbr. **Mal.**

Malayalam, language of Malabar coast, SW. India.

Malaysia, since 1957, independent state within the Commonwealth; consists of Malaya, Sabah, and Sarawak; adj. **Malaysian.**

malcontent, *not* male-.

Malcuzzinski (Witold), b. 1914, Polish pianist.

mal de mer (Fr. m.), seasickness.

Malden, Surrey.

mal de tête (Fr. m.), headache.

Maldive Islands, elective Sultanate SW. of Ceylon.

Maldon, Essex.

mal du pays (Fr. m.), home-sickness.

male, abbr. **m.** (bot., zool.), sign ♂.

malee, *use* **mallee.**

malemute, malamute, Eskimo dog.

malentendu (Fr. m.), misunderstanding (one word).

mal entendu (Fr.), misunderstood (two words).

Malesherbes (C. G. de L. de), 1721–94, French statesman. *See also* **Malherbe.**

Malet (Lucas), pen-name of Mrs. M. St. L. Harrison.

malgré (Fr.), in spite of; — *elle,* ditto herself; — *eux,* — *elles,* ditto themselves; — *lui,* ditto himself; — *moi,* ditto myself.

Malherbe (François de), 1555–1628, French writer. *See also* **Malesherbes.**

mali, *use* **mallee.**

Mali, republic in NW. Africa, 1962, *formerly* Soudan (French).

Malines, Belgium, *not* Mechlin, q.v.

malleable, *not* male-.

mallee, Indian gardener, *not* mal/ee, -i.

Mallow, Co. Cork.

Malmaison, near Paris (one word).

Malmesbury, Glouc.

malmsey, a sweet wine, *not* -sie, -esie, -asye.

Malone (Edmond, *not* -und*), 1741–1812*, British lit. critic.

Malplaquet (battle of), 1709.

malpractice, misbehaviour, *not* -se.

malstrom, *use* **mael-.**

Maltese cross, ✠. *See also* **cross, crux.**

Malthus (T. R.), 1766– 1834, writer on population.

Malton, Yorks.

mal/um (Lat.), an evil, *pl.* **-a;** *malum/ in se,* an intrinsic evil; — *prohibi-tum,* a prohibited wrong.

Malvernshire, new county, proposed 1971, to replace Herefordshire and Worcestershire.

m. à m. (Fr.), *mot à mot* (word for word).

mameluco, in Brazil, off-spring of white and Indian.

mameluke, Egyptian mounted soldier, *not* mama-, mamlouk, memlook.

mamill/a, nipple; *pl.* **-ae;** adj. **-ary.**

mamm/a, breast; *pl.* **-ae;** adj. **-ary.**

mamma, mother, *pref. to* mama; *pron.* mah-mah'.

mammon, riches. (not cap.).

Mammon, god of riches (cap.).

M.Am.Soc.C.E., Member of the Amalgamated Society of Civil Engineers.

Man., Manila; Manitoba.

man., manual.

Man (Isle of), abbr. **I.o.M.,** *not* I.M.

manacle, fetter, *not* -icle.

Manacles, rocks off Cornish coast.

manage/able, -ment.

man/akin, trop. American bird. *For* dwarf *use* **-ikin.**

mañana (Sp.), tomorrow.

Manassas, Virginia, scene of American Civil War battles.

Manasseh (tribe of).

Manasses (Prayer of), Apocr.

manatee, the sea-cow; in Sp. *manati.*

manche (Fr. m.), a handle; (f.) a sleeve.

Manche (La) (Fr.), the English Channel.

Manchester, abbr. **Manch.,** *or* **M/C.**

man-child, *pl.* **men-children** (hyphens).

Manchu (noun), an inhabitan or the language of Man-churia; (adj.), of the land, people or language of Manchuria; *not* -choo, -chow, -tchoo, -tchu.

Manchukuo, an empire of NE. Asia, 1932–45, formed by the Japanese out of Manchuria, Chinese Jehol, and part of Inner Mongolia.

Manchuria, region in E. Asia, named (1643) from an invading Mongolian people; re-embodied in China, 1945.

Mancunian (inhabitant) of Manchester.

Mandalay, Burma, *not* Mande-.

mandamus, writ issued from a higher court to a lower, *not* -emus (not ital.).

mandarin, Eur. name for a Chinese official; Chinese official language; a small Chinese orange; *not* -ine.

mandatary, one to whom a mandate is given.

mandatory (adj.), command-ing, compulsory.

M and B (*also* **M and B 693**), sulphonamide drug

(from initials of manufacturers May and Baker).

mandioc, *use* **manioc.**

mandolin, stringed instrument, *not* -ine.

mandrel, a spindle, *not* -il.

mandrill, a baboon.

manège (Fr. m.), horsemanship, riding-school; trick. *See also* **ménage.**

Manet (Édouard), 1832–83, French painter.

man/et (Lat., theat.), he, *or* she, remains; *pl.* **-ent.**

manganese, (chem.) symbol **Mn** (no point).

mangel-wurzel, a large beet, *not* mangle-, mangold-.

Mangnall's Questions, school-book by *Mangnall (Richmal),* 1769–1820, English schoolmistress.

mango/, Indian fruit, *not* -oe; *pl.* **-es.**

mangold-wurzel, *use* **mangel- —.**

mangosteen, tropical fruit, *not* -an, -ine.

manhaden, *use* **men-.**

Manhattan Island, New York.

Manhattan Project, the production of the first atomic bombs in U.S.

Manichaean, pertaining to the **Manichees,** religious followers of the Persian **Mani,** *c.* 216–76; *not* -ean.

manicle, a fetter, *use* **-acle.**

manifesto/, declaration of policy; *pl.* **-s.**

manikin, a dwarf, anatomical model, *not* mana-, manni-; in Fr. m. *mannequin. See also* **manakin** *and* **mannequin.**

Manila, Philippine Islands, abbr. **Man.**

manioc, the cassava plant, *not* -dioc, -ihoc, -ihot, -iocca.

maniplies, *use* **many-.**

manipulator, *not* -er.

Manipur, NE. India, *not* Munnepoor.

Manitoba, Canada; abbr. **Man.**

mannequin, dressmaker's (live) model. *See also* **manakin** *and* **manikin.**

Mannheim, Baden, *not* Manh-.

Mannlicher rifle.

manœuvr/e, -ed, -ing (U.S. **maneuver/, -ed, -ing**).

man-of-war, armed ship; *pl.* **men———** (hyphens).

man-of-war's-man (apos., hyphens).

manqu/é (Fr.), *fem.* **-ée,** unsuccessful.

Mansard (François), 1598–1666, French architect.

mansard roof, lower part steeper than upper (not cap.).

Mansfield (Katherine), 1888–1923, N.Z.-born British writer of short stories, pseud. of Katherine Beauchamp, later Murry. *See* **Murry.**

mantel, shelf above fireplace.

mantelet, short cloak; movable screen to protect belligerents, *not* mantlet.

mantelpiece, *not* mantle-.

mantilla (Sp.), a short mantle; a veil covering head and shoulders.

mantle, cloak.

mantlet, *use* **mantelet.**

manual, organ keyboard; abbr. **man.**

manufactur/e, -er, abbr. **mfr.; -ed, mfd.; -ers, -es, mfrs.; -ing, mfg.**

manu forti (Lat.), by main force.

manumit/, to set (slave) free; **-ted, -ting.**

manu propria (Lat.), with one's own hand.

manus (Lat. f.), the hand; *pl. same.*

manuscript, abbr. **MS.**
(**a,** *not* an), *pl.* **MSS.** (point
at end only). It should be
written (or, better, typed)
on one side of paper which
should be of one size
throughout. One inch blank
margin on left-hand side.
Caps. *I, J, S, T,* and l.c. *e, i,*
l, m, n, t, u, if written, to be
clear. Each leaf to be paged
in consecutive order from
the first to the last: not each
chapter separately. Never
place corrections on *back*
of a leaf, but put in an
extra leaf and mark it, say,
23 A, B, or C. If a leaf
is deleted, say 24, mark
previous one 23–24.
Adhesive tape should be
used as little as possible, and
pins and staples should not
be used. Copy for extracts
and footnotes should be
incorporated in sequence
with the text. *See also*
footnotes.

manuscrit (Fr. m.), MS.

Manuskript (Ger. n.), MS.;
also printer's copy.

Manutius/ (Aldus), 1450–
1515, in It. **Aldo**
Manuzio; — — 'the
younger', 1547–97; —
(**Paulus**), 1511–74; Italian
printers.

Manx/, of the Isle of Man;
-man, -men, -woman,
-women (each one word).

manyplies (zool.), the
omasum or third stomach of
ruminants, *not* mani, mony-.

Manzanilla, a dry sherry.

Maori/, member or language
of native race of New
Zealand; *pron.* mowr'ē;
pl. **-s.**

Mao Tse-Tung, b. 1893,
Chairman of Chinese
Communist Party, 1954– .

ma petite (Fr. f.), my little
(girl).

maquereau (Fr. m.),
mackerel.

Maquis, the resistance
movement in France in
Second World War; from
Corsican *maquis,*
scrubland.

mar/, -red, -ring.

mar., maritime.

Mar (Earl of), family name
Goodeve-Erskine. *See also*
Mar and Kellie.

marabou/ feather, —
stork, *not* -bout, -bu.

marabout, N. African monk
or hermit, *not* -but.

marabout (Fr. m.), a very
large coffee-pot or kettle.

Maracaibo, Venezuela, *not*
-ybo.

maranatha (Syriac), 'our
Lord cometh'.

Mar and Kellie (Earl of),
family name Erskine. *See*
also **Mar.**

maraschino, a liqueur.

Marat (Jean Paul), 1743–93,
French revolutionary leader,
assassinated by Charlotte
Corday.

Maratha, an Indian race,
not Mahratta.

Marathi, Indian language,
not Mahratti.

Marazion, Cornwall; *pron.*
marazi'on.

marbleize (U.S.), to colour
like marble, *not* -ise.

marbling (bind.), staining
endpapers or book edges to
resemble marble.

marbré (Fr.), marbled;
also marbled edges of
books.

March (month of)
abbr. **Mar.**

Märchen (Ger. n.), a fairy-
tale; *pl.* same.

marches/e (It.), marquis;
fem. **-a,** marchioness.

marchioness, abbr. **march.**
(cap. as title).

Marcobrunner, a hock.

Marconi (Guglielmo), 1875–1937, inventor of wireless telegraphy.

marconigram, wireless telegraph message.

mardi gras (Fr. m.), Shrove Tuesday.

maréchal/ (Fr. m.), Field-Marshal; his wife, *-e.*

Maréchal Niel, a rose.

mare's-tail (bot.), a marsh plant (apos., hyphen).

marg., margin, *-al.*

margarine, the alternative to butter, *not* -in; *pron.* should be mar′-gar-in, *but* mar-jer-ēn′ is now established, together with abbr. **marge** (no point).

margarite, a mineral; *pron.* mar′-gar-īt.

Margaux (Château-), a claret (hyphen).

marge (Fr. f.), margin.

marginalia, marginal notes, *pl.* (not ital.).

margins (typ.), the four are called back (at binding), head (top), foredge (opposite the binding), and tail (foot of page). An acceptable ratio for the size of margins, in the orders as above, is 1 : 1½ : 2 : 2½.

Margoliouth (David Samuel), 1858–1940, British orientalist.

marguerite, ox-eye daisy; *pron.* mar-ger-ēt′.

mariage de convenance (Fr. m.), marriage of convenience, *not* marr-.

Mariamne, wife of Herod the Great.

Marie de′ Medici, 1573–1642, wife of Henry IV of France (*not* de); in Fr. **de Médicis.**

marijuana (Sp.), hemp, *not* -huana.

marinade (Fr. cook.), a pickle.

Marines ('Blue'), Royal Marine Artillery; — **('Red'),** Royal Marine Light Infantry; *now simply* The Corps of Royal Marines.

Mariolatry, undue worship of the Virgin Mary, *not* Mary-.

marionette, a puppet, *but* Fr. **marionnette.**

maritime, abbr. **mar.**

marivaudage (Fr. m.), daintily affected style, from **Marivaux (Pierre C. de Chamblain de),** 1688–1763, French dramatist and novelist.

Marjoribanks, *pron.* march′-banks.

mark, German coin, *pl. same;* the currency of the Federal Republic of Germany is based on the **Deutsche Mark,** q.v.

market/, abbr. **mkt.;** **-ed.**

Market/ Drayton, Salop; — **Harborough,** Leics. (no hyphens).

market overt (law), open market.

market-place (hyphen).

market town (two words).

marks of correction, *see* **proof correction marks.**

marks of reference (typ.), * † ‡ § ‖ ¶. *See also* **footnotes** *and* **reference marks.**

marline-spike, for separating strands of rope in splicing, *not* -in, -ing (hyphen).

Marlow (Great), Bucks.

Marlowe (Christopher), 1564–93, English dramatist.

marmoset, a monkey.

Marocco, *use* **Morocco.**

maroon, very dark red, *not* morone.

Marprelate Controversy (the), war of pamphlets, 1588–9, between puritan

Marprelate Controversy
(*cont.*):
'Martin Marprelate' and
defenders of the
Established Church.
marque de fabrique (Fr.
f.), trade-mark.
marque (**letters of**), those
authorizing reprisals at sea.
Marquesas Islands,
S. Pacific.
marquetry, inlaid work; in
Fr. f. *marqueterie.*
mar/quis, -quess, abbr.
M., *or* **marq.;** *fem.* **marchioness,** abbr. **march.;**
caps. as titles; in Fr.
marquis/, *fem.* **-e.**
**marquois/ scale, —
triangle,** drawing apparatus,
not Marquoi's, Marquois's.
Marrakesh, Morocco, *not*
Mara-, -kech.
marriage, in Fr. m.
mariage (one *r*).
marriageable, *not* -gable.
married, abbr. **m.**
marron (Fr. m.), chestnut.
marrowfat, a pea.
'Marseillaise (La)', French
national song.
Marseilles, S. France; in
Fr. **Marseille.**
marshal/, -led, -ler, -ling
(U.S. **-ed, -er, -ing**).
Marsham (Viscount),
eldest son of Earl Romney.
See also **Masham.**
marten, a weasel. *See also*
martin.
Martha's Vineyard, an
island, Mass., U.S.
Martial, Rom. poet, abbr.
Mart.
martial, warlike.
Martian, of Mars.
martin, a bird. *See also*
marten.
Martineau (Harriet), 1802–
76, English writer.
martingale, strap from
horse's nose-band to girth,
not -gal.

Martinique, W. Indies.
Martinmas, 11 Nov.
martyrize, etc., *not* -ise.
marvel/, -led, -ling, lous
(U.S. **-ed, -ing, -ous**).
Marvell (Andrew), 1621–78,
English poet and satirist.
Marx/ (Karl), 1818–83,
German socialist, author of
Das Kapital; **-ian; -ism,** *not*
-ianism.
Maryland, U.S., off. abbr.
Md.
Marylebone, London,
formerly Mary-le-bone;
obsolescent pron. mă′-rĭ-bŭn,
current pron. mă′-rĭ-la-bŏn.
Marymass, 25 Mar.
Maryolatry, *use* **Mari-.**
Marzials (Sir F. T.), 1840–
1912, English writer.
mas (Lat.), a male; *pl.*
mares.
mas (Sp.), but.
más (Sp.), more.
**Masaryk (Thomas
Garrigue),** 1850–1937, first
president of Czechoslovakia;
— (**Jan Garrigue**), his son,
1886–1948, Czechoslovak
politician.
masc., masculine.
Mascagni (Pietro), 1863–
1945, Italian composer.
masculine, abbr. **m.,** *or*
masc.
Masefield (John), 1878–
1967, Poet Laureate 1930–67.
maser, microphone amplification by stimulated
emission of radiation
(acronym). *See also* **laser.**
mashallah! (Arab., Pers.,
Turk.), an exclamation of
wonder.
Masham (Baron), family
name Lister. *See also*
Marsham.,
mashie, a golf club, *not* -y.
Mashona/, -land, Rhodesia,
not Mashu-.
masjid (Arabic), a mosque,
not mus-.

mask, cover for the face, etc. *See also* **masque.**

masochism, a sexual perversion which delights in being cruelly treated; from **Leopold von Sacher-Masoch,** 1835–95, Austrian novelist.

Mason (Freemasonry) (cap.).

Mason-Dixon line, U.S., separated slave-owning South from free North; surveyed 1763–67 by Englishmen Charles Mason and Jeremiah Dixon (hyphen).

Masor/ah, Heb. tradition, *not* the many variations; **-etic Text,** abbr. **M.T.**

mass (mech.), abbr. **m.**

Mass., Massachusetts, U.S. (off. abbr.).

massé (Fr. m.), stroke at billiards.

Masséna (André), 1758–1817, French marshal.

Massenet (Jules Émile Frédéric), 1842–1912, French composer.

Massereene (Viscount).

masseu/r, *fem.* **-se** (not ital.).

massif (geol.), mountain mass (not ital.).

Massora, *use* **Masorah.**

master-at-arms (naut.), first-class petty officer (hyphens).

master mariner, captain of a merchant vessel (two words).

Master of, The, title of eldest son of certain Scottish peers, e.g. The Master of Lovat.

Master of the Rolls, abbr. **M.R.**

masterpiece (one word).

master printer, the head of a printing establishment.

Master Printers Association, abbr. **M.P.A.**

mast-head (hyphen).

mastic, a gum-resin, *not* ich, -ick.

masurium, symbol **Ma** (no point), *now* **technetium.**

mat, dull, lustreless; **matt** (I.E.E.) is displacing it in technical use.

Matabele/, *pl. same;* **-land,** S. Africa (one word).

matador, bull-fighter, *not* -ore.

matchwood (one word).

maté, Paraguay tea, *not* mate (not ital.).

matelot (Fr. m.), a sailor.

matelote (Fr. cook. f.), a rich fish stew.

mat/er (Lat.), mother; *pl.* **-res.**

materialize, *not* -ise.

materia medica, science of drugs (not ital.).

matériel (mil.), everything except personnel (ital.).

math., mathemat/ics, -ical, -ician.

mathematics (typ.), references to footnotes in math. works to be marks of reference (†, ‡, etc.), and not superior figures, as these may be mistaken in the text for indices. When letters are required for formulae, caps. and l.c. (not s.caps.) are usual. A formula, if detached from the text, is generally set in the middle of the line; and if it has to be carried on to the next, the break is made at an *equals, minus,* or *plus* sign, which is carried over. Abbr. **math.** *See also* **B.S.I., figures, fractions.**

Mathew (Lord Justice), 1830–1909.

Mathews (Charles), 1776–1835, English actor; — **(Charles James),** 1803–78, English actor and dramatist, son of former; — **(Elkin),** publisher; — **(Shailer),** 1863–1941, American educator and theologian. The usual

Mathews (*cont.*):
spelling of the name is
Matthews.

matin (Fr. m.), morning.

mâtin (Fr. m.), mastiff.

matinée, entertainment by
day (before evening, and gen.
in afternoon); *matinée
musicale,* ditto with music.

matins, sometimes in
Prayer Book **mattins.**

matriculator, *not* -er.

Matrimonial Causes Acts
(law) (no apos.).

matr/ix (typ.), individual die
for casting type; *pl.* **-ices.**

Matt., St. Matthew's Gospel.

Mattei (Tito), 1841–1914,
Italian composer.

matter (typ.), MS. or copy
to be printed, type that has
been set; **live** *or* **standing** —,
type that is still needed.

Matthews, the usual
spelling, *but see* **Mathews.**

Mau, Uttar Pradesh, India.
See also **Mhow.**

maud (Sc.), shepherd's
woollen wrap, *not* -e.

**Maugham (William
Somerset),** 1874–1965,
English novelist and
dramatist.

Maugrabin (Hayraddin),
in Scott's *Quentin Durward.*

Maulmain, Burma, *use*
Moulmein.

maulstick, painter's hand-
rest, *not* mahl-.

Mau Mau, a Kikuyu secret
society in Kenya, rebelled
1952 (two words).

maund, Indian weight.

Maundy Thursday, day
before Good Friday, *not*
Maunday (two words).

Maupassant (Guy de),
1850–93, French writer.

Mauresque, *use* **Mor-.**

Mauretania, name of two
successive Cunard liners.

Maurist, member of the
reformed Benedictine

congregation of St. Maur
(Fr.).

Mauritania, NW. Africa,
independent 1960.

Mauritius, former British
colony, French-speaking, in
Indian Ocean; independent
1968.

mausoleum/, a magnificent
tomb; *pl.* **-s.**

mauvaise honte (Fr. f.)
shyness.

mauvais/ goût (Fr. m.),
bad taste; — *pas,* a difficulty; — *quart d'heure,*
bad quarter of an hour,
a short unpleasant time;
— *sujet,* a ne'er-do-well;
— *ton,* bad style.

maverick (Western U.S.),
an unbranded animal,
masterless person, rover.

Max., Maximilian I or II,
Holy Roman emperors.

max., maxim, maximum.

maxill/a, the jaw; *pl.* **-ae.**

maxim/um, the greatest;
pl. **-a;** abbr. **max.** (not ital.).

maxwell, unit of magnetic
flux; abbr. **Mx** (no point).

Maxwell (J. Clerk),
1831–79, physicist, *not*
Clerk-Maxwell.

**Maxwell-Lyte (Sir Henry
Churchill),** 1848–1940,
English hist. writer.

May (month of), not to be
abbreviated.

may (tree) (not cap.).

maya (Hindu philos.),
illusion.

Maya/, one of an Indian
people of cent. America
and S. Mexico; *pl.* **-s;**
adj. **-n.**

maybe, perhaps (one word).

May Day, 1 May (caps.,
two words).

mayday, international radio-
telephonic distress signal
(one word, not cap.).

Mayence on the Rhine,
use **Mainz am Rhein.**

Mayfair, London (one word), *but* **May Fair Hotel,** London.

mayhem, (legal and U.S.) maiming.

mayonnaise (Fr. f.), a salad dressing (not ital.).

mayst (no apos.).

mazagran (Fr. m.), black coffee served in a glass.

Mazarine Bible, 42-line, first book printed from movable type, by Gutenberg and Fust, *c.* 1450. **Cardinal Mazarin,** 1602–81, had twenty-five copies.

Mazeppa (**Ivan**), 1644–1709, Cossack chief, hero of Byron's poem.

mazurka, a Polish dance, *not* mazou-.

Mazzini (**Giuseppe**), 1805–72, Italian patriot.

M.B., *Medicinae Baccalaureus* (Bachelor of Medicine).

M.B.E., Member of (the Order of) the British Empire.

Mc, *see* **Mac.**

M.C., Master of Ceremonies, — of Surgery, (U.S.) Member of Congress, — of Council, Military Cross.

M/C., Manchester, machine.

M.C.C., Marylebone Cricket Club, Middlesex County Council.

M.Ch., M.Chir., *Magister Chirurgiae* (Master of Surgery).

M.C.P., Member of the College of Preceptors.

M.C.R., Middle Common Room.

M.C.S., Military College of Science.

Md, mendelevium (no point).

Md., Maryland, U.S. (off. abbr.).

MD, Middle Dutch.

M.D., *Medicinae Doctor* (Doctor of Medicine),

(It. mus.) *mano destra* (right hand), (Fr. mus.) *main droite* (right hand).

m.d., month's date.

Mdlle, *use* **Mlle** (Mademoiselle).

Mdme, *use* **Mme** (Madame).

MDN., *Mark der Deutschen Notenbank,* E. German coin.

M.D.S., Master of Dental Surgery.

M.E., Marine Engineer, Mechanical Engineer, Military Engineer, Mining Engineer, Most Excellent.

ME., Middle English.

Me., Maine, U.S. (off. abbr.).

Me (Fr.), *maître* (title of French advocate).

me (**it is**), **it is I,** both used in speech, but former should not be printed, except as a colloquialism.

mea culpa (Lat.), by my fault.

meagre, scanty (U.S. **-er**).

mealie/ (S. Afr.), ear or grain of maize; *pl.* **-s.**

mealy-mouthed, hypocritical (hyphen).

mean/time, -while (one word).

measur/e, -able, abbr. **meas.;** (typ.) the width to which type is set, usu. stated in 12 pt. (pica) ems; **-ements** (*see* figures).

M.E.C., Member of Executive Council.

Mecca, cap. of Hejaz, and one of the federal capitals of Saudi Arabia, *not* Mekka, -ah, -eh. *See* **Riyadh.**

Mecenas, *use* **Mae-.**

mech., mechan/ics, -ical.

mechanics is *singular.*

Mechlin lace, etc., *but see* **Malines.**

Mecklenburgh Square, London, W.C.

Mecklenburg/-Schwerin, — **-Strelitz,** Germany.

M.Ed., Master of Education.
med., medical, medicine, medieval, medium.
medal/, -led, -lion, -list (U.S. **-ed, -ist**).
Médecin malgré lui (*Le*), by Molière, 1666.
medical, abbr. **med.;** — **signs,** ʒ drachm, ♍ minim, M *misce* (mix), ʒ ounce. O pint, ℞ *recipe*, Ɖ scruple.
Medic/i, Florentine ruling family, fifteenth century; *pron.* mĕ′-dĭ-tshĭ; adj. **-ean.**
medicinae (Lat.), of medicine; abbr. **M.**
medieval/, abbr. **med.;** **-ism, -ist, -ize,** etc., *not* -ae-.
Medina, river, I.W.
Medina, *properly* **El Medina,** Arabia.
Medit., Mediterranean.
meditatio fugae (Lat., Sc. law), contemplation of flight.
medi/um, *pl.* **-a,** in spiritualism **-ums** (not ital.); abbr. **med.**
medium/ former standard size of paper, 18 × 23 in.; — **4to,** 11½ × 9 in., — **8vo,** 9 × 5¾ in. (untrimmed). *See* **book sizes.**
Medjidie, Turkish order of knighthood, founded by Sultan Abdu'l Majid; (not cap.) Turkish coin.
med. jur., medical jurisprudence.
Médoc (Fr. m.), a claret.
Meerut, Uttar Pradesh, India, *not* Mirat.
meetings, in news reports, speakers' names usu. s.caps., resolutions quoted.
Meffert (**Peter**) (Ger.), Mr. What's-his-name.
mega-, prefix meaning a million times, abbr. **M** (no point).
megalomania, the delusion of grandeur.
megavolt (elec.), a million volts; abbr. **MV** (no point).

megilp, an artist's medium, vehicle for oil-colours, *not* mag-, -ilph.
megohm (elec.), a million ohms; abbr. **MΩ** (no point).
megrim/, -s, headache, 'the blues'.
Meilhac (**Henri**), 1831–97, French dramatist.
mein Herr (Ger.), a form of address, as Sir; *pl.* **meine Herren.**
meiosis (rhet.), diminution, understatement.
Meiringen, Switzerland, *not* Mey-.
Meissen porcelain, from German town.
Meissonier (**Jean Louis Ernest**), 1815–91, French painter; — (**Juste Aurèle**), 1693–1750, French goldsmith, architect, furniture designer.
Meistersinger von Nürnberg (*Die*), opera by Wagner, 1867.
me judice (Lat.), in my opinion.
Mekk/a, -ah, -eh, *use* **Mecca.**
Melanchthon (**Philip**), grecized form of Philipp Schwarzerd, 1497–1560, Luther's associate.
Melanesia, the islands between the Equator and the Tropic of Capricorn, and between New Guinea and Fiji (a bishopric, not a political unit).
mélange (Fr. m.), a mixture.
Melchior (**Lauritz**), 1890–1973, Danish tenor.
Melchi/zedek, king of Salem, O.T.; N.T., **-sedec,** but **-zedek** in N.E.B.
mêl/é (Fr.), *fem.* **-ée,** mixed.
mêlée, a fray (not ital.); U.S. no accents.
Meliboean (poetry), alternating, *not* -aean, -ean.

melodrama, romantic and sensational drama.

Melpomene (Gr.), the muse of tragedy.

melting-point (hyphen).

Melton Mowbray, Leics. (no hyphen).

mem., memento, memorial.

Member, abbr. **M.** For membership of certain bodies with royal charters *see* entries beginning **M.R.** Initials indicating membership of other bodies may be deduced from the initials of the body (e.g. **M.I.C.E.** from **I.C.E.**) or from analogous entries beginning **F.** (e.g. **M.I.O.B.** from **F.I.O.B.**).

Member of Parliament (caps.); abbr. **M.P.,** *pl.* **M.P.s.**

memento/, a souvenir, *pl.* **-es,** abbr. **mem.** (not ital.); in Fr. m. *mé-.*

memento mori (Lat.), remember that you must die.

meml/ook, -uk, *use* **mameluke.**

memo/, memorandum, *pl.* **-s** (no point).

mémoire (Fr. m.), bill, report, treatise; (f.) memory.

memorabilia (Lat.), noteworthy things, is *pl.*

memorand/um, abbr. **memo,** a written note, *pl.* **-ums;** *pl.* **-a,** things to be made a note of.

memorialize, to petition by a memorial, *not* -ise.

memoria technica (Lat.), mnemonics.

memorize, to commit to memory, *not* -ise.

Menad, *use* **Mae-.**

ménage (Fr. m.), a household. *See also* **manège.**

menagerie, (place for) a collection of wild animals, *not* -ery.

Mencken (Henry Louis), 1880–1956, U.S. author.

mendacity, falsehood.

Mendel/ (Gregor Johann), 1822–84, Austrian botanist; **-ian, -ism.**

mendelevium, symbol **Md** (no point).

Mendeleyev (Dmitri Ivanovich), 1834–1907, Russian chemist.

Mendelssohn-Bartholdy (Felix), 1809–47, German composer.

mendicity, begging.

meneer (Afrik.), mister, sir.

Menelek II (Sahala Mariem), 1844–1913, emperor of Abyssinia.

Ménestrel (Le), French musical periodical.

menhaden, a N. American fish of herring family, *not* man-.

meno (It. mus.), less.

mensa (Lat.), a table; *a mensa et toro,* from bed and board (a kind of divorce), *not* thoro.

Menshevik, member of a minority group of the Russian Social Democratic Party before 1917. *See* **Bolshevik.**

mens sana in corpore sano (Lat.), a sound mind in a sound body.

menstru/um (Lat.), a solvent; *pl.* **-a.**

mensur., mensuration.

menthe (Fr. cook. f.), mint, *not* mi-.

Menton, Fr. Riviera, often given It. spelling **Mentone** and pron. men-tō´-ně.

menu/ (Fr. m.), bill of fare, *pl.* **-s;** — (**order of**), *hors-d'œuvre* (same in *sing.* and *pl.*), appetizers; *potages,* soups; *poissons,* fish; *relevés,* removes; *entrées,* 'made' dishes; *rôtis,* joints; *légumes,* vegetables;

Menu (*cont.*):
entremets, side dishes; *gelées*, jellies; *crèmes*, creams; *fromages*, cheeses; *dessert*, dessert; *glaces*, ices; *café*, coffee; *liqueurs*.

menu gibier (Fr. cook. m.), small game, as grouse, etc.; **menus plaisirs,** small pleasures.

m.ep., mean effective pressure.

Mephistophelean, malicious, cynical, *not* -ian.

mépris (Fr. m.), contempt.

méprise (Fr. f.), mistake.

mer., meridian, meridional.

Merano, Italian Tirol.

Merath, *use* **Meerut.**

Mercator's projection, a method of map-making, from latinized form of **Gerhard Kremer,** 1512–94, Flemish-born German cartographer.

Mercedes, German motor car; **Mercédès** (Fr.), **Mercedes** (Sp.), girl's name.

merchandise, *not* -ize.

Merchant/ Company Schools, Edin.; — **Taylors Company;** *but* — **Taylors' School** (apos.).

merci (Fr. m.), thanks; no, thank you; (f.) mercy.

mercury, (chem.) symbol **Hg** (no point).

Meredith (George), 1828–1909, English novelist and poet; — **(Owen),** *see* **Bulwer-Lytton (Edward Robert).**

meretricious, tawdry.

Mergenthaler (Ottmar), 1854–99, inventor of Linotype, q.v.

meridian, a great circle passing through the poles of a sphere and any given place; esp. that which cuts the observer's horizon at due north and south, and which the sun crosses at (local) noon; abbr. **m.** *or* **mer.;** (metaph.) the highest point.

meridies (Lat.), noon; abbr. **m.**

meridional, of a meridian, abbr. **m.** *or* **mer.;** (in the northern hemisphere) southern; of S. Europe; (noun) an inhabitant of S. Europe, esp. of S. France.

Mérimée (Prosper), 1803–70, French novelist and historian.

meritorious, deserving reward or praise.

merlan (Fr. m.), whiting.

merle, the common blackbird, *not* merl.

Merovingian, (king) of a Frankish dynasty in Gaul and Germany, *c.* 500–700, *not* -j-.

merry-andrew, buffoon (hyphen, not cap.).

merry-go-round (hyphens).

merrythought, the wishbone (one word).

Merseyside, new metropolitan area, proposed 1971, including Liverpool, Bootle, St. Helens, Birkenhead, Wallasey, Southport.

Merthyr Tydfil, S. Wales (no hyphen).

mesa (Western U.S.), flat-topped mountains; *pron.* mā′sa.

mésalliance (Fr. f.), marriage with an inferior; *use* **misalliance.**

Mesdemoiselles, abbr. **Mlles,** *not* Mdlles.

mesjid, *use* **mas-.**

mesmerize, to hypnotize, fascinate, *not* -ise.

Mesolongi, *use* **Missolonghi.**

Messageries Maritimes, 'La Compagnie des Services Maritimes des Messageries', a French shipping company.

Messiaen (Olivier E.P.C.), b. 1908, French organist and composer.

Messiah, Messianic.

Messieurs (Fr.), abbr. **MM.**; *sing.* **Monsieur.**

Messrs., *sing.* **Mr.** (point).

mestee (W. Ind.), an octoroon; *not* mustee.

mestiz/o, one of Spanish and American-Indian blood, *not* -ino; *pl.* **-os;** *fem.* **-a,** *fem. pl.* **-as.**

met., metronome.

metal/, -led, -ling (U.S. **-ed, -ing**).

metallurgy.

metal rule (typ.), a type-high strip of metal for printing a line on paper: en rule, em rule, two-em rule, and longer.

metamorphose, to transform, *not* -ise, -ize.

metaph., metaphys/ics, -ical, -ically, -ician, metaphor, -ical, -ically.

meteor., meteorology.

meter, measuring device.

Meth., Methodist.

methodize, *not* -ise.

métier (Fr. m.), a handicraft.

metonymy, change of name; abbr. **meton.**

Met.R., Metropolitan Railway (London).

metre, SI unit of length, 39·37 in.; abbr. **m** (no point).

Métro (Le) (no point), abbr. of *Le Métropolitain,* the Paris underground railway.

metrology, science of weights and measures; abbr. **metrol.**

metronome (mus.), instrument for fixing tempi; abbr. **M.** *or* **met.;** Maelzel's —, **M.M.**

metronymic, name taken from female ancestor, *not* ma-.

metropol/is, *pl.* **-ises; -itan;** abbr. **metrop.**

mettre/ au net (Fr.), to make a fair copy; — **à la question,** to torture; — **en question,** to doubt.

meum/ (Lat.), mine; — **and tuum,** mine and thine, not *et tuum.*

Meux, *pron.* mūz.

mews, a street of stables, now converted into garages or houses; *pl. same.*

Mex., Mexic/o, -an.

Meynell/ (Alice), 1847–1922, English poet; — **(Sir Francis),** b. 1891, English typographer.

M.E.Z. (Ger.), *Mitteleuropäische Zeit,* time of the Middle European zone, one hour in advance of G.M.T.

mezereon (bot.), a spring-flowering shrub, *not* -eum.

mezzanine, a low storey between two others.

mezz/o (It. mus.), *fem.* **-a,** half, medium; abbr. **M.;** *pron.* med'so.

mezzo-rilievo, mezzo-soprano (hyphens).

mezzotint (typ.), intaglio technique from a roughened plate.

M.F. (paper), machine finish; (typ.) modern face.

mf (mus.), *mezzo forte* (rather loud).

mfd., manufactured.

mfg., manufacturing.

M.F.H., Master of Foxhounds.

M.Fr., Middle French.

mfr., manufactur/e, -er.

mfrs., manufactur/es, -ers.

m.ft., *mistura fiat* (let a mixture be made).

M.G. (mus.), *main gauche* (left hand); (paper) machine glazed.

Mg, magnesium (no point).

mg, milligramme (no point).

M.Gr., Middle Greek.

Mgr., Monsignor, Monseigneur, *pl.* **Mgrs.**

M.H., Master of Hounds
(usu. beagles or harriers).

MHG., Middle High German
(one point only).

M.H.K., Member of the
House of Keys (I.o.M.).

mho (elec.), unit of conduc-
tance. *See also* **ohm** (opp.).

M.Hon., Most Honourable.

Mhow, Madhya Pradesh,
India. *See also* **Mau.**

M.H.R., Member of the
House of Representatives.

MHz, megahertz, a million
hertz (no point, two caps.).

M.I., Military Intelligence,
Mounted Infantry.

M.I.5, Secret Service
Division.

miasm/a (Gr.), noxious
emanation; *pl.* **-ata.**

Mic., Micah (O.T.).

micaceous, pertaining to
mica; *not* -ious.

mi-carême (*la*) (Fr.),
Mid Lent; *pl.* **les**
mi-carêmes (hyphens).

Micawber/ (**Wilkins**), in
David Copperfield; **-ish,**
unpractical but hopeful;
-ism.

Mich., Michaelmas;
Michigan, U.S. (off. abbr.).

Michel (**Louise**), 1830–1905,
French anarchist.

Michelangelo Buonarroti,
1475–1564, Italian sculptor,
painter, architect, poet (two
words, not three).

Michelson/ (**Albert
Abraham**), 1852–1931,
German-American
physicist; — **-Morley**
experiment.

Michigan, off. abbr. **Mich.**

Mickey (**Finn**), (U.S.)
a drugged drink.

Mickiewicz (**Adam**), 1798–
1855, Polish poet.

micky (to take the — out of)
to annoy.

Micmac, a tribe of N.
American Indians (one word).

micro-, prefix meaning a
millionth, symbol μ, e.g.
microhm, μΩ; **micro-
metre** (preferred to **micron**),
μm; **microvolt,** μV.

microcosm, the little
world. *See also* **macrocosm.**

microfiche, a sheet of
microfilm, suitable for
filing, containing a number
of separate images.

microfilm, film bearing
miniature photographic
copy of printed or other
graphic matter.

micrography, description or
delineation of microscopic
objects.

micrometer, instrument for
measuring minute distances
or angles. *See also* **micrometre,** *under* **micro-.**

micromillimetre *or*
millimicron, symbol **mμ,**
use **nanometre,** symbol **nm.**

micron, *use* **micrometre,**
q.v. *under* **micro-.**

micro-organism (hyphen).

microphotography, strictly,
reducing a photograph to
microscopic size; erron. for
photomicrography, q.v.

micros., microscop/y, -ist.

mid., middle.

midbrain (one word).

Mid Calder, Midlothian
(caps., no hyphen).

midday (one word).

middle, abbr. **M.** *or* **mid.**

middle age (two words).

middle-aged (hyphen).

Middle Ages (**the**), roughly
from the fall of the Western
Roman empire to the
Renaissance and the
Reformation (two words,
caps.).

middle class (two words,
but hyphenated as adjective).

Middle English, abbr. **ME.**

middleman (one word).

Middlesbrough, Yorks., *not*
-borough.

Middlesex, abbr. **Middx.**
Middleton (Baron), family
    name Willoughby. *See also*
    Midleton, Mydd-.
Middx., Middlesex.
Mid Glamorgan, new
    county, proposed 1971,
    comprising Merthyr Tydfil,
    Rhondda, parts of Brecon-
    shire and Monmouthshire.
midinette, Parisian shop-girl
    (not ital.).
Midland Bank, Ltd.
Mid Lent, fourth Sunday
    in Lent (caps., no hyphen).
Midleton (Earl), family
    name Brodrick. *See also*
    Midd-, Mydd-.
Midlothian (one word).
midnight (one word).
midrib (one word).
midships (one word).
Midsomer Norton, Som.
midsummer (one word).
Midsummer Day, 24 June
    (two words, caps.).
Midwest, the North-Central
    states of U.S. (one word).
midwinter (one word).
Miehle (typ.), a printing-
    press; *pron.* mē′lē.
Miers (Sir H. A.), 1858–
    1954, English mineralogist.
    See also **Myers, Myres.**
mightest, *not* mightst.
mignonette, a fragrant
    plant;
    in Fr. *mignonnette.*
migraine (med.), a severe
    headache (not ital.).
M.I.J., *use* **M.J.I.**
mijnheer, ordinary Dutch
    form of address—as Sir;
    in Ger. *mein Herr.*
mijoter (Fr.), to cook
    slowly, to simmer.
mil, one-thousandth of an
    inch (no point).
mil., military, militia.
mile/, -s, abbr. **m.;** geogr.
    or naut. **—,** 6,080 feet;
    statute —, 5,280 feet;
    in Fr. m. *mille/, -s.*

mileage, *not* milage.
milestone (one word).
milieu, environment (not
    ital.). *See also* **le juste milieu.**
military, abbr. **mil.**
Military Academy, abbr.
    M.A.
Militia, abbr. **M.,** *or* **mil.**
milk-run, milkman's morning
    round, a routine flight.
Milky Way (astr.) (caps.).
mill, abbr. **m.**
Mill (James), 1773–1836,
    Scottish historian and
    economist; — **(John
    Stuart),** 1806–73, English
    economist and polit.
    philosopher, son of former.
Millais (Sir John Everett),
    1829–96, English painter,
    P.R.A.
Millay (Edna St. Vincent),
    1892–1951, American poet.
mille (Fr. m.), a thousand
    (no *s* in plural), abbr. **M.;**
    also a mile, *pl.* **milles.**
millenary, of a thousand;
    the thousandth anniversary.
millennium/, a thousand
    years, *pl.* **-s** (two *l*'s, two *n*'s).
mille passus (Lat.), 1,000
    paces of five feet, or the
    Roman mile; abbr. **M.P.**
millepede (zool.), *not* -ed,
    milli-.
Millers Dale, Derby. (no
    apos.).
Milles-Lode, family name of
    Earl Sondes. *See also* **Mills.**
Millet (Aimé), 1819–91,
    French sculptor; — **(Jean-
    François),** 1814–75, French
    painter.
milli- (prefix), one-
    thousandth (symbol **m**), e.g.
    **milliampere, mA;
    millilitre, ml; millimetre,
    mm.**
milliard, a thousand millions.
millibar, one-thousandth
    of a bar, q.v.; abbr. **mbar,**
    or **mb** in meteorological
    usage (no point).

millicurie, a measure of radioactivity; abbr. **mCi** (no point).

milligramme, one-thousandth of a gramme, 0·015 grains; abbr. **mg** (no point).

millimicron (mμ), *use* **nanometre (nm).**

million, abbr. **m.** For millions of pounds use, for example, £150 m.

millionaire, *not* -onnaire.

millipede, *use* **mille-.**

Mills, family name of Baron Hillingdon. *See also* **Milles-Lade.**

Milne-Edwards (Alphonse), 1835–1900, — **(Henri),** 1800–85, French zoologists of English extraction.

Milngavie, Dumbartonshire.

milreis, 1,000 reis, Portuguese gold coin superseded by the escudo; Brazilian coin, now the cruzeiro; *not* mill-, -rei.

Milwaukee, Wis., U.S.

mimic/, **-ked,** **-king.**

min., minim, minimum, mining, minister, minor, minute, -s.

mina, a starling of SE. Asia, *not* myn-, -ah.

minac/ious, threatening; **-ity.**

minatory, threatening.

minauderie, affected, simpering behaviour (*not* ital.).

mincemeat (one word).

Mindanao, one of the Philippine Islands, *not* -oa.

Mindererus/, Latinized name of R. M. Minderer (*c.* 1570–1621), German physician; — **spirit,** a diaphoretic.

mineralog/y -ical, abbr. **mineral,** (of) the study of minerals; *not* minerolog/ical, -y.

minever, *use* **mini-.**

mingy, mean, *not* -ey.

minibus (one word).

minicab (one word).

Minié (Claude Étienne), 1814–79, inventor of rifle, etc.

minikin, a diminutive person or thing. *See also* **manikin.**

minim, a drop, one-sixtieth of fluid drachm; abbr. **min.,** sign ℳ.

minimize, *not* -ise.

minim/um, *pl.* **-a** (not ital.); abbr. **min.**

mining, abbr. **min.**

minion (typ.), old name for a size of type, about 7 pt.

minister, abbr. **min.**

Ministry of Technology (abbr. **Min. Tech.**), absorbed in Department of Trade and Industry, 1970.

minium, red oxide of lead.

miniver, a fur, *not* -ever.

Minn., Minnesota, U.S. (off. abbr.).

Minneapolis, U.S.

Minnehaha, wife of Hiawatha.

minnesinger, one of a school of medieval German lyric poets (*not* ital.).

Minoan, pertaining to ancient Crete, its people, or its language (from King Minos).

minor, abbr. **min.**

Minories, a street in London.

Minotaur, monstrous offspring of a bull and Pasiphaë, wife of King Minos.

Min./ Plen. *or* **Plenip.,** Minister Plenipotentiary; — **Res.,** ditto Residentiary.

Min. Tech., Ministry of Technology, q.v.

Mint (the) (cap.).

minuet, a dance, or its music, *not* -ette.

minus (Lat.), less (not ital.), sign —.

minuscule, a small, or lower-case, letter.

minute/, -s, abbr. **m.,** *or*
min., sign ´; — **mark** (´),
symbol for feet, minutes,
also placed after a syllable
on which the stress falls.
minuti/ae (Lat.), small
details; *sing.* **-a** (not ital.).
mirabile/ dictu (Lat.),
wonderful to relate; —
visu, ditto see.
mirky, dark, *use* **murky.**
miry, mire-like, *not* -ey.
Mirzapur, Uttar Pradesh,
India, *not* -pore.
misadvice, bad counsel.
misadvise, to give bad
counsel.
misalliance, marriage with
an inferior, *not mésalliance.*
misc., miscellaneous,
miscellany.
miscall (one word).
miscegenation, interbreeding
between white and Negro,
or white and oriental races.
miscellanea (Lat.),
miscellanies, is *pl.*
mischievous, *not* -ious.
miscible, capable of being
mixed.
miscue (billiards) (one word).
misdemeanour (U.S. **-or**).
Mise (Fr.), *marquise*
(marchioness), *not Mise.*
mise en scène (Fr. f.),
scenery, stage-effect.
Miserere, (musical setting
of) the 50th Psalm of the
Vulgate.
miserere, a misericord,
bracket on turn-up seat
used as support for person
standing.
misfeasance, a wrongful
act; (law) a trespass.
misfire (one word).
Mishnah, a collection of
Jewish precepts.
misle, *use* **mizzle** q.v.
misletoe, *use* **mistle-.**
mismanagement.
misogam/y, hatred of
marriage; **-ist.**

misogyn/y, hatred of
women; **-ist.**
misprint (typ.),
a typographical error.
Miss., Mission, -ary;
Mississippi, U.S. (off. abbr.).
missa/ (Lat.), a religious
Mass; — *cantata,* sung
Mass, without deacon
and subdeacon; —
catechumenorum, first
part of the service of the
Mass; — *fidelium,* Mass of
the faithful.
missel-thrush, *not* mistle-.
misseltoe, *use* mistle-.
mis/send, to send
incorrectly; **-sent.**
misshapen (one word).
Mission, -ary, abbr. **Miss.**
Mississippi, river and State,
U.S.; off. abbr. **Miss.**
Missolonghi, Greece, *not*
Mesolongi.
Missouri, river and State,
U.S.; off. abbr. **Mo.**
mis/ -spell, — **-spend,** —
-spent, — **-state** (hyphens).
mist (naut.), abbr. **m.**
mistakable, *not* -eable.
Mister, abbr. **Mr.** (point
in *Hart's Rules,* no point in
publications by H.M.S.O.,
most newspapers, and most
publishers).
**Mistinguett (Jeanne Marie
Bourgeois),** 1873–1956,
French entertainer, *not* -e.
mistle, *use* **mizzle.**
mistle-thrush, *see* **missel-.**
mistletoe, *not* missel-, misle-.
mistral (Fr. m.), cold
NW. wind in S. France.
Mistress, abbr. **Mrs.**
(point, *but see* **Mister**).
M.I.T., Massachusetts
Institute of Technology.
Mithridates (VI, 136–63
B.C.), king of Pontus,
not Mithra-.
Mitilini, Lesbos, Greece; the
trad. English spelling is
Mytilene.

mitring, *not* mitreing.

mixable, *not* -eable, -ible.

mizen-mast, the aftermost mast of a three-masted ship; **mizen,** the aftermost of the fore-and-aft sails; *not* mizz-.

mizzle, fine rain, *not* misle, mistle.

M.J.I., Member of the Institute of Journalists.

Mk., mark (Ger. coin), *use* **RM** or **DM.**

Mkt., Market.

M.L., Licentiate in Midwifery, Medieval Latin, Middle Latin, motor launch.

Ml., mail.

ml, millilitre, -s (no point).

M.L.A., Member of the Legislative Assembly, Modern Languages Association.

M.L.C., Member of the Legislative Council.

MLG., Middle Low German (one point only).

M.Litt., Master of Letters.

Mlle, -s, Mademoiselle, Mesdemoiselles (in Fr. no point after abbr.).

M.M., Military Medal, (mus.) Maelzel's metronome.

MM, 2,000.

MM., (Their) Majesties, (Fr.) *Messieurs* (Sirs).

mm, millimetre, -s (no point).

m.m., *mutatis mutandis* (with the necessary changes).

Mme (Fr.), Madame, *pl.* **Mmes** (in Fr. no point after the abbr.).

m.m.f., magneto-motive force.

M.N., Merchant Navy.

Mn, manganese (no point).

Mnemosyne, (Gr. myth.) goddess of memory, mother of the Muses.

M.O., mass observation, Medical Officer, money order.

Mo., Missouri (off. abbr.).

Mo, molybdenum (no point).

mob/, -bed, -bing.

mobilize, *not* -ise.

moccasin, American Indian shoe, N. American venomous snake (not the many variants).

Mocha, a coffee (in Fr. m. *moka*) from Mocha, Arabian port on Red Sea.

mock-turtle soup (one hyphen).

M.o.D., Ministry of Defence, including, from 1964, the Admiralty, the War Office, and the Air Ministry.

M.O.D., Ministry of Overseas Development, formed 1964.

mod., moderate, modern.

mod., *moderato* (mus.).

mode (Fr. m.), method, (gram.) mood; (f.) fashion.

model/, -led, -ler, -ling (U.S. -ed, -er, -ing).

moderate, abbr. **mod.**

moderato (mus.), in moderate time; abbr. ***mod.***

Modér/é, *fem. -ée,* a Moderate in French politics.

modern, abbr. **mod.**

modern face (typ.), a type design with contrasting thick and thin strokes, abbr. **M.F.**

modern figures (typ.), lining figures, q.v.

modernize, *not* -ise.

modicum/, a small quantity; *pl.* **-s** (not ital.).

modif/y, -ied, -ying.

Modigliani (Amedeo), 1884–1920, Italian painter and sculptor.

modiste, a milliner, dress-maker (not. ital.).

Modjeska (Helena), 1844–1909, Polish actress.

modo praescripto (Lat.), as directed.

Mods., Moderations, the First Public Examination, Oxford University.

modus/ operandi (Lat.), a plan of working; —

vivendi, a way of living, a temporary compromise.

moelle de bœuf (Fr. cook. f.), beef marrow.

Moët et Chandon, champagne manufacturers.

mœurs (Fr. f. pl.), manners, customs.

Mogul, a Mongolian, *not* Mog/hal, -hul, Mughal.

M.O.H., Master of Otter Hounds, Medical Officer of Health, Ministry of Health (since 1968 the Ministry of Health and Social Security).

Mohammed, *use* **Mahomet** (trad. Eng. form) or **Muhammad** (correct).

Mohammedan, *use* **Muhammadan.** *See also* **Islam, Muslim.**

Mohave Desert, *use* **Moj-.**

Mohawk, N. Amer. Indian, *not* Mohock.

Mohegan, (member of) eastern branch of Mahican Indian tribe, formerly in lower Conn. and Mass., U.S.

Mohican, (member of) western branch of Mahican Indian tribe, formerly on both sides of the Hudson River, U.S.

Mohocks, London ruffians (18th cent.).

M.O.I., Ministry of Information, *later* **C.O.I.**

moire (noun), a watered fabric, usu. silk, orig. mohair (not ital.).

moiré (adj.), (of silk, etc.) watered; (noun) the watered surface (not ital.).

mois (Fr. m.), month, abbr. *m/.* *See also* **month.**

Mojave Desert, Calif., U.S., *not* Moh-.

Moka (Fr. m.), the best coffee; in Eng. **Mocha.**

M.o.L., Ministry of Labour, merged, 1968, in **Department of Employment and Productivity, D.E.P.**

mol (chem.), abbr. of **mole,** q.v.

molasses, syrup from sugar, *not* moll-.

Moldavia, a Soviet Socialist Republic. *See* **U.S.S.R.**

mole (chem.), SI unit of amount of substance; abbr. **mol** (no point).

Molière, stage-name of Jean-Baptiste Poquelin, 1622–73, French dramatist.

Moll (Ger. mus.), minor.

mollah, *use* **mu-.**

mollasses, *use* **mola-.**

Molnar (Férenc), 1878–1952, Hungarian playwright.

Moloch, Canaanite idol to whom children were sacrificed (often fig.), *not* -eck.

Moltke (Count Helmuth Karl Bernard von), 1800–91, Prussian field-marshal; — **(Helmuth Johannes Ludwig von),** 1848–1916, German general in First World War, nephew of preceding.

molto (mus.), much, very.

mol. wt., molecular weight.

molybdenum, symbol **Mo** (no point).

Mombasa, Kenya, *not* -assa.

moment/um, impetus, mass × velocity; *pl.* **-a** (not ital.).

Mommsen (Theodor), 1817–1903, German historian.

Mon., Monday; Monmouthshire.

Monaco, principality adjoining Mediterranean France; adj. **Monégasque.**

Mona Lisa, portrait by Leonardo da Vinci, also called *La Gioconda.*

mon/ ami (Fr.), *fem.* — *amie,* my friend.

mon cher (Fr. m.), *fem.* *ma chère,* my dear.

Monck (Viscount). *See also* **Monk.**

Monckton (Lionel), 1861–1924, English composer; — **(Walter Turner, Viscount)**, 1891–1963, British lawyer and politician.

Moncreiff (Baron).

Moncreiffe (Sir R. Iain K., Bt.).

Moncrieff, more frequent spelling.

Monday, abbr. **M.**, or **Mon**.

monde (Fr. m.), the world, society.

mon Dieu! (Fr.), an ejaculation, not necessarily expressing more than astonishment.

Monet (Claude), 1840–1926, French painter.

monetary.

money/, *pl.* **-s**, *not* -ies; **-ed**, *not* monied; — **order**, abbr. **M.O.** See also **figures**.

Monghyr, Bihar, India.

mongoos/e, an Indian animal, *pl.* **-es**.

Monk Bretton (Baron). See also **Monck**.

Monmouthshire, abbr. **Mon**.

Mono, see **Monotype**.

monochrome, (picture) in one colour (one word).

monocle, a single eyeglass.

monogamy, marriage with one person.

monogyny, marriage with one wife.

Monophoto (typ.), a film-setting system adapted from Monotype principles.

monopol/ism, -ist, -ize, -y.

Monotype, a composition system, using separate keyboard and caster, for casting single types; abbr. **Mono** (no point).

Monroe Doctrine, that European powers should not interfere in American affairs, from **James Monroe**, 1758–1831, U.S. president.

Mons., this abbr. for Monsieur is regarded as impolite in France.

Monseigneur (Fr.), abbr. **Mgr**; *pl.* **Messeigneurs, Mgrs.** See also **Monsignor**.

Monserrat, Spain. See also **Mont-**.

Monsieur/ (Fr.), Mr., Sir, abbr. (to be used in third person only) **M.**; *pl.* **Messieurs**, abbr. **MM.**; — **Chose**, Mr. What's-his-name. See also **Mons**.

Monsignor/, R.C.C. title, abbr. **Mgr.**; *pl.* **-s**, abbr. **Mgrs.**; It. **-e**, *pl.* **-i**.

Mont., Montana, U.S. (off. abbr.).

montage, mounting photographs and other objects on a surface to make a design; selecting, cutting, and combining separate 'shots' to make a continuous film.

Montagu-Chelmsford Report (India), *not* -gue.

Montagu of Beaulieu (Baron).

Montagu (Lady Mary Wortley), 1689–1762, English writer.

Montague, Romeo's family in *Romeo and Juliet*.

Mont Blanc (caps.).

mont-de-piété (Fr. m.), Government pawnshop; *pl.* **monts-** — — (hyphens).

Monte Cristo, *not* — Christo.

Montefiascone, Italian wine, *not* -sco (one word).

Monterey, Calif., U.S.

Monte Rosa, Switzerland (caps., two words).

Monterrey, Mexico.

Montesquieu (Charles de Secondat), 1689–1755, French jurist and philos. writer.

Montesquiou (J. F. de), assassinated the Prince of Condé, 1569; — **(Madame de)**, guardian of Napoleon's son.

Montevideo, cap. of
Uruguay (one word).

Montgomerie, family name
of Earl of Eglinton; —
(**Alexander**), 1556–1610,
Scottish poet.

Montgomery, second title
of Earl of Pembroke, town
and county in Wales, also
towns in Ala. and W.Va.,
U.S., and W. Pakistan.

**Montgomery of Alamein
(Bernard Law, Viscount),**
b. 1887, British field-marshal
in Second World War.

month/, -s, abbr. **m.,**
— (**day of the**) (typ.), to
be thus, 25 Jan., *not* Jan.
25. When necessary, months
to be abbreviated thus:
Jan., Feb., Mar., Apr., Aug.,
Sept., Oct., Nov., Dec.;
May, June, July to remain
in full. In Fr. the names
of the months do not take
caps., as **janvier.**

Montpelier, Vermont, U.S.

Montpellier, French town.

Mont-Saint-Michel, dép.
Manche, France (caps.,
hyphens); in Cornwall,
Mount Saint Michael, *use*
St. Michael's Mount.

Montserrat, Leeward
Islands. *See also* **Mons-.**

Montyon prizes, of French
Academy, *not* Month-.

monyplies, *use* **ma-.**

Mooltan, *use* **Mu-.**

moon, abbr. **m.;** sign for
new, ●; first quarter ☽;
full, ○; last quarter ☾.

moonlight (one word).

moonshee, use **munshi.**

Moore (George), 1852–
1933, Irish novelist; — (**Sir
John**), 1761–1809, British
general, killed at Corunna;
— (**Thomas**), 1779–1852,
'the bard of Erin'. *See also*
More.

Moosonee (Bp. *of*),
Ontario, Canada.

mop/e, -ed, -ing, -ish.

moped, *pron.* mō-ped,
a bicycle with a low-powered
engine.

moqueu/r (Fr.), *fem. -se,*
a mocker, mocking.

Mor., Morocco.

moral, Eng. adj., concerned
with the principles of
right and wrong (e.g. —
philosophy), virtuous (opp.
to immoral); Eng. noun,
a moral lesson or principle,
in Fr. f. **morale.**

morale, Eng. noun, *pron.*
mor-ahl', state of mind, in
respect of confidence and
courage, of groups of
combatants or others under
stress; in Fr. m. **moral.**

moralize, *not* -ise.

Moray, Scottish county,
formerly Elginshire; *not*
Morayshire.

morbidezza (It. art),
extreme delicacy.

morbilli (med.), measles,
not -bilia.

morbus (**cholera**) (ital.).

morceau/ (Fr. m.), a morsel,
also short mus. piece; *pl. -x.*

mordant, (adj.) biting;
(noun) a dye fixer.

Mordaunt (Sir O. L'E.).

mordent (mus.), a type of
ornament.

More (Hannah), 1745–1833,
English religious writer;
— (**Sir Thomas**), 1478–
1535, English writer,
beheaded by Henry VIII,
canonized 1935. *See also*
Moore.

morel, an edible fungus,
not -lle.

morello cherry, *not* -a.

more maiorum (Lat.), in
the style of one's ancestors.

morendo (mus.), dying away.

mores (Lat.), social customs
and conventions.

Moresque, Moorish, *not*
Mau-.

more suo (Lat.), in his, *or* her, own peculiar way.

Moreton-in-Marsh, Glos. (hyphens, *not* -in-the-Marsh).

Morgagni (Giovanni Battista), 1682–1771, Italian anatomist.

morganatic marriage, between royalty and commoner, the children being legitimate but not heirs to the higher rank (not cap.).

Morghen (Raffaello Sanzia), 1758–1833, Italian engraver.

morgue, a mortuary.

morgue (Fr. f.), haughtiness.

Morison (James), 1816–93, Scottish founder of the Evangelical Union, 1843; — **(James Augustus Cotter),** 1832–88, English hist. writer; — **(Stanley),** 1889–1967, typographer.

Morisot (Berthe), 1841–95, French Impressionist painter.

Morland (George), 1763–1804, English painter.

Mormon, member of Church of Jesus Christ of Latter-day Saints (*not* -an).

morn., abbr. of **morning.**

Mornay (Duplessis-), 1549–1623, French Huguenot leader.

Morny (duc de), 1811–65, French statesman.

Morocc/o, abbr. **Mor.; -an;** *not* Ma-; independent 1956.

morocco leather (bind.) (not cap.); **french —** **—,** a low grade with small grain; **levant —** **—,** high grade with large grain; **persian** **—** **—,** the best, usu. finished on the grain side.

morone, *use* **maroon.**

morph., morphology, the study of forms (bot. or linguistics).

Morpheus, god of sleep, *not* -æus.

morphia, a drug (pop. for **morphine**).

morphoea, a skin disease; pop. **morphew.**

Morris (Gouverneur), 1752–1816, American statesman; — **(William),** 1834–96, English craftsman, poet, and socialist.

Morrison (Robert), 1782–1834, Scottish missionary and Chinese scholar.

mortgag/ee, one to whom a mortgage is granted; **-er,** one who mortgages; in law, **-or.**

mortice, *use* **-ise.**

mortifié (Fr. cook.), well hung (of meat, etc.).

mortis causa (Lat., Sc. law), in contemplation of death.

mortise and tenon, a joint for wood, *not* -ice — —.

Morvan (Le), French district.

Morven, Argyl., *not* Morvern.

Mosaic, of Moses.

mosaic, inlaid.

Moseley, a Birmingham suburb. *See also* **Mosl-.**

Moseley (Henry Gwyn-Jeffreys), 1887–1915, English physicist.

Moselle, river, France–Germany; in Ger. **Mosel.**

Moselle, a white wine.

Mosely Education Commission, 1903. *See also* **Moz-.**

Moses' law.

Moslem, *use* **Muslim,** q.v.

Mosley (Sir Oswald). *See also* **Mose-, Moz-.**

mosquito/, *pl.* **-es.**

Mossley, Lancs.

mosso (mus.), 'moved' (e.g. *più mosso*, more moved = quicker).

Most High, as Deity (caps.).

Moszkowski (Moritz), 1854–1925, Polish composer.

M.O.T., Ministry of Transport, merged, 1970, in Department of the Environment; **M.O.T. Test,** for motor vehicles.

mot (Fr. m.), a word; *mot à mot,* word for word, abbr. *m. à m.*

motet (mus.), a sacred composition for several voices, *not* mott-, -ett, -ette, -etto.

Mother Carey's chicken, the storm petrel.

Mother Hubbard, a character in a nursery-rhyme; a gown such as she wore.

Mother Hubberds Tale, by Spenser, 1591.

Mothering Sunday, fourth in Lent.

mother-in-law, *pl.* **mothers — —** (hyphens).

motherland (one word).

mother-of-pearl (hyphens).

mother tongue (two words).

motif, dominant idea in artistic expression; ornament of lace, etc. (not ital.).

motley, a mixture, *not* -ly.

moto (It. mus.), motion; *con —,* with more rapid motion; *— continuo,* constant repetition; *— contrario,* contrary motion; *— obbliquo,* oblique motion; *— perpetuo,* a piece of music speeding without pause from start to finish; *— precedente,* at the preceding pace; *— primo,* at the first pace; *— retto,* direct or similar motion.

motor car, motor cycle (two words when nouns, hyphened when adjs.).

motorized, *not* -ised.

motorway (one word).

mottl/-ed, -ing.

motto/, *pl.* **-es.**

motu proprio (Lat.), of his own accord.

mouchard (Fr. m.), a police spy.

mouchoir (Fr. m.), pocket-handkerchief.

mouezzin, *use* **mue-.**

mouflon (Fr. m.), a wild sheep, *not* mouff-, muf-.

mouillé (Fr.), softened, wet.

moujik, Russian peasant, *not* mujik.

mould (U.S. **mold**).

moule (Fr. f.), mussel.

Moulmein, Burma, *not* Maulmain.

moult, a shedding, *not* molt.

Mount/, -ain, abbr. **Mt.;** *pl.* **Mts.**

Mount Auburn, Mass., U.S., noted cemetery.

Mount Edgcumbe (Earl of) (two words).

Mountgarret (Viscount) (one word).

Mount Saint Michael, Cornwall, *use* **St. Michael's Mount,** in Fr. **Mont-Saint-Michel,** dép. Manche.

Mourne Mountains, Ire.

mousseline/ (Fr. f.), fine muslin; *— -de-laine,* untwilled woollen cloth.

mousseu/x (Fr.), *fem.* **-se,** foaming, as wine.

moustache (U.S. **mus-**).

mousy, mouse-like, *not* -ey.

moutarde (Fr. f.), mustard.

mouthpiece (one word).

mouton (Fr. m.), mutton.

movable, in legal work **moveable.**

moyen/ (Fr. m.), medium; *— âge (le),* the Middle Ages.

moyenne (Fr. f.), average.

Mozart (Wolfgang Amadeus), 1756–91, Austrian composer.

Mozartian, *not* -ean.

Mozley (James Bowling), 1813–78, English theologian.

M.P., Madhya Pradesh (India), *formerly* Central Provinces, Member of

M.P. (*cont.*):
Parliament, Metropolitan Police, Military Police, *mille passus* (a thousand paces, the Roman mile).

m.p., melting-point.

mp (It. mus.), *mezzo-piano*.

M.P.B.W., Ministry of Public Building and Works, absorbed in Dept. of the Environment, 1970.

M.P.F., Master Printers Federation.

m.p.g., miles per gallon.

m.p.h., miles per hour.

M.P.N.I., Ministry of Pensions and National Insurance, merged, 1968, in **Department of Health and Social Security.**

M.P.O., Metropolitan Police Office ('Scotland Yard').

M.P.T., Ministry of Post and Telecommunications. *See also* **Post Office, The.**

M.P.U., Medical Practitioners' Union.

M.R., Master of the Rolls, Municipal Reform.

Mr., Mister, q.v., *pl.* **Messrs.**

M.R.A.C., Member of the Royal Agricultural College.

M.R.A.S., Member of the Royal Asiatic Society, ditto Royal Astronomical Society.

M.R.Ae.S., Member of the Royal Aeronautical Society.

M.R.B.M., medium-range ballistic missile.

M.R.C., Medical Research Council.

M.R.C.C., Member of the Royal College of Chemistry.

M.R.C.O., Member of the Royal College of Organists.

M.R.C.O.G., Member of the Royal College of Obstetricians and Gynaecologists.

M.R.C.P., Member of the Royal College of Physicians.

M.R.C.S., Member of the Royal College of Surgeons.

M.R.C.V.S., Member of the Royal College of Veterinary Surgeons.

M.R.G.S., Member of the Royal Geographical Society.

M.R.H., Member of the Royal Household.

M.R.I., Member of the Royal Institution.

M.R.I.A., Member of the Royal Irish Academy.

M.R.I.C.S., Member of the Royal Institution of Chartered Surveyors.

M.R.I.N.A., Member of the Royal Institution of Naval Architects.

Mrs., Missis, Missus, which are corruptions of Mistress (for point at end *see* **Mister**).

M.R.San.I., Member of the Royal Sanitary Institute, *now* **M.R.S.H.**

M.R.S.H., Member of the Royal Society for the Promotion of Health.

M.R.S.L., Member of the Royal Society of Literature.

M.R.S.M., Member of the Royal Society of Medicine, ditto Royal Society of Musicians.

M.R.S.T., Member of the Royal Society of Teachers.

M.R.V.O., Member of the Royal Victorian Order.

MS., *manuscriptum* (manuscript), *pl.* **MSS.** (caps., one point). *See also* **manuscript.**

M.S., Master of Science, ditto Surgery, *memoriae sacrum* (sacred to the memory of), (It. mus.) *mano sinistra* (the left hand).

M.S.A., Member of the Society of Apothecaries (of London), *also* of Arts, ditto Architects, Mutual Security Agency (replacing **E.C.A.**).

M.Sc., Master of Science.

M.S.H., Master of
Staghounds.

m.sl., mean sea-level.

M.S.M., Meritorious Service
Medal.

MSS., *manuscripta*
(manuscripts). *See also*
manuscript.

M.S.V., Marine Services
Vessel.

M.T., Masoretic Text (of
O.T.), Mechanical (Motor)
Transport.

Mt., Mount, -ain.

M.T.B., motor torpedo-boat.

M.T.C., Mechanical
Transport Corps.

M.T.O., Mechanical
Transport Officer.

Mts., Mountains.

mucous (adj.).

mucus (noun).

mud/, -died, -dying.

Mudki, E. Punjab, India,
not Moodkee.

muezzin, Muslim crier,
not mou-.

muffetee, a wristlet.

mufti (Arab.), a magistrate,
not -tee (ital.).

mufti (in), in civilian dress
(not ital.).

Mughal, *use* **Mogul.**

mugwump, an Indian chief,
one who thinks himself
important, (U.S. politics) a
politician critical of his party.

Muhammad, now correct
for the traditional English
form **Mahomet.**

Muhammadan, pertaining
to, a follower of, Muhammad
(Mahomet); *not*
Mohammedan. *See* **Muslim.**

Mühlhausen, Thuringia,
Germany.

mujik, Russian peasant, *use*
moujik.

mulatto/, offspring of a
European and a Negro;
pl. **-es.**

mulch, half-rotten vegetable
matter, *not* -sh.

mulet (Fr. m.), grey mullet,
also he-mule.

Mulhouse, Alsace, France;
in Ger. **Mülhausen.**

mull (bind.), coarse muslin
glued to backs of books.

mullah (Muslim), a learned
man, *not* cap., moll-, mool-,
-a.

mullein, tall yellow-flowered
plant, *not* -en.

Müller (Friedrich Max),
1823–1900, English
philologist.

mulligatawny, a soup, *not*
muli-, mulla-.

**Mulock (Dinah Maria,
Miss),** *later* **Mrs. Craik,**
1826–87, English novelist.

mulsh, *use* **mulch.**

Multan, W. Pakistan, *not*
Moo-.

multimillionaire, a possessor
of several million dollars
(one word).

multiple mark (typ.), the
sign of multiplication ×.

multiplepoinding (Sc. law),
a process which safeguards
a person from whom the
same funds are claimed by
more than one creditor (one
word).

multiracial (one word).

multum in parvo (Lat.),
much in small compass.

mumbo-jumbo, an object
of popular homage (hyphen).

Munchausen (Baron),
1720–97, Hanoverian nobleman whose extravagant
adventures are the theme
of *Adventures of Baron
Munchausen,* collected by
Rudolph Eric Raspe; in
Ger. **Münchhausen.**

München, German for
Munich.

mungoose/, *use* mon-; *pl.* **-s.**

municipalize, etc., *not* -ise.

Munnepoor, *use* **Manipur.**

munshi (Ind.), a writer or
teacher, *not* moonshee.

Munster, Ireland.

Münster, W. Prussia, Germany; Switzerland.

muntjak, a S. Asian deer, *not* -jac, -jack.

Muntz (metal), alloy of copper and zinc for sheathing ships, etc., *not* Muntz's.

mur (Fr. m.), a wall.

mûr (Fr. adj.), ripe.

murano glass, from island near Venice.

Murdoch (John), 1747–1824, friend of Burns.

Murdock (William), 1754–1839, inventor of coal-gas lighting, *not* -och.

mûre (Fr. f.), mulberry.

murky, dark, *not* mi-.

Mürren, Oberland, Switzerland.

murrhine, fluorspar ware; *not* murrine, myrrhine.

Murrumbidgee, river in N.S.W., Australia.

Murry (John Middleton), 1889–1957, English hist. writer, *not* -ay; — **(Katherine),** wife of above, *see* **Mansfield.**

Murshidabad, W. Bengal, India.

mus., museum, music, -al.

Musalman, *use* Mussul-.

Mus.B. *or* **Bac.,** Bachelor of Music.

musc/a (Lat.), a fly; *pl.* *-ae.*

Muscadet, a dry white wine from Brittany. *See* **muscatel.**

Muscat, S. Arabia.

muscatel, general name for a wine made from the muscat-grape (musk-flavoured).

Muschelkalk (geol.), shell limestone (cap.).

Musc/i, the true mosses; *sing.* *-us.*

Mus.D. *or* **Doc.,** *Musicæ Doctor* (Doctor of Music)

museography, museum cataloguing, *not* musae-.

Muses (the nine), Calliope, Clio, Erato, Euterpe, Melpomene, Polyhymnia, Terpsichore, Thalia, Urania.

museum, abbr. mus.

Music (Bachelor of), abbr. **Mus.B.** *or* **Bac., B.Mus.;** — **(Doctor of),** abbr. **Mus.D.** *or* **Doc., D.Mus.** — **(Master of),** Camb., abbr. **Mus.M.**

music/, -al, abbr. **mus.;** — **paper,** that ruled for writing music upon.

Musigny, a red Burgundy wine.

musjid (Arab.), a mosque, *use mas-.*

Muslim, (a member) of the faith of **Islam,** q.v.; *not* Moslem. Preferred to **Muhammadan** in general usage, as connoting the religion rather than the prophet.

muslin-de-lain, use **mousseline-de-laine.**

Mus.M., Master of Music (Cambridge).

musquito, *use* mos-.

Mussalman, *use* Mussul-.

Musselburgh, Midlothian, *not* -borough.

Mussorgsky (Modest Petrovich), 1839–81, Russian composer.

Mussul/man, a Muslim, from Pers. **Musulman** (not the many variants); *pl.* **-mans,** *not* -men.

mustache, *use* mous-.

Mustafa, Algeria.

Mustafabad, Uttar Pradesh, India.

mustang (Western U.S.), small, half-wild horse.

mustee (W. Ind.), *use* me-.

mustn't, to be close up.

Musulman, Pers. form of **Mussulman.**

mutand/um (Lat.), anything to be altered; *pl.* *-a.*

mutatis mutandis (Lat.), with the necessary changes; abbr. **m.m.**

mutato nomine (Lat.), with the name changed.

mutton (typ.), colloquial term for an em quad.

'mutual' friend, often objected to, though used by Burke, Dickens, Lytton, Sterne, and others; the alternative 'common' is ambiguous.

Muzaffarabad, Kashmir.

Muzaffarpur, Bihar, India.

muzhik, Russian peasant, *use* **moujik**.

Muzio gambit, a chess opening.

M.V., motor vessel, (*or* **m.v.**) muzzle velocity.

m.v. (It. mus.), *mezza voce* (with half voice-power).

mv, microvolt (no point).

M.V.O., Member (of fourth or fifth class) of the (Royal) Victorian Order.

M.V.Sc., Master of Veterinary Science.

M.W., Most Worshipful, — Worthy.

M.W.B., Metropolitan Water Board.

myalism, W. Indian Negro witchcraft; adj. **myal**.

myall, a wild Australian Aboriginal.

myall-wood, hard violet-scented Australian wood (hyphen).

myceli/um (bot.), the thallus of a fungus; *pl.* **-a**.

Mycenaean, of Mycenae (Anc. Greece) or its civilization.

Myddelton Square, Clerkenwell, London. *See also* **Mi-**.

Myddleton (Sir Hugh), 1560–1631, London merchant.

My dear Sir, (in letters, two caps. only, comma at end).

Myers (Frederic William Henry), 1843–1901, English poet, essayist, spiritualist; — **(Leopold Hamilton)**, 1881–1944, English novelist.

myna (bird), *use* **mina**.

mynheer (Du.), Sir, Mr.; a Dutchman.

myop/ia, shortness of sight; adj. **-ic**.

my/osis, contraction of the pupil of the eye; adj. **-otic**.

myosotis, the forget-me-not.

Myres (Sir John Linton), 1869–1954, English archaeologist. *See also* **Miers, Myers**.

Myriapoda, the centipedes and millepedes, *not* Myrio-.

myrobalan, a plum, *not* -bolan.

myrrhine, *use* **murr-**.

myrtille (Fr. f.), bilberry.

myrtle, *not* -tel.

Mysore, Deccan, India, *not* the more correct Maisur.

myst., mysteries.

myth., motholog/y, -ical.

mythopoeic, myth-making, *not* -paeic, -peic.

Mytilene, Lesbos, Greece; **Mitylene** in N.T., **Mitilini** in modern Greek.

myxomatosis, a contagious and destructive infection of rabbits.

N

N, nitrogen, the thirteenth in a series.

N., Norse, north, -ern, all proper names with this initial, (Fr.) *nord* (north), (Lat.) *nom/en, -ina* (name, -s), *noster* (our), (mag.) symbol of magnetic flux.

(N.) (naval), navigat/ing, -ion.

n., nail (2¼ inches), name, nephew, neuter, new, nominative, noon, note, -s, noun.

n., (Fr.) *nous* (we, us), (Lat.) *natus* (born), *nocte* (at night).

n, (math.) an indefinite integer; as prefix, nano-, *see* **nm.**

n/ (Fr.), before a verb, *nous* (we, us).

ñ (Sp.), called '*n* with the tilde', or 'Spanish *n*'; *pron.* as ni in onion; follows all other *n*'s in Spanish alphabetical arrangement.

N.A., National Academ/y, -ician, Native Administration, Nautical Almanac, Naval Auxiliary, North America, -n.

Na, *natrium* (sodium) (no point).

n/a (banking), no account.

NAAFI *or* **Naafi,** Navy, Army, and Air Force Institutes.

Naas, Kildare, N.I., *pron.* Nās; *also* Norway, the home of Sloid, q.v.

nabob, a rich Anglo-Indian (orig. same as **nawab,** but now differentiated).

Nabuchodonosor, *see* **Nebuchadnezzar.**

N.A.C., Noise Abatement Council.

nach Christi Geburt (Ger.), = A.D.; abbr. *n. Chr.* See *also vor — —*).

Nachdruck (Ger. typ. m.), reprint, pirated edition; **nachdrucken** to reprint, or pirate.

Nachmittag (Ger. m.), afternoon; abbr. **Nm.**

nachmittags (Ger. adv.), p.m.; abbr. **nachm.**

Nachtmaal (Du.), the Lord's Supper; in Afrik. **Nagmaal.**

nach und nach (Ger., mus.), by little and little.

nacre, mother-of-pearl (not ital.).

nacré (Fr.), like mother-of-pearl (ital.).

nadir, the lowest point, opp. to **zenith.**

naenia, *use* ne-.

naev/us, a skin blemish, 'mother's mark'; *pl.* **-i.**

Naga Hills, Assam.

Nagaland, Indian state.

Nagar, W. Bengal, Mysore, E. Punjab, Kashmir.

-nagar (Indian suffix), a town, as Ahmadnagar, *not* -naggore, -nagore, -nugger, -ur.

Nagasaki, Japan, *not* Nang-.

Nagmaal, *see* **Nachtmaal.**

Nagpur, Madhya Pradesh, India, *not* -pore.

Nahum, O.T., abbr. **Nah.**

naiad/, river-nymph, *not* naid; *pl.* **-s** *or* **-es.**

naif, artless, *use* **naïve;** in Fr. **naïf/f,** *fem.* **-ve.**

nail, 2¼ inches; abbr. **n.**

Naini Tal, Uttar Pradesh, India.

nainsook, Indian muslin, *not* -zook.

Nairne (**Baroness,** *née* Caroline Oliphant), 1776–1845, Scottish poetess.

Nairnshire, Scotland.

naïve/, artless, *not* nai-, naïf; **-ty.**

naïveté (Fr. f.), artlessness.

N.A.L.G.O., *commonly* **NALGO** *or* **Nalgo,** National Association of Local Government Officers.

Nalson (John), 1638–86, English theologian and historian.

Nama (S. Afr.), Hottentot tribesman.

namable, *use* name-.

Namaqualand (off. spelling), S. Africa (one word).

namby-pamby, weakly sentimental (hyphen).

name, abbr. **n.**

nameable (U.S. nam-).

namely, *pref. to* viz.

namesake (one word).

names of books and ships (typ.), to be italic.

N. & Q., *Notes and Queries.*

nankeen, fabric, *not* -kin.

nano-, prefix signifying the sub-multiple 10^{-9}.

nanometre, one-thousandth part of a micrometre; abbr. **nm** (no point); use in preference to millimicron ($m\mu$).

Nansen (Fridtjof), 1861–1930, Norwegian Arctic traveller.

Nantasket Beach, Mass., U.S.

Nantucket Island, Mass., U.S.

Naoroji (Dadabhai), 1825–1907, Indian politician, first Parsee M.P. (for Central Finsbury).

Nap., Napoleon.

nap/, -ped, -ping.

nap, a card game.

naphtha, an inflammable oil, *but* **Felsnaptha.**

Napierian logarithms, from **John Napier,** 1550–1617, Scottish mathematician; *not* -perian.

napoleon, in Fr. m.

napoléon, 20-franc coin of Napoleon I.

napolitaine (à la) (Fr. cook.), in Neapolitan style (not cap. *n*).

Narbada, Indian river, *not* Nerbudda.

narciss/us, flower, *pl.* **-i** (bot.), **-uses** (non-tech.); **-ism,** admiration of one's own body.

narcos/is, stupor induced by narcotics; *pl.* **-es.**

narghile, a hookah, *not* -gile, -gili; in Pers. **nargileh.**

Narragansett Bay, Rhode I., U.S., *not* -et.

narrow measure (typ.), type composed in narrow widths, as in columns.

narwhal, the sea-unicorn, *not* -e, -wal; — **tusk,** *not* horn.

N.A.S., National Association of Schoolmasters, Noise Abatement Society.

NASA, National Aeronautics and Space Administration (U.S.).

nasalize, *not* -ise.

N.A.S.D., National Amalgamated Stevedores and Dockers.

Nash (Richard, *or* **'Beau'),** 1674–1762, Bath Master of Ceremonies.

Nash *or* **Nashe (Thomas),** 1567–1601, English pamphleteer and dramatist.

Nasirabad, W. Pakistan.

Nasmith (James), 1740–1808, English theologian and antiquary.

Nasmyth (Alexander), 1758–1840, Scottish painter; — **(James),** 1808–90, Scottish engineer; **Nasmyth hammer,** *not* -th's.

nasturtium/ (bot.), *not* -ian, -ion; *pl.* **-s.**

N.A.T., National Arbitration Tribunal.

Nat., Natal (prov. of S. Africa), Nathanael, -iel, National.

nat., natural, -ist.

nat. hist., natural history.

National/, abbr. **Nat.;** — **Academ/y, -ician,** abbr. **N.A.;** — **Assemblies** (*see* **Assemblies**); — **Graphical Association,** abbr. **N.G.A.**

nationalize, *not* -ise.

National Physical Laboratory, Teddington; abbr. **N.P.L.**

National Westminster Bank, Ltd.

nations and places, as adjectives or nouns, in frequent commercial use, need no cap., as french polish, -er, morocco leather, plaster of paris, prussian blue, turkey red, and many others.

native oyster, one raised on an artificial bed.

NATO, *commonly* **Nato,** North Atlantic Treaty Organization.

nat./ ord., natural order; — **phil.,** — philosophy.

NATSOPA, National Society of Operative Printers and Assistants.

nattier blue, a soft blue, from **Jean Marc Nattier,** 1685–1766, French painter.

natt/y, trim; **-ier, -ily.**

natura (Lat.), nature.

natural/, -ist, abbr. **nat.**

natural (mus.), sign ♮.

naturalia (Lat.), the sexual organs.

naturalize, *not* -ise.

natura/ naturans (Lat.), creative nature; — *naturata,* created nature.

natura non facit salt/um, -us (Lat.), Nature makes no leap/, -s.

nature, the processes of the material world; cap. only when personified.

naturel (*au*) (Fr. cook.), plainly prepared.

natus (Lat.), born; abbr. *n.*

naught, nothing; *not* nought, q.v., except in arithmetic.

Nauheim (Bad), Hesse, Germany.

nause/a, sickness; **-ate, -ous.**

nautch/, Indian dancing entertainment; — **-girl;** *not* nach, natch.

nautical/, abbr. **naut.;** — **mile,** (U.K.) 1,853·18 m., (international) 1,852 m.

Nautical Almanac, abbr. **N.A.**

nautil/us, a shell; *pl.* **-i.**

nav., naval, navigation.

Navaho/, N. American Indian; *pl.* **-s.**

navarin (Fr. cook. m.), a stew of mutton or lamb.

Navarrese, of Navarre.

navet (Fr. m.), turnip.

navigat/ing, -ion, abbr. (N.), *or* **nav.**

Navy, Army, and Air Force, in toasts, etc., the Navy precedes, being the senior service.

'Navy List', (not hyphen).

nawab, Indian title. *See* **nabob.**

Naz/arene, -arite, native of Nazareth, *not* -irite, q.v.

Nazi, member of the German National Socialist Party (abbr. of *N*ational-so*zi*alist); **Nazism.**

Nazirite, an anc. Hebrew who had taken vows of abstinence, *not* -arite, q.v.

N.B., New Brunswick (Canada), North Britain (a name for Scotland offensive to Scots), *nota bene* (Lat., mark well).

Nb, niobium (no point).

n.b. (cricket), no ball.

N.B.C., National Book Council, *now* **N.B.L.;** (U.S.) National Broadcasting Company.

n.b.g., no bloody good.

N.B.L., National Book League.

N.B.P.I., National Board for Prices and Incomes.

n.Br. (Ger.), *nördliche Breite* (north latitude).

N.B.S., National Broadcasting Service (of New Zealand).

N.C., North Carolina, U.S. (off. abbr.).

n.c., nitrocellulose.

N.C.B., National Coal Board.

N.C.C., Non-Combatant Corps.

N.C.C.V.D., National Council for Combating Venereal Disease.

n.Chr. (Ger.), *nach Christo* or *nach Christi Geburt* (= A.D.).

N.C.O., Non-commissioned Officer.

N.C.R., no carbon (paper) required.

N.C.U., National Cyclists' Union.

N.C.W., National Council of Women.

N.D. (Fr.), Notre Dame.

Nd, neodymium (no point).

n.d., no date.

N. Dak., North Dakota, U.S. (off. abbr.).

N.E., new edition (*also* **n/e**), New England.

NE., north-east, (Fr.) *nord-est* (north-east). *See also* **compass.**

Ne, neon (no point).

né (Fr. m.), *fem.* **née,** born.

n/e (banking), no effects.

Neal (**Daniel**), 1678–1743, English Puritan writer; — (**John**), 1793–1876, American writer.

Neale (**John Mason**), 1818–66, English hymnologist.

Neanderthal skull, of a supposed Palaeolithic man, found in 1857 in a cave near Düsseldorf.

Neapolitans, inhabitants of Naples.

neap tide, that of smallest range (two words).

near, abbr. **nr.; near by** (adv.), two words; **near-by** (adj.), hyphen.

Nearctic, of northern N. America, *not* Neoarctic.

neat's-foot oil (one hyphen).

N.E.B., NEB, New English Bible.

Nebr., Nebraska, U.S. (off. abbr.).

Nebuchad/nezzar, king of Babylon, destroyed Jerusalem in 586 B.C. (**Nabuchodonosor** in A.V. Apocr. and the Vulgate; **-rezzar,** in Jer. 43:10, etc.).

nebula/, *pl.* **-s.**

nécessaire (Fr. m.), dressing-case.

necess/ary, -ity.

Neckar, river, Württemberg.

Necker (**Jacques**), 1732–1804, French statesman.

nec pluribus impar (Lat.), a match for many (motto of Louis XIV).

N.E.D., New English Dictionary, use **O.E.D.** (*Oxford English Dictionary*).

N.E.D.C., National Economic Development Council, colloq. **Neddy.**

née (Fr. f.), born (U.S. not ital.).

needlework (one word).

Neele (**Henry**), 1798–1828, English poet.

neelghau, an antelope, *use* **nylghau.**

ne'er/, never; — **-do-well** (hyphens).

ne exeat regno (law), a writ to restrain a person from leaving the kingdom.

nefasti (*dies*) (Lat.), blank days.

neg., negative, -ly.

neglectable, *use* **negligible.**

négligé (Fr. m.), (lingerie) easy undress, a diaphanous dressing-gown (U.S. **negligee**).

negligible, *not* eable.

negotiate, *not* -ciate.

Negretti & Zambra, instrument makers, London.

negrillo/, one of a dwarf Negro people in Cent. or S. Africa; *pl*. **-s.**

Negri Sembilan, *see* **Malaya, Federation of.**

negrito/, one of a dwarf negroid people in the Malayo-Polynesian region; *pl*. **-s.**

Negr/o, *pl*. **-oes,** *fem.* **-ess** (cap.).

negroid, *not* -rooid.

Negus, title of Emperor of Abyssinia.

negus, wine punch.

Neh., Nehemiah.

Nehru (Jawaharlal, 'Pandit'), 1889–1964, Indian nationalist leader, Prime Minister from 1947.

n.e.i., *non est invent/us, -a, -um* (he, she, *or* it, has not been found).

neige (Fr. cook. f.), whisked white of egg.

neighbour/, -hood (U.S. **-or**).

Neilgherry Hills, S. India, *use* **The Nilgiris.**

Neill (Patrick), d. 1705, first printer in Belfast, of Scottish birth; — **(Patrick),** 1776–1851, Scottish naturalist.

neither (of two), *sing.*; **neither he nor she** (*sing.*), **neither he nor they** (*pl.*), **neither these nor those** (*pl.*).

Nejd ('the plateau'). *See* **Saudi Arabia.**

nekton, free-swimming organic life, as opp. to **plankton.**

nematode (noun *or* adj.), (of) round-worm or thread-worm, *not* -oid.

nem. con., nemine contra-dicente; — *diss.,* — *dissentiente.*

Nemean/ (adj.), of the vale of Nemea in anc. Argolis; — **games,** one of the four Pan-hellenic festivals; — **lion,** slain by Hercules.

Nemesis (cap.).

nemine/ contradicente (Lat.), unanimously, abbr. *nem. con.*; — *dissentiente*, no one dissenting, abbr. *nem. diss.*

nemo/ (Lat.), nobody; — *me impune lacessit* (Lat.), no one attacks me with impunity (motto of Scotland, and of the Order of the Thistle).

nemophila (bot.), a garden flower.

N.Eng., New England.

nenia, an elegy, *not* nae-.

ne nimium (Lat.), shun excess.

nenuphar, the great white water-lily; not cap. when not generic name. *See Nuphar.*

neo-Christianity (cap. C only).

Neocomian (geol.) (cap.).

neo-Darwin/ian, -ism.

neodymium, symbol **Nd** (no point).

neo-Lamarckian (hyphen, one cap.).

neolog/ize, to use new terms, *not* ise; **-ism,** abbr. **neol.**

neon, symbol **Ne** (no point).

neo-Platon/ic, -ism (hyphen, one cap.).

Nep., Neptune.

Nepal, kingdom between Tibet and India, *not* -aul.

nephew, abbr. **n.**

ne plus ultra (Lat.), perfection.

neptunium, symbol **Np** (no point).

ne quid nimis (Lat.), be wisely moderate.

Nerbudda, Indian river, *use* **Narbada.**

nereid/, a sea-nymph; *pl.* -s *or* (with cap.) -es.

Neri (Saint Philip), 1515–95, founder of the Congregation of the Oratory.

Nernst, electric lamp, from **Walther Hermann Nernst,** 1864–1941, German physicist and chemist.

nero-antico (It.), a black marble.

nerve-racking, *not* wr-.

Nesbit (Evelyn), pen-name of Mrs. Edith (Hubert) Bland, 1858–1924, English writer.

Nesbitt (Cathleen), b. 1890, English actress; — **(Hon. Wallace),** 1858–1930, Canadian advocate (K.C.) and judge.

Nessler's reagent (chem.), from **Julius Nessler,** 1827–1905, German chemist.

n'est-ce pas? (Fr.), is it not so?

net, not subject to deduction, *not* nett.

net/, -ted, -ting.

Neth., Netherlands.

netsuke, Japanese ornament.

nett, not subject to deduction, *use* **net.**

nettle rash (two words).

network (one word).

Neuchâtel, Switzerland.

Neufchâtel, Aisne, France; Seine-Maritime, France; a kind of cheese.

Neuilly, dép. Seine, France.

neuralgia, pain in a nerve (a symptom, not a disease).

neurasthenia, nervous prostration, chronic fatigue.

neurine, a poisonous ptomaine, *not* -in.

neuritis, inflammation of fibres.

Neuropter/a, an order of insects (lacewings, etc.); *sing.* -on.

neuros/is, a functional derangement through nervous disorder; *pl.* -es.

neuter, abbr. n., *or* neut.

neutralize, *not* -ise.

neutron/ (sci.), an uncharged particle; *pl.* -s.

Nev., Nevada, U.S. (off. abbr.).

névé (Fr. m.), glacier snow (not ital.).

never/-ending, — -failing (hyphens).

never/more, -theless (one word).

never-to-be-forgotten (hyphens).

Nevill, family name of Marquess of Abergavenny.

Neville, family name of Baron Braybrooke.

new, abbr. n.

Newbegin, Whitby, Yorks.

Newbiggin, Durham, Northumb., Westmorland, Yorks.

Newbigging, Aberdeen, Angus, Lanark.

Newborough (Baron).

New Brunswick, Canada, abbr. N.B.

Newburgh, Fife **(Countess of).**

Newcastle/ upon Tyne; — **under Lyme** (no hyphens).

newcomer (one word).

Newdigate (Sir Roger), 1719–1806, founder of Oxford prize for poem.

new edition, abbr. N.E., n/e. *See also* title-pages.

New English Bible (The), first part (the New Testament) publ. 1961, complete 1970; abbr. N.E.B., NEB.

newfangled (one word).

New Forest, Hants (two words).

Newfoundland (one word), Canada, abbr. NF., Nfld.

New Hampshire, U.S., N.H., *never* abbr. as — Hants.

New Haven, Connecticut, U.S. (two words).

Newhaven, near Edinburgh; *also* Sussex (one word).

New Hebrides, abbr. **N.Heb.**

New Jersey, U.S., abbr. **N.J.**

New Mexico, abbr. **N.Mex.**

Newmilns, Ayrshire.

Newnes (Sir George), 1851–1910, publisher.

New Orleans, U.S., abbr. **N.O.**

new paragraph (typ.), abbr. **n.p.,** symbol ⌷.

New Quay, Cardigan (two words).

Newquay, Cornwall (one word).

New Red Sandstone (geol.) (caps.).

New South Wales, Australia (three words, caps., no hyphen); abbr. **N.S.W.**

Newspaper Publishers' Association, abbr. **N.P.A.**

newspapers (titles of) (typ.), when cited, to be in italic; s.caps. only when in the paper itself.

newsprint, paper on which newspapers are printed.

New Style, according to the Gregorian calendar, adopted in Britain on 14 Sept. 1752 (omitting 3–13 Sept.), and in Russia in 1917; abbr. **N.S.** *See also* **Old Style.**

newsvendor, *not* -er.

New Testament, abbr. **N.T.;** for abbr. of books in, *see* their names.

Newtonabbey, Co. Antrim (one word).

Newton Abbot, Devon.

Newton-le-Willows, Lancs., (hyphens).

Newtonmore, Inverness (one word).

Newton Poppleford, Devon.

Newton Stewart, Kirkcudbright (two words). *See also* **Newtownstewart.**

Newtownards, Co. Down (one word).

Newtownbutler, Fermanagh (one word).

Newtowncunningham, Co. Donegal (one word).

Newtownforbes, Co. Longford (one word).

Newtownmountkennedy, Wicklow (one word).

Newtownsands, Limerick (one word).

Newtownstewart (one word), Tyrone. *See also* **Newton Stewart.**

New Year's Day (caps.).

New York, the U.S. state, abbr. **N.Y.;** the city, often abbr. **N.Y.C.,** but officially **New York, N.Y.**

New Yorker, inhabitant of New York.

New Yorker, magazine (ital.).

nex/us (Lat.), a tie, a linked group; *pl.* **-us** (pedantic) *or* **-uses** (pop.), *not* -i.

Ney (Michel), 1769–1815, French marshal.

nez retroussé (Fr. m.), a turned-up nose.

NF., Newfoundland.

N.F., New French, Norman-French.

Nfld., Newfoundland.

N.F.P.W., National Federation of Professional Workers.

N.F.S., National Fire Service (during Second World War).

N.F.U., National Farmers' Union.

N.F.W.I., National Federation of Women's Institutes.

N.G., National Giro, National Guard, New Granada.

n.g., no good.

N.G.A., National Graphical Association.

N.Gr., New Greek.

N.H., New Hampshire, U.S. (off. abbr.).

N.Heb., New Hebrew, — Hebrides.

NHG, New High German (one point only).

N.H.I., National Health Insurance.

n.h.p., nominal horse-power.

N.H.R.U., National Home Reading Union.

N.H.S., National Health Service.

Ni, nickel (no point).

Niagara, river separating Ontario, Canada, from New York State, U.S.

Niagara Falls, waterfalls of R. Niagara; town, N.Y.; town, Ontario.

Nibelungenlied, German epic, twelfth–thirteenth century, *not* Nie- (one word).

niblick, a golf club.

NIBMAR *or* **Nibmar,** 'No independence before majority rule'.

N.I.C., National Incomes Commission, colloq. **Nicky.**

Nicar., Nicaragua.

Nicene Creed, based on decisions formulated at Nice (Nicaea) in Asia Minor, A.D. 325; *not* Nicaean. (Academically known for accuracy as the Niceno-Constantinopolitan creed.)

niche, a recess, *not* -ch.

Nicholas, anglicized spelling of five popes, two Russian emperors, and the patron saint of Russia; in Russ. **Nikolai.**

Nicholls (Sir George), 1781–1865, English Poor Law administrator.

Nichols, family of English printers and antiquaries stemming from **John Nichols,** 1745–1826.

Nichols (Robert Malise Bower), 1893–1944, English poet.

Nicholson, the usual spelling, *but see* **Nicolson.**

nicht wahr? (Ger.), is it not so?

nick (typ.), a groove cast in the shank of a type.

nickel/, (chem.) symbol **Ni** (no point); — **-plating** (hyphen); — **silver** (two words).

nickel (U.S.), a five-cent coin.

nicknack, *use* **knick-knack.**

nickname (one word).

Nicobar Islands, Indian Ocean, *not* Nik-.

Nicole (François), 1683–1758, French mathematician; — **(Pierre),** 1625–95, a Portuguese Royalist.

Nicoll (Robert), 1814–37, Scots poet; — **(Sir William Robertson),** 1851–1923, Scottish man of letters.

Nicolle (Charles Jean Henri), 1866–1936, French physicist and bacteriologist.

Nicol prism, from **William Nicol,** 1768–1851, Scottish physicist.

Nicolson (Hon. Sir Harold George), 1886–1968, British politician and man of letters.

Nicomachean Ethics, by Aristotle.

Nicosia, Cyprus (Gr. **Levkosia**), Sicily, *not* Nik-.

N.I.D., Naval Intelligence Division.

nid/us (Lat.), a nest; *pl.* **-i.**

Niebelungenlied, use *Nib-.*

Niebuhr (Barthold Georg), 1776–1831, German historian and philologist; — **(Karsten),** 1733–1815, German traveller.

niece, a relation, *not* nei-.

niell/o, Italian metal work; *pl.* **-i** (not ital.).

Niepce (Joseph Nicephore), 1765–1833, French physicist,

originator of photography (*see* **Daguerre**); — **de Saint-Victor (C.M.F.),** 1805–70, nephew of above, inventor of heliography; *pron.* nē-ĕps´.

Niersteiner, a hock (wine).

Nietzsche (Friedrich Wilhelm), 1844–1900, German polit. philosopher; *pron.* nēts´-shĕ.

Nièvre, dép. France.

Niger (Republic of), W. Cent. Africa, independent 1960.

Nigeria (Republic of), W. coast of Africa, independent 1960.

night/-cap, — **-dress** (hyphens).

nightfall (one word).

night-gown (hyphen).

nightshade (bot.) (one word).

night/-shirt, — **-time** (hyphens).

nihil/ (Lat.), nothing; — *ad rem,* nothing to the purpose; — *debet,* he owes nothing; — *dicit,* he says nothing; — *obstat,* no objection is raised (to publication, etc.).

Nijni Novgorod, Russian city (no hyphen), now named **Gorky.**

Nikobar Islands, *use* **Nic-.**

Nikolaev, Russian Black Sea naval base, *not* -aiev.

nil/ (Lat.), nothing; — *admirari,* wondering at nothing (*not* admiring nothing); — *conscire sibi,* to be conscious of no fault; — *desperandum,* despair of nothing, *not* never despair.

nilgau, an antelope, *use* **nylghau.**

Nilgiris, The, hills, S. India, *not* Neilgherry Hills.

nil nisi cruce (Lat.), nothing but by the cross.

Nilsson (Christine), 1843–1921, Swedish singer.

ni l'un (*or* **une** *fem.*) **ni l'autre** (Fr.), neither the one nor the other.

nimbus/, a halo, a rain cloud; *pl.* **-es.**

niminy-piminy, affectedly delicate, *not* -i -i.

n'importe! (Fr.), never mind!

nincompoop, a simpleton (one word).

ninepins, game (one word).

ninth, *not* -eth.

niobium, symbol **Nb** (no point).

nip/, **-ped,** **-per,** **-ping.**

nipping (bind.), crushing air out of book before casing-in.

Nippon, native name for Japan.

ni. pri., *nisi prius.*

nirvana (Budd.), cessation of sentient existence.

nisi/ (Lat.), unless; — *prius,* unless before, abbr. *ni. pri.*

nis/us (Lat.); an effort; *pl.* **-us.**

nitrate, a salt of nitric acid.

nitrite, a salt of nitrous acid.

nitrogen, symbol **N** (no point).

nitrogenize, *not* -ise.

nitrogenous, *not* -eous.

nitro-glycerine (U.S. **-in**), an explosive (hyphen).

Nitzsch, a family of German writers.

nizam, a Turkish soldier, (cap.) title of ruler of Hyderabad; *pl.* same.

Nizhni-Novgorod, Russia, *use* **Nijni Novgorod.**

N.J., New Jersey, U.S.

N.K.G.B., U.S.S.R. 'People's Commissariat of/ State Security', 1943, succeeded by **M.G.B.** ('Ministry of — —'), 1946, and **K.G.B.** ('Committee of — —'), 1953. *See* **O.G.P.U., N.K.V.D., K.G.B.**

Nkrumah (Dr. Kwame), 1909–72, Ghanaian politician (President, 1960–6).

N.K.V.D., U.S.S.R., 'People's Commissariat for Internal Affairs', 1934–43. *See* **O.G.P.U., N.K.G.B., K.G.B.**

N.L., Navy League, New Latin.

n.l., *non licet* (Lat., it is not allowed), *non liquet* (Lat., it is not clear), (typ.) new line.

N. lat., north latitude.

N.L.C., National Liberal Club.

N.L.F., National Liberation Front (S. Arabia), *see* **FLOSY.**

Nm. (Ger.), *Nachmittag* (afternoon), *nachmittags* (p.m.).

nm, nanometre.

N. Mex., New Mexico, U.S. (off. abbr.).

N.M.U., National Maritime Union.

NNE., north-north-east.

NNW., north-north-west (*see also* **compass**).

No, nobelium (no point).

N.O., Navigation Officer, New Orleans, (bot.) natural order, -s, (Fr.) *nord-ouest* (north-west).

N.O., n.o. (cricket), not out.

No., from It. *numero* (number); *pl.* **Nos.;** in Fr. **n°** (no point).

no (the negative), *pl.* **noes.**

Noachian, pertaining to Noah.

Nobel (Alfred Bernard), 1833–96, Swedish inventor of dynamite; — **prizes** (five), awarded annually for Physics, Chemistry, Physiology and Medicine, Literature, Peace.

nobelium, abbr. **No** (no point).

nobis (Lat.), for, *or* on, our part; abbr. **nob.**

noblesse/ (Fr. f.), nobility; — **oblige,** — imposes obligations.

nobody (one word).

nocte (Lat.), at night; abbr. **n.**

'Noctes Ambrosianae', articles in *Blackwood's Magazine*.

nocturne, (painting) a night scene, (mus.) a night piece (not ital.).

N.O.D., Naval Ordnance Department.

nod/, -ded, -ding.

Noël (Fr. m.), Christmas; Eng. **Nowel(l),** obs. except in carols.

noetic, of the intellect.

nœud (Fr. m.), a knot.

noisette (Fr. f.), a hazel-nut; (cook.) in *pl.* **-s,** small choice pieces of meat.

noisette (bot.), a hybrid between China and moss rose.

noisome, noxious, ill-smelling (no connection with noise).

noisy, *not* -ey.

nolens volens (Lat.), unwilling or willing; *pl.* **nolentes volentes.**

noli me tangere (Lat.), don't touch me (no hyphens).

noli-me-tangere (bot.), a balsam, (med.) an erosive ulcer (hyphens, not ital.).

nolle prosequi (Lat.), plaintiff's relinquishment of suit; abbr. **nol. pros.**

nolo/ (Lat.), I will not; — **contendere,** I plead guilty; — **episcopari,** I do not wish to be a bishop (formula for avoiding responsible office).

nol. pros., *nolle prosequi.*

nom., nominal, nominative.

no-man's-land, unclaimed territory (apos., hyphens).

nom de guerre (Fr. m.), assumed name.

nom de plume, pen-name (an Eng. formation; in Fr. **nom de lettres** *or* **pseudonyme**).

nom de théâtre (Fr. m.), stage-name.

nom/en (Lat.), a name, *pl.* **-ina,** abbr. N.; *nomen/ genericum,* a generic name; — *specificum,* a specific name.

nomic, conventional, esp. of spelling. *See also* **gnomic.**

nomin., nominative.

nominative, the case of the subject; abbr. **n., nom.,** *or* **nomin.**

non/ (Lat.), not; — *assumpsit,* a denial of any promise.

nonce-word, one coined for the occasion (hyphen).

nonchalance, indifference (not ital.).

nonchalant/, indifferent; in Fr. f. *-e.*

non-commissioned officer/, -s (U.S. colloq. **non-com**); abbr. **N.C.O.**

non compos mentis (Lat.), of unsound mind.

non con., non-content, dissentient.

Nonconformist, an English Protestant separated from the Church of England (cap. only in this sense).

non constat (Lat.), it is not clear.

non coupé (Fr.), uncut leaves.

non-ego (metaph.), the not-self (ital.).

nones (Rom. calendar), the ninth day, counting inclusively, before the ides.

non est/ (Lat.), it is wanting; — —*invent/us, -a, -um,* he, she, *or* it has not been found, abbr. **n.e.i.**

nonesuch (strictly correct), **nonsuch** (usual), person or thing that is unrivalled.

Nonesuch Press, founded by Sir Francis Meynell.

nonet (mus.), composition for

nine performers; in It. *nonetto.*

none the less (three words).

non-Euclidean (hyphen, one cap.)

non/ inventus (Lat.), not found; — *libet,* it does not please (me); — *licet,* it is not permitted, abbr. **n.l.;** — *liquet,* it is not clear; — abbr. **n.l.;** — *mi ricordo* (It.), I do not remember; — *nobis* (Lat.), not unto us; — *obstante,* notwithstanding, abbr. *non obst.;* — *obstante veredicto,* not-withstanding the verdict.

nonpareil, unequalled; (typ.) old name for a size of type, about 6 pt.

non placet (Lat.), it does not commend itself.

nonplus/, to perplex; **-sed, -sing** (U.S. **-ed, -ing.**)

non plus ultra (Lat.), perfection.

non/ possumus (Lat.), we cannot; — *prosequitur,* he does not prosecute, abbr. *non pros.;* — *sequitur* it does not follow logically, abbr. *non seq.*

non-stop (hyphen; U.S., one word).

nonsuch, now usual for **nonesuch,** q.v.

nonsuit, stoppage of suit by judge when plaintiff has failed to make a case (one word).

non-U, not upper-class (no point).

noon, abbr. **n.**

noonday (one word).

no one (two words).

n.o.p., not otherwise provided for.

no par. (typ.), matter to run on, and have no break.

Nor., Norman.

nord (Fr. m.), north; abbr. **N.**

Nordau (Max Simon), 1849–1923, physician, philosopher, Zionist, born in Budapest.

Norddeutscher Lloyd (two words); abbr. **N.D.L.**

Nordenfeldt gun.

Nordenskjöld (Nils Adolf Erik, Baron), 1832–1901, Swedish Arctic explorer.

nord/-est (Fr.), north-east, abbr. **NE.;** — *-ouest,* north-west, abbr. **N.O.** (no caps. except for abbrs.).

Norge, Norw. for **Norway.**

norm, an authoritative standard.

norm/a (Lat.), a rule or measure; *pl. -ae.*

normalize, to standardize, *not* -ise.

Normanby (Marq. of).

normande (à la) (Fr. cook.), apple-flavoured (not cap.).

Noronha (Fernando de), Brazilian penal colony in S. Atlantic.

Norroy, the third King-of-Arms.

Norse, abbr. **N.**

north, abbr. **N.** *See also* **compass.**

north., northern.

North (Christopher), pen-name of **Prof. John Wilson,** 1785–1854, Scottish poet.

Northallerton, Yorks. (one word).

North Americ/a, -an, abbr. **N.A.** *or* **N.Amer.**

Northamptonshire, abbr. **Northants** (no point).

North Britain, or Scotland, abbr. **Scot.,** *not* N.B.

North Carolina, U.S., abbr. **N.C.**

North Dakota, U.S., abbr. **N.Dak.**

north-east, abbr. **NE.** *See also* **compass.**

northern, abbr. **N.** *or* **north.**

Northern Rhodesia, abbr. **N.R.;** *now* **Zambia.**

Northern Territory (Australia), abbr. **N.T.**

North-German Gazette (one hyphen).

North Pole (caps.).

Northumb., Northumberland.

North Wales, abbr. **N.W.**

north-west, abbr. **NW.** *See also* **compass.**

North Yorkshire, new county name, proposed 1971.

Norvic., signature of Bp. of Norwich (full point).

Norw., Norway, Norwegian.

Norway, in Norw. **Norge;** in Fr. **Norvège.** *See also* **Assemblies, Norway.**

Norwegian typography, practically as Danish.

n^{os} (Fr.), *numéros* (numbers).

nosce teipsum (Lat.), know thyself.

nos/e, -ey.

nose dive (two words).

nose-piece (U.S. one word).

Nosey Parker, an inquisitive person (two caps.).

nostalgia, home-sickness, *not* -gy.

noster (Lat.), our, our own; abbr. **N.**

Nostradamus (Michel de Nostredame), 1503–66, French astrologer.

nostrum/, a quack remedy; *pl. -s* (not ital.).

nota bene (Lat.), mark well; abbr. **N.B.**

notabilia (Lat.), notable things.

notand/um (Lat.), a thing to be noted; *pl. -a.*

Notary Public, law officer (caps., two words); *pl. -ies —;* abbr. **N.P.**

notation, *see* **figures.**

note/, -s, abbr. **n.,** *pl.* **nn.** *See also* **footnotes, shoulder-notes, side-notes.**

notebook (one word).

note of/ admiration *or* **exclamation** (!); —— **interrogation** (?).

notic/e, -eable, -ing.

notif/y, -ied, -ying.

notiti/a (Lat.), a list; *pl. -ae.*

not proven, *see* **proven.**

notre (Fr. adj.), our; *nôtre* (*le, la*) (pronoun), ours; *les nôtres,* our folk.

Notre-Dame (Our Lady), abbr. **N.-D.,** French name of many churches, *not* Nô- (hyphen).

Nottinghamshire, abbr. **Notts** (no point).

not/um (Lat.), the back (of an insect); *pl. -a.*

n'oubliez pas (Fr.), don't forget.

nougat, a confection; *pron.* nōō'gah.

nought, the figure o (*see also* **naught**).

noumen/on, an object of intellectual intuition, not perceptible by the senses, *opp.* to **phenomenon**; *pl. -a.*

noun, abbr. **n.**

nouns (collective), if regarded as a whole to be treated as singular, e.g. the army *is,* the committee *meets.* If regarded as a number of units, to be treated as plural, e.g. the French (people) *are* thrifty.

nouns (German), all have initial caps.

nouns *or* **adjectives of nation or place,** in common use, need no caps., as french polish, -er, morocco leather, plaster of paris, prussian blue.

nous (Fr.), we; abbr. *n.,* before a verb *n/.*

nous (Gr.), shrewdness; *pron.* nows (not ital.).

nous avons changé tout cela (Fr.), we have changed all that.

nous verrons (Fr.), we shall see.

nouveau/ riche/ (Fr. m.), parvenu; *pl. -x -s.*

nouveautés (magasin de) (Fr. m.), linen-draper's shop, *not — des —.*

nouvelles (Fr. f. pl.), news.

Nov., November.

Nova/ Scotia, Canada, abbr. **N.S.;** **— Zembla,** *use* Novaya Zemlya, Arctic islands (two words, caps.).

Noveboracensian, of New York, *not* Nova-.

novelette, a small novel.

November, abbr. **Nov.**

noviciate, the state or period of being a novice.

novus homo (Lat.), a self-made man; *pl. novi homines.*

nowadays (one word).

Nowel(l), *see* **Noël.**

nowhere (one word).

noyau, a liqueur; also a sweetmeat.

Np, neptunium (no point).

N.P., New Providence, Notary Public.

n.p., net personalty, (typ.) new paragraph, (bibliographical) no place of publication given.

N.P.A., Newspaper Publishers' Association.

N.P.F.A., National Playing Fields Association.

N.P.L., National Physical Laboratory, Teddington.

N.P.O., New Philharmonia Orchestra.

n.p.p., no passed proof.

Nr. (Ger.), *Nummer* (number).

nr., near.

N.R., Northern Rhodesia, North Riding.

N.R.A., (U.S.) National Recovery Act, **—** Rifle Association.

N.R.S., National Rose Society.

N.S., New Series, New Side, Newspaper Society, New Style (after 1752), Nova Scotia.

N.-S., *Notre-Seigneur* (Our Lord).

n.s., not specified.

n/s (banking), not sufficient.

N.S.A., National Service Acts, — Skating Association, Nursery School Association.

N.S.P.C.C., National Society for the Prevention of Cruelty to Children.

N.S. Tripos, Natural Science Tripos.

N.S.W., New South Wales.

N.T., National Theatre, New Testament, (Australia) Northern Territory.

n.t.p., normal temperature and pressure.

n.u., name unknown.

nuance, shade of difference (not ital.).

Nubecul/a, the Magellanic clouds; *pl.* **-ae.**

nuclear fission.

nucle/us, *pl.* **-i.**

nudis verbis (Lat.), in plain words.

nugae (Lat.), trifles.

-nugger, Indian suffix. *See also* **-nagar.**

N.U.G.M.W., National Union of General and Municipal Workers.

N.U.I., National University of Ireland.

N.U.J., National Union of Journalists.

nul/ (Fr.), *fem.* **-le,** none, not one.

nullah (Ind.), a dry watercourse (not ital.).

nulla-nulla, Australian wooden club, *not* -ah -ah.

nullif/y, -ied, -ying.

nulli secundus (Lat.), second to none.

nullo (typ.), the o, *or* zero.

Num., Numbers (O.T.), *not* Numb.

N.U.M., National Union of Mineworkers.

num., numeral, -s.

number, abbr. **No.** *or* **no.,** *pl.* **Nos.** *or* **no.**

number (house), in road or street, no point following, as, 6 Fleet Street.

numerals (roman), caps. I, II, V, X, L, C, D, M, not to be followed by a point. For kings, rulers, etc., the name should be in upper and lower case, and the numeral in caps. as Henry V, Edward VII (no point). Lower case i, ii, etc., is often used for pagination of preliminary matter. In Fr. no full point after. In Ger. full point with arabic and roman ordinal numbers, but not cardinal. Abbr. **num.**

numérateur (Fr. m.), numerator.

numér/o (Fr. m.), number, abbr. **no,** *pl.* **nos;** **-oter,** to number (e.g. pages); **-oteur,** numbering machine.

numis., numismatic, -s, numismatology.

Nummer (Ger. f.), number, abbr. **Nr.**

numskull, a dunce, *not* numb-.

nunc aut nunquam (Lat.), now or never.

Nunc Dimittis (Lat.), Simeon's canticle.

nunc est bibendum (Lat.), now is the time to drink.

nuncheon, a midday meal, *not* -ion.

nuncio/, a papal ambassador; *pl.* **-s.**

nunquam (Lat.), never.

N.U.P.B. & P.W., National Union of Printing, Bookbinding, and Paper Workers, *now* **SOGAT,** q.v.

N.U.P.E., National Union of Public Employees.

Nuphar, yellow water-lily genus, also spelt *Nenuphar. See also* **nenuphar.**

N.U.R., National Union of Railwaymen.

nur, nurr, a hard knot in wood, *use* **knur.**

Nuremberg, *not* -burg; in Ger. **Nürnberg.**

Nureyev̆ (Rudolf Hametovich), b. 1938, Russian ballet-dancer.

nurl, *use* **kn-.**

Nürnberg, anglicized as **Nuremberg.**

nurs/e, -ing, -eling.

nurseryman (one word).

N.U.S., National Union of Seamen; ditto Students.

N.U.S.E.C., National Union of Societies for Equal Citizenship.

N.U.T., National Union of Teachers.

nut/, -ted, -ting.

nut/crackers; -hatch, a bird; **-shell** (one word).

N.U.T.G., National Union of Townswomen's Guilds.

nux vomica, seed of E. Indian tree, source of strychnine (two words, not ital.); abbr. **nux vom.**

N.V., New Version.

N.V.M., Nativity of the Virgin Mary.

NW., north-west. *See also* **compass.**

N.W., North Wales.

N.W.F.P., North-West Frontier Province (Pakistan).

N.W.T., North-West Territories (Canada).

N.Y., New York city or state, U.S. *See* **New York.**

Nyasaland, Cent. Africa, *not* Nyassa- (one word); *now* **Malawi.**

N.Y.C., New York City, (New York, U.S.).

nylghau, short-horned Indian antelope, *not* nilgau.

nymph/ae (anat.), the *labia minora; sing.* **-a.**

Nymphaea (bot.), the white water-lily genus.

N.Z., New Zealand.

O

O, oxygen (no point), (Lat.)
octarius (a pint), the
fourteenth in a series.

O., Odd Fellows, old, Order
(as D.S.O.), (naut.) overcast,
owner, all proper names
with this initial, (Fr. m.) *ouest*
(west), (Ger. m.) *Osten* (east).

O! *see* **Oh!**

O', Irish name prefix;
use apos. as O'Neill, *not*
turned comma; **o** or **ó,**
followed by thin space, also
used, thus: ó Brian.

o' abbr. for of.

Ö (Sw.), island.

Ø, Scandinavian-
Norwegian principally.

%, per cent; **‰,** per mille.

o/a, on account of.

Oak-apple Day, 29 May.

O.A.P., Old Age Pension(er).
The pension is officially
Retirement Pension, the
pensioner now commonly a
'senior citizen'.

oarweed, *use* ore-.

oas/is, *pl.* **-es.**

O.A.S., Organization of
American States,
Organisation de l'Armée
Secrète.

oatcake (one word).

Oates (Titus), 1649–1705,
false informer of the Popish
Plot, 1678.

oatmeal (one word).

Oaxaca, Mexico.

O.B., Old Boy, outside
broadcast.

ob., oboe.

ob., *obiit* (he, she, *or* it died).

Obadiah, abbr. **Obad.**

obbligato (It. mus.),
(compulsory) accompani-
ment, *not* obl-; abbr. **obb.**

O.B.E., Officer (of the Order)
of the British Empire.

obeah, Negro witchcraft,
not -ea, -eeyah, -i.

obeisance, courtesy bow.

obelisk, *not* -isc; (typ.) the
dagger mark (†); **double
obelisk,** ‡.

obel/us, critical mark,
pl. **-i;** in ancient MSS. —,
÷, *or* †.

Oberammergau, Bavaria.

obi, witchcraft, *use* **obeah.**

obi, Japanese sash.

obiit/ (Lat.), he, she, *or* it
died, abbr. **ob.;** — *sine
prole,* died without issue,
abbr. **ob.s.p.**

obit, date of death, funeral
or commemoration service
(not ital.).

obiter/ dictum (Lat.),
a thing said by the way, *pl.*
— *dicta; — script/um,*
ditto written, *pl.* — *-a.*

object/, -ion, -ive, -ively,
abbr. **obj.**

object-glass, lens nearest
the object.

objet d'art (Fr. m.), a work
of artistic value; *pl.* **objets**
— (ital.).

obl., oblique, oblong.

obligato, *use* **obb-.**

obliger, one who does a
favour.

obligor (law), one who binds
himself to another.

oblique, abbr. **obl.**

obliviscence, forgetfulness.

oblong, abbr. **obl.**

obo/e (mus.), *not* hautbois,
-boy; abbr. **ob.;** **-ist,** *not*
-eist.

obol, small silver coin or
weight of anc. Greece.

obol/us, an **obol;** also used
for various small coins in
medieval European
countries; *pl.* **-i.**

O'Brien (William Smith),
1803–64; — **(William),**
1852–1928, Irish patriots.

O'Bryan (W.), 1778–1868,
founder Bible-Christians;
his followers **Bryanites,**
not O'Bryanites.

obs., observation,
observatory, observed,
obsolete.

obsequies, funeral rites, the
sing. -y not used.

observanda (Lat.), things to
be observed.

observat/ion, -ory, abbr.
obs.

obsession, a morbid
preoccupation.

obsidian (mineral.).

obsolescen/ce, -t,
becoming obsolete.

obsolete, abbr. **obs.**

ob.s.p., obiit sine prole (died
without issue).

obstetrics, midwifery; abbr.
obstet.

obstructor, *not* -er.

obverse, that side of a coin
with the head or main
device.

O.C., Officer Commanding.

o.c., *use* **op. cit.**

o/c, overcharge.

ocarina, porcelain wind-
instrument, *not* och-.

Occam/ (William of),
1280–1349, English
Franciscan philosopher;
-ism, -ist; *not* Ockham.

Occidental, Western (cap.).

occip/ut, back of head (not
ital.); **-ital.**

**occur/, -red, -rence, -rent,
-ring.**

ocell/us (entom.), simple
(as opp. to compound) eye
(of insect); *pl.* **-i.**

ochlocracy, mob-rule.

ochone, *use* **ohone.**

ochr/e, yellow pigment,
-eous, -y (U.S. **ocher,
ochreous, ochery**); *not*
oker.

Ockham, Surrey. *See also*
Occam.

o'clock (typ.), close up (not
to be abbreviated in print).

O'Connell (Daniel), 1775–
1847, Irish statesman.

**O'Connor (Feargus
Edward),** 1794–1855, Irish-
born Chartist leader;
— **(Rt. Hon. Thomas
Power),** 1848–1931, Irish-
born journalist and British
politician.

O'Conor (Charles Owen),
styled **The O'Conor Don**
(cap. T), 1838–1906, Irish
politician; — **(Sir Nicholas
Roderick),** 1843–1908,
British diplomatist.

O.C.R., Optical Character
Recognition (reading of
print by electronic eye).

ocra, *use* **okra.**

Oct., October.

octahedr/on, solid figure
with eight faces, *pl.* **-a; -al;**
not octae-, octoe-, octoh-.

octaroon, *use* **octo-.**

octastyle, having eight
columns, *not* octo-.

Octateuch, first eight books
of O.T., *not* Octo-.

octavo/ (typ.), a book based
on eight leaves, sixteen
pages, to the basic sheet;
pl. **-s,** abbr. 8vo (no point).
See **book sizes.**

octet (mus.), *not* -ett, -ette,
ottett (not ital.).

October, abbr. **Oct.**

octopus/, *pl.* **-es.**

octoroon, person of one-
eighth Negro blood, *not*
octa-.

octroi (Fr. m.), municipal
customs duties (not ital.).

O.C.T.U., *commonly* **OCTU**
or **Octu,** Officer Cadets
Training Unit.

Oculi Sunday, third in Lent.

ocul/us (Lat.), an eye; *pl.* **-i.**

O.D., Old Dutch, Ordnance
datum.

O/D, on demand, overdraft.

od, a hypothetical force.

odal, land held in absolute ownership, *not* udal.

odalisque (Turk.), female slave, *not* -isk (not ital.).

O.Dan., Old Danish.

odd, used as suffix requires hyphen (e.g. twenty-odd).

Odd Fellows, Independent Order of (official, separate words, caps.); abbr. **I.O.O.F.**

oddments (typ.), the parts of a book separate from the main text, such as contents, index; a section containing the oddments.

odd pages (typ.), the right hand, or recto, pages.

Odelsting, lower house Norwegian Parliament.

Odendaalsrus (off. spelling), Orange Free State, *not* -st.

Odéon, Paris theatre.

Oder–Neisse line, between Poland and E. Germany.

odeum, building for musical performances.

Odeypore, *use* Udaipur.

odi profanum vulgus (Lat.), I loathe the common herd.

odium, hatred, unpopularity.

odium/ aestheticum (Lat.), the bitterness of aesthetic controversy; — *medicum,* ditto medical; — *musicum,* ditto musical; — *theologicum,* ditto theological.

odometer, *use* h-.

O'Donoghue of the Glens (The) (cap. T).

O'Donovan (The) (cap. T).

odontoglossum/, an orchid; *pl.* **-s;** italics (cap. *O*) as genus.

odor/iferous, -ize, -izer, -ous.

odour/, -less (U.S. **odor/, -less).**

Odysseus, Greek for Ulysses.

Odyssey, Greek epic; **Odyssean.**

OE., Old English.

œ (ligature). *See also* **diphthongs.**

Oe (Dan., Sw.), old form for island, *use* **Ö.**

O.E.C.D., Organization for Economic Co-operation and Development.

oecist, the founder of a Greek colony, *not* oek-, oik-.

oecology, the science dealing with the relations of organisms to their surroundings, *use* **ec-.**

oecumenic/, -al, world-wide (of church councils) (U.S. **ec-).**

Oecumenical Patriarch, head of the Orthodox Church of Constantinople.

O.E.D., the *Oxford English Dictionary; N.E.D.* (New English Dictionary) is incorrect.

oedema/, swelling; **-tous** (U.S. **ed-).**

Oedipus/, the Theban hero, *not* Edi-; — **complex** (psych.), a boy's unconscious attachment to his mother and hostility to his father (two words).

O.E.E.C., Organization for European Economic Co-operation, *now* **O.E.C.D.,** q.v.

Oehlenschläger (Adam), 1779–1850, Danish writer.

œil (Fr. m.), eye, *pl.* **yeux; œil-de-bœuf,** a small round window, *pl.* **œils- — —; œil-de-perdrix,** a soft corn, *pl.* **œils- — —.**

o'er (typ.), to be close up.

oersted, unit of magnetic field strength, from **Hans C. Oersted,** 1777–1851, Danish physicist.

oesophag/us, the gullet; *pl.* **-i; -eal** (U.S. **e-**) (not ital.).

Oesterley (Revd. William), 1866–1950, English writer on biblical subjects.

Oesterreich (Ger.), Austria, use **Ös-**.

œuf (Fr. m.), egg; *œufs/ à la coque*, boiled eggs; — *à la neige*, whisked eggs; — *à l'indienne*, curried eggs? — *de Paques*, Easter eggs; — *sur le plat*, fried eggs.

œuvres/ (Fr. f. pl.), works; — *inédites*, unpublished works; — *mortes*, — *posthumes*, posthumous works; — *vives*, bottom of a ship.

O.F., Odd Fellows, Old French, (typ.) old face type.

O.F.C., Overseas Food Corporation.

off., official, officinal.

Offaly, Ireland, *formerly* King's County.

Offa's Dike, between England and Wales (apos.).

offcut (typ.), a piece cut off a sheet to reduce it to the appropriate size (one word).

Offenbach (Jacques), 1819–80, French composer, German-born.

offence (U.S. -se).

offer/, -ed, -ing, -tory.

offg., officiating.

off-hand/, -ed, casual, extempore (hyphen).

official/ (abbr. **off.**, *or* **offic.**).

officiating, abbr. **offg.**

officina (Lat.), a workshop. *See also* **oficina**.

officinal, used in a shop, used in medicine, sold by druggists; abbr. **off.**

offprint (typ.), a separately printed copy, or small edition, of an article which originally appeared as part of a larger publication.

offset (typ.), transfer of ink from its proper sheet (now commonly **set-off**, q.v.);

— **-litho**, — **-lithography**, a planographic printing process in which ink is transferred from its plate on to an intermediate blanket cylinder and then offset on to the paper.

offshoot (one word).

off shore (adv., two words); **off-shore** (adj., hyphen).

offside (football) (one word).

oficina (Sp.), a S. American factory. *See also* **off-**.

O'Flaherty (Liam), b. 1896, Irish novelist.

Oflag, German prison camp for officers.

O.F.M., Order of Friars Minor.

O.F.S., Orange Free State (South Africa).

oft-times (hyphen).

O.Gael., Old Gaelic.

ogee, a moulding; adj. **ogee'd**.

og/ham, ancient alphabet, *not* -am, -um, -hum.

ogiv/e, diag. rib of vault, pointed arch; **-al**.

O.G.P.U. *or* **Ogpu**, U.S.S.R. 'United state administration for struggle against espionage and counter-revolution', 1922–34. *See* **N.K.V.D.**

O'Grady (The) (cap. T).

ogr/e, man-eating giant, *pl.* **-es**; *fem.* **-ess**, *f. pl.* **-esses**; adj. **-eish**, *not* **-ish**.

Oh!, to be used when it is an exclamation, independent of what follows, as in a cry of pain. Use **O** with vocatives or when there is no stop after it, as *O for the wings of a dove! O who will o'er the downs so free?*

O.H.B.M.S., On Her, *or* His, Britannic Majesty's Service.

O. Henry, *see* **Henry**.

OHG., Old High German.

Ohio, U.S., off. not abbr.

ohm (elec.), SI unit of electrical resistance; abbr. Ω; *see also* **mho** (opp.); from **G. S. Ohm,** 1787–1854, German physicist.

O.H.M.S., On Her, *or* His, Majesty's Service.

oho! exclamation of surprise, *not* O ho, Oh ho, etc.

ohone, Gaelic and Irish cry of lamentation, *not* och-.

oidium, a fungus, *not* oï-.

oie (Fr. f.), goose.

oignon (Fr. m.), onion.

oikist, *use* oecist.

oil/cake, -can, -cloth (one word).

oil/-colour, — -painting (hyphens).

oil/skin, -stone (one word).

oi polloi (Gr.), the people, *use* **hoi —**.

O.Ir., Old Irish.

oison (Fr. m.), gosling.

Oistrakh/ (David), b. 1908, Russian violinist; **— (Igor),** b. 1931, Russian violinist, son of above.

O.K., 'all correct'; *not* okay.

okapi, giraffe-zebra-like animal.

Okehampton, Devon.

O'Kelly (The) (cap. T).

Oken (Lorenz), 1779–1851, German naturalist.

Oklahoma, U.S.; abbr. **Okla.**

okra, pods used for thickening soup; *not* oc(h)-, okro.

Ol., Olympiad.

Olaf (St.), patron of Norway.

old/, abbr. **O.; — -clothes-man, — -clothes-shop** (hyphens).

Old English (typ.), black letter, q.v.

old face (typ.), a type design based on the original roman type of the fifteenth century; abbr. **O.F.**

old-fashioned (hyphen).

'Old Glory', U.S. stars-and-stripes flag.

Old Hickory (U.S. colloq.), Andrew Jackson, President of U.S.

'Old Hundredth', hymn-tune, *not* '— Hundred'.

Old Man of the Sea, in *Arab. Nights* (caps.).

Oldmeldrum, Aberdeen (one word).

Old Red Sandstone (geol.) (caps.).

Old Style, according to the Julian calendar, abbr. **O.S.** *See* New Style.

old style (typ.), a type design, being a regularized old face; abbr. **O.S.**

Old Testament, abbr. **O.T.,** *or* **Old Test.;** for abbr. of books, *see* each title.

oleiferous, oil-producing, *not* olif-.

oleography, a method of chromolithography.

OLG., Old Low German.

Olifants River, S. Africa (no apos.).

Oligocene (geol.) (cap., not ital.).

olive/-branch, — -oil (hyphens).

Olivetan, an order of monks, *not* -ian.

Olivier (Laurence Kerr, Baron), b. 1907, English actor. *See also* **Ollivier.**

olla podrida, Spanish national dish, *also* a medley (not ital.).

Ollivier (Olivier Émile), 1825–1913, French statesman and writer. *See also* **Olivier.**

Olympiad, period of four years between celebrations of Olympic games; abbr. **Ol.**

Olympian, of Olympus, the abode of the Greek gods.

Olympic, of Olympia, *or* of the games originally held there.

O.M., (Member of the) Order of Merit.

o.m., old measurement.

omadhaun, Irish term of contempt (not the many variants).

Omagh, Co. Tyrone.

Omaha, city in Nebraska, U.S.

Oman, *see* Muscat.

Omar Khayyám, 1050?–1122, Persian poet.

Ombudsman, Parliamentary Commissioner to investigate complaints against government departments, of Scandinavian origin, first appointed in Britain in 1965.

Omdurman, Sudan.

omega, the Greek long *o*, last letter of Greek alphabet (ω, Ω).

omelet, in Fr. f. *omelette*; *omelette soufflée,* a puff omelet.

omicron, the Greek short *o*, (o, O), *not* omik-.

omissions (typ.), *see deleatur,* elision, ellipsis.

omit/, -ted, -ting.

omnibus/, *pl.* -es; abbr. **bus,** *not* 'bus, *pl.* **buses.**

omnium gatherum, a confused medley (U.S., hyphen, *not* ital.).

O.N., Old Norse.

on-coming (hyphen).

on dit (Fr. m. sing./pl.), gossip ('men say').

one (**a,** *not* an).

one-and-twenty, etc. (hyphens).

one-eighth, *see* fractions.

Oneida, socialistic community started at L. Oneida, N.Y., U.S., 1847.

one-idea'd (hyphen).

O'Neill (Eugene Gladstone), 1888–1953, American playwright;— **(Moira),** pseud. of Agnes Higginson Skrine, Irish poet.

oneiro/critic, -mancy, interpreter of, divination by dreams, *not* oniro-.

oneness (**a,** *not* an) (one word).

oneself is reflexive or intensive; **one's self,** one's personal entity.

one-sided (hyphen).

O.N.F., Old Norman-French.

onlook/, -er, -ing (one word).

on ne passe pas (Fr.), no thoroughfare.

o.n.o., or near(est) offer.

onomasticon, a vocabulary of proper names.

onomatopoe/ia, -ial, -ian, -ic, -ical, -ically, word formation by imitation of sound; abbr. **onomat.**

onomatopo/ësis, -etic, -etically, *not* -poiesis.

onrush (one word).

on shore (adv., two words); **on-shore** (adj., hyphen).

onside (football) (one word).

Ontario, Canada; abbr. **Ont.**

on to (two words).

ontolog/y, metaphysical study of the essence of things; **-ize,** *not* -ise.

onus, burden (not ital.).

onus probandi (Lat.), burden of proof (ital.).

%, per cent, -age.

‰, per mille.

Oodeypore, India, *use* **Udaipur.**

oolong, a tea, *not* ou-.

oomiak, Eskimo boat (not the many variants).

oopak, a tea, *not* -ack.

Ootacamund, Madras, India, *not* Utakamand; colloq. abbr. **Ooty.**

oozy, muddy, *not* -ey.

O.P., observation post, *Ordinis Praedicatorum* (of the Order of Preachers, or Dominicans).

o.p., overproof; (theat.) opposite the prompter's

side, or the actor's right;
(typ.) out of print.

op., optime, q.v.

op. (Lat.), *opus* (work), *opera*
(works).

op art, art in geometrical
form giving the illusion of
movement (no point).

op. cit., *opere citato* (in
the work quoted) (not
ital.).

O.P.E.C., Organization of
Petroleum Exporting
Countries.

Open Door policy,
opportunity for free trade
(U.S. **open-door**).

open/-hearted, — **-mouthed**
(hyphens).

Open Sesame (caps., two
words).

open-work/, -ed, -ing
(hyphens).

opera buffa (It.), comic
opera; in Fr. *opéra bouffe*.

Opéra-Comique, Paris
theatre (hyphen).

opera-glass (hyphen).

opercul/um (biol.), a cover;
pl. **-a** (not ital.).

opere/ citato (Lat.), in the
work quoted, abbr. **op. cit.;**
— *in medio,* in the midst
of the work.

ophicleide, (mus.) serpent,
bass or alto key-bugle,
not -eid.

ophiology, study of serpents,
not ophid-.

ophthalmic, of the eye.

Opie (Amelia), 1769–1853,
English novelist, wife of —
(John), 1761–1807, English
painter.

o.p.n., *ora pro nobis* (pray
for us).

opodeldoc, a liniment.

opopanax, a perfume.

opp., opposed, opposite.

oppress/or, *not* -er.

opt., optative, optical,
optician, optics.

optime (Camb.), one next

in merit to wranglers (not
ital.); abbr. **op.**

optimize, to make the best
of, *not* -ise.

opus/ (Lat.), a work, *pl.*
opera, abbr. *op.*; —
magnum, a great work,
pl. *opera magna.* Cf.
magnum opus.

opuscul/um (Lat.), a small
work, an essay; *pl.* **-a;** in
Eng. **opuscule/,** *pl.* **-s.**

opus number (mus.), the
one by which a work is
known (two words).

opus/ operantis (Lat.), the
effect of a sacrament resulting
from the spiritual disposition
of the recipient (the Protestant
view); — *operatum,* ditto
resulting from the grace
flowing from the sacrament
itself (the R.C. view).

O.R., other ranks.

o.r., owner's risk.

or, two or more singular
subjects joined by *or* take
the verb in the singular
number, e.g. John *or* William
is going. Where *or* joins the
last two words of a list,
practice varies, but O.U.P.
inserts a comma, e.g.
black, white, or green.

or (her.), gold.

ora (Lat. pl.), mouths. *See os.*

ora e sempre (It.), now and
always.

orangeade, *not* -gade.

Orange Free State, prov. of
S. Africa (three words),
abbr. **O.F.S.**

Orange/ism, extreme Irish
Protestantism, *not* -gism;
-man (one word, cap.).

Orangeman's Day,
12 July. Bank holiday in
Northern Ireland.

orang/-utan, *formerly* —
-outang, *but not* ourang-,
-utang (hyphen, not ital.).

**Oranmore and Browne
(Baron).**

ora pro nobis (Lat.), pray for us; abbr. **o.p.n.**

orat., orator, -ical, -ically.

oratio/ obliqua (Lat.), indirect speech; — **recta,** direct speech. Manner of reporting speech, e.g. 'I am glad', said he, 'to see you again' (*recta*); He said that he was glad to see me again (*obliqua*).

oratorios (titles of) (typ.), when cited, to be in ital.

orc, a dolphin, *not* ork.

Orcadian, of Orkney.

ord., ordained, order, ordinal, ordinance, ordinary.

Order, abbr. **O.;** when referring to a society, to be cap., as the Order of Jesuits.

order/, abbr. **ord.;** — **-book** (hyphen).

orders (bot. and zool.), caps. but not italic.

ordin/al, -ance (a regulation), **-ary,** abbr. **ord.**

ordnance, artillery, mil. stores.

Ordnance/ Survey Department (caps.), abbr. **O.S.D.;** — **datum** (one cap.), the standard sea-level of the Ordnance Survey, abbr. **O.D.**

ordonnance, the proper disposition of parts of a building or picture (not ital.).

ordre du jour (Fr. m.), agenda of a meeting.

öre, coin of Sweden, Denmark, and Norway, one hundredth of Kron/a, -e; Ice. equivalent, **Eyrir,** *pl.* **Aurar.**

Oreg., Oregon, U.S. (off. abbr.)

O'Rell (Max), 1848–1903, pen-name of Paul Blouet, French author and journalist.

oreo/graphy, -logy, *use* **oro-.**

ore/ rotundo (Lat.), well-turned, imposing speech; — **tenus,** from the lips and not the heart.

ore-weed, seaweed, *not* oar-.

orfèvrerie (Fr. f.), goldsmith's work.

orfray, *use* **orphrey.**

org., organ, -ic, -ism, -ized.

organdie, dress fabric, *not* -i (U.S. **-y**); in Fr. m. *organdi.*

organize, etc., *not* -ise.

organon, a system of rules.

orge (Fr. f.), barley.

orgeat (Fr. m.), barley-water.

org/y, *not* -ie; *pl.* **-ies.**

oriel, small room built out from a wall; its window.

Oriental/, -ist (cap.); abbr. **Or.** *or* **Orient.**

orientalize, *not* -ise (not cap.).

oriflamme, banner, *not* -flamb.

orig., origin, -al, -ally, -ate, -ated.

Origen, 185–253, a Father of the Church.

original (Sp. typ.), copy.

Origin of Species, by C. Darwin, 1859.

orinasal, of the mouth and nose, *not* oro-.

Orinoco, river, S. America. *See also* **oro-.**

oriole, a bird.

Orléans (House of) (**é**); **Orlean/ism, -ist** (no accent in Eng.).

Orme's Head, Caernarvon (apos.).

ormolu, a gold-coloured alloy (not ital.).

Ormonde (Marquess of).

Ormuzd, the Zoroastrian spirit of Good (not the many variants).

orn/é (Fr.), *fem.* **-ée,** adorned.

ornith., ornitholog/y, -ical.

Ornithorhynchus, the duck-billed platypus.

oro/graphy, -logy, mountain description and science, *not* oreo-.

oronoco, a Virginian tobacco.

Orotava, *properly* **La Orotava,** Canary Islands, *not* Ora-.

orotund, magniloquent.

Orphe/us (Gr. myth.), a Thracian lyrist; **-an.**

Orphic, pertaining to **Orphism,** the mystic cult connected with Orpheus.

orphrey, an ornamental border, *not* orfray.

orris-root, used for perfume (hyphen).

Or San Michele, church at Florence, *not* — Saint —.

orthoepy, word pronunciation.

orthopaedic, concerned with the cure of bone deformities, usu. in the young (U.S. **-edic**).

ortolan, an edible bird (not ital.).

Orvieto, Italian white wine.

O.S., Old Saxon, — school, — series, — side, — Style (before 1752), — style type, ordinary seaman, Ordnance Survey, (cloth.) outsize.

o.s., only son.

o/s, out of stock, outstanding.

Os, osmium (no point).

os (Lat.), a bone; *pl.* **ossa.**

os (Lat.), a mouth; *pl.* **ora.**

O.S.A., Order of St. Augustine.

Osaka, Japan, *not* Oz-.

O.S.B., Order of St. Benedict.

Osborn (Sherard), 1822–75, British rear-admiral and Arctic explorer.

Osborne, Isle of Wight.

Osborne, family name of Dukes of Leeds.

Osbourne (Lloyd), 1868–1947, writer (stepson of R. L. Stevenson).

oscill/ate, to fluctuate; **-ation, -ator, -atory, -ogram, -ograph.**

Oscott College (R.C.), Warwickshire.

oscul/ate, to kiss, adhere closely; **-ant, -ation, -atory.**

oscul/um (Lat.), a kiss, *pl.* **-a;** *osculum pacis,* the kiss of peace.

O.S.D., Ordnance Survey Department, Order of St. Dominic.

O.S.F., Order of St. Francis.

O.Sl., Old Slavonic.

Osler (Sir William), 1849–1919, Canadian physician.

Oslo, *formerly* **Christiania,** capital of Norway.

Osmanli, of the family of Osman (founder of the Ottoman empire), *not* -lee, -lie, -ly (not ital.).

osmium, symbol **Os** (no point).

o.s.p., *use* **ob.s.p.,** q.v.

ossa, see *os.*

ossein, bone cartilage, *not* -ine.

Ossett, Yorks., *not* Oset, Osset.

ossia (It. mus.), or.

Ossory, Ferns, and Leighlin (Bishop of).

o.s.t. (naut.), ordinary spring tides.

Ost (Ger. m.), east (cap.); abbr. **O.**

Ostend, Belgium; in Fr. **Ostende,** in Fl. **Oostende.**

ostensibl/e, outwardly professed; **-y.**

osteomyelitis, inflammation of the marrow of the bone (one word).

osteria (It.), an inn.

Österreich (Ger.), Austria, *not* Oe-.

Ostiaks, *use* **Osty-.**

ostiole, a small opening, *not* -eole.

ostler, a groom (U.S. **h-**).

ostracize (*not* -ise), in anc. Greece, to banish a dangerous citizen by votes recorded on potsherds (*ostrak/on,* pl. *-a*).

ostreiculture, oyster culture, *not* ostra-, ostrea-, ostreo-, ostri-.

ostreophagous (adj.), oyster-eating.

Ostrovsky (Alexander Nikolaevich), 1823–86, Russian dramatist.

Ostyaks, of W. Siberia, *not* Osti-.

Oswaldtwistle, Lancs., *not* -sle.

O.T., Old Testament.

Otaheite, *now* **Tahiti.**

O.T.C., *now* **S.T.C.**

O.Teut., Old Teutonic.

otherworld/liness, -ly (one word).

otium/ (Lat.), leisure; — *cum dignitate,* leisure with dignity; — *sine dignitate,* leisure without dignity.

otolith, an ear-bone, *not* -lite (not ital.).

ototoi (Gr.), alas! *not* otototoi, ottotoi.

ottava rima (It.), stanza of eight lines, as in Byron's *Don Juan.*

Ottawa, Canada, *not* Otto-.

Otterspool, Lancs. (one word).

Ottoman/, a Turk; *pl.* **-s** (cap.).

ottoman/, a sofa, a fabric; *pl.* **-s** (not cap.).

Otto (of roses), *use* **attar.**

Otway (Thomas), 1652–85, English dramatist.

O.U., Oxford University.

ouananiche, the Labrador salmon; *pron.* wa´nanish.

oubliette (Fr. f.), a dungeon (not ital.).

Oudenarde, Belgium; battle of —, 1708. In mod. Belg., **Audenarde.**

Oudh, India, *not* Oude; *pron.* owd.

O.U.D.S., Oxford University Dramatic Society.

ouest (Fr. m.), west; abbr. **O.**

ought, should. *See* **naught, au-.**

Ouida, pen-name of Louise de la Ramée (1839–1908), English novelist.

ouï-dire (Fr. m. sing./pl.), hearsay.

ouija, a board with an alphabet, used with a planchette, q.v.

oukaz, *use* **ukase.**

Ouless (W. W.), 1848–1933, British painter.

ounce/, -s, abbr. **oz.,** sign ℥; 437½ grains avoirdupois, 28·35 grammes approx.

O.U.P., Oxford University Press, the whole printing and publishing organization owned by Oxford University. *See also* **Clarendon Press.**

ourang-outang, *see* **orang-outang.**

ours (no apos.).

ousel, *use* **ouz-.**

out (typ.), an accidental omission of copy in composition.

out-and-out, unreserved(ly) (hyphens).

out/board, -come, -door (one word).

Outeniqua Mountains, S. Africa.

out/fit, -ted, -ter, -ting; -general; -grow/, -th (one word).

out-Herod (hyphen, cap.).

outhouse (one word).

outl/ie, -ier, -ying.

outmanœuvre (one word) (U.S. **outmaneuver**).

outmoded (one word).

out/-of-date (attributive adj., hyphens); — **-of-doors** (hyphens); — **of print,** abbr. **o.p.;** — **of sorts**

(typ.), when any letter in a fount is all used.

out-patient (hyphen).

outrance (*à*) (Fr.), to the bitter end, *not* à l'-.

outr/é (Fr.), *fem.* **-ée**, eccentric.

outspan (S. Afr.), to unyoke; unyoking place.

outstanding (one word).

outstrip/, -ped, -ping.

outv/ie, -ier, -ying (one word).

outward-bound (adj., hyphen).

Outward Bound Trust (no hyphen).

outweigh (one word).

outwit/, -ted, -ting.

ouvert/ (Fr.), *fem.* **-e**, open.

ouvri/er (Fr.), a workman; *fem.* **-ère**.

ouzel, a bird, *not* ous-.

over all (adv., two words); **over-all** (adj., hyphen).

overall/, -s (noun, one word).

overboard (one word).

overburden, *not* -then.

overburdensome (one word).

overcast (naut.), abbr. **O.**

overcharge, abbr. **o/c.**

Over Darwen, Lancs., *use* **Darwen.**

over-glad (hyphen).

overboard (one word).

over/land, -leaf, -mantel (ornamental mirror, etc., above mantel-shelf), **-mantle** (garment), **-night, -rate, -reach, -ride, -rule** (one word).

overrun (typ.), to turn over words from one line to the next (one word).

oversea/, -s (one word).

overvalue (one word).

ovol/o, a moulding; *pl.* **-i.**

ov/um, an egg; *pl.* **-a** (not ital.).

O.W., Office of Works.

Owens College, Manchester (no apos.).

owner, abbr. **O.**

Ox., Oxford.

Oxbridge, Oxford or Cambridge University.

Oxford Alman/ack, not -ac.

Oxford English Dictionary (*The*), abbr. **O.E.D.,** *not N.E.D.*

Oxford hollow (bind.), paper-lined hollow back.

Oxfordshire, abbr. **Oxon.**

Oxford University Press, abbr. **O.U.P.,** q.v.

oxide, *not* -id, -yd, -yde.

oxidization, oxidation, *not* oxy-.

oxidize, etc., *not* -ise, oxy-.

Oxon., Oxfordshire, *Oxonia* (Oxford), *Oxoniensis* (of Oxford).

Oxon., signature of Bp. of Oxford (full point).

oxy-acetylene (hyphen).

oxychloride, *not* oxi-.

oxygen/, (chem.) symbol **O** (no point; *pl.* **-ize,** *not* -ise.

oyer and terminer (law), royal commission to judges on circuit to hold courts.

oyez! hear ye! *not* oyes.

oz., ounce, **-s.**

P

P, (car) park, pedestrian (crossing), phosphorus, (chess) pawn, the fifteenth in a series.

P., pastor, post, president, prince, proconsul, proper names with this initial, (Fr.) *Père* (father), (Lat.) *Papa* (Pope), *Pater* (Father), *pontifex* (a bishop), *populus* (people).

P, (mech.) power.

p, penny, pennies, pence (*see* **decimal currency**); prefix (pico-) meaning 10^{-12}.

p., page, participle, (naut.) passing showers, past, (ichth.) pectoral, pipe, (Fr.) *passé* (past), *pied* (foot), *pouce* (inch), *pour* (for), (Lat.) *partim* (in part), *per* (through), *pius* (holy), *pondere* (by weight), *post* (after), *primus* (first), *pro* (for).

p, (mech.) pressure; (It. mus.) *piano* (softly).

℔, *per* (by, for).

¶ (typ.), the paragraph mark, used to denote the commencement of a new paragraph (but in proof correction use symbol [ ]); also sixth footnote reference mark.

Π, π (Gr.), *see* **pi**.

P.A., personal assistant, Press Association, Publishers Association.

Pa., Pennsylvania, U.S. (off. abbr.).

p.a., *par amitié* (by favour), per annum (yearly).

Pa, protactinium (no point).

Paarl, Cape Province, S. Africa.

pabulum, food (not ital.).

pace/ (Lat.), with the consent of; — *tua*, with your consent.

pacha, *use* **pasha.**

pacha (Fr. m.), pasha.

Pacha of Many Tales, by Marryat, 1836.

pachymeter, instrument for measuring small thicknesses, *not* pacho-. *See also* **micrometer.**

package/, -s, abbr. **pkg.**

pack-drill (hyphen).

packet/, -ed, -ing.

pack-horse, — -saddle (hyphens).

packthread (one word).

pad, sheets of paper fastened on one edge, and removable singly.

Paderewski (Ignace Jan), 1860–1941, pianist, first Premier of Polish Rep., 1919.

padishah, a title applied to the Shah of Persia, the Sultan of Turkey, the Great Mogul, and the (British) Emperor of India; in Pers. *padshah.*

padlock (one word).

padre (It., Port., Sp.), father, applied also to a priest.

padre (colloq.), a chaplain.

padron/e (It.), a master, employer; *pl.* **-i.**

p. ae., *partes aequales* (equal parts).

paean, a song of triumph. *See also* **paeon, peon.**

paedagogy, *use* pe-.

paedeutics, science of education (U.S. **pai-**).

paediatrics, science of children's diseases (U.S. **pedi-**).

Paedobaptists, *not* Pe-.

paenology, *use* pe-.

paeon (Gr. and Lat. prosody), a foot of one long and three shorts. *See also* **paean, peon.**

paeony, *use* **peony.**

Paganini (Nicolò), 1784–1840, Italian violinist and composer.

paganize, *not* -ise.

page (typ.), type, or type and blocks, arranged for printing on one side of a leaf; *abbr.* **p.,** *pl.* **pp.** (*see also* **pagination**).

page (Fr. m.), a page-boy; (f.) page of a book.

paginate, to number pages consecutively.

pagination (typ.), the numbering of the pages of a book, journal, etc.; may be in headline or at foot of page; generally omitted on opening pages of chapters, main sections, etc. *See also* **preliminary matter.**

pag/ing, -inal.

Pagliacci, I, opera by R. Leoncavallo.

Pahang, *see* **Malaya, Federation of.**

Pahlanpur, Rajasthan, India, *use* **Pal-.**

paid, *abbr.* **pd.**

paideutics, *use* **paed-.**

paillasse (Fr. m.), a clown; (f.) a straw-mattress, in Eng. **palliasse.**

pailles/ (Fr. cook. f.), straws; *— de parmesan,* cheese-straws.

Pain (Barry Eric Odell), 1865–1928, English humorous writer. *See also* **Paine, Payn, Payne.**

pain (Fr. m.), bread.

Paine (Thomas), 1739–1809, English-born political philosopher and American patriot, author of *The Rights of Man. See also* **Pain, Payn, Payne.**

painim, a pagan, *use* **pay-.**

paint, painting.

paintings (titles of), when cited, to be in italic.

pair/, -s, *abbr.* **pr.**

pais (trial per), by the jury.

Paisano/ (Mex.), nickname for a Spaniard; *pl.* **-s.**

pajamas, U.S. form of **pyjamas.**

Pak., Pakistan, -i.

pakeha (Maori), a white man (not ital.).

Pakistan/, independent rep. 1956; **-i;** *abbr.* **Pak.** *See* **Bangladesh.**

Pal., Palestine.

palaeo-, prefix (= ancient) (U.S. **paleo-**).

palaeography, study of anc. modes of writing; *abbr.* **palaeog.**

palaeontology, study of fossils; *abbr.* **palaeont.;** (typ.) genera, species, and varieties to be italic, other divisions roman (*see also* **botany**).

palaeozoic, of the first geological period.

palaestra, a wrestling school, *not* pale-.

palais (Fr. m.), palace,

palankeen, *use* **palanquin.**

Palanpur, Rajasthan, India, *not* Pahl-.

palanquin, *not* -keen.

palate, roof of the mouth, sense of taste. *See also* **palette, pallet.**

palazz/o (It.), a palace; *pl.* **-i.**

pal/e, -ish.

paleo-, prefix, *use* **palaeo-.**

Palestine, *abbr.* **Pal.**

paletot, an overcoat (no accent, not ital.).

palette, artist's thin portable board for colour-mixing. *See also* **palate, pallet.**

palindrome, word or phrase reading the same backwards as forwards.

Palladian, of the Greek goddess **Pallas** (Minerva), hence characterized by wisdom or learning; also a Renaissance modification of the classic Roman style of architecture, from **Andrea Palladio,** 1518–80, Italian architect.

palladium, symbol **Pd** (no point).

pallet, straw-mattress, projection on a machine or clock, valve in an organ, platform for carrying bulk loads of paper, etc. *See also* **palate, palette.**

pallette, piece of armour; *use* **pallet.**

palliasse, a straw-mattress; in Fr. f. *paillasse.*

palliat/e, to alleviate, minimize; **-or.**

palm-oil (U.S. two words).

Palm Sunday, one before Easter (two words, caps.).

Palomar, Mount (observatory, telescope), Calif., U.S.

pam., pamphlet.

Pamir, tableland in Cent. Asia, *not* -irs.

pampas-grass (hyphen).

Pan., Panama.

panacea, a cure-all (not ital.).

Pan/-African, — -American (but **Pan American Airways, — — Union**), — **-Anglican** (hyphen, caps.).

panais (Fr. m.), parsnip.

Pandean pipes, *not* -aean (cap.).

pandect, a treatise covering the whole of a subject; (pl. cap.) the digest of Roman law made under the Emperor Justinian in the sixth century A.D.

pandemonium, utter confusion, *not* pandae-.

pandit/, a learned Hindu, *fem.* **-a; Pandit** (cap.) is used as a title. *See also* **pundit.**

P. & O., Peninsular and Oriental Steam Navigation Company.

panegyr/ic, a formal speech or essay of praise; **-ize,** *not* -ise.

panel/, -led, -ling (U.S. **-ed, -ing**).

panem et circenses (Lat.), bread and circus games.

paner (Fr. cook.), to dress with eggs and breadcrumbs.

panhandle (U.S.), a narrow projection of land; (colloq.) to beg.

Panhellen/ic, -ism (one word, cap.).

panic/, -ked, -ky.

Panislam (one word).

Panizzi (Sir Antonio), 1797–1879, Italian-born English librarian.

Panjab, *use* **Punjab.**

panjandrum, a mock title.

pannel, *use* **panel.**

pannikin, a little pan, *not* pana-, pani-, -can.

Pan-pipe, *not* Pan's — (cap., hyphen).

pans (Fr. dress. m. pl.), long floating ends of ribbon, also coat-tails.

Panslavic, *not* Panscl-.

pantagraph, *use* **panto-.**

Pantaloon, the lean old man of Italian comedy.

panta rhei (Gr.), all things are in a state of flux.

Pantheon, Rome.

Panthéon, Paris (**é**).

pantograph, a mechanical drawing machine, *not* panta-, penta-.

pantomime.

pantoufle (Fr. f.), a slipper; in Eng. **pantofle.**

Panzer/(Ger.), armoured; **— division.**

paon/ (Fr.), peacock; *fem.* **-ne.**

Papa (Lat.), Pope; abbr. **P.**

papal/, -ly.

Papandreou (Georgios), 1888–1968, Greek statesman.

papaw, *not* pawpaw, a small N. American deciduous tree, or its edible fruit. Also used, incorrectly, for **papaya.**

papaya, a trop. American evergreen tree, or its edible fruit. *See also* **papaw.**

paperback, a type of book (one word).

paper sizes, *see* **crown, demy, DIN, elephant, foolscap, imperial, large crown, medium, post, pott, royal, small royal.** *See also* **book sizes.**

papet/ier (Fr.), *fem. -ière,* a stationer.

Papier (Ger. n.), paper (cap.).

papier (Fr. m.), paper (not cap.).

papier mâché, moulded paper pulp (two words, U.S. **hyphen**).

papill/a, a small protuberance on a living surface; *pl.* **-ae** (not ital.).

papillon (Fr. m.), butterfly.

papoose, N. American Indian infant, *not* papp-.

Papst (Ger. m.), Pope (cap.).

papyr/us, a MS. on papyrus; *pl.* **-i.**

par, of exchange, etc. (no point).

par., paragraph, parallel, parenthesis, parish.

par (Fr.), by, out of, in, through.

Para., Paraguay.

para(s)., paragraph(s).

Parable of the Ten Virgins (caps.).

par/ accès (Fr.), by fits and starts; — *accident,* accidentally; — *accord,* by agreement.

paradisaical, *not* -iacal.

paraffin, *not* parra-, -fine.

paragon (typ.), old name for a size of type, about 20 pt.

paragraph, the matter between one break-line and the next; (typ.) in conversation, one for each fresh speaker or interruption. First line usually indented

one em. Last line should have more than five letters. When numbered 1, 2, clauses (1), (2). Abbr. **par., para.,** *pl.* **pars., paras.,** sign ¶, proof correction symbol [.

paragraph mark (¶) (typ.), may be used to indicate a new paragraph, but in proof correction use symbol [; sixth footnote reference mark.

Paraguay, *pron.* pa′ragwĭ, abbr. **Para.**

paraît pas (il n'y) (Fr.), there is no appearance of it.

paraît plus (il n'y) (Fr.), there remains no trace of it.

parakeet, *not* paraquet, -oquet, -okeet, parroquet.

paralipsis, drawing attention to a subject by affecting not to mention it, *not* -leipsis, -lepsis, -lepsy.

parallel/, abbr. **par.; -ed, -ing.**

parallèle (Fr. f.), parallel geom. lines; a fortification; in all other senses masc.

parallelepiped, a solid figure bounded by six parallelograms, *not* -ipiped, -opiped.

parallel mark (‖) (typ.), fifth footnote reference mark.

paralogize, to reason falsely, *not* -ise.

paralyse (U.S. **-yze**), *not* -ise, -ize.

Paramatta, *use* **Parra-.**

Paramecium (zool.), *not* -aecium, -oecium.

par amitié (Fr.), by favour; abbr. **p.a.**

para/noia *or* **-noea,** insanity characterized by delusions.

paraph, the flourish at the end of a signature.

paraphernalia, *pl.,* miscellaneous personal belongings.

paraquet, *use* **parakeet.**

paratroops, airborne soldiers trained to land by parachute.

par avance (Fr.), in advance.

parbleu! (Fr. colloq.), an exclamation of surprise.

parcel/, -led, -ling (U.S. -ed, -ing).

parcel post, *not* parcels.

parcen/ary (law), joint heirship; -er, joint heir.

parchment, inner split sheepskin prepared for writing; — -paper, imitation parchment.

parcimony, *use* parsi-.

par/ ci, par là (Fr.), here and there; — *complaisance*, out of politeness; — *dépit*, out of spite.

parenthes/is, *pl.* -es, abbr. parens., the upright curves ( ). *See also* brackets, punctuation X.

parenthesize, to insert as a parenthesis, *not* -ise.

parerg/on, a subsidiary work; *pl.* -a (not ital.).

par/ excellence (Fr.), pre-eminently; — *exemple*, for example, abbr. *p. ex.*; — *exprès*, by express; — *faveur*, by favour; — *force*, by superior strength.

pargana (Ind.), a parish, *not* pergunnah.

par hasard (Fr.), by chance, *not* — haz-.

parheli/on, a mock sun; *pl.* -a.

pariah (Ind.), one of low or no caste; a social outcast.

pari mutuel, a method of betting on horses (Fr. equivalent of totalisator).

pari passu (Lat.), at the same rate.

parish/, abbr. par.; — priest, abbr. P.P.

Parisian, of Paris (cap.); *Parisienne* (Fr. f.), a woman of Paris (cap.).

park, abbr. P, pk.

Park (Mungo), 1771–1806, Scottish traveller in Africa.

parka, Eskimo hooded jacket.

Parkinson's disease, shaking palsy, studied by James Parkinson (1755–1824).

Parkinson's Law, the law, facetiously expounded by C. N. Parkinson, that work expands to fill the time available for it.

Parl., parliamentary.

Parliament/ (cap.), abbr. Parl.; — House, Edin., the Scottish Law Courts. *See also* Assemblies.

parlour (U.S. -or).

Parmesan, a cheese made at Parma.

parochialize, *not* -ise.

parokeet, *use* parakeet.

parol (law), oral, not written, *not* -le.

parole (mil.), a watchword, prisoner's promise not to escape.

paroquet, *use* parakeet.

paroxysm, a fit of pain, passion, laughter.

par/ parenthèse (Fr.), by the way; — *précaution*, as a precaution.

parquetry, inlaid flooring; in Fr. f. *parqueterie*.

Parr (Thomas, 'Old'), 1483–1635, English centenarian.

parr, a young salmon, *not* par.

parrakeet, *use* parakeet.

Parramatta, N.S.W., *not* -mata, Para-.

Parratt (Sir Walter), 1841–1924, English organist.

parricide, murder(er) of a near relative or of a revered person. *See also* patri-.

Parrish's chemical food.

parroquet, *use* parakeet.

pars., paragraphs.

parsec (astron.), a unit of distance, 3·26 light years.

Parsee/, a descendant of the Zoroastrians who fled from Persia to India in the eighth century; *pl.* **-s**; *not* -si.

Parsifal, opera by Wagner, 1879.

parsimony, meanness, *not* parci-.

parsnip (hort.), *not* -ep.

part, abbr. **pt.**

part., participle.

parterre, a flower-bed, or garden (not ital.); also area in theatre between orchestra and audience.

partes aequales (Lat.), equal parts; abbr. **p. ae.**

Parthenon, temple at Athens.

Parthian arrow, shaft, *or* **shot,** one delivered when turning away (one cap.).

parti (Fr. m.), party (faction), match (marriage), resolution (good or bad).

particeps/ (Lat.), an accomplice; — *criminis,* a participator in crime.

participator, *not* -er.

participle, a verbal adjective; abbr. **p.** *or* **part.**

particoloured, variegated, *not* party- (one word).

particularize, *not* -ise.

particulier (Fr. m.), a private citizen.

partie/ (Fr. f.), part; — *carrée,* a party of two men and two women.

partim (Lat.), in part; abbr. **p.**

parti pris (Fr. m.), foregone conclusion, prejudice; *de* — —, deliberately.

partisan, an adherent of a party, (mil.) a member of a resistance movement, *not* -zan.

partout (Fr.), everywhere.

part/-song, — **-time** (hyphens).

party (Conservative, Labour, Liberal, etc.) (not cap.).

party-coloured, *use* **parti-.**

parure, a set of jewels.

parvenu/, *fem.* **-e,** *pl.* **-s,** an upstart (not ital.).

Pasadena, Calif., U.S.

Pas-de-Calais, dép. N. France (hyphens).

pas de/ deux (Fr. m.), dance for two: — — *quatre,* ditto four; — — *trois,* ditto three.

Pas de zèle! (Fr.), Don't be too zealous!

pasha (Turk.), a title placed *after* the name, *not* -cha, -shaw, bashaw; in Fr. m. *pacha.*

Pasha of three tails, the highest rank; then two tails, then one tail.

Pashtu, Afghan language, *use* **Pushtu.**

Pas possible! (Fr.), You don't say so!

pas redoublé (Fr. m.), doubled pace, a quickstep.

pass., passive.

passable, may be passed (*see also* **passi-**).

Passchendaele, Belgium, battle (1917).

pass/é (Fr.), *fem.* **-ée,** past, faded; abbr. **p.**

passementerie (Fr. f.), embroidery, *not* passi-.

passe-partout (Fr. m.), a master-key, permit, mount for picture (**passe-partout,** the anglicized form, incorrect and now obsolescent, meant the dark adhesive strip surrounding the picture).

pas seul (Fr. m.), dance for one person.

passible, susceptible. See also **passa-.**

passim (Lat.), here and there throughout.

Passion Week, follows Passion Sunday (fifth in Lent). Holy Week follows Palm Sunday.

pass-key (hyphen).

password (one word).

past, abbr. **p.**

pastel/, artist's crayon; **-list** (U.S. **-ist**). *See also* **pastille.**

Pasternak (Boris Leonidovich), 1890–1960, Russian novelist and poet. Nobel prize for literature (declined), 1958.

pasteurize, to sterilize, *not* -ise.

pastiche, medley.

pastille, confection, odorizer, *not* -il. *See also* **pastel.**

pastoral/e (mus.), a pastoral composition; *pl.* **-i.**

pat., patented.

Pata., Patagonia.

patchouli, perfume from Indian plant, *not* -ly.

pâte/ (Fr. cook. f.), paste; — *d'Italie,* vermicelli, macaroni; — *feuilletée,* puff pastry; — *frisée,* short pastry.

pâté/ (Fr. m.), a pie; — *de foie gras,* a spiced paste of goose-liver.

pâté (Eng.), a liver paste (not ital.).

patell/a (anat.), knee-cap; *pl.* **-ae;** adj. **patellar.**

paten, Eucharist bread-plate, *not* -in, -ine.

Patent Office, *pron.* păt′-ent; abbr. **Pat. Off.**

Pater (Lat.), Father; abbr. **P.**

paterfamilias, father of a family; *pl.* **patres-.**

paternoster (a), a muttered prayer, esp. the Lord's Prayer (one word).

pater patriae (Lat.), father of his country.

Paterson (William), 1658–1719, British founder of the Bank of England.

Paterson, N.J., U.S.

path., patholog/y, -ical.

Patiala, E. Punjab, India.

patin/, -e, *use* **paten.**

pâtiss/erie (Fr. f.), pastry; **-ier,** *fem.* **-ière,** pastry-cook.

patois, a dialect of the common people (not ital.).

Patres/ (Lat.), fathers, abbr. **PP.;** — *Conscripti,* Conscript Fathers, abbr. **PP.C.**

patria potestas (Rom. law), father's power over his family.

patricide, murder(er) of a father. *See also* **parri-.**

patrol/, -led, -ling.

patronize, *not* -ise.

patte/ (Fr. dress. f.), a decorative strap; — *de collet,* shoulder-strap.

Pattenmakers Company, *not* Pattern-.

Patteson (John Coleridge), 1827–71, British ecclesiastic, bishop of Melanesia, and there martyred.

Pattison (Mark), 1813–84, Rector of Lincoln Coll., Oxford.

Patton (George Smith), 1885–1945, U.S. general.

P.A.U., Pan American Union.

pauca verba (Lat.), few words.

pauperize, etc., *not* -ise.

Paus., Pausanias, Greek geographer, second century B.C.

pavan, a dance, *not* -ane, -en, -ian, -in; Fr. f. *pavane.*

pavé (Fr. m.), pavement, jewellery setting with stones close together.

pavement (U.S.), roadway; English pavement is U.S. sidewalk.

pavilion, *not* pavill-.

pavillon (Fr. m.), flag, bell of a trumpet, etc.

paviour, one who lays pavements, *not* -er, -ier; U.S. **-ior;** *also* **Paviors Company.**

Pavlova (Anna), 1885–1931, Russian ballet dancer.

pawn (chess), abbr. **P.**

pawpaw, *use* **papaw.**

pax vobiscum! (Lat.), peace be with you!

paxwax, the neck cartilages (not the many variations).

P.A.Y.E., pay as you earn.

paymaster, abbr. **paymr.,** *or* **P.M.** (one word).

Paymaster-General (caps., hyphen); abbr. **P.M.G.**

payment, abbr. **pt.**

Payn (James), 1830–98, English novelist and editor.

Payne (Edward John), 1844–1904, English historian; — **(John Howard),** 1791–1852, American playwright, wrote 'Home, Sweet Home'.

paynim, a pagan, *not* pai-.

pays (geog.), the country (not ital.).

Pays-Bas (Fr. m. pl.), the Netherlands (caps., hyphen).

P.B., *Pharmacopoeia Britannica,* Plymouth Brethren, Prayer Book.

Pb, *plumbum* (lead) (no point).

P.B.I. (mil. slang), (poor bloody) infantry(man).

P.C., Panama Canal, Parish Council, -lor, Police Constable (q.v.), Privy Council, -lor.

p/c, petty cash, prices current.

p.c., per cent, postcard.

P.C.S. (Sc.), Principal Clerk of Session.

P.D., *Pharmacopoeia Dublinensis* (Dublin Pharmacopoeia), Postal District (London), (Ger.) *Privatdozent* (university teacher).

Pd, palladium (no point).

pd., paid.

p.d., *per diem,* (elec.) potential difference.

P.D.A.D. (law), Probate, Divorce, and Admiralty Division.

P.D.S.A., People's Dispensary for Sick Animals.

P.E., *Pharmacopoeia Edin-*

burgensis (Edinburgh Pharmacopoeia), Port Elizabeth (Cape Province), Protestant Episcopal.

p.e., personal estate.

P.E.A., Portuguese East Africa.

peace/maker, -time (one word).

pea/cock, *fem.* **-hen;** (*young*) **-chick** (one word).

pea-green (hyphen).

pearl (in knitting), *use* **purl.**

pearl (typ.), old name for a size of type, about 4¾ pt.

Pearl Harbor, U.S. naval base, Hawaii, *not* Harbour.

Peary (Robert Edwin), 1856–1920, American Arctic explorer, first at N. Pole, 1909.

pease-pudding (hyphen).

peat-hag, a peat pit.

pebbl/e, -y.

P.E.C. *or* **pec** (no point), photo-electric cell.

peccadillo/, a trifling offence; *pl.* **-es.**

peccary, S. American mammal, *not* -i.

peccav/i (Lat.), I have erred; *pl.* **-imus.**

pêche (Fr. f.), fish/ery, -ing, peach; **pêche melba,** ice-cream and peaches, flavoured with liqueurs (not ital.).

péché (Fr. m.), a sin; *pécher,* to sin.

pêcher (Fr.), to fish.

peck/, -s, abbr. **pk** (no point).

pectoral (ichth.), abbr. **p.**

peculat/e, -or, embezzl/e, -er.

Ped. (mus.), pedal.

pedagog/ue, schoolmaster (derogatory); **-y, -ics,** science of teaching.

pedal/, -led, -ling (U.S. **-ed, -ing**).

pedlar, travelling vendor of small wares, *not* -er; U.S. **peddler.**

Pedobaptists, *use* **Pae-.**

Peeblesshire, abbr. **Peebles.**

peep-show (hyphen).

peewit, bird; *use* **pewit.**

Peggotty, in *David Copperfield.*

P.E.I., Prince Edward Island, Canada.

peignoir (Fr. m.), a woman's loose dressing-gown.

peine forte et dure (Fr. f.), severe punishment, a medieval judicial torture.

Peirce (Charles Sanders), 1839–1914, American mathematician, founder of philosophical pragmatism.

Peirse (Sir Richard H.), 1860–1940, British Admiral.

Peking/, China, *not* Peip-, -kin; **-ese,** a small dog, abbr. **peke** (not cap., no point).

pekoe, a black tea, *not* peckoe, pecco (not cap.).

pell-mell, confusedly; in Fr. *pêle-mêle.*

Peloponnesus, the modern Morea.

Pembrokeshire, abbr. **Pemb.**

pemmican, dried meat for travellers, *not* pemi-.

pen., peninsula.

penalize, *not* -ise.

Penang/, *see* **Malaya;** — **lawyer,** a type of walking-stick.

penchant, bias (not ital.).

pencil/, -led, -ling (U.S. -ed, -ing).

P.E.N. Club, an international association of writers (= Poets, Playwrights, Essayists, Editors, Novelists).

pendant, anything hanging.

pendent (adj.), suspended.

pendente lite (Lat.), during the suit.

pendule (Fr. m.), pendulum; (f.) clock.

pendulum/, *pl.* **-s.**

penetralia (Lat.), secrets.

pen-feather, quill, feather, *not* pin-, q.v.

penguin, a bird. *See also* **pinguin.**

penicillin (med.).

Penicilli/um (bot.), a genus of fungi, mould; *pl.* **-a** (ital.).

Penicuik, Midlothian.

Peninsular/ Campaign, SE. Virginia, 1862, in American Civil War; — **War,** Spain and Portugal, —1808–14, in Napoleonic Wars.

Penmaenmawr, Caernarvon.

pen-name (hyphen).

pennant (naut.), a piece of rigging, a flag.

pennon (mil.), a long narrow flag.

penn'orth (colloq.), a pennyworth.

Pennsylvania, off. abbr. **Pa.,** *not* Penn.

penny, *pl.* **pennies** when meaning the number of coins: **pence,** their value; abbr. *s.* and *pl.* **d.; new penny,** abbr. **p** (no point). *See* **decimal currency.**

penn/y, -iless.

penny-a-liner (hyphens).

pennyroyal (bot.), a kind of mint (one word).

pennyweight, 24 grains (approx. 1·55 g); abbr. **dwt** (no point).

penology, science of punishment, *not* pae-.

Penrhyn, Caernarvon, *also* Baron —.

Penryn, Cornwall.

pensée (Fr. f.), thought, maxim, *also* pansy; *arrière/-* —, a mental reservation, *pl.* — *-pensées.*

pension/ (Fr. f.), a boarding-house, school; *en* —, on boarding terms; *pensionnat* (m.), a boarding-school.

Pent., Pentecost.

pentagraph, *use* **panto-.**

Pentateuch/, first five books of the O.T.; **-al** (cap.).

Pentecost, Whit-Sunday; abbr. **Pent.**

pentecostal (not cap.).

pentstemon (bot.), *not* pens-.

penumbr/a, lighter shadow round dark shadow of an eclipse; *pl.* **-ae.**

peon, a servant. *See also* **paean, paeon.**

peony, a flower, *not* pae-.

P.E.P., Political and Economic Planning.

pepsin, an enzyme in gastric juice, *not* -ine.

Pepys (Samuel), 1633–1703, diarist and civil servant; *pron.* pēps.

per., period.

per (Lat.), by, for; abbr. **p.,** *or* ℔ ; *per accidens,* by accident; **per annum,** yearly, abbr. **p.a.,** *or* **per ann.** (not ital.); *per capita,* by the number of individuals.

Perak, *see* **Malaya, Federation of.**

perceiv/e, -able, -er.

per cent (two words), *see* **per cento.**

percentage (one word).

per/ cento (It.), per cent; — *centum* (Lat.), by the hundred, abbr. **per cent** (no point) *or* %; **per mille,** by the thousand, abbr. %₀.

perceptible, *not* -able.

Perceval, one of King Arthur's knights; — **(Spencer),** 1762–1812, English statesman.

perch, (rod or pole), 5·092 m; do not abbreviate.

perchance, perhaps.

perche (Fr. f.), perch (a fish), pole (stick).

percolat/e, -ing, -or.

per/ consequens (Lat.), consequently; — *contra,* on the other hand; — *curiam,* by the court.

perdendosi (mus.), dying away.

per diem (Lat.), daily.

perdreau/ (Fr. m.), a year-old partridge; *pl.* **-x.**

perdrix/ (Fr. f.), partridge, *pl. same;* — *blanche,* ptarmigan.

perdu/ (Fr.), *fem.* **-e,** concealed, lost.

Père (Fr. m.), R.C.C. father; abbr. **P.**

Père Lachaise, a Paris cemetery (two words, caps.).

per/ essentiam (Lat.), essentially; — *eundem,* by the same (judge).

perf., perfect, (stamps) perforated.

per fas aut (*or et*) *nefas* (Lat.), by fair means or (and) foul.

perfect, abbr. **perf.**

perfect binding, unsewn binding, q.v.

perfecter, one who perfects, *not* -or; (typ.) a printing press which prints both sides of the paper at one pass.

perfecting (typ.), printing the second side of a sheet.

perforated, abbr. **perf.**

perforce, of necessity (one word).

pergunnah (Ind.), parish; *use* **pargana.**

peridot, gem, *not* -te.

perigee/ (astr.), point of planet's, moon's, or satellite's orbit nearest the earth; *pl.* **-s;** abbr. **perig.**

Périgord (Fr. cook.), cooking based on truffles.

perine/um, -al (anat.).

per interim (Lat.), in the meantime.

period, abbr. **per.;** in typ. called the full point, or point (*see* **punctuation V**).

periodicals (**titles of**), when cited, to be italic.

peripatetic, walking about; (cap. P) Aristotelian (school of philosophy).

peripeteia, sudden reversal of fortune, *not* -tia (not ital.).

periphras/is, circumlocution; *pl.* **-es.**

periton/eum (anat.), **-eal, -itis.**

periphlitis (path.).

periwig, *not* perri-.

periwinkle, plant, and mollusc.

Perlis, *see* **Malaya.**

per mark (typ.), ℔.

per mensem (Lat.), monthly.

permis de séjour (Fr. m.), permit for residence.

permissible.

permit/, -ted, -ting.

per pais (Norman Fr.), by jury (= by the county).

per/ procurationem (Lat.), by procuration, abbr. *per pro.* or *p.p.;* — *quod* (Lat.), whereby.

Pers., Persia, -n.

pers., person, -al, -ally.

per saltum (Lat.), at a leap; — *se,* by himself, herself, itself, *or* themselves.

Persia/, -n, abbr. **Pers.**

persian morocco (bind.) (no caps.).

Persian type has four forms, Naskhi, Tâleek, Nustâleek, Shekestah.

persiflage, banter (not ital.).

per sign (typ.), ℔.

persil (Fr. m.), parsley.

persimmon (bot.), the date-plum, *not* -simon.

persist/ence (in Fr. f. *-ance*), **-ency, -ent.**

persona/ grata (Lat.), an acceptable person; — *gratissima,* a most acceptable person; — *ingrata,* — *non grata,* unacceptable person.

personalty (law), personal estate, *not* -ality.

personnel, staff of persons employed in any service.

persp., perspective.

perspicac/ity, clearness of understanding; adj. **-ious.**

perspicu/ity, clearness of statement; adj. **-ous.**

per stirpes (Lat.), by the number of families.

persuasible.

per thousand, abbr. ‰.

per totam curiam (Lat.), unanimously.

Peru., Peruvian.

peruke, a wig, *not* -que.

per viam (Lat.), by way of.

pes (Lat.), a foot; *pl.* **pedes.**

Peshawar, W. Pakistan, *not* -ur.

peshwa, a Maratha chief (not ital.).

peso, Spanish dollar.

pessimi exempli (Lat.), likely to prove a bad example.

Pestalozzi (Johann Heinrich), 1745–1827, Swiss educationist.

Pesth, *use* **Budapest.**

Pet., 1, 2, First, Second Epistle of Peter (N.T.).

Pétain (Henri Philippe) 1856–1951, French Marshal.

petal/, -led (U.S. **-ed**).

Peterlee, Co. Durham, 'new town' 1948.

Peter Schlemihl, a well-meaning unlucky fellow (title of a novel by Chamisso).

Peter's pence, a small tax on English R.C.s, abolished by Henry VIII; now a world-wide voluntary contribution to the Pope on St. Peter's Day.

petit/ (Fr.), *fem.* **-e,** small; — *bourgeois,* lower middle class; — *comité,* a small party; — *curé,* French curate; — *déjeuner,* breakfast; — *four,* a small fancy cake (*pl.* —*s fours*).

petitio principii (Lat.), begging the question.

petit/*-lait* (Fr.), whey;
— *-maître*, a fop;
-e-maîtresse, a female
dandy, *pl.* **-es-maîtresses**;
— *pain*, a roll.
petits/ *pois* (Fr. m.),
green peas; — *soins*, little
attentions.
petit verre (Fr. m.), a glass
of liqueur.
Petrarc/h (Francesco),
1304–74, Italian scholar and
poet; adj. **-an.**
petrel, a bird, *not* -erel.
Petriburg., signature of
Bp. of Peterborough (full
point).
Petrograd, name given to
St. Petersburg during the
First World War; now
called Leningrad.
petrol, refined petroleum
(U.S. **gasoline, gas**).
petrology, abbr. **petrol.**
Pettie (John), 1839–93,
Scottish painter.
pettifog/, to cavil in legal
matters; **-ger, -gery, -ging.**
petty/ cash, abbr. **p/c;**
— **officer** (two words),
abbr. **P.O.**
peu à peu (Fr.), little by little.
peut-être (Fr.), perhaps.
pewit, a bird, *not* pee-.
p. ex. (Fr.), *par example* (for
instance).
P.F., Procurator-fiscal.
Pf. (Ger.), *Pfennig.*
p.f. (Fr.), *pour féliciter* (to
congratulate).
pf (It. mus.), *più forte* (a little
louder) or *piano forte* (soft,
then loud).
pfennig, a small German
coin, $\frac{1}{100}$ of a mark; Ger. m.,
cap., *Pfennig.*
Pfingsten (Ger.), Whitsun-
tide; *Pfingstmontag*,
Whit-Monday.
Pfleiderer (Edmund),
1842–1903; — **(Otto)**,
1839–1908, German
philosophers.

p.f.s.a., *pour faire ses adieux*
(to say good-bye).
Pfund (Ger. n.), pound
(cap.); abbr. *Pfd.*
p.f.v., *pour faire visite* (to
make a call).
P.G., paying guest.
pg, picogramme (no point).
P.G.A., Professional Golfers'
Association.
P.G.M. (Freemasonry, Odd
Fellows), Past Grand
Master.
pH, measure of hydrogen
ion concentration.
phaenogam (bot.), *not* phe-;
but use **phanerogam.**
phaenomenon, *use* phe-.
Phaethon (Gr. myth.), son
of Helios, *not* Phaë-, -ton,
but pron. fā'-i-thon (not a
diphthong).
phaeton, a carriage; *pron.*
fā'-i-tn *or* fā'-tn.
phalan/x, a compact body of
men; *pl.* **-xes**; bot. or
biol. *pl.* **-ges.**
phall/us (bot. and comp.
relig.), *pl.* **-i.**
phantasmagoria/, a shifting
scene of real or imagined
figures; *pl.* **-s.**
phantasy, etc., *use* **fan-.**
phantom, *not* f-.
Phar., pharmacopoeia.
Pharaoh, *not* -oah.
pharisaic/, -al (not cap.).
Pharisee/, one of an anc.
Jewish sect, strict observers
of religious forms, hence a
self-righteous person; *pl.* **-s.**
pharm., pharmaceutical,
pharmacy.
pharmacol., pharmacology.
pharmacopoeia/, a book
describing drugs, abbr. **P.**
(*see* **B.P.**) *or* **Phar.**; —
Dublinensis (of Dublin),
abbr. **P.D.**; —
Edinburgensis (of
Edinburgh), abbr. **P.E.**;
— *Londiniensis* (of
London), abbr. **P.L.**

pharyn/x, the cavity behind the larynx; *pl.* **-ges; -gal, -geal, -gitis.**

Ph.B., *Philosophiae Baccalaureus* (Bachelor of Philosophy).

Ph.D., *Philosophiae Doctor* (Doctor of Philosophy).

Phèdre, by Racine, 1677.

Phenician, *use* **Phoe-.**

phenix, *use* **phoe-.**

phenogam, *see* **phaeno-.**

phenomen/on, an appearance; *pl.* **-a,** *not* phae- (not ital.).

Phidias, 500–432 B.C., Athenian sculptor; in Gr. **Pheid-.**

Phil., Philippine, Epistle to Philippians (N.T.).

Philadelphia, abbr. **Phila.**

philatel/y, stamp-collecting; **-ic, ically, -ist.**

Philem., Philemon (N.T.).

philhellenic, friendly to the Greeks (not cap.).

philibeg, *use* **filibeg.**

Philip (George) & Son, map publishers. *See also* **Phill-.**

Philippe, Kings of France.

Philippians, Epistle to, abbr. **Phil.**

philippic, any of the speeches of Demosthenes against Philip of Macedon or of Cicero against Antony, a bitter invective (not cap.).

philippina, a game of forfeits, *not* fillipeen, philipena, phillipine, philopoena.

Philippine Islands, abbr. **P.I.**

Philippines, The, independent 1946, inhabited by **Filipinos.**

Philippopolis, Bulgaria; in Bulg. **Plovdiv.**

Philipps, family name of Viscount St. Davids. *See also* **Phill-.**

Philips (Ambrose), 1675–1749, English writer of

pastoral and nursery poems, hence 'namby-pamby'; — **(Edward,** 1630–94, and **John,** 1631–1706), Milton's nephews; — **(John),** 1676–1709, parodist of Milton. *See also* **Phill-.**

Philister (Ger.), a townsman, a non-student; *pl. same* (cap.).

Philistin/e, an anc. inhabitant of SW. Palestine; (not cap.) a person indifferent to culture; **-ism.**

Phillip (Colin B.), 1855–1932, English painter; — **(John),** 1817–67, English painter. *See also* **Philip.**

phillipina, *use* **philipp-.**

Phillipps (James Orchard), 1820–89, English antiquary and Shakespearian scholar; — **(Sir Thomas),** 1792–1872, English book-collector. *See also* **Philipps.**

Phillips (Sir Claud), 1846–1924, English art critic; — **(John Bertram),** b. 1906, English Bible translator; — **(Stephen),** 1864–1915, English poet; — **(Wendell),** 1811–84, American abolitionist. *See also* **Philips.**

Phillpotts (Eden), 1862–1960, English novelist and dramatist; — **(Henry),** 1778–1869, Bp. of Exeter. *See also* **Philpott.**

philosophers' stone, to change base metals to gold, *not* 's.

philosophize, *not* -ise.

Philpott (Henry), 1807–92, Bp. of Worcester. *See also* **Phillpotts.**

Phil. Soc., Philological Society of London, Philosophical Society of America.

Phil. Trans., the *Philosophical Transactions of the Royal Society of London.*

philtre (love), U.S. **-er.**

Phiz, illustrator of Dickens, *see* **Browne (Hablot Knight).**

phlebitis, inflammation of the veins.

phobia/, a morbid fear; *pl.* **-s.**

Phoebus, Apollo.

Phoenician, *not* Phe-.

phoenix, myth. bird, rose rejuvenated from its own ashes, *not* phen-.

phon., phonetics.

phone, *net* 'phone.

phonol., phonology.

phosphor/us, symbol **P** (no point); adj. **-ous.**

phosphuretted, *not* -eted, -oretted.

photo/, photograph (no point); *pl.* **-s.**

photo/composition, -setting (typ.), setting copy photographically.

photog., photograph/y, -ic.

photograph/e (Fr. m. and f.), photographer; *-ie* (f.), photograph, -y.

photogravure (typ.), intaglio printing process; abbr. **gravure.**

photolithography (typ.), the photographic processes for making a plate for printing by offset-lithography; abbr. **photolitho** (no point).

photom., photometr/y, -ical.

photomicrography, photography of objects enlarged under a microscope. *See* **microphotography.**

photomontage, *see* **montage.**

phr., phrase.

phren., phrenology, study of surface of cranium as index of mental faculties.

phrenetic, delirious, frantic, *not* fren-.

phrenitic, affected with phrenitis, inflammation of the brain.

phrensy, *use* **frenzy.**

phthisis, tuberculosis.

phyl/um, a main division of the animal or vegetable kingdom; *pl.* **-a.**

phys., physical, physician, physics.

physic/, -ked, -king.

physiol., physiolog/y, -ical, -ist.

physique, constitution (not ital.).

physique (Fr. f.), physics (natural philosophy).

P.I., Philippine Islands.

pi (typ.), *use* **pie.**

pi, Gr. *Π*, (math.) continued product; π, ratio of circumference to diameter of circle, or 3·14159265 . . .

pianissimo (It. mus.), very soft; abbr. *pp.*

pianississimo (It. mus.), as softly as possible; abbr. *ppp.*

piano (mus.), softly; abbr. *p.*

pianoforte/, mus. instrument, *pl.* **-s;** usu. abbr. **piano/** (no point), *pl.* **-s.**

piast/re, small Egyptian, Spanish, Turkish coin (not ital.); U.S. **-er.**

Piat (P.I.A.T.), Projector Infantry Anti-Tank (portable weapon).

piazz/a (It.), an open square, *pl.* **-e** (not ital.); U.S., a veranda, *pl.* **-as.**

P.I.B., Prices and Incomes Board.

pibroch, an air on the bagpipe, *not* the bagpipe itself.

Pica, the ordinal of the Latin Church (formerly printed in pica type).

pica (typ.), the standard for typographic measurement, equals 12 pt. or about one-sixth of an inch; also an old name for a size of type, about 12 pt.

picaresque, of a style of fiction describing the life of an (amiable) rogue (not ital.).

Picasso (Pablo), 1881–1973, Spanish painter.

picayune, a small U.S. coin pre-1857, any trifling coin, person, or thing; (adj.) trifling.

piccalilli, a pickle.

piccaninny, Negro infant, *not* pica-; U.S. **picka-**.

piccolo/, the smallest flute; *pl.* **-s.**

pick (typ.), a dirty letter; also a measurement of the surface strength of paper.

pickaxe (one word).

Pickelhaube (Ger. f.), former infantry helmet (cap.).

picket/, (mil. or in industrial disputes) a man or men placed to watch for approaching enemies, *not* piq-, picq-; *also* verb, **-ed, -ing.**

pick-me-up, a stimulant (hyphens); *pl.* **-ups.**

pickpocket (one word).

picnic/, -ked, -king.

pico-, prefix meaning 10^{-12}, abbr. **p** (no point).

pictures (titles of), when cited, to be in italic.

pidgin English, Chinese jargon, from *pidgin* (business), *not* pigeon — (two words, one cap.).

pie (typ.), type which has been upset, *not* pi.

piebald, of two colours in irregular patches, usu. of horses, usu. black and white; *not* pye-. *See also* **skewbald.**

pièce/ (Fr. f.), a piece, play, etc.; — *de conviction*, document used as evidence; — *de résistance*, the principal dish at a meal; — *d'occasion*, a work composed for a special occasion; — *justificative*, document used as evidence in favour.

piecemeal, one portion at a time (one word).

pied/ (Fr. m.), a foot, abbr. **p.**; — *-à-terre*, an occasional residence, *pl.* *pieds-* — - — (hyphens).

Pierce (Franklin), 1804–69, President of U.S. 1853–7.

Pierce the Ploughman's Crede, anon. about 1394. *See also* **Piers.**

Pierian Spring, the fountain of the Muses in Thessaly.

Pierides, the nine Muses.

pierr/ot, seaside entertainer derived from French pantomime; *fem.* **-ette.**

Piers Plowman (*The Vision of William concerning*), by W. Langland, first ed. 1362. *See also* **Pierce.**

pietà, representation of dead Christ in his Mother's arms.

Pietermaritzburg, S. Africa.

pietr/a dur/a (It.), a stone mosaic; *pl.* **-e, -e.**

pigeon-hol/e, -ed (hyphen).

pigmy, one of a dwarf race of Cent. Africa, a dwarf. (This spelling is displacing the more correct **pygmy**, cf. **gipsy**.)

pigst/y, *pl.* **-ies** (one word).

Pike's Peak, Rocky Mountains, U.S. (apos.).

Piketberg (off. spelling), Cape Province, *not* Piquet-.

pilaff, admissible spelling for the Mediterranean version of **pilau**, q.v.

pilau, Oriental or Turkish dish of rice boiled with fowl, meat, or fish, and spices and raisins, *not* pill-, -aw, -ow (not ital.).

pilot/, -ed, -ing.

Piloty (K. von), 1826–86, German painter.

Pilsen (Czechoslovakia); in Czech. **Plzeň.**

Pilsener, a light beer (cap.).

Pilsudski (Joseph), 1867–1935, Polish general, first President of Poland, 1918.

pimento, allspice, *not* -a.

Pinakothek (Ger. from Gr.), picture-gallery.

pince-nez, spring eye-glasses (not ital., hyphen).

pincers, a tool, *not* pinch-.

Pindar, 522–443 B.C., Greek poet; abbr. **Pind.**

Pindar (**Peter**), 1738–1819, pen-name of Dr. J. Wolcot.

pineapple (one word).

Pinero (**Sir Arthur Wing**), 1855–1934, dramatist; *pron.* pin-ēr′ō.

pin-feather, small feather, *not* pen-, q.v.

pinguin, W. Indian plant or fruit.

pinscher, a breed of dog, *not* pinch-.

Pinsuti (**Ciro**), 1829–88, Italian composer.

pint/, -s, abbr. **pt.**

pintade (Fr. f.), guineafowl; Eng. **pintado/,** *pl.* **-s,** is also a kind of petrel.

Pinturicchio, nickname of **Bernardino di Betto,** 1454–1513, Italian painter.

pinxit (Lat.), he, *or* she, painted it; abbr. *pnxt.* or *pinx.*

pipe, a cask, a wine measure of about 100 galls.; abbr. **p.**

Pippa Passes, by R. Browning, 1841.

pipy, like, *or* having, pipes, *not* -ey.

piquant/ (Fr.), *fem.* **-e,** sharp.

pique, resentment; a score in piquet.

piqué, a thick cotton fabric (not ital.).

piqué (Fr.), (of wine) slightly sour; (mus.) short, detached; (cook.) larded.

piquet, a card game, *not* picq-.

Piquetberg, *use* **Piket-.**

P.I.R.A., Paper and Board, Printing and Packaging Industries Research Association.

piragua, S. American dug-out canoe, *not* periagua, pirogue.

piranha, ferocious S. American fish, *not* per-, -ai, -aya.

pirrauru, Australian aborigine's supplementary husband or wife.

pis aller (Fr. m.), a makeshift.

piscin/a, a fish-pond; stone basin and drain in a niche in church, for disposing of water used in washing the chalice, etc.; *pl.* **-ae.**

Pissarro (**Camille**), 1831–1903, French painter.

pistachio/, a nut; *pl.* **-s;** not -acho.

pitance, *use* **pitt-.**

pit-a-pat, with palpitation, *not* pitpat, pity-, pittypat (hyphens).

pitchfork (one word).

pitchstone (geol.) (one word).

Pitman (**Sir Isaac**), 1813–97, English inventor of shorthand.

pittance, an allowance, esp. a small one, *not* pita-.

Pitti (**Palazzo**), art gallery, Florence.

Pittsburgh, Pa., U.S., *not* -burg.

più (It.), more.

pius (Lat.), holy; abbr. **p.**

Pix, *use* **Pyx.**

pix/y, a small fairy, *not* -ie; **-ilated,** bewildered, *not* pixy-led.

pizzicato (mus.), pinched, plucked; abbr. *pizz.*

P.J., presiding judge, Probate Judge.

pk., park, peak, peck, -s.

PK, psychokinesis (no point).

pkg., package, -s.

P.K.T.F., Printing and Kindred Trades Federation.

P.L., Paymaster Lieutenant, *Pharmacopoeia Londiniensis* (London Phar.), Poet Laureate, Primrose League.

P/L. (one point), Profit and Loss.

Pl., Plate, -s.

pl., place, plural.

P.L.A., Port of London Authority.

place aux dames! (Fr.), ladies first!

placebo/, vespers for the dead; (med.) a medicine given to humour the patient; *pl.* -s.

placet (Lat.), it pleases, permission granted.

Place Vendôme, a square in Paris.

placket (dress.), an opening.

plafond, a ceiling, esp. decorated (not ital.).

plagiarize, adopt another's writings, *not* -ise.

plagu/e, -ily, -y.

Plaid Cymru, Welsh nationalist party.

plain sailing, (fig.) easy work. *See also* **plane sailing** (naut.).

plain-song, vocal music, unison, in medieval modes (hyphen).

plaintiff, abbr. plf.

plaister, *use* plas-.

planchet, a coin-blank.

planchette, small board on castors and a pencil-point, used as a medium for automatic writing and 'spirit-messages'.

Planck constant, h $(6 \cdot 6256 \times 10^{-34} \text{Js})$.

Planck's Law of Radiation, the quantum theory, from **Max Planck,** 1858–1947, German physicist.

plane, *not* 'plane.

plane sailing (naut.), calculation of a ship's position on the assumption that it is moving on a plane surface (two words). *See also* **plain sailing.**

planetary signs, *see* **astronomy.**

plankton, microscopic drifting organic life found in water. *See* **benthos** *and* **nakton.**

planographic (typ.), a printing process based on a flat surface, as offset, q.v.

Plantagenet, patronymic of the English sovereigns from 1154 to 1485.

Plantin (Christophe), 1518–89, French printer.

plaster (sticking-), *not* plaist-.

plastron (Fr. dress. m.), a bodice front.

Plate/, -s, (cap. when enumerated in book, etc.), abbr. **Pl.**

plate, (typ.) an electro, stereo, or illustration; (photog.) **whole —,** $8\frac{1}{2} \times 6\frac{1}{2}$ in., **half- —,** $6\frac{1}{2} \times 4\frac{3}{4}$, **quarter- —,** $4\frac{1}{4} \times 3\frac{1}{4}$.

plateau/, an elevated plain; *pl.* -x (not ital.).

plate-glass (hyphen).

platinize, to coat with platinum, *not* -ise.

platinum, symbol Pt (no point).

Platonic (cap. when in hist. or philos. contexts); **platonic love** (not cap.).

Platt-Deutsch, Low German.

platypus/, the Australian duck-bill; *pl.* -es.

platyrrhine, broad-nosed (of monkeys), *not* -yrhine.

plausible, *not* -able.

Plautus (Titus Maccius), 254–184 B.C., Roman dramatist; abbr. **Plaut.**

play/bill, -goer (one word).

plays (titles of), when cited to be in italic. *See also* **quotations.**

playwright (one word).

play-writer (hyphen).

plaza/ (Sp.), a public square; *pl.* -s (not ital.).

pleasur/e, -able.

plebeian, vulgar, common, *not* -bian.

plebiscite, a vote of the people (no accent, not ital.); in Fr. m. **plé-.**

plebiscit|um (Lat.), a decree of the *plebs*; *pl.* **-a.**

plebs (Lat.), the populace.

Pleiad (Gr. myth.), one of the seven daughters of Atlas; any brilliant group of seven, such as the French poets of the late sixteenth century (in Fr. f. *pléiade*); *pl.* **Pleiades,** a constellation.

plein air (Fr. m.), the open air.

Plen., plenipotentiary.

pleno jure (Lat.), with full authority.

plethora, unhealthy repletion.

pleur|a, a membrane lining the thorax or enveloping the lungs; *pl.* **-ae; -isy,** inflammation of same.

pleuro-pneumonia (hyphen).

plexus|, a network (of nerves, etc.); *pl.* **-es.**

plf., plaintiff.

plie (Fr. f.), plaice.

Plimsoll line (naut.).

plimsolls, rubber-soled canvas shoes.

Plinlimmon, *use* **Plynlimon.**

plis creux (Fr. dress. m. pl.), box-pleats.

plissé (Fr. m.), gathering, kilting, or pleating.

plod|, -der, -ding.

plough, (U.S.) **plow.**

plum|, -my.

plumb, vertical.

plum pudding (two words).

Plunket, family name of Baron Plunket.

Plunkett, family name of Earl of Fingall, and of Barons Dunsany and Louth.

pluperfect, abbr. **plup.**

plural|, abbr. **pl.; -ize.** *not* -ise.

plurals of abbreviations, as M.P.s, B.Litt.s (no apos.).

plus| (Lat.), more; — **mark,** that of addition, +.

plus tôt (Fr.), sooner.

Pluto (Rom. myth.), the god of the underworld.

PLUTO (no points), Pipe Line under the Ocean (Second World War).

plutonium, symbol **Pu** (no point).

plutôt (Fr.), rather.

Plutus (Gr. myth.), personi. fication of riches.

pluvier (Fr. m.), plover.

pluviometer, rain-gauge, *not* pluvia-.

Plymouth Brethren, religious sect; abbr. **P.B.**

Plynlimon, Welsh mountain, *not* Plin-, -limmon.

P.M., paymaster, postmaster, post-mortem, Prime Minister, Provost-Marshal.

p.m. (Lat.), *post meridiem* (afternoon) (not ital.)

Pm, promethium (no point).

pm., premium, premolar.

pm, picometre (no points).

P.M.G., Paymaster-General, Postmaster-General.

p.m.h., production per man-hour.

p.n., promissory note.

P.N.E.U., Parents' National Educational Union.

pneumatic, relating to air or gases, abbr. **pneum.**

pneumon|ic pertaining to the lungs; **-ia,**

pnxt., *pinxit* (he, *or* she, painted it).

Po, polonium (no point).

P.O., petty officer (R.N.), pilot officer (R.A.F.), postal order, post office.

pocket envelope, one in which the entry is on the short side.

pocket-handkerchief (hyphen).

poco| (It.), a little; — *a poco,* little by little.

pococurante, apathetic, careless (one word, not ital.).

P.O.D., pay on delivery, Post Office Department.

P.O.D., *Pocket Oxford Dictionary.*

podestà, an Italian municipal magistrate.

Podsnappery, British philistinism, from Mr. Podsnap in Dickens's *Our Mutual Friend.*

podzol/, acid sandy soil deficient in humus, *not* -sol; **-ization,** *not* -isation.

Poe (Edgar Allan), 1809–49, American writer.

poêle (Fr. m.), pall, stove; (f.) frying-pan.

poems (titles of), when cited, to be roman quoted; but those long enough to form a separate publication should be in italic. *See also* **quotations.**

poet., poetic, -al, poetry.

Poet Laureate (caps., two words); abbr. **P.L.,** *see* **Austin, Betjeman, Bridges, Cibber, Masefield, Southey, Tennyson.**

poetry (typ.), to be centred on longest line, unless such line is disproportionately long, in which case centre poetry optically; turn-over lines to be one em more than greatest indention of poem; a grave-accented *è* may be used to show that an otherwise mute syllable is to be separately pronounced, as *raisèd*; when verses are numbered, no point after the figure; **poetry quotations** should usually be set in a smaller size type and without quotation marks.

Poets' Corner, Westminster Abbey (caps.).

pogrom, an organized massacre, esp. of Russian Jews.

poignard, *use* **poniard.**

poilu, name for the French soldier.

poinsettia (botany), *not* point-.

point (typ.), all marks of punctuation, especially the full stop. *See also* **compass, point system, punctuation VI.**

point-blank (hyphen).

point/ d'appui (Fr. m.), a basis of operations; — ***d'attaque,*** basis of offensive operations.

Point-de-Galle, Ceylon (hyphens).

point et virgule (Fr.), the semicolon.

point system (typ.), the Anglo-American standard by which the bodies of all types shall be multiples, or divisions, of the twelfth of a pica, which is theoretically the sixth of an inch (72 metric points = 1 inch); abbr. **pt.**

pois (Fr. m. sing. and pl.), pea.

poisson (Fr. m.) fish; — ***d'avril,*** April fool.

poivre (Fr. m.), pepper.

Pol., Poland, Polish.

Poland, abbr. **Pol.;** in Pol. **Polska,** in Fr. **Pologne,** in Ger. **Polen.**

polarize, to restrict vibrations of light or other electromagnetic waves to one plane; (elec., mag., chem.), to separate positive and negative charges; (fig.) to give special meaning or unity of direction to; *not* -ise.

pole, *see* **perch.**

Pole Carew, *pron.* pool kā′rĭ.

polecat (one word).

pol. econ., political economy.

Police (Ger.), ***police*** (Fr.), policy of insurance. *See also* ***Polizei.***

police/ constable, — sergeant (no hyphens), abbr. **p.c., p.s.** Caps. when preceding a name, but newspapers usually print **P.c.** or **P/C,** to avoid confusion with initials.

police state (two words), a totalitarian one controlled by political police.

polichinelle (Fr. m.), puppet, buffoon.

poliomyelitis, infantile paralysis; abbr. **polio** (no point).

Polish, abbr. **Pol.**; (typ.) has 24 letters as in Eng. without *q* and *v*; ą, ç, ć, ń, ó, ś, ź, ż, and ł, both l.c. and caps. In dividing words the letters *ch, cz, dz (dż), rz,* and *sz* should not be separated.

polit., political, politics.

politesse (Fr. f.), politeness.

political economy, abbr. **pol. econ.**

polity, organization as a state, esp. in a particular form, e.g. monarchy, republic, confederation; *not* = policy.

Polizei (Ger. f.), police (cap.). *See also* **Police.**

pollock *or* **pollack,** sea-fish.

Pollock (Sir Frederick), 1845–1937, Prof. of law; — **(Walter Herries),** 1850–1926, writer.

Pollok (Robert), 1799–1827, Scottish poet.

Pollokshaws, near Glasgow.

pollster, sampler of public opinion (*see also* **psephologist**).

polonium, symbol **Po** (no point).

polyanthus/ (bot.), *not* -os; *pl.* **-es.**

Polybius, Greek historian, 200–120 B.C.; abbr. **Polyb.**

polyglot, *not* -ott.

polyhedr/on, *not* polye-; *pl.* **-a.**

Polyhymnia (Gr.), muse of rhetoric.

Polyolbion, by Drayton, 1613–22.

polyp/ *or* **polype/** (zool.), *pl.* **-s.**

polyp/us (path.), *pl.* **-i.**

polytechnic/, concerned with many technical subjects; — **school;** — **institution** (caps. when the title of a particular college).

polythene, commercial name for polyethylene.

polyzo/on (zool.), *pl.* **-a.**

pomade, preparation for the hair, *not* pomm-.

pomelo, a fruit, the shaddock, *not* pumm-.

Pommard, *not* Pomard; a Burgundy wine.

pommel/ -led, -ling (verb.), to pound with the fists; *often* **pummel.**

pommel (noun), knob, saddle-bow; *not* pummel.

pommes/ (Fr. f. pl.), apples; — *de terre,* potatoes.

Pompeian, of Pompeii.

ponctuation (Fr. f.), punctuation.

pondere (Lat.), by weight; abbr. **p.**

Pondicherry, India; in Fr. **Pondichéry.**

poniard, a dagger, *not* poign-, poin-.

pons/ (Lat.), a bridge, *pl.* *pontes;* — *asinorum,* bridge of asses, Euclid, i. 5.

Pontacq, a white wine.

Pontefract, *obsolesc. pron.* pomfret.

pontif/ex (Lat.), a bishop. abbr. **P.;** *pl.* **-ices.**

pont/iff -ifical.

Pont-l'Évêque, a French town; (m.) a cheese.

pood (Russ.), 36 lb. Eng.

Pool, Leeds.

Poole, Dorset.

Poole (W. F.), 1821–94, of *Poole's Index.*

Poona, Bombay, *not* -ah.
poorhouse (one word).
Poor Law (two words, caps.).
poor-rate (hyphen, no caps.).
pop., popular, population.
pop (noun), popular music;
(adj.) popular, *as in* **pop art**
(no point).
Pope (**the**) (cap.).
Pope-Joan, a card game
(hyphen, two caps.).
popularize, *not* -ise.
population, abbr. **pop.**
populus (Lat.), people;
abbr. **P.**
porc (Fr. m.), pork, pig.
Porchester Terrace, London. *See also* **Port-.**
Porson, a Greek type-face.
Porson (**Richard**), 1759–
1808, English Greek scholar.
Port., Portug/al, -uese.
Port au Prince, Haiti.
Port aux Basques,
Newfoundland.
Portchester, Hants. *See also*
Porch-.
Porte, the Turkish Court
and Government; more
fully **the Sublime —.**
porte/-cochère (Fr. f.),
a carriage entrance; —
-***crayon*** (Fr. m.), a pencil-
holder.
Port Elizabeth, Cape
Province; abbr. **P.E.**
portentous, *not* -ious.
Porter (**William Sydney**),
see **Henry** (**O.**).
Port Glasgow, Renfrew.
portico/, *pl.* **-es; -ed.**
portière (Fr. f.), door-
curtain, a portress, carriage
door, *or* window.
portmanteau/, *pl.* **-x** (not
ital.).
Porto Bello, Panama, *use*
Puerto Bello.
Portobello, near Edinburgh
(one word).
Porto Rico, *use* **Puerto Rico.**
Portpatrick, Wigtown (one
word).

portray, *not* pour-.
Port-Royal, monastery
(hyphen).
Port Royal, Jamaica; *also*
S. Carolina, U.S. (no
hyphen).
Port Salut, a cheese (no
hyphen).
Portugal, abbr. **Port.** (*see
also* **Assemblies**).
Portuguese, abbr. **Port.;**
(typ.) alphabet has 25 letters
as in Eng., without *w*. The
vowels *a*, *o* may have a til
(curved mark) over, as João,
põem. The acute accent, the
circumflex, and ç as in Fr.,
are used sometimes.
Portuguese East Africa,
abbr. **P.E.A.**
pos., positive.
P.O.S.B., Post Office Savings
Bank.
pos/e, -ed, -ing.
Posen, Poland; in Pol.
Poznań.
poseu/r (Fr.), *fem.* **-se,**
a prig, one who poses.
posology (med.), study of
dosages.
poss., possess/ion, -ive.
posse comitatus (Lat.), the
county force.
possessive case:
1. The apostrophe for this
must be used only for
nouns; not for the
pronouns hers, its, ours,
theirs, yours.
2. For nouns in the singular
and plural that end in any
letter but *s*, the apostrophe
must *precede* the *s*, as
President's house, men's
hats.
3. For nouns in the singular
number that end in *s*, **the**
possessive is usually formed
by adding the *'s*, as in
octopus's tentacles.
4. For nouns in the plural
number that end in *s*, the
apostrophe must follow

possessive case (*cont.*):
the *s*, as in octopuses'
tentacles.

5. When the *s* would be
silent *in speech*, it is
generally omitted, as for
conscience' sake.

6. In English names and
surnames add *'s* as in Burns's
poems, St. James's Street.

7. *Ancient* words ending
in *-es* usually make the
possessive in *-es'*, as
Ceres' rites, Moses' law.

8. French names ending in
silent *-s* or *-x* take an
additional *'s*.

post, former size of paper
with several variations: —,
$19 \times 15\frac{1}{4}$ in.; pinched —,
$18\frac{1}{2} \times 14\frac{1}{2}$ in.; large —,
$16\frac{1}{2} \times 21$ in.

post (Lat.), after; abbr. **p.**

post, abbr. **P.**

postage stamp (two words).

postal order, abbr. **P.O.**

postcard/, -s (one word);
abbr. **p.c.**

post code (two words).

poste restante, P.O. dept.
where letters remain till
called for.

posteriori (*a*) (adj.),
reasoning from experience,
not à (ital.).

postgraduate (one word).

post-haste (hyphen).

post hoc (Lat.), after this.
See **propter hoc.**

posthumous, occurring after
death, *not* postu-.

Posthumus, in *Cymbeline.*

postilion, one who guides
post- or carriage-horses,
riding the near one, *not*
-llion.

post litem motam (Lat.),
after litigation began.

postmark (one word).

postmaster (one word);
abbr. **P.M.**

postmaster, a scholar at
Merton Coll., Oxford.

Postmaster-General
(hyphen, caps.); abbr.
P.M.G.

post meridiem (Lat.),
afternoon; abbr. **p.m.** (not
caps., or s. caps.).

post mortem (Lat.), after
death.

post-mortem (adj. and
noun), abbr. **P.M.**

postnatal (one word).

post-obit, a bond payable
after a death (hyphen, not
ital.).

Post Office, The (caps.,
no hyphen), public
corporation, replaced the
govt. dept. in 1969.
See also **M.P.T.**

post office (l.c., no hyphen),
a local office of the above,
abbr. **P.O.**

post paid, abbr. **p.p.**

postscript (one word); abbr.
PS., *pl.* **PSS.**

post terminum (Lat.), after
the conclusion.

postumous, *use* posth-.

posy, a nosegay, *not* -ey.

pot., potential.

potage/ (Fr. m.), soup;
— *à la queue de bœuf,*
oxtail soup; — *de levraut,*
hare soup; — *printanier,*
soup with spring vegetables;
— *à la tête de veau,*
mock-turtle soup.

potassium, symbol **K** (no
point).

potato/, *pl.* **-es.**

pot-au-feu (Fr. cook. m.),
a meat broth.

poteen, illicit whisky, *not*
pott., poth-.

potential, abbr. **pot.**

potlatch, N. American
Indian feast at which gifts
are given, *not* -lach, -lache
(not ital.).

potpourri, a medley.

potsherd, a piece of broken
earthenware, *not* -ard,
-are.

pott/, former standard size of paper, $12\frac{1}{2} \times 15\frac{1}{2}$ in.; — **4to**, $7\frac{3}{4} \times 6\frac{1}{4}$ in.; —**8vo**, $6\frac{1}{4} \times 3\frac{7}{8}$ in. (untrimmed).

pouce (Fr. m.), an inch; a thumb; abbr. **p.**

pouding (Fr. cook. m.), pudding.

poudr/é (Fr.), *fem.* **-ée,** powdered.

Poughkeepsie, New York State, U.S.; *pron.* pō-kĭp′-sǐ.

poularde (Fr. f.), fat pullet.

poule/ (Fr. f.), a ; hen — *de neige,* white grouse; — *faisane,* hen-pheasant.

poulet/ (Fr. m.), a young chicken; — *de grain,* a corn-fed chicken.

Poulett (Earl, *not* of); *pron.* pawl′et.

poulette (Fr. f.), young hen.

pound, avoirdupois, approx. 453 g; abbr. **lb,** *pl.* same (no point).

pound mark (money), **£** (sing. and pl.), q.v.

pour/ (Fr.), for, abbr. **p.;** — *ainsi dire,* so to speak.

pourboire (Fr. m.), gratuity, tip.

pour/ dire adieu (Fr.), to say good-bye, abbr. **p.d.a.;** — *faire ses adieux,* ditto, abbr. **p.f.s.a.;** — *faire visite,* to make a call, abbr. **p.f.v.**

pourparler (Fr. m.), preliminary discussion (one word, ital.).

pour prendre congé (Fr.), to take leave; abbr. **p.p.c.**

pour rendre visite (Fr.), to return a call; abbr. **p.r.v.**

pour tout dire (Fr.), in a word.

pourtray, *use* por-.

pousse-café (Fr. m.), a liqueur (after coffee).

Poussin (Nicolas), 1594–1665, French painter.

poussin (Fr. m.), a very young chicken.

P.O.W., prisoner of war.

Powis (Earl of), family name Herbert; *pron.* pō′is (*see also* **Powys**).

powwow, N. American Indian conference, *not* pawaw.

Powys, family name Baron Lilford; *pron.* pō′is. See also **Powis.**

Powys, new Welsh county, proposed 1971, comprising Montgomeryshire, Radnorshire, and parts of Breconshire.

PP. (Lat.), *Patres* (fathers).

P.P., parish priest, Past President.

pp., pages.

pp (It. mus.), *pianissimo* (very soft) or *più piano* (softer).

p.p., past participle, post paid, (Fr.) *publié (-ée) par* (published by), (Lat.) *per procurationem* (by authority of).

p.p.c., *pour prendre congé* (to take leave, to pay a parting call).

P.P.E., Philosophy, Politics, and Economics (Oxford degree subject).

p.p.i., policy sufficient proof of interest.

P.P.I.T.B., Printing and Publishing Industry Training Board.

p.p.m., parts per million.

P.P.P., Psychology, Philosophy, and Physiology (Oxford degree subject).

ppp (It. mus.), *pianississimo,* as softly as possible.

P.P.P.I.T.B., Paper and Paper Products Industry Training Board.

P.P.S., Parliamentary *or* principal private secretary.

P.PS., *post-postscriptum,* further postscript.

P.P.U., Peace Pledge Union (of the 1930s).

P.Q., previous (*or* preceding) question; Province of Quebec, Canada.

P.R., prize ring, Proportional Representation, Public Relations, Puerto Rico, (Lat.) *Populus Romanus* (the Roman people).

pr., pair, -s, price.

Pr, praseodymium (no point).

P.R.A., President of the Royal Academy.

praam, a boat, *use* **pram**.

Prachtausgabe (Ger. typ. f.), de luxe edition.

practice (noun; U.S. also verb).

practise (verb).

praemunire, a writ, *not* pre-.

praenomen, a Latin first name, *not* pren-.

praepostor, a school prefect, *not* prep-, -itor.

praeter propter (Lat.), about, nearly; abbr. **pr. pr.**

praetor, a Roman magistrate, *not* pre-.

Praga, suburb of Warsaw.

Prager (Ger.), inhabitant of Prague.

Präger (Ger.), a coiner.

Prague, Czechoslovakia; Eng. and Fr. for Czech **Praha;** Ger. **Prag.**

pram, a boat, *not* praam.

praseodymium, symbol **Pr** (no point).

pratique, a limited quarantine, *not* -ic.

Prayer Book (caps., no hyphen); abbr. **P.B.**

Prayer of Manasses (Apocr.), abbr. **Pr. of Man.**

P.R.B., Pre-Raphaelite Brotherhood (group of artists), 1848.

pre-Adamite (hyphen, cap. A).

Préault (A. A.), 1809-79, French sculptor.

preb., prebend, -ary.

prec., preceding, precentor.

precentor, choir director; abbr. **prec.**

preceptor, a teacher.

preces (Lat.), prayers.

precession (astr.), earlier occurrence (of the equinoxes); (dyn.), the resultant rotation of the axis of a spinning body revolving about another body (like a 'sleeping' top).

pre-Christian (hyphen, cap. C).

Précieuses ridicules (*Les*), play by Molière, 1659.

précieu/x (Fr.), an affected man; *fem.* **-se.**

précis/, a summary, *pl.* same (not ital.); — **-writing.**

precisian, one who is rigidly precise, esp. (hist., in hostile sense) a Puritan.

precisionist, one who makes a practice of precision.

pre-Columbian (hyphen, cap. C).

precursor, forerunner, *not* -er.

pred., predicative, -ly.

predicant, a preacher, esp. Dominican.

predictor, *not* -er.

predikant (Afrik.), a preacher of the Dutch Protestant church, esp. in S. Africa.

predilection, partiality.

pre/-eminence, -eminent, -emption, -engage, -establish, -exist (all hyphened).

pref., preface, preference, preferred, prefix, -ed.

preface, the introductory address of the author to the reader, in which he explains the purpose and scope of the book. Abbr. **pref.** *See also* **preliminary matter.**

préfecture/ (Fr. f.), county-hall in a French town; — *de police,* office of commissioner of police.

prefer/, -able, -ably, etc.

prefer/ence, -red, abbr. **pref.**

préfet (Fr. m.), prefect.

prefix/, -ed, abbr. **pref.**
prehistoric (one word).
Preignac, a white wine.
Prejevalski, *use* **Prjevalski.**
prejudge/, -ment (one
  word).
prejudice (bias) **against; —
  in favour of; without — to,**
  without abandoning a
  claim to.
prelim., preliminary.
preliminary matter (typ.),
  giving *identification* and any
  explanations desirable for
  bibliographical and trade
  purposes, or to 'prepare' the
  reader of a book; the order
  should be: series title;
  publisher's announcements,
  e.g. list of other titles in the
  same series; book half-title;
  frontispiece; title-page,
  including publisher's
  imprint; copyright notice,
  publisher's agencies, I.S.B.N.,
  impression lines, country of
  origin, printer's imprint (this
  is sometimes printed
  elsewhere, e.g. on the last
  page of the book);
  dedication; acknowledge-
  ments; foreword (introducing
  the author, and usually
  written by someone else);
  preface (written by the
  author, introducing the book
  and stating its purpose);
  contents, list of illustrations/
  maps/tables/graphs/ etc.;
  introduction.
pre-makeready (typ.),
  careful preparation of the
  forme before it goes to the
  machine.
premier (*au*) (Fr. m.), on
  the first floor; *première
  danseuse,* principal fem.
  dancer in a ballet; *en
  première,* in a first-class
  carriage; *première qualité,*
  first quality.
première, first performance
  of a film or play (not ital.).

premise (verb), to say or
  write as introduction; *pron.*
  prĕm-īz′; *not* -ize.
premises (noun, pl.),
  building(s) with grounds and
  appurtenances; (law) the
  aforesaid building(s), etc.
premiss/ (logic),
  a proposition; *pl.* **-es** (an
  accepted, but unnecessary
  and unwarranted
  differentiation in spelling
  from premis/e, -es).
premium/, abbr. **pm.;** *pl.* **-s.**
premolar, a tooth; abbr. **pm.**
premunire, *use* **prae-.**
prendre l'habit (Fr.), to
  become a monk or nun.
prenomen, *use* **praenomen.**
prentice, an apprentice
  (no apos.).
pre/occupy, -ordain (one
  word).
prep., preparat/ion, -ory,
  preposition.
pre/paid, -pay (one word).
prepositor, *use* **praepostor.**
Pre-Raphaelite/ (hyphen,
  caps.); — **Brotherhood,**
  abbr. **P.R.B.**
Pres., president.
présalé (Fr. m.), salt-marsh
  sheep or mutton (one word);
  pl. *prés-salés* (hyphen).
Presb., Presbyterian.
presbyopia, a failing of near
  sight in the elderly.
Presbyterian (cap.); abbr.
  Presb.
pre-select (hyphen).
preselective (of motor-car
  gears) (one word).
preses (Sc.), president, *or*
  chairman.
president, abbr. **Pres.**
**President of the United
  States,** etc. (caps.).
Press (the), newspapers,
  etc. (cap.).
press agent (two words).
press-box, shelter for
  reporters at outdoor functions
  (hyphen).

Pressensé (E. D. de), 1824–91, French theologian and statesman.

Press (freedom of the).
Every person who prints anything for hire or reward must, under a penalty of £20, keep for six months one copy at least of the matter printed, and write on it the name and place of abode of the person who employed him to print it.

Every person who prints any paper meant to be published must print on the first or last leaf his name and usual place of business; on failing to do so he forfeits the sum of £5, and so does any person publishing the same.

Papers printed by Parliament, or in Government offices, engravings, auction lists, bills of lading, receipts, and a few similar forms, are exempt.

press-gallery, esp. in House of Commons (hyphen).

pressman (one word).

press/-mark, that which shows the place of a book in a library (hyphen); *now usu.* **shelf-mark;** — **-proof,** the last one examined before going to press, or taking electro or stereo (**machine-revise,** after **make-ready,** may follow).

press-work (typ.), the operating, adjustment, or management of a printing press; also the work done by the press.

pressure (mech.), symbol *p* (no point).

Prester John, mythical medieval priest-king of Cent. Asia or Abyssinia; *Prester John*, novel by John Buchan.

prestige, renown (not ital.).

prestige (Fr. m.), enchantment (ital.).

presto (mus.), quickly.

Preston/kirk, -pans, Haddington (one word).

Prestwich, Lancs.

Prestwick, Ayr.

presum/e, -able, -ably, -ing.

pret., preterite.

pretence (U.S. **-se**).

preten/sion, -tious.

preterite, past tense, *not* -it; abbr. **pret.**

preternatural, etc. (one word).

prêter serment (Fr.), to take the oath.

pretium/ affectionis (Lat., Sc. law), a fancy price; — *periculi,* premium for insurance.

pretor, use **prae-**.

pretzel (Ger.), a salted biscuit (not ital.).

Preussen, Ger. n. for **Prussia**.

preux chevalier (Fr. m.), a brave knight.

prevail/, -ed, -ing.

preventive, *not* -tative, -titive.

Prévost (Marcel), 1862–1941, French novelist.

Prévost d'Exiles (Antoine François), 1679–1765, French novelist, known as **Abbé Prévost**.

Prévost-Paradol (L. A.), 1829–70, French writer.

prévôt (Fr. m.), provost.

P.R.I., President of the Royal Institute (of Painters in Water-Colours).

P.R.I.B.A., President of the Royal Institute of British Architects.

price list (two words).

prie-dieu, kneeling stool (hyphen, not ital.).

priest, abbr. **Pr.**

prim., primary, primate, primitive.

prima (typ.), the first part of the next page, sheet,

or slip to the one being
read; also mark on copy
where reading is to be
resumed after interruption.

prima/ (It. f.), first; —
buffa, first female singer in
a comic opera; — *donna*,
first ditto in opera, *pl.*
prime donne; **prima facie**
(Lat.), at first sight (two
words, not ital.); *di (or a)*
prima vista (It.), at first
sight; *prima volta* (It.
mus.), the first time.

Prime Minister (two
words, caps.); abbr. **P.M.**

primer, that which primes,
a first coat of paint, an
elementary school-book;
pron. prī'-.

primer (typ.), *see* **great —,
long —** (sizes of type); *pron.*
prĭm'-.

primeur (Fr. f.), early fruit
or vegetables, early love,
bloom.

primeval, of the first age of
the world; *not* -aeval.

primigenial, original, *not*
primo-.

primo (It. mus.), upper part
in a duet.

primo (Lat.), in the first
place; abbr. **1⁰**.

primum cognitum (Lat.),
the first thing known.

primus/ (Lat.), first, abbr.
p.; — *inter pares*, first
among equals.

prince, abbr. **P.**; **Prince/ of
Glory, Life,** *or* **Peace,** as
Deity (caps.); — **of Wales/;**
— — — **Island,**
off. Penang.

princeps (Lat.), the first, *pl.*
principes; *editio —*, the
first edition of a work, *pl.*
editiones principes.

princess, a long close-fitting
gown; in Fr. *princesse* (f.).

Princeton University, N.J.,
U.S.

Princetown, Devon.

principal, adj., chief; noun,
the chief person (cap. when
the title of an office).

principle, a fundamental
truth, moral basis.

print., printing.

print (in), still on sale; —
(out of), new copies no
longer obtainable, abbr.
o.p.

printani/er (Fr. cook.), *fem.*
-ère, with early spring
vegetables.

printer, abbr. **pr.**; **King's**
or **Queen's Printer,** may
print Bibles (A.V.), Prayer
Books, Statutes, and Acts
of State, to the exclusion of
all other presses, except (in
the case of Bibles and
Prayer Books) those of the
Universities of Oxford and
Cambridge. Special licence
may be given to print
Bibles in Scotland and
Ireland.

printer's error, *pl.* **print/-
er's**, *or* **-ers', errors.**

printer's mark, an imprint.

printing, abbr. **ptg.**, *or*
print.

Prinz/ (Ger. m.), prince
(usu. of the blood royal),
pl. **-en**; *fem.* **-essin**, *pl.*
-essinnen (cap.).

prior to, *before,* or *previous to,*
preferred.

prise, to force open, *not* -ize.

priv., privative.

Privatdozent (Ger. m.),
a university teacher paid only
by students' fees (one word,
cap.); abbr. **P.D.**

Private (mil.), abbr. **Pte.**

privative, denoting the loss
or absence of something;
esp. in linguistics; abbr.
priv.

Privy Council/, -lor (two
words, caps.), abbr. **P.C.**;
Privy Seal, **P.S.**

prix/ (Fr. m.), prize, price; —
fixe, fixed price.

prize, to force open, *use* **-ise.**

p.r.n., *pro re nata* (as occasion may require).

P.R.O., Public Record Office, — Relations Officer.

pro (Lat.), for; abbr. **p.**

proa, Malay vessel, *not* the many variations.

pro and con, *pro et contra* (for and against); *pl.* **pros and cons** (not ital., no points).

Prob., Probate (Division).

prob., probab/le, -ly, problem.

probatum est (Lat.), it has been proved.

pro bono publico (Lat.), for the public good.

probosc/is, long flexible trunk or snout; *pl.* **-ises.**

Proc., proceedings, proctor.

procès (Fr. m.), lawsuit.

process blocks (typ.), those made by photographic and etching processes, for printing illustrations by letterpress.

process-coated paper, a paper coated on machine, and used for general illustration work and packaging.

procès/-verbal (Fr.), official report, minutes; *pl.* — *-verbaux.*

proconsul (one word); abbr. **P.**

Procter (Adelaide Anne), 1825–64, English poet; — (**Bryan Waller,** *not* Walter), 1787–1874, pen-name 'Barry Cornwall', English poet.

proctor, a university official, an attorney in spiritual courts; abbr. **Proct.; King's (Queen's) Proctor,** an official who can intervene in divorce cases.

Proctor (Richard Anthony), 1837–88, British astronomer.

Procurator-fiscal, Scottish law officer (cap. P, hyphen).

procureur/ (Fr. m.), an attorney; — *de la république,* — *du roi,* or — *général,* public prosecutor.

prodrom/us, a preliminary treatise; *pl.* **-i.**

producible, *not* -able.

pro et contra (Lat.), for and against (*see also* **pro and con**).

Prof(s)., professor(s).

professoriate, *not* -orate.

proffer/, -ed, -ing.

pro forma/ (Lat.), as a matter of form; (noun, not ital.) an account showing the market prices of specified goods; *pl.* **-s.**

progr/amme (U.S. **-am**); in computing, usu. **-am.**

pro hac vice (Lat.), for this occasion, *not* — hâc —.

projector, *not* -er.

prolegomen/a, preliminary remarks; *sing.* (rare) **-on.**

proletariat, the poorest class in a community, *not* -te (not ital.).

prologize, etc., to deliver a prologue, *not* -uize.

prolonge (mil.), a rope for a gun-carriage; *pron.* pro-lonj′.

prom (no point), a promenade (at seaside), a promenade concert; **The Proms,** the Henry Wood Promenade Concerts at the Royal Albert Hall or elsewhere.

prom., promontory.

Promethean, of Prometheus (Gr. myth.).

promethium (*formerly* -**eum**), symbol **Pm** (no point).

promissory note, abbr. **p.n.**

pron., pronominal, pronoun, pronounced, pronunciation.

prononc/é (Fr.), *fem.* **-ée,** strongly marked.

pronoun, abbr. **pron.;** when relating to Deity, l.c. unless caps. specified.

pronounc/e, -eable, -ed, -ement, -ing; abbr. **pron.**

pronunciamento/, a manifesto; *pl.* **-s** (not ital.).

pronunciation, *not* -nounc-.

proof (typ.), a trial copy from type or film, taken for correction; **author's —,** a clean proof as corrected by the compositor, supplied to the author, and later returned by him with his corrections, abbr. **a. p.;** **clean —,** one having very few printer's errors; **first —,** lit. the proof first produced after typesetting or filmsetting; **foundry —,** the final one taken from type prepared for plating; **galley** *or* **slip —,** a proof taken before the matter is made up into pages: usu. about 18 in. long; **page-on-galley** *or* **slip-page —,** one having type made up into pages but not yet imposed (i.e. in sheets); **page —,** *or* **— in sheets,** one made up into pages; **slip —** (*see* galley, above); **— marks** (*see* **proof correction marks**); **— paper,** that used for taking proofs; **plate —,** one taken from a plate; **press —,** the final one passed by author, editor, or publisher, for the press; **— -reader,** one who reads and corrects printers' proofs; **rough —,** one taken without special care.

proof correction marks. For a comprehensive treatment see BS 1219. *Hart's Rules* contains an article on Proof Correction. The following are the commonest marks:

cap., change to capital letters those trebly under-lined.

ital., change to italic letters those underlined.

l.c., change to lower-case letters (small, not caps. or s.caps.) those encircled.

n.p., begin a new paragraph with the word after the mark [.

press, print off.

Qy., *or* **?,** added by reader to mark something about which he is uncertain.

revise, submit another proof.

rom., change to roman letters those encircled.

run on, and a line drawn from the last word of the first paragraph to the first word of the second, no new paragraph.

s.caps., change to small capitals those doubly underlined.

stet, let the cancelled word which is dotted underneath remain.

trs., transpose letters, words, etc., as marked.

w.f., wrong fount, alter.

× bad letter (i.e. damaged type), substitute good type.

⌿ delete what is crossed out.

∧ the caret mark, insert matter in margin.

▢ indent first word.

insert space, or equalize spacing.

less #, reduce space where marked ⌴.

℘ a type inverted, turn.

⌒ remove space, close up.

√ to be put under all apos., quotes, and superior letters (as *r* in M^r) to be added.

⊥ a space to be pushed down.

⌐ move to the left.

¬ move to the right.

‖ make parallel at sides.

. . . . . *see* **stet,** above.

≡ lines to be straightened.

⊙ full point needed where indicated, ⊙ colon ditto.

/ a stroke as this to be put

proof correction marks
(cont.):
    after each correction in the
margin to show that it is
concluded, to separate it
from others, and to call
attention to it.
    ALL corrections to be made
in *ink or ball pen*, and
attention called to them *in
the margin*, as otherwise they
are liable to be overlooked.

prop., proposition.

propaganda, an activity for
the spread of a doctrine or
practice, is singular.

pro patria (Lat.), for one's
country.

propel/, **-led**, **-ler**, **-ling**.

propell/ant (noun); **-ent**
(adj.).

Propertius (**Sextus**), *c.* 50
B.C.–A.D. 14, Roman poet;
abbr. **Prop.**

prophe/cy (noun); **-sy** (verb).

propitiat/e, appease; **-or**, *not*
-er.

proposition, abbr. **prop.**

proprio motu (Lat.), of
one's own accord.

propter hoc (Lat.), because
of this. *See post hoc.*

pro/ rata (Lat.), in
proportion; — *re nata*, as
occasion may require, abbr.
p.r.n.

pros., prosody.

pro salute animae (Lat.),
for the good of the soul.

pros and cons, *pl.* of **pro and
con** (not ital., no points).

prosceni/um, the front part
of the stage; *pl.* **-a**.

proselyt/e, a religious
convert; **-ize**, to convert,
not -ise.

prosit! (Lat.), your good
health! (used by German
students and others).

prosody, the laws of poetic
metre; abbr. **pros.**

prospector, *not* -er.

prospectus/, a circular,

available to the public,
describing a school, a forth-
coming book, or a commercial
enterprise; *pl.* **-es.**

Prot., Protestant.

protactinium, symbol **Pa**
(no point).

protagonist, leading
character in a play, novel,
or cause (not the opp. of
antagonist).

pro tanto (Lat.), to that
extent.

protean, assuming different
shapes, from Proteus (Gr.
myth.), *not* -ian.

protector, *not* -er.

protég/é, one under the
protection of a patron, *fem.*
-ée (not ital.).

pro tempore (Lat.), for the
time being; abbr. *pro tem.*,
or *p.t.*

Protestant/, abbr. **Prot.**;
-ism (cap.).

protester, *not* -or.

protocol, first draft of a
diplomatic document,
diplomatic etiquette.

protomartyr, the first
martyr in a cause, esp. St.
Stephen.

protonotary, a chief clerk,
esp. to some lawcourts, *not*
protho-.

prototype, an original model.

protozo/on, *pl.* **-a** (not ital.),
single-cell form of life.

protractor, drawing instrument, *not* -er.

Proudhon (**Pierre Joseph**),
1809–65, French socialist.

Prov., Proven/ce, -çal, Proverbs, province, Provost.

prov., proverbially, provincial, provisional.

prov/e, **-able**, **-ing**.

proven (*not*) (Sc. law),
a verdict intermediate
between guilty and not guilty,
equalling acquittal; but no
further trial possible on the
same charge.

provenance, (place of) origin (not ital.).

provençale (à la) (Fr. cook.), with garlic or onions (not cap.).

Proven/ce, S. France (no cedilla), **-çal;** abbr. **Prov.**

Proverbs, O.T., abbr. **Prov.**

provinc/e, abbr. **Prov.;** **-ial,** abbr. **prov.**

Province of Quebec, Canada, abbr. **P.Q.**

proviso/, stipulation; *pl.* **-s** (not ital.).

Provost/, abbr. **Prov.;** — **-Marshal** (caps., hyphen), abbr. **P.M.**

prox., see *proximo.*

proxime/ accessit (Lat.), he, *or* she, came nearest (to winning a prize, etc.); abbr. *prox. acc.;* *pl.* — *accesserunt.*

proximo (Lat.), in, *or* of, the next month; abbr. *prox.,* this abbr. not to be printed.

pr. pr., *praeter propter* (about, nearly).

P.R.S., President of the Royal Society (London).

P.R.S.A., President of the Royal Scottish Academy.

P.R.S.E., President of the Royal Society of Edinburgh.

prud'homme (Fr. m.), (*formerly*) good and true man; (*now*) expert, umpire.

Prudhomme, see **Sully-Prudhomme.**

prunella, a throat affliction; a strong silk or worsted material; (with cap. P) a genus of plants (the self-heal).

prunello, a kind of prune.

Pruss., Prussia, -n.

p.r.v., *pour rendre visite* (to return a call).

Przemyśl (Poland).

PS., *postscriptum,* postscript (one full point only); *pl.* **PPS.** (see also **P.PS.**).

P.S., permanent secretary, Police Sergeant (see also **Police Constable**), private secretary, Privy Seal, (theat.) prompt side (two points).

Ps., see **Psalm.**

P.S.A., Pleasant Sunday Afternoon, a church or chapel meeting (late Victorian or Edwardian).

Psalm, abbr. **Ps.; Psalms** (*pl.*), abbr. **Pss.; Psalms** (O.T.), abbr. **Ps.**

Psalmist (the) (cap.).

Psalter (the), the Book of Psalms, separately printed (cap.).

psaltery, an anc. and medieval plucked instrument.

p's and q's (apos., no points).

psephologist, an analyst of election results.

pseudonym, an assumed name; abbr. **pseud.**

pshaw! an exclamation, *not* psha, -h.

psi, Greek letter ψ, symbol for seaport (bar through tail).

P.S.N.C., Pacific Steam Navigation Company.

PSS., *postscripta* (postscripts).

Pss., see **Psalm.**

P.S.T. (U.S.), Pacific Standard Time.

psych., psychic, -al.

psychedelic, (of drugs) inducing fantastic mental pictures, *not* psycho-.

psychokinosis, movement by psychic agency; abbr. **PK** (no points).

psychol., psycholog/y, -ical.

P.T., physical training, post town (*also* **p.t.**), pupil teacher.

Pt. (geog.), Point, Port.

Pt, platinum (no point).

pt, part, payment, pint, -s, (math.) point, (typ.) point system.

p.t., *pro tempore* (for the time being).

P.T.A. *or* **p.t.a.,** Parent-Teacher Association.

Ptah (Egypt.), creator.

Pte. (mil.), private.

pterodactyl, *not* -le.

ptg., printing.

ptisan, medicated drink, *not* tisane.

P.T.O., please turn over, Public Trustee Office.

ptomaine poisoning, former name of 'food poisoning'.

Pu (no point), plutonium.

pub./, public, -an, publish, -ed, -er, -ing; — **doc.,** public document.

publice (Lat.), at the expense, on behalf of the state (*not* publicly).

public house (two words).

publicize, to advertise what is published.

Public School (caps.), English private school, i.e. not owned or maintained by state or local government, but usu. by board of governors as trustees.
In U.S. (not caps.) a school run by public funds.

publié(-e) par (Fr.), published by; abbr. **p.p.**

publish/, -ed, -er, -ing, abbr. **pub.**

Publishers Association, The (no apos.); abbr. **P.A.**

publisher's binding, usu. that in cloth.

Puebla, Mexico.

Pueblo, Colorado.

pueblo (Sp.), a village, any inhabited place.

Puerto Bello, Panama; — **Rico,** W. Ind. island; *not* Porto —.

puff-adder (hyphen).

puff-ball (hyphen).

pug-dog (hyphen).

puggaree, a hat-scarf, *not* the many variations.

puin/é (Fr.), *fem.* **-ée,** younger, opposed to *aîné,* senior; *pron.* pwē'-ne.

puisne (law), *pron.* pū'nĕ.

pukka, *pref. to* pucka, pukkah.

pul/e, to whine; **-ing.**

pull (typ.), a proof.

pull a proof (typ.), take an impression.

Pullman, (U.S.) sleeping-car, (G.B.) a specially luxurious and fast train, a type of railway carriage with tables.

pulque, Mexican beverage.

pulsimeter, a pulse measurer.

pulsometer, a pumping engine.

pulverize, *not* -ise.

pumice, pumice-stone, *not* variants.

pummel (verb), common form of **pommel.**

pummel (noun), *use* **pommel.**

pummelo, pumelo, *use* **pomelo.**

pumpernickel, Westphalian rye-bread.

Punakha, cap. of Bhutan.

Punchinello (cap.), principal character in Italian puppet-show; hence **Punch** (no point).

punctatim (Lat.), point for point.

punctilio/, (scrupulous observance of) a point of behaviour; *pl.* **-s.**

punctuation.

I. **General purpose.**
Punctuation in the written word corresponds to pauses, inflexions, and emphasis in the spoken word, the aim being to make the sense clear. One cannot be dogmatic about punctuation, as the style of it varies from age to age, and from one type of writing to another. For example, Shakespeare's commas told the actors where best to pause, prose

writers of the eighteenth century used commas freely on a logical grammatical basis, most modern writers punctuate as lightly as possible, and legal documents are designed to make the meaning clear without punctuation. Within any piece of writing the style of punctuation should be consistent. The punctuation in the copy should be followed by the compositor when so ordered, and always when printing extracts or quotations from other works.

The common uses of the various punctuation marks now follow, in the order: II, **comma**; III, **semi-colon**; IV, **colon**; V, **period**; VI, **question mark**; VII, **exclamation mark**; VIII, **apostrophe**; IX, **turned comma**; X, **parentheses**; XI, **brackets**; XII, **dashes**; XIII, **hyphen**; XIV, **brace**; XV, a note on **duplication of points**.

II. **comma** (,)

This is the slightest of the separating marks. It should be used:

1. To separate main clauses when the second is not closely identified with the first, e.g. 'Cars will turn here, and coaches will go straight on'. But cf. 'He turned and ran.'

2. When, without the comma, the eye or tongue would run on and momentarily mistake the sense, e.g. 'Saul and Jonathan were lovely and pleasant in their lives, and in their death they were not divided.'

3. To separate subordinate clauses from the rest of the sentence when a slight pause seems natural, e.g. 'When you have finished, come to me.' But cf. 'Come to me when you have finished.'

4. When the sentence would mean something different without the comma, e.g. 'He didn't go to church, because he was playing golf.'

5. Between adjectives which each qualify a noun in the same way, e.g. 'a cautious, eloquent man.' But cf. 'a distinguished foreign author'.

6. To separate items in a list, e.g. potatoes, peas, and carrots. (The comma after *peas* is O.U.P. practice, and logically justified.)

7. After salutations and vocatives, e.g. My Lord, Dear Sir, O God, and also before them if they do not begin the sentence.

8. To mark the beginning and end of a parenthetical word or phrase, e.g. 'I am sure, however, that it will not happen.' 'Syracuse, once the world's largest city, is now only a small town.' ' "Go home", he said, "to your father." ' ' "I am," he said, "and always shall be." '

9. Before a quotation. Note the increasing importance of the break before the quotation in the following: 'You say "It cannot be done." I boldly cried out, "Woe to this city!" Then he wrote these words: "I have named none to their disadvantage." '

10. Before e.g., i.e., viz., and the like, and after the

punctuation (*cont.*):
following phrase or clause,
making the whole a
parenthesis.

11. In numbers of four or
more figures, to separate
each three consecutive
figures, starting from the
right, e.g. 10,135,793. This
does not apply to
mathematical work or
dates.

III. **semicolon** (;)
This separates those parts
of a sentence between
which there is a more
distinct break than would
call for a comma, but
which are too intimately
connected to be made
separate sentences. Ideally
the clauses or phrases
which it separates should
be similar in importance
and in grammatical
construction, e.g. 'To err is
human; to forgive, divine.'
See also **Greek.**

IV. **colon** (:)
This is used:

1. When the preceding
part of the sentence is
complete in sense and
construction, and the
following part naturally
arises from it in sense
though not in construction,
e.g. 'The universe would
turn to a mighty stranger:
I should not seem part of
it.'

2. To lead from
introduction to main
theme, from cause to effect,
or from premiss to
conclusion, e.g. 'Country
life is the natural life: it is
there that you will find real
friendship.'

3. After such expressions
as namely: for example:
this maxim: to resume: to
sum up: the following:

(a dash should not be added
to a colon which
introduces a list).

V. **period, full point, full
stop** (.)
This is used:

1. At the end of all
sentences which are not
questions or exclamations.
The next word should
generally begin with a
capital letter.

2. After most
abbreviations (q.v.) and
initials. But see the
Preface to this edition, and
individual entries.

3. Three full points,
separated by the normal
space of the line, mark
omissions. When the
preceding sentence ends in
a full point, the first of the
additional three should be
close up. *See* **ellipsis.**
See also **abbreviations,
capitalization, decimal
coinage, time of day.**

VI. **question mark, note
of interrogation** (?)

1. This should follow every
question which expects a
separate answer. It is not
used after indirect
questions, e.g. 'He asked
why I was there.' The next
word should generally
begin with a capital letter.

2. [?] in brackets, added to
a quotation, expresses the
editor's doubt.
See also **Greek, quotation
marks, Spanish.**

VII. **exclamation mark,
note of exclamation** (!)
This is used:

1. After an exclamatory
word, phrase, or sentence
expressing absurdity,
command, contempt,
disgust, emotion,
enthusiasm, irony, pain,
sorrow, a wish, wonder.

2. At the editor's discretion, after an impressive or striking remark or thought.

3. After a rhetorical question (not expecting an answer).

4. In mathematics, as the factorial sign.

5. [!] in brackets, added to a quotation, to express the editor's amusement, dissent, or surprise; or in chess commentaries, to denote a good move.

See also **quotation marks, Spanish.**

VIII. apostrophe (')

This is used:

1. To show the possessive case, q.v.

2. To show an omission, e.g. e'er, tho', we'll, he's (he is, he has), it's (it is), '69 (1969).

3. In Irish names, such as O'Connor. *But see* **Mac.**

4. In giving the plural of a single letter, e.g. p's and q's, or other plurals which might otherwise be unintelligible, e.g. do's and dont's, set-to's, *Faust*'s (versions of the opera). But the apostrophe is not in itself a sign of the plural, and is not needed in M.P.s, the 1970s.

5. As the 'closing quote'.

See **quotation marks.**

IX. turned comma (')

This is used:

1. As the 'opening quote'.

See **quotation marks.**

2. In Scottish names like M'Gregor. *See* **Mac.**

X. parentheses ( )

These enclose:

1. Interpolations and remarks made by the writer of the text himself, e.g. 'He is (as he always was) a rebel.'

2. An authority, definition, explanation, reference, or translation.

3. In the report of a speech, interruptions by the audience.

4. Reference letters or figures, e.g. (1), (a). These do not need a point as well as the parentheses. *See also* XV below.

XI. brackets, crotchets [ ]

These enclose comments, corrections, explanations, interpolations, notes, or translations, which were not in the original text, but have been added by subsequent authors, editors, or others, e.g. 'For Quarels [*sic*], they are to be avoided.'

XII. dashes

(*a*) The **en rule** (–) is used:

1. To join dates, as 1914–18, and joint authors.

2. Where a dash is needed in place-names or technical terms.

(*b*) The **em rule** (—) is used:

1. Like parentheses or a pair of commas, before and after a parenthetical clause.

2. Like a colon. *See* IV, 1, 2, above.

3. To indicate faltering, hesitant, of stammering speech.

4. After a quotation, before the name of the author (as an alternative to parentheses).

5. In dictionaries, etc., to represent the catchword, and so save space.

(*c*) The **two-em rule** (——) is used:

1. To show that a sentence is left unfinished.

2. To denote the omission of a part or the whole of an undesirable word.

punctuation (*cont.*):

XIII. hyphen (-)

This is used:

1. To join two or more words so as to make one indivisible expression, e.g. rear-guard (noun), never-to-be-forgotten (adj.). *See* Preface to this edition.

2. To join a prefix to a proper name, e.g. anti-Darwinian.

3. To prevent misconceptions by linking words, e.g. a poor-rate collection, a poor rate-collection.

4. To prevent misconceptions by separating a prefix from the main word, e.g. recover, re-cover (an umbrella); (a footballer) resigns, re-signs.

5. To separate two similar consonant or vowel sounds in a word, as a help to understanding and pronunciation, e.g. sword-dance, Ross-shire, co-operate (the hyphen here is preferable to a **diaeresis**, q.v.).

6. To represent a common second element in all but the last word of a list, e.g. two-, three-, or fourfold.

7. At the end of a line of print, to indicate that a word has been divided. *See* **division of words.**

XIV. brace (⏜)

This is used (usually vertically) to connect words, lines, staves of music, etc., and in mathematical and tabular work. When used to show that one thing comprises several others, the brace should point towards the single item, which should be central, e.g.

Biology $\begin{cases} \text{Botany} \\ \text{Zoology.} \end{cases}$

XV. duplication of points

This should be avoided where possible. For instance, if the second of a pair of commas comes at the end of a sentence, it is absorbed in the full point, question mark, or exclamation mark. A comma should not precede or follow a dash. If a sentence which is a statement ends with quoted matter which is itself a statement, the full point before the final quote will be sufficient. There are many complications (see *Hart's Rules*, pp. 43–6), but, as in all punctuation, clarity is the object, and logic and common sense the touchstones.

punctus (Lat.), a point; *pl. same.*

pundit (now facetious or slightly contemptuous), a learned man. *See also* **pandit.**

Punica fides (Lat.), Punic faith, treachery.

Punjab, India and Pakistan, *not* -aub, Panjab, Penjab.

Punjabi, Punjab inhabitant, or dialect, *not* -bee.

punkah (Anglo-Ind.), a large fan, *not* -a.

Punkt (Ger. typ. m.), point, dot, a full stop (cap.); *punktieren,* to point, dot, or punctuate; *Punktierung* (f.), punctuation.

punteggiatura (It.), punctuation.

punto e virgola (It.), semicolon.

P.U.O. (med.), pyrexia (fever) of unknown origin.

pup/a (entom.), a chrysalis; *pl.* -ae (not ital.).

pupillage (two *l*'s).

-pur (Ind.), a city, as Nagpur, Kanpur.

Purchas (**Samuel**), 1577–1626, English compiler of voyages.

purchasable, *not* -eable.

purdah (Ind.), (curtain for) seclusion of women of rank.

purée/ (Fr. cook., f.), sieved pulp, a thick soup; — *de pois*, pea soup.

pur et simple (Fr.), unqualified.

purgatory, place of temporary suffering and purification of souls of the dead (not cap.).

Puritan/ (cap.), a member of a branch of English Protestants (late sixteenth to mid-seventeenth century) who desired simpler forms of worship; (not cap.) one who is strict in religion or morals; **-ism**.

purl, in knitting, *not* pearl.

Purleigh, Essex.

Purley, Berks., Surrey.

purlieus, surroundings.

purpose/, **-ful**, **-less**, **-ly**.

purr, as a cat, *not* pur.

pur sang (Fr. m.), pure blood; adj., thoroughbred, total.

purslane (bot.), a salad herb, *not* -lain.

purveyor, one whose business is to supply meat or meals, *not* -er.

Pushtu, Afghan language, *not* Pashtu, Pushto, or Pushtoo.

put down (typ.), to alter from caps. to lower case.

putrefy, to go rotten, *not* -ify.

putrescible, liable to putrefy.

putsch, a revolutionary attempt.

puttees, strips of cloth worn round the lower leg for protection, *not* -ies.

put up (typ.), to alter from lower case to caps.

Puy-de-Dôme, dép. France (hyphens, two caps.). In phrases, *puy* (Fr. m.), a small volcanic cone, to have lower-case *p* and no hyphens, as *le puy de Dôme*.

P.V.C., polyvinyl chloride (plastic).

p.v.t. (Fr.), *par voie télégraphique* (by telegraph).

P.W.A. (U.S.), Public Works Administration.

P.W.D., Public Works Department.

Pwllheli, Caernarvon.

pwt., pennyweight, *use* **dwt** (no point).

P.X., please exchange; (U.S.) post exchange.

pyaemia (med.), a type of blood-poisoning, *not* pyem-.

pye (typ.), *use* **pie**.

pyebald, *use* pie-.

pygmy, correct, *but use* **pigmy**, q.v.

pyjamas, *not* the many variations; U.S. **pa-**.

pyknic, of short, squat stature.

pyramids, pl. only, a type of billiards.

Pyrénées/ (**Basses-**); **Hautes-** —; — **-Orientales**, déps. France.

pyrotechnics, the art of fireworks; abbr. **pyrotech.**

pyrrhic (victory), one won at great cost, from Pyrrhus, king of Epirus, 318–272 B.C.

Pytchley Hunt (**the**); *pron.* pītsh′lĭ.

pyx (**trial of the**), at the Royal Mint, *not* pix (not cap.).

Q

Q, (chess) queen, queue, the sixteenth in a series.

Q., pen-name of Sir Arthur Thomas Quiller-Couch, q.v.

Q., queen, question, all proper names with this initial.

q is used to transliterate the Arabic letter *qaf* and the Hebrew letter *qof*, which generally represent a guttural sound pronounced deeper in the throat than *k* (*kaf*).

q., query, quintal, quire, -s, (naut.) squalls.

q. (Lat.), *quaere* (inquire); quasi.

Q.A.B., Queen Anne's Bounty.

Qantas, Queensland and Northern Territory Aerial Service (the Australian Commonwealth airline).

Qatar, Arabia.

QB (chess), queen's bishop (no points).

Q.B., Queen's Bench.

Q.B.D., Queen's Bench Division.

Q-boat (First World War), a merchant-vessel with concealed guns.

QBP (chess), queen's bishop's pawn (no points).

Q.B.S.M. (Sp.), *que besa su mano* (who kisses your hand). Precedes the signature in a letter, and commonly follows **S.S.S.,** q.v.

Q.C., Queen's, *or* Queens', College, Queen's Counsel.

q.d., *quasi dicat* (as if one should say), *quasi dictum* (as if said).

q.e., *quod est* (which is).

Q.E.D., *quod erat demonstrandum* (which was to be demonstrated).

Q.E.F., *quod erat faciendum* (which was to be done).

Q.E.I., *quod erat inveniendum* (which was to be found out).

QKt (chess), queen's knight (no points).

QKtP (chess), queen's knight's pawn (no points).

q.l., *quantum libet* (as much as you please).

Qld (no point), Queensland (Australia).

Q.M., Quartermaster.

qm., *quomodo* (by what means).

Q.Mess., Queen's Messenger.

Q.M.G., Quartermaster-General.

Q.M.S., Quartermaster-Sergeant.

Q.O.C.H., Queen's Own Cameron Highlanders.

QP (chess), queen's pawn (no points).

q.pl., *quantum placet* (as much as seems good).

qq.v., *quae vide* (which see; refers to plural).

QR (chess), queen's rook (no points).

qr., quarter (28 lb.), quire; pl. **qrs.**

QRP, queen's rook's pawn (no points).

Q.S., quarter-sessions, Queen's Scholar.

q.s., *quantum sufficit* (as much as suffices).

Q.S.O. *or* **QSO** (no points), quasi-stellar object, quasar.

qt., quantity, quart, -s.

q.t., (on the) quiet.

qu., question.

qua (Lat.), in the character of, *not* -à, -â.

quad (colloq.), quadrangle; a quadruplet; (typ.) a piece of spacing material, usually

quad (*cont.*):
of size em, 2-em, 3-em, or 4-em (originally quadrat); (paper) a size of printing paper four times (quadruple) the basic size; (no point in any sense).

quad., quadrant.

Quadragesima, first Sunday in Lent

quodrenni/um, a period of four years; *pl.* **-a; -al;** *not* quadrie-.

quadroon, offspring ef white and mulatto, with quarter-Negro blood.

quaere (Lat.), inquire; abbr. *q.*

quaeritur (Lat.), it is asked.

quaesit/um (Lat.), something sought; *pl.* **-a.**

quaestio/ vexat/a (Lat.), an unsolved problem, *pl.* **-nes -ae.**

quaestor, anc. Roman magistrate. *See also* **que-.**

quae vide (Lat.), which see: refers to plural; abbr. **qq.v.**

quagga (S. Afr.), zebra-like animal.

quai (Fr. m.), quay, railway platform.

quaich, Scots drinking vessel, *not* -gh.

Quai d'Orsay, Paris, the French Foreign Office.

Quaker, a member of the Society of Friends.

quale (Lat.), the quality of a thing.

quam/ primum (Lat.), without delay; — *proxime,* as nearly as possible.

quand même (Fr.), notwithstanding, all the same.

quantity, abbr. **qt.**

quant/um (not ital.), a natural minimum quantity of an entity; *pl.* **-a;** *hence* **quantum theory,** theory of the emission and absorption of energy in finite steps. *See also* **Planck.**

quant/um (Lat.), a concrete quantity, *pl.* **-a; quantum/ libet,** as much as you please, abbr. **q.l.;** — *meruit,* as much as he, *or* she, deserved; — *placet,* as much as seems good, abbr. **q.pl.;** — *sufficit,* as much as suffices, abbr. **q.s.,** *or* **quant. suff.;** — *valeat,* whatever it may be worth; — *valebat,* as much as it was worth; — *vis,* as much as you will, abbr. **q.v.**

Qu'Appelle (Bp. of), Rupert's Land, Canada.

quarrel/, ed, -ler (*not* -lor), **-ling, -some** (U.S. **-ed, -er, -ing**).

quart/, -s, abbr. **qt.**

quart/, -e (fencing), *use* carte.

quart., quarterly.

Quart (Ger. n.), quarto (cap.).

quarter/, -s, abbr. **qr., qrs.**

quarter-binding, the spine in a different material from the rest of the case.

quarter/-day, — -deck (hyphens).

Quartermaster/ (one word), abbr. **Q.M.;** — **-General** (hyphen, caps.), abbr. **Q.M.G.;** — **-Sergeant** (hyphen, caps.), abbr. **Q.M.S.**

quarter-sessions (not caps.), abbr. **Q.S.**

quartet, *not* -ette, -etto.

quartier/ (Fr. cook. m.), quarter; — *d'agneau,* — of lamb; (mil.) *quartier-général,* headquarters.

quarto/ (typ.), a book based on four leaves, eight pages, to the basic sheet; *pl.* **-s;** abbr. **4to** (no point). *See* **book sizes.**

quasar, a quasi-stellar object; abbr. **Q.S.O.,** *or* **QSO** (no points).

quasi, in certain sense, almost (not ital.); abbr. *q.*

quasi/ dicat (Lat.), as if one should say, abbr. *q.d.;* — *dictum,* as if said, abbr. *q.d.;* — *dixisset,* as if he had said.

Quasimodo, first Sunday after Easter (one word, cap.).

quass (Russ.), rye beer; *use* **kvass.**

quater-cousin, *use* **cater-.**

Quatre-Bras (battle of), 1815.

quatrefoil, an ornament, *not* quater-, quarter-.

Quattrocento (It.), 1400–99, the early Renaissance period of art and literature.

quay, wharf, *not* key.

Q.U.B., Queen's University, Belfast.

Quebec, Canada, abbr. **P.Q.**

queen, abbr. **Q.;** (chess, no point).

Queen Anne's Bounty, formerly for augmenting C. of E. livings (apos.); abbr. **Q.A.B.**

Queenborough, Sheerness, Kent. *See also* **Queens-.**

Queen Mary College, London, *not* Mary's.

Queens, borough of New York City (no apos.).

Queensberry (Marquess of).

Queensborough, Drogheda. *See also* **Queenb-.**

Queensbury, Bradford, Yorks.

Queen's College, Oxford, London (named after one queen).

Queens' College, Camb. (named after two queens).

Queen's Counsel, abbr. **Q.C.**

Queen's County, Ireland, now **Leix.**

Queensland (Australia), abbr. **Qld** (no point).

Que faire? (Fr.), What is to be done?

Quelle affaire! (Fr. f.), What a to-do!

quelque chose (Fr. m.), something, a trifle.

Quel temps/ fait-il? (Fr.), What is the weather like? — — *il fait!* What weather this is!

quenelle (Fr. cook. f.), a force-meat ball (ital.).

Quentin Durward, by Sir W. Scott, 1823.

query, abbr. **q., qy.,** *or* **?**

Quesnay (François), 1694–1774, French economist.

question, abbr. **Q.** *or* **qu.**

questionnaire, a formulated series of questions (not ital.).

questor, R.C.C. *or* French Assembly. *See also* **quae-.**

Quételet (L. A. J.), 1796–1874, Belgian mathematician.

Quetta, Baluchistan.

quetzal, currency unit of Guatemala.

Quetzalcoatl, trad. culture-hero of the Aztecs.

queue, persons in line, *not* cue; abbr. on signs **Q** (no point).

queue/ (Fr. f.), tail; — *de bœuf,* ox-tail; *faire —,* to stand in a queue.

Que voulez-vous? (Fr.), What do you want?

quick/lime, -sand, -set, -silver (one word).

quicumque vult (Lat.), whosoever will (first words of the Athanasian Creed).

quid (Lat.), that which a thing is.

quidam, an unknown person, *pl. same.*

quid faciendum? what is to be done?

quidnunc, a gossip (not ital.).

quid pro quo, something in return, an equivalent (not ital.).

¿ Quién sabe? (Sp.), Who knows? (turned interrog. before, unturned after).

quietus, a settlement, finishing stroke (not ital.).

Quiller-Couch (Sir Arthur Thomas), 1863–1944, English novelist and essayist (hyphen); *pron.* kootsch; pen-name **Q.** (full point).

Qu'importe? (Fr.), What does it matter? *Que m'importe?* What is that to me?

quincentenary, five-hundredth anniversary (one word).

quincunx/, five arranged as on dice; *pl.* **-es.**

quinine, specific against malaria and fevers, *not* -in.

Quinquagesima, the Sunday before Lent.

quinquenni/um, a five-year period; *pl.* **-a.**

quinsy, tonsillitis, *not* -cy, -sey, -zy.

quint/al, 100 kilos, 220½ lb., 1·968 cwt., *not* kentle, kintle; *pl.* **-als** (in French *-aux*); abbr. **q.**

quintet (mus.), *not* -ette.

quintillion, cardinal number, 1 with 30 ciphers; (U.S.) 1 with 18 ciphers.

quiproquo (Fr. m.), mistake.

quipu (Peru), the language of knotted cords, *not* -po, -ppo, -ppu.

quire, part of a church, *or* church singers, *use* **choir.**

quire, 24 or 25 sheets of paper; abbr. **q.,** *pl.* same; **quires,** books in sheet form.

Qui s'excuse s'accuse (Fr.), to excuse oneself is to accuse oneself.

quisling, traitor, from **Vidkun Quisling,** 1887–1945, pro-Nazi leader in Norway.

quisque (Lat.), everyone.

quit/, -ter (*not* -tor).

Quito, cap. of Ecuador.

Qui va là? (Fr.), Who goes there?

Qui vive? (Fr.), who goes there? **qui vive** (**on the**), on the alert (not ital.).

quixotic (not cap.), like Don Quixote, hero of the romance by Cervantes (1547–1616), extravagantly romantic and visionary.

quiz/, to interrogate (mockingly), a competition by interrogation, **-zed, -zer, -zes, -zing.**

Qumran, Jordan, site associated with Dead Sea Scrolls.

quoad/ (Lat.), as far as; — *hoc,* to this extent; — *omnia,* in respect of all things; — *sacra,* as regards sacred things; — *ultra,* as regards things further back in time.

quod erat demonstrandum, etc., *see* **Q.E.D.,** etc.

quod est (Lat.), which is; abbr. **q.e.**

quodlibet (mus.), a medley.

quod vide (Lat.), which see (sing.); abbr. **q.v.**

quoins (typ.), wedges or expanding devices which secure type, blocks, and furniture in the chase; *pron.* coins.

quoique (Fr.), although.

quoi que (Fr.), whatever.

quoits, a game, *not* coits.

quo jure? (Lat.), by what right?

quomodo (Lat.), by what means; abbr. **q.m.**

quondam (adj.), former, from Lat. *quondam* (adv.), formerly.

quorum/, the number of members whose presence is needed to make proceedings valid; *pl.* **-s** (not ital.).

quot., quot/ation, -ed.

quota/, a share; *pl.* **-s.**

quotation marks (typ.), in English, one turned comma at the beginning and one apostrophe at the end; abbr. **quotes.** The apostrophe at the end of the quotation should come before all punctuation marks unless these form part of the quotation itself. Quotes are to be used when citing titles of articles in magazines, chapters of books, essays, poems (*but see* **poems, titles of**), and songs.

They are *not* to be used for the titles of the books of the Bible; where the substance only of an extract is given; or where the tense or person has been altered. *See also* **authorities,** and *Hart's Rules*, pp. 42–8.

quotations, *all* extracts in the exact words of the original, if set in the text type, to have 'quotes' at the commencement, and at the beginning of each paragraph (*not* each line, except in special cases); and at the end of the quotation only.

If the extract is set in smaller type than the text, quotation marks are not required, except in conversational matter. A space both before and after adds importance and emphasis.

Punctuation of the extract to be *exactly* as in the original. The concluding point to be outside the last quotation mark if not in the original. *See also* **ellipsis.**

quotations within quotations to have double quotation marks within the single. Quotations within the double quotation to be single-quoted.

quote (typ.), to enclose within quotation marks.

quotes (typ.), quotation marks, q.v.

quot homines, tot sententiae (Lat.), there are as many opinions as there are men.

quousque (Lat.), how long?

quo vadis? (Lat.), where are you going?

Qur'ān, *use* **Koran.**

q.v., *quantum vis* (as much as you will), *quod vide* (which see: refers to sing.).

Q.V.R., Queen Victoria Rifles.

qy, query (no point).

R

R, radius, *retarder* (on time-piece regulator = to retard), (chess) rook, the seventeenth in a series.

R (elec.), symbol for resistance.

R., rabbi, Radical, railway, rector, registered, reply, republican, river, Royal, all proper names with this initial, (Fr.) *Rue* (street), (Ger.) *Recht* (law), (Lat.) *regina* (queen), *respublica* (commonwealth), *rex* (king), (naut.) run (deserted), (theat.) right (from actor's point of view), (thermom.) Réaumur.

®, registered trade mark.

r., rare, recto, residence, resides, rises, rouble, (naut.) rain.

ρ (Gr.) (math.), rho, radius of curvature.

R, rupee, *use* **Re** (no point).

℞, *recipe* (take).

℟, response (to a versicle).

Rᵒ (math.), radius of a circle in degrees of arc; **R'**, ditto in minutes of arc; **R''**, ditto in seconds of arc.

r months, Sept. to Apr.

Ra, radium (no point); — (**Re**), Egyptian god of the sun.

R.A., Rear-Admiral, Referees' Association, Road Association, Royal Academ/y, — -ician, — Artillery, (astr.) right ascension.

R.A.A., Royal Academy of Arts.

R.A.A.F., Royal Auxiliary Air Force.

Rabat, cap. of Morocco.

rabat (Fr. m.), clerical, academical neckband.

rabbet/, -ed, -ing, groove in woodwork; *also* **rebate**; *not* rabbit.

rabbi/, Jewish expounder of the law; *pl.* **-s**; abbr. **R.** (cap.); **Chief Rabbi** (caps.).

rabbin/, *usually pl.*, **-s**, authorities on the law, mainly of second to thirteenth centuries.

rabbinic (adj.).

Rabbinic (cap.) (noun), late Hebrew; abbr. **Rabb.**

rabbit/, a rodent; **-er**, **-ing**; — -warren (hyphen). *See also* **rabbet**, **rebate**.

rabdomancy, *use* **rhab-**.

Rabelais/ (**François**), 1483–1553, French writer; **-ian** (cap.).

rabi, spring grain harvest in India.

R.A.C., Royal Agricultural College, — Armoured Corps, — Automobile Club.

raccoon, *use* **racoon**.

rac/e, **-y**.

race/-course, — **-horse** (hyphens).

R.A.C.S., Royal Arsenal Co-operative Society.

rach/is (bot., zool.), *more usual than* rhachis; *pl.* (incorrectly formed) **-ides**.

rachitis, rickets.

Rachmaninov (S. V.), 1873–1943, Russian composer.

Rachmanism, slum land-lordism (from 1963).

rack and ruin. *But use* **wrack** for destruction, sea-weed.

racket/, *not* racquet; **-eer**, **-s** (game), **-y**.

raconteur (not ital.).

racoon (U.S. **racc-**).

racquet, *use* **racket**.

13

rad., radix (root).
Rad., Radical.
R.A.D.A., Royal Academy of Dramatic Art.
radar, *radio detection and ranging* (not cap.).
R.A.D.C., Royal Army Dental Corps.
Radcliffe (**Ann**), 1764–1823, writer; — (**John**), 1650–1714, physician; — **College,** Mass., U.S.; — **Camera, Infirmary, Library,** *and* **Observatory,** Oxford. *See also* **Rat-.**
radian, SI unit of plane angle (approx. 57·296°).
radiator, *not* -er.
Radical (polit.), abbr. **R.**
radical (chem.), *not* -cle; — **sign** (math.), √.
radicle (botany).
radio/, -s (no point).
radioactiv/e (one word); **-ity.**
radiograph, X-ray photograph.
radio-isotope (hyphen).
radium, symbol **Ra** (no point).
rad/ius, *pl.* **-ii,** abbr. **R** (no point).
rad/ius vect/or, *pl.* **-ii; -ores.**
rad/ix, a root; *pl.* **-ices;** abbr. **rad.**
radon, previously known as radium emanation, symbol **Rn** (no point).
R.A.E., Royal Aircraft Establishment(s).
Rae (**John**), 1813–93, Scottish Arctic traveller. *See also* **Ray, Reay.**
Rae Bareli, Uttar Pradesh, India, *not* Ray Bareilly.
Raeburn (**Sir Henry**), 1756–1823, Scottish painter.
R.A.E.C., Royal Army Educational Corps.
R.Aero.C., Royal Aero Club of the United Kingdom.

R.Ae.S., Royal Aeronautical Society.
R.A.F., Royal Air Force.
R.A.F.A., Royal Air Forces Association.
raffia, a palm-fibre, *not* -f-.
R.A.F.O., Reserve of Air Force Officers, *now* **R.A.F.R.O.,** q.v.
R.A.F.R., Royal Air Force Regiment.
rafraîchissements (Fr. m. pl.), cooling drinks, fruit, etc.
R.A.F.R.O., Royal Air Force Reserve of Officers.
R.A.F.V.R., Royal Air Force Volunteer Reserve.
rag/, ged, -ging.
R.A.G.C., Royal and Ancient Golf Club, St. Andrews.
ragee, a coarse Indian grain, *not* ragg-, -i.
rag/out, a rich meat stew; in Fr. m. **-oût.**
Ragusa, It. for **Dubrovnik** (Yugoslavia); *also* a town in Sicily.
raie (Fr. f.), skate (fish).
Raiffeissen/ (**Friedrich Wilhelm**), 1818–88, German founder of agricultural co-operative banks, from 1846, and — Credit Banks, from 1865.
raifort (Fr. m.), horse-radish.
Raikes (**Robert**), 1735–1811, English originator of Sunday Schools.
rail/road, -way (one word); abbr. **R.**
rain/, abbr. **r.; -bow, -drop, -fall** (each one word); — **-water** (hyphen).
raison/ de plus (Fr.), all the more reason; — *d'État,* a reason of State; — *d'être.* purpose of existence.
raisonn/é (Fr.), *fem.* **-ée,** reasoned out; *catalogue* —, explanatory catalogue (ital.).

raj (Hind.), sovereignty.

raja/, Indian title, commonly but less correctly **-h** (not cap.); *fem.* **rani.**

Rajagopalachari (Chakravarti), 1878–1972, last Gov.-Gen. of India, 1948–50.

Rajasthan, Indian state.

Rajput/, member of Hindu soldier caste, *not* -poot; **-ana,** Indian state.

Rajshahi, E. Pakistan, *not* Rajeshaye.

râle/, noise made in difficult breathing; *pl.* **-s.**

Ralegh (Sir Walter), 1552–1618, English courtier, colonizer, soldier, and writer -eigh usual but erroneous.

Raleigh (Prof. Sir Walter), 1861–1922, English writer. *See also* **Rayleigh.**

Ralfs (John), 1807–90, English botanist.

rallentando (mus.), with decreasing pace, abbr. *rall.*

Ralph, *elegant pron.* rāf, in U.S. rălf.

R.A.M., Royal Academy of Music (London).

ram/, **-med, -ming.**

Ramadhan (Fast of), also ninth Muslim month; Pers. and Turk. **Ramazan.**

Ramayana, Hindu epic.

Rambouillet, dép. Seine-et-Oise.

R.A.M.C., Royal Army Medical Corps.

ramchuddar, Indian shawl.

rame (Fr. typ. f.), ream.

Ramée (Marie Louise de la), 1839–1908, French writer of English novels; pen-name **Ouida.**

ramekin, a cheese-cake, *not* -quin.

ramier (Fr. m.), wood-pigeon.

Ramillies (battle of), 1706.

Rampur, Uttar Pradesh, India.

Ramsay (Allan), 1686–

1758, Scottish poet; **(Allan)**, 1713–84, Scottish painter; — **(Sir William)**, 1852–1916, Scottish chemist.

Ramsey, Hunts., and I. of M.

Ramsey (Sir Alfred), b. 1920, English footballer and manager; — **(Arthur Michael)**, b. 1904, Bp. of Durham 1952–6, Abp. of York 1956–61, Abp. of Canterbury 1961–73; — **(Ian Thomas)**, 1915–72, Bp. of Durham 1966–72.

ram/**us** (Lat.), a branch; *pl.* **-i.**

rancher/**o** (Sp.), *fem.* **-a,** a small farmer.

rancour, spite, *but* **-orous.**

Randolph-Macon College, Virginia.

Randvermerk (Ger. m.), marginal note, *also Marginalie.*

ranee, use **rani.**

ranging figures (typ.), lining figures, q.v.

Rangoon, Burma, *not* -un.

rani, Indian queen or princess, *not* ranee, rannee, ranny.

Ranjit Singh, 1780–1839, founder of Sikh kingdom.

Ranjitsinhji (Kumar Shri), 1872–1933, cricketer; Maharaja Jam Sahib of Nawanagar 1906–33.

Ranke (L. von), 1795–1886, German historian.

rann/**ee, -y,** use **rani.**

ranuncul/**us,** a buttercup, *pl.* **-uses;** (bot.), the genus, including buttercups (cap. and ital.), *pl.* **-i.**

ranz-des-vaches, Swiss alpenhorn melody.

R.A.O.B., Royal Antediluvian Order of Buffaloes.

R.A.O.C., Royal Army Ordnance Corps.

rap/, -ped, -ping.

R.A.P.C., Royal Army Pay Corps.

Raphael/ (in It. **Raffaello Sanzio**), 1483–1520, Italian painter; **-esque.**

raphi/s (bot., zool.), a needle-like crystal; *pl.* **-des;** *not* rha-.

Rappahannock, river, Virginia.

rapparee, a seventeenth-century Irish freebooter.

rappee, a coarse snuff.

rapport (en) (Fr. m.), in harmony, in keeping (with).

rapprochement (Fr. m.) establishment or renewal of friendly relations.

rapscallion, rascal, *not* rabs-.

rar/a av/is (Lat.), a prodigy, lit. a rare bird; *pl.* **-ae, -es.**

rare, abbr. **r.**

rarebit, *see* **Welsh rabbit.**

rarefaction, *not* -efication.

rarefy, *not* rari-.

rarity, *not* -ety.

Rarotonga, Cook Islands, New Zealand.

R.A.S., Royal Agricultural, Asiatic, *or* Astronomical Society.

Rasalas (astr.), star in Leo.

R.A.S.C., Royal Army Service Corps, *now* **R.C.T.**

rase, to destroy, *use* **raze.**

Raskolnik (Russ.), a dissenter from the Orthodox Church.

Rasoumowsky Quartets (the), by Beethoven; *properly* **Razumovsky.**

Rasselas, by S. Johnson, 1759.

rat/, -ting.

rata (Lat.), individual share; *pro* —, in proportion.

rat/able, *see* **-eable.**

ratafia, a cordial, cake, biscuit, *or* cherry, *not* -ifia, -ifie.

ratan, *use* **rattan.**

ratany (bot.), *use* rh-.

Ratcliff Highway, *not* -e, *now* The Highway. *See also* **Rad-.**

rateable (U.S. **ratable**).

ratepayer (one word).

Rathaus (Ger. n.), town hall.

ratio/, arith. relation; *pl.* **-s.**

rationale, logical cause, reason.

rationalize, *not* -ise.

Ratisbon, Bavaria, *use* **Regensburg.**

ratline (naut.), the ladder-rope on the shrouds, *not* -in, -ing.

rattan, a cane, *not* ratan.

rattlesnake (one word).

Raumer (Friedrich L. G. von), 1781–1873, German historian; — **(R. von),** 1822–1905, German philologist.

R.A.V.C., Royal Army Veterinary Corps.

ravel/, -led, -ling (U.S. **-ed, -ing**).

Rawalpindi, Punjab, Pakistan, *not* Rawul-, colloq. Pindi.

Ray (John), 1627–1705, English naturalist, spelt Wray till 1670. *See also* **Rae, Reay.**

Ray Bareilly, *use* **Rae Bareli.**

Rayleigh, Essex.

Rayleigh (John William Strutt, Baron), 1842–1919, English physicist. *See also* **Raleigh.**

raze, to destroy, *not* rase.

Razumovsky, *see* **Rasoumowsky.**

R.B., Rifle Brigade.

Rb, rubidium (no point).

R.B.A., Royal (Society of) British Artists.

R.B.S., Royal (Society of) British Sculptors.

R.C., Red Cross, Roman Catholic.

R.C.A., Royal College of Art.

R.C.C., Roman Catholic Church.

R.C.M., Royal College of Music (London).

R.C.N.C., Royal Corps of Naval Constructors.

R.C.O., Royal College of Organists.

R.C.O.G., Royal College of Obstetricians and Gynaecologists.

R.C.P., Royal College of Physicians, ditto Preceptors.

R.C.S., Royal College of Science, ditto Surgeons, Royal Commonwealth Society; Royal Corps of Signals.

R.C.T., Royal Corps of Transport.

R.C.V.S., Royal College of Veterinary Surgeons.

R.D., Royal Dragoons, Rural Dean.

R/D, refer to drawer (of a cheque).

Rd., road.

R.D.C., Royal Defence Corps, Rural District Council.

R.D.F., Radio Direction-Finding.

R.D.I., Royal Designer for Industry (Royal Society of Arts).

R.D.S., Royal Drawing Society.

R.D.Y., Royal Dockyard.

Re (il) (It.), the King (no accent).

Re, rhenium (no point); rupee (no point).

R.E., Reformed Episcopal, Right Excellent, Royal Engineers, — Exchange, — Society of Painter-Etchers and Engravers.

re (Lat.), with regard to.

re- (the prefix), when followed by *e* and separately sounded, to have hyphen, as re-echo.

react, etc. (one word).

readdress (one word).

Reade (Charles), 1814–84, English novelist. *See also* **Rede, Reed, Reid.**

reader (typ.), a corrector of the press; one who reports on MSS. to a publisher (l.c.).

Reader, a university teacher, in some universities intermediate between Lecturer and Professor (cap. when title).

Reader's Digest Association Ltd., publishers.

readers' marks, *see* proof correction marks.

reading-room (hyphen).

readjourn, readjust, readmission, readmit/, -ted, -ting (one word).

ready-made (hyphen)

reafforest (one word) (U.S. reforest).

reagent (one word).

real, former Portuguese and Brazilian coin; *pl.* **reis.**

real/, Spanish and Mexican coin, formerly current in U.S. (a 'bit', value 12½ cents); *pl.* **-es.**

realiz/e, -able, *not* -ise.

Realpolitik (Ger.), practical politics (cap., not ital.).

real tennis, the original game, no longer just tennis, nor royal tennis.

realty (law), landed property.

ream of paper, 480, 500, 504, or 516 sheets; abbr. **rm.**

reanimate, reappear, reappoint (one word).

Rear-Admiral, abbr. **R.A.** *or* **Rear-Adm.** (hyphen, caps.).

rear-guard (hyphen).

rearm (one word).

rearmouse, *use* reremouse.

reassemble, reassert/, -ed, -ing, reassur/e, -ance (one word).

Réaumur (René Antoine F. de), 1683–1757, inventor of thermom. scale; the scale itself, abbr. **R.**, *or* **Réaum.** *See also* **Raumer.**

reaver, a robber (Sc. **reiver**).

reawake, etc. (one word).

Reay (Donald James Mackay, Baron), 1839–1921, Scottish (Dutch-born) Governor of Bombay and first president of the Brit. Academy. *See also* **Rae, Ray.**

rebaptize, *not* -ise (one word).

rebate, to reduce, a reduction, *also* a hard freestone. *See also* **rabbet.**

rebel/, **-led, -ling.**

rebound, to bound back (one word).

re-bound (bookbinding) (hyphen).

rebus/, a puzzle; *pl.* **-es.**

rebut/, **-ted, -ting.**

rec., receipt, recipe, record, -ed, -er.

recall, in Scots law **recal.**

Récamier (Jeanne Françoise J. A., Madame), 1777–1849, a leader of French Society.

recast (one word).

recd., received.

receipt, abbr. **rec.**

receivable, *not* -eable.

Rechabite, a total abstainer.

réchauffé, a warmed-up dish, (fig.) a re-hash.

recherch/é (adj.), *fem.* **-ée,** choice (not ital.).

recidivist, one who habitually relapses into crime.

recipe/, *pl.* **-s,** abbr. **rec.;** — **mark** (typ.), ℞.

réclame (Fr. f.), notoriety by advertisement; (journ.) editorial announcement; (typ.) catchword, prima.

Reclus (Jean Jacques Élisée), 1830–1905, French geographer, *not* Ré-.

recoal (one word).

recognizance, a bond given to a court, *not* -sance.

recognize, *not* -ise.

recommit/, **-ted, -ting.**

recompense (noun and verb).

recompose (one word).

reconcilable, *not* -eable.

reconciler, *not* -or.

reconnaissance, preliminary survey, *not* reconnoi- (not ital.).

reconnoitre, to make a preliminary survey (U.S. **-er**).

reconsider (one word).

record-player (hyphen).

recoup, to recompense, recover, make up for.

recover, to regain possession of, to revive (one word).

re-cover, to cover again (hyphen).

recreat/e, to refresh; **-ion,** amusement, pastime (no hyphens).

re-creat/e, to create again; **-or,** *not* -er (hyphen).

rect., rectified.

rectif/y, -ied, -ier, -ying.

recto (typ.), the right-hand page, usu. having an odd page number, 1, 3, 5, etc.; abbr. ᵃ, ʳ, r., rᵒ (not ital.).

rector/, incumbent of a parish, originally one whose tithes were held by the parson; abbr. **R.**; adj. **-ial.**

Rector (cap. as title), head of Scottish universities, some university colleges, some Scottish and German schools, some R.C. missions, seminaries, etc.

rectoral (adj.), of God as ruler.

rect/um (anat.), *pl.* **-a.**

rect/us (anat.), *pl.* **-i.**

reçu (Fr. m.), a receipt.

recueil (Fr. m.), a literary compilation.

reculer pour mieux sauter (Fr.), to withdraw to await a better opportunity.

recur/, -red, -ring.
recut, to cut again (one word).
rédact/eur (Fr.), editor; *fem.* **-rice.**
rédaction (Fr. f.), editing, editorial department.
Redakteur (Ger. m.), editor (cap.).
Redbourn, Herts.
Redbourne, Lincs.
redbreast, a robin.
redecorate (one word).
Rede Lecture, Camb. Univ. *See also* **Reade, Reed, Reid.**
redeliver, redemand (one word).
Redemptionists, an order of Trinitarian friars devoted to the redemption of Christian captives from slavery.
Redemptorists, an order of missionaries founded in 1732 by Alfonso Liguori.
Redgauntlet, by Sir W. Scott, 1824 (one word).
red-hot (hyphen).
red lead (two words).
red-letter day (one hyphen).
redoubt (fort.), *not* -out.
redress, to remedy (one word).
re-dress, to dress again (hyphen).
red-tap/e, official routine; **-ism, -ist** (hyphen).
reducible, *not* -eable.
reductio ad/ absurdum (Lat.), an obviously absurd conclusion; — — *impossibile,* an impossible conclusion.
red-water, cattle disease (hyphen).
re-dye, to dye again (hyphen).
reebok (Afrik.), an antelope, *not* rhe-.
re-echo (hyphen).
Reed (Alfred German), 1847–95, English actor; — **(Edward Tennyson),** 1860–1933, English caricaturist;

— **(Talbot Baines),** 1852–93, English typefounder and writer of boys' books;
— **(Walter),** 1851–1902, American army surgeon (mosquitoes and yellow fever). *See also* **Reade, Rede, Reid.**
Reekie (Auld), Old Smoky, that is Edinburgh.
re/-elect, -embark (*not* reim-), **-enact, -enforce** (to enforce again), **-enslave, -enter, -enthrone, -establish, -exchange, -exhibit** (hyphens).
Ref., the Reformation.
ref., referee, referred, reference, reform/ed, -er, refractor.
refait (Fr. m.), a drawn game; new horns or antlers.
Ref. Ch., Reformed Church.
refer/, -able, -ence, -red, -rer, -ring.
refer/ee, -eed, abbr. **ref.**
reference marks (typ.), may be used as an alternative to superior figures for footnote references in the order * (except in math. works) † ‡ § ‖ ¶, repeated in duplicate as ** etc. if necessary. *See also* **footnotes.**
referend/um, an appeal to the people to decide on certain laws, etc.; *pl.* **-a.**
refer/rible, *use* -able.
refill (one word).
refit/, -ted, -ting.
refl., reflect/ion, -ive, -ively, reflex, -ive, -ively.
reflectible, *use* **reflexible.**
reflection (the general spelling, to be used); **reflexion** (etym. correct); abbr. **refl.;** in Fr. f. *réflexion.*
reflective, (of surfaces) giving back a reflection, (of people) meditative.
reflector, *not* -er.

reflex/ible, able to be reflected. *not* reflect-.

reflexion, etym. correct, but *use* **reflection.**

reflexive (gram.), implying that the action is reflected upon the doer.

reforest/, -ation, U.S. for **reafforest/, -ation.**

reform, to improve, correct.

re-form, to form again.

Reformation (the) (cap.); abbr. **Ref.**

Reform Bills, 1832, 1867, 1884-5.

reform/ed, -er, abbr. **ref.**

refractor, a type of telescope; abbr. **ref.**

refrangible, that can be refracted.

Reg., Regent, *regina* (queen).

reg., regis/ter, -trar, -try, regular, -ly.

regalia, is *plural.*

regd., registered.

regenerator.

Regensburg, Bavaria, *not* Ratisbon.

Regent, abbr. **Reg.**

Regent's Park, London (apos.).

Reg.-Gen., Registrar-General.

Régie, governmental control of articles paying duty in Aus., Fr., It., Sp., Turk.

regime (not ital., no accent when thus anglicized); in Fr. m. *régime.*

regimen/, *pl.* **-s** (not ital.).

regiment, abbr. **regt.**

regina (Lat.), queen; abbr. **R.** *or* **Reg.**

register (binding), a book-marker; (typ.) when pages back one another exactly, or when the separate colour printings of an illustration fit exactly, they are said to be '*in* register', otherwise '*out of* register'.

registered, abbr. **regd.**

register marks (typ.),

crosses used to help achieve good register.

Register Office, *not* Registry.

registrable, *not* -erable.

registr/ar, -y, abbr. **reg.**

Registrar-General (hyphen, caps.); abbr. **Reg.-Gen.**

Registrary, official of Cambridge University (*not* Registrar).

regium donum (Lat.), a royal grant.

Regius Professor, abbr. **Reg. Prof.**

règle (Fr. f.), a rule.

réglé, -e (Fr.), settled, regular; ruled (of paper).

Règne Animal (Le), by Cuvier, 1817.

regn/um (Lat.), a kingdom, or badge of royalty; *pl.* **-a.**

Reg. Prof., Regius Professor.

regrater (hist.), one who buys to sell at a profit (once a criminal offence), *not* -or.

regret/, -ful, -fully, -table, -tably, -ted, -ting.

regt., regiment.

regul/a (Lat.), a book of rules; *pl.* **-ae.**

regular/, -ly, abbr. **reg.**

regulator, *not* -er.

Reichs/anstalt, German off. institution (1871-1945); *Reichsanzeiger,* German Gazette; **-kanzler,** German Chancellor; **-mark,** abbr. **R.M.; -tag,** German legislative body (cap.).

Reid (Sir George), 1841-1913; Scottish painter; — **(Rt. Hon. Sir George Houston),** 1845-1819, Australian politician; — **(Capt. Thomas Mayne),** 1818-83, British novelist; — **(Thomas),** 1710-96, Scottish metaphysician; — **(Whitelaw),** 1837-1912, American journalist and diplomat. *See also* **Reade, Rede, Reed.**

Reikiavik, *use* **Reykj-.**

reim, *see* **riem.**

reimbark, *use* **re-em-.**

reimburse, to pay for loss or expense (one word).

réimpression (Fr. f.), a reprint.

Reims, Fr., *not* Rh-.

reine-Claude (Fr. f.), greengage; *pl.* *reines-.*

re infecta (Lat.), with the object not attained.

reinforce/, -ment (mil.), *not* reen-.

Reinhardt (Max), 1873–1943, German theatrical producer.

reinstate (one word).

reis, pl. of *real,* a Portuguese coin.

Reis Effendi (Turk.), title of former Secretary of State for Foreign Affairs.

reissue, *see* **title-pages.**

reiver, a robber, Scottish form of **reav-.**

Réjane (Gabrielle Charlotte, real name **Réju),** 1857–1920, French actress.

rel., relative, -ly, religion, religious, *reliquiae* (relics).

relâche (Fr. m.), respite, rest, interruption; (theat.) performances suspended; (f.) a port, harbour.

relat/er, one who relates; **-or** (law), one who lays information before the Attorney-General.

relationship, the state of being related.

relative/, -ly, abbr. **rel.**

relativity, the state of being relative.

releas/er, one who releases; **-or** (law), one who grants a release.

re-let/, -ting (hyphen).

relev/é (Fr.), *fem.* **-ée,** exalted, noble; (cook.) highly seasoned, *not* ré-.

relic, *not* -ique.

relief-printing (typ.), process such as letterpress.

relievo, *use* **rilievo.**

religieuse/ (Fr. f.), a nun; *pl.* **-s.**

religieux (Fr. m.), a monk; *pl. same.*

relig/ion, -ious, abbr. **rel.**

religious/ denominations (typ.), as Baptist, Protestant, to have caps.; — **marks,** *see* **ecclesiastical signs.**

relique, *use* **relic.**

reliquiae (Lat.), relics, is *plural;* abbr. **rel.**

rel/y, *not* -ie; **-ied, -ying.**

rem., remarks.

remainder (typ.), that part of an edition which is unsaleable at its original price.

Remarque (Erich Maria), 1898–1970, German-born naturalized American novelist.

Rembrandt/ (in full, — **Harmenszoon van Rijn Ryn),** 1607–70, Dutch painter; adj. **-esque.**

R.E.M.E., Royal Electrical and Mechanical Engineers.

remerciment (Fr. m.), thanks, *not* -iement.

rem/ex (Lat.), wing quill feather; *pl.* **-iges.**

Reminiscere Sunday, the second in Lent.

remisier, a half-commission man on the Stock Exchange.

remissible, capable of being forgiven.

remit/, -tance, -ter.

remonstrator, *not* -er.

rémoulade or *rémolade* (Fr. f.), salad dressing, kind of sauce.

removable, *not* -eable.

remplissage (Fr. m.), padding.

Rémusat (Charles François Marie, comte de), 1797–1875, French politician and writer; — **(Jean Pierre),** 1788–1832, French Chinese scholar.

Renaissance (the), *not* -ascence (cap.).

renard, the fox, *use* **rey-**.

rendezvous, *sing.* and *pl.* (one word, not ital.); Fr. *rendez-vous* (hyphen).

Renoir (Auguste), 1841–1919, French painter.

renomm/é (Fr.), *fem.* **-ée,** celebrated.

renommée (Fr. f.), renown, acclaim.

Renouf (Sir Peter le Page), 1822–97, English Egyptologist.

renouncement, *use* **renunciation**.

renovator, *not* -er.

rentes/ (Fr. f.), independent income, *also* government stocks; — *sur l'État,* interest on government loans.

rent/ier (Fr.), *fem.* **-ière,** one whose income is derived from investments.

renvoi (Fr. m.), dismissal, adjournment; (law) sending before another court; (typ.) a reference mark.

reometer, *use* **rhe-**.

reopen (one word).

reorganize, *not* -ise.

Rep., U.S. Republican (party).

rep., report, -er, representative, republic, -an.

rep, a fabric, *now usually* **repp**.

rep/air, -airable (of material things), **-aration** (amends).

reparable (of loss, etc.), that can be made good.

repartee, (the making of) witty retorts (not ital.); in Fr. f. *repartie*.

repartir (Fr.), to reply, to start again.

répartir (Fr.), to divide.

repel/, -led, -lent, -ler.

repertoire (not ital.).

repertorium (Lat.), a catalogue.

repetatur (Lat.), let it be repeated; abbr. *repet*.

répétiteur, one who rehearses opera-singers (not ital.).

repetitorium (Lat.), a summary.

replaceable, *not* -cable.

replica/, a duplicate by the artist himself; *pl.* **-s** (not ital.).

réplique (Fr. f.), a reply.

repl/y, -ies, -ier, -ying.

report/, -er, abbr. **rep.**

repoussé, ornamental metal work hammered from the reverse side (not ital.).

repp, a fabric, *now more usual than* **rep**.

repr., representing.

reprehensible, open to rebuke, *not* -able.

representable, *not* -ible.

representative, abbr. **rep.**

Representatives (House of), lower division of U.S. Congress (caps.).

repress/, -ible, -or (*not* -er).

reprint (typ.), a second or new impression of any printed work; a reimpression; printed matter taken from some other publication for reproduction; also printed 'copy' (one word); abbr. **R.P.** *See also* **title-pages**.

reprisal, act of retaliation, *not* -izal.

reprise, (law) a yearly charge or deduction, (mus.) a return to an earlier theme, *not* -ize.

reprize, to prize anew.

reproducible.

reproof (noun), a rebuke.

reproof (verb), to make waterproof again.

reprove, to rebuke.

republic/, -an, abbr. **R.**

Republican, U.S. political party, abbr. **Rep.**

République française (l.c. *f*), French Republic; abbr. **R.F.**

repudiator.

reputable, respectable.
requiem/, the Mass for the dead; *pl.* **-s.**
requies/cat in pace (Lat.), may he, *or* she, rest in peace, abbr. **R.I.P.,** *pl.* *-cant* — —; *-cit* — —, he, *or* she, rests in peace.
reredos/ (two syllables), ornamental screen or panelling behind altar, *not* -dorse, -dosse, rerdos; *pl.* **-es.**
reremouse, a bat, *not* rear-.
res., reserve, resid/es, -ence, resigned.
res/ (Lat.), a thing or things; — *adjudicata,* a matter already decided; — *angusta domi,* scanty means at home.
rescuable.
reserve, abbr. **res.**
Reserve (Army) (caps.).
reserv/er, in law **-or.**
reservist, *not* -eist.
res gestae (Lat. *pl.*), things done, matters of fact.
resid/es, -ence, abbr. **r.,** *or* **res.**
residu/um, *pl.* **-a.**
resigned, abbr. **res.**
resin, *pron.* rĕz'in, gum from trees or synthetically produced. *See also* **rosin.**
resist/ance, -ant, *not* -ence, -ent.
resist/er, person; **-or,** thing.
res/ judicata (Lat.), a thing already decided; — *nihili,* a nonentity.
Resnik (Regina), b. 1922, American mezzo-soprano.
resolv/able, -er.
resonator, an instrument responding to a note.
resource, in Fr. f. *ress-.*
resp., respondent.
resp. (Ger.), *respektiv.*
respecter.
Respighi (Ottorino), 1879–1936, Italian composer.
respirator, *not* -er.
response mark (typ.), ℞.

responsible, in Fr. *responsable.*
res publica (Lat.), public property (two words).
respublica (Lat.), the commonwealth (one word).
restaurateur (Fr. m.), restaurant-keeper.
restor/able, -ator.
Restoration (the) (cap.).
resum/e, -able.
résumé, a summary (not ital.).
resurgam (Lat.), I shall rise again.
resuscitat/e, -or.
Reszke (Édouard de), 1856–1917, Polish bass; — **(Jean de),** 1850–1925, Polish tenor.
ret., retired.
retable, the super-altar.
retd., returned.
R. et I. (Lat.), *Rex et Imperator,* king and emperor; *Regina et Imperatrix,* queen and empress.
retin/a, inner membrane of the eyeball; *pl.* (anat.) **-ae,** (gen.) **-as.**
retired, abbr. **ret.**
retraceable.
retract/able, -ability, *not* -ible, -ibil-.
retractor, *not* -er.
retree, slightly defective paper.
retriever, a dog.
retrouss/é (Fr.), *fem.* **-ée,** turned up.
returned, abbr. **retd.**
Reuben (Bib.), son of Jacob.
Reubens, *use* **Ru-.**
reunion, a social gathering; in Fr. f. *réunion.*
Réunion (Île de), Indian Ocean.
Reuters Ltd., reporting agency; *pron.* roi'-ters.
Rev., Book of Revelation (N.T.), Review. *See* **Reverend.**

rev., revenue, reverse, revis/e, -ed, -ion, revolution, -s.

Reval (Estonian S.S.R.), *use* **Tallinn.**

Revd., *see* **Reverend.**

réveil (Fr. m.), an awaking, a morning call.

reveille, morning call to troops; *pron.* rĕ-văl′-ĭ (no accents and not ital.).

réveillon (Fr. m.), a midnight repast on Christmas eve or New Year's eve.

Revel (Estonian S.S.R.), *use* **Tallinn.**

revel/, -led, -ler, -ling (U.S. -ed, -er, -ing).

Revelation, Book of (N.T.), *not* -ions; abbr. **Rev.**

revenons à nos moutons (Fr.), let us return to our subject.

revenue, abbr. **rev.**

Reverend, standard abbr. **Rev.**; elegant abbr. **The Revd.**; *pl.* **Revds.**; Very Revd. (dean), Right Revd. (bishop), Most Revd. (archbishop).

reverie, day-dream, *not* -y.

revers (Fr. dress.), the front turned back showing the inner surface; *pl.* same.

reverse, abbr. **rev.**

reversed block (typ.), a design in which the illustration or wording appears in white against a background.

reversi, a game, *not* ri-.

reversible, *not* -able.

reverso (typ.), *see* **verso.**

rêveu/r (Fr.), *fem.* -se, (day) dreamer.

revidieren (Ger.), to revise.

Review, abbr. **Rev.**

Reviews (titles of) (typ.), when cited, to be italic.

revise (typ.), second or subsequent proof; abbr. **rev.**

revis/e, -able, -ing.

revis/e, -ed, -ion, abbr. **rev.**

Revised Standard Version, the (caps.), abbr. **R.S.V.**

Revised Statutes, abbr. **R.S.** *or* **Rev. Stat.**

Revised Version, the, (caps.), abbr. **R.V.**

reviv/er, one who revives; (law) -or, a proceeding to revive a suit.

revoir (à) (Fr.), to be revised.

revoir! (au), till we meet again! (not ital.).

revo/ke, -cable, -cation.

Revolution (the), Amer. 1775–83, Chin. 1911–12, Eng. 1688–9, Fr. 1789–95, 1830, 1848, 1870, Russ. 1905, 1917 (cap.).

revolution/, -s, abbr. **rev.**

revolutionize, *not* -ise.

Rev. Stat., Revised Statutes.

revue, a theatrical entertainment (not ital.).

rex (Lat.), king; abbr. **R.**

Reykjavik, Iceland, *pron.* rā′kyăvek; *not* Reiki-.

reynard, the fox, *not* ren-.

Reynolds News (no apos.).

Reynolds numbers (two words, no apos.).

rez-de-chaussée (Fr. m.), ground floor (hyphens).

R.F., *République française* (Fr. Republic), Royal Fusiliers.

rf., *see* **rinforzando.**

R.F.A., Royal Field Artillery.

R.F.C., Royal Flying Corps (*since* 1918 **R.A.F.**), Rugby Football Club.

R.G.A., Royal Garrison Artillery.

R.G.S., Royal Geographical Society.

R.H., Royal Highness.

Rh, rhodium (no point).

r.h., right hand.

R.H.A., Royal Hibernian Academy, — Horse Artillery.

rhabdomancy, divination by rod, *not* ra-.

Rhadamanth/ine, stern, like -us, judge of the Greek Hades, *not* Ra-, -tine.

Rhaet/ia, -ian, -ic, (of) Austrian Tyrol, *not* Rae-, Rhe-.

rhapsodize, to be enthusiastic, *not* -ise.

rhatany (bot.), S. American shrub with astringent root, *not* rat-.

Rheims, *use* **Reims.**

Rhein (Ger. m.), the Rhine.

Rheingold (*Das*), opera by Wagner, 1869.

Rheinisches Museum für Philologie, a German periodical.

rhenium, symbol **Re** (no point).

rheology (phys.), science of flow.

rheo/meter, -stat, -trope, instruments for (respectively) measuring, regulating, reversing electric current.

Rhesus factor, (in the blood), abbr. **Rh-factor** (hyphen, no point); **Rh-positive,** reacting to blood tests like rhesus monkeys; **Rh-negative,** not ditto.

rhet., rhetoric.

R.H.G., Royal Horse Guards (the Blues).

rhinoceros/, *pl.* **-es;** abbr. **rhino/,** *pl.* **-s** (no point).

R. Hist. S., Royal Historical Society.

Rhode Island, U.S., off. abbrev. **R.I.**

Rhodes Scholar (at Oxford).

Rhodesia, S. Africa, U.D.I. Nov. 1965, republic by unilateral declaration, Mar. 1970.

rhodium, symbol **Rh** (no point).

rhododendron/, *pl.* **-s.**

rhodomontade, *use* **rodo-.**

rhomb/us (geom.), *pl.* **-i.**

Rhondda Valley, Glam.

Rhône, dép. and river, *not* Rhone.

R.H.S., Royal Horticultural Society, — Humane —.

rhumb/ (naut.), a loxodromic curve, *not* rho-, ru-; — **-line, -course, -sailing** (hyphen).

rhym/e, to versify, *not* rime; **-er** (**-ester** is derogatory).

rhythm/, -ic.

R.I., Rhode Island, U.S. (off. abbr.), Royal Institute of Painters in Water-Colours, Royal Institution.

R.I.A., Royal Irish Academy.

Rialto, Venice (cap.).

riant, laughing, cheerful, pleasant (not ital.).

rib/, -bed, -bing.

R.I.B.A., Royal Institute of British Architects.

riband, *see* **ribbon.**

ribband, a light spar used in shipbuilding.

rib/bon, *not* -and, except in sport and heraldry.

R.I.C., Royal Institute of Chemistry, Royal Irish Constabulary (pre-1922).

Ricardo (David), 1772– 1823, English economist.

Richelieu (Cardinal), 1585– 1642, French statesman.

Richepin (Jean), 1849–1926, French writer.

Richter (Hans), 1843–1916, German conductor of Wagnerian opera and the Hallé Orchestra; — (**Johann Paul Friedrich**), 1763–1825, German writer, pen-name Jean Paul.

Richthofen (Baron Manfred von), 1892–1918, German flying ace.

rick, *see* **wrick.**

rickets, a bone disease.

rickettsi/a, a micro-organism such as causes typhus, *pl.* **-ae;** from Howard Taylor Ricketts, 1871–1910, American pathologist.

rickety, shaky, *not* -tty.

rickshaw, abbr. of **jinricksha.**

ricochet/, skip (of projectile), **-ed, -ing** (not ital.).

R.I.C.S., Royal Institution of Chartered Surveyors.

rid/, **-ded, -ding.**

rid/**e, -eable, -den, -ing.**

ridg/**e, -y.**

riem (Afrik.), thong, *not* reim.

Riemann/(**Georg Friedrich Bernhard**), 1826–66, German mathematician; adj. **-ian.**

Riesling, a white wine.

Rievaulx Abbey, Yorks.

rifaciment/**o** (It.), a remaking; *pl.* **-i.**

riff-raff (hyphen).

rifl/**e, -ing.**

right (theat., from actor's point of view), abbr. **R.**

right angle, symbol ⌐.

right ascension (astr.), abbr. **R.A.**

righteous.

right/**-hand, -handed,** adjs. (hyphens).

right-hand pages (typ.), the recto pages, usu. with odd page numbers.

Right Reverend (for bishops and moderators in Presbyterian churches and Church of Scotland), abbr. **The Right Revd., Rt. Revd.**

Rigi, Switzerland, *not* -hi.

rigor (med.), a shivering-fit, *pron.* rī′-gor (not ital.).

rigor mortis (Lat.), stiffening of death (not ital.).

rigorous, *not* rigour-.

rigour, severity (U.S. **-or**).

Rigsdag, the Danish parliament.

Rigsmaal, the literary language of Norway; *see* **Landsmaal.**

Rig-Veda, Sanskrit religious book (caps., hyphen).

R.I.I.A., Royal Institute of International Affairs.

Riksdag, Swedish Parliament.

riliev/**o** (It.), raised or embossed work, *not* re-; *pl.* **-i.**

Rilke (**Rainer Maria**), 1875–1926, Austrian poet.

rim/, **-med, -ming.**

rima (It.), verse.

rim/**e,** hoar-frost; **-y.** *See also* **rhyme.**

Rimsky-Korsakov (**Nicholas Andreievich**), 1844–1908, Russian composer.

R.I.N.A., Royal Institution of Naval Architects, *formerly* **I.N.A.**

rinderpest, pleuro-pneumonia in cattle (one word).

rinforz/*ando,* **-ato** (It. mus.), with more emphasis; abbr. **rf.,** *or* **rinf.**

Ring der Nibelungen (*Der*), by Wagner, 1876.

Rio de Janeiro, Brazil, *not* Rio Janeiro.

Rio Grande, river, Brazil.

R.I.P., *Requiescat* (or **-ant**) *in pace* (may he, she (*or* they) rest in peace!).

R.I.P.H. & H., Royal Institute of Public Health and Hygiene.

Ripman (**Prof. Walter**), 1869–1947, English educationist.

riposte, a retort (U.S. **ripost**).

rippl/**e, -y.**

Rip Van Winkle, by Washington Irving, 1820 (three caps.).

ris de veau (Fr. cook. m.), sweetbread.

rises, abbr. **r.**

risible, provoking laughter; *not* -able.

risqu/*é* (Fr.), *fem.* **-ée,** risky, indelicate.

rissole, cake of minced meat fried in batter (not ital.).

rissolé (Fr. cook.), well-browned.

ritardando (mus.), holding back; abbr. *rit.* or *ritard.*

ritenuto (mus.), held back; abbr. *riten.*

ritornell/o (mus.), a short instrumental passage in a vocal work; return of full orchestra after a solo passage in a concerto; *pl.* *-i.*

ritualist/, one devoted to ritual (adj. *-ic*); (cap.) one of the High Church party in the C. of E.

Riv., river.

rival/, *-led*, *-ling* (U.S. *-ed*, *-ing*).

Rivaulx, *see* Rie-.

rivel/, to corrugate; *-led*, *-ling.*

River, when with name to have cap., as Yellow River, River Dart; abbr. R., *or* Riv.

Rivera y Orbaneja (Miguel Primo de), 1870–1930, Spanish general, dictator 1923–30.

riverside.

Rivesaltes, a French wine.

rivet/, *-ed*, *-er*, *-ing.*

Riviera, the coast of France and Italy from Nice to La Spezia.

Rivière (Briton), 1840–1920, English painter.

rivière (Fr. f.), river, (of diamonds) collar.

Rivingtons (Publishers), Ltd.

rix-dollar, coin once current in various European countries, *not* ricks- (hyphen); abbr. Rx.

Riyadh, cap. of Nejd, and one of the federal capitals of Saudi Arabia. *See* Mecca.

riz (Fr. m.), rice.

Rizzio (David), 1540–66, Italian musician, favourite of Mary Q. of Scots, assassinated, *not* Ricc-.

R.L.O., Returned Letter Office (*formerly* Dead — —).

R.L.S.S., Royal Life Saving Society.

R.M., Reichsmark, Resident Magistrate, Royal Mail, — Marines.

rm., ream.

R.M.A., Royal Marine Artillery, — Military Academy (Sandhurst, *formerly* Woolwich).

R.M.C., Royal Military College (Sandhurst), *now* R.M.A.

R.Met.S., Royal Meteorological Society.

R.M.L.I., Royal Marine Light Infantry.

R.M.S., Royal Mail Service, — — Steamer, — Microscopical Society, — Society of Miniature Painters.

R.M.S.M., Royal Military School of Music.

Rn (chem.), radon (no point).

R.N., Royal Navy.

R.N.A.S., Royal Naval Air Service, since 1918 incorporated in R.A.F.

R.N.C., Royal Naval College.

R.N.L.I., Royal National Lifeboat Institution.

R.N.R., Royal Naval Reserve.

R.N.V.R., Royal Naval Volunteer Reserve, combined with R.N.R. in 1957.

R.O., Receiving Office, -r, Relieving Officer, Returning —, Royal Observatory.

ro., rood.

r⁰ (typ.), recto.

Road (typ.), *after* name to be cap., as Fulham Road; abbr. Rd.

road/side, *-stead*, *-way* (no hyphen).

roan (binding), a soft and flexible sheepskin, often imitating morocco.

Roanoke, Virginia, U.S.

roast (to rule the), to exercise leadership, *not* roost.

Robben Island, S. Africa.

Robbia (Luca della), 1399–1482, Italian sculptor. *See also* **Della-Robbia**.

robbin (E. Ind.), a package.

Robbins Report, 1963, on Higher Education (no apos.).

robe de/chambre (Fr. f.), morning-gown; — — *cour*, Court-dress.

Robens (Alfred, Lord), 1910– , Chairman of the National Coal Board till 1971.

Robespierre (Maximilien F.M. Isidore de), 1758–94, French revolutionary.

robin, the bird. *See also robbin*.

Robin Goodfellow, a sprite (caps).

Robin Hood/, hero of medieval legend; — —'s Bay, a town, Yorks. (apos., three words).

robin redbreast.

Robinson Crusoe, by Defoe, 1719.

robot, automaton, *not* robb-.

Rob Roy, Robert ('the Red') Macgregor, 1671–1734, Scottish outlaw (caps., two words).

Robt, Robert (no point).

roburite, an explosive.

R.O.C., Royal Observer Corps.

roc, a fabulous bird, *not* rock, rok, ruc, ruck, rukh.

Roch (St.), *pron.* rŏk.

Roche, *pron.* rōsh.

Rochefoucauld, *see* La —.

Rochelle, France, *use* La —.

roches moutonnées (geol.), *pl.*, a glaciated type of rock-surface (not ital.).

rochet, a surplice-like linen garment, *not* rotch-, -ette.

Rocinante, Don Quixote's steed, usu. anglicized as **Rosinante**.

Rock (the), Gibraltar.

Rockefeller/ (John Davison), 1840–1937, head of family of U.S. capitalists; — **Center**, nexus of office skyscrapers, N.Y.; — **Foundation**, 1913, philanthropic; — **Institute**, 1901, for medical research, a university since 1965.

Rockies (the) (N. Amer.), the Rocky Mountains.

'Rock of Ages' (caps).

rococo, a frivolous baroque of reign of Louis XV of France, *not* rocc-.

rod, *see* perch.

Rod (Édouard), 1857–1910, French writer.

Rodd (James Rennell, first Baron Rennell), 1858–1941, English diplomat and scholar.

Roderic, d. 711, last king of the Visigoths, *not* -ick.

Rodin (Auguste), 1840–1917, French sculptor.

rodomontade, bragging talk, *not* rh-.

roebuck (one word).

roe-deer (hyphen).

Roffen., signature of Bp. of Rochester (point).

Rogation Sunday, that before Ascension Day.

Rogers (Bruce), 1870–1951, American typographer.

Roget (Peter Mark), 1779–1869, compiled *Thesaurus*.

rognons (Fr. m.), kidneys.

Rohilkhand, Uttar Pradesh, India, *not* Rohilc-, -und.

R.O.I., Royal Institute of Oil Painters.

roi fainéant (Fr.), do-nothing king.

roisterer, noisy reveller, *not* roy-.

rok, *use* roc.

Rokitansky (Karl, Baron von), 1804–78, Czech-born Austrian anatomist.

role, actor's part, in Fr. m. *rôle*.

roll-call (hyphen).

Rolls-Royce (hyphen).

Rölvaag (Ole Edvart), 1876–1931, Norw.-Amer. novelist.

roly-poly, a pudding, *not* the many variants.

Rom., Roman, Romance, Romans (Epistle to the).

rom., roman type.

Romaic, modern Greek.

romaika, a national dance of mod. Greece.

roman (typ.), ordinary upright letters as distinct from bold or italic; abbr. **rom.**

Roman Catholic/ (caps.), abbr. **R.C.;** —— **Church** (caps.), abbr. **R.C.C.**

Roman de la Rose, thirteenth-cent. French allegorical verse romance, source of *Romaunt of the Rose,* attributed to Chaucer.

Romanée-Conti, a red Burgundy wine.

Romanes, gipsy language, *pron.* rŏ′-măn-ĕz.

Romanes lectures, at Oxford Univ., *pron.* rō-mahn′-ĕz.

Romanesque, style of architecture between classical and Gothic.

Romania/, -n, the official Romanian spelling, now preferred to the traditional English Roum- or Rum-.

romanize, *not* -ise (cap. in hist. and cult. senses).

roman numerals, *see* **numerals (roman).**

Romanov, Russian dynasty, 1613–1917, *not* -of, -off; *pron.* rō-mahn′-ŏf.

Romans (the Epistle to the); abbr. **Rom.** (N.T.).

Romansh, Rhaeto-Romanic, dial. of E. Switzerland, *not* Rou-, Ru-, -ansch, -onsch.

Romany, a gipsy, *not* -ncy, -mmany (cap.).

Romaunt of the Rose, see Roman de la Rose.

Romney (George), 1734–1802, English painter.

Romney Marsh, Kent.

Romsey, Hants.

Ronda, Spain.

ronde (typ.), a form of script.

rondeau/, a form of poem; *pl.* **-x.**

rondel, a special form of the rondeau.

rondo/ (mus.), a movement whose main theme recurs at regular intervals; *pl.* **-s.**

rone, a water-pipe.

Röntgen (Julius), 1855–1934, Dutch composer; — **(Wilhelm Konrad von),** 1845–1923, German physicist, discoverer of Röntgen (or X-) rays.

rood, abbr. **ro.**

Rooinek (Afrik.), an Englishman, *not* Roi-.

rook (chess), abbr. **R,** *also* a bird.

Rooke (Sir George), 1650–1709, English admiral.

Roosevelt (Franklin Delano), 1882–1945, U.S. President 1933–45; — **(Theodore),** 1858–1919, U.S. President 1901–9.

roost (to rule the), *use* **roast.**

rop/e, -y.

Roquefort, a Fr. cheese.

rorqual, a whale.

rosaceous, of the rose family.

Rosalind, in *As You Like It,* and Spenser's *Shepheardes Calendar.*

Rosaline, in *Love's Labour's Lost, Romeo and Juliet.*

rosary, a rose-garden, a string of beads for prayers, *not* -ery.

Roscommon, Ireland.

ros/e, -y.

rose (Fr. m.), pink colour; (f.) a rose; *couleur de —,* roseate, attractive.

Rosebery (Earl of), *not* -berry, -bury.

rosemary, evergreen fragrant shrub, *not* rosm-.

Rosencrans (William Starke), 1819–98, U.S. general.

Rosencrantz and Guildenstern, in *Hamlet*.

Rosenkranz (J. K. F.), 1805–79, German metaphysical philosopher.

Rosenkreuz, *see* **Rosicrucian.**

Rosentreter, a chess opening.

rosery (error), *use* **-ary.**

rose-water (hyphen).

rosewood (one word).

Rosh Hashama, the Jewish New Year's Day.

Rosicrucian, (a member of) an order devoted to occult lore, founded by Christian Rosenkreuz, 1484.

rosin, a solid residue from turpentine distillation, used esp. on strings of musical instruments; *pron.* roz'-in. *See also* **resin.**

Rosinante, anglicized spelling of Don Quixote's steed, in Sp. **Rocinante.**

Roskilde/, Denmark; — **(Treaty of),** 1658, between Denmark and Sweden.

Roslin, Midlothian.

Rosny (Joseph Henry), pseudonym covering collaboration of French novelist brothers Joseph Henri Boëx, 1856–1940, and Séraphin Justin François Boëx, 1859–1948.

rosolio, a sweet cordial of S. Europe, *not* -oglio, -oli (not cap.).

R.o.S.P.A., Royal Society for the Prevention of Accidents.

Ross (Sir James Clark), 1800–62, English Arctic explorer; — **(Sir John),** 1777–1856, Scottish explorer, uncle of preceding; — **(Sir Ronald),** 1857–1932, physician (malaria-mosquito).

Rosse (Earl of), *pron.* rŏs.

Rossetti (Christina Georgina); 1830–94, English poet, sister of next; — **(Dante Gabriel),** 1828–82, English painter and poet; — **(Gabriele),** 1783–1854, Italian poet and liberal, father of the other three; — **(William Michael),** 1829–1919, English author and critic, son of preceding.

rossignol (Fr. m.), nightingale, skeleton key.

Rosslyn (Earl of). *See also* **Roslin.**

Ross-shire (hyphen); *now* **Ross and Cromarty.**

Rostand (Edmond), 1868–1918, French dramatist.

roster, a list of persons, showing rotation of duties.

Rostropovich (Mstislav), b. 1927, Russian cellist.

rostr/um, speaker's platform, *pl.* **-a** (not ital.).

rosy, *not* -ey.

rot/, **-ted,** **-ting.**

rota/, a roster; *pl.* **-s.**

Rotarian, a member of a Rotary Club (cap.).

rotary, revolving, *not* rotatory; (typ.) printing machine in which the plate(s) are mounted on a cylinder.

Rotary Club, a branch of the world-wide Rotary Movement, aiming at service to humanity (caps.).

rotator, a revolving part, (anat.) a muscle that rotates a limb.

rotatory, *use* **rotary.**

rote, mechanical memory or performance.

Rothamsted, Herts., agric. station for soil research.

Rothe (Richard), 1799–1867, German theologian.

Rothes (Earl of), *pron.* rōth′iz.

Rothschild, European family of bankers.

rôti (Fr. m.), roast meat.

rotifer/, minute aquatic animal, *pl.* **-s;** *rotifera* (Lat.) is pl.

rôtir (Fr. cook.), to roast.

rotogravure (typ.), web-fed photogravure.

rotondo (It. typ.), roman type.

rotor (math.), a vector of definite position; (mech.) a revolving part.

rottenstone (one word).

Rottingdean, Sussex (one word).

rotund/a, a domed circular building or hall, *not* -o; *pl.* **-as.**

roturi/er (Fr.), *fem.* **-ère,** of mean birth.

Rouault (Georges), 1871–1958, French painter.

Roubiliac (Louis François), 1695–1762, French sculptor, *not* -lliac.

rouble, Russian coin and monetary unit, *not* ru-; abbr. **r.**

roué, a debauchee (not ital.).

rouelle de veau (Fr. f.), fillet of veal.

rouge-et-noir, a game of chance (hyphens, not ital.).

rouget (Fr. m.), red mullet.

rough, to trump, *use* **ruff.**

rough-and-ready (adj.), — **-dry,** — **-hew,** — **-rider,** — **-shod** (hyphens).

roulade (mus.), a florid passage (not ital.).

rouleau/, a roll of money; *pl.* **-x** (not ital.).

Roumania/, -n, *use* **Romania,** q.v.

Roumelia/, -n, *use* **Rum-.**

roundabout (one word).

rounding (bind.), shaping back of book into a convex curve.

round-robin, a petition (hyphen).

Rouse (William Henry Denham), 1863–1950, English educationist.

Rousse (Edmond), 1817–1906, French writer.

Rousseau (Henri), 1844–1910, French painter, called *Le Douanier;* — **(Jean Baptiste),** 1670–1741, French poet; — **(Jean Jacques),** 1712–72, Geneva-born French philosopher; — **(Pierre Étienne Théodore),** 1812–67, French painter.

Roussillon, a red wine.

rout (verb), to put to flight; (noun) a rabble.

Routledge & Kegan Paul, Ltd., publishers.

rowlock (naut.), *not* roll-, rull-; *pron.* rŭl′uk.

Roxburgh, Scotland.

Roxburghe Club, exclusive club for bibliophiles.

Roxburghe (Duke of).

Royal/ (cap.), abbr. **R.;** — **Academ/y,** — **-ician,** — **Artillery,** abbr. **R.A.;** — **Highness, R.H.**

royal, former standard size of paper, 20 × 25 in.; — **4to,** 12½ × 10 in., — **8vo,** 10 × 6¼ in. (untrimmed). *See* **book sizes.**

Royal Society, abbr. **R.S.**

Royal Welch Fusiliers, Welch Regt. (but **Welsh Guards).**

roysterer, *use* **roi-.**

R.P., read for press, Reformed Presbyterian, reply paid, reprint, (Fr.) *Révérend Père* (Reverend Father), Royal Society of Portrait Painters.

R.P.E., Reformed Protestant Episcopal.

r.p.m., revolutions per minute. In scientific work **rev/min** (no points) is preferred.

R.P.O., Royal Philharmonic Orchestra.

r.p.s., revolutions per second. *See* **r.p.m.**

R.P.S., Royal Photographic Society.

R.Q.M.S., Regimental Quartermaster-Sergeant.

R.S., Revised Statutes, Royal Society.

Rs, rupees.

r.s., right side.

R.S.A., Royal Scottish Academ/y, -ician, Royal Society of Arts.

R.S.D., Royal Society of Dublin.

R.S.E., Royal Society of Edinburgh.

R.S.F., Royal Scots Fusiliers.

R.S.F.S.R., Russian Soviet Federated Socialist Republic, one (and by far the largest) of the republics forming the Union of Soviet Socialist Republics (**U.S.S.R.,** q.v.).

R.S.H., Royal Society for the Promotion of Health.

R.S.I., Royal Sanitary Institute, *now* **R.S.H.**

R. Signals, Royal Corps of Signals.

R.S.L., Royal Soc. London (usu. **R.S.** only), Royal Society of Literature.

R.S.M., Regimental Sergeant-Major, Royal School of Mines, Royal Society of Medicine.

R.S.O., railway sub-office, — sorting office.

R.S.P.B., Royal Society for the Protection of Birds.

R.S.P.C.A., Royal Society for Prevention of Cruelty to Animals.

R.S.S., *Regiae Societatis Sodalis* (Fellow of the Royal Society; Royal Statistical Society (*see* **F.S.S.**).

R.S.V., Revised Standard Version.

R.S.V.P., *répondez, s'il vous plaît* (please reply) (not to be used in writings in the third person).

R.T., radio-telegraphy, radio-telephony, received text.

R.T.C., Royal Tank Corps.

Rt. Hon., Right Honourable.

R.T.O., Railway Transport Officer.

R.T.R., Royal Tank Regiment.

Rt. Revd., Right Reverend (of a bishop or moderator).

R.T.S., Religious Tract Society (now incorporated in **U.S.C.L.**), Royal Toxophilite Society.

R.T.Y.C., Royal Thames Yacht Club.

R.U., Rugby Union.

Ru, ruthenium (no point).

Rubáiyát (*The*), by Omar Khayyám; in Persian poetry *Rubá'iyát, pl.*, are four-lined stanzas.

rubella (med.), German measles.

Rubens (Peter Paul), 1577–1640, Flemish painter, *not* Reu-.

rubican, a horse flecked white or grey.

rubicelle, a variety of ruby.

Rubicon (to cross the), to take an irretraceable step (cap.).

rubicund, red (of flesh).

rubidium, symbol **Rb** (no point).

Rubinstein (Anton Gregor), 1829–94, Russian composer and pianist; — **(Artur),** b. 1886, Polish pianist.

ruble, *use* **rouble.**

rubric, instruction in church book, originally printed in red.

ruby (typ.), old name for a size of type, about 5½ pt.

ru/c, -ck, -kh, *use* **roc.**

R.U.C., Royal Ulster Constabulary.

ruche (Fr. dress.), a quilling or frilling, *not* rou-.

rucksack, bag carried on back by walkers, etc., *not* rucsac.

rudd, a fish, *not* rud.

Rüdesheimer, a Rhine wine.

rue, to regret; **rueful, ruing.**

R.U.E. (theat.), right upper entrance.

ruff, a bird, *fem.* **reeve;** a fish (*not* ruffe); a frill worn round the neck; (cards) to trump.

rug/a (Lat.), a wrinkle; *pl.* -ae.

Ruhmkorff/ (H.D.), 1803–77, electrician; — **coil.**

rule (typ.), a line:
  dotted, ... ;
  double, ========;
  em, —;
  en, –;
  French, ——◆——;
  parallel, ========;
  single, ———;
  spread *or*
  swelled, ———————— ;
  total, ========;
  wavy, ∿∿∿∿∿.

'Rule, Britannia!' (comma).

rule-work (typ.), composition with many rules, as in tabular matter (hyphen).

rum/, -my.

Rumania/, -n, *use* **Romania/, -n,** q.v.

rumb, *use* rh-.

Rumelia/, an area of the Balkans, mainly in Bulgaria; -n; *not* Rou-.

rumin/ant, an animal that chews the cud; **-ator,** one who ponders, *not* -er.

Rumpelstiltskin, a dwarf in German folklore.

run (naut.), deserted; abbr. R.

Runeberg (Johan L.), 1804–77, Swedish poet.

runners (typ.), figures or letters placed down the margin of a page to identify the lines.

running/ headline *or* — **title** (typ.), *see* **headlines.**

Runnymede, meadow on R. Thames where K. John signed Magna Charta, 1215.

runoff (noun, one word).

run on/ (typ.), (matter) to (be) run on without break or paragraph; — — **solid,** to continue without break or leads.

runway (one word).

rupee, abbr. **Re,** *pl.* **Rs.**

Rupert's Land (Abp. of), Canada.

R.U.R., Royal Ulster Rifles.

ruralize, *not* -ise.

rus/é (Fr.), *fem.* **-ée,** artful.

ruse de guerre (Fr. f.), a war stratagem.

R.U.S.I., Royal United Services Institute (for Defence Studies), *formerly* Royal United Service Institution.

rus in urbe (Lat.), the country within a town.

Russ., Russia, -n, *see* R.S.F.S.R.

Russel (Alexander), 1814–76, a well-known editor of the *Scotsman.*

russel-cord, a fabric.

Russell (Earl), 1872–1970, Bertrand Russell, English philosopher and mathematician; — **(Baron, of Liverpool)**; *also* family name of Dukes of Bedford; — **(George),** *see* **A.E.**

Russia/, *see* R.S.F.S.R.; **-n,** abbr. **Russ.;** (typ.) 36 letters, of which 4 were abolished in the New Orthography of 1918; for details see *Hart's Rules.*

rut/, -ted, -ting, -ty.

Ruth (the Book of), abbr. **Ruth** (O.T.).

ruthenium, symbol **Ru** (no point).

Rutherford (Mark), 1831–1913, pseud. of **William Hale White,** English writer.

Ruthven (Baron), *pron.* rĭvn′.

Rutli, meadow near L. Lucerne, legendary meeting-place of founders of Swiss freedom.

Ruwenzori, mountain, Cent. Africa.

Ruy Lopez, chess opening.

Ruysdael (Jakob), 1628–82, Dutch painter, *pron.* rois′dahl.

R.V., Revised Version.

R.V.S.V.P., *répondez vite, s'il vous plaît* (please reply quickly).

R.W., Right Worshipful, — Worthy.

Rwanda, Cent. Africa, ind. 1962.

R.W.F., Royal Welch Fusiliers.

R.W.S., Royal Society of Painters in Water Colours.

Rx., rix-dollar; tens of rupees.

Ry., railway.

R.Y.A., Royal Yachting Association, formed from **Y.R.A.,** q.v.

Rye House Plot, 1682–3 (no hyphens, three caps.).

R.Y.S., Royal Yacht Squadron (a club).

Ryun (Jim), American runner, b. 1948.

S

S, (chem.) sulphur, (math.) scalar, (on timepiece regulator) slow, the eighteenth in a series.

S., Sabbath, Saint, school, series, Signor, Socialist, Society, soprano, south, -ern, sun, Sunday, surplus, all proper names with this initial, (Fr.) *saint* (saint), (Ger.) *Sankt* (saint), *Seite* (page), *Süd* (south), (Lat.) *sepultus* (buried), *socius* or *sodalis* (Fellow), (It. mus.) *sinistra* (left hand).

s., second, -s (of time) (no point in scientific work), section, see, set, sign, -ed, singular, (meteor.) snow, solidus (shilling), solo, son, spherical, stem, (meteor.) stratus cloud, substantive, succeeded, (Fr.) *siècle* (century), *sud* (south), (Ger.) *siehe* (see), (Lat.) *semi* (half).

s., shilling, -s.

s (Fr.), *sur* (on), e.g. Boulogne s/M = sur-mer.

's, abbr. for Du. *des* (of the), as 's Gravenhage (The Hague.)

𝕊. (It. mus.), the repeat mark.

$, the dollar mark; (typ.) to be *before*, and close up to, the figures.

∫ (math.), sign of integration.

Σ (Gr.) (math.), sum.

S.A., the Salvation Army, sex-appeal, South Africa, South Australia, *Sturm Abteilung* (Nazi Storm-troops).

s.a. (Lat.), *sine anno* (without date.)

Sabah, part of Malaysia.

Sabaoth (Scrip.), armies.

Sabbatarian/, -ism (caps.).

sabretache, bag for cavalry, *not* -tash, -tasche.

Sabreur (Le Beau), Joachim Murat, 1767–1815, brother-in-law of Napoleon, French marshal, King of Naples.

sac (med. and biol.), a baglike cavity.

saccharimeter, instrument for testing sugar concentrations, *not* -ometer.

Sacheverell (Henry), 1672–1724, English ecclesiastic and politician.

Sachs (Hans), 1494–1576, German poet; — **(Julius),** 1832–97, German botanist. *See also* **Sax, Saxe.**

Sachsen, Ger. n. for **Saxony.**

sackcloth (one word).

sacque, a loose coat, *use* **sack.**

sacr/é (Fr.), *fem.* **-ée,** sacred.

sacrilegious, profane, *not* sacre-, -ligious.

saddle-stitch (bind.), inset pages wire-stitched together.

sadism, a sexual perversion with love of cruelty, from comte D. A. F. de Sade, 1740–1814, French soldier and writer.

Sadleir (Michael), 1888–1957, English author and publisher, son of following.

Sadler (Sir Michael Ernest), 1861–1943, English educationist.

s.a.e., stamped and addressed envelope.

safari (Swahili), hunting expedition.

Saffron Walden, Essex (no hyphen).

saga/, Norse (spec. Icelandic) romance; *hence* any body of legends, any long romantic story; *pl.* **-s.**

sagesse (Fr. f.), wisdom.

Saghalien Island, *use* **Sakhalin** —.

sagou (Fr. m.), sago.

sahib (Ind.), master, gentleman; (cap.) an honorific affix, as Smith Sahib; *fem.* **mem-sahib; pukka sahib,** perfect gentleman.

S.A.I. (Fr.), *Son Altesse Impériale* (Her, *or* His, Imperial Highness); *pl.* **SS.AA.II.**

Saidpur, India, *not* Sayyid-.

saignant/, *fem.* *-e* (Fr. cook.), underdone.

sailcloth (one word).

sailed, abbr. **sld.**

Sailors' Home, *not* -'s.

sainfoin (bot.), a leguminous fodder-plant, *not* saint-.

Saint, abbr. **S.,** *or* **St.,** *pl.* **SS.;** in alphabetical arrangement always place under Saint, *not* under St-.; (typ.) if avoidable St. should not end line. In Fr. small *s* and space after if relating to the person of a saint, as saint Jean, but cap. S and hyphen if relating to the name of a place or person or saint's day: as Saint-Étienne, Saint-Beuve, la Saint-Barthélemy. Fr. abbr. **S.,** *fem.* **Ste,** for the persons of saints; **St-,** *fem.* **Ste-,** in names of places, of persons other than saints, or of saints' days. In Ger. **Sankt,** abbr. **St.**

St. Abbs, Berwick; **St. Albans,** Herts. (no apos.); **St. Albans** (Bp. of); **St. Aldwyn (Viscount),** *see* **Hicks-Beach; St. Andrew's Cross,** ×; **St. Andrew's Day,** 30 Nov.; **St. Andrews, Dunkeld, and Dunblane** (Bp. of); **St. Andrews**

University, Fife (no apos.); **St. Anne's Day,** 26 July; **St. Anne's on the Sea,** Lancs. (no hyphens, apos.); **St. Anthony's fire,** erysipelas; **St. Antony's College,** Oxford; **St. Arvans,** Mon. (no apos.); **St. Aubin,** Jersey, *not* n's; **St. Augustine** (of Canterbury), converted England; **St. Augustine** (of Hippo), author of *The Confessions;* **St. Barnabas's Day,** 11 June; [St.] **Bartholomew Day,** 24 Aug.; **St. Bees** (St. Begha's), Cumberland (no apos.); **St. Boswells,** Roxburghshire (no apos.); **St. Catharine's College,** Cambridge; **St. Catherine's College,** *formerly* **Society,** Oxford; **St. Clears,** Carms. (no apos.); **St. Clement's Day,** 23 Nov.; **St. Crispin's Day,** 25 Oct.; **St. Davids,** Fife, Pembs. (no apos.); **St. David's Day,** 1 Mar.; **St. Denis's Day,** 9 Oct.; **St. Dunstan's Day,** 19 May; **St. Edm. and Ipswich,** signature of present Bp. of St. Edmundsbury and Ipswich; **St. Edmund Hall,** Oxford; **St. Edmund's House,** Cambridge; **St. Elmo's fire,** an electric discharge; **Saint Émilion,** a claret; **Saint Éstèphe,** a claret; **Saint Étienne,** dép. Loire; **St. Fillans,** Perth (no apos.); **St. George's Channel** (apos.); **St. George's Day,** 23 Apr.; **St. Gotthard,** Switz., *not* Goth-; **St. Helens,** Lancs. (Merseyside from 1972), I.O.W. (no apos.); **St. Ives,** Corn., Hunts. (no apos.); **St. James's,** the British court; **St. James's Day,**

25 July; **St. James's Palace, Park, Square, Street,** London; **St. John,** as proper name *pron.* sin'-jun; **Saint John,** New Brunswick; **St. John Ambulance Association, Brigade,** *not* John's; **St. John's,** Newfoundland, Quebec; **St. John's College,** Oxford, Cambridge; **St. John the Baptist's Day,** 24 June; **St. John the Evangelist's Day,** 27 Dec.; **St. John's Wood,** London; **St. John's-wart,** hypericum (hyphen); **Saint Julien,** a claret; **St. Just,** Cornwall; **St.-Just-in-Roseland,** Cornwall (hyphens); **Saint-Just (Louis Antoine Léon de),** 1767–94, French revolutionist; **St. Katharine's (of Alexandria) Day,** 25 Nov.; **St. Kitts** (no apos.), St. Christopher Island, W.I.; **St. Lambert's Day,** 17 Sept.; **St. Lawrence River,** Canada; **St. Lawrence's Day,** 10 Aug.; **St. Leger,** a race; as surname *pron.* sill'-in-jer *or* sent'-lej-er; **St. Leonards,** Hants; **St. Leonards-on-Sea,** Sussex (hyphens, no apos.); **St. Luke's Day,** 18 Oct.; **St. Luke's summer,** mid-Oct.; **St. Margaret's Day,** 20 July; **St. Mark's Day,** 25 Apr.; **St. Martin-in-the-Fields,** London church, *not* Martin's (hyphens); **St. Martin's summer,** mid-Nov.; **St. Mary Abbots,** Kensington (no apos.); **St. Mary Church,** Torquay suburb (three words); **St. Mary Cray,** Kent (no 's); **St. Matthew's Day,** 21 Sept.; **St. Matthias's Day,** 24 Feb. (s's); **St. Mawes,** Corn.; **St. Michael and All Angels' Day,** 29 Sept.; **St. Michael's,** Azores, *use* **São Miguel; St. Michael's Mount,** Corn.; **Mont-Saint-Michel,** Fr. (hyphens); **St. Mungo's Well,** Knaresborough, Yorks.; **St. Neot,** Corn.; **St. Neots,** Hunts. (no apos.); **St. Nicholas's clerks,** thieves; **St. Nicolas,** patron of Russia, town in Belgium; **St. Olaf,** patron of Norway; **St. Patrick's Day,** 17 Mar.; **St. Paul,** Minnesota, U.S.; **St. Paul de Loanda,** W. Africa, *use* **Loanda; St. Paul's,** London; **St. Paul's Cray,** Kent; **St. Paul's Day,** 25 Jan.; **St. Peter Port,** Guernsey, *not* Peter's; **St. Peter's,** Rome; **St. Peter's Day,** 29 June; **St. Petersburg** (Petrograd), *now* **Leningrad; St. Philip and St. James's Day,** 1 May; **Saint-Pierre,** a claret; **Saint-Pierre (Jacques Henri B. de),** 1737–1814, French author; **St. Rollox,** Glasgow; **Saint-Saëns (Charles Camille),** 1835–1921, French composer; **St. Sepulchre (Church of); Saint-Simon (Claude Henri, comte de),** 1760–1825, founder of French socialism; **Saint-Simon (Louis de Rouvroy, duc de),** 1675–1755, French diplomat and writer; **St. Simon and St. Jude's Day,** 28 Oct.; **St. Stephen,** Corn.; **St. Stephen's,** the Houses of Parliament; **St. Stephen's Day,** 26 Dec.; **St. Swithun's Day,** *not* in's, 15 July; **St. Thomas's Day,** 21 Dec.; **St. Valentine's Day,** 14 Feb.; **St. Vitus's dance,** chorea (s's).

Sainte-Beuve (Charles Augustin), 1804–69, French literary critic.

Sainte-Claire Deville (H. É.), 1818–81, French chemist (one hyphen).

Saintsbury (George Edward Bateman), 1845–1933, English literary critic.

Sakandarabad, Hyderabad, *use* **Secunder-**; Uttar Pradesh, India, *use* **Sikandarabad**.

sake, *pron.* sah´-kĭ, a Japanese fermented liquor, *not -ké, -ki*.

Sakhalin, northern half of island, E. Asia, but *use* **Karafuto** for southern half.

saki, a S. American monkey.

Saki, pen-name of Hector Hugh Munro, 1870–1916, English writer.

Sakyamuni, Buddha.

salaam, Oriental salutation, *not -lam* (not ital.).

salable, *use* sale-.

salade (Fr. f.), salad.

salami/, *pl.* **-s**, anglicized form of It. **salam/e**, *pl.* **-i**, a highly seasoned sausage.

sale (Fr.), dirty.

salé (Fr. cook.), salted.

saleable (U.S. **salable**).

Salem, Madras; Mass. (U.S.); a Nonconformist chapel.

Salempur, Uttar Pradesh, India.

Salesian, (member of) an order founded by Don Bosco in honour of St. Francis de Sales.

Salic law, limiting succession to certain lands among the Salian Franks to males, *not* -ique.

salicylic acid.

salle/ (Fr. f.), hall; — **à manger**, dining-room (not ital.); — **d'attente**, waiting-room.

Sallust (Caius Sallustius Crispus), 86–35 B.C., Roman historian; abbr. **Sall.**

Sally Lunn, a tea-cake (caps., two words) (U.S. **sally-lunn**).

salmagundi, a medley; also a seasoned dish.

salmi, a ragout, esp. of game; in Fr. m. *salmis*.

Salmon (George), 1819–1904, Irish mathematician and theologian.

Salmond (Stewart Dingwall Fordyce), 1838–1905, Scottish theologian.

salon (Fr. m.), reception-room, exhibition, fashionable society.

Salop, abbr. for Shropshire (no point); *also* new name for a revised Shropshire, proposed 1971.

Salpêtrière (La), hospital for the aged or insane, Paris.

salpicon (Sp. m.), cold minced meat, *not* -çon.

salsify (bot.), purple goat's-beard, *not* -afy.

salt-cellar (hyphen).

Salt Lake City, Utah, U.S. (caps., no hyphen).

Saltoun (Baron).

saltpetre (one word).

saltus (Lat.), a jump; *pl. same*.

Saluki, Arabian gazelle-hound.

salutary, beneficial, *not* -ory.

salutatory, welcoming, *not* -ary.

Salvador, *properly* **El Salvador**, rep. of Cent. America.

salvage, rescue of ship or contents from shipwreck, goods from fire, etc.

salver, a tray (*see* **salvor**).

Salvio gambit, a chess opening.

salvo/, simultaneous discharge of guns, bombs, cheers; *pl.* **-es**.

salvo jure (Lat.), reserving the right.

sal volatile, ammonium carbonate, smelling-salts.

salvor, one who salves property, *not* -er (*see* **salver**).

Salzkammergut, Austria.

Sam., Samaritan.

Sam. (1, 2), Samuel, First, Second Book of (O.T.).

samarium, symbol **Sm** (no point).

Samarkand, Uzbekistan, U.S.S.R., *not* -cand, -qand.

sambok (Afrik.), *use* **sjambok.**

Sambourne (E. Linley), 1845–1910, *Punch* artist.

Sam Browne (belt), officer's, with shoulder strap.

S. Amer., South America, -n.

Samoyed, a Mongolian of NW. Siberia, a breed of dog, *not* -oied, -oide, -oyede.

sampan, Chinese boat, *not* san-.

Sampson (Dominie), in *Guy Mannering.*

Samuel, First, Second Book of (O.T.), abbr. **Sam. (1, 2).**

Samurai, Japanese mil. class (*sing.* and *pl.*).

sanatorium/, *not* -arium; *pl.* **-s** (U.S. **sanitarium**).

sanatory, healing. *See also* **sanitary.**

Sancho Panza, Don Quixote's squire.

Sancho-Pedro, card game (caps., hyphen).

sanctum/, a retreat, *pl.* **-s;** — **sanctorum** (Lat.), a special retreat, *pl.* **sancta** — (not ital.).

Sand (George, *not* Georges), Madame Amandine A. L. Dudevant, 1804–76, French novelist.

sandal/, -led (U.S. -ed).

Sandars Reader, Camb.

Sanday (Prof. William), 1843–1920, English theologian.

Sandeau (L. S. Jules), 1811–83, French writer.

S. & M., signature of Bp. of Sodor and Man.

sandpaper (one word).

sandpiper, a bird (one word).

sandstone (one word).

Sandys, *pron.* sandz.

sang-de-bœuf (Fr. m.), a deep-red colour.

sang-froid, self-possession (hyphen, not ital.).

Sanhedrin, supreme Jewish council, *not* -im.

sanitary, healthy, *not* -ory. *See also* **sanatory.**

Sankt (Ger.), saint; abbr. **St.**

sannup (Amer.-Ind.), husband of a squaw, *not* -op.

sanpan, *use* **sam-.**

sans (Fr.), without.

San Salvador, cap. of El Salvador.

sans/ appel (Fr.), without appeal; — *cérémonie,* informally; — *changer,* without changing.

Sanscrit, *use* **Sansk-.**

sansculott/e, in Fr. Rev., a man of the lower classes; a strong republican or revolutionary; **-es, -erie, -ism, -ist** (one word); in Fr. m. *sans-culott/e* (hyphen), *-isme.*

sans doute (Fr.), without doubt.

Sansevieria (bot.), a genus of lily.

sans/ façon (Fr.), informally; — *faute,* without fail; — *gêne,* free-and-easy (hyphen if used as a noun).

Sanskrit, *not* -crit, abbr. **Skt.;** (typ.) 34 consonants, 10 vowels, 4 diphthongs, all special forms.

sans/ pareil (Fr.), un-equalled; — *peine,* without difficulty; — *peur*

sans/ (*cont.*):
et sans reproche, fearless
and blameless; — *phrase,*
without circumlocution.
sans serif (typ.), a typeface
without serifs.
sans/ *souci* (Fr.), without
cares; — *tache,* stainless.
Santa (It., Sp.), female
saint; abbr. **Sta** (no point).
Santa Claus, *not* — Kl-.
Santa Fé, Argentina, New
Mexico.
Santander, N. Spain (one
word).
Santenot, a Burgundy wine.
Santo Domingo, former
name of the Dominican
Republic, W.I., and of its
capital Ciudad Trujillo.
Santos-Dumont (Alberto),
1873–1932, Brazilian
aeronaut.
Sâo, saint, in Brazilian
place-names, as **Sâo Paulo.**
Saône/, French river, *pron.*
sōn; **Haute- —,** dép.
(hyphen), **— -et-Loire,** dép.
(hyphens).
Saorstat Eireann (Erse),
Irish Free State.
Sapho, novel by Daudet,
opera by Gounod, 1851.
Sapph/**o,** *c.* 600 B.C., Greek
poetess of Lesbos; adj. **-ic.**
S.A.R. (Fr.), *Son Altesse
Royale* (His *or* Her Royal
Highness); *pl.* **SS.AA.RR.**
Sar., Sardinia, -n.
Saragossa, Spain; in Sp.
Zaragoza.
Sarawak, part of Malaysia.
sarcenet, *use* sars-.
sarcom/**a** (path.), a tumour;
pl. **-ata.**
sarcophag/**us,** stone coffin;
pl. **-i.**
Sardinia, in It. **Sardegna;**
abbr. **Sar.**
Sardou (Victorien), 1831–
1908, French dramatist.
Sargent (John Singer),
1856–1925, American

painter; — **(Sir H.
Malcolm W.),** 1895–1967,
English conductor.
sari, Indian female garment,
not -ee, -y.
sarong, a Malay petticoat
for man or woman.
sarsaparilla, (med.) dried
root of a tropical American
Smilax.
sarsenet, a fabric, *not* sarc-.
Sartor Resartus, 'the tailor
re-tailored', by Carlyle,
1833–4.
Sarum., signature of Bp. of
Salisbury (full point).
Saskatchewan, Canada;
abbr. **Sask.**
sassafras (bot. and med.),
N. American tree; an
infusion from its bark, *not*
sasse-.
Sat., Saturday.
Satan (cap.).
satanic, devilish (not cap.
unless referring to Satan).
S.A.T.B., soprano, alto,
tenor, bass.
sateen, a shiny fabric, *not*
satt-.
satinet, a thin satin, *not*
-ette.
satire, literary work holding
up folly or vice to ridicule.
See also **satyr.**
satirize, *not* -ise.
satrap/, anc. Persian viceroy;
-y, his province or office.
sat sapienti (Lat.), sufficient
for a wise man.
Satsuma, Japanese pottery.
Saturday, abbr. **Sat.**
Saturnalia/ (Lat.), a time of
licence and merrymaking in
honour of Saturn, strictly
pl. but used in Eng. as
sing.; **-n** (not cap.), riotously
merry.
Saturnian, of the god or
planet Saturn.
satyr/, *pron.* săt'-er, (class.
myth.) a woodland deity,
goat-footed; a lascivious

man; adj. **-ic,** type of Greek comedy with chorus of satyrs. *See also* **satire.**

sauce piquante (Fr. f.), a sharp sauce.

Sauchiehall Street, Glasgow (two words).

saucisse (Fr. f.), fresh pork sausage.

saucisson (Fr. m.), large highly seasoned sausage.

Saudi Arabia, *formerly* Hejaz, Nejd, and Asir.

Sauerkraut (Ger. n.), chopped and fermented cabbage (cap.).

saumon (Fr. m.), salmon.

Saumur, a champagne.

sauté/, -e (Fr.), lightly fried.

Sauterne, a white Bordeaux wine from Sauternes.

sauve qui peut (Fr.), let him save himself who can.

savannah, a treeless plain of sub-trop. America.

Savannah, river and town, Georgia, U.S.; *also* town in Tennessee.

savant/, man of learning, *pl.* **-s;** *fem.* **-e,** *pl.* **-es** (not ital.).

Savigny, a red Burgundy.

Savile/, family name of Earl of Mexborough; — (**Baron**); — **Club,** — **Row,** London; — (**Sir Henry**), 1549–1622, founder of Savilian chairs at Oxford, *not* -ille.

savings bank (no apos.).

savoir/-faire (Fr.), skill, tact; — *-vivre,* good breeding (hyphens).

Savonarola (**G.**), 1452–98, Italian religious reformer.

Savoyard, of Savoy.

Sax., Saxon, Saxony.

Sax (**Adolphe J.**), 1814–94, Belgian inventor of saxhorn and saxophone. *See also* **Sachs, Saxe.**

Saxe (Saxony), in Ger. **Sachsen.**

Saxe (**Hermann Maurice, comte de**), 1696–1750,

French marshal; — (**John Godfrey**), 1816–87, American poet and humorous writer. *See also* **Sachs, Sax.**

Saxe/-Altenburg, — -Coburg-Gotha, — -Meiningen, — -Weimar (hyphens), former duchies in E. Germany, incorporated in Thuringia (Coburg in Bavaria), 1919; in Ger. **Sachsen-.**

saxhorn, brass wind-instrument with long winding tube and bell opening.

Saxon/, -y, abbr. **Sax.**

saxophone, mil. and dance-band instrument with reed, metal tube, and many finger-keys.

S.A.Y.E., save as you earn.

Saye and Sele (**Baron**).

Sayyidpur, India, *use* **Saidpur.**

Sb, *stibium* (antimony) (no point).

S.B.N., Standard Book Number, *now* **I.S.B.N.,** International ditto.

S.C., South Carolina (U.S.), Staff College, — Corps, Supreme Court, (Lat.) *Senatus Consultum* (a decree of the Senate), (law) same case, (paper) super-calendered.

Sc., Scotch, Scots, Scottish.

Sc, scandium (no point).

s.c. (typ.), small capitals.

sc., scene, scruple.

sc. (Lat.) scilicet (namely).

sc., sculpsit (he, *or* she, carved, *or* engraved it).

S.C., Special Constable.

Sca Fell, English mountain, *not* Scaw—; *pron.* skaw′fel (two words).

Scafell Pikes, highest English mountain, *not* Pike (two words).

scagliola, imitation marble, *not* scal-.

scal/a (anat.), a canal in the cochlea; *pl.* **-ae.**

Scala (La), theatre, Milan.

scalable, *not* -eable.

scalar (math.), a real number; symbol **S** (no point).

scaler, one who, *or* that which, scales.

Scaliger (Joseph Justus), 1540–1609, French philologist; — **(Julius Caesar),** 1484–1558, Italian scholar, father of preceding.

scaliola, *use* scagl-.

scallop, a shell, also used in cook. and dress., *not* sco-, escalop.

scan/, to examine closely (not casually), **-ned, -ning, -sion.**

Scand., Scandinavia, -n.

scandalize, *not* -ise.

scandal/um magnatum (Lat.), defamation of high personages, *pl.* **-a —;** abbr *scan. mag.*

Scandinavia/, -n, abbr. **Scand.**

scandium, symbol **Sc** (no point).

S.C.A.P.A. *or* **SCAPA,** Society for Checking the Abuses of Public Advertising.

scape/goat, -grace (one word).

s.caps. (typ.), small capitals.

Scarborough, Yorks.

Scarbrough (Earl of).

scarecrow (one word).

scarlatina, scarlet fever, *not* scarlet-.

Scarlatti (Alessandro), 1659–1725, father; — **(Domenico),** 1685–1756, son; Italian composers.

Scarlett, family name of Baron Abinger.

scathe/, to injure; **-less,** *not* scathless.

Sc.B., *Scientiae Baccalaureus* (Bachelor of Science).

S.C.C., Sea Cadet Corps.

Sc.D., *Scientiae Doctor* (Doctor of Science).

scélérat (Fr. m.), a scoundrel.

scen/a (It., Lat.), scene in a play or opera, *pron.* shā′na; It. *pl.* **-e,** Lat. *pl.* **-ae.**

scenario/, outline of a play or film; *pl.* **-s.**

scène (Fr. f.), scene, stage; *en —,* on the stage.

Scenes of Clerical Life, by George Eliot, 1858, *not* from.

sceptic, one inclined to disbelieve; *pron.* sk- (U.S. **sk-**).

S.C.G.B., Ski Club of Great Britain.

sch., scholar, school, schooner.

Schadow (Friedrich), 1789–1862, German painter; — **(Johann Gottfried),** 1764–1850, German sculptor, father of Rudolph and Friedrich; — **(Rudolph),** 1786–1822, German sculptor.

Schäfer (E. A.), *see* **Sharpey-Schafer** (hyphen).

Schaumburg-Lippe, Germany (hyphen).

Scheele/ (Karl Wilhelm), 1742–86, German chemist; **—'s green** (apos., no hyphen).

Scheffel (Joseph Victor von), 1826–86, German poet.

Scheffer (Ary), 1795–1858, Dutch painter; — **(H. T.),** 1710–59, Swedish chemist. *See also* **Schoe-.**

Scheherazade, the relator in *The Arabian Nights.*

Schelde, river, Belgium–Holland; in Fr. **Escaut;** (*not* -dt).

Schelling (Friedrich Wilhelm Joseph von), 1775–1854, German philosopher.

schelm, a rascal, *not* skelm (Sc. **skellum**).

schem/a (Gr.), an outline;
pl. **-ata.**

scherzo/ (mus.), a playful
piece; *pron.* skārt′so; *pl.* **-s;**
scherzando, in a playful
manner.

Schiedam (cap.), Holland
gin, schnapps.

Schiehallion, Mt., Perth.

Schiller (Friedrich von),
1759–1805, German poet.

**Schimmelpenninck (Mary
Ann, Mrs.),** 1788–1856,
English writer.

schipperke, a breed of
dogs; *pron.* skip-er′-kĕ.

schirocco, *use* **si-.**

schizanthus (bot.), the
butterfly-flower.

Schläger (Ger. m.), student's
duelling sword (cap.).

Schlagintweit, German
family of five brothers,
travellers, mid-nineteenth
century.

**Schleiermacher (Friedrich
Ernst Daniel),** 1768–1834,
German theologian.

Schlemihl (*Peter*), tale by
Chamisso.

Schleswig-Holstein,
Germany (hyphen).

Schliemann (Heinrich),
1822–90, German archaeo-
logist.

Schloss (Ger. n.), a castle,
lock; *pl. Schlösser* (cap.).

Schluss/ (Ger. m.),
conclusion; — *folgt,*
concluded in our next.

schnapps (Du.), gin, *not* -aps.

Schnitzler (Arthur), 1862–
1931, Austrian playwright.

Schobert (Johann), *c.* 1720–
67, German composer.

Schoeffer (Peter), 1425–
1502, German-born printer.
See also **Sche-.**

scholi/um (Lat.), a scholar's
note in a manuscript; *pl.* **-a;**
-ast.

**Schomberg (Friedrich
Hermann, Duke of),**

14

1615–90, German-born
French marshal and
English mercenary officer.

**Schomburgk (Sir Robert
Hermann),** 1804–65,
German traveller.

school/, abbr. **S.;** — **board**
(two words).

**school/boy, -girl, -master,
-mistress, -room** (one
word).

schooner, abbr. **sch.**

Schopenhauer (Arthur),
1788–1860, German
philosopher.

schottische, dance, etc., *not*
-ich, -ish.

Schreiner (Olive), 1862–
1920, S. African authoress.

Schrödinger (Erwin),
1887–1961; Austrian
physicist.

Schubart (Daniel), 1739–91,
German poet.

Schubert (Franz Peter),
1797–1828, Austrian
composer.

Schulze-Delitzsch (H.),
1808–83, founder of German
People's Banks.

Schumann (Robert), 1810–
56, German composer.

Schutzstaffel, Hitler's
bodyguard, abbr. **S.S.** *or*
SS.

Schuyler (E.), 1840–90,
American writer; —
(Philip John), 1735–1804,
American statesman and
soldier; *pron.* skī′ler.

Schuylkill, Pa., U.S.;
pron. skool-kil.

Schwalka (F.), 1849–92,
American traveller.

Schwann (Theodor), 1810–
82, German naturalist and
anatomist.

schwanpan, more correctly
suanpan, but use anglicized
swanpan.

schwärmerie (Ger.),
a sentimental enthusiasm
(not ital.).

Schwarzkopf (Elisabeth, Mrs. Walter Legge), b. 1915, Polish-born soprano.

Schwarzwald, the Black Forest.

Schweinfurt/, Bavaria; — -blue, — -green, etc.

Schweinfurth (Georg August), 1836–1925, German traveller in Africa.

Schweitzer (Albert), 1875–1965, German philosopher, theologian, organist, med. missionary at Lambaréné, Fr. Equatorial Africa (now Gabon).

Schweiz (die), Ger. for Switzerland.

Schwyz, canton in Switz.

scia/graphy, the perspective of shadows; **-gram**; *not* scio-, *not* (in this sense) skia-. *See* **skiagraphy**.

science, abbr. **Sci.**

scienter (Lat.), knowingly.

scilicet (Lat.), namely; abbr. **sc.**

scimitar, Turkish sword, *not* the many variants.

Scind, Pakistan, *use* Sind.

scintilla/, a spark, trace; *pl.* **-s.**

sciograph, *use* scia-.

scirocco, *use* si-.

scissel, scrap metal, *not* -il, -ile, sizel.

Sclav, etc., *use* Sl-.

sclerom/a, *pl.* **-ata**, **scleros/is**, *pl.* **-es** (med.), hardening, *not* scler-.

S.C.M., State Certified Midwife, Student Christian Movement.

scollop, *use* sca-.

Scone, Perth; *pron.* skoon.

scone, a soft cake, *not* scon, skon; *pron.* skŏn.

score (bind.), to break the surface of board to help folding.

score, three-, four-, five-, etc. (one word).

scori/a, slag; *pl.* **-ae.**

Scot, native of Scotland. *See also* **Scottish**.

Scot., Scotch, Scotland, Scottish.

Scotch, in Eng. and U.S., now increasingly reserved for phrases — (whisky), — broth, — mist, etc.; disliked by Scots people; for general use, therefore, **Scots** *or* **Scottish** to be preferred; abbr. **Sc.**, *or* **Scot.**

Scotchman, in Sc. **Scotsman**, *see* **Scotch**.

scot-free (hyphen).

scotice, in Scots dialect.

Scotism, the doctrine of Duns Scotus.

Scots/, in Scotland preferred to **Scottish**; abbr. **Sc.**; — **Greys**, — **Guards** (no apos.).

Scotsman, in Scotland preferred to **Scotchman**.

Scotticism, a Scottish expression, *not* Scoti-.

Scottish, *not* Scotish; abbr. **Sc.**, *or* **Scot.**

scow, a flat-bottomed boat, *not* skew, skow.

S.C.R. (Oxf. Univ.), Senior Common Room; (Camb. Univ.), — Combination Room.

scratch comma, short shilling mark /, formerly used as a comma.

scratch-cradle, a game, *use* **cat's-cradle**.

screamer (typ.), exclamation mark !

screen (typ.), a fine grating on film or glass which breaks an illustration with various tones into dots of the appropriate size.

screen printing, *see* **silk screen**.

scribes and Pharisees (cap. P only).

scrips/it (Lat.), he, *or* she, wrote it; *pl.* **-erunt**, *or* **-ere.**

script (typ.), type resembling handwriting.

script., Scriptur/e, -al.
scriptori/um, a writing room; *pl.* **-a.**
Scriptures (the) (cap.).
scrivener's palsy, writer's cramp (apos.).
scrot/um (anat.), *pl.* **-a.**
scruple, 20 grains; abbr. **sc.,** sign ℈.
scrutator, a scrutineer.
scrutin/ d'arrondissement (Fr. m.), voting for a single candidate; — *de liste,* ditto group of candidates.
scrutinize, *not* -ise.
scud/o, an old Italian coin; *pl.* **-i.**
sculduddery (Sc.), grossness, lewdness (*see also* **skul-duggery**).
sculk, *use* **sk-.**
scull, oar, and form of rowing, *not* sk-.
sculp., sculpt/or, -ural, -ure.
sculps/it (Lat.), he, *or* she, engraved, *or* carved, it; *pl.* **-erunt,** *or* **-ere;** abbr. **sc.,** *or* **sculps.**
sculptures (titles of) (typ.), when cited, to be in italic.
scutcheon, *use* **escut-.**
Scylla and Charybdis (class. myth.), personified rock and whirlpool in Straits of Messina.
scymitar, *use* **scim-.**
s.d., shillings, pence, *sine die* (indefinitely).
sd. (books), sewed.
S. Dak., South Dakota, U.S. (off. abbr.).
SE., south-east.
S.E., *Son Excellence* (Fr.) (His Excellency).
S/E., Stock Exchange.
Se, selenium (no point).
sea, when with name, to be cap., as North Sea, Sea of Marmara.
sea-bed (hyphen).
seaboard (one word).
S.E.A.C., South-East Asia Command.

seafar/er, -ing (one word).
Seaford, Sussex.
Seaforde, Co. Down.
sea/-going, -gull, -island (of cotton), **-kale** (hyphens).
Seal, Sevenoaks, Kent.
Seale, Farnham, Surrey.
sea-level (hyphen).
sealing-wax (hyphen).
seamstress, sewing-woman, *not* semp-.
Seanad Eireann, Erse for Senate (of Eire).
seance, a sitting (not ital., no accent).
seaport (symbol Ψ) (one word).
seascape (one word).
sear, wither(ed), *not* sere.
sea-serpent (hyphen).
sea-shore (law), the land between high and low water (hyphen).
sea-sickness (hyphen).
seaside (one word).
S.E.A.T.O., South-East Asia Treaty Organization.
sea-urchin (hyphen).
seaweed (one word).
sebaceous, fatty, *not* -ious.
Sebastopol, the spelling generally used in contemporary accounts of the Crimean War. *But see* **Sevastopol.**
sec (Fr.), *fem. sèche,* dry (ital.).
sec., secant, second, -s (of time, not used in scientific work), secretary.
sec., see secundum.
Sec.-Gen., Secretary-General.
Sechuana, language of the Bechuanas.
Secker (Martin) & Warburg, Ltd., publishers.
second (adj.), abbr. **2nd** (no point.)
second/, -s, abbr. **s** (no full point in scientific work), *or* **sec.; — mark,** ". *See also* **secund.**

seconde (Fr. f.), a fencing parry, (rail.) second class, (typ.) second proof.

second-hand (adj., hyphen).

Second World War, 1939–45, *not* World War II.

secrecy, *not* -sy.

sec. reg., secundum regulam (according to rule).

secretaire, a writing-table (not ital.).

Secrétan (Charles), 1815–95, Swiss philosopher.

secretariat, a secretary's office, *not* -ate.

Secretary, head of State department (cap.).

secretary, a writer; abbr. **sec.**

secret/e, to hide, to form and separate (of blood, sap, etc.); **-ion, -ory.**

section (typ.), a chapter subdivision, abbr. **s., sect.,** *or* §; — **mark,** §, fourth ref. mark for footnotes; *pl.* §§.

secularize, *not* -ise.

secund (biol.), on one side only. *See also* **second.**

Secunderabad, Hyderabad, *not* Sak-, Sek-; *but* **Sikandarabad,** Uttar Pradesh, India.

secundo (Lat.), in the second place; abbr. 2°.

secundum/ (Lat.), according to, abbr. *sec.;* — *artem,* ditto art, abbr. *sec. art.;* — *legem,* ditto law, abbr. *sec. leg.;* — *leges regni,* ditto laws of the kingdom; — *naturam,* naturally, abbr. *sec. nat.;* — *quid,* in some respects only; — *regulam,* according to rule, abbr. *sec. reg.;* — *veritatem,* universally valid.

S.E.D., Scottish Education Department.

se defendendo (Lat.), in defending himself, *or* herself.

sederunt (Lat.), a meeting, *or* sitting (not ital.).

Sedgemoor, Somerset; — (**battle of**), 1685 (one word).

Sedlitz powder, *use* Sei-—.

seducible.

séduisant/ (Fr.), *fem.* -e, bewitching.

See (the Holy), the Papacy.

see (verb), abbr. **s.**

Seefried (Irmgard), b. 1919, German soprano.

Seeley (Sir John Robert), 1834–95, English hist. writer.

Seely (Sir John Edward Bernard), 1868–1947, British politician, created **Baron Mottistone,** 1933.

see-saw (hyphen).

seethe, to boil, *not* -th.

S.E. & O. (Fr.), *sauf erreur et omission, see* **s.e.o.o.**

segue (It.), follows.

seiche, a fluctuation in the level of a lake; in Fr. f. *sèche.*

Seidlitz powder, an aperient, *not* Sed-.

seigneur (Fr. m.), a person of rank; *le Seigneur,* God.

Seine/-et-Marne, — -et-**Oise,** — -**Maritime** (*formerly* **Inférieure**), French déps. (hyphens).

seise (law), to put in possession of, *not* -ze.

seisin (Sc. law), taking possession, *not* -zin.

seismology, study of earthquakes.

Seit/e (Ger. f.), a page, abbr. **S.,** *sing.* and *pl.;* but *pl.* with article, *die Seiten.*

seize, to grasp. *See also* **seise.**

séjour (Fr. m.), sojourn.

Sekunderabad, *see* Sec-.

sel., selected.

sel (Fr. m.), salt.

sel. (Ger.), *selig* (deceased, late).

Selangor, *see* **Malaysia.**

Selassie (Haile), *see* **Haile Selassie.**

Selborne (Earl of).

Selborne (*Natural History of*), by Gilbert White, pub. 1789.

selector, *not* -er.

selenium, symbol **Se** (no point).

self-made (hyphen).

selfsame (one word).

selig (Ger.), deceased, late; abbr. *sel.*

selle de mouton (Fr. f.), saddle of mutton.

seller's option, abbr. **s.o.**

Sellindge, Hythe, Kent.

Selling, Faversham, Kent.

selon les règles (Fr.), according to the rules.

Selous (**Frederick Courtney**), 1851–1917, British African explorer and hunter; *pron.* seloo´.

Selsey, Sussex, *not* -sea.

seltzer, a Prussian mineral water.

selvage, an edging of cloth, *not* -edge.

Selw., Selwyn Coll., Camb.

Sem., Semitic.

sem., semicolon.

semant/ic (adj.), concerning the meaning of words; (noun) **-ics.**

semaphore, signalling apparatus.

semeio/graphy, -logy, -tics, science of symptoms, *not* semio-.

semester, a college course of half a year.

se mettre en frais (Fr.), to make efforts to please.

semi (Lat.), half; abbr. *s.*

semi-barbar/ian, -ic, -ism, -ous (hyphen).

semi-bold (typ.), a weight between roman and bold.

semicircle (one word).

semicolon (one word), abbr. **sem.** *See* **punctuation III.**

semi-monthly, -weekly = twice —. Cf. **bi-monthly, -weekly.**

Seminole, *s.* and *pl.*, Amer. Indian.

semi-official (hyphen).

semiology, *use* **semeiol-.**

Semite, *not* Sh-.

Semitic, abbr. **Sem.**

semp. (It. mus.), *sempre* (the same style throughout).

semper/ eadem (Lat. f. s., and n. pl.), always the same; **—** *fidelis*, always faithful, *pl.* **—** *fideles*; **—** *idem* (m. and n. sing.), always the same.

Sempill (**Baron**).

sempre (mus.), always.

sempstress, *use* **seams-.**

Sen., Senat/e, -or, Seneca, senior.

sen. (It.), *senza* (without).

sen, $\frac{1}{100}$ of Japanese gold yen.

Senat/e, -or, abbr. **Sen.**

Senatus (Lat.), the Senate.

Senatus Academicus, the governing body in Scottish universities (not ital.).

Senatus Consultum, a decree of the Senate; abbr. **S.C.**

Seneca (**Lucius Annaeus**), 3 B.C.–A.D. 65, Roman stoic philosopher and statesman; abbr. **Sen.**

Senefelder (**Alois**), 1771–1834, discoverer, in 1796, of the lithographic principle.

Senegal, W. Africa, rep. 1959; in Fr. **Sénégal.**

senhor/ (Port.), Mr.; *fem.* **-a.**

senior, abbr. **Sen.**

seniores priores (Lat.), elders first.

se non è vero, è ben trovato (It.), if it be not true, it is well invented.

señor/ (Sp.), Mr.; **-es**, Messrs.; **-a**, Mrs.; **-ita**, Miss.

sensible, in Fr. *sens/é*, *fem.* **-ée.**

sensible (Fr.), sensitive.

sensori/um (Lat.), grey matter of brain and spinal cord; *pl.* **-a.**

sensual, concerned with gratification of the senses, lewd.

sensualize, *not* -ise.

sensuous, pertaining to or affected by the senses.

sentimentalize, to regard as tinged with emotion, *not* -ise.

senza (It.), without.

s.e.o.o. (Fr.), *sauf erreur ou omission* (errors or omissions excepted).

Seoul, cap. of S. Korea, *not* Seul, Soul; in Jap. **Keijō.**

separator, *not* -er.

separat/um (typ.), a reprint of one of a series of papers; *pl.* **-a.**

Sephardim, *pl.,* the Spanish and Portuguese Jews.

sepoy (hist.), Indian soldier in European service (not cap.).

Sept., September, Septuagint, *not* Sep.

septemvir/ (Lat.), one of a committee of seven; *pl.* **-i.**

septicaemia, blood-poisoning, *not* -emia.

Septuagesima Sunday, third before Lent.

Septuagint, Greek version of O.T., *c.* 270 B.C., abbr. **Sept.; — Version,** abbr. **LXX** (no point).

sept/um (biol.), a partition; *pl.* **-a.**

Sepulchre (Church of St.), *not* -'s.

sepultus (Lat.), buried; abbr. *S.*

seq., (*sing.*), *sequens* (the following), *sequente* (and in what follows), *sequitur* (it follows).

seqq., (*pl.*), *sequentes, sequentia* (the following), *sequentibus* (in the following places).

sequel/a (path.), a symptom following a disease; *pl.* **-ae.**

sequen/s, -te, see **seq.**

sequent/es (m. f.), **-ia** (n.), **-ibus,** *see* **seqq.**

sequitur (Lat.), it follows; abbr. **seq.**

sérac/ (Fr. m.), a castellated mass of ice in a glacier; *pl.* **-s** (not ital.).

seraglio/, a harem; *pron.* se-rahl'yo, *pl.* **-s.**

seraph/, a celestial being; *pl.* **-s;** Heb. *pl.* **-im,** *not* -ims.

Serb., Serbian.

sere, wither; *use* **sear.**

serecloths, *use* cere-.

serge, large candle, *use* **cierge.**

Sergeant (mil.; but -j- in official Army Lists, etc.), abbr. **Sgt.**

seriatim, serially, point by point.

series, abbr. **S., ser.**

serifs (typ.), short lines across the ends of arms and stems of letters.

Seringapatam, Mysore.

serio-comic (hyphen).

Serjeant (legal).

sermonize, *not* -ise.

serra (Port.), sierra, mountain range.

ser/um (*pl.* **-a**), the fluid that separates from clotted blood; specially prepared sera are used medicinally.

serviceable, *not* -cable.

serviette, table-napkin (not ital.).

servitor, an attendant, *not* -er.

sesquipedalian, (of words) one and a half (metrical) feet long; cumbrous.

sess., session.

Session (Court of), supreme Scottish Court, *not* — — Sessions; — **(Parliamentary)** (caps.).

sesterce, Roman coin, symbol **HS** (no point).

sestet, last six lines of a sonnet. *See also* **sextet.**

Sesuto, language of the Basutos.

set, abbr. **s.**

S.E.T., Selective Employment Tax.

set-back (noun, hyphen).

S.-et-L., dép. France, Saône-et-Loire; **S.-et-M.,** dép. France, Seine-et-Marne; **S.-et-O.,** dép. France, Seine-et-Oise.

set-off (typ.), accidental transfer of ink from one sheet to another.

Settlement (Stock Ex.) (cap.).

settler, one who settles. *See also* **settlor.**

settlor (law), one who makes a settlement. *See also* **settler.**

Seul, Korea, *use* **Seoul.**

Sevastopol, Crimea, U.S.S.R., *not* Seb-.

Sevenoaks, Kent (one word).

Seven Years War, 1756–63 (no apos.).

Sévigné (Madame de, Marie de Rabutin-Chantal), 1626–96, French writer.

Sèvres porcelain.

sewage, the refuse that passes through sewers.

sewerage, the system of sewers.

sewin, salmon-trout, *not* -en.

Sexagesima Sunday, the second before Lent.

sextet (mus.), (a work for) a group of six performers, *not* ses-, -ett, -ette. *See also* **sestet.**

sexto (typ.), a book based on 6 leaves, 12 pages, to the basic sheet; abbr. **6to** (no point); — **-decimo,** *see* **sixteenmo.**

sexualize, to attribute sex to, *not* -ise.

s.f., *sub finem* (towards the end).

Sforza/, Milanese ducal

family, notably — **(Ludovico),** 1451–1508; — **(Carlo, Count),** 1873–1952, leader of anti-Fascist opposition in Italy.

sforz/ando, **-ato** (mus.), with sudden emphasis on a chord or note; abbr. *sfz.*

S.G., Solicitor-General.

Sganarelle, a character in Molière's comedies.

s.g.d.g. (Fr.), *sans garantie du gouvernement* (without government guarantee).

sgraffit/o, decorative work in which different colours are got by removing outer layers; *pl.* **-i.** *See also* **graffito.**

's Gravenhage, Dutch for **The Hague.**

Sgt., Sergeant.

shadoof, Egyptian water-raising apparatus; in Egypt. Arabic *shaduf.*

S.H.A.E.F., Supreme Headquarters, Allied Expeditionary Force.

shagreen, tanned skin of fish, sharks, etc.

Shahabad, Bengal, Hyderabad, Punjab, Uttar Pradesh (India).

Shairp (John Campbell), 1819–85, Scottish educator and critic.

Shakespear/e (William), 1564–1616, abbr. **Shak.;** **-ian,** *not* the many variants.

Shakespeare Society (the), *but* the **New Shakspere Society.**

shako/, mil. head-dress, *not* sch-; *pl.* **-s.**

shallot, a kind of onion, *not* esch-, sch-, schalot.

Shalott (The Lady of), by Tennyson.

shammy-leather, *use* **chamois- —.**

shandrydan, a rickety vehicle, *not* -dery-.

Shanghai, China; **shanghai/** (not cap.), to make drunk and ship as a sailor; **-ed.**

shan't, to be close up, one apos. only.

shanty, sailor's song, *not* ch-.

shapable, *not* shape-.

shareholder (one word).

sharp (mus.), sign ♯.

Sharp (Becky), in *Vanity Fair;* — **(Cecil James),** 1859–1924, English collector of folk-songs; — **(Granville),** 1734–1813, English abolitionist; — **(James),** 1618–79, English architect; — **(William),** 1856–1905, Scottish poet and novelist, pen-name **Fiona McLeod.**

Sharpe (Charles Kirkpatrick), 1781–1851, Scottish antiquary and artist; — **(Samuel),** 1799–1881, English Egyptologist and biblical scholar.

Sharpey-Schafer (Sir Edward Albert), *né* **Schäfer,** 1850–1935, English physiologist.

Shaw (George Bernard), 1856–1950, Irish-born English playwright; adj. **Shavian;** — **(Aircrafts-man),** *see* **Lawrence, T. E.**

shaykh, *use* **sheikh.**

sheaf, *pl.* **sheaves.**

shear/, to cut (*see also* **sheer**); — **-hulk,** — **-legs,** etym. correct, but displaced by **sheer-,** q.v.

shearwater, a bird (one word).

sheath (noun).

sheathe (verb).

shebeen (Ir.), unlicensed house selling spirits.

sheepshank, a type of knot (one word).

sheepskin, a rug, a book-binding leather, a parchment (one word).

sheer, (adj.) mere, vertical, (adv.) quite, vertically,

(verb) to deviate, swerve. *See also* **shear.**

sheer-hulk, a dismasted ship (hyphen).

sheer-legs, hoisting apparatus for masts (hyphen).

Sheer Thursday (Maundy Thursday), *not* Shere —.

sheet (typ.), a piece of paper of a definite size; a signature of a book.

sheets (in) (typ.), not folded, or, if folded, not bound.

sheet work (typ.), printing the two sides of a sheet from two formes.

sheikh (Arab.), a chief; *pron.* shāk; *not* sha-, -ik, -yk.

sheiling, *use* **shieling.**

sheldrake, a water-bird, *not* shell-.

shellac, a gum, *not* -ack, shelac, shelack.

Shelley (Percy Bysshe), 1792–1822, English poet.

Shelta, a cryptic jargon used by tinkers.

shelv/e, -ing, -y.

Shemite, *use* **Semite.**

Shepheard's Hotel, Cairo.

Shepherd Market, London.

Shepherd's Bush, London.

shepherd's/ needle, — **purse** (apos.).

Sheppard (Jack), 1702–24, highwayman.

Sheppey (Isle of), Kent.

Shepton Mallet, Somerset.

Sheraton (Thomas), English furniture designer.

Sherborne (Baron).

Sherborne, Dorset, Glos.

Sherbourne, Warwick.

Sherburn, Dur., or Malton, Yorks.

Sherburn-in-Elmet, Yorks.

Shere, Surrey.

Shere Thursday, *use* **Sheer —.**

sherif, Muslim title, *not* -eef.

sheriff, county officer.
Sheringham, Norfolk.
Sherpa, one of a Himalayan people from borders of Nepal and Tibet, *not* -ah.
Sherpur, E. Pakistan.
Sherrington (Sir Charles Scott), 1857–1952, English physiologist.
shew, *use* **show** except in Scottish law, and biblical and Prayer Book citations.
shewbread, *use* **show-** except in Scrip.
sheyk, *use* **sheikh.**
shieling, Highland hut or sheep-shelter, *not* sheil-.
Shifnal, Salop.
Shiites, followers of Ali.
shikari (Ind.), a hunter, *not* the many variants.
Shikarpur, Pakistan.
shillelagh, Irish cudgel, *not* the many variants.
shilling/, -s, abbr. *s. or* /-; — **mark** (typ.), /.
shilly-shally/, -ing.
Shinto/, -ism, indigenous Japanese religion, *not* Sintoo, -u.
'ship (typ.), *see* **companionship.**
ship/building, -owner, -shape (one word).
ships' names (typ.), to be italic.
Shipston on Stour, War. (no hyphens).
Shipton, Glos.
Shipton under Wychwood, Oxon. (no hyphens).
Shire/brook, Derby; **-coates,** Notts.; **-hampton,** Glos.; **-newton,** Mon. (one word).
shoe/, -ing.
Sholapur, Bombay.
Shooter's Hill, Kent.
short and (typ.), the ampersand, &.
short circuit (noun); **short-circuit** (verb).
short/ letters (typ.), ă, ĕ,

etc.; — **ton,** 2,000 lb.; abbr. **s.t.;** — **vowel** (typ.), ă, ĕ, etc.
Shostakovich (Dmitri), b. 1906, Russian composer.
shoulder-notes (typ.), marginal notes at the top outer corner of the page.
shouldst, to be close up, no apos.
shovel/, -led, -ler, -ling, -ful, *pl.* **-fuls** (U.S. **-ed, -er, -ing**).
show, *see* **shew.**
showbread, Jewish offering; **shew-** only in Scrip.
show business (two words), colloq. **showbiz** (one word, no point).
showroom (one word).
show-through (typ.), the degree to which the printed ink film is visible through the paper.
s.h.p., shaft horse-power.
shriek (typ.), exclamation mark:!
shrillness.
shrivel/, -led, -ling (U.S. **-ed, -ing**).
Shropshire, *see* **Salop.**
Shrovetide, from the Saturday evening before to Ash Wednesday morning.
Shrove Tuesday, day before Ash Wednesday.
shumac, *use* **sumac.**
s.h.v., *sub hac voce or hoc verbo* (under this word).
shwanpan, Chinese abacus; *use* **swanpan.**
shy/, -ly, -ness, *not* shi-.
SI, Système International d'Unités, a coherent system of scientific units based on the metre, kilogramme, second, ampere, kelvin, and candela; adopted by the General Conference of Weights and Measures (CGPM) and endorsed by the International Standards Organization (ISO).

S.I., Sandwich Islands, Staten Island (N.Y.).

Si, silicon (no point).

S.I.A., Society of Industrial Artists.

sialagog/ue, an agent inducing a flow of saliva, *not* sialo-; **-ic.**

Siam, *use* **Thailand.**

Sib., Siberia, **-n.**

sibilant, (adj.) hissing; (noun) the letter *s* or *z*.

sibyl/, a prophetess; **-line.** *See also* **Sybil.**

Sic., Sicil/y, **-ian.**

[*sic*] (Lat.), thus, so (print in brackets).

sice, *use* **syce.**

Sicilian Vespers, massacre of the French in Sicily, 1282.

sicilienne (à la) (Fr.), in Sicilian style (not cap.).

sic passim (Lat.), like this throughout.

sicut ante (Lat.), as before.

sic vos non vobis (Lat.), thus you labour, but not for yourselves.

side/-arms, — -bet (hyphens).

sideboard (one word).

side/-car, — -chapel, — -drum (hyphens).

side/light, -long (one word).

side-notes (typ.), those in margin, generally outer (hyphen).

side/-saddle, — -show, — -slip, — -step, — -stroke, — -track (hyphens).

sidewalk (U.S.), pavement (one word).

sideways (one word).

Sidgwick & Jackson, Ltd., publishers.

Sidney (Sir Philip), 1554–86, English soldier, courtier, writer. *See also* **Syd-.**

siècle (Fr. m.), century; abbr. **s.**

Siegfried/, a *Nibelungenlied* hero, *not* Sig-; **— line,**

German fortified line on Franco-German border prior to 1939.

siehe (Ger.), see; abbr. **s.**

siehe dies (Ger.), see this (= q.v.); abbr. **s.d.**

Siemens (Werner), 1816–92, German founder of the electrical firm; **— (Sir William, Karl Wilhelm),** 1823–83, German-born British engineer, brother of preceding.

Sienkiewicz (Henryk), 1846–1916, Polish novelist.

Sienna, Italy; in It. **Siena.**

sierra, a mountain-chain.

Sierra/ Leone, W. Africa, independent 1961; **— Madre,** Mexican mountain-chains; **— Nevada,** mountain-chain in E. California, U.S.

siesta/ (Sp.), afternoon rest; *pl.* **-s.**

Sieveking (Sir Edward Henry), 1816–1904, English physician.

Sieyès (Emmanuel-Joseph), 1748–1836, French statesman.

si fait! (Fr.), yes, indeed!

Sig., *Signor,* **-i.**

sig., signature.

Sigfried, *use* **Sieg-.**

sightseeing (one word).

sigill/um (Lat.), a seal; *pl.* **-a,** *pron.* si-jil´-.

sign/, -ed, abbr. **s.**

signal/, -ize, -led, -ler, -ling, -ly (U.S. **-ed, -er, -ing**).

signatory, one who has signed, *not* -ary.

signature/ (mus.), the key sign at beginning of the stave; (typ.) complete part of a book, usu. 4, 8, 16, 32, or 64 pp.; these are given letters of the alphabet at foot of first page; text begins with B, omits J, V, W; when the alphabet is

exhausted, duplicate the
letters as Aa, 3A, etc.; a, b,
c, etc., are used for prelims.;
abbr. **sig.**

signed, abbr. **s.**

Signor/ (It.), Mr., *pl. -i,*
abbr. *Sig.; -a,* Mrs., *pl. -e;*
-ina, Miss, *pl. -ine.*

signs, *see* **astronomy,**
ecclesiastical, proof corr.
marks.

Sikandarabad, Uttar
Pradesh, India; *but*
Secunderabad, Hyderabad.

Sikes (Bill), in *Oliver Twist,*
not Sy-.

Sikkim, E. Himalayas.

Sikorski (Gen. Wladyslaw),
1881–1943, Polish Prime
Minister.

Silbe (Ger. f.), syllable
(cap.).

silhouette, shadow-outline.

siliceous, of silica, *not* -ious.

silicon, symbol **Si** (no
point).

silk screen (typ.), process
based on a stencil supported
on a fine mesh.

sill (of door, window), *not*
cill.

sillabub, milk or cream
curdled with wine, *not*
silli-, sy-.

Sillery, a champagne.

silo/, air-tight chamber for
storing grain; *pl.* **-s.**

silvan, of woods, *not* sy-.

silver, (chem.) symbol **Ag**
(*argentum*) (no point).

silvicultur/e, -ist, *not*
sylvi-.

s'il vous plaît (Fr.), if you
please; abbr. *s.v.p.*

simile/, a (literary) likening
of one thing to another; *pl.*
-s, *not* -ies.

simile (mus.), in the same
manner.

similia similibus curantur
(Lat.), like cures like.

similiter (Lat.), in like
manner.

simitar, *use* **scimitar.**

Simla, cap. of Himachal
Pradesh, India.

Simonds (Viscount).

Simonstown, Cape Province
(one word).

simoom, a hot desert wind,
not -oon.

simpatico (It.), congenial.

simpliciter (Lat.), absolutely,
without qualification.

simulacr/um, an image,
a deceptive substitute; *pl.* **-a.**

simultaneous, *not* -ious.

sin, sine (no point).

sin. (It. mus.), *sinistra* (left
hand).

Sind, Pakistan, *not* -e, -h,
Scinde.

Sindbad, the sailor, *not*
Sinb-.

Sindhia of Gwalior
(Maharajah).

Sindi/, Sind native; *pl.* **-s.**

sine (math.), abbr. **sin** (no
point).

sine/ (Lat.), without; —
anno, without the date,
abbr. *s.a.;* — *cura,*
without office; — *die,*
without a day (being
named), abbr. *s.d.;* —
dubio, — doubt; —
invidia, — envy; — *loco,*
anno, vel nomine, —
place, year, or name, abbr.
s.l.a.n.; — *loco et anno,*
— place and date (said of
books without imprints,
abbr. *s.l.e.a.);* — *mora,* —
delay; — *nomine,* —
(printer's) name, abbr. *s.n.;*
— *odio,* — hatred; —
prole, — issue, abbr. *s.p.;*
— *qua non,* an
indispensable condition, *not*
— quâ —.

sing., singular.

Singakademie, Berlin
(f. one word, cap.).

Singapore, island off south
end of Malay Peninsula.

sing/e, to scorch, **-ed, -eing.**

Singh, Indian title, as Ranjit Singh, *not* -ng.

singillatim (Lat.), one by one.

singular, abbr. **s.,** *or* **sing.**

sinh, hyperbolic sine (no point).

Sinhalese, (native or language) of Ceylon, *not* Sing-, Cing-; U.S. **Singhalese.** *But see* **Ceylon.**

sinistra (mus.), left hand; abbr. *S.,* or *sin.*

Sinn Fein/, the movement for Irish independence; *pron.* shĭn fān; **-er, -ism.**

sinus/ (anat.), cavity in bone or tissue; *pl.* **-es.**

Sioux, N. American Indian; *pl. same, pron.* soo.

siphon, *not* sy-.

si quis (Lat.), if anyone.

sirdar, (Ind., Egypt) a commander; (Egypt) the Commander-in-chief (cap.).

siren, a sea-nymph, *also* steam whistle or similar warning device, *not* sy-.

sirocco/, in S. Italy a hot, dusty wind from the Sahara; further north the same wind, now sultry and moist; *pl.* **-s;** *not* sci-.

sirup, *use* **sy-.**

sister-in-law (hyphens).

Sistine Chapel, in the Vatican, *not* Six-.

Sisyph/us, in Gr. myth.; **-ean,** condemned to eternal punishment.

sit (Lat.), let it be so.

Sitapur, Uttar Pradesh, India.

sitting-room (hyphen).

situs (Lat. *s.* and *pl.*), a site.

Sitwell (Dame Edith), 1887–1964, English poet; — **(Sir Osbert),** 1892–1969, English poet, novelist, essayist; — **(Sir Sacheverell),** b. 1897, English poet and art critic.

Siwalik Hills, India, *not* Siv-.

Six Mile Bottom, Cambs. (three words).

Sixmilebridge, Co. Clare, *also* Limerick (one word).

Six Road Ends, Co. Down (three words).

sixte, a fencing parry, etc.

sixteenmo (typ.), a book based on 16 leaves, 32 pages, to the basic sheet; abbr. **16mo** (no point).

sixty-fourmo (typ.), a book based on 64 leaves, 128 pages, to the basic sheet (hyphen); abbr. **64mo** (no point).

sizable, *use* **sizea-.**

sizar, an assisted student.

sizeable, *not* -able.

sizes of type, for the original names *see* **bourgeois, brevier, canon, double pica, emerald, english, gem, great primer, long primer, minim, nonpareil, paragon, pearl, pica, ruby, small pica.**

S.J., Society of Jesus (Jesuits).

S.J.A.A., St. John Ambulance Association.

S.J.A.B., St. John Ambulance Brigade.

sjambok (Afrik.), ox-hide whip.

S.J.C. (U.S.), Supreme Judicial Court.

Skagerrak, arm of the North Sea between Denmark and Norway (one word), *not* Skager Rack.

skean-dhu (Sc.), dirk worn in the stocking.

skee, *see* **ski.**

skein, of silk, etc., *not* -ain.

skelm, *use* **schelm.**

Skelmersdale, Lancs., 'new town', 1962.

skeptic, *use* **sc-.**

Skerryvore lighthouse, off Argyllshire, Scotland.

skewbald, of two colours in

irregular patches, usu. of horses, usu. white and a colour not black. *See also* **piebald.**

ski/, a runner attached to the foot for snow, *not* skee; *pl.* **-s.**

skia/graph, an X-ray photograph, *not* scia-, scio-, skio-; **-gram.** *See also* **scia-.**

skiing, using skis (no hyphen).

skilful, *not* skill-.

skinflint, a miser (one word).

skiver (bind.), the grain side of a split sheep skin.

Skt., Sanskrit.

skulduggery (U.S.), underhand practices. *See also* **sculduddery.**

skulk, to lurk, *not* sc-.

skull, to row, *use* sc-.

skull-less (hyphen, three *l*'s).

Skutari, *use* Sc-.

Skye terrier (cap. S).

skyey, *not* skiey.

skylight, small upper window (one word).

S.L., serjeant-at-law, solicitor-at-law.

S.L.A.D.E., Society of Lithographic Artists, Designers, and Engravers.

slaked lime, *not* slack- —.

Slamannan, Stirlingshire.

s.l.a.n., sine loco, anno, vel nomine (without place, year, or name).

slapdash, off-hand (one word).

S. lat., south latitude.

Slav/ic, -onian, -onic, of the Slavs, *not* Sc-; abbr. **Slav** (no point).

sld., sailed.

s.l.e.a., sine loco et anno (without place or date).

sled, sledge, a narrow cart on runners, for use on snow or bare ground.

sleigh, a carriage on runners, for use on snow.

sleight, of hand, *not* sli-; *pron.* slīt.

Slesvig, Germany, *use* **Schleswig.**

sleuth-hound (hyphen).

slew round, to rotate, *not* slue —.

slip proofs, *see* **proof, galley** *or* **slip.**

slipshod (one word).

Sloane (Sir Hans), 1660–1753, English naturalist.

sloid, manual training, *not* -jd, -yd.

sloot, *use* **sluit.**

sloping fractions (typ.), those with an oblique stroke as ¹/₂. *See also* **fractions.**

sloth, laziness; *also* (zool.) an animal.

Slough, near Windsor; *pron.* slow (ow as in how).

slough, to shed; *pron.* sluf.

slow-worm, *not* sloe-.

sloyd, *use* **sloid.**

s.l.p., sine legitima prole (without lawful issue).

slue round, *use* **slew** —.

sluit (S. Afr.), a narrow channel, *not* sloot.

slyly, *not* sli-.

slype, a passage between walls, esp. between south transept and chapter house.

S.M., Sergeant- or Staff-Major, (mus.) short metre, (Fr.) *Sa Majesté,* (Ger.) *Seine Majestät,* (It.) *Sua Maestà,* (Sp.) *Su Magestad* (His Majesty).

Sm, samarium (no point).

small capitals, *see* **capitals (small);** abbr. **s.c.** *or* **s.caps.**

small pica (typ.), old name for a size of type, about 11 pt.

smallpox (one word).

small royal, former standard size of paper, 19 × 25 in.; — **4to,** 12½ × 9½ in.; — **8vo,** 9½ × 6¼ in. (untrimmed); basis for

small royal (*cont.*):
size of **metric royal**,
960 × 1272 mm. *See* **book sizes.**

Smalls, Oxford 'Responsions' Examination.

S.M.D. (mus.), Short Metre Double.

S.M.E., *Sancta Mater Ecclesiae* (Holy Mother Church).

Smelfungus, Sterne's name for Smollett (one *l*).

smelling-salts (hyphen).

smell-less (hyphen, three *l*'s).

smelt, *not* smelled.

smelt, a small sea-fish. *See also* **smolt.**

S.M.I. (Fr.), *Sa Majesté Impériale* (His, *or* Her, Imperial Majesty).

Smith (Sydney), 1771–1845, English clergyman and wit; — **(Sir William Sidney),** 1764–1840, English admiral, defender of St. Jean d'Acre.

Smithsonian Institution, Washington, D.C., U.S.; abbr. **Smith. Inst.;** founded 1846 from funds left by **James Smithson,** 1765–1829, English chemist.

S.M.Lond.Soc., *Societatis Medicae Londiniensis Socius,* Member of the London Medical Society.

S.M.M., *Sancta Mater Maria* (Holy Mother Mary).

smok/e, -able, -y.

Smollett (Tobias George), 1721–71, Scottish physician and novelist.

smolt, a young salmon. *See also* **smelt.**

smooth/, -s, *not* -e, -es.

smorgasbord, Scandinavian hors-d'œuvres (not ital.).

smorzando (mus.), gradually dying away.

smoulder, *not* smol-.

s.m.p., *sine mascula prole* (without male issue).

Smyoniot, (native) of Smyrna.

Smyth (Dame Ethel), 1858–1944, English composer; — **(John),** 1586–1612, founder of the English Baptists.

Smythe (Francis Sydney), 1900–49, English mountaineer.

Sn, *stannum* (tin) (no point).

s.n., *sine nomine* (without name).

snapdragon, a Christmas game; (bot.) antirrhinum (one word).

snipe, a gamebird, *sing.* and *pl.*

snivel/, -led, -ler, -ling (U.S. **-ed, -er, -ing**).

snoek (Afrik.), a sea-fish.

Snorri Sturluson, 1178–1241, Icelandic historian and poet. *See also Heimskringla.*

snow (meteor.), abbr. **s.**

S.O., Staff Officer, Stationery Office, sub-office.

s.o., seller's option, substance of.

So-and-so (Mr.), (cap., hyphens).

Soane's (Sir John) Museum, London.

S.O.A.S., School of Oriental and African studies.

Sobranje, Bulgarian National Assembly, *not* -ie, -ye.

sobriquet, nickname, *not* sou- (not ital.); *pron.* sŏ′-brē-kā.

Soc., Socialist, Society, Socrates.

so-called (adj., hyphen).

Socialist (cap. when name of polit. party); abbr. **S., Soc.**

socialize, *not* -ise.

société/ (Fr. f.), society; — *anonyme,* limited liability company; *Société des Bibliophiles françois,* founded 1820, *not* français (l.c. *f*); abbr. **Sté.**

Society, abbr. **S.**, *or* **Soc.**

sociol., sociology.

Soc. Isl., Society Islands, S. Pacific.

socius/ (Lat.), Fellow, Associate, abbr. *S.*; — *criminis,* associate in crime.

Socotra, Indian Ocean, *not* -ora, Sok-.

Socrates, 469–399 B.C., Greek stonemason and philosopher, *not* Sok-; abbr. **Soc.**

sodium, symbol **Na** (*natrium*) (no point).

Sodom and Gomor/rah, O.T.; in N.T. (A.V.) **-rha.**

Sodor and Man (Bp. of).

S.O.E., Special Operations Executive.

S.O.E.D., Shorter Oxford English Dictionary.

sœur de charité (Fr. f.), a Sister of Mercy.

Sofar, sound firing and ranging (under water). *See also* **Sonar.**

soffit, under-surface of arch.

sofi, *use* **sufi.**

S. of S., Song of Solomon.

softa, Muslim student of sacred law (not ital.).

SOGAT *or* **SoGAT**, Society of Graphical and Allied Trades. *See also* **N.U.P.B. & P.W.**

soi-disant, self-styled (hyphen, not ital.).

soirée/, an evening party; — **dansante,** ditto with dancing; — **musicale,** ditto music (not ital.).

Sokrates, *use* **Soc-.**

Sol (Lat.), the sun (cap.).

Sol., Solomon.

sol., solicitor, solution.

solan goose, the gannet, *not* -and, -en, -ent.

solati/um (Lat.), compensation; *pl.* **-a.**

sola topi (Ind.), a sun helmet, *not* solar-.

sold/o, former Italian coin, $\frac{1}{20}$ of a lira; *pl.* **-i** (not ital.).

solecism, a blunder in speaking, writing, *or* behaviour.

solecize, *not* -ise.

solemnize, *not* -ise.

solen, a mollusc.

sol-fa (mus.) (hyphen).

solfeggio (mus.), a sol-fa exercise for the voice.

Solicitor-General (caps., hyphen); abbr. **Sol.-Gen.**

solicitude, anxiety, concern; in Fr. f. *soll-.*

solid (typ.), text matter set without spacing between lines.

solid/us (Lat.), shilling; *pl.* **-i**, abbr. **s.**; (typ.) the shilling stroke, /; also used for fractions.

soliloqu/ize, *not* -ise; **-y.**

solmization (mus.), solfaing, *not* -sation.

sol/o, abbr. **s.**; *pl.* **-os**, It. mus. *pl.* **-i.**

Solon, 638–558 B.C., Athenian lawgiver.

sol/us (theat.), *fem.* *-a*, alone.

solvable, *not* -eable, -ible.

solvitur ambulando (Lat.), the question settles itself naturally.

Solzhenitsyn (Alexander Isayevich), b. 1918, Russian writer, Nobel Prize for Literature, 1970.

Somalia, NE. Africa, independent 1960.

Somaliland (one word).

sombrero/, broad-brimmed hat; *pl.* **-s.**

somebody, somehow, someone (one word).

Somerby, Leics., Lincs.

somersault, *not* -set.

Somersby, Lincs., birthplace of Tennyson.

Somers Town, London (two words).

some/thing, -what, -where (one word).

Son (the), as Deity (cap.).

son, abbr. **s.**

Sonar, sound navigation and ranging, *cf.* **Asdic, Sofar.**

sonata/ (mus.), *pl.* **-s.**

Sondes (Earl, *not* of).

Song/ of Solomon, abbr. **S. of S.**; **— of Songs**, same as preceding.

songs (titles of) (typ.), roman quoted when cited.

son-in-law (hyphens); *pl.* **sons- — —.**

Son of/ God, — — Man (caps.).

soochong, *use* **sou-.**

Sop., soprano, -s.

Sophocles, 495–406 B.C., Greek dramatist; abbr. **Soph.**

sophomore (U.S.), second-year student, *not* sophi-.

Sophy, a Persian shah, orig. of the Cafi or Safawi dynasty, 1502–1736.

sopra (It.), above; *come —*, as above.

sopran/o (mus.), Eng. *pl.* **-os**, It. *pl.* **-i**; abbr. **S.**, *or* **Sop.**

Sorbonne, medieval theological college of Paris, now a university with faculties of science and arts also.

s'orienter (Fr.), to take one's bearings, to gain information about.

sortes/ (Lat.), (divination by) lots; **—** *Biblicae or Sacrae, Homericae, Vergilianae*, (divination from) random passages of Scripture, Homer, Virgil.

sorts (typ.), pieces of type.

SOS, signal for help.

so-so, passable (hyphen).

sostenuto (mus.), sustained.

Sotheby, Wilkinson, & Hodge (Messrs.), auctioneers, *now* **Sotheby's.**

sotto/ (It.), under; *— voce*, in an undertone.

sou/ (Fr. m.), former French coin of small value, half-penny; *pl.* **-s**; *gros —*, penny.

soubrette, maid or other pert fem. part in (musical) comedy.

soubriquet, *use* sob-.

souchong, a black tea, *not* soo-.

Soudan/, -ese, *use* Sud-.

soufflé (Fr. m.), very light milk pudding.

souffleur (Fr. m.), theat. prompter.

souk, a Muslim market-place.

Soult (Nicolas Jean de Dieu), 1769–1851, French marshal, Duke of Dalmatia.

soupçon, a taste, a very small quantity (not ital.).

soupe (Fr. f.), broth.

soupe de l'Inde (Fr. f.), mulligatawny soup.

souper (Fr. m.), supper, *not* -pé.

souris (Fr. m.), smile; (f.) mouse.

south/, -ern, abbr. **S.** *See also* **compass**).

South Africa/, -n, abbr. **S.A.**; **— America/, -n**, abbr. **S. Amer.**; **— Arabia**, *see* **Southern Yemen People's Republic; South Australia/, -n**, abbr. **S.A. — Carolina**, U.S., abbr. **S.C.**; **— Dakota**, U.S., abbr. **S.Dak.** (off.).

Southdown, sheep and mutton (one word).

South Downs, Hants. etc.

south-east (hyphen), abbr. **SE.** (*see also* **compass**).

South-East Lancashire and North-East Cheshire, *or* **Greater Manchester**, new metropolitan area, proposed 1971, includes Manchester, Salford, Oldham, Stockport, Wigan, Bolton, Bury,

Rochdale, Sale, Ashton-under-Lyne.

southern, abbr. **S.**

Southern Africa, geog. term, incl. Rhodesia and other countries as well as Republic of South Africa.

Southern Yemen People's Republic, independent Nov. 1967, *previously* South Arabia (Brit.).

Southey (Robert), 1774–1843, Poet Laureate.

South Glamorgan, new county, proposed 1971, comprising Cardiff and parts of Glamorgan and Monmouthshire.

Southwark, *or* 'The Borough', formerly in Surrey; *pron.* súdh-urk.

Southwell (Bp. of), *pron.* súdh-ul.

south-west (hyphen), abbr. **SW.** *See also* **compass.**

South West Africa (no hyphen).

South Yorkshire, new metropolitan area, proposed 1971, including Barnsley, Doncaster, Sheffield, Rotherham.

sou'wester, sailor's hat.

sovereign/, -s, abbr. **sov.**

soviet (Russ.), an elected council, the basis of Russian governmental machinery since 1917; adj. (cap.), as in Soviet Russia. *See also* **U.S.S.R.**

Sp., Spain, Spanish.

sp., specimen, spelling, spirit.

sp, *pl.* **spp** species.

s.p., self-propelled, starting price.

s.p., *sine prole* (without issue).

space/craft, -man, -suit (one word).

spaces (typ.), blanks for placing between words or letters.

spaghetti, a kind of macaroni (not ital.).

spahi, Turkish horse-soldier, Algerian French cavalryman; in Turk. **sipahi.**

Spain, abbr. **Sp.**

Spalato (Yugoslavia), *pron.* spa'lato; *now called* **Split.**

spandrel, space between curve of an arch and enclosing mouldings, *not* -il.

Spanish, abbr. **Sp.;** (typ.) alphabet consists of 27 letters including the sounds *ch, ll,* and *ñ,* but does not include *k* and *w. ch, ll,* and *rr* must not be separated. The portion carried over to begin with a consonant. Notes of exclam. and interrog. are inverted before and upright after their phrases. Caps. much less used than in English. *n* must never be substituted for *ñ.* Small caps. and italic as in English. Accents are much used.

Spanish n (*ñ*), 'curly *n*', or '*n* with the tilde'; *pron.* as ni in onion.

S.P.A.T.C., South Pacific Air Transport Council.

S.P.C., Society for the Prevention of Crime.

S.P.C.K., Society for Promoting Christian Knowledge.

spec., special, -ly, specific, -ally, -ation.

spécialité (Fr. f.), a speciality (ital.).

speciality, *not* -lty.

specialize, *not* -ise.

species, *sing.* and *pl.*; abbr. **sp,** *pl.* **spp** (no point). *See also* **botany, zoology.**

specific gravity, abbr. **sp. gr.;** (typ.) print in figures.

specimen, abbr. **sp., spec.**

Spectaclemakers Society (no hyphen, no apostrophe).

spectr/um, *pl.* **-a.**

speculat/e, -or.

specul/um, a mirror, (surg.) instrument for viewing

specul/um (*cont.*):
body cavities, bright patch
on a bird's wing; *pl.* **-a.**
speech (**break in**), *see*
punctuation XII (*a*).
spele/an, cave-dwelling
(adj.); **-ologist, -ology.**
The etymologically correct
spelaean, etc., have been
abandoned by most national
associations and technical
periodicals.
spelt, *not* spelled.
spencer, short double-
breasted overcoat, woollen
jacket.
Spencer (**Earl,** *not* of).
Spen/cer (**Herbert**), 1820–
1903, English philosopher;
-cerian, -cerism.
Spengler (**Oswald**), 1880–
1936, German philosopher
of history.
Spen/ser (**Edmund**), 1552–
99, English poet; **-serian,**
of the poet, his style, *or* his
stanza.
Spetsai, Greece, *not* Spezzia.
spew, to vomit, *not* spue.
Speyer, Germany, *not*
Spires.
Spezzia, *use* **Spetsai**
(Greece), *or* **La Spezia**
(Italy).
S.P.G., Society for the
Propagation of the Gospel;
now **U.S.P.G.**
sp. gr., specific gravity.
spherical, abbr. **s.**
sphinx/, *not* sphy-; *pl.* **-es.**
spick-and-span (adj.,
hyphens).
spiegando (mus.), 'un-
folding', becoming louder.
spiky, *not* -ey.
spina bifida (med.),
condition arising from
failure of two parts of the
spine to unite at embryo
stage.
spinach, *not* -age.
spine (bind.), that part of
the case protecting the back

of a book, and bearing —
lettering.
spinney, a thicket, *not* -ny.
Spinoz/a (**Baruch**), 1632–
77, Dutch Jewish
philosopher; **-ism.**
spiraea (hort.), an
ornamental shrub.
Spires, Germany; *use*
Speyer.
spirit, abbr. **sp.**
spirito (mus.), life, spirit,
energy.
spiritual, of the spirit.
spiritualize, *not* -ise.
spirituel, marked by
refinement and quickness
of mind; fem. the same
in Eng. (not ital.).
spirt, *use* spu-.
Spithead, strait between
I.O.W. and Portsmouth.
Spitsbergen, Arctic Ocean,
not Spitz-; in Norw.
Svalbard.
split fractions, *see*
fractions.
split infinitive, the separation of 'to' from the verb by
an adverb, as 'he used to
often say'. Objected to by
many, but numerous
examples in *O.E.D.*
Spode/ (**Josiah**), 1754–
1827, maker of — **china** at
Stoke.
Spohr (**Louis**), 1784–1859,
German composer.
spolia (Lat.), spoils; —
opima, the richest spoils;
also trophy won by generals
of opposing armies in single
combat.
spoliation, *not* spoil-.
spond/ee, foot of two
syllables (– –), **-aic.**
spontane/ity, -ous.
spoonful/, *pl.* **-s.**
spoony, foolishly fond, *not*
-ey.
sporran, the kilt pouch.
spos/a (It.), a bride, *pl.* **-e;**
-o, bridegroom, *pl.* **-i.**

S.P.Q.R., *Senatus Populusque Romanus* (the Senate and Roman people); small profits and quick returns.

S.P.R., Society for Psychical Research.

sprightly, lively, *not* spritely.

spring (season of) (not cap.).

springbok (Afrik.), an antelope, *not* -buck.

sprinkled edges (bind.), cut edges of books finely sprinkled with colour.

spruit (Afrik.), watercourse.

spry/, active; **-er, -est, -ly, -ness.**

s.p.s., sine prole superstite (without surviving issue).

spue, *use* **spew.**

spurt, *not* -irt.

sputnik, a Russian earth-satellite.

sput/um, expectorated matter; *pl.* **-a.**

sq./, square; — **ft.,** — feet; — **in.,** — inches; — **m.,** — metres; — miles; — **yd.,** — yards (each *s.* and *pl.*). These are not used in scientific work.

Sqn. Ldr., *or* **Sqn/Ldr,** Squadron Leader.

squalls (naut.), abbr. **q.**

square (bind.), that part of the case which overlaps the edges of a book.

square back (bind.), a book that has not been rounded, sometimes one in paper covers.

square root (two words).

squeegee, rubber-edged implement for sweeping wet surfaces, *not* squil-.

squirearchy, government (influenced) by landed proprietors, *not* -rarchy.

S.R., Southern Railway (prior to nationalization), Southern Rhodesia.

Sr, strontium (no point).

S.R.B.P., synthetic resin-bonded paper.

S.R.C., Science Research Council, Students' Representative Council.

S.R.I., *Sacrum Romanum Imperium* (the Holy Roman Empire).

Sri Lanka, 'Resplendent Island', new name for Republic of Ceylon, 1972.

Srinagar, Kashmir, *not* Ser-.

S.R.N., State Registered Nurse.

S.R.O., statutory rules and orders.

S.R.S., *Societatis Regiae Sodalis* (Fellow of the Royal Society).

S.S., Sunday school, Secretary of State, steamship, (Fr.) *Sa Sainteté* (His Holiness).

S.S. *or* **SS.,** *Schutzstaffel* (Ger.), Hitler's bodyguard.

SS., Saints, (Lat.) *sanctissimus* (most holy).

ss. (med.), half.

s.s., screw steamer, (mus.) *senza sordini* (without mutes).

SS.D., *Sanctissimus Dominus* (Most Holy Lord, i.e. the Pope).

SSE., south-south-east. *See also* **compass.**

S.S.G.G., letters of the *Femgericht*, q.v.: *Stock, Stein, Gras, Grein* (stick, stone, grass, groan).

S.Sgt., S/Sgt., Staff Sergeant.

S.S.R., Soviet Socialist Republic.

S.S.S. (Sp.), *su seguro servidor* (your faithful servant). Commonly followed by **Q.B.S.M.,** q.v., preceding the signature in a letter.

SSW., south-south-west. *See also* **compass.**

St., Saint, always in alphabetic arrangement to be placed under Saint, not St; strait, -s; street; in Slavonic languages, Stair, old.

s.t., short ton (2,000 lb.).

st., stanza, stone, strophe, (typ.) stet (let it remain), (cricket) stumped.

S.T.A., Scottish Typographical Association.

Sta (It., Sp., Port.), *santa* (female saint) (no point).

Staäl (baron de), 1822–1907, Russian diplomatist;
— **(Marguerite Jeanne Cordier Delaunay, baronne de)**, 1684–1750, French writer. *See also* Staël, Stahl.

'Stabat Mater', 'the Mother was standing' (Catholic hymn).

stabbed (bind.), with wire-stitching through the side of a booklet.

staccato, distinct (not ital.).

Stadtholder, Dutch governor, *not* Stadh-.

Staël (Madame de), 1766–1817, (in full, **Staël-Holstein, Anne Louise Germaine, baronne de**, *née* Necker), French writer. *See also* Staäl, Stahl.

staff, a pole; (mus.) set of lines on which music is written, *pl.* **staffs** *or* **staves**; a body of persons in authority, *pl.* **staffs**. *See* **stave**.

Staffs., Staffordshire.

staghound (one word).

Stagirite (the), Aristotle, *not* Stagy-; *pron.* staj-′ĭ-rīt.

stagy, *not* -ey.

Stahl (Friedrich Julius), 1802–61, German lawyer and politician. *See also* Staäl, Staël.

staid, solemn, *not* stayed.

stalactite, deposit on cave roofs.

Stalag, German P.O.W. camp.

stalagmite, deposit on cave floors.

stalemate (chess) (one word).

Stalingrad, Russian city, *previously* Tsaritsyn, *now* **Volgagrad**.

stamen/ (bot.), *pl.* -s.

stamina, power of endurance.

stampat/o, -a (It.), printed; *-ore*, a printer.

Stamp Office (two words).

stanch (verb,) to check a flow, *not* staun-.

standardize, *not* -ise.

stand/point, -still (one word).

Stanhope (Earl), 1753–1816, inventor of first iron press, 1800.

stannary, a tin mine.

stannum, tin; symbol **Sn** (no point).

Stanstead, Suffolk.

Stansted, Essex, Kent.

stanz/a, a group of rhymed lines; *pl.* -as, It. *pl.* -e; abbr. **st.**

star (typ.), the asterisk *.

star/, -red, -ry, -ring.

Starcross, Devon (one word).

starfish (one word).

stark (Ger., mus.), loud, vigorous.

Stars and Stripes, U.S. flag.

'Star-Spangled Banner, The', U.S. National Anthem.

starting-point (hyphen).

stat., statics, statuary, statute.

stat., *statim* (immediately).

State (cap. in place-names).

Staten Island, New York, *not* Staa-; abbr. **S.I.**

stater, an anc. Greek coin.

statics, the science of forces in equilibrium, is treated as sing.

statim (Lat.), immediately; abbr. *stat*.

stationary, fixed.

Stationers' Hall, London (apos. after s).

stationery, paper, etc.

statistics, the subject, *sing.*; numerical facts systematized, *pl.*

stator (mech.), a stationary part within which something revolves.

statuary, abbr. **stat.**

statuette, a small statue.

status, rank (not ital.).

status quo/ (Lat.), the same state as now; —— *ante,* ditto as before.

statute, a written law; abbr. **stat.**

staunch (adj.), firm, loyal, *not* stan-.

stave/, staff (mus.), a snatch of song, a piece of wood in the side of a barrel; *pl.* **-s.** *See also* **staff.**

stayed, stopped, *not* staid.

S.T.B., *Sacrae Theologiae Baccalaureus* (Bachelor of Theology).

S.T.C., Senior (Officers') Training Corps.

S.T.D., *Sacrae Theologiae Doctor* (Doctor of Theology), Subscriber Trunk Dialling.

Ste (Fr. f.), *sainte* (female saint) (no point).

steadfast, *not* sted-.

steamboat (one word).

steam/-**engine,** —— -**hammer** (hyphen).

steamship (one word), abbr. **S.S.**

Steel (Flora Annie), 1847–1929, Scottish novelist; —— **(Sir James),** 1830–1904, Scottish dignitary.

Steele (Sir Richard), 1672–1729, English essayist and dramatist.

Steell (Gourlay), 1819–94, Scottish painter; —— **(Sir John),** 1804–91, Scottish sculptor, brother of preceding.

steenbok (Afrik.), a small antelope, *not* steinbuck.

steeplechase/, cross-country horse-race; **-r,** horse *or* rider.

steeplejack (one word).

Steevens (George), 1736–1800, English Shakespearian commentator. *See also* **Stephen, Stephens, Stevens.**

Stefansson (Vilhjalmur), 1879–1962, Canadian Arctic explorer.

Steinbeck (John Ernst), 1902–68, American novelist.

Steinberg, a hock (wine).

stem, abbr. **s.**

stemm/**a,** a pedigree; *pl.* **-ata.**

stencil/, **-led, -ler, -ling** (U.S. **-ed, -er, -ing**).

Stendhal, pen-name of **Marie Henri Beyle,** 1783–1842, French novelist.

step/**brother, child, -daughter, -father, -mother, -sister, -son** (each one word).

Stephen (Sir Leslie), 1832–1904, English biographer and critic. *See also* **Steevens, Stephens, Stevens.**

Stephens (Alexander Hamilton), 1812–83, American statesman; —— **(James),** 1882–1950, Irish poet and novelist. *See also* **Steevens, Stephen, Stevens.**

Stephenson (George), 1781–1848, English locomotive engineer; —— **(Robert),** 1803–59, English engineer (tubular bridges), son of preceding. *See also* **Stev-.**

steppe, treeless plain, esp. of Russia.

stepping-stone (hyphen).

stereotype (typ.), a plastic, lead alloy, or rubber duplicate plate cast from a matrix moulded from original relief printing material; abbr. **stereo** (no point).

sterilize, to destroy micro-organisms in or on, to make incapable of reproduction, *not* -ise.

Sterling (John), 1806–44, Scottish writer.

sterling, (of money) of standard value; abbr. **stg.**

Sterne (Laurence, *not* Law-), 1713–68, English novelist.

stet (typ.), a Latin word meaning 'let it stand', written in the proof margin to cancel an alteration, dots being placed under what is to remain.

stetson, wide-brimmed felt hat.

Steuart (Sir Alan Henry Seton-), 1856–1913, Scottish dignitary; — **(Sir James Denham),** 1712–80, Scottish economist; — **(John Alexander),** 1861–1932, Scottish journalist and novelist.

Stevens (Alfred), 1818–75, English sculptor; — **(Thaddeus),** 1792–1868, American abolitionist. *See also* **Steevens, Stephen, Stephens.**

Stevenson (Adlai Ewing), 1835–1914, U.S. Vice-President; — **(Adlai Ewing),** 1900–65, U.S. politician, grandson of preceding; — **(Robert),** 1772–1850, English lighthouse engineer; — **(Robert Louis),** 1850–94, Scottish novelist, essayist, and poet, abbr. **R.L.S.** *See also* **Steph-.**

Stewart, family name of Earl of Galloway; — **(Dugald),** 1753–1828, Scottish metaphysician; — **(Sir Harry Jocelyn Urquhart),** 1871–1945, Scottish dignitary; — **(James),** 1831–1905,

Scottish African missionary. *See also* **Steuart, Stuart.**

stg., sterling.

stibium, antimony, symbol **Sb** (no point).

stich, a verse; *pron.* stĭk.

stichometry, division into or measurement by lines of verse, *not* stycho-.

stichomythia, dialogue in alternate lines of verse, *not* stycho-.

Stieglitz (Alfred), 1864–1946, U.S. photographer.

stigma/, a brand; *pl.* **-ta.**

stigmatize, *not* -ise.

stile, over a fence. *See also* **style.**

stiletto/, a dagger; *pl.* **-s.**

stillborn (one word).

still life (two words).

stillness.

Stilton cheese (cap.).

stimie (golf), *use* **sty-.**

stimul/us, *pl.* **-i.**

stip., stipend, -iary.

stirk, a yearling ox or cow, *not* sterk, sturk.

Stirling, Stirlingshire.

Stirling (J. Hutchison, *not* -inson), 1820–1909, Scottish metaphysician; — **(William Alexander),** 1567–1640, Scottish poet, usu. called William Alexander. *See also* **Ster-.**

stirp/s (Lat.), lineage; *pl.* **-es.**

Stock Exchange (caps.); abbr. **S/E, St. Ex., Stock Ex.**

stockholder (one word).

stockinet, an elastic fabric, *not* -ette, -inget.

stockpile (one word).

stoep (Afrik.), platform of stone, brick, cement, etc., attached to outer wall(s) of a house, (U.S. **stoop).**

stoicheio/logy, the doctrine of elements, *not* stoechio-, stoichio-; **-metric** (chem.), having elements in fixed proportions; **-metry** (chem.), the proportion in which elements occur in a compound.

stokehold (naut.), *not* -hole.

ston/e, abbr. **st.; -y.**

stone (typ.), surface on which pages of type are imposed.

Stonyhurst College, Lancs.

stoop (U.S.), stoep.

stoop, flagon; *use* **stoup.**

stopgap (one word).

stop-press (hyphen).

stop valve (two words).

storey/, a horizontal division of a building; *pl.* **-s;** *not* story, -ies; **-ed.**

storied, celebrated in story, *not* -yed.

storiolog/y, scientific study of folklore; **-ist.**

Storting, legislative assembly of Norway.

story (of a building), *use* **storey.**

story/-book, — -teller, — -telling (hyphens).

stoup, flagon, holy-water basin, *not* stoop.

stowaway (one word).

Stow-on-the-Wold, Glos. (hyphens).

S.T.P., *Sacrae Theologiae Professor* (Professor of Sacred Theology); a powerful hallucinatory drug.

str., stroke (oar).

Strachan, *pron.* strawn.

Strachey, family name of Baron O'Hagan and Baron Strachie; **— (Giles Lytton),** 1880–1932, English biographer.

Stradbroke (Earl of).

Stradivarius, a violin or other stringed instrument made by **Antonio Stradivari** or **Antonius Stradivarius,** of Cremona, 1650–1737.

Strafford (Earl of).

straight accents (typ.), the long accents, as *ā, ē.*

straightforward (one word).

strait/, -s, when with name to be cap.; abbr. **St.**

strait/-laced, — -waist-coat, *not* straight- **—** (hyphens).

Straits Settlements, now a component of Malaysia.

Stranraer, Wigtown.

Strasburg, English form of Fr. **Strasbourg,** Ger. **Strassburg.**

Stratford de Redcliffe (Viscount), 1786–1880, diplomatist.

Stratford-upon-Avon, War., *not* -on- (hyphens).

strathspey, Scottish dance.

strato-cirrus (meteor.), *use* **cirro-stratus.**

stratosphere, the upper atmosphere, where temp. is constant.

strat/um, a layer; *pl.* **-a.**

strat/us, a low layer of cloud, *pl.* **-i;** abbr. **s.**

Strauss (Johann I), 1804–49, Austrian composer of Viennese waltzes; **— (Johann II),** 1825–99, the best known of the family, son of above; **— (Joseph),** 1827–70, and **— (Eduard),** 1835–1916, also sons of Johann I; **— (Johann III),** 1866–1939, son of Johann II; **— (Richard Georg),** 1864–1949, German composer of operas, songs, and orchestral works.

Streatfeild, family name, *not* -field.

street (typ.), name of, to have initial caps., as Regent Street; spell out when a number, as Fifth Avenue; number of house in, not to be followed by any point, as 6 Fleet Street; abbr. **St.**

stri/a (anat., geol.), a stripe; *pl.* **-ae.**

strike-through (typ.), the penetration of ink into paper.

stringendo (mus.), pressing, accelerating the speed.

strontium, symbol Sr (no point).

Struwwelpeter, German child's book.

strychnine, *not* -in.

Stuart (House of); — (Leslie), 1866–1924, English composer. *See also* **Steuart, Stewart.**

stucco/, (to apply) plaster coating to wall surfaces; **-es,** **-ed.**

Stück (Ger. n.), a piece.

studio/, *pl.* **-s.**

stumbling-block (hyphen).

stupefy, *not* -ify.

Sturluson, *see* **Snorri.**

Sturm und Drang (Ger.), storm and stress (no hyphens).

Sturm-und-Drang-Periode, German romanticism of the late eighteenth century (three hyphens).

Stuttgart, Germany, *not* Stü-, -ard.

sty, inflamed swelling on eyelid; enclosure for pigs; *not* stye; *pl.* **sties.**

Stygian, of the River Styx.

style, custom, manner; *but* **stile** over a fence.

style of the house (typ.), the custom of a printing establishment as to both the lit. aspect (use of capitals, spellings, abbreviations, italics, word-division, punctuation, etc.) and the general layout and design.

stylize, *not* -ise.

stymie, (golf) one ball directly between the other and the hole, (metaph., noun and verb) block; *not* sti-, -my.

Styx, a river in Hades.

Suabia, *use* **Swa-.**

Suakin, Sudan, *not* -im.

suaviter in modo (Lat.), gently in manner. *See* *fortiter in re.*

sub., subaltern, subscription, substitute, suburb, -an.

sub (Lat.), under.

subahdar (Ind.), a native captain.

subaltern, officer below rank of captain; abbr. **sub.**

subaudi (Lat.), understand, supply; abbr. *sub.*

sub-bass (hyphen).

sub/committee, -deacon, -dean, -divide (one word).

sub-edit/, -or, -orial (hyphen).

subfusc/, -ous, dark.

sub-genus (hyphen).

sub-headings, *see* **headings** (sub-).

subj., subject, -ive, -ively, subjunctive.

sub judice (Lat.), under consideration.

subjunctive, abbr. **subj.**

sub-kingdom (hyphen).

sublet (one word).

Sub-Lieutenant (hyphen), abbr. **Sub-Lt.**

Sublime Porte, Turkish Court and Government.

sub modo (Lat.), in a qualified sense.

subpoena/, (to serve) a writ commanding attendance; *pl.* **-s;** *not* -pena (one word, not ital.).

sub rosa (Lat.), under the rose, privately.

subscription, abbr. **sub.**

subsection (one word); abbr. **subsec.**

subsidence, a sinking of ground; *pron.* sub'-sĭdence.

subsidize, to pay a subsidy to, *not* -ise.

subsidy, a grant of public money.

sub sigillo (Lat.), in the strictest confidence.

sub silentio, in silence.

sub-species (hyphen).
substantive, abbr. **s.,** *or*
  subst. (*see* **nouns**).
substitute, abbr. **sub.**
substrat/um, *pl.* **-a.**
subtil/, -e, *use* **subtle** in all
  senses.
subtilize, to rarefy, *not* -ise.
sub-title, a minor heading.
subtl/e, fine, rarefied,
  elusive, cunning; **-er, -est,**
  -ety, -y, *not* subtil-.
subtopia, suburban development with every modern
  excrescence.
suburb/, -an, abbr. **sub.**
sub/ voce or — *verbo* (Lat.),
  under a specified word;
  abbr. **s.v.**
subway (one word), an
  underground passage, (U.S.
  and Glasgow) an under-
  ground railway.
succeeded, abbr. **s.**
succès/ d'estime (Fr. m.),
  success with more honour
  than profit; — *fou,*
  extravagant success.
suchlike (one word).
sucking-pig (hyphen).
sud (Fr. m.), south; abbr. **s.**
Süd (Ger. m.), south; abbr.
  S. (cap.).
Sudan/, independent 1956;
  -ese; *not* Sou-.
su/e, -ed, -ing.
suede, dull-dressed kid, as
  for gloves (no accent).
suédoise (*à la*), in Swedish
  style (*é,* not cap.).
Suetonius (Caius
  Tranquillus), *c.* 70–140,
  Roman historian; abbr.
  Suet.
suff., suffix.
suffic/it (Lat.), it is
  sufficient; *pl.* **-*iunt.***
sufi, a Muslim mystic, *not*
  sofi, soofee, sophy.
suggestible, open to
  suggestion, *not* -able.
suggestio falsi (Lat.), an
  indirect lie.

Suidas, *c.* 1100, Greek
  lexicographer, abbr. **Suid.**
sui/ generis (Lat.), (the only
  one or ones) of his, her, its,
  or their own kind; — *juris,* of
  full age and capacity.
Suisse/ (Fr.), (native) of
  Switzerland; *also* (not cap.)
  a porter of a mansion,
  beadle of a church; *fem.*
  -*sse*; la Suisse, Fr. for
  Switzerland.
suite, a set of rooms,
  attendants, *or* musical pieces
  (not ital.).
suite/ (Fr. f.), continuation;
  — *et fin,* conclusion.
suivez (mus.), follow the
  soloist.
suivre/ (*à*) (Fr.), to be
  continued; *faire* — (letters
  and parcels) to be forwarded,
  (typ.) to run on.
Sully-Prudhomme (René
  François Armand), 1839–
  1907, French poet and
  critic.
sulphur, symbol **S** (no
  point); U.S. **sulfur.**
sulphuretted, U.S.
  sulfureted.
sultan/, a Muslim ruler,
  fem. **-a; Sultan (the),**
  of Turkey, till 1922; abbr.
  Sult.
Sultanpur, India.
sum (math.), symbol Σ.
sumac (bot.), an ornamental
  tree, *not* sh-, -ach, -ack.
summarize, *not* -ise.
summer (not cap.).
summer-time, the summer
  season (hyphen); **British
  summer time,** one hour
  in advance of G.M.T., in
  summer only, 1922–67, and
  from 1972 (separate words).
  See also **B.S.T.**
summum bonum (Lat.),
  the supreme good.
sun, abbr. **S.**
sun/beam, -bonnet, -burn
  (one word).

sundae, ice-cream with crushed fruit and nuts.

Sunday, abbr. **Sun.**

sun/dial, -flower (one word).

sunn, E. Indian fibre.

Sunna, traditional Muslim law, *not* -ah.

Sunni, an orthodox Muslim, *not* -ec.

sun/rise, -set, -shade, -shine, -spot, -stroke (one word).

suo/ jure (Lat.), in one's own right; — *loco,* in its own place.

sup., superior, supine.

sup. (Lat.), *supra* (above).

super, as colloq. for superfine or supernumerary (no point).

super-calendered paper, highly polished but not coated; abbr. **S.C.**

supercargo/, person in a ship managing the commercial transactions, *pl.* **-es** (one word).

superexcellen/ce, -t (one word).

superficies, a surface, *sing.* and *pl.*

superfine, abbr. **super** (no point).

superintendent, abbr. **supt.**

superior, abbr. **sup.**

superiors (typ.), small characters set above ordinary characters, as in maths. and chem., ^{1}, ^{2}, ^{a}, ^{b}.

superl., superlative.

supermarket (one word).

supersede, to take the place of, *not* -cede.

supersonic, above the speed of sound.

supervise, *not* -ize.

supervisor, *not* -er.

supine, abbr. **sup.**

supplement, abbr. **suppl.**

suppos/ititious, conjectural, spurious, *not* -itious.

suppository, a medicated plug, *not* -ary.

suppressio veri (Lat.), suppression of the truth.

suppressor, *not* -er.

supr., supreme.

supra (Lat.), above, formerly; abbr. *sup.*

suprême (Fr. f.), a method of cooking, with a rich cream sauce.

Supreme Court (U.S.).

supt., superintendent.

sur (Fr. prep.), upon; abbr. *s/* in addresses; (adj.) sour, *fem.* **sure.**

sûr, -e (Fr.), sure, safe.

sura, a chapter of the Koran (cap. for particular chapters).

surah, a thin silk fabric.

Surat, Bombay.

surcingle, a belt.

Sûreté, Paris, the French C.I.D.

surfeit/, excess; **-er, -ing.**

surg/eon, -ery, -ical, abbr. **surg.**

Surgeons (Royal College of), abbr. **R.C.S.**

surmise, conjecture, *not* -ize.

surplus, abbr. **S.**

surprise, *not* -ize.

surrenderer (law), *not* -or.

sursum corda (Lat.), (lift) up your hearts.

Surtees (Robert Smith), 1805–64, English fox-hunting novelist.

surtout, an overcoat.

surv., survey/ing, -or, surviving.

Surv.-Gen., Surveyor-General.

survivor, *not* -er.

Susanna (Apocr.), abbr. **Sus.**

suspender, *not* -or; *pl.,* straps to support socks, (U.S.) braces.

sus. per coll. (Lat.), *suspen/sio (-sus, -datur) per collum,* hanging (hanged, let him be hanged) by the neck.

Susquehanna River, New York State, U.S., *not* -ana.

Sutlej, Punjab river.

suttee, custom of Hindu widow immolating herself on husband's pyre, *not* sati.

suum cuique (Lat.), let each have his own.

Suwannee River, U.S., *not* Swa-.

S.V., *Sancta Virgo* (Holy Virgin), *Sanctitas Vestra* (Your Holiness).

s.v., *sub voce,* or *verbo* (under a word or heading, as in a dictionary); sailing vessel.

S.V.A., Incorporated Society of Valuers and Auctioneers.

svastika, *use* **sw-.**

svelte (Fr.), elegant.

Svendsen (**Johan Severin**), 1840–1911, Norwegian composer.

Sverige, Swedish for **Sweden.**

s.v.p. (Fr.), *s'il vous plaît* (if you please).

S.W., South Wales.

SW., south-west. *See also* **compass.**

Sw., Swed/en, -ish.

Swabia, Germany, *not* Su-.

Swahili, a people and language of Zanzibar and the coast opposite.

Swammerdam (**Jan**), 1637–80, Dutch naturalist.

swanpan, Chinese abacus, anglicized from **suanpan,** *not* schwan-.

swansdown (one word).

swap, to exchange, *use* **-op.**

swaraj, self-govt. for India, *not* su-.

swash (typ.), letters with tails or flourishes.

swastika, a religious symbol, adopted by the German Nazi party, *not* sv-.

swat, to hit sharply. *See also* **swot.**

swath, a line of cut grass.

swathe, to bind.

Swazi/, -land, S. Africa.

swede, a root (not cap.).

Sweden, abbr. **Sw.,** in Swed. **Sverige** (*see also* **Assemblies**).

Swedish, abbr. **Sw.;** (typ.) alphabet contains Ger. *ä, ö.* Also the peculiar 'Swedish *a*' (*Å, å*) *pron.* somewhat as *aw.* In alph. arrangement *å, ä, ö,* are put after *z.* The acute accent may be used to mark an accented syllable.

sweepback (of aircraft's wings), noun and adj. (one word).

Sweet (**Henry**), 1845–1912, English philologist. *See also* **Swete.**

sweetbread (cook.) (one word).

sweetbrier, *not* -briar (one word).

sweet/-oil, — -pea (hyphens).

sweet-william (bot.) (hyphen, not caps.).

swelled rule (typ.), a rule wider in centre than at ends. *See* **rule.**

Swete (**Henry Barclay**), 1835–1917, English biblical scholar. *See also* **Sweet.**

Swinburne (**Algernon Charles**), 1837–1909, English poet.

Swindon, Wilts.

swingeing, hard (blow).

swing-wing (of aircraft) (hyphen).

Swinton, Lancs., Yorks.

Swithun/ (**St.**), Bp. of Winchester 852–62; **-'s Day,** 15 July.

Switzerland, abbr. **Switz.;** in Fr. **la Suisse,** in Ger. **die Schweiz,** in It. **Svizzera** (*see also* **Assemblies**).

swop, to exchange, *not* swap.

swot, to study hard. *See also* **swat.**

swung dash (typ.), a dash which represents the stem of a word, ~.

Sybil, Christian name. *See also* **sibyl**.

sycamine (N.T., A.V.), the mulberry-tree.

sycamore (bot.), (Bib., A.V.) a kind of fig-tree, *Ficus sycomorus* (**sycomore** in N.T., N.E.B.); (Eur. and Asia) an ornamental shade-tree, the sycamore maple, *Acer pseudoplatanus*; (U.S.) a plane tree, *Platanus*.

syce (Anglo-Ind.), a groom, *not* sice.

sycomore, *see* **sycamore**.

Sydney, N.S.W., Australia. *See also* **Sidney**.

Sydney Heads, two cliffs.

Sykes, *see* **Si-**.

syllabub, *use* **si-**.

syllabus/, *pl.* **-es**.

syllogism, a logical argument of two premisses and a conclusion.

syllogize, to argue by syllogism, *not* -ise.

sylvan, *use* **si-**.

sylvicultur/e, -ist, *use* **si-**.

symbolize, *not* -ise.

sympathique (Fr.), congenial, having the right artistic feeling for.

sympathize, *not* -ise.

symposi/um, a drinking-party (obs. in this sense except, with cap., as title of one of Plato's Socratic dialogues), a conference, a collection of views on a topic; *pl.* **-a**

syn., synonym, -ous.

synaeresis, gram. contraction, *not* -eresis.

synagog/ue, an assembly of Jews for worship, their place of worship; **-al, -ic**.

synchronize, to (cause to) coincide in time, *not* -ise.

syncope, a cutting short, a fainting; *pron.* sĭn′-kup-ĕ.

syndrome, a collection of symptoms.

Syne (Auld Lang), the days long ago, a sentimental Scottish song, now widely adopted.

synonym/, a word with the same meaning as another; **-ous**, abbr. **syn.; -ize**, *not* -ise; **-y**, *not* -e, -ey.

synops/is, a summary; *pl.* **-es**. But *see* **Synoptic Gospels**.

Synoptic Gospels, Matt., Mark, and Luke, whose text can be laid out in a synopsis, i.e. *in full* in parallel columns.

synthesize, to make a whole out of parts, *not* -ise.

syphon, *use* **si-**.

Syr., Syria, -c, -n.

syren, *use* **si-**.

Syriac, abbr. **Syr.**; has 22 letters, besides vowel points, reads from right to left, and is set as Hebrew. There are three forms of type, Estrangelo, Jacobite, Nestorian.

Syringa, (bot.) the lilac genus.

syringa, (pop.) the mock orange.

syringe/, instrument for squirting or injecting; **-ing**; *not* si-.

syrin/x, Pan-pipe, (anat.) a narrow tube from throat to ear-drum, the vocal organ of birds, a narrow gallery in rock; *pl.* **-ges** *or* **-xes**.

syrup, *not* sirop, -up; abbr. **syr.**

syst., system.

systematize, *not* -ise.

syzygy (astr.), the moon being in conjunction or opposition.

Szigeti (Joseph), 1892–1973, Hungarian violinist.

T

T, tera- (10^{12}); the nineteenth in a series.

T., Tenor, Territory, Testament, Titus (Roman praenomen), all proper names with this initial, (It. mus.) *tace* (be silent).

T, temperature.

t., ton, -s, town, -ship, tun, -s, (Fr.) *tome* (volume), *tonneau* (ton), (Lat.) *tempore* (in the time of), (mus.) *tempo* (time), *tenor/e, -i* (tenor, -s), (naut.) thunder.

't (Du.), *het* (the, n.), as Van 't Hoff.

Ta, tantalum (no point).

T.A., Territorial Army.

T.A.A.V.R., Territorial, Auxiliary, and Volunteer Reserve.

Tabago, use **To-.**

tabasheer, a plant opal, *not* -ir, -achir.

table/ alphabétique (Fr. typ. f.), index; — *des matières*, table of contents.

tableau/ (Fr. m.), a picture, etc., *pl. -x; tableau/ vivant/*, 'living picture' by motionless actors in costume, *pl. -x -s.*

tableau/, often in Eng. for *tableau vivant*, q.v., but also for a suddenly perceived situation; *pl.* **-x.**

table d'hôte, common table for guests at hotel (*pl.* **tables** —; a set meal, as distinct from *à la carte.*

tables of contents, *see* contents (**tables of**).

tablespoonful/, *pl.* **-s.**

tablier (Fr. m.), apron.

taboo, forbidden, *not* -u.

tabor, small drum, *not* -our.

tabouret, drum-shaped stool, *not* -oret.

tabul/a (Lat.), a document, *pl.* **-ae; *tabul/a ras/a,*** a blank surface, *pl.* **-ae -ae.**

tabulat/e, -or.

tac-au-tac (fencing), parry and riposte (hyphens, not ital.); but *du tac au tac* (Fr., fig.), from defence to attack (no hyphens, ital.).

tace (It. mus.), be silent; abbr. **T.**

Tacitus (Caius Cornelius), *c.* 55–120, Roman historian; abbr. **Tac.**

tacks/man (Sc.), a lessee, *not* tax-; *pl.* **-men.**

Tadjikistan, a Soviet Socialist Republic. *See* **U.S.S.R.**

taedium vitae (Lat.), weariness of life.

tael, former Chinese monetary unit, one Chinese ounce of silver.

Tae-ping, *use* **Taiping** (one word).

taffeta, a fabric, *not* the many variations.

tagetes (bot.), a type of marigold, *not* -ete; *pl. same.*

Tagore (Rabindranath), 1861–1941, Indian poet.

tail (typ.), foot of the page.

tailladé (Fr. cook.), crimped.

taille/ (Fr. f.), engraving, also size, etc.; — *douce,* copperplate engraving.

tail-piece (typ.), the design at end of a section, chapter, or book.

tailzie (Sc. law), entail, succession.

Tain, Ross and Cromarty.

Taine (Hippolyte Adolphe), 1828–93, French historian and lit. critic.

Taipei, capital of Taiwan, q.v.

Taiping rebellion, 1850–64, *not* Tae-.

Tait (Archibald Campbell), 1811–82, Abp. of Canterbury; — **(Peter Guthrie)**, 1831–1901, Scottish mathematician and physicist. *See also* **Tate.**

Taiwan, *formerly* Formosa.

Taj Mahal, mausoleum at Agra, India, *not* — Me-.

take/-off, -over (hyphen).

Tal (Ger. n.), valley, *not now Th-*.

Talbot de Malahide (Baron).

Taler (Ger. m.), coin, *formerly Th-*; abbr. **Tlr.**

tales (law), a suit for summoning jurors to supply a deficiency; **tales/man,** one so summoned, *pl.* **-men.**

Talfourd (Sir Thomas Noon), 1795–1854, English dramatist, biographer, and author of the Copyright Act of 1842.

talisman/, a charm, amulet; *pl.* **-s.**

talis qualis (Lat.), such as it is.

Talleyrand-Périgard (Charles Maurice de, prince of Benevento), 1754–1838, French politician.

Tallinn, Estonian S.S.R., *formerly* Reval.

Tallis (Thomas), *c.* 1510–85, English composer, *not* Talys, Tallys; **Tallis's canon,** a hymn-tune.

tallness.

Talmud, Hebrew laws.

Talweg (before 1900 *Thalweg*), centre of a river channel, used as boundary between two countries.

Tam., Tamil.

TAM, Television Audience Measurement.

tambourin, a long narrow drum of Provence, a dance accompanied by it.

tambourine, a small drum, with jingling metal discs, played on with the hand.

tameable, *not* -mable.

Tamil, S. Indian language, *not* -ul; abbr. **Tam.**

Tammany Hall, Democratic Party H.Q., New York, *not* Tama-.

'Tam o' Shanter', poem by Burns (caps., small *o*, apos., no hyphen).

tam-o'-shanter, a woollen cap (hyphens, apos.).

tan, tangent, -s (no point).

tangerine orange, *not* tangier-.

tangible, *not* -able.

Tangier, Morocco, *not* -iers.

tanh, hyperbolic tangent (no point).

Tanjor/, -e, India, *use* Thanjavur.

Tannhäuser, opera by Wagner, 1845.

tantalize, to torment with hopes unfulfilled, *not* -ise.

tantalum, symbol Ta (no point).

tant/ mieux (Fr.), so much the better; — *pis,* so much the worse.

Tanzania (Tanganyika and Zanzibar), independent rep. 1963.

Taoism, doctrine of Lao-tsze, *not* Tâ-, Taö- (one word).

tapis (sur le) (Fr.), under consideration, *or* discussion.

tapisserie (Fr. f.), tapestry.

tar/, -ry.

tarantella, an Italian dance, or its music.

tarantula, a spider.

Tarbert, Argyl., Harris, Co. Kerry.

Tarbet, Loch Lomond.

tariff, duty on particular goods, *not* -if.

tarlatan, a muslin, *not* -etan.

tarpaulin, waterproof cloth, orig. of tarred canvas, *not* -ing.

Tarpeian Rock, anc. Rome.

tartar/, a deposit on the teeth; adj. **-ic**.

Tartar, an inhabitant of Tartary, *properly, but less usually*, **Tatar**; an intractable person.

tartare (*à la*) (Fr. cook.), with cold mustard sauce.

Tartar/us, the anc. Greek underworld; adj. **-ean**.

Tartary, *properly, but less usually*, **Tatary**, a region of W. Asia and E. Europe.

Tartuffe, Le, play by Molière, 1669.

Tartuffe, religious hypocrite (Fr. m. *tartufe*).

Tas., Tasmania.

taseometer, instrument for measuring strains.

tasimeter, instrument for measuring changes in pressure.

Tasmania, abbr. **Tas.**

Tass, the Soviet news agency.

ta-ta! good-bye! (hyphen).

Tatar, *see* **Tartar**.

Tate/ (Nahum), 1652–1715, Irish poet and dramatist; — **(Sir William Henry)**, 1842–1921, English industrialist; — **Gallery**, London. *See also* **Tait**.

tatterdemalion, a ragged fellow, *not* -ian.

Tattersalls, London (apostrophe only in the possessive case).

tattoo/, design on the skin, *not* tattoo, tatow, tatu; **-ed, -er, -ing, -s**.

tattoo/, drum-beat, call to quarters, mil. parade by night; *pl.* **-s**.

Tauchnitz (Karl Christoph), 1761–1836, founded at Leipzig, 1796, publishing firm famous for editions of Latin and Greek authors; — **(Christian Bernard, Baron von)**, 1816–95, founded at Leipzig the

Librairie Bernhard Tauchnitz, famous for reprints of British and American authors, banned in Britain and U.S. because of copyright infringements.

tau cross, the **T**.

taut (naut.), tight, in good condition, *not* -ght.

tautologize, to use too many expressions with the same meaning, *not* -ise.

taverns (names of), *see* **inns (names of)**.

tawny, tan-colour, *not* -ey.

tax-collector, tax-free (hyphen).

taxiing.

taxman, *see* **tacks-**.

taxpayer (one word).

Taylor Institution, Oxford, *not* Taylorian, *not* Institute.

Taylour, family name of Marquess of Headfort.

tazz/a (It. f.), bowl or cup, *pron.* tăt′să; *pl.* **-e**.

T.B., torpedo-boat, tuberculosis (tubercle bacillus).

Tb, terbium (no point).

T.B.D., torpedo-boat destroyer.

T.C., Town Councillor.

Tc, technetium (no point).

T.C.D., Trinity College, Dublin.

Tchad (Lake), *use* **Chad**.

Tchaikovsky (Peter Ilich), 1840–93, Russian composer.

Tchekoff (Anton), *use* **Chekhov**.

Tchertkoff, *use* **Chertkov**.

Te, tellurium (no point).

Teall (Sir Jethro Justinian Harris), 1849–1924, English geologist.

teapot (one word).

tease, *not* -ze.

teasel (bot.), *not* -sle, -zel, -zle.

teaspoonful/, *pl.* **-s** (one word).

tech., technical, -ly.

technetium, symbol **Tc** (no point).

technol., technological, -ly.

techy, peevish, *use* **tetchy.**

tedesc/o (It. adj.), *fem. -a,* German (not cap.).

teed (golf).

teenager (one word).

Teesside, new county, proposed 1971. (New name **Cleveland,** proposed 1972.)

teetotal/, abstaining from intoxicants; **-ism, -ler, -ly.**

teetotum/, a four-sided top spun by the fingers; *pl.* **-s.**

Tegnér (Esaias), 1782–1846, Swedish poet.

Tehran, cap. of Persia, *not* -heran.

Teignmouth, Devon, *pron.* tĭn′muth. *See also* **Tyne-.**

Teil (Ger. m.), a part; *pl. -e, not now Th-* (cap.).

telecommunications (one word).

televis/e, -ion (one word).

Telford, Salop, 'new town', 1963.

Telford (Thomas), 1757–1834, Scottish engineer.

tell-tale (hyphen).

tellurian, of the earth.

tellurion, orrery, *not* -ian.

tellurium, symbol **Te** (no point).

Telugu, Indian language, *not* -egu, -oogoo.

Téméraire (The Fighting), picture by Turner.

temp., temporary.

temp., tempore (in the time of).

temperature, symbol *T* (no point). In scientific work the unit of temperature is the kelvin (K), although °C is still used; —, **degrees of** (typ.), to be in arabic figures, as 10 °C, 50 °F.

Templar, member of a religious order, the **Knights Templars;** student or lawyer living in the Temple, London.

tem/plate, *use* **-plet.**

Temple Bar, London.

templet, a mould or pattern, *not* -plate.

temp/o (It. mus.), time; *pl. -i,* abbr. **t.**

tempora mutantur (Lat.), times are changing.

temporary, abbr. **temp.;** adv. **temporarily.**

tempore (Lat.), in the time of; abbr. **t.,** *or* **temp.**

temporize, to avoid immediate decisions, *not* -ise.

Tenasserim, Burma, *not* **Tenn-.**

Ten Commandments (the) (caps.).

Tenerife (peak and island of), Canary Is., *not* -iffe.

Teniers (David), 1582–1649, and 1610–90, Dutch painters, father and son.

Tenison (Thomas), 1636–1715, Abp. of Canterbury. *See also* **Tennyson.**

Tennasserim, *use* **Tena-.**

Tennessee, U.S., off. abbr. **Tenn.**

Tenniel (Sir John T.), 1820–1914, English cartoonist and caricaturist.

tennis, it is no longer necessary to use 'lawn tennis', *but see* **I.L.T.F.** *See also* **real tennis.**

Tennyson (Alfred Lord), 1809–92, Poet Laureate 1850–92. *See also* **Tenison.**

tenor, settled course, *not* -our.

tenor/e (It. mus. m.), tenor voice; *pl. -i,* abbr. **t.**

tenuto (mus.), held on, sustained.

Ter., Terence, Terrace.

ter (Lat.), thrice.

tera-, prefix, 10^{12}; abbr. **T** (no point).

terat., teratology, study of malformations.

terbium, symbol **Tb** (no point).

tercel, *use* **tier-.**

Terence (Publius Terentius Afer), 190–159 B.C., Roman comic playwright; abbr. **Ter.**

Teresa (St.), *not* Th-.

tergiversat/e, to change one's principles; **-ion, -or.**

termagant, a brawling woman.

termination, abbr. **term.**

terminator, *not* -er.

terminology, study of the proper use of terms; abbr. **term.**

termin/us, end; *pl.* **-i.**

terminus/ ad quem (Lat.), the finish; — *a quo*, the starting-point.

Terpsichore (Gr.), muse of dancing; *pron.* terp-sĭ′-kor-ĭ.

Terr., Territory.

terrace, cap. when with name; abbr. **Ter.**; in Fr. f. **terrasse.**

terracotta, (an object of art made of) kiln-burnt clay and sand (one word).

Terra del Fuego, *use* **Tierra — —.**

terrae/ filius (Lat.), son of the soil; *pl.* — *filii.*

terra firma, dry land (two words, not ital.).

terr/a incognit/a (Lat.), unexplored region; *pl.* -ae -ae (ital.).

terret, ring for driving-rein, *not* -it.

Territory (cap. in geog. names), abbr. **T.** *or* **Terr.**

terrorize, *not* -ise.

tertio (Lat.), in the third place; abbr. **3°.**

tertium quid (Lat.), a third something, an intermediate course.

terz/a rim/a (It.), a rhyming scheme; *pl.* -e -e.

tesla, unit of magnetic polarization, from **Tesla (Nikola)**, 1856–1943, Yugoslav-American physicist.

tessellate(d), pave(d) with tiles, *not* -elate(d).

tesser/a, small square tile; *pl.* **-ae** (not ital.).

tessitura (mus.), the ordinary compass of the voice.

Testament, abbr. **T.**, *or* **Test.**

testamur (Lat.), examination certificate.

test/is (anat.), *pl.* **-es.**

test/-match, — -paper, — -tube, — -types (for vision testing) (hyphens).

tetchy, peevish, *not* tec-.

tête (Fr. f.), head; *tête-à-tête* (m., s. and pl., not ital. in Eng. usage), private interview; *but tête à tête* (without hyphens), privately; *tête/ de veau*, calf's head; — *dorée* (bind.), gilt top.

tet. tox., tetanus toxin.

Teufelsdröckh (Herr), in Carlyle's *Sartor Resartus.*

Teut., Teuton, -ic.

Tex., Texas, U.S. (off. abbr.), Texan.

textbook (one word).

textus receptus (Lat.), the received text; abbr. *text. rec.*

t.g., type genus.

T.G.W.U., Transport and General Workers' Union.

Th., Thomas, Thursday.

Th, thorium (no point).

Thailand, *formerly* Siam.

Thal (Ger.), valley, *use* **Tal.**

Thaler (Ger.), *use now* **Ta-.**

Thalia (Gr.), muse of comedy; *pron.* thălī′a.

thalidomide, a sedative drug, withdrawn 1961 because it caused malformations in foetus during pregnancy.

thallium, symbol **Tl** (no point).

Thanjavur, India, *not* Tanjor, -e.

Thanksgiving Day (U.S.), last Thursday in November.

Tharrawaddy, Burma, *not*
Tharawadi.

that, refers to a person or
thing first mentioned, or
further in order or place
than when *this, these* are
used; *pl.* **those.**

thé (Fr. m.), tea.

Theaetetus, dialogue by
Plato, named after disciple of
Socrates.

theat., theatrical.

theatre, U.S. theater, Fr.
théâtre (m.); *Théâtre
français,* Paris (one cap.).

thec/a (anat., bot.), case,
sheath, sac, *pl.* **-ae.**

theirs (no apos.).

Thellusson Act, 1800,
prohibiting bequests designed
to accumulate.

them/a (Gr.), a theme; *pl.*
-ata.

Theo., Theodore.

theocracy, a priest- or god-
governed state, *not* **-sy.**

theocrasy, mingling of
several divine attributes in
one god, *not* **-cy.**

Theocritus, Greek poet, third
century B.C.; abbr. **Theoc.**

theol., theolog/y, -ian, -ical.

theologize, *not* **-ise.**

Theophrastus, *c.* 380–290
B.C., Greek philosopher;
abbr. **Theoph.**

theor., theorem.

theoret., theoretic, -al, -ally.

theorize, *not* **-ise.**

theosoph/y, a philosophy
professing knowledge of God
by inspiration; **-ical, -ist,
-ize.**

therapeutic/, healing; **-s,**
study of healing agents;
abbr. **therap.**

Theresa (St.), *use* **Ter-.**

Thérèse (Fr.).

thermodynamics, the
mathematical treatment of
the relationship between
heat and other forms of
energy (one word).

thermomet/er, -ric, abbr.
thermom.

thermonuclear (one word).

Thermopylae (Pass of),
Greece; battle, 480 B.C.

these, *see* **this.**

thes/is, *pl.* **-es.**

Thess., 1, 2 Thessalonians
(N.T.), Thessaly.

Thibet, *use* **Ti-.**

thibet (woollen fabric), *use*
ti-.

thimblerig/, a trick; **-ger,
-ging** (one word).

thin/, -ner, -nish.

Thirty-nine Articles (the)
(hyphen, two caps.).

thirty-twomo (typ.), a book
based on 32 leaves, 64
pages, to the basic sheet;
abbr. **32mo** (no point).

Thirty Years War, 1618–48
(caps., no apos.).

this, refers to a person or
thing which was last men-
tioned, or which is nearer in
order or place; *pl.* **these.**
See also **that.**

thole-pin (naut.), one of two
which keep an oar in position, *not* **-owl, -owel**
(hyphen).

Thomas, abbr. **T., Th.,** *or*
Thos.

Thom/ism, doctrine of St.
Thomas Aquinas; **-ist.**

**Thompson (Sir Benjamin,
Count von Rumford),**
1753–1814, American-born
founder of Royal Institu-
tion, London; — **(Sir
D'Arcy Wentworth),** 1860–
1948, Scottish biologist; —
(Sir Edward Maunde),
1840–1929, English librarian
and palaeographer; —
(Francis), 1859–1907,
English poet; — **(Sir
Henry),** 1820–1904, English
surgeon, advocate of
cremation; — **(Silvanus,**
not Sy-, **Phillips),** 1851–
1916, English physicist.

Thomsen's disease, muscular spasm.

Thomson (Prof. Arthur), 1858–1935, Scottish anatomist; — **(Sir Charles Wyville),** 1830–82, Scottish zoologist; — **(James),** 1700–84, Scottish poet, 'The Seasons'; — **(James),** 1834–82, Scottish poet, 'B.V.', 'City of Dreadful Night'; — **(Prof. Sir John Arthur),** 1861–1933, Scottish zoologist and writer; — **(Joseph),** 1858–95, Scottish African traveller; — **(Prof. Sir Joseph John),** 1856–1940, English physicist; — **(Sir William, Lord Kelvin),** 1824–1907, British mathematician and physicist (hence **kelvin,** q.v.).

Thomson's electrometer, galvanometer, etc.

thor/ax (anat., zool.), the part of the body between neck and abdomen or tail; *pl.* **-aces.**

Thoreau (Henry David), 1817–62, U.S. author and philosopher.

thorium, symbol **Th** (no point).

thorn, (Þ þ), *pron.* th as in 'think', used in Anglo-Saxon and Icelandic works.

thorough, *not* thoro'.

thorough-bass (mus.), bass indicated by system of numerals (hyphen).

thorough/bred, -going (one word).

Thos., Thomas.

those, *see* **that.**

though, abbr. **tho'.**

thowel, *use* **thole.**

thrall, slave, bondage; **thraldom,** bondage.

thrash, to beat soundly; — **out,** to discuss exhaustively. *See* **thresh.**

Threadneedle Street, London (two words).

three-quarter(s) (hyphen).

three R's (the), reading, writing, arithmetic (no point).

threescore, sixty (one word).

threescore and ten, seventy (three words).

thresh, to beat out corn (specialized use of **thrash,** q.v.).

thresher/-shark, — **-whale** (hyphens).

threshing/-floor, — **-machine** (hyphens).

threshold, *not* -hhold.

thro', *use* **through.**

Throckmorton (Sir Nicholas W.G.), 1515–71, English diplomat.

throes, violent pangs.

Throgmorton Avenue, *also* **Street,** London, E.C.

Throndhjem, *use* **Trondheim.**

through, *not* thro'; **Monday through Friday** (U.S.), from Monday to Friday inclusive.

throw out (bind.), to mount a diagram, map, etc., upon a guard so that it may remain in view while other pages are read.

Thucydides, *c.* 470–400 B.C., Greek historian; abbr. **Thuc.**

thug/ (Ind.), member of religious fraternity of murderers, a ruffian; **-gee** (*not* thagi), **-gery, -gism.**

thuja, accepted English form of bot. *Thuya,* the arbor-vitae genus.

thulium, symbol **Tm** (no point).

thunder (naut.), abbr. **t.**

Thür (Ger.), *use* **Tür.**

Thursday, abbr. **Th.**

thuya, *see* **thuja.**

T.H.W.M., Trinity High-Water Mark.

thyme, herb.

Thynne, family name of Marquis of Bath.

Ti, titanium (no point).

Tiberias, anc. Palestine, *now* **Tubariya,** Israel.

Tiberius (in full, **Tib. Claudius Nero Caesar**), 42 B.C.–A.D. 37, second emperor of Rome, 14–37.

Tibet, Cent. Asia, *not* Th-.

tibet, a woollen fabric, *not* th-.

tic douloureux, facial neuralgia, *not* dol- (two words).

ticket/, -ed, -ing.

Ticonderoga, New York.

t.i.d. (med.), *ter in die* (three times a day).

tidbit, *use* tit-.

tie, tying, *not* tieing.

Tientsin, port of Peking (one word).

tiercel, a male falcon, *not* ter-.

Tierra del Fuego, S. America, *not* Terra — —.

tiers état (Fr. m.), third estate, the common people (not caps.).

Tietjens (Therese Cathline Johanna), 1831–77, German-born Hungarian soprano, *not* Titiens.

tiffany, a gauze muslin.

Tiffany (Charles Lewis), 1812–92, American jeweller.

tiffin (Anglo-Ind.), light lunch, *not* -ing.

tigerish, *not* tigr-.

Tighnabruaich, Argyl.

tight back (bind.), the cover fastened solidly to the back, so that it does not become hollow when open.

tigrish, *use* tiger-.

T.I.H., Their Imperial Highnesses.

tike, *use* ty-.

tilde, the mark as over the Sp. *n*, *ñ*; in Port. til.

Tilsit (Treaty of), 1807, *not* -tt.

Tim., 1 and 2 Timothy (N.T.).

timbre, characteristic quality of sounds of a voice or instrument (not ital.).

timbre-poste (Fr. m.), postage-stamp; *pl.* ***timbres- —***, abbr. **t.p.**

Timbuktu, W. Africa, *not* -buctoo; *but* **'Timbuctoo'**, Tennyson's prize-poem, 1829.

time of day (typ.), to be in figures with full point where time includes minutes as well as hours: 9.30 a.m. (or 09.30 hrs.); 10 a.m. (or 10.00 hrs.); 4.30 p.m. (or 16.30 hrs.). Such phrases as half-past two, a quarter to four, are better spelt out. *See also* **date.**

time-lag (hyphen).

Times (The), established 1788 (caps.). *The* (cap. *T*, ital.) should always be part of title.

timpan/o (mus.), the orchestral kettle-drum, *not* ty-; *pl.* **-i** (*see also* **tympanum**).

tin (*stannum*), symbol **Sn** (no point).

tinct., tincture.

Tindal (Matthew), 1656–1733, English theologian, *not* -all (*see also* **Tyn-**).

tin-foil (hyphen).

tingeing, *not* -ging.

tin-plate (hyphen).

tinsel/, -led, -ling (U.S. **-ed, -ing**).

Tintagel, Cornwall, *not* -il.

-tion (typ.), if necessary at end of lines, carry over this and not -ation, -ition, etc.

tip in (bind.), method of inserting plates, etc.

tipo (It., Sp.), type.

Tipperary, Ireland.

tippet, a cape, *not* tipet.

tipstaff/, a bailiff; *pl.* **-s.**

tip/toe, -toeing, -top (one word).

TIR, Transports Internationales Routiers.

tirade, a long declamation.

tirailleur (Fr. m.), a sharp-shooter (not ital.).

tire (of a wheel) is correct, but now usu. **tyre.**

tirer (Fr. typ.), to print.

tiret (Fr. typ. m.), dash, *or* rule.

tiro, *pl.* **-s,** *not* tyro.

Tirol, *see* **Tyrol.**

'tis, for 'it is' (apos., close up).

Tit., Titus.

tit., title.

titanic (not cap., except ref. to Titans).

Titanic, **the,** liner sunk by iceberg, 1912.

titanium, symbol **Ti** (no point).

titbit, *not* tid- (one word).

Titel/ (Ger. typ. m.), the title; *-blatt* (n.), title-page; *-zeile* (f.), headline (caps.).

Titian (**Tiziano Vecellio**), 1477–1576, Venetian painter.

Titiens, *use* **Tietjens.**

titillate, to excite pleasurably.

titivate, to smarten up, *not* titt-.

title-deed (hyphen).

title-page (typ.), should contain: name of book, author, publisher, place of publication, date of publication, copyright symbol ©. *See also* **preliminary matter.**

title-pages. The Publishers' Association and the Book-sellers' Association of Great Britain and Ireland jointly recommend and urge the adoption of the following as the invariable practice of the book trade.

'(1) DATE. (*a*) That the title-page of every book should bear the date of the year of publication, i.e. of the year in which the im-pression, or the reissue, of which it forms a part, was first put on the market.

(*b*) That when stock is reissued in a new form, the title-page should bear the date of the new issue, and each copy should be described as "a reissue", either on the title-page or in a bibliographical note. (*c*) That the date at which a book was last revised should be indicated either on the title-page or in a bibliographical note.

'(2) BIBLIOGRAPHICAL NOTE. That the bibliographical note should, when possible, be printed on the back of the title-page, in order that it may not be separated there-from in binding.

'(3) IMPRESSION, EDITION, REISSUE. That for biblio-graphical purposes definite meanings should be attached to these words when used on a title-page, and the follow-ing are recommended:

'*Impression.*—A number of copies printed at any one time. When a book is reprinted without change it should be called a new *impression,* to distinguish it from an *edition* as defined below.

'*Edition.*—An impression in which the matter has under-gone some change, or for which the type has been reset. (The term "Revised Edition" should be used where there has been some material change in the text.)

'*Reissue.*—A republication at a different price, or in a different form, of part of an impression which has already been placed on the market.

'(4) LOCALIZATION. When the circulation of an impression of a book is limited by agreement to a particular area, that each

title-pages (*cont.*):
copy of that impression should bear a conspicuous notice to that effect.

'ADENDDUM. In cases where a book has been reprinted many times, and revised a smaller number of times, it is suggested that the intimation to that effect should be as follows, e.g.:

'FIFTEENTH IMPRESSION (THIRD EDITION).

This would indicate that the book had been printed fifteen times, and that in the course of those fifteen impressions it had been revised or altered twice.'

title-role (hyphen).

titles (cited), of articles in periodicals, chapters in books, shorter poems, and songs, to be roman quoted, not italic; of books, periodicals, newspapers, plays, long (book-length) poems, paintings, and sculptures, to be italic.

title-sheet (typ.), that containing the preliminary matter.

titles of honour, as LL.D., F.R.S., are usually in caps. Frequently s.caps. give a better general effect. *See also* **compound ranks.**

titre (Fr. typ. m.), title.

tit-tat-to, a game (hyphens).

tittivate, *use* **titi-.**

Titus/, Epistle to (N.T.), abbr. **Tit.;** — (Roman praenomen), abbr. **T.**

Tl, thallium (no point).

T.L.S., *Times Literary Supplement.*

T.L.W.M., Trinity Low-Water Mark.

Tm, thulium (no point).

T.N.T., trinitrotoluene.

T.O., Telegraph Office.

Tobago, W. Indies, *not* Ta-. *See* **Trinidad.**

Tobermore, Londonderry, N. Ireland.

Tobermory, Isle of Mull, Argyl.

Tobit (Apocr.), not to be abbreviated.

toboggan/, *not* -ogan; **-ing.**

Toc H, Talbot House (no point).

Tocqueville (Alexis C. H. M. C. de), 1805–59, French statesman and polit. writer.

tocsin, alarm-bell.

today (no hyphen).

to-do, commotion (hyphen).

toffee, *not* -y.

toga/, the Roman mantle; *pl.* **-s.**

Togo, Cent. W. Africa, independent 1960.

toile (Fr. f.), linen-cloth.

toilet, *not* -ette.

toilette (Fr. f.), toilet.

Toison d'or (Fr. f.), the golden fleece.

Tokai, a white wine from NE. Italy.

Tokay, a Hungarian wine; in Hung. **Tokaj.**

Tokyo, cap. of Japan, *not* -io; *formerly* Yeddo.

Toler, family name of Earl of Norbury.

Tolstoy (Count Leo), 1828–1910, Russian novelist, *not* -oi.

tomalley, so-called liver of lobster, *not* -ly.

tomato/, *pl.* **-es.**

tome (Fr. m.), a volume; abbr. **t.**

tomorrow (no hyphen).

tomtit, a small bird (one word).

tomtom, Indian drum (one word).

ton/ (weight), **-s,** abbr. **t.**

ton (Fr. m.), style.

Tonbridge, *but* **Tunbridge Wells,** Kent.

Tongking, North Vietnam, *not* Tun-, Tonkin, Tonquin.

Tonic Sol-fa (one hyphen).

tonight (no hyphen).

tonn., tonnage.

tonne, metric ton (1000 kilogrammes).

tonneau, the rear part of a motor-car body.

tonneau (Fr. m.), ton, tun, or cask; abbr. **t.**

tonsillitis, inflammation of the tonsils, *not* -ilitis.

tooling (bind.), impressing the design on the binding by hand.

toothpick (one word).

topgallant/ mast, — sail (one word); *naut. pron.* t'gallant.

topinambour (Fr. m.), Jerusalem artichoke.

topmast (one word).

topog., topograph/y, -ical.

topsail (one word); *naut. pron.* tops'l.

tops and tails (typ.), prelims. and index.

topside (paper), the side of paper opposite to the wireside; (naut.), ship's side between waterline and deck.

topsy-turvy (hyphen).

Tor (Ger. m.), fool; (n.) gate, *not now* Th- (cap.).

torc, *use* torque.

tormentor, *not* -er.

tornado/, *pl.* -es.

torniquet, *use* tour-.

torpedo/, *pl.* -es.

Torphichen (Baron), *pron.* tor′fi-ken.

torque, a gold ornament, (mech.) turning movement, *not* torc.

Torquemada (Tomás de), 1420–98, Spanish Inquisitor.

Torres Vedras, fortified town near Lisbon, Portugal; battle, 1810.

torso/(sculp.), the trunk; *pl.* -s.

tortue/ (Fr. f.), turtle; — *claire*, clear turtle soup.

Toscanini (Arturo), 1867–1957, Italian conductor.

totalisator, betting device, abbr. **tote** (no point); *also* **Totalisator Horserace Board**; *not* -izator. *But see* **totalize.**

totalize, to collect into a total, *not* -ise.

totidem verbis (Lat.), in so many words.

toties quoties (Lat.), the one as often as the other.

toto caelo (Lat.), diametrically opposed, *not* — coe-.

totum (Lat.), the whole.

toujours/ *perdrix* (Anglo-Fr.), always partridge, too much of one good thing; — *prêt*, always ready.

toupee, a wig, *not* -ée, -et.

tour/ (Fr. m.), a tour; (f.) tower; *tour à tour*, alternately, in turn; — *d'adresse* (m.), legerdemain; — *de force*, a feat of strength or skill; — *de main*, sleight of hand.

tourmaline, a mineral, sometimes cut as a gem, *not* -in.

Tournai, Belgium.

Tournay, France.

tourney, a tournament.

tourniquet, bandage, etc., for stopping flow of blood, *not* torn-.

tournure (Fr. f.), contour, figure, (dress) bustle.

tourte (Fr. f.), tart.

Toussaint L'Ouverture (François), 1743–1803, Haitian Negro general and liberator; in Fr. **Louverture** (no apos.).

tout/ *à coup* (Fr.), suddenly; — *à fait*, entirely; — *court*, abruptly; — *de même*, all the same; — *de suite*, immediately; — *d'un coup*, all at once; — *ensemble*, the general effect; — *le monde*, all the world (no hyphens).

tovarich/, comrade, *pl.* **-i;** anglicized from Russ. *tovarishch.*

towel/, -ling (U.S. **-ing**).

town, abbr. **t.**

town/ councillor, *not* -ilor; abbr. **T.C.;** — **hall** (two words).

Townshend (Marquess.

township, abbr. **t.**

toxicol., toxicolog/y, -ical.

toxin, a poison, *not* -ine.

toxophilite, (student, lover) of archery.

Tr., trustee.

traceable, *not* -cable.

trache/a, the windpipe; *pl.* **-ae.**

Tractarian/; -ism, the Oxford or High-Church Movement of mid-nineteenth century (cap.).

tractor, *not* -er.

trad., traditional.

trad (no point), used of a style, esp. of jazz of the 1920s.

trade-mark (hyphen).

trade/ union (two words), *pl.* — **unions;** in Brit., but not in U.S., often **trades/ union,** *pl.* — **unions;** abbr. **T.U.;** always **Trades Union Congress,** abbr. **T.U.C.**

trade wind (two words).

traduction (Fr. f.), translation.

Trafalgar, *pron.* -gar' for Sp. pron. of the Cape.

traffic/, -ked, -ker.

trafic (Fr. m.), trade.

trag., tragedy, tragic.

tragedi/an, a tragic actor; *fem.* **-enne.**

Trail (James William Helenus), 1851–1919, Scottish botanist.

Traill (Henry Duff), 1842–1900, English journalist and biographer.

traipse, to trudge, *now usual for* **trapes.**

trait, a characteristic.

trait d'union (Fr. typ. m.), the hyphen.

trammel/, to entangle; **-led, -ling** (U.S. **-ed, -ing**).

trampoline, acrobats' spring-mattress, *not* -in.

tranquil/, -lity, -lize, -ly.

trans., transactions, transitive, translat/ed, -ion, -or.

transact/, -or.

transalpine (one word, not cap.).

transatlantic (one word, not cap.).

Transcaucasia, *formerly* Transcaucasian Soviet Federated Socialist Republic, one of the republics forming the Union of Soviet Socialist Republics (*see* **U.S.S.R.**), but now divided into three constituent republics of the Union: Armenian S.S.R., Azerbaijan S.S.R., and Georgian S.S.R.

transf., transferred.

transfer/, -able, -ence, -red, -rer, -ring.

transgress/, to pass beyond the limit of; **-ible, -or.**

tranship/, -ment (one word), *not* transs-.

transitive (gram.), taking a direct object; abbr. **transit.**

translat/ed, -ion, -or, abbr. **trans.; -able.**

transmissible, *not* -able.

transpose (typ.), to move letters, words, lines, etc., from one place to another; **trs./** being written in the margin, and a line put round the matter pointing to where it is to be transferred. *See also* **proof correction marks.**

Transvaal, prov. of S. Africa; abbr. **Tvl.**

trapes, to trudge, *now usu.* **traipse.**

tratto d'unione (It. typ.), the hyphen.

trattoria (It. f.), Italian-style restaurant.

travel/, -led, -ler, -ling (U.S. **-ed, -er, -ing**).

Travellers' Club, London (apos. after *s*).

T.R.C., Thames Rowing Club, tithe rent charge (abolished 1936).

Treas., treasurer, treasury.

treatise, a systematic written study.

trecent/o, (It. art of) the period 1300–99; **-ist** (not ital.).

tre corde (mus.), three strings; in pianoforte music indicates that soft pedal must be released.

Treitschke (Heinrich G. von), 1834–96, German historian.

trek/ (Afrik.), journey (verb and subst.); *not* -ck; **-ked, -ker, -king.**

Trelawny, *not* -ey.

tremor, *not* -our.

Trengganu, *see* **Malaya, Federation of.**

trente-et-quarante (Fr. m.), a gambling game.

Tresco, Scilly.

Trescowe, Cornwall.

trestle, a table support, *not* tressel.

Trèves, *use* **Trier.**

trevet, *use* **tri-.**

T.R.H., Their Royal Highnesses.

tribrach, foot of three syllables ($\cup \cup \cup$).

trichologist, a practitioner of hair treatment.

tricolour, the French flag, *not* -or, except U.S.; in Fr. m. *drapeau tricolore*.

Trier, Germany, *not* Trèves.

trigesimo-secundo, *use* **thirty-twomo,** q.v.

trigon., trigonometr/y, -ical.

trill (mus.), *not* th-.

trillion, (U.K.) 10^{18}; (U.S. and France) 10^{12}.

trimmed edges, *see* **edges.**

Trin., Trinity.

Trinidad and Tobago, W. Indies, independent 1962.

Trinity Sunday, the one after Whit-Sunday.

triphthong, three vowels in a single syllable as *eau* in *beau.*

Triple Alliance (the), England, Sweden, Netherlands against France, 1668; Britain, France, Holland against Spain, 1717; Germany, Austria, Italy, 1883–1915, counterbalanced by the **Triple Entente,** Britain, France, Russia.

tripos/, Cambridge examination; *pl.* **-es.**

triptych, set of three painted or carved panels, hinged together.

triptyque, an international pass for a motor car.

Tristan da Cunha, S. Atlantic, *not* — d'Acunha.

Tristan und Isolde, opera by Wagner, 1865.

Tristram, knight of the Round Table (usual Eng. form of Tristan).

triturat/e, to grind finely; **-or.**

triumvir/, one of a committee of three; Eng. *pl.* **-s;** Lat. *pl.* (ital.) **-i;** collective noun **-ate.**

trivet, iron bracket hooked to a grate, *not* tre-.

trocar (med.), instrument for withdrawing fluid from the body, *not* troch-.

troche (med.), a medicated lozenge.

troch/ee, a foot of two syllables, long short; adj. **-aic.**

troika, Russian vehicle drawn by three horses abreast; (fig.) a committee of three.

troll/ey, the usual spelling; **-y** in elec. (I.E.E.).

trollop, a slatternly woman.

Trollope (Anthony), 1815–82, English novelist.

trompe-l'œil (Fr.), an illusion, esp. in still-life painting or plaster ornament.

trompette (Fr. m.), trumpeter; (f.) trumpet.

Trondheim, Norway, *formerly* **Trondhyem**, *not* Th-.

troop/, of soldiers; **-er**.

tropaeolum/, a trailing plant; *pl.* **-s**. As bot. genus, *Tropaeolum*.

tropical (not cap.).

troposphere, the lower atmosphere, where temperature falls with rise in height. *See also* **stratosphere**.

troppo (mus.), too much.

Trotsky (Leon), pseud. of Lev Davidovich Bronstein, 1879–1940, Russian revolutionary, *not* -tz-, -ki.

trottoir (Fr. m.), footway, pavement.

troup/e, of performers; **-er**.

trousseau/, bride's outfit; *pl.* **-x** (not ital.).

trouvaille (Fr. f.), a lucky find.

troy weight (not cap.): 1 troy pound (approx. 373 g) = 12 troy ounces; 1 troy ounce = 20 pennyweights.

Trs., Trustees.

Trucial States, Arabia, seven independent sheikhdoms.

truite/ (Fr. f.), trout; — *au bleu*, brook trout; — *de lac*, lake trout; — *saumonée*, salmon trout.

Truman (Harry S), 1884–1972, U.S. politician, President 1945-52 (no point after the S).

trumpet/, **-ed**, **-ing**.

Truron., signature of Bp. of Truro (full point).

trustee, abbr. **Tr.**, *pl.* **Trs.**

T.S. (paper), tub-sized.

Tsad (Lake), *use* — **Chad.**

Tsar of Russia; **Tsarevich**, his son; **Tsarevna**, his dau.; **Tsarina**, his wife (in Russ. **Tsaritsa**); *not* Cz-, Tz-.

Tsarevich, heir to Russian throne, *not* Cesarevitch.

Tsarskoe Selo, *pron.* tsar'-skŏ-yĕ syĕlah', near St. Petersburg (now Leningrad), imperial residence; renamed Detskoe Selo and, later, Pushkin; *not* Tz-.

Tschaikowsky (P. I.), *use* **Tchaikovsky.**

Tschigorin, *use* Ch-.

Tschudi (Aegidius), 1505-72, Swiss historian; — **(Johann Jakob von)**, 1818-89, Swiss naturalist.

tsetse fly, African fly, *not* tzetze; *pron.* tset'-sĭ.

T.S.H., Their Serene Highnesses.

t.s.v.p., *tournez s'il vous plaît* (Fr.), please turn over, P.T.O.

T.T., Tourist Trophy, tuberculin tested.

t.t.l. *or* **T.T.L.**, to take leave.

T.T.S. (typ.), teletypesetting, line-casting machines controlled by perforated tape.

T.U., trade union, -s.

tub/a, bass saxhorn; *pl.* **-as**.

Tübingen, German town and university.

T.U.C., Trades Union Congress.

Tuesday, abbr. **Tue.**

Tuileries, Paris (one *l.*).

tulle, fine silk fabric.

tumbrel, a cart, *not* -il.

tum/our, a morbid growth; U.S. **-or.**

tumul/us, burial mound; *pl.* **-i** (not ital.).

tun/ (cask), **-s**, abbr. **t.**

Tunbridge Wells, *but* **Tonbridge**, Kent.

tungsten, wolfram, symbol W (no point).

Tunisia, N. Africa, independent 1956.

tunnel/, -led, -ling (U.S. **-ed, -ing**).

tu quoque! (Lat.), thou also!

Tür (Ger. f.), door, *not now* Th- (cap.).

Turco/ (hist.), French Algerian soldier; *pl.* **-s;** *not* -ko.

Turcophil, one friendly to the Turks.

Turgenev (Ivan Sergeivich), 1818–83, Russian novelist, *not* the many variants; *pron.* toor-gān′-yef.

Turk., Turk/ey, -ish.

turkey red (not cap.).

Turkistan, a region of cent. Asia, *not* Turke-.

Turkmenistan, a Soviet Socialist Republic. *See* **U.S.S.R.**

Turkoman/, an inhabitant of Turkmenistan, *not* Turco-; *pl.* **-s.**

turned commas (typ.), *see* **quotation marks, punctuation IX.**

Turner (Joseph Mallord William, *not* Mall/ad, -ard), 1775–1851, English painter.

turning-point (hyphen).

Turnour, family name of Earl Winterton.

turn over, abbr. **T.O.**

Tuskar Rock, lighthouse, Co. Wexford.

Tuskegee Institute, Ala., U.S.

tussock-grass, *not* -ac.

Tutankhamun, Egyptian pharaoh, reigned *c.* 1358–1350 B.C.; *not* -amen.

tutti (mus.), all.

tuum (Lat.), thine. *See also* *meum.*

TV, television (no points).

T.V.A. (U.S.), Tennessee Valley Authority.

Tvl., Transvaal.

Twain (Mark), *see* **Clemens.**

Tweeddale (Marquis of).

tweeny(-maid), a servant subsidiary to two others, esp. cook and housemaid, *not* 't.

Twelfth Day, 6 Jan.

twelvemo *or* **duodecimo** (typ.), a book based on 12 leaves, 24 pages, to the basic sheet; abbr. **12mo** (no point).

twenty-fourmo (typ.), a book based on 24 leaves, 48 pages, to the basic sheet; abbr. **24mo** (no point).

twentymo (typ.), a book based on 20 leaves, 40 pages, to the basic sheet; abbr. **20mo** (no point).

Twisleton-Wykeham-Fiennes, family name of Lord Saye and Sele.

twofold (one word).

two/-foot, -inch, -mile, -pound, -ton (adjs., hyphens).

T.Y.C., Thames Yacht Club.

tyke, a dog, *not* ti-.

Tyler (John), 1790–1862, American President 1841–5; — **(Wat),** d. 1381, English rebel.

Tylor (Sir Edward Burnett), 1832–1917, English anthropologist.

tympan/um, the ear-drum; *pl.* **-a.** *See also* **timpano.**

Tyndale (William), 1484–1536, English priest, translated Bible, burned at stake.

Tyndall (John), 1820–93, English physicist.

Tynemouth, Northumb.; *pron.* tĭn′muth. *See also* **Teign-.**

Tyneside-Wearside, new metropolitan area, proposed 1971, including Newcastle upon Tyne, Tynemouth, Gateshead, South Shields, Sunderland.

typ., typograph/er, -ic, -ical, -ically.

type, a piece of metal having on one end a letter or character in relief, used in letterpress printing. *See* **height to paper.**

type metal, an alloy of lead, antimony, and tin.

typewriter, the machine.

typist, the user of a typewriter.

typography, the design of printed matter.

Typophiles, The (U.S.), a group devoted to the graphic arts.

tyrannize, *not* -ise.

tyre (of a wheel), now the usual spelling, esp. when of rubber, but **tire** was formerly correct.

tyro, *use* **tiro.**

Tyrol, region of Austria and Italy, in Ger. **Tirol,** in It. **Tirolo.**

Tyrwhitt, *pron.* tir′rit.

Tzar/, -evich, -evna, -ina, *see* **Tsar,** etc.

Tzarskoye Selo, *use* **Tsarskoe** —.

tzetze fly, *use* **tsetse** —.

U

U, upper-class, uranium (no point), the twentieth in a series.

U., Unionist, (film) universal, all proper names with this initial, (Ger.) *Uhr* (clock, o'clock).

u., (Ger.) *und* (and), *unter* (among), (naut.) ugly, threatening weather.

U.A.R., United Arab Republic.

ubique (Lat.), everywhere.

ubi supra (Lat.), in the place above (mentioned); abbr. *u.s.*

U.C., University College.

u.c. (typ.), upper case, (It. mus.) *una corda* (on one string).

U.C.C.A., Universities' Central Council on Admissions.

U.C.D., University College, Dublin.

U.C.L., University College, London.

U.C.L.A., University of California at Los Angeles.

U.C.S., University College School.

U.C.W., University College of Wales.

Udaipur, India, *not* Odeypore, Oodey-, Ude-.

udal, *use* **odal.**

U.D.C., Urban District Council.

U.D.I. *or* **UDI,** unilateral declaration of independence.

U.F.C., United Free Church (of Scotland).

U.F.O. *or* **UFO,** unidentified flying object.

Uffizi Gallery, Florence, *not* -izzi.

Uganda, Africa, independent 1962, republic 1963.

U.G.C., University Grants Committee.

Ugley, village in Essex.

U.H.F., ultra-high frequency.

uhlan, a Prussian lancer, in Ger. **Ulan.**

Uhland (Johann Ludwig), 1787–1862, German poet.

Uhr/ (Ger. f.), clock, o'clock; *pl. -en,* abbr. **U.** (cap.).

u.i., ut infra (as below).

uitlander (Afrik.), foreigner.

U.J.D., *Utriusque Juris Doctor* (Doctor of both Laws).

U.K., United Kingdom.

U.K.A., Ulster King-of-Arms, United Kingdom Alliance.

ukase, in Russ. *ukaz,* an edict, *not* oukaz.

Ukraine, *properly* **Ukrainian Soviet Socialist Republic,** one of the republics forming the Union of Soviet Socialist Republics (*see* **U.S.S.R.**); *not* Little Russia.

Ulan, *use* **uhlan.**

Ullswater, Cumberland, *not* Ulles-.

Ulster, Ireland.

ulster, a coat (not cap.).

Ulster King-of-Arms, *not* -at-; abbr. **U.K.A.**

ult. (should not be printed), *ultimo* (last [month]).

ultima/ (Lat. f.), final; — *ratio,* the last resource; — *ratio regum,* resort to arms; — *Thule,* a remote island in the N. Atlantic vaguely known to the ancients, the furthest limit.

ultimatum/, final proposal; *pl. -s.*

ultimo (Lat.), last month; better not abbreviated.

ultimum vale (Lat.), the last farewell.

ultimus haeres (the final heir), the crown or the state.

ultra/ (Lat.), beyond, extreme; — **vires**, beyond legal power.

ultra-violet (hyphen).

Umbala, -balla, use **Ambala**.

umbr/a (astr.), a shadow; *pl.* **-ae**.

umlaut, *see* **Ä, ä** *and* **accents and diacritical marks.**

Umritsar, *use* **Amritsar.**

U.N., United Nations, *not* UN, U.N.O., UNO, Uno.

U.N.A., United Nations Association.

una corda (mus.), one string; in pianoforte music indicates that soft pedal must be depressed.

unanimous (a, *not* an).

unauthorized, *not* -ised.

una voce (Lat.), unanimously.

unbaptized, *not* -ised.

unbiased, *not* -ssed.

uncanny, *not* -ie.

unchristian (one word).

unciatim (Lat.), ounce by ounce.

uncircumcised, *not* -ized.

unclench, *see* **clench.**

unclinch, *see* **clinch.**

uncooperative (one word).

uncoordinated (one word).

UNCTAD, United Nations Conference on Trade and Development.

unctuous, greasy, *not* -ious.

underestimate (one word).

underhand (one word).

underlay (typ.), to make type, etc., type-high.

underlie, *not* -ly.

underline (typ), use single line for italic; double, for small capitals; treble, for large capitals; wavy, for bold type; (typ.), caption to illustration, diagram, etc., usually below it.

under-runners (typ.), excess of marginal notes which are continued below body of

text, generally at foot of page. *See* **runners.**

under/sell, -tone (one word).

underwater (adj.), (one word).

under way, moving, *more correct than* — weigh (two words).

unenclosed, *not* unin-.

UNESCO *or* **Unesco,** United Nations Educational, Scientific, and Cultural Organization.

ungarisch (Ger.), Hungarian; abbr. **ung.** (not cap.).

Ungarn, Ger. n. for **Hungary.**

unguent, ointment.

unheard-of (hyphen).

UNICEF *or* **Unicef,** United Nations International Children's Emergency Fund.

unicorn, uniform, union, unison (a, *not* an).

Unionist, abbr. **U.**

Union Jack (two words).

uni/son, in Fr. **-sson.**

Unit., Unitarian, -ism.

unit (a, *not* an).

Unitas Fratrum (Lat.), off. for **Moravian Church.**

United Arab Republic, 1958, Egypt and Syria; 1961, Syria seceded; abbr. **U.A.R.**

United/Free Church of Scotland (caps.), abbr. **U.F.C.;** — **Kingdom/** (caps.), abbr. **U.K.;** — — **Alliance** [for the suppression of the liquor traffic] (caps.), abbr. **U.K.A.;** — **Presbyterian/,** abbr. **U.P.;** — — **Church** (caps.), abbr. **U.P.C.;** — **Service Club** (*not* Services). *See also* **U.S., U.S.I., U.S.S.R.**

Univ., University; (in Oxford) University College.

universal (a, *not* an); abbr. **univ.**

Universal Copyright Convention, drafted at Geneva 1952 and signed by forty-three countries; ratified by the required minimum of twelve countries (including U.S.A.) by mid-1955 and effective there from 16 Sept. 1955.

universalize, *not* -ise.

unlicensed, *not* -ced

unm., unmarried.

unmistakable, *not* -eable.

unmould, *not* -mold.

U.N.O., UNO, *or* **Uno,** United Nations Organization, *use* **U.N.**

uno animo (Lat.), unanimously.

unparalleled.

unridable, *not* -eable.

unrival/led, U.S. -ed.

U.N.R.R.A., UNRRA, Unrra, United Nations Relief and Rehabilitation Administration.

U.N.R.W.A., UNRWA, Unrwa, United Nations Relief Works Agency.

unsalable, *use* **-eable.**

unscalable, *not* -eable.

unselfconscious.

unserviceable, *not* -cable.

unsewn binding (bind.), a glueing technique which replaces sewing, used on paperbacks, etc.

unshakeable, *not* -kable.

unskilful.

until (typ.), should, if possible, not be divided.

untrammel/led (U.S. -ed).

untravel/led (U.S. -ed).

u.ö. (Ger. *und öfters*), and often.

U.P., United Presbyterian; United Press; Uttar Pradesh (formerly United Provinces), India.

u.p., under proof.

up., upper.

upanishad, a Sanskrit philosophical treatise.

upper case (typ.), the case containing capitals, small capitals, figures, and signs; hence the capitals A–Z; abbr. **caps.,** indicated in MS. by three lines underneath; for small capitals abbr. **s. caps.** or **s.c.,** indicated by two lines underneath.

Upper Volta, W. Africa, independent 1960.

Uppsala, Sweden, *not* Ups-.

upstairs (one word).

up-to-date (attributive adj., hyphens).

U.P.U., Universal Postal Union.

U.P.W., Union of Postal Workers.

uraemia (path.), *not* ure-.

Urania (Gr.), muse of astronomy.

uranium, symbol **U** (no point).

Uranus, Greek mythology and astronomy.

urari, *use* curare.

urbi et orbi (Lat.), to the city (Rome) and the world.

urethr/a (anat.), *pl.* -ae.

U.R.I., Upper Respiratory Infection.

urim and thummim, Exod. 28:30, are plurals.

Urquhart, *pron.* urk′urt.

Uru., Uruguay.

U.S., United Service, — States.

u.s., ubi supra (in the place above [mentioned]), *ut supra* (as above).

U.S.A., United States of America.

usable, *not* -eable.

U.S.C., United States of Colombia.

U.S.C.L., United Society for Christian Literature.

U.S.D.A.W., Union of Shop, Distributive, and Allied Workers.

useful (**a,** *not* an).

usf. (Ger.), *und so fort* (and so on).

U.S.I., United Service Institution (*not* Services).

U.S.P.G., United Society for the Propagation of the Gospel.

usquebaugh (Gaelic), whisky.

Ussher (James), 1581–1656, Irish divine, Abp. of Armagh.

U.S.S.R., Union of Soviet Socialist Republics, comprising the Russian Soviet Federated Socialist Republic (R.S.F.S.R.) and the Armenian, Azerbaijan, Estonian, Finno-Karelian, Georgian, Kazakh, Kirghiz, Latvian, Lithuanian, Moldavian, Tadjik, Tukmen, Ukrainian, Uzbek, and White Russian (Belorussian) Soviet Socialist Republics.

usu., usual, -ly.

usurper (a, *not* an).

Utah, officially not abbr.

Utakamand, *use* **Ootacamund.**

ut dictum (Lat.), as directed; abbr. *ut dict.*

U.T.H., ultra-heat tested (long-keeping milk).

utilize, *not* -ise.

ut infra (Lat.), as below.

uti possidetis (Lat.), as you now possess (opposed to *status quo ante*).

Utopia/, -n (caps.).

ut supra (Lat.), as above; abbr. *u.s.*

Uttar Pradesh, India, *formerly* United Provinces.

ut videtur (Lat.), as it seems.

U/W, underwriter.

uxor (Lat.), wife; abbr. *ux.*

Uzbekistan, a Soviet Socialist Republic, *not* Uzbeg-. *See* **U.S.S.R.**

Uzès (Marie Clémentine Rochechouart-Mortemart, duchesse d'), 1848–1933, French novelist, dramatist, huntsman, campaigner for women's rights.

V

V, five, vanadium (no point), (elec.) volt, (math.) potential energy, (Ger.) *Vergeltungswaffe* (reprisal weapon: V1, flying bomb; V2, rocket); not used in the numeration of series.

V., Vice-, Volunteers, all proper names with this initial.

v., ventral, verse, verso, versus, (Ger.) *von* (of).

v. (Lat.), *vice* (in place of), *vide* (see), (mus.) *violino* (violin), *voce* (voice).

℣, sign for versicle.

V.A., Vicar-Apostolic, Vice-Admiral, (Order of) Victoria and Albert (for ladies).

Va., Virginia, U.S. (off. abbr.); (mus.) viola.

v.a., verb active; (Lat.) *vixit . . . annos* (lived [so many] years).

vaccinat/e, to inoculate with cowpox against smallpox; (in general) to inoculate; **-ion, -or.**

vacillat/e, to move from side to side; **-ion, -or.**

vacu/um, *pl.* **-a.**

V.A.D., Voluntary Aid Detachment (for nursing in First World War).

vade-mecum/, a handbook or other article carried on the person; *pl.* **-s** (hyphen).

vae victis! (Lat.), woe to the vanquished!

vaille que vaille (Fr.), whatever it may be worth, at all events.

vainglor/y, -ious (one word).

valance, short curtain or drapery, *not* -ence.

vale! (Lat.), farewell!, *pl. valete!* **vale** (noun), a farewell (not ital.).

valence, valency, q.v.

Valencia, Ireland, Spain.

Valenciennes lace.

valency (chem.), the combining power of an element.

Valentia (Viscount), *not* -cia.

Valentine's Day (St.), 14 Feb. (apos.).

valet/, man-servant; — **de chambre,** a body-servant (not ital.); *valet/ de pied*, footman; — *de place*, a local guide (ital.).

valeta, a waltz; *use* **vel-.**

Valetta, Malta; *use* **Vall-.**

Valhalla (Norse myth.), palace in which souls of dead heroes feasted, *not* W-. *See also* **Hel.**

valkyrie (Norse myth.), one of Odin's handmaidens, *not* w-.

Valladolid, Spain.

Valletta, Malta, *not* Val-, -eta.

Vallombrosa, N. Italy, *not* Vallam-.

valour, *but* **valorous.**

Valparaiso, Chile; *pron.* ĭz′-o.

valse/ (Fr. f.), waltz; — *à deux temps, à trois temps* (no hyphens), variations of the waltz.

Vambéry (Arminius), 1832–1913, Hungarian traveller and philologist.

van, *or* van der, this prefix usually l.c., but copy signature.

vanadium, symbol **V** (no point).

Vanbrugh, *pron.* van′brŭ.

Van Diemen's Land, not — Dieman's — (apos.); *now* **Tasmania,**

Van Dyck (Sir Anthony),
1599–1641, Flemish painter
(two words); anglicized
form **Vandyke** (one word),
used to denote a work by
him. *See also* **vandyke**.

vandyke/ (adj.), in the style
of Van Dyck; hence —
beard, pointed; — **brown;**
— **collar,** deeply cut (hence
verb, **to vandyke,** to notch);
— **edge;** — **lace** (all two
words).

Vane-Tempest-Stewart,
family name of Marquess
of Londonderry (hyphens).

Van Gogh (Vincent), 1853–
90, Dutch painter.

Vanhomrigh (Esther),
1692–1723, Swift's 'Vanessa'.

**Van Nostrand-Reinhold
Co.,** publishers.

**Van't Hoff (Jacobus
Hendricus)**, 1852–1911,
Dutch physicist and chemist.

vaporize, *not* -ise.

vapour, *but* **vaporous.**

var., (biol.) variety, (math.)
variant.

vari/a lectio/ (Lat.),
a variant reading, abbr. **v.l.;**
pl. **-ae -nes,** abbr. **vv.ll.**

variant (math.), abbr. **var.**

variegated, diversified (usu.
in colour).

variety (biol.), abbr. **var.**
See also **botany.**

variorum edition, one
with notes by various
commentators.

variorum notae (Lat.),
notes by commentators.

vas/ (anat.), a duct; *pl.* **-a.**

vascul/um, bot. specimen
case; *pl.* **-a.**

vas deferens, spermatic duct.

vasectomy, excision of *vas
deferens.*

Vaseline (trade name, cap.).

vassal, feudal retainer.

Vassar College, New York.

V.A.T., Value Added Tax.

Vat., Vatican.

v.aux., verb auxiliary.

vb, verb.

V.C., Vice-Chairman,
— -Chancellor, — -Consul,
Victoria Cross.

v. Chr. (Ger.), *vor Christus,
vor Christo,* or *vor Christi
Geburt* (B.C.).

V.D., venereal disease,
Volunteer (officers) Decoration.

v.d., various dates.

v. dep., verb deponent.

V.D.H., valvular disease of
the heart.

V.D.U., Visual Display Unit.

VE, victory in Europe
(VE day, 8 May 1945).

v^e (Fr.), *veuve* (widow).

veau (Fr. m.), calf, (cook.)
veal, (bind.) calf, calf-skin.

vedette, mounted sentinel,
patrol boat, *not* vi-.

Vega (Garcilaso de la), *see*
Garcilaso.

**Vega Carpio (Lope Felix
de)**, known as **Lope de
Vega,** 1562–1635, Spanish
dramatist and poet.

Vehmgericht/, German
medieval tribunal, *pl.* **-e**
(not ital.); adj. **Vehmic.**

veille (Fr. f.), the day before,
eve. *See also vielle, vieille.*

**Velázquez (Diego
Rodriguez de Silva y)**,
1599–1660, Spanish painter,
not Velas-; Sp. *pron.*
vĕ-lath′-keth.

veld (Afrik.), open country;
pron. felt; *not* -dt.

veldschoen, a shoe made of
raw hide (corruption of Du.
vel schoen, skin shoe); in
Afrik. **velskoen.**

veleta, a waltz; *not* val-.

vellum/, very smooth
parchment; — **-paper,**
that imitating vellum.

veloce (mus.), quickly.

velocity (phys.), abbr. **v.**

velskoen, *see* **veldschoen.**

velvety.

Ven., Venerable (used for archdeacons only).

venaison (Fr. f.), venison.

venal, of a vein; sordid. *See also* **venial.**

Vendée (La), dép. France; adj. **Vendean,** of the royalist party, 1793–5.

vend/er, in law **-or.**

vendetta, a blood feud (not ital.).

Vendôme, town in north-cent. France; **Colonne —,** and **Place —,** Paris.

venerat/e, -or.

venere/al, -ous.

venesection, blood-letting.

Venet., Venetian.

venetian blind (not cap.).

Venezuela, S. American rep.; abbr. **Venez.**

venial, pardonable. *See also* **venal.**

ventilat/e, -or.

ventral, of the belly; abbr. **v.**

ventre à terre (Fr.), at full speed.

ventriloquize, *not* -ise.

vera causa (Lat.), a true cause.

veranda, *not* -ah.

verb, abbr. **vb.**

verb. (Ger.), *verbessert* (improved, revised).

verbalize, to put into words, *not* -ise.

verbatim (Lat.), word for word (not ital.); *verbatim, literatim, et punctatim,* word for word, letter for letter, and point for point (ital.).

verbum satis sapienti (Lat.), a word to the wise suffices; abbr. *verb. sap.* (*or sat.*).

verd-antique, a stone, *not* verde- — (hyphen).

verderer, forester, *not* -or.

verdigris, green rust on copper, *not* verde-.

Verein (Ger. m.), Association (cap.).

Vereinigte Staaten, Ger. for **United States** (of America); abbr. *Ver. St.*

Vereshchagin (Vasili Vasilievich), 1842–1904, Russian painter.

verger, an attendant in a church. *See also* **virger, virgir.**

Vergil (Polydore), 1470–1555, Italian humanist.

Vergilius (Publius — Maro), 70–19 B.C., Roman poet, usu. anglicized as **Virgil.**

vergleich (Ger.), compare; abbr. *vgl.*

Verlagsbuchhändler (Ger. m.), publisher, -s (cap.).

vermilion, *not* -llion.

Vermont, U.S., off. abbr. **Vt.**

vermouth, an appetizer; in Fr. m. *vermout,* in Ger. m. *Wermuth.*

Veronese (Paolo), 1528–88, Italian painter, real name **Cagliari.**

Verrocchio (Andrea del), 1435–88, Italian painter and sculptor, *not* the many variations.

Versailles, near Paris.

vers de société (Fr. m.), society verses.

verse, abbr. **v.** *or* **ver.,** *pl.* **vv.**

versicle, short verse in liturgy said or sung by minister, followed by people's (or choir's) response; (typ.) the sign ℣ used in religious works. *See also* ℟.

vers libre, free verse.

verso (typ.), the left-hand page, having an even page number, as 2, 4, 6; not ital.; abbr. **ᵃ, ᵛ, v., vᵒ.**

versus (Lat.), against (not ital.); abbr. **v.**

Vertebr/a, a segment of the backbone; *pl.* **-ae** (not ital.).

Vertebrata (*pl.*), animals with a spinal column; abbr. **Vert.**

vert/ex, highest point; *pl.*
-ices.

vertu, *use* **vi-.**

Vertue (George), 1684–1756,
English engraver.

verve, spirit (not ital.).

**Verwoerd (Hendrik
Frensch),** 1901–66, Prime
Minister of Republic of
South Africa, 1958–66.

Very light, a flare fired from
a pistol.

Very Revd., Very Reverend
(for deans, provosts, and
former moderators).

vespiary, a nest of wasps.

Vespucci (Amerigo), 1451–
1512, Italian navigator.

vessels' (ships') **names,** to
be in italic.

vestigia (Lat. *pl.*), traces.

vet, veterinary surgeon (no
point).

veto/, ban; *pl.* **-es.**

vettur/a (It.), a carriage,
cab, or car, *pl.* **-e**; **-ino**, its
driver or proprietor, *pl.*
-ini.

veuf (Fr. m.), widower.

veuve (Fr. f.), widow; abbr.
v^e.

Vevey, Switzerland, *not* -ay.

vexata quaestio (Lat.),
a disputed question.

v.f., very fair.

V.G., Vicar-General.

v.g., very good.

vgl. (Ger. for cf.), *vergleich*,
compare.

V.H.F., very high frequency.

V.I. (map-making), vertical
interval.

v.i., verb intransitive.

via (Lat.), by way of, *not*
-â (not ital.).

via media (Lat.), a middle
course (ital.).

Vic., vicar, -age, Victoria.

vicar/, incumbent of a parish
who is not a **rector**, q.v.;
adj. **-ial.**

Vicar/-Apostolic, abbr.
V.A.; — **-General, V.G.**

vicarious, exercised or
suffered by one person for
another.

Vicars' College, a cathedral
residence.

vice, a tool, *not* -se.

Vice/, abbr. **V.;** — **-Admiral,**
abbr. **V.A.;** — **-Chairman,**
V.C.; — **-Chamberlain;** —
-Chancellor, V.C.; —
-Consul, V.C.; —
-President, V.P.; —
-Regent (hyphens, caps.
when used as titles).

Viceroy (cap.), **viceregal.**

vice versa (Lat.), the order
being reversed (no hyphen
or accent, not ital.).

victimize, *not* -ise.

Victoria/, abbr. **Vic.;** —
and Albert (Order of), for
ladies, abbr. **V.A.;** —
Cross, abbr. **V.C.;**
— **Nyanza,** *use* **Lake
Victoria.**

victoria, a carriage.

victual/ (*pron.* vĭt'l), **-led,**
-ler, -ling (U.S. **-ed, -er,**
-ing).

vide/ (Lat.), see, abbr. *v.*;
— *ante,* see before; — *infra,*
— below; *videlicet,* namely
(one word), abbr. **viz.;**
vide/ post, see below; —
supra, — above, abbr. *v.s.*

vide (Fr. mus.), open (of
strings).

vidette, *use* **ve-.**

videtur (Lat.), it seems.

vide ut supra (Lat.), see as
above.

vie (rival), **vying.**

vieille (Fr. f.), an old woman.
See also **veille, vielle.**

vielle (Fr. f.), a hurdy-gurdy.
See also **veille, vieille.**

Vienna, in Ger. **Wien,** in Fr.
Vienne.

Vienne, town in dép. Isère,
France; tributary of R.
Loire, rising in Haute-
Vienne. *See also* **Haute-
Vienne.**

viennoise (*à la*) (Fr.), in Viennese style (not cap.).

Vientiane, *see* **Laos.**

Vierkleur (Afrik.), flag of Transvaal Republic.

vi et armis (Lat.), by force and arms.

Vietcong, the anti-govt. guerrilla force in S. Vietnam.

Vietnam: Southern Zone, cap. Saigon; Northern Zone, cap. Hanoi.

vieux/ *français*, Old French (not cap.); — *jeu*, an outworn subject.

view-hallo (hunt.), *not* the many variations.

vif (Fr., mus.), lively, briskly.

vigesimo, *see* **twentymo.**

vigesimo-quarto, *see* **twenty-fourmo.**

vignettes (typ.), illustrations with undefined edges.

vigour, *but* **vigorous.**

viking, northern sea robber of eighth to tenth centuries.

vilayet, Turkish prov. or dist.; abbr. **vila.**

vilify, to disparage.

village, abbr. **vil.**

villageoise (*à la*) (Fr.), in village style.

villain/, an evil-doer; **-ous,** **-y.** *See also* **villein.**

Villa-Lobos (Hector), 1887–1959, Brazilian composer.

villeggiatura (It. f.), country holiday.

villégiature (Fr. f.), country holiday.

villein/ (orig. -ain, but now usefully differentiated), a serf; **-age.** *See also* **villain.**

Villiers, family name of Earls of Clarendon and Jersey; *pron.* vil′lers.

vinaigrette, smelling-bottle, *not* vinegar-.

Vinci, Leonardo da, *see* **Leonardo.**

vincul/**um** (typ.), a brace, or horizontal line, for linking in mathematics; *pl.* **-a.**

vin du pays (Fr. m.), wine of the neighbourhood.

violat/**e, -or.**

violino (It.), violin; abbr. *v.*

Viollet-le-duc (Eugène Emmanuel), 1814–79, French architect and archaeologist.

violoncell/**o,** *not* violin-; *pl.* **-i,** abbr. **'cello; -ist.**

V.I.P., very important person.

virago/, termagant; *pl.* **-es.**

Virchow (Rudolf), 1821–1902, German pathologist.

virger, verger at certain cathedrals, such as St. Paul's and Winchester. *See also* **virgir.**

Virgil, 70–19 B.C., Roman poet; in Lat. **Vergilius.**

Virginia, U.S., off. abbr. **Va.**

virginia creeper (bot.), *not* -ian — (not cap.).

virginibus puerisque (Lat.), for girls and boys.

virgir, verger at Canterbury Cathedral. *See also* **virger.**

viritim (Lat.), man by man.

virtu (articles of), artistic articles of interesting workmanship, antiquity, or rarity, *not* ve-, -ue (not ital.).

virtuos/**o,** one skilled in an art, *pl.* **-i.**

virus/, a sub-microscopic infective agent; *pl.* **-es.**

vis/ (Lat. f.), force, *pl.* **vires;** — *a tergo,* force from behind.

visa/, endorsement on a passport (not ital.); *pl.* **-s.**

vis-à-vis (Fr.), face to face (hyphens).

visc/**era,** *pl.,* interior organs, esp. in the abdomen; *sing.* **-us.**

viscount/, **-ess** (cap. as title); abbr. **Visc.**

viscount/**cy, -ship,** the rank or jurisdiction of a viscount.

viscounty, (obs.) viscount.

viscous, sticky.

vise, a tool, *use* **vice.**

visé, older form of **visa.**

Vishnu, second person of the Hindu triad.

vis/ inertiae (Lat.), force of inanimate matter; —
major, superior force; —
medicatrix naturae, nature's power of healing.

visor, a cap peak, *not* viz-.

vista/, a view; *pl.* **-s.**

visualize, *not* -ise.

vis viva (Lat.), living force.

vitalize, *not* -ise.

vitiat/e, to spoil; **-or.**

viticulture, culture of vines.

vitriol/, oil of, sulphuric acid; **blue** —, copper sulphate; **green** —, ferrous sulphate; **white** —, zinc sulphate.

vituperat/e, to revile; **-or.**

viva! (It.), long live!

vivace (mus.), lively, quickly.

vivandi/er (Fr.), *fem.* *-ère,* army sutler.

vivant rex et regina! (Lat.), long live the King and Queen!

vivari/um, enclosure for living things; *pl.* **-a.**

vivat/ regina! (Lat.), long live the Queen! — *rex!* ditto the King!

viva/ voce, orally, *not* vivâ; also noun, an oral examination, Eng. *pl.* — **voces** (not ital.).

*vive/! (*Fr.), long live! — *la bagatelle!* ditto trifles! — *la différence!* ditto the difference! — *la République!* ditto the Republic!

vivisect/, -ion, -or.

vixit . . . annos (Lat.), lived (so many) years; abbr. **v.a.**

viz., *videlicet* (namely) (not ital.); (typ.) comma before.

vizier, a Muslim official, *not* -ir, -sier.

vizor, *use* vis-.

VJ, victory over Japan (VJ day 15 Aug. 1945; in U.S. 2 Sept. 1945) (no points).

v.l., *varia lectio* (a variant reading).

v.M. (Ger.), *vorigen Monats* (last month).

v.n., verb neuter.

V.O., Veterinary Officer, (Royal) Victorian Order.

vᵒ, verso (left-hand page).

voc., vocative.

vocab., vocabulary.

vocalize, *not* -ise.

vocative, abbr. **voc.**

voce (It. mus.), voice; abbr. *v. See also* **vox.**

vogue la galère! (Fr.), happen what may!

Vogüé (Eugène Melchior, vicomte de), 1848–1910, French essayist.

voilà/ (Fr.), see there! — *tout,* that is all.

vol., volume.

volaille (Fr. f.), fowl, poultry.

volant (Fr. dress. m.), a flounce.

Volapük, an artificial international language, invented by J. M. Schleyer, 1879.

vol-au-vent (Fr. cook. m.), filled puff-pastry case (not ital.).

volcano/, *pl.* **-es.**

Volgagrad, U.S.S.R., *formerly* Tsaritsyn, *then* Stalingrad.

Volksausgabe (Ger. f.), popular edition.

Volkslied/ (Ger. n.), a folk-song; *pl.* **-er** (cap.).

Volksraad (Afrik.), legislative assembly, esp. of the Transvaal or Orange Free State before 1900.

vols., volumes.

volt (elec.), symbol **V** (no point), SI unit of potential difference.

Voltaic Republic, *use* **Upper Volta.**

volte-face (Fr. f.), a turning about.

volti subito (It. mus.), turn over quickly; abbr. *v.s.*

volume, abbr. **vol.,** *pl.* **vols.**

Volunteers, abbr. **V.**

von, this prefix usu. l.c., but copy signature.

voortrekker (Afrik.), pioneer.

vor Christi Geburt, or vor Christus, or vor Christo (Ger.), B.C.; abbr. *v. Chr.*

vort/ex, whirlpool; *pl.* **-exes.**

vouch/er, in law **-or.**

vox/ (Lat. f.), voice, *pl.* *voces*; — *et praeterea nihil,* voice and nothing else; — *populi,* public sentiment.

voyez! (Fr.), see! look! abbr. *v.*

V.P., Vice-President.

V.R., *Victoria Regina* (Queen Victoria), Volunteer Reserve.

vraisemblance, appearance of truth (not ital.).

V.R. et I., *Victoria Regina et Imperatrix* (Victoria Queen and Empress).

v.refl., verb reflexive.

V.S., Veterinary Surgeon.

v.s. (Fr. chron.), *vieux style* (old style), (Lat.) *vide supra* (see above); (It. mus.) *volti subito* (turn over quickly).

V.S.O., Voluntary Service Overseas.

V.T., *Vetus Testamentum* (Old Test.).

v.t., verb transitive.

Vt., Vermont, U.S. (off. abbr.).

V.T.C., Volunteer Training Corps.

V.T.O.L., vertical take-off and landing.

Vuillard (**Jean Édouard**), 1868–1940, French painter.

Vuillaume (**J. B.**), 1798–1875, most important of French family of makers of bowed instruments.

vulcanize, to treat rubber with sulphur at high temperature, *not* -ise.

Vulg., the Vulgate.

vulg., vulgar, -ly.

vulgar fractions, *see* **fractions.**

vulgarize, *not* -ise.

Vulgate, the Latin Bible of the R.C.C.; abbr. **Vulg.**

vulgo (Lat.), commonly.

vv., verses, (mus.) first and second violins.

vv. ll., *variae lectiones* (variant readings).

V.W., Very Worshipful.

v.y. (bibliog.), various years.

vying.

Vyrnwy Lake, Wales.

W

W, watt; wolfram (tungsten) (no point); not used in the numeration of series.

W., Wales, warden, Wednesday, Welsh, west, -ern, all proper names with this initial.

w., week, -s, (cricket) wide, wife, (naut.) wet dew.

W.A., Western Australia.

W.A.A.C., Women's Army Auxiliary Corps, *later* Q.M.A.A.C. (Queen Mary's — — —).

W.A.A.E., World Association for Adult Education.

W.A.A.F., Women's Auxiliary Air Force, *earlier and later* **W.R.A.F.**

W.A.A.S., Women's Auxiliary Army Service.

wadi/ (Arab.), the dry bed of a torrent, *not* -y; *pl.* **-s.**

W.A.E.C., War Agricultural Executive Committee (Second World War).

w.a.f., with all faults.

W. Afr., West Africa.

wagon/, -er, -ette, *not* wagg-.

wagon/ (Fr. m.), a railway carriage; — **-lit,** sleeping-car, *pl.* **wagons-lits** (hyphen, not ital. in Eng. usage).

wagtail, a bird (one word).

Wahabi, a sect formed by Abd-el-Wahhab (1691–1787) to restore primitive Islam, *not* Wahh-, -bees.

Wahrheit (Dichtung und) (Ger.) (Fiction and Truth), by Goethe.

Waiapu (Bp. of), New Zealand.

Wai-hai-wei, *use* **Wei-haiwei** (no hyphens).

Waikiki Beach, Hawaii.

Wain (Charles's) (astr.).

wainscot/, panelled woodwork on an interior wall; **-ed, -ing.**

Wakley (Thomas), 1795–1862, English doctor, founded *The Lancet* in 1823. *See also* **Walkley.**

Wal., Walloon.

Walachian, one of a non-Slav people of SE. Europe, *not* Wall-.

Waldegrave, surname; *pron.* Wawgrāv.

waldgrave, an old German title of nobility; in Ger. *Waldgraf.*

Waldteufel (Émile), 1837–1912, French composer.

wale, a flesh mark, *use* **weal.**

waler, a N.S.W. horse.

Wales, abbr. **W.**

Walhalla, *use* **V-.**

walkie-talkie, portable radiotelephone, *not* -y -y.

walking-stick (hyphen).

Walkley (Arthur Bingham), 1855–1926, English dramatic critic. *See also* **Wakley.**

walk-over, no competition (hyphen); abbr. **w.o.**

Walküre (Die), second part of Wagner's *Nibelungen-Ring,* 1870.

walkyrie, *use* **v-.**

walla (Ind.), a man, *not* -ah.

wallaby, a small kangaroo, *not* the many variations.

Wallace (Alfred Russel, *not* -ell), 1823–1913, English naturalist; — **(Sir Donald M.),** 1841–1919, English writer; — **(Henry Agard),** 1888–1965, American politician; — **(Lewis, 'Lew'),** 1827–1905,

Wallace (*cont.*):
American general and
author; — (**Sir Richard**),
1818–90, English art
collector and philanthropist
(The Wallace Collection,
London); — (**Prof.
Robert**), 1853–1939,
Scottish agricultural
writer; — (**Sir William**),
1272–1305, Scottish hero;
— (**William Vincent**),
1812–65, Irish composer. *See
also* **Wallas, Wallis.**
Wallachian, *use* **Wala-.**
Wallas (**Graham**), 1858–
1932, English socialist
writer. *See also* **Wallace,
Wallis.**
wall-eyed (hyphen).
wallflower (one word).
Wallis (**George Harry**),
1847–1936, English art
writer; — (**John**), 1616–
1703, English mathe-
matician, a founder of the
Royal Society. *See also*
Wallace, Wallas.
Walloon, (a speaker of) a
French dialect of S. Belgium
and parts of N. France;
abbr. **Wal.**
Wallop, family name of Earl
of Portsmouth.
wall-paper (hyphen).
Wall Street, New York.
Walpurgis night, the one
preceding 1 May.
Walton (**Izaak,** *not* Isaac),
1593–1683, English author
of *Compleat Angler*.
waltz, a dance (not ital.);
in Fr. f. *valse*; in Ger. m.
Walzer (ital.).
W. & M., William and
Mary (King and Queen).
wapiti, American elk, *not*
wapp-.
War., Warwickshire.
Warboys, Huntingdonshire.
war/-cloud, — **-cry**
(hyphens).
Ward (**Artemas**), 1727–

1800, American
Revolutionary general; —
(**Artemus**), pseud. of
Charles Farrar Browne,
1834–67, American
humorist; — (**Mrs.
Humphry,** *not* -rey),
1851–1920, English
novelist (Mary Augusta
Arnold).
war-dance (hyphen).
warden, abbr. **W.**
war/-god, — **-head,** —
-horse (hyphens).
Warlock (**Peter**), pseud. of
Philip Heseltine, 1894–
1930, English composer.
war-lord (hyphen).
warmonger (one word).
War Office, abbr. **W.O.,**
see **M.o.D.**
war/-paint, — **-path**
(hyphens).
warrant/er, one who
authorizes or guarantees;
-or (law), one who gives
warranty.
warrant-officer (hyphen).
Warre (**Edmond**), 1837–
1920, Provost of Eton.
warship (one word).
wartime (one word).
Warwickshire, abbr. **War.**
Wash., Washington, U.S. (off.
abbr. of State).
wash-drawing, one made
with a brush and black or
neutral tint.
washhouse (one word).
Washington, a state of U.S.
on Pacific seaboard, abbr.
Wash.
Washington, D.C., U.S.
capital, near Atlantic coast.
wasn't, to be close up.
Wassermann, blood test for
syphilis, from **August von
Wassermann,** 1866–1925,
German bacteriologist.
watch/case, -maker, -word
(one word).
water-closet (hyphen),
abbr. **W.C.** (s.caps.).

water/course, -fall (one word).

watering-place (hyphen).

water/-level, — -lily, — -line (hyphens).

watermark (typ.), a design in the paper itself (one word).

water/proof, -tight, -works (one word).

Watling Street, a Roman road in England.

watt (elec.), unit of power; abbr. **W** (no point).

wattling, wattle work, twig structure.

Watts-Dunton (Walter Theodore), 1836–1914, English man of letters.

waul, a cat-cry, *not* -wl.

wav/e, -y.

wavelength (one word), symbol λ (lambda).

Wavertree, surname; *pron.* Wawtree.

way (under), moving, *more correct than* — weigh (two words).

Waynflete (William of), 1395–1486, Bp. of Winchester, Lord Chancellor.

wayzgoose/, name given formerly to printers' annual dinner, etc.; *not* the many variations; *pl.* **-s.**

Waziristan, formerly NW. Frontier Province of India, *not* Wazar-.

W.C., Western-Central postal district, London.

w.c., water-closet, without charge.

W.D., War Department, Works ditto.

W.D.C., War Damage Commission (during and after Second World War).

W.E.A., Workers' Educational Association.

weal, a flesh mark, *not* wale.

wear, of a river, *use* weir.

Wearside, *see* Tyneside-Wearside.

weasand, the gullet, *not* wez-.

weathercock (one word).

Webb (Beatrice), 1858–1943, wife of — **(Sidney James, Lord Passfield),** 1859–1947, English economists and sociologists; — **(Mary),** 1881–1927, English novelist.

web/-fed (typ.), presses which receive paper from a reel and not as separate sheets; — **-letterpress, — -offset.**

Webster (Daniel), 1782–1852, U.S. statesman and orator; — **(Noah),** 1758–1843, U.S. lexicographer.

Wedgwood ware, *not* Wedge-, a superior kind of pottery, invented by Josiah Wedgwood, 1730–95.

Wednesday, abbr. **W.,** *or* **Wed.**

week/, -s, abbr. **w.,** *or* **wk.**

week-day (hyphen); in Fr., not cap., as *lundi.*

week-end (hyphen).

weever, a fish.

Weidenfeld (George) & Nicolson, Ltd., publishers.

weigh (under), moving, *use* — way.

weight, abbr. **wt.**

weights, use figures; abbreviations as cwt., qr., lb., oz., *not* to have s added for the plural.

Weihaiwei, *not* Wai-hai-wei.

Weingartner (Paul Felix), 1863–1942, German conductor and composer.

weir, a dam across a river, *not* -ar.

Weismann (August), 1834–1914, German zoologist.

Weissnichtwo, (Ger. for Know-not-where), in *Sartor Resartus.*

Weizmann/ (Chaim), 1874–1952, Polish-born chemist and Zionist leader; — **Institute,** Israel.

Weizsäcker (Julius), 1828–89, German historian; — **(Karl),** 1822–99, German theologian.

welcher (turf), *use* **-sher.**

Welch Fusiliers (Royal), Welch Regt. (but **Welsh Guards).**

welk, *use* **wh-.**

well/-being, — **-born,** — **-bred** (hyphens).

Wellhausen (Julius), 1844–1918, German biblical scholar.

well-known, hyphen only when a noun follows immediately.

wellnigh (one word).

well-to-do (hyphens).

Welsh, abbr. **W.;**
alphabet has 26 letters; *ch, dd, ff, ng, ll, th,* being each counted as one. No *j, k, q, v, x, z.* In addition to the usual accents, *w* (= oo) and *y* may have the circumflex. Accent always on the last or penultimate syllable, never on the antepenultimate. *Pron.* dd as dh; ll as hl; u as öi; î as ē; y as u *or* öi.

welsher, one who decamps from a race-course without paying the winning betters, *not* **-cher.**

Welsh Guards. *See also* **Welch.**

welsh rabbit, melted cheese on toast, *not* — **rarebit.**

Welt/anschauung (Ger.), world-philosophy; ***-politik; -schmerz,*** world-sorrow.

Wemyss/ Bay, Renfrews.; — **Castle,** Fife; — **(Earl of),** *pron.* wēmz.

werewolf (myth.), a human capable of turning into a wolf, *not* **wer-.**

Wergeland (Henrik), 1808–45, Norwegian poet.

wergild, a fine, *not* **were-.**

werwolf, *use* **were-.**

west/, -ern, abbr. **W.** *See also* **compass.**

West Africa, abbr. **W. Afr.**

West Bridgford, Notts., *not* Bridge-.

West End, London (caps.).

westeria, *use* **wistaria.**

Westermarck (Edward Alexander), 1862–1939, Finnish anthropologist.

Western Australia, abbr. **W.A.**

West Glamorgan, new Welsh county, proposed 1971, including Swansea, Neath, Port Talbot.

Westhoughton, Lancs. (one word).

Westmeath, Co., Ire.; — **(Earl of)** (one word).

West Midlands, new metropolitan area, proposed 1971, including Wolverhampton, Walsall, Dudley, West Bromwich, Solihull, Coventry, most of Birmingham.

Westmorland, off.; — **(Earl of),** *not* -eland.

West Virginia, abbr. **W. Va.**

West Yorkshire, new metropolitan area, proposed 1971, including Bradford, Keighley, Leeds, Halifax, Dewsbury, Huddersfield, Wakefield.

w.f. (typ.), wrong fount. *See* **proof correction marks** *and* **wrong fount.**

W.F.T.U., World Federation of Trade Unions.

W.G., W. G. Grace, 1848–1915, English cricketer.

Wg-Comdr., Wg/Cdr, Wing-Commander.

whalebone (one word).

whallabee, *use* **wallaby.**

whar/f, landing-stage; abbr.

whf.; *pl.* usu. **-fs** (U.S. usu. **-ves**).

Wharfedale, Yorks.

what-d'ye-call-it? (colloq.) (hyphens, apos.).

Whately (Richard), 1787–1863, Abp. of Dublin, *not* -ey.

Whatman paper, a first-quality English hand-made drawing-paper (cap.).

whatnot, a piece of furniture with shelves (one word).

wheatear, a bird (one word).

wheat-ear, an ear of wheat (hyphen).

wheelbarrow (one word).

Wheeler (James Talboys), 1824–97, English historian of India.

whelk, a mollusc, *not* we-.

whereas (law), a word which introduces the recital of a fact (one word, usu. cap.).

whether or not (*not* — — no).

whf., wharf.

which (gram.), now refers exclusively to things; **who,** to persons.

whiffletree, *use* **whipple-.**

whilom, former(ly), *not* -ome.

whimbrel, a bird, *not* wim-.

whimsy, caprice, *not* -ey.

whipper/-in of hounds; *pl.* **-s-in.**

whippletree, the cross-piece to which the traces of a harness are attached, *not* whiffle- (one word).

whip-poor-will, American bird (hyphens).

whirl/pool, -wind (one word).

whisky, *not* -ey (except Irish).

Whistler (James Abbott McNeill, *not* -eil), 1834–1903, American painter and etcher.

Whitaker & Sons, publishers of *Almanack* (*not* ac-), etc.

white (typ.), any space of paper not printed upon; **— line,** a line not printed upon.

Whitefield (George), 1714–70, English preacher, *not* Whitf-; *but pron.* Whit′-.

Whitehall, London (one word).

Whiteing (Richard), 1840–1928, English journalist and novelist.

whiteout (one word), Antarctic blizzard.

White Russian Soviet Socialist Republic, a Soviet Socialist Republic (*but use* **Belorussia**). *See* **U.S.S.R.**

White's Club, London.

whitewash (one word).

whitish.

Whitman (Walt), 1819–92, American poet.

Whit/ Monday, Sunday, historically seventh after Easter, not necessarily coincident with Spring Bank Holiday (U.K.).

Whittier (John Greenleaf), 1807–92, American poet.

Whittlesey, Cambs., *not* -sea.

whiz/, *not* whizz; **-zed, -zing.**

who (gram.), now refers exclusively to persons; **which,** to things.

W.H.O., World Health Organization.

whoa! stop!

whodunit, a novel or play of crime detection, *not* -nnit (one word).

whole-bound, bound wholly in leather.

whooping-cough, *not* hoop- — (hyphen).

who's, who is (apos.).

whose, of whom.

Who's Who, Who Was Who, reference books.

Whyte-Melville (George John), 1821–78, Scottish novelist (hyphen).

W.I., West Ind/ies, -ian; Women's Institute.

wich/-elm, -hazel, *use* **wy-**.

Wicliffe, *see* **Wyclif**.

widdershins, *use* **withershins**.

wide awake (two words), fully awake.

wide-awake (hyphen), adj., alert; noun, a type of hat.

widespread (one word).

widgeon, a bird, *not* wig-.

widow (typ.), a break-line at top of page or column — to be avoided.

Wieland (Christoph Martin), 1733–1813, German poet and novelist.

Wien, in Eng. **Vienna**.

Wiener (Norbert), 1894–1964, U.S. mathematician and writer on cybernetics.

Wiener-Neustadt, Austria (hyphen).

wienerschnitzel, veal cutlet dressed with bread-crumbs and eggs (one word, not ital.; in Ger. two words, caps.).

Wieniawski (Henri), 1835–80, Polish violinist and composer; — (**Joseph**), 1837–1912, Polish pianist and composer, brother of preceding.

Wiesbaden, German resort (one word).

wife, abbr. **w.**

wigeon, *use* **widg-**.

Wiggin (Kate Douglas), 1856–1923, American educator and novelist.

Wight (Isle of), abbr. **I.W.**

Wigorn., signature Bp. of Worcester (full point).

Wigton, Cumberland.

Wigtown, Scotland.

Wilamowitz-Moellendorf (Ulrich von), 1848–1931, German classical scholar.

Wilde (Henry), 1833–1919, English physicist; — (**Oscar Fingall O'Flahertie Wills**), 1856–1900, Irish playwright and poet.

wildebeest, a gnu; in Afrik. *wildebees/*, *pl.* *-te*.

wild-fowl (hyphen).

wilful/, -ly, -ness, *not* will-.

Wilhelmj (August Emil D. F.), 1845–1908, German violinist.

Wilhelmshaven, former German naval station (one word).

Wilhelmstrasse, Berlin, the former German Downing Street.

Williams & Glyn's Bank, Ltd.

will-o'-the-wisp, the *ignis fatuus* (apos., hyphens).

Wiltshire, abbr. **Wilts**.

Wimborne (Viscount).

Wimborne Minster, Dorset.

wimbrel, *use* **wh-**.

wincey, a cloth, *not* -sey.

Winchelsea, Sussex.

Winchilsea (Earl of).

Winckelmann (Johann Joachim), 1717–68, German art critic.

wind (naut.), Beaufort Scale: 1, light air; 2, light breeze; 3, gentle —; 4, moderate —; 5, fresh —; 6, strong —; 7, moderate gale; 8, fresh —; 9, strong —; 10, whole —; 11, storm; 12, hurricane.

Windhoek, SW. Africa.

Wind. I., Windward Islands.

win/e, -y.

winepress (one word).

winsey, *use* -cey.

wint/er, -ry (not cap.).

wintergreen, an aromatic plant (one word).

Winton., signature Bp. of Winchester (full point).

wire-side, the side of paper formed on the wire of a paper-making machine.

Wis., Wisconsin, U.S. (off. abbr.); Wisdom of Solomon (Apocr.).

Wisbech, Cambs., *not* -each.

Wisdom of Solomon (Apocr.), abbr. **Wis.** *or* **Wisd.**

wiseacre (one word).

Wislicenus (Johannes), 1835–1902, German chemist.

wistaria (bot.), not wisteria.

witch/-elm, — -hazel, *use* wych- —.

witenagemot, Anglo-Saxon Parliament.

withal.

with/e, *pl.* -es, *or* **with/y,** *pl.* -ies, a flexible twig, often of willow, *not* wy-.

withershins, contrary to the direction of the sun, *not* widder-.

withhold, etc. (one word, two *h*'s).

witness-box (hyphen).

Wittenberg, Germany.

Witwatersrand University, Johannesburg, S. Africa.

wivern, *use* wy-.

wizard, *not* wis-.

wk., week, -s.

W.L.A., Women's Land Army (Second World War).

W. long., west longitude.

Wm, William (no point).

W.M.O., World Meteorological Organization.

WNW., west-north-west (*see also* **compass**).

W.O., War Office (*see* **M.O.D.**), Warrant Officer, Wireless Operator.

w.o., walk-over.

Wodehouse, *pron.* wood-, family name of Earl of Kimberley; — **(Pelham Grenville),** 1881–, English humorous novelist. *See also* **Woodhouse.**

Wolcot (John), 1738–1819, 'Peter Pindar'.

Wolcott (Oliver), 1726–97, American statesman.

Wolf (Friedrich August), 1759–1824, German classical scholar; — **(Hugo),** 1860–1903, Austrian composer.

Wolfe (Charles), 1791–1823, Irish poet; — **(Humbert),** 1886–1940, English poet; — **(James),** 1727–59, English general, took Quebec; — **(Thomas Clayton),** 1900–38, American novelist.

Wolff (Sir Henry Drummond Charles), 1830–1908, British politician and diplomat; — **(J. Christian von),** 1679–1754, German philosopher and mathematician; — **(Joseph),** 1795–1862, German-born English-domiciled traveller; — **(Kaspar Friedrich),** 1733–94, German embryologist; adj. **Wolffian.**

Wolf-Ferrari (Ermanno), 1876–1948, Italian composer.

wolverine, American animal, *not* wool-, -ene.

Woman's/Journal; — *Own.*

women's rights (apos.).

won't, to be close up, one apos. only.

woo/, -ed, -er, -s.

Woodard Foundation, of a number of English public schools, named after **Nathaniel Woodard,** 1811–91, English Anglican priest, *not* Woodw-.

woodbine, honeysuckle, *not* -ind.

Woodburytype, a photo-mechanical process for forming a matrix for printing (cap.).

woodchuck, N. American marmot (one word).

woodcock/, bird, m. and f.; *pl.* **-s.**

woodcut (typ.), design cut in the side grain of a type-high block of wood (one word).

wood engraving (typ.), design cut in the end grain of a type-high block of wood (two words).

Woodhouse, surname of Emma in Jane Austen's *Emma. See also* **Wodehouse.**

woodpecker (one word).

woodruff (bot.), *not* -roof.

woodwork (one word).

wool/, -len, -ly (U.S. **-en**).

Woolf (Adelaide Virginia), 1882–1941, English novelist and essayist.

Woollcott (Alexander), 1887–1943, American author and dramatic critic.

Woolloomooloo, Sydney, Australia.

Woolsack (House of Lords) (one word).

woolsorter's disease, anthrax, *not* -ers'.

Worcestershire, abbr. **Worcs.**

Worde, *see* **Wynkyn.**

Word of God (the) (caps.), but in N.T. l.c. *w.*

workaday (one word).

work and turn (typ.), printing the two sides of a sheet of paper from one forme.

work/house, -man (one word).

work off (typ.), actually to print the paper.

World War I, 1914–18; — — **II,** 1939–45; *use* **First World War; Second World War.**

wormwood, (bot.) *Artemisium Absinthium,* (fig.) bitterness.

Wormwood Scrubs, London.

worship/, -ped, -per, -ping (U.S. **-ed, -er, -ing**).

worthwhile, attrib. adj.

(one word); predicatively, two words.

Wotton (Sir Henry), 1568–1639, English diplomat and poet.

would-be, adj. (hyphen).

wouldst (typ.), to be close up, no apos.

Woulfe/ (Peter), 1727–1803, English chemist; hence — -**bottles,** for distillation (one cap., hyphen).

wove paper, that which does not show wire marks: distinct from laid —.

w.p.b., waste-paper basket.

w.p.c., woman police constable (caps. when used before a name); **W.P.c.** usual in newspapers, to avoid confusion with initials.

W.R., West Riding, Yorks.

W.R.A.C., Women's Royal Army Corps.

wrack, a seaweed, *not* r-.

W.R.A.F., Women's Royal Air Force.

Wrangler (Cambridge University), one placed in first class of mathematical tripos.

wrap round (bind.), to wrap pages containing plates (illustrations) round a section of text.

wrap round plate (typ.), flexible relief plate (e.g. of rubber or plastic, to replace metal).

wrasse, a fish, *not* -ass.

wrath (noun), great anger (*see also* **wroth**).

Wray, *see* **Ray.**

wreath (noun).

wreathe (verb).

W.R.I., Women's Rural Institute.

wrick, a twist or sprain, *not* rick.

writer's cramp, *not* -ers' cramp.

W.R.N.S., Women's Royal Naval Service.

Wroclaw, Poland; in Ger. **Breslau.**

wrongdo/er, -ing (one word).

wrong fount (typ.), when the wrong kind of type has been used; abbr. **w.f.**

wrong'un (cricket), a googly (apos., close up).

wroth (adj.), wrathful (*see also* **wrath**).

Wrottesley (**Baron**).

W.R.V.S., Women's Royal Voluntary Services, *formerly* **W.V.S.**

wryneck, a bird (one word).

wry-necked (adj., hyphen).

W.S. (Sc.), Writer to the Signet (= attorney).

WSW., west-south-west. *See also* **compass.**

W.T. (*or* **W/T**), wireless telegraphy.

wt., weight.

Württemberg, State, SW. Germany (two *t*'s).

Wuthering Heights, by Emily Brontë, 1846.

W. Va., West Virginia, U.S. (off. abbr.).

W.V.S., Women's Voluntary Services, *now* **W.R.V.S.**

Wyandotte, N. American Indians; l.c. a fowl, *not* -ot.

wych-/-elm, — -hazel, *not* wich-, witch-.

Wycherley (**William**), 1640–1716, English dramatist.

Wyclif (**John**), *c.* 1324–84, English religious reformer and translator of the Bible; *not* the many variants.

Wycliffe Hall, Oxford, a theological college.

Wymondham, Norfolk; *pron.* wind'um.

Wyndham/, family name of Baron Leconfield; — (**Sir Charles**), 1837–1919, English actor; — (**George**), 1863–1913, English statesman; —'s **Theatre,** London.

Wyndham-Quin, family name of Earl of Dunraven.

Wynkyn de Worde, 1471–1534, early printer in London.

Wyo., Wyoming, U.S. (off. abbr.).

wyth/e, -y, *use* **withe.**

Wythenshawe, Manchester.

wyvern, heraldic dragon, *not* wi-.

X

X, ten, certain kinds of beer, the twenty-first in a series.

X., motion-picture certificate barring under-16's, all proper names with this initial.

X (usu. *XP* or **Xt.**, qq.v.), the Gk. letter chi, for *Christos*, Christ.

x (math.), the first unknown quantity.

Xanthippe, wife of Socrates.

Xavier, St. Francis.

X^bre (Fr.), December.

XC, 90.

XCIX, 99.

x.cp., ex (without) coupon.

x.d. *or* **ex div.,** ex (without) dividend.

Xe, xenon (no point).

Xenocrates, 396–314 B.C., Greek philosopher.

xenon, symbol **Xe** (no point).

Xenophanes, 538–500 B.C., Greek philosopher and poet.

Xenophon, 435–355 B.C., Greek historian; abbr. **Xen.**

Xeres, Spain, *use* **Jerez.**

Xérez (Francisco de), b. 1504, Spanish historian of conquest of Peru.

xerography, an electrostatic printing process.

xerox/, dry-copying process, or machine, for documents; a copy made thereby, *pl.* **-es** (from the trade name Rank Xerox, Ltd.).

Xerxes, 519–465 B.C., king of Persia.

x-height (typ.), height of short letters in fount.

x.i. *or* **ex int.,** ex (without) next interest.

Xmas, Christmas (no point).

Xn., Christian; **Xnty.,** Christianity.

x.n. *or* **ex n.,** (ex new) ex (without) the right to new shares.

XP (as monogram ☧), the Greek letters *chi rho*, first two of *Christo*).

X-ray (hyphen).

Xt., Christ.

XX, ale of double strength.

XXX, ale of triple strength.

xylography, the printing of wood-block books.

xylonite, a plastic.

xylophone (mus.), a percussion instrument of wooden bars vibrating when struck.

Y

Y, yen (q.v.), yttrium, the twenty-second in a series.

Y, riv. Holland, *use* **IJ.**

Y., all proper names with this initial.

y in Dutch, *use* **ij,** as Nijmegen, Ijmuiden.

y., year, -s.

y (math.), the second unknown quantity.

yacht.

yager, anglicized form of Ger. **Jäger,** a huntsman, rifleman.

Yahoo, in Swift's *Gulliver's Travels,* an animal with human form but brutish instincts.

Yahveh, the probable pronunciation of the Hebrew consonants YHWH which are traditionally transliterated as **Jehovah;** *not* Jahveh.

Yakutsk, Siberia, *not* J-.

Yale, U.S. University, at New Haven, Conn.

Yangtze Kiang, Chinese river (*kiang* = river).

Yankee, a citizen of the New England States or of the North of U.S., *not* -i.

yaourt, *see* **yogurt.**

yapp (bind.), a soft case with overlapping edges.

yard/, -s, abbr. **yd., yds.;** number of, to be in figures.

yard-arm (naut.), hyphen.

Yarde-Buller, family name of Baron Churston.

Yarkand, Cent. Asia, *not* -end, -und.

yarl, *use* j-.

Yaroslavl, Russia, *not* Jaroslav.

yashmak, Muslim woman's veil.

Y.B., Year Book, q.v.

Yb, ytterbium (no point).

yclept, called, named (one word).

yd., yds., yard, -s.

y^e, = the, through confusing the Anglo-Saxon þ (= th) with Old-Eng. ÿ (y).

Yeames (William Frederick), 1835–1918, English painter; *pron.* yāmz.

year/, -s, abbr. **y.**

year-book (hyphen); **Year Book** (law reports) (caps., two words), abbr. **Y.B.**

years, in giving the first and last of a series use the fewest figures sufficient to match the spoken word, as 1892–8, 1855–80, 1890–1904, 1911–18.

Yeats (William Butler), 1865–1939, Irish poet; *pron.* yāts.

Yeats-Brown (Francis), 1886–1944, English author.

yelk, *use* yo-.

yellow-hammer, a bird (hyphen), *not* — -ammer.

Yellowplush (one word) *Papers,* by Thackeray, 1841.

Yellowstone/ (one word) **Park;** — **River.**

Yemen, S. Arabia.

yen, the dollar of Japan, abbr. **Y.**

Yeniseisk, Siberia, on R. Yenisei, *not* Jenisesi.

Yeo., Yeomanry.

Yerkes telescope, Chicago, U.S. (no apos.).

Y.E.S., Youth Employment Service.

yeux, see œil.

Yezo, Japan, *now called* **Hokkaido.**

Yggdrasil (Scan. myth.), the tree binding heaven, earth, and hell, anglicized from O.N. *yggrdrasill*; *not* Ygd-.

Y.H.A., Youth Hostels Association.

Yiddish/, corrupt German and Hebrew dialect; **-er,** speaker of same.

ylang-ylang, (perfume from) Malayan tree (hyphen).

Y.M.C.A., Young Men's Christian Association.

Y.M.P., Young Master Printer.

Ynca, *use* **Inca.**

yodel/, falsetto song; **-led, -ling,** *not* -dle, jodel.

yog/**a,** Hindu system of philosophic meditation; **-i,** a devotee of yoga.

yogh(o)urt, *see* **yogurt.**

yogurt, sour fermented milk, orig. of the Levant (the commonest Eng. spelling of many).

Yokohama, Japan (one word).

Yom Kippur (Jewish relig.), Day of Atonement.

Yonge (Charles Duke), 1812–91, English historian; — **(Charlotte Mary),** 1832–1901, English novelist; *pron.* yŭng. *See also* **Young.**

Yorke, family name of Earl of Hardwicke.

Yorkshire, abbr. **Yorks.**

Yosemite Valley, U.S.; *pron.* yō-sĕm′-ĭ-tĕ.

Youghal, Co. Cork, Ireland; *approx. pron.* yawl.

Youl (Sir James Arndell), 1809–1904, Tasmanian colonist.

you'll, to be close up.

Young (Brigham), 1801–77, American Mormon leader. *See also* **Yonge.**

younger, abbr. **yr.**

Young Men's Christian Association, abbr. **Y.M.C.A.;** ditto **Women's, Y.W.C.A.**

your, abbr. **yr.**

yours (no apos.).

Yquem (Château-d'), a Sauterne (hyphen).

yr., younger, your.

Y.R.A., Yacht Racing Association, *now* **R.Y.A.,** q.v.

Yriarte (Charles), 1832–98, French writer.

Ysaye (Eugène), 1858–1929, Belgian violinist; *pron.* ē-sī′-ye.

Yseult/, **-e, Ysolde, Ysolt, Ysoude,** *use* **Iseult.**

Y.T., Yukon Territory, Canada.

ytterbium, symbol **Yb** (no point).

yttrium, symbol **Y** (no point).

Yugoslavia, *not* J-; adj., **Yugoslav,** *not* -avian.

Yuit, Eskimo of NE. Siberia. *See also* **Ennuit.**

Yukon/ **River,** Alaska, U.S., and Canada; — **province,** Canada, *not* Youcon, -kon.

-yse. In words like **analyse, catalyse, paralyse, -lys-** is part of the Greek, and not a suffix like -ize. The spelling -yze is therefore incorrect, though common in U.S.

Yvetot, Normandy.

Y.W.C.A., Young Women's Christian Association.

Z

Z, (elec. and mag.) symbol for impedance (no point), the twenty-third of a series.

Z., all proper names with this initial.

z (math.), the third unknown quantity.

Z.A., Zuid Afrika.

Zach., Zachary.

Zaehnsdorf (Joseph), 1819–86, Austrian-born English-domiciled bookbinder.

Zagreb, Yugoslavia, *not* -ab, Agram.

Zaharoff (Sir Basil), 1849–1936, Greek-born British financier.

Zaïre, new name (1971) for **Congo, Democratic Republic of,** q.v.; also the unit of currency.

Zambezi, African river, *not* -si.

Zambia, *formerly* N. Rhodesia, independent rep. 1964.

zanana, *use* **ze-.**

Zangwill (Israel), 1864–1926, English novelist and dramatist.

Zanzibar, *see* **Tanzania.**

Zaragoza, Spain, *use* **Saragossa.**

zariba (Arab.), fortified camp, *not* the variations.

Zarskoe, *use* **Tsarskoe Selo.**

zart (Ger., mus.), tenderly.

Zealand, Denmark, *not* Zeeland.

Zech., Zechariah.

Zeeland, Holland, *not* Zea-.

Zeitgeist (Ger. m.), the spirit of the time (cap.).

Zeltinger, a Moselle wine.

zenana (Ind.), the women's apartments, *not* za-.

zenith, the highest point, opp. to **nadir.**

Zeph., Zephaniah.

zero/, *pl.* **-s.**

Z.E.T.A., Zero energy thermonuclear assembly.

Zetinje, *use* **Cetinje.**

Zeus, *pron.* zūs.

Z.G., Zoological Gardens.

zigzag/, **-ging** (one word).

Zimbabwe, group of ruins in S. Rhodesia.

Zimmermann (Agnes Marie), German-born nat.-British composer; — **(Johann Georg),** 1728–95, Swiss doctor and writer, author of *Solitude.*

Zimmern (Sir Alfred), 1879–1957, English writer on international affairs.

zinc, symbol **Zn** (no point).

zinco/ (typ.), a relief block, usu. in line, made from zinc; *pl.* **-s.**

zincography, the art of engraving and printing from zinc.

zingara (*à la*) (Fr. cook.), in gipsy style.

zingar/o (It.), a gipsy, *pl.* **-i;** *fem.* **-a,** *pl.* **-e.**

zirconium, symbol **Zr** (no point).

Zn, zinc (no point).

zodiac, *see* **astronomy.**

Zoffany (John), 1734–1810, German-born English-domiciled painter.

Zollverein (Ger. m.), customs union.

zoochem., zoochemistry.

zoogeog., zoogeography.

zool., zoolog/y, **-ical, -ist.**

zoology, *not* zoöl-, but *pron.* zo-ol'-; abbr. **zool.;** (typ.) genera, species, and varieties to be italic, other divisions roman.

zo/on, an animal; *pl.* **-a.**

zoon politikon (Gr.),
the political animal,
man.

zouave, French soldier.

Zr, zirconium (no point).

Z.S., Zoological Society.

zugzwang (chess),
a blockade, a position
in which any move is
disastrous.

Zuider Zee, Holland; *pron.*
zöider zā.

Zululand (one word),
annexed by S. Africa, 1897.

Zurich, Switzerland; in
Ger. **Zürich.**

zwieback, a kind of biscuit
rusk (not ital.).

Zwingli (Ulrich), 1484–
1531, Swiss Protestant
reformer.

Z NOTES